A Companion to Tourism

Blackwell Companions to Geography

Blackwell Companions to Geography is a blue-chip, comprehensive series covering each major subdiscipline of human geography in detail. Edited and contributed by the disciplines' leading authorities each book provides the most up to date and authoritative syntheses available in its field. The overviews provided in each Companion will be an indispensable introduction to the field for students of all levels, while the cutting-edge, critical direction will engage students, teachers, and practitioners alike.

Published

1. *A Companion to the City*
Edited by Gary Bridge and Sophie Watson

2. *A Companion to Economic Geography*
Edited by Eric Sheppard and Trevor J. Barnes

3. *A Companion to Political Geography*
Edited by John Agnew, Katharyne Mitchell, and Gerard Toal (Gearoid O Tuathail)

4. *A Companion to Cultural Geography*
Edited by James S. Duncan, Nuala C. Johnson, and Richard H. Schein

5. *A Companion to Tourism*
Edited by Alan A. Lew, C. Michael Hall, and Allan M. Williams

Forthcoming

6. *A Companion to Feminist Geography*
Edited by Joni Seager and Lise Nelson

7. *Handbook to GIS*
Edited by John Wilson and Stewart Fotheringham

A Companion to Tourism

Edited by

Alan A. Lew
Northern Arizona University, USA

C. Michael Hall
University of Otago, New Zealand

and

Allan M. Williams
University of Exeter, UK

Blackwell Publishing

350 Main Street, Malden, MA 02148-5020, USA
108 Cowley Road, Oxford OX4 1JF, UK
550 Swanston Street, Carlton, Victoria 3053, Australia

First published 2004 by Blackwell Publishing Ltd

Library of Congress Cataloging-in-Publication Data

A companion to tourism / edited by Alan A. Lew, C. Michael Hall, Allan M. Williams.
p. cm. – (Blackwell companions to geography)
Includes bibliographical references (p.).
ISBN 0-631-23564-7 (alk. paper)
1. Travel. I. Lew, Alan A. II. Hall, Colin Michael, 1961– III. Williams, Allan M. IV. Series.

G155.A1C5347 2004
910′ .01–dc22

2003017016

A catalogue record for this title is available from the British Library.

Set in 10 on 12pt Sabon
by Kolam Information Services Pvt. Ltd, Pondicherry, India
Printed and bound in the United Kingdom
by TJ International Ltd, Padstow, Cornwall

For further information on
Blackwell Publishing, visit our website:
http://www.blackwellpublishing.com

Contents

Contributors

Gregory J. Ashworth studied economics and geography at the universities of Cambridge, Reading, and London. He is currently Professor of Heritage Management and Urban Tourism in the Faculty of Spatial Sciences at the University of Groningen, The Netherlands. His special interests are in urban tourism and urban conservation planning.

Irena Ateljevic is a Senior Lecturer in Tourism Management at Auckland University of Technology, New Zealand. She received her Ph.D. in Geography at the University of Auckland. Her research interests include issues of backpacker travel; tourism entrepreneurship; discourse analysis of tourist experiences; and tourism representations as constructed and interpreted in the context of various social conditions (gender, class, ethnicity, etc.).

Stephen Boyd is currently based at the University of Otago in New Zealand. He has an eclectic range of interests in tourism with recent projects focusing on tourism and national parks, tourism and world heritage sites, and heritage tourism in general.

Bill Bramwell is Reader in Tourism in the Centre for Tourism and Cultural Change at Sheffield Hallam University, UK. He has edited books on rural tourism, collaboration and partnerships in tourism, and sustainable tourism in Europe, and he is working on a book on Southern European tourism. In 1992 he co-founded the *Journal of Sustainable Tourism*, which he still co-edits. His research interests include discourses of sustainable tourism, tourism and environmental policies, cultural responses to tourism, tourism growth management, and tourism in Southern Europe.

Richard Butler was born in England and educated at Nottingham (BA Hons.) and Glasgow (Ph.D.) universities. He taught at the University of Western Ontario from 1967 to 1997, specializing in the geography of tourism and recreation. He is past president of the International Academy for the Study of Tourism and a past president of the Canadian Association for Leisure Studies. His main fields of research have been the evolution cycle of resorts, the social impact of tourism, sustainable tourism, and tourism on islands.

Erlet Cater is Senior Lecturer in Tourism and Development in the Department of Geography, University of Reading, UK. She edited the book *Ecotourism: A Sustainable Option* (1994) and was an Advisory Editor for *The Encyclopaedia of Ecotourism*. She is an advisor for the Society and Environment Forum of the RGS-IBG and Coral Cay Conservation, and has judged the British Airways Tourism for Tomorrow Awards. She is on the editorial boards of *Tourism Geographies* and the *Journal of Ecotourism.*

T. C. Chang is an Associate Professor at the Department of Geography (National University of Singapore). His research interests are in urban tourism, regional (Southeast Asia) tourism, arts, culture, and heritage. He was co-editor (with Peggy Teo and K. C. Ho) of *Interconnected Worlds: Tourism in Southeast Asia* (Pergamon, 2001).

Andrew Church is Professor of Human Geography at the University of Brighton, UK. He is Honorary Secretary for Research at the Royal Geographical Society–Institute of British Geographers and is also Chair of the Society's Geography of Leisure and Tourism Research group. His research interests include tourism policy, employment in the tourism and leisure sector, and human–nature relations in everyday leisure spaces. His recent publications on tourism and leisure have appeared in a wide range of scholarly journals, including *Tourism Geographies*, *Sociology*, and *Leisure Studies.*

Tim Coles is Lecturer in Human Geography and University Business Fellow at the University of Exeter, UK. His research interests are in tourism and restructuring, tourism, diasporas, and transnationalism, tourism, retailing, and shopping, and e-tourism. He is the Honorary Secretary of the Geography of Leisure and Tourism Research Group of the Royal Geographical Society (with IBG). Among his recent publications are "Urban Tourism, Place Promotion and Economic Restructuring: The Case of Post-Socialist Leipzig," in *Tourism Geographies* (2003), and "The Emergent Tourism Industry in Eastern Germany a Decade after Unification," in *Tourism Management.*

Mike Crang is a Lecturer in Geography at Durham University, UK. He has worked on issues of culture, identity, and belonging which led him to study cultural tourism. He has been especially interested in issues around visual media and their influence on tourists. He is the co-editor of the journal *Tourist Studies*, and of the books *Tourism: Between Place and Performance* (with Simon Coleman), *Thinking Space* (with Nigel Thrift), and *Virtual Geographies* (with Phil Crang and Jon May).

David Crouch is Professor of Cultural Geography, Tourism, and Leisure at the University of Derby, UK, and Visiting Professor of Geography and Tourism at the University of Karlstad, Sweden. He has written widely on cultural geography, tourism and leisure, and research approaches, including recent papers in Tourist Studies and Social and Cultural Geography, and numerous book chapters. His edited books include *Leisure/Tourism Geographies* (Routledge, 1999) and *Visual Culture and Tourism* (with Nina Lubbren; Berg, 2003).

Keith G. Debbage is an Associate Professor of Urban-Economic Geography in the Department of Geography at the University of North Carolina at Greensboro, USA. His major research interests include the economic geography of the air transportation industry, the resort cycle, and urban planning. Dr. Debbage has published in the *Annals of Tourism Research*, *Tourism Management*, the *Journal of Transport Geography*, and the *Journal of Air Transport Management*, amongst others. In 2002 he received the thirteenth Roy Wolfe Award in Tourism Geography from the AAG Recreation, Tourism, and Sport Specialty Group.

Anne-Marie d'Hauteserre is Tourism Program Coordinator in the Department of Geography at the University of Waikato. She obtained her BA from the University of Madagascar and her other higher degrees from the University of Paris I, La Sorbonne. Her research interests stem from her background in geography and lie in the application of critical social science theories to tourism issues. She uses tourism destinations she has had the opportunity to know in depth, such as Monaco or Foxwoods Casino Resort, to support and illustrate her work. She is also very keen to spread knowledge of the French Pacific to the English-speaking community in the hope of establishing more communication between the two.

Stephen Doorne is a Lecturer in the School of Social and Economic Development at the University of South Pacific in Suva, Fiji. He received his Ph.D. in Tourism at the Victoria University of Wellington, New Zealand. His research interests include cultural and ethnic tourism, tourism and development, tourism imagery, and tourism entrepreneurship.

Yianna Farsari is a Research Associate at the Regional Analysis Division of the Foundation for Research and Technology-Hellas (FORTH) in Heraklion, Greece. She is a Ph.D. candidate at the University of Surrey, School of Management, in collaboration with FORTH. Her research interests include sustainable tourism indicators, policy-making for sustainable tourism in mass Mediterranean destinations, and GIS-based support for tourism policy-making.

Donald Getz is a Professor of Tourism and Hospitality Management at the Haskayne School of Business, University of Calgary, Canada. He has authored two books on event management and event tourism, and was co-founder of the research journal *Event Management*. His doctorate is in Social Sciences (Geography) from the University of Edinburgh.

Alison Gill is a Professor with a joint appointment with the Department of Geography and the School of Resource and Environmental Management at Simon Fraser University in Vancouver, British Columbia, Canada. Her research interests lie in resort development, especially in mountain environments, and on the impacts of tourism in rural areas and small towns. She has conducted extensive research on changing community–resort relationships in Whistler, BC. Her research appears in numerous book chapters as well as journals such as *Tourism Management*, *Environment and Planning A*, and *The Professional Geographer*. She serves on the editorial boards of *Tourism Geographies* and the *Journal of Architectural and Planning Research*.

Jon Goss is a Professor in the Department of Geography at the University of Hawaii. His research interests include urbanization and development in Southeast Asia and real and imaginary landscapes of popular culture, including shopping malls, theme parks, and film. He has conducted research on various tourist landscapes in Hawaii, including Waikiki, the Arizona Memorial, and the Polynesian Culture Center.

C. Michael Hall is Professor and Head of the Department of Tourism, at the University of Otago, Dunedin, New Zealand, and Honorary Professor, Department of Marketing, University of Stirling, Scotland. He is co-editor of *Current Issues in Tourism* and associate editor for Asia and the Pacific for *Tourism Geographies*. For the period 2000–4 he was Chairperson of the IGU Commission on Tourism, Leisure and Global Change.

Julia Hasse holds a Ph.D. in Tourism Management from Victoria University of Wellington in New Zealand and has worked as a lecturer at the University of the West of England and the University of Applied Sciences Eberswalde, in Germany. She has recently accepted a Post-doctoral Fellowship at the Auckland University of Technology in New Zealand, where her work focuses on the application of participatory approaches and Geographical Information Systems in sustainable tourism planning.

Tom D. Hinch is an Associate Professor with the Faculty of Physical Education and Recreation at the University of Alberta. His research interests focus on the relationship between travelers and the places that they visit. He has examined this relationship in the context of tourism and indigenous people, sport tourism, and tourism seasonality. Tom is particularly interested in unique issues that indigenous people face in their attempts to harness tourism for their own objectives.

Shirlena Huang is an Associate Professor at the Department of Geography, National University of Singapore. Her research areas include gender issues, with a particular focus on migrant labor flows within the Asia-Pacific region, as well as urbanization and conservation. She has recently edited (with Brenda S. A. Yeoh and Peggy Teo) a volume on *Gender Politics in the Asia-Pacific Region* (Routledge, 2002).

George Hughes is a Senior Lecturer in Geography within the School of GeoSciences at Edinburgh University, UK. His research explores the uses of leisure and tourism in the socio-economic production of geographical space. This includes analysis of environmentally orientated types of tourism with an empirical focus on Belize. Relevant papers include "Environmental Indicators," *Annals of Tourism Research* (2002), "The Cultural Construction of Sustainable Tourism," *Tourism Management* (1995), and, with Furley, "Threshold, Carrying Capacity and the Sustainability of Tourism: A Case Study of Belize," *Caribbean Geography* special issue (1996).

Dimitri Ioannides is Associate Professor of Planning and Tourism Development at Southwest Missouri State University and, since January 2003, has also been a Senior Research Fellow at the Centre for Regional and Tourism Development in Bornholm, Denmark. He has co-edited *The Economic Geography of the Tourist Industry* (Routledge, 1998) and *Mediterranean Islands and Sustainable Tourism Development* (Continuum, 2001), and has also written a number of articles relating, among other topics, to the structure and organization of the travel industry.

John Jenkins is a Senior Lecturer in the Department of Leisure and Tourism Studies at the University of Newcastle, Australia. He is book reviews editor of *Current Issues in Tourism* and co-editor of *Annals of Leisure Research*. He is also co-editor of the *Encyclopedia of Leisure and Outdoor Recreation*, published by Routledge.

Alan A. Lew is a Professor and Chair in the Department of Geography, Planning and Recreation at Northern Arizona University. He is the editor-in-chief of the journal *Tourism Geographies*; among his edited books are *Tourism in China* (1995 and 2003), *Tourism and Gaming on American Indian Lands* (1998), and the forthcoming *Seductions of Place* (with Carolyn Cartier; Routledge, 2004). He is a member of the American Institute of Certified Planners, and is the webmaster for the Association of American Geographers' Recreation, Tourism and Sport Specialty Group, and the International Geographical Union's Commission on Tourism, Leisure and Global Change.

David Mason is a Senior Lecturer with the School of Information Management at Victoria University, Wellington, New Zealand, specializing in database design and e-commerce applications. He has extensive consultancy experience internationally, and is the author of numerous articles and books on information systems implementation. His current research interests centre on the adoption and application of ICT within the tourism industry, with particular emphasis on community informatics for tourism.

Bob McKercher is an Associate Professor in Tourism in the School of Hotel and Tourism Management at the Hong Kong Polytechnic University. He completed his undergraduate degree in geography at York University, Canada, his master's degree at Carleton University in Canada, and his Ph.D. at the University of Melbourne in Australia. Dr McKercher has broad research interests and has published more than a hundred scholarly papers and research reports on a variety of tourism issues.

Kevin Meethan is Senior Lecturer in Sociology at the University of Plymouth, UK. His research interests in tourism encompass sociocultural change and global–local relations, genealogy, and diasporic identity. Recent publications include *The Changing Consumer* (edited with S. Miles and A. Anderson; Routledge, 2002), and *Tourism in Global Society: Place, Culture, Consumption* (Palgrave, 2001).

David Mercer is Associate Professor in the School of Social Science and Planning at RMIT University in Melbourne, Australia. He is responsible for the postgraduate program in International Urban and Environmental Management and is the author of over 120 papers, book chapters, and books on natural resource management, tourism, and environmental policy, mainly with an Australian focus.

Klaus Meyer-Arendt is the Chair of the Department of Environmental Studies at the University of West Florida in Pensacola. His research interests include the interaction of physical and cultural processes in coastal environments of the USA and Latin America, especially the Gulf of Mexico. He is past recipient of a Senior Scholar Research Award to Mexico funded by the Fulbright Commission and the García-Robles Foundation, and the Roy Wolfe Award of the Recreation Tourism and Sport Specialty Group of the Association of American Geographers.

Simon Milne is Professor of Tourism and Associate Dean of Research in the Business Faculty, Auckland University of Technology. Simon now coordinates the New Zealand Tourism Research Institute (www.nztri.org). His research focuses on creating stronger links between tourism and surrounding economies. In recent years he has focused on the ability of information technology to improve the marketing, economic performance, and sustainability of tourism firms, products, and destinations.

Claudio Minca is Professor of Human Geography at the University of Newcastle. He has written widely on geographical representations, tourism, and postmodernism in geography, and is the author of *Spazi effimeri* (1996) and the editor of *Introduzione alla geografia postmoderna* (2001), *Postmodern Geography* (2001), and *Orizzonte mediterraneo* (2003).

Nigel Morgan is based in the Welsh Centre for Tourism Research in the Welsh School of Hospitality, Tourism and Leisure Management, University of Wales Institute, Cardiff, UK. His research interests embrace destination marketing, seaside resort development, tourism sociology, and tourism and leisure advertising and branding. His most recent book is *Destination Branding: Creating the Unique Place Proposition* (Butterworth, 2002), and he is currently working on *Creating Tourism Identities* and *Cultures Through the Post: Essays on Tourism and Postcards*.

Dieter K. Müller is an Assistant Professor at the Department of Social and Economic Geography, Umeå University Sweden. His main research interest is in tourism in peripheral and rural areas, and particularly second-home tourism. Recently he has co-edited the book *Mobility, Tourism and Second Homes* (with C. Michael Hall; Channelview, 2004).

Tim Oakes is Associate Professor of Geography at the University of Colorado at Boulder, and a visiting research scholar at the University of Technology, Sydney. He is the author of *Tourism and Modernity in China* (Routledge, 1998), and has written extensively on the cultural geography of Chinese regional development. He is currently co-editing *Travels in Paradox*, with Claudio Minca, and *Translocal China*, with Louisa Schein, while preparing a new book titled *Trading in Places*. His current research examines the cultural and ethnic politics of heritage tourism in China.

Stephen Page is Scottish Enterprise Forth Valley Chair in Tourism, University of Stirling, Scotland and associate editor of the journal *Tourism Management*. He has published extensively in the area of tourism and transport and is the author of *Transport and Tourism* (Pearson Education) and the co-editor of the new research monograph, *Progress in Tourism and Transport* (Elsevier Science).

Thomas W. Paradis is Associate Professor in the Department of Geography, Planning and Recreation at Northern Arizona University, Flagstaff. He teaches a wide variety of geography and planning courses, and his research interests include small-town growth and change, downtown redevelopment, and heritage tourism. He has recently authored his first book, *Theme Town: A Geography of Landscape and Community in Flagstaff, Arizona* (2003).

Poulicos Prastacos is Director of Research at the Foundation for Research and Technology-Hellas (FORTH) in Heraklion, Greece. His areas of expertise include geoinformatics (GIS, databases, spatial methods) and spatial decision support systems. He has published more than thirty scientific papers in the areas of forecasting mathematical models, integration of GIS tools in decision support, and environmental information systems.

Richard Prentice holds the Chair of Heritage Interpretation and Cultural Tourism at the University of Sunderland, UK. His interests are in lifestyle formation, tourism and arts marketing, consumer imaginings and experiences of cultural and heritage tourism, and market-based product design. Sample publications include "Journeys for Experiences," in P. Keller and T. Bieger (eds), *Tourism Growth and Global Competition* (2001) and (with V. A. Andersen) "Festival as Creative Destination," *Annals of Tourism Research* (2003).

Robert Preston-Whyte is Professor of Geography at the University of Natal in Durban, South Africa. His research interest in coastal tourism emerged out of controversial ecotourism and dune mining issues relating to the Lake St Lucia wetland prior to its emergence as a World Heritage Site. This was followed by his current interest in seaside tourism that is largely motivated by the social, cultural, and political changes in seaside tourism that have taken place in Durban since the end of the apartheid regime. Some of these are reported in the *Annals of Tourism Research* and *Tourism Geographies.*

Annette Pritchard is Director of the Welsh Centre for Tourism Research in the Welsh School of Hospitality, Tourism and Leisure Management at the University of Wales Institute, Cardiff, UK. Her research interests include tourism sociology (especially the interplay between human status characteristics such as gender, sexuality, and race and the power dimensions of tourism), and destination marketing branding. Her books include *Tourism Promotion and Power* (Wiley, 1998), *Power and Politics at the Seaside* (University of Exeter, 1999), and *Tourism and Leisure Advertising* (Butterworth, 2000).

Michael Riley is Professor of Organizational Behaviour at the School of Management, University of Surrey, UK where he is Director of Postgraduate Research. Initially trained in hotel management, he studied labor economics, industrial relations, and human resource planning at the University of Sussex, UK, and was awarded a doctorate at the University of Essex. His work over two decades centres on the labor aspects of tourism and hospitality, and he has written extensively on human resource management and labor market issues. His current research interests are concerned with pay, knowledge accumulation, and the relationship between industrial culture and managerial cognition.

Mike Robinson holds the Chair of Tourism Studies and is Director of the Centre for Tourism and Cultural Change at Sheffield Hallam University, UK. His research interests lie in the relationship between tourism and culture(s), with specific interests in heritage meanings, tourism's relationship with the arts and popular culture, identity-making, image, sustainable tourism development, and tourist behavior. Previous books include *Tourism and Cultural Conflicts* (with Boniface) and his latest book is *Literature and Tourism: Essays in the Reading and Writing of Tourism Texts* (with Andersen). He is editor-in-chief of the *Journal of Tourism and Cultural Change* and an associate editor of the *Scandinavian Journal of Hospitality and Tourism*.

Jarkko Saarinen is Professor of Geography in the Department of Geography at the University of Oulu, Finland. His research and teaching interests include tourism development and its sociocultural impacts in peripheral regions, tourism sustainability, and nature-based tourism in wilderness environments. His publications include "Social Constructions of Tourist Destinations," in G. Ringer (ed.), *Destinations: Cultural Landscapes of Tourism* (1998) and "The Regional Economics of Tourism in Northern Finland," *Scandinavian Journal of Hospitality and Tourism* (2003).

Richard Sharpley is Reader in Travel and Tourism Management at Northumbria University, UK. The author of a number of tourism books and journal articles, his research interests lie in the field of the rural tourism, the sociology of tourism, and sustainable tourism development, with a particular focus on tourism development in Cyprus.

Gareth Shaw is Professor of Human Geography at the University of Exeter, UK. His research interests include behavioral and consumption studies, small firms and economic development, and tourism and disability. He is co-author of *Critical Issues in Tourism* (with Allan Williams; Blackwell, 2002), and co-editor of *Tourism and Economic Development: European Experiences* (with Allan Williams; Wiley, 3rd edn 1998), as well as being book review editor for *Tourism Geographies.*

Stephen L. J. Smith is a Professor in the Department of Recreation and Leisure Studies, University of Waterloo. His research interests include tourism statistics and tourism economics. He works with the Canadian Tourism Commission, Statistics Canada, and numerous other organizations on improving the quality of tourism statistics.

Patricia A. Stokowski is an Associate Professor with the School of Natural Resources, University of Vermont. Her teaching and research interests center around outdoor recreation behavior, tourism planning, and rural and resource-dependent communities, and she has written extensively about social impact of tourism, sense of place, and community social networks. She is the author of *Riches and Regrets: Betting on Gambling in Two Colorado Mountain Towns* (University Press of Colorado, 1996) and *Leisure in Society: A Network Structural Perspective* (Mansell Press, 1994). Beyond the halls of academia, Stokowski is a professional ice-dance coach.

Theano S. Terkenli is an Assistant Professor at the Department of Geography and at the Interdepartmental Program of Graduate Studies in Tourism Planning, Administration and Policy, both at the University of the Aegean, Lesvos, Greece. Her academic interests include geographies of everday life; spatialities of contemporary social life and culture from the transnational to the local scale; cultural landscape theory and analytical approach; critical perspectives in tourism and recreation; ideas of home and identity; and geographies of the Aegean and the Mediterranean. She is the author of *The Cultural Landscape: Geographical Perspectives* (Greek; Papazissis Publishers, 1996) and various articles and book chapters on cultural geography, tourism, and the cultural landscape.

Victor B. Teye is Associate Professor of Tourism and Coordinator of the Travel and Tourism Program at Arizona State University in the United States. His research interests include the political dimensions of tourism development, human resource issues, and heritage tourism, especially in developing countries. He has presented research papers at several international conferences and has published in leading refereed tourism journals. He was a Fulbright Teaching and Research Scholar at the University of Cape Coast in Ghana and has also served as a Tourism Consultant in a number of African countries. He is presently a Visiting Professor at the International Management Center in Krems, Austria.

Dallen J. Timothy is Associate Professor at Arizona State University and Visiting Professor of Heritage Tourism at Sunderland University, UK. He has published extensively in tourism books and scholarly journals on political boundaries, supranationalism, planning in the developing world, heritage, shopping and consumption, rural and peripheral regions, ethnic diasporas, and community-based development. Dr. Timothy is also on the editorial boards of seven international tourism journals and recently finished his term as the Chair of the Recreation, Tourism and Sport Specialty Group of the Association of American Geographers.

John E. Tunbridge studied at the universities of Cambridge, Bristol, and Sheffield and is currently Professor of Geography and Environmental Studies at Carleton University, Ottawa, Canada. His special interests are in heritage and waterfront issues, with particular reference to Canada, South Africa and Central Europe.

D. Jim Walmsley is Professor of Geography and Planning in the School of Human and Environmental Studies at the University of New England, Armidale, Australia. He has worked in Australia for thirty years. His early research interests were in how individuals cope with living in cities and with how and why human well-being varies from place to place. This has led in recent years to a concern with the role of leisure, recreation, and tourism in human well-being, and with cognitive imagery in tourism.

David B. Weaver is Professor of Tourism and Events Management in the Department of Health, Fitness and Recreation Resources at George Mason University, Virginia. He is a specialist in ecotourism, sustainable tourism, and destination life-cycle dynamics, and has authored or co-authored five books and over sixty refereed articles and book chapters on related topics. Dr. Weaver is also the editor of *The Encyclopedia of Ecotourism* (CABI Publishing, 2001). He has held previous appointments at Griffith University (Australia) and the University of Regina (Canada).

Allan M. Williams is Professor of Human Geography and European Studies at the University of Exeter. His research interests embrace the relationships between economic development and different forms of mobility, including both tourism and migration. He is author or editor of a number of books including *Critical Issues in Tourism* (with Gareth Shaw), *Tourism in Transition: Economic Change in Central Europe* (with Vlado Balaz; I. B. Tauris, 2000), and *Tourism and Migration* (with Michael Hall; Kluwer, 2002). He is co-editor of *European Urban and Regional Studies*, and associate editor of *Tourism Geographies*.

Poh Poh Wong is Associate Professor in the Department of Geography, National University of Singapore. His research interests focused on tourism–environment relationships with reference to Southeast Asia and small island states in the Indian Ocean. He is the editor of *Tourism vs Environment: The Case for Coastal Areas* (Kluwer, 1993) and author of *Coastal Tourism in Southeast Asia* (ICLARM, 1991). He has recently completed overviews on tourism development, ecotourism trends, coastal environment, and coastal zone management of Southeast Asia.

Preface

Travel, touring, going away, coming home, visiting attractions, sunbathing, buying souvenirs, seeing, recreating, experiencing, learning, relaxing, sharing: these are all activities and experiences which increasingly weave together the lives of individuals, at least in the developed world. Whether or not we all share the same understanding of tourism, or whether a clearly definable tourism industry exists, the tourism phenomenon has been encompassing in its impacts on landscapes and how we live our lives in the 20th and 21st centuries. It is probably the complexity and fascination of tourism issues, along with shared personal interests in landscape, place, and social relationships, both at home and in distant places, which have drawn the three editors of this volume both into the discipline of geography, and into the field of tourism studies. We have, each from our own distant corner of the globe, devoted much of our professional lives to the study of tourism and have collaborated on a variety of projects over the years, most notably the journal, *Tourism Geographies*. So when the invitation came to develop this *Companion to Tourism*, as part of Blackwell's Companions to Geography series, we did not need to think long before accepting the opportunities it presented – perhaps at that stage underestimating the challenges that it would also pose.

This *Companion* was initially conceived as an exploration and review of the contributions of geographers and geography to our understanding of tourism. We recognize, of course, that geography does not have a monopoly on tourism studies. But we do believe that tourism is intrinsically of concern to geography and geographers in the centrality that it gives to places and spatial relationships (both physical and cognitive), as well as environmental issues and the landscapes of tourism. Tourism studies, however, has evolved as a multidisciplinary and interdisciplinary field, and we certainly did not wish to be regimented by overly narrow disciplinary concerns in this volume. Instead, we defined what we perceived to be the major research and theoretical subject areas of tourism studies, and then sought out leading scholars who have written on these themes within a geographical framework. We believe that the result has been the assembly of discerning reviews by a distinguished group of scholars, some of whom are affiliated with geography departments, but many more of whom are based in interdisciplinary, tourism-related programs. Their disciplinary affiliations have been of far less concern to us than what they have to say on particular issues.

We also made some efforts to balance contributions from different parts of the world. It must be admitted at the outset that, because this work is published in English, scholars from English-speaking countries predominate, and the book makes no pretence to cover all the vast research undertaken outside the English language community of researchers. However, we have included a mix of representatives from Europe, North America, and the Pacific, along with some representation from other regions.

The result reflects broader social science and interdisciplinary perspectives, while still reflecting the inherent nature of geography. We believe that the contributors have presented some of the best in tourism thought and research, and while not as fully comprehensive of either tourism geography or tourism studies, as we might have naively sought at the outset, we believe that the outcome is a coherent series of insights that effectively capture some of the most innovative, challenging, and rewarding areas of contemporary tourism research.

With any book, there are a large number of people who must be thanked for their support. Michael would like to acknowledge the help of Sarah Stevens in undertaking the analysis of CAB abstracts; Mel Elliott and Frances Cadogan for their organizational brilliance; Dick Butler, Nick Cave, Chris Cooper, Elvis Costello, David Duval, Thor Flognfeldt, Stefan Gössling, Derek Hall, Tuija Härkönen, Bruno Jansson, Dieter Müller, Stephen Page, Jarkko Saarinen, Anna Dóra Sæflórsdóttir, Brian Wheeler, and Geoff Wall and his fellow editors for the opportunity to discuss their various insights into tourism geography; and, most importantly, Jody for her support and coping with getting confused about which Al(l)an he was referring to. Allan would like to acknowledge the assistance of his secretary Jan Thatcher, the day-to-day academic collaboration with his colleagues Tim Coles and Gareth Shaw, a fellowship provided by the University of Otago in 2003, and – above all – the support of his wife Linda. And the other Alan would like to thank his administrative assistant, Debbie Martin, for her ongoing support of his research efforts; his colleagues Dawn Hawley, Tina Kennedy, and Carolyn Daugherty for their assistance on *Tourism Geographies* during some hectic times at the university; his graduate assistant, Alisa Wenker, for her help with his classes while this project was going on; his children Lauren, a budding scholar in her own right, Chynna, and Skylan, for allowing their Dad space to work at home and during family vacations; and the constant and devoted support of his wife, Mable.

Alan A. Lew, Flagstaff, Arizona, USA
C. Michael Hall, Dunedin, New Zealand
Allan M. Williams, Exeter, UK

Part I Introduction

Chapter 1

Tourism: Conceptualizations, Institutions, and Issues

C. Michael Hall, Allan M. Williams, and Alan A. Lew

Introduction

At the beginning of the twenty-first century, tourism as an industry had probably achieved a higher profile in the public consciousness of the developed world than ever before. There has, of course, been a steady growth in the numbers of tourists over several decades, but the critical reasons were the impacts on international tourism of (1) the terrorist attacks of September 11 2001, (2) the American-led invasion of Iraq, (3) airline financial failures, and (4) government and traveler responses to the SARS virus. Destinations and tourism-related businesses around the world experienced a profound shift in consumer confidence and travel behavior. Arguably, these impacts, and their subsequent media reporting, gave the tourism industry an unprecedented high-policy profile as government and governance at all levels wrestled with travel and security issues, and resultant shifts in the economic and employment impacts of tourism.

These recent events have led to a questioning of many of the assumptions about tourism, and tourism researchers are reassessing the relevance of their work, not only in terms of policy and other applications, but also, more fundamentally, in the ways in which the subject is theorized and conceptualized. A history of the sociology of tourism knowledge, unlike a history of tourist activity, has yet to be completed. Whilst this was not explicitly the aim of this volume, the range and depth of the chapters do provide an opportunity to reassess many of the key themes and issues in contemporary tourism studies, as well as the intellectual context within which they were prepared.

This introductory chapter is, therefore, divided into three main sections. First is a brief account of some of the issues surrounding the definition of tourism and, hence, its study. Second is a discussion of some of the key themes and issues that have emerged in tourism as a field of social scientific endeavor. Third, and finally, are some comments regarding the relationships between areas of tourism research, their ebb and flow, and the selection of chapters in this volume. These issues are revisited in the concluding chapter.

Conceptualizing Tourism

Although many may sympathize with the sentiments of Williams and Shaw's observation that "the definition of tourism is a particularly arid pursuit" (1988: 2), it is, as they also acknowledged, "crucially important." This is largely because of the continuing need to determine tourism's economic impacts, but it also has broader economic and policy ramifications. Undoubtedly, a substantial amount of research effort has gone into the determination of "supply side" or industry approaches to the definition of tourism, such as the development of Tourism Satellite Accounts (TSAs), which have become significant policy tools for organizations such as the World Travel and Tourism Council (Smith, chapter 2). From a supply-side perspective, the tourism industry may be defined as "the aggregate of all businesses that directly provide goods or services to facilitate business, pleasure, and leisure activities away from the home environment" (Smith 1988: 183). However, such production-oriented approaches, while useful for comparative economic research and studies of tourism's economic impact, fail to convey the manner in which the production and consumption of tourism are interwoven. They also do not address the implications that this has for understanding the broader social, environmental, and political dimensions of tourism, as well as fundamental economic issues of commodification, distribution, tourism labor, and the appropriate role of the state in tourism (Williams, chapter 5).

An adequate conceptualization of tourism, therefore, clearly requires that we go beyond the narrowly economic. Most obviously, there is a need to appreciate the relationships of leisure, recreation, and tourism with other social practices and behavior (figure 1.1). As Parker (1999: 21) observed,

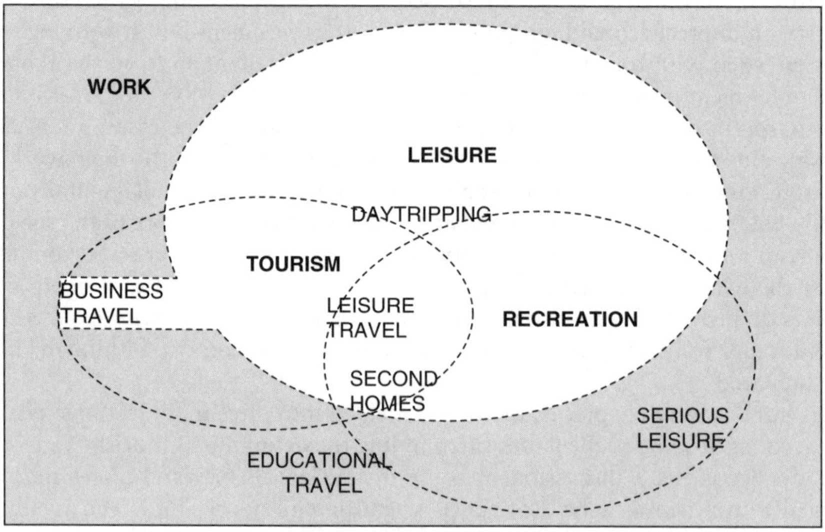

Figure 1.1 Relationships between leisure, recreation, and tourism
Source: After Hall 2003.

> It is through studying leisure as a whole that the most powerful explanations are developed. This is because society is not divided into sports players, television viewers, tourists and so on. It is the same people who do all these things.

Furthermore, Featherstone (1987: 115) argued that tourism research should be socially situated:

> The significance and meaning of a particular set of leisure choices . . . can only be made intelligible by inscribing them on a map of the class-defined social field of leisure and lifestyle practices in which their meaning and significance is relationally defined with reference to structured oppositions and differences.

There is, therefore, considerable value in viewing tourism and recreation as part of a wider conceptualization of leisure (Shaw and Williams 1994, 2002; Hall and Page 2002). In figure 1.1 broken lines are used to illustrate that the boundaries between the concepts are "blurred." Work is typically differentiated from leisure, but there are two main realms of overlap: first, business travel, which is often seen as a work-oriented form of tourism; and, second, "serious leisure," which refers to the breakdown between leisure and work pursuits and the development of leisure career paths with respect to hobbies and interests (Stebbins 1979, 1982).

In addition to being defined in relation to its production and consumption, tourism is increasingly being interpreted as but one, albeit highly significant, dimension of temporary mobility and circulation (Bell and Ward 2000; Urry 2000; Williams and Hall 2000, 2002) (see figure 1.2). A merging of leisure, recreation, and tourism research (Aitcheson 1999; Crouch 1999a, 1999b; Aitcheson, Macleod, and Shaw 2000; Hall and Page 2002), along with the emerging study of migration (Williams and Hall 2000; Williams et al. 2000; Hall and Williams 2002), circulation, and mobility (Urry 2000), are having a profound influence on how tourism studies are perceived as an area of academic interest. Indeed, it is only recently that temporary movements away from home (such as tourism, but also including travel for work or education, travel for health reasons, and even going overseas after finishing university) have begun to catch the awareness of migration researchers (Bell and Ward 2000). It is increasingly evident to those seeking wider perspectives on tourism that all forms of mobility are highly interrelated. Thus, the inclusion of same-day travel "excursionists" within technical definitions of tourism makes the division between recreation and tourism even more arbitrary. Indeed, there is increasing international agreement that "tourism" refers to all visitor activities, including those of both overnight and same-day visitors (UN 1994: 5). Given innovations in transport technology, same-day travel is becoming increasingly important at widening spatial scales, an exemplification of geographic "space-time compression." This has led the UN (1994: 9) to observe that "day visits are important to consumers and to many providers, especially tourist attractions, transport operators and caterers." This emphasizes the need for those interested in tourism to address the arbitrary boundaries between tourism and leisure, and tourism and migration. Tourism constitutes just one form of leisure-oriented temporary mobility, and in being part of that mobility, it is also both shaped by and shaping it.

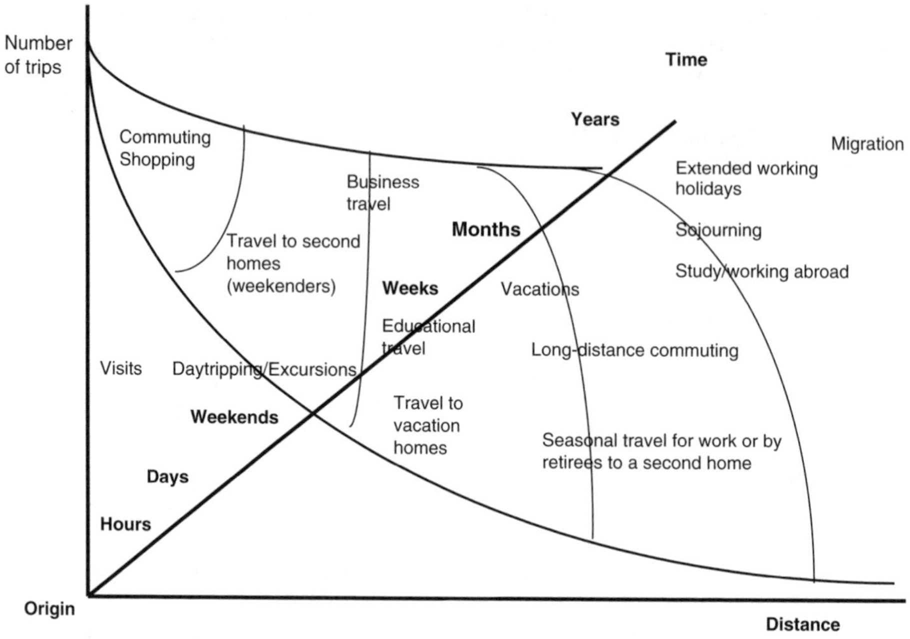

Figure 1.2 Extent of temporary mobility in space and time
Source: After Hall 2004a, 2004b.

While stressing the need to conceptualize tourism in terms of mobility, Flavell (2001: 391–2) reminds us that "to assess really the extent or nature of movement, or indeed even see it sometimes, you have in fact to spend a lot of the time 'studying things that stand still': the borders, institutions and territories of nation states; the sedimented 'home' cultures of people that do not move." This directs our attention to the non-mobile. Although there is a well-established literature on leisure constraints (e.g. Jackson, Crawford, and Godbey 1993; Jackson and Scott 1999) such notions have been relatively little applied to tourism (Shaw and Williams 2002), with the possible exception of discussions of seasonality (Hinch and Jackson 2000; Baum and Lundtrop 2001). Nevertheless, geographers have long recognized that a basic precondition for tourism mobility is that absences from the stations of the daily world are, for certain periods of time, socially and institutionally sanctioned. The opportunity to travel has always depended on the right to be absent from home and work, with such rights having historically been reserved for very few groups in the (usually male) population (Frändberg 1998). Indeed, Hägerstrand (1984), describing the breakaway from the time-space prism of everyday life that tourism represents, refers to this as an "escape from the cage of routines." Similarly, the growing recognition of the role of spatial settings by sociologists has direct implications for understanding tourism as a social practice, with Giddens (1984: xxv) observing, "Time-space 'fixity' also means social fixity; the substantially 'given' character of the physical milieux of day-to-day life interlaces with routine and is deeply influential in the contours of institutional reproduction."

Clearly, the embeddedness of tourism in modern social and economic practices has created a significant space for social science research which may not only be of relevance for tourism itself but for a deeper understanding of the everyday, as well as wider patterns of mobility. Nevertheless, the notion of tourism is open to multiple conceptualizations which rest on the ontological, epistemological, and paradigmatic assumptions of the viewer. This means that the conceptualization of tourism remains open to substantial contestation that may almost seem at odds with a popular lay understanding of what tourism represents.

Before we proceed further with the contested notions of how tourism should be conceptualized, it should be noted that some commentators question the utility of tourism as a concept at all.

> We will begin by interrogating the very category of "tourism." Is there such an entity? Does the term serve to demarcate a usefully distinct sphere of social practice? Where does tourism end and leisure or hobbying and strolling begin? This book [*Touring Cultures*] is based on the view that tourism is a term that is waiting to be deconstructed. Or as Marx might have said it is a chaotic conception, including within it too wide a range of disparate phenomena... It embraces so many different notions that it is hardly useful as a term of social science, although this is paradoxical since Tourism Studies is currently being rapidly institutionalized within much of the academy. (Rojek and Urry 1997: 1)

The next section of the introduction takes up this theme of the institutionalization of tourism.

The Institutionalization of Tourism Studies: Tourism as a Discipline?

Despite contestation over key concepts, tourism studies, as Rojek and Urry (1997) recognized, is becoming institutionalized in academic terms. Arguably, one of the reasons for conceptual confusion is because of the multiplicity of disciplinary and paradigmatic approaches that have been brought to bear on tourism phenomena (Mowforth and Munt 1998; Meethan 2001), as indeed is true of many of the phenomena which are studied in the social sciences. As Jafari and Ritchie (1981: 22) recognized, tourism studies, "like its customers who do not recognize geographical boundaries, does not recognize disciplinary demarcations." Furthermore, Tribe (1997: 638) described tourism analysis as interdisciplinary, multidisciplinary, and "conscious of its youthfulness." Yet while such statements about the state of tourism studies are widespread, they fail to understand that the study of tourism within the social sciences has a far longer history than is often imagined, and is less "youthful" than Tribe implies. For example, with respect to the geography of tourism, Hall and Page (2002) chart an Anglo-American and European tradition of social scientific scholarship on tourism that dates to the 1920s and 1930s.

The predominant attitude among many tourism researchers is perhaps best summed up by Bodewes (1981: 37), who argued that "tourism is usually viewed as an application of established disciplines, because it does not possess sufficient doctrine to be classified as a full-fledged academic discipline." Tribe (1997) even suggests that the search for tourism as a discipline should be abandoned, and that the diversity of the field should be celebrated. Nevertheless, this has to be set against the increasing recognition that tourism is becoming seen as a legitimate area of study in its own right (Ryan 1997), and that – at least superficially – it has many of the characteristics of a discipline (Hall 2004b). Johnston (1991), in his landmark review of Anglo-American Geography, identified three key characteristics of a discipline:

- a well-established presence in universities and colleges, including the appointment of professorial positions;
- formal institutional structures of academic associations and university departments; and
- avenues for academic publication, in terms of books and journals. Indeed, "It is the advancement of knowledge – through the conduct of fundamental research and the publication of its original findings – which identifies an academic discipline; the nature of its teaching follows from the nature of its research." (Johnston 1991: 2)

These characteristics clearly apply to the field of tourism studies. There are departments and degree programs established throughout the world, although in countries such as Australia and the United Kingdom they are less common in older established universities. The first undergraduate degree program in tourism in the United Kingdom was established at the University of Surrey in 1973. The first programs in Australia were established at Gatton College (now a part of the University of Queensland) and Footscray CAE (now a part of the Victoria University of Technology) in the late 1970s. Many universities also have professorial positions in tourism.

There are also a number of institutional structures for tourism both within universities and colleges of higher learning (e.g., departments and schools of tourism), and through national and international forums. For example, at a national level institutions such as the Council for Australian University Tourism and Hospitality Education (CAUTHE) and the Tourism Society in the United Kingdom run annual research conferences and provide a forum for discussion on tourism education. Specialty tourism research groups also operate within national academic associations, such as the Association of American Geographers, the Canadian Association of Geographers, the Institute of British Geographers, and similar groups in Germany, China, and elsewhere.

At the international level social scientific unions in the fields of anthropology and ethnology, economic history, geography, history, and sociology have tourism commissions or working groups. For example, the International Geographical Union's Commission on Tourism, Leisure and Global Change, which was established in 2000, has existed in various guises as a commission or study group since 1972. A number of other international tourism research and education organizations also exist which have made substantial contributions to tourism studies. For example, the first refereed academic journal on tourism, *Revue de Tourisme/The Tourist Review*, was established as early as 1946 as the official organ of the Association Internationale d'Experts Scientifiques du Tourisme (AIEST) based in Switzerland. The Council of Hotel, Restaurant and Institutional Education (CHRIE), which has a strong tourism component, was also established in 1946 in the United States. The Tourism and Travel Research Association (TTRA) had its beginnings in the merger in the US of the Western Council of Travel Research and the Eastern Travel Research Association in 1970. Although it retains a strong North American base, TTRA is now a substantial international network with a European chapter and over 800 members. In Europe, the Association for Tourism and Leisure Education (ATLAS) was established in 1991 to develop transnational educational initiatives in tourism and leisure. Since that time ATLAS has expanded rapidly to include chapters from the Asia-Pacific region, Africa, and the Americas. With an institutional membership of over 300 and an active conference, research, and publishing program, ATLAS is now one of the most significant international tourism education and research organizations.

In terms of the advancement of knowledge, there is now a substantial body of tourism literature as evidenced in journals, books, conference proceedings, and electronic publications. The growth of tourism journals is indicated in table 1.1 and figure 1.3. Some 77 journals, published in English either in full or in part, are identified as having had a substantial academic component devoted to tourism research. Figure 1.3 makes clear the highly uneven geographical distribution of editorships, and therefore of the locations of the gatekeepers to journal publishing (see Hall 2004c for a discussion on the role of gatekeepers in tourism studies). In analyzing the list of journals, it is also noticeable that the journal field has been marked by increased specialization in subject matter. For example, there are specific journals on geography, ecotourism, sports tourism, and tourism planning, as well as regionally oriented academic journals. To academic tourism journals can be added the many trade publications in which some research may be reported, while many researchers also publish their tourism work in non-tourism, discipline-based journals. These include substantial contributions to the tourism literature, such as Butler's (1980) often cited life-cycle model published in the *Canadian Geographer* and Britton's (1991) fundamental critique of the geography of tourism published in *Environment and Planning D: Society and Space.*

Two questions follow from this review. First, does tourism studies constitute a discipline? This is a difficult question, and it is not one that the editors were able to agree on, even amongst themselves. However, we do take note of Johnston's (1991: 9) reflections that:

> there is no fixed set of disciplines, nor any one correct division of academics according to subject matter. Those disciplines currently in existence are contained within boundaries established by earlier communities of scholars. The boundaries are porous so that disciplines interact. Occasionally the boundaries are changed, usually through the establishment of a new discipline that occupies an enclave within the pre-existing division of academic space.

The growth of tourism studies helps to reshape such boundaries, as well as being influenced by them.

The second, and in most ways more important, question is whether the field of tourism studies is in good health. The answer is of course contingent. It could be argued that the high level of research activity implies that it is in excellent health and

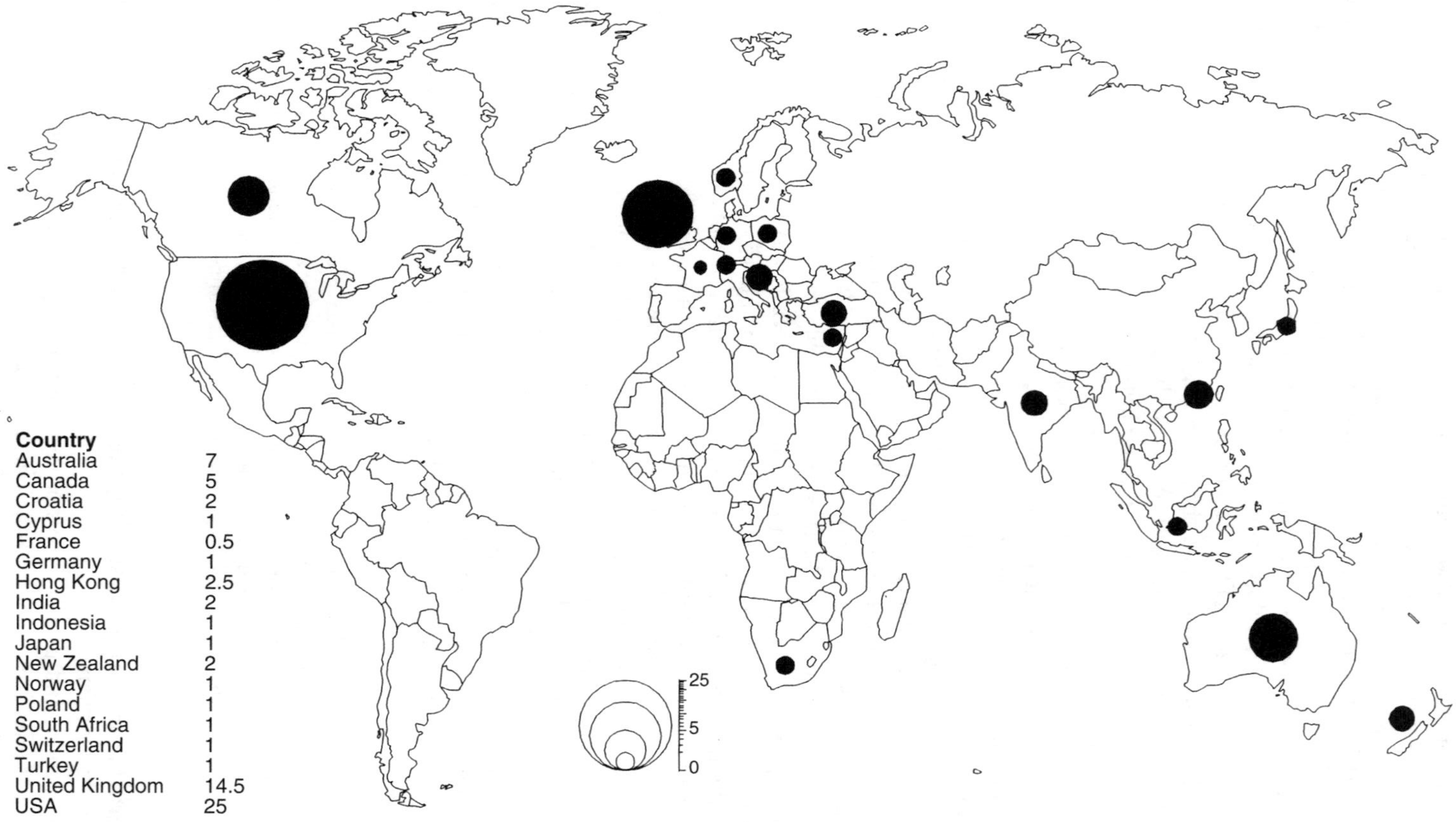

Figure 1.3 Global distribution of tourism journal editors

Table 1.1 Academic tourism journals

Journal title	Date established	Country of publication (2003)	Editor based in (2003)
TOURISM: An International Interdisciplinary Journal (formerly Turizam)	1952	Croatia	Croatia
The Tourist Review/Revue de Tourisme	1956	Switzerland	Switzerland
World Leisure & Recreation Association Journal	1958	Canada	Australia
Cornell Hotel and Restaurant Administration Quarterly	1960	USA	USA
Journal of Leisure Research	1969	USA	USA
Journal of Travel Research	1972	USA	USA
Annals of Tourism Research	1974	UK	USA
Journal of Leisurability	1974	USA	Canada
Tourism Recreation Research	1975	India	India
Journal of Hospitality & Tourism Research (formerly Hospitality Research Journal and Hospitality Education and Research Journal)	1976	USA	Hong Kong
Leisure Sciences	1978	UK	USA
Loisir et Societe/Society and Leisure	1978	Canada	Canada
Tourism Management	1979	UK	New Zealand/UK
Leisure Studies	1981	UK	UK
Teoros International	1981	Canada	Canada
Visions in Leisure and Business	1982	USA	USA
International Journal of Hospitality Management	1982	UK	UK
FIU Hospitality Review	1983	USA	USA
Journal of Park and Recreation Administration	1983	USA	USA
Turyzm	1986	Poland	Poland
Journal of Hospitality & Tourism Education (formerly Hospitality and Tourism Educator)	1988	USA	USA
ACTA Turistica	1989	Croatia	Croatia
International Journal of Contemporary Hospitality Management	1989	UK	UK

Cont'd

Table 1.1 *Cont'd*

Journal title	Date established	Country of publication (2003)	Editor based in (2003)
ANATOLIA: An International Journal of Tourism and Hospitality Research	1990	Turkey	Turkey
Journal of the International Academy of Hospitality Research	1990	USA	USA
Journal of Tourism Studies	1990	Australia	Australia
Leisure Options: Australian Journal of Leisure and Recreation	1991–6	Australia	Australia
Journal of Hospitality Financial Management	1992	USA	USA
Journal of Hospitality & Leisure for the Elderly	1992	USA	USA
Journal of Travel & Tourism Marketing	1992	USA	Hong Kong
Event Tourism (formerly Festival Management & Event Tourism)	1993	USA	USA
Journal of Sustainable Tourism	1993	UK	UK
Journal of Restaurant & Foodservice Marketing	1994	USA	USA
Australian Journal of Hospitality Management	1994	Australia	Australia
Journal of Vacation Marketing	1994	USA	Australia
Annals of Leisure Research	1995	Australia	New Zealand
Journal of Hospitality & Leisure Marketing	1995	USA	USA
Journal of Sport Tourism	1995	UK	USA
Managing Leisure	1995	UK	UK
Progress in Tourism and Hospitality Research	1995–7	UK	UK
Tourism Analysis	1995	USA	USA/Australia
Tourism Economics	1995	UK	UK
Asia Pacific Journal of Tourism Research	1996	Korea	Hong Kong
Journal of International Hospitality, Leisure and Tourism Management	1997	USA	USA
Tourismus	1997	Germany	Germany
Current Issues in Tourism	1998	UK	Australia/New Zealand
Information Technology & Tourism	1998	USA	Austria
Journal of Convention & Exhibition Management	1998	USA	USA
Tourism Review International (formerly Pacific Tourism Review)	1998	USA	USA
Praxis – The Journal of Applied Hospitality Management	1998	USA	USA

Tourism, Culture & Communication	1998	USA	Australia
International Journal of Tourism Research	1999	UK	UK
Tourism Geographies	1999	UK	USA
Tourism and Hospitality Research: The Surrey Quarterly Review	1999	UK	UK
International Journal of Hospitality and Tourism Administration	2000	USA	Canada
Journal of Leisure Property	2000	USA	UK
Journal of Quality Assurance In Tourism & Hospitality	2000	USA	USA
Journeys: The International Journal of Travel and Travel Writing	2000	USA	France/UK/USA
Journal of Travel and Tourism Research	2001	Turkey	Turkey
Journal of Teaching in Travel & Tourism	2001	USA	Hong Kong/USA
Tourism Today	2001	Cyprus	Cyprus
Tourist Studies	2001	UK	Australia/UK
Scandinavian Journal of Hospitality and Tourism	2001	Norway	Norway
Tourism Forum – Southern Africa Tourism Forum – Southern Africa	2001	South Africa	South Africa
ASEAN Journal on Hospitality and Tourism	2002	Indonesia	Indonesia
International Travel Law Journal Online	2002	UK/USA	USA
Japanese Journal of Tourism Studies	2002	Japan	Japan
Journal of Ecotourism	2002	UK	Canada
Journal of Hospitality, Leisure, Sport & Tourism Education	2002	UK	UK
Journal of Human Resources in Hospitality & Tourism	2002	Canada	USA
PASOS – Journal of Tourism and Cultural Heritage	2002	USA	Spain
Journal of Tourism and Cultural Change	2003	UK	UK
Tourism Research Journal (TJR)	2003	India	India
Journal of Quality of Life Research in Leisure and Tourism	2004	UK	USA
Tourism and Hospitality Planning and Development	2004	UK	UK
Tourism in Marine Environments	2004	USA	Canada

has become solidly institutionalized in the academy. However, the field has also been substantially criticized in terms of its theoretical base. As Meethan (2001: 2) commented, "for all the evident expansion of journals, books and conferences specifically devoted to tourism, at a general analytical level it remains under-theorized, eclectic and disparate." The comments of Franklin and Crang (2001: 5) are similarly astringent:

> The first trouble with tourism studies, and paradoxically also one of its sources of interest, is that its research object, "tourism," has grown very dramatically and quickly and that the tourism research community is relatively new. Indeed at times it has been unclear which was growing more rapidly – tourism or tourism research. Part of this trouble is that tourist studies has simply tried to track and record this staggering expansion, producing an enormous record of instances, case studies and variations. One reason for this is that tourist studies has been dominated by policy led and industry sponsored work so the analysis tends to internalize industry led priorities and perspectives... Part of this trouble is also that this effort has been made by people whose disciplinary origins do not include the tools necessary to analyze and theorize the complex cultural and social processes that have unfolded.

Their assessment does point at one of the persistent tensions in tourism research, between the often contradictory requirements of critical social science and the extent to which industry and policy-makers influence the research agenda, particularly through funding and commercialization strategies (Ryan 2001; Cooper 2002; Hall and Page 2002). There are similar contradictions in several of the social sciences, but they are particularly sharp in tourism, because of the very nature of the subject matter (which is often regarded as "fun") and the weak institutionalization of tourism early on within those academic centers that were at the forefront of critical social science. Nevertheless, it is possible to be too pessimistic. As already noted, the field of tourism has a considerably longer history than is often realized and there is a substantial and growing volume of research funded by national research councils and others beyond the direct influence of the tourism industry. Indeed, we believe that the contents of this volume bear testimony not only to the breadth of tourism studies, but also to the growth of critically engaged tourism research. This is not to say that there is theoretical and methodological convergence in tourism studies. Rather, the understanding of a field as complex and multi-scalar as tourism is unlikely to be the sole domain of either a single paradigm or a single discipline.

Issues

Disciplines and fields of study change over time, and areas of specialization come and go depending on intrinsic and extrinsic factors. For example, issues such as "sustainability" or "safety and security" rise or fall on the tourism agenda of academics, as well as governments, in response to external factors such as terrorism or environmental concerns, as well as on the availability of specific funding opportunities. There are also shifts in research priorities arising out of debates in tourism studies, and in surrounding areas of study and established disciplines. Tables 1.2 and 1.3 illustrate some of the changing concerns within tourism studies as indicated by a

Table 1.2 Keyword search of *CABI Leisure, Recreation and Tourism Abstracts* 1976–2002: geography-oriented keywords

Year	Space	Place	Environment	Geography	Geographic Information System (GIS)
1976	0	1	1	0	
1977	4	3	11	0	
1978	12	12	53	5	
1979	22	22	59	6	
1980	14	22	57	4	
1981	18	13	55	6	
1982	11	27	44	4	
1983	22	44	56	7	
1984	21	30	72	7	
1985	18	25	74	2	
1986	22	64	76	7	
1987	31	47	74	6	
1988	22	58	75	5	
1989	19	74	108	3	
1990	27	84	152	8	2
1991	30	83	143	12	1
1992	19	77	111	7	3
1993	35	89	152	5	2
1994	30	106	141	5	4
1995	27	70	148	3	2
1996	32	110	138	7	1
1997	26	87	113	4	5
1998	30	107	121	7	3
1999	23	67	147	2	5
2000	34	56	152	10	4
2001	45	90	167	10	6
2002	35	73	93	16	6

key word search of journals abstracted in *CABI Leisure, Recreation and Tourism Abstracts*. This is necessarily selective, and prone to the misinterpretations that are intrinsic to such automatic scanning. However, they do provide insights into the changing concerns in tourism research. Table 1.2 reflects some of the fundamental concerns of geographers, and illustrates the relative importance of place and environment as key concepts in tourism research, although this analysis does not distinguish between geographers and non-geographers as authors of these articles. The most obvious feature of this table is the large number of articles that can be classified as concerned with the "environment." Arguably, this may be a function of the appearance of new journals, such as the *Journal of Sustainable Tourism*, rather than necessarily an increase in overall interest in the subject area. However, there is a long history of concern with environmental topics in tourism, which predates the appearance of this particular journal. In contrast, specific concerns with space and spatiality have only received limited attention, perhaps reflecting the relative shift away from positivism. But there has been significant growth since 1998, which might be attributed to the establishment of the journal *Tourism Geographies*. Interestingly, an analytical tool such as Geographical Information Systems (GIS), which is attracting increased attention from social science disciplines other than geography, has had only limited reference within tourism journals, although it has considerable potential for tourism research (see Farsari and Prastacos, chapter 47).

Table 1.3 indicates the impact of several new themes in the tourism studies literature as well as the persistence of more established themes. The idea of sustainability has been a major research theme in tourism studies and was eagerly adopted from the late 1980s as a focal point for journal articles, many of which appeared in the *Journal of Sustainable Tourism*. Perhaps surprisingly, other concepts which have been significant in the broader social sciences, such as postmodernity and globaliza-

Table 1.3 Keyword search of *CABI Leisure, Recreation, and Tourism Abstracts* 1976–2002: social science keywords

Year	Sustainable	History	Heritage	Ancient monuments/ Historic buildings	Destination/ Resort life cycle	Ethnicity/ Ethnic groups	Gay/ Sexuality/ Sexual roles	Post-modernity
1976								
1977		1	2	2				
1978		5	13			1		
1979	1	21	27			1		
1980		20	24			3		
1981		16	12			9		
1982		16	5			14	1	
1983	1	25	6			10		
1984		52	13			24	3	
1985	2	56	11	8		19	3	
1986	1	58	15			8	1	
1987	2	58	28	2		13		
1988	2	59	17	1		18	6	
1989	9	88	40		1	24	11	
1990	18	90	29			41	21	
1991	19	22	32	6		28	22	
1992	33	91	29		3	30	13	
1993	36	83	37	7		38	16	3
1994	62	105	59	8	1	47	19	4
1995	44	104	54	9	1	47	43	2
1996	56	118	81	10		70	28	1
1997	49	109	76	18	3	51	9	5
1998	52	85	69	14	1	74	10	3
1999	93	75	66	5	1	86	8	5
2000	79	104	69	3	1	60	9	4
2001	119	106	89	7	2	37	14	6
2002	83	114	68	4		57	8	6

tion appear to have had less or no impact on tourism studies (see Oakes and Minca, chapter 22), at least in terms of being recorded as key words for journal articles. For example, globalization did not appear as a key word for journal articles in the period examined. This is not to argue that they are not important, indeed there is a significant and substantial body of literature on globalization (e.g. Urry 1990; Cooper and Wahab 2001; Meethan 2001; Page and Hall 2003; Hall 2004b; Ashworth and Tunbridge, chapter 17; Chang and Huang, chapter 18), and postmodernism is also an explicit theme in the contents of many of the articles on heritage. But they have not become central unifying concepts in tourism. Similarly, concerns over sexuality and gay-related issues in tourism, although significant for post-structural "cultural" approaches to tourism (Aitcheson et al. 2000; Crang, chapter 6; Crouch, chapter 7; Debbage and Ioannides, chapter 8), appear as a relatively marginal topic in tourism journals. Ethnic tourism and ethnicity have a higher profile, in part because of interest in cultural tourism, related to the role of heritage as an important object of tourism studies.

Table 1.4 provides an overview of the extent to which some economic concepts and approaches have been the subject of journal articles. As with geography, the economics field has a specialist journal, *Tourism Economics*, with economic analyses also being significant in a number of other journals. Studies of the economic impact of tourism appear to dominate while the significance of the subject of economic evaluation appears to ebb and flow. Nevertheless, in terms of sheer volume, the economic analysis of tourism does not appear any greater than studies of the physical environment within the main tourism journals, although there are considerably more economically oriented studies than those concerned with the cultural turn.

Such studies of keywords in abstracts can only provide a partial picture of the relative significance of particular issues in tourism research. As already noted, much research is published outside the immediate realm of tourism, leisure, and recreation journals, and the analysis presented here also excludes the enormous amount of material published in books, whether they be authored or edited contributions, and presented at conferences. Nevertheless, such snapshots do help illustrate some of the rich diversity of subject matter that exists in tourism and which is also represented in the contributions in this present volume.

As emphasized earlier, this book does not aim to determine whether tourism studies is a discipline or not. Rather, it aims to explore some of the key themes found in the substantial field of research and scholarship on tourism, with an emphasis on research emanating from the broadly defined discipline of geography. The study of tourism now occupies a significant academic space in the same way that tourism as an industry and as a social practice occupies significant economic and sociocultural space. Yet its boundaries are constantly changing and will continue to change in light of internal discourses, engagement with debates across boundaries, and exogenous factors. For good or bad, it is also almost inevitable that, given how academic institutions function in capitalist societies, industry and government agencies (including research funding) will continue to shape the agenda of tourism research, alongside the tradition of critical social and theoretical social

Table 1.4 Keyword search of *CABI Leisure, Recreation, and Tourism Abstracts* 1976–2002: economic-oriented keywords

Year	Economic development	Economic impact	Economics	Economic analysis / evaluation / situation	Economic policy	Economic depression / growth
1976						1
1977	2	2		7		3
1978	11	6	8	12		2
1979	9	5	19	10		
1980	14	3	14	12		
1981	3	8	14	13		2
1982	7	5	13	32		2
1983	6	13	26	28		3
1984	8	8	11	29		6
1985	11	9	19	28	1	4
1986	10	11	28	22		5
1987	4	10	13	27	3	6
1988	10	10	25	44	4	7
1989	24	17	27	38	3	12
1990	32	37	36	31	2	5
1991	29	33	28	21		12
1992	11	31	25	19		11
1993	13	34	26	47	4	17
1994	34	38	29	79	1	30
1995	33	37	32	75	6	19
1996	35	62	37	59	3	17
1997	29	83	42	60	1	12
1998	36	87	43	61	3	4
1999	14	86	29	59	3	8
2000	39	82	54	46	7	11
2001	30	96	39	26	9	18
2002	38	82	20	26	3	11

scientific enquiry. These permeable boundaries, and the space within them, lie at the heart of this work. The present volume is therefore a snapshot of some of the dominant discourses in the social science of tourism: where it has come from, where it is now, and some thoughts on where it might go in the future. The outcome, inevitably, is that the collection of essays in this book illustrates that tourism is a diverse field, in terms of its concerns, theories, and methodologies. But they also demonstrate that it is characterized by substantive debate and continuing innovation, and that it is also increasingly engaged in some of the major debates that characterize social science. The recent increased attention given to mobility (including emergent work on non-mobility) in contemporary social science can only serve to reinforce this.

REFERENCES

Aitcheson, C. (1999). New cultural geographies: The spatiality of leisure, gender and sexuality. *Leisure Studies* 18, 19–39.

Aitcheson, C., Macleod, N. E., and Shaw, S. J. (2000). *Leisure and Tourism Landscapes: Social Constructions of Space and Place*. London: Routledge.

Baum, T., and Lundtrop, S. (eds) (2001). *Seasonality in Tourism*. Oxford: Pergamon.

Bell, M., and Ward, G. (2000). Comparing temporary mobility with permanent migration. *Tourism Geographies* 2(1), 87–107.

Bodewes, T. (1981). Development of advanced tourism studies in Holland. *Annals of Tourism Research* 8, 35–51.

Britton, S. G. (1991). Tourism, capital and place: Towards a critical geography of tourism. *Environment and Planning D: Society and Space* 9, 451–78.

Butler, R. W. (1980). The concept of a tourist area cycle of evolution: Implications for management of resources. *Canadian Geographer* 24(1), 5–12.

Cohen, E. (1992). Pilgrimage and tourism: Convergence and divergence. In A. Morinis (ed.), *Sacred Journeys: The Anthropology of Pilgrimage* (pp. 47–61). Westport, CT: Greenwood Press.

Cooper, C. (2002). Knowledge management and research commercialization agendas. *Current Issues in Tourism* 5(5), 375–7.

Cooper, C., and Wahab, S. (eds) (2001). *Tourism in the Age of Globalization*. London: Routledge.

Crouch, D. (1999a). Introduction: Encounters in leisure / tourism. In D. Crouch (ed.), *Leisure / Tourism Geographies: Practices and Geographical Knowledge* (pp. 1–16). London: Routledge.

Crouch, D. (ed.) (1999b). *Leisure / Tourism Geographies: Practices and Geographical Knowledge*. London: Routledge.

Featherstone, M. (1987). Leisure, symbolic power and the life course. In J. Horne, D. Jary, and A. Tomlinson (eds), *Sport, Leisure and Social Relations* (pp. 113–38). London: Routledge & Kegan Paul.

Flavell, A. (2001). Migration, mobility and globaloney: Metaphors and rhetoric in the sociology of globalization. *Global Networks* 1(4), 389–98.

Frändberg, L. (1998). *Distance Matters: An Inquiry into the Relation between Transport and Environmental Sustainability in Tourism*, Humanekologiska skrifter 15. Göteborg: Department for Interdisciplinary Studies of the Human Condition.

Franklin, A., and Crang, M. (2001). The trouble with tourism and travel theory? *Tourist Studies* 1(1), 5–22.

Giddens, A. (1984). *The Constitution of Society: Outline of the Theory of Structuration*. Berkeley: University of California Press.

Hägerstrand, T. (1984). Escapes from the cage of routines: Observations of human paths, projects and personal scripts. In J. Long and R. Hecock (eds), *Leisure, Tourism and Social Change* (pp. 7–19). Dunfermline: Dunfermline College of Physical Education.

Hall, C. M. (2003). *Introduction to Tourism: Dimensions and Issues*, 4th edn. Melbourne: Pearson Education.

Hall, C. M. (2004a). Space-time accessibility and the tourist area cycle of evolution: The role of geographies of spatial interaction and mobility in contributing to an improved understanding of tourism. In R. Butler (ed.), *The Tourism Area Life-Cycle*. Clevedon: Channel View.

Hall, C. M. (2004b). *Tourism*. Harlow: Prentice-Hall.

Hall, C. M. (2004c). Reflexivity and tourism research: Situating myself and/with others. In J. Phillimore and L. Goodson (eds), *Qualitative Research in Tourism*. London: Routledge.

Hall, C. M., and Page, S. J. (2002). *The Geography of Tourism and Recreation: Space, Place and Environment*, 2nd edn. London: Routledge.

Hall, C. M., and Williams, A. M. (eds) (2002). *Tourism and Migration: New Relationships Between Consumption and Production*. Dordrecht: Kluwer.

Hinch, T., and Jackson, E. L. (2000). Leisure constraints research: Its value as a framework for understanding tourism seasonality. *Current Issues in Tourism* 3(2), 87–106.

Jackson, E. L., Crawford, D. W., and Godbey, G. (1993). Negotiation of leisure constraints. *Leisure Sciences* 15(1), 1–11.

Jackson, E. L. and Scott, D. (1999). Constraints to leisure. In E. L. Jackson and T. L. Burton (eds), *Leisure Studies at the Millennium* (pp. 299–321). State College: Venture Publishing.

Jafari, J., and Ritchie, J. R. B. (1981). Toward a framework for tourism education problems and prospects. *Annals of Tourism Research* 8, 13–34.

Johnston, R. J. (1991) *Geography and Geographers: Anglo-American Human Geography Since 1945*, 4th edn. London: Edward Arnold.

Meethan, K. (2001). *Tourism in Global Society: Place, Culture and Consumption*. London: Palgrave.

Mowforth, M., and Munt, I. (1998). *Tourism and Sustainability: New Tourism in the Third World*. London: Routledge.

Page, S., and Hall, C. M. (2003). *Urban Tourism Management*. Harlow: Prentice-Hall.

Parker, S. (1999). *Leisure in Contemporary Society*. Wallingford: CAB International.

Rojek, C., and Urry, J. (1997). Transformations of travel and theory. In C. Rojek and J. Urry (eds), *Touring Cultures: Transformations of Travel and Theory* (pp. 1–19). London: Routledge.

Ryan, C. (1997). Tourism – a mature subject discipline? *Pacific Tourism Review* 1, 3–5.

Ryan, C. (2001). Academia–industry tourism research links: States of confusion. *Pacific Tourism Review* 5(3/4), 83–96.

Shaw, G., and Williams, A. M. (1994). *Critical Issues in Tourism: A Geographical Perspective*. Oxford: Blackwell.

Shaw, G., and Williams, A. M. (2002). *Critical Issues in Tourism: A Geographical Perspective*, 2nd edn. Oxford: Blackwell.

Smith, S. L. J. (1988). Defining tourism: A supply-side view. *Annals of Tourism Research* 15, 179–90.

Stebbins, R. A. (1979). *Amateurs: On the Margin Between Work and Leisure*. Beverley Hills: Sage Publications.

Stebbins, R. A. (1982). Serious leisure: A conceptual statement. *Pacific Sociological Review* 25, 251–72.

Tribe, J. (1997) The indiscipline of tourism. *Annals of Tourism Research* 24, 638–57.

UN (United Nations) (1994) *Recommendations on Tourism Statistics*. New York: United Nations.

Urry, J. (1990). *The Tourist Gaze: Leisure and Travel in Contemporary Societies*. London: Sage Publications.

Urry, J. (2000). *Sociology Beyond Societies: Mobilities for the Twenty-First Century*. London: Routledge.

Williams, A. M., and Hall, C. M. (2000). Tourism and migration: New relationships between production and consumption. *Tourism Geographies* 2(1), 5–27.

Williams, A. M., and Hall, C. M. (2002). Tourism, migration, circulation and mobility: The contingencies of time and place. In C. M. Hall and A. M. Williams (eds), *Tourism and*

Migration: New Relationships Between Consumption and Production (pp. 1–52), Dordrecht: Kluwer.

Williams, A. M., King, R., Warnes, A., and Patterson, G. (2000). Tourism and international retirement migration: New forms of an old relationship in southern Europe. *Tourism Geographies* 2, 28–49.

Williams, A. M., and Shaw, G. (1988). Tourism and development: Introduction. In A. M. Williams and G. Shaw (eds), *Tourism and Economic Development: Western European Experiences* (pp. 1–11). London: Belhaven Press.

Part II Perspectives on Tourism

Chapter 2

The Measurement of Global Tourism: Old Debates, New Consensus, and Continuing Challenges

Stephen L. J. Smith

Introduction

That tourism is a global phenomenon is not debated. However, the definition and nature of the phenomena collectively known as global tourism are frequently debated and misunderstood. "Global," as a term, is not the major source of confusion. In the context of this chapter, it refers to the fact that visitor flows, tourism advertising, flows of spending by visitors and tourism enterprises, the ownership of tourism enterprises, and the collection and reporting of tourism statistics reach around the world and form a complex web of interconnections and dependencies among tourism businesses and organizations. The confusion stems from the nature of "tourism" itself, which we will explore in this chapter.

Tourism and travel have been part of the human experience for millennia. Chatwin (1988) hypothesizes that travel, in the form of nomadism, was the norm for *Homo sapiens* for much of our species' history. That biological heritage, Chatwin argues, shaped the human psyche to consider travel to be not only normal but even, under the right conditions, pleasurable. Tourism has grown in importance over recorded human history, and it takes a wide variety of forms in response to diverse motivations, including religion, education, pleasure, romance, business, health, social status, escape, self-discovery, and more. The full history of tourism is not the focus of this chapter, but it is useful to note that, despite its long history and that fact that a small number of people have traveled to distant lands for centuries, tourism did not become a truly global phenomenon until the development of commercially viable jet aircraft capable of trans-oceanic flights in the 1950s.

The word, "tourism" has been part of the English lexicon for nearly two centuries and traditionally had a negative connotation. One of the first recorded uses of the word "tourism" is reported by the *Oxford English Dictionary* (*OED* 1971: 3363) as appearing in England's *Sporting Magazine* in 1811. A disparaging article in the magazine on the growing tendency of working-class English families to travel for pleasure referred to "sublime Cockney tourism." "Tourist" has an even older provenance, dating back, at least, to a reference in a 1780 advertisement carrying the phrase, "He throws the piece only into the way of actual tourists" (*OED* 1994). Samuel Pegge, ca. 1800, also provided an early reference to "tourist" in an essay in *Anecdotes of the English Language* where he observed: "A Traveller is now-a-days called a Tour-*ist*" (*OED* 1971: 3363). The context was one of disapproval of the increase in rising trend in working-class pleasure travelers. Even today, some people still tend to make invidious distinctions between their own activities as a "traveler" (which they see as "good") and those of the great mass of "tourists" (which they see as "bad"). An excellent illustration of the modern invidious use of "tourist" can be seen in Boorstin (1962). Despite such cavils against tourism, it is now recognized as a source of substantial economic, environmental, and social consequence and a topic worthy of objective, scientific research. As the title implies, this chapter looks at conceptual and analytical challenges related to understanding tourism as well as to issues of data collection and analysis.

The Conceptual Challenge of Tourism

Why does the measurement of tourism involve such conceptual and analytical difficulties? There are several reasons. The first is the tendency of researchers to propose different definitions to meet their needs or justify their perspective on an issue. Jafari (1992) summarizes these differences as four "platforms." The first is (in Jafari's terminology) the "advocacy" platform, which focuses on tourism's contributions to job creation and economic development. The "cautionary platform" takes an opposing view by pointing out the costs of tourism. The "adaptancy" platform recognizes both benefits and costs of tourism and argues that proper planning and management can ameliorate problems while still achieving benefits of tourism. Finally, the "scientific" platform focuses on the objective understanding of tourism as a phenomenon. Given the diversity of fundamental perspectives on the nature of tourism – intrinsically good, intrinsically bad, a management and planning problem, or a subject for scientific research – a diversity of definitions should not be surprising.

However, tourism poses conceptual and analytical challenges even for those whose goal is only to measure its size. The challenges stem from a core question: is tourism an industry? Before answering this question, it may be useful to explain why it needs to be asked.

The phrase "tourism industry" typically is used in any discussion of the contribution of tourism to a nation's economy. The World Travel and Tourism Council is frequently cited as claiming tourism is "the world's largest industry"; policy-makers, analysts, and scholars often speak of the size of tourism compared to that of other industries. If such comparisons are to be made, they must be made by defining and measuring tourism in a way that is consistent with the conventions and tools used in macro-economics: the International Standard Industrial Classification, the Central Product Classification, and Systems of National Accounts (SNA – the analytical framework used by virtually all nations to collect, order, and analyze macro-economic data on the performance of their economies) (UN Statistics Division 1990). But, again, is tourism an industry and if not, how can it be defined and measured in a way to permit credible measurement?

An industry is a set of businesses defined by their primary product. For example, the auto industry is the set of businesses that manufacture cars; the gaming industry is the set of businesses that offer gambling opportunities. A set of businesses must meet three criteria to be considered an industry:

1 They produce essentially the same product.
2 They use essentially the same technology.
3 The output is large enough to warrant data collection and reporting.

Is there a collection of tourism businesses that meet these criteria? However tourism is defined, most people would include the elements of movement (transportation), of remaining temporarily in one place (such as staying in accommodation), being entertained, and consuming food and drink as aspects of tourism. There is no obvious logic that one can use to meaningfully aggregate these diverse products into a single generic product that would characterize something called the tourism industry.

So, if tourism is not an industry, what is it? Let us turn to a brief examination of the evolution of definitions of tourism and related concepts. Our focus will be on formal international conventions rather than academic debates about the nature of tourism because these conventions represent the cutting edge of work on defining and measuring global tourism as an economic phenomenon in ways that will shape future academic debates.

Towards a definition of tourism

The first global attempt to formally define tourism was in 1937. The Committee of Statistical Experts of the League of Nations (OECD 1973) defined an "international tourist" as anyone visiting a country other than his/her usual residence for more than 24 hours, excluding workers, migrants, commuters, students, and travelers who did not stop while *en route* through a country on their way to a third country. However, little was done with this definition for nearly two decades as a result of the demise of the League of Nations and the outbreak of World War II.

In 1950, the International Union of Official Travel Organizations (IUOTO) revived the 1937 definition and included students on study tours as "tourists." IUOTO also defined two new terms: "international excursionist" (an individual visiting another country for pleasure for less than 24 hours) and "transit travelers" (persons traveling through a country without stopping *en route*). In 1953, the UN Statistical Commission (UNSC) organized a Convention Concerning Customs Facilities for Tourism that further modified the IUOTO definition by setting a maximum stay of six months. The 1963 UN Conference on International Travel and Tourism again drew a distinction between "tourists," who stayed 24 hours or more, and "excursionists" or "day visitors," who stayed less than 24 hours. The combination of tourists and excursionists was called "visitors." Then, in 1968, the Expert Statistical Group of the UNSC endorsed the term "tourist" and suggested dropping "day visitor" in favor of "excursionist" for those staying less than 24 hours. They also recommended classifying "transit travelers" as "excursionists." These recommendations were ratified in 1978 at a conference with representatives of the World Tourism Organization (WTO), the UN Conference on Trade and Development, the Conference of European Statisticians, the East Caribbean Common Market, and the Caribbean community.

The IUOTO definition and its subsequent modifications left undefined a number of terms and did not provide direction for the international harmonization of tourism statistics and concepts. These limitations were addressed by the WTO at an international conference on tourism statistics in Ottawa, 1991. The work of the Ottawa conference was predicated on the observations that:

1 Tourism statistical requirements and users vary substantially.
2 There were wide variations in the levels of national tourism statistical infrastructure development.
3 Some core concepts, including tourism itself, still had alternative interpretations.

Accordingly, the Ottawa conference adopted a set of relatively narrow objectives. These were to reach agreement on key concepts that would: (a) have global applications, (b) be as simple and as clear as possible, (c) be focused on statistical applications, and (d) be as consistent as possible with international standards and conventions in areas such as SNA. The conference was successful in reaching agreement on a number that became the basis for recommendations on defining and measuring international tourism. These recommendations were approved by the UNSC in 1993 (WTO 1994).

Concurrent with this progress, the WTO began searching for a new analytical framework to make the economic measurement of tourism consistent with the statistics used for more conventional industries. They wanted, in particular, to integrate tourism into the SNA. Measuring tourism's contribution to a nation's economy is a particular challenge because, for reasons noted earlier, tourism is not an industry in the SNA.

French national accountants were the first to explore how to analyze aspects of a nation's economy, such as tourism, that are not adequately represented within the SNA. To do this they developed a concept called *comptes satellites* (satellite accounts) (Sebbar 2001). The phrase refers to a subset of national accounts that contains data on an economic activity that is conceptually and technically linked to the SNA, but separate from them.

In 1982, the WTO commissioned a study on the feasibility of Tourism Satellite Accounts (TSAs) and the recommendations were endorsed at its General Assembly in New Delhi (WTO 1983). This document became the foundation for subsequent work by the WTO on TSAs. The Organization for Economic Cooperation and Development (OECD) independently began work on the integration of tourism in SNAs in 1985. Progress on their work roughly paralleled that of the WTO but remained independent. The National Task Force on Tourism Data (1987) also explored the potential of TSAs and recommended the creation of one for Canada. The OECD published its *Manual on Tourism Economic Accounts* in 1991, the same year that Statistics Canada presented a concept paper on TSAs at the Ottawa conference (Lapierre 1991).

The decade following the 1991 Ottawa conference saw a dramatic increase in the volume and pace of work related to tourism definitions and statistical tools. These included approval by the UNSC in 1993 of the Ottawa conference definitions. The

UNSC also accepted the WTO's Standard International Classification of Tourism Activities (a list of tourism-related industries) as a provisional classification system. The Statistical Office of the European Community (Eurostat) developed a number of data-collection and analysis programs based on the 1993 recommendations approved by the UN. Statistics Canada published the results of the first TSA in 1994 (Lapierre and Hayes 1994). The World Travel and Tourism Council (WTTC) began to promote what it called a "simulated travel and tourism satellite account" (Boskin 1996). Smith and Wilton (1997) critiqued the WTTC approach, noting the numerous ways in which it fell short of being a TSA and why that approach exaggerates the size of tourism in an economy.

From 1995 to 1998 Eurostat, the WTO, and the OECD continued exploring the potential of TSAs, and published a number of reports. Guidelines developed by WTO and OECD were presented at the Enzo Paci World Conference on the Measurement of the Economic Impact of Tourism in Nice, France in 1999. At that meeting, the WTO guidelines were endorsed by delegates from 160 nations, but the WTO also was directed to work with the OECD to resolve remaining technical differences. These differences were resolved in the months following the conference and finally, in 2000, the UN Statistics Division approved a joint submission by the WTO, OECD, and Eurostat entitled *Tourism Satellite Account: Recommended Methodological Framework* (OECD Statistical Office of the European Communities, United Nations, and World Tourism Organization 2001).

The balance of this chapter describes the definitions and tools that are considered to be "state of the art" in measuring tourism's role in the global economy as well as some of the areas in which work is still needed.

The State of the Art

The fundamental concept in measuring tourism is, of course, *tourism*:

> Tourism is the set of activities engaged in by persons temporarily away from their usual environment, for a period not more than one year, and for a broad range of leisure, business, religious, health, and personal reasons, excluding the pursuit of remuneration from within the place visited or long-term change of residence. (WTO 1994)

There are several important features of this definition. First, it is demand-side. Tourism is something that people do, not something businesses produce. When measuring the magnitude of tourism as an economic activity, one focuses on expenditures made by visitors in the course of a trip (or on behalf of a visitor, such as contracts with a hotel made by a tour operator in assembling a tour for sale). Certain exceptions to the restriction to expenditures made during a trip are possible. For example, the purchase of consumables made immediately before departure, such as gas for the car, can be tallied as tourism expenditures. Expenditures such as dry cleaning made immediately after the trip and linked to trip activities may also be counted.

Items not to be measured under this definition are as important as those that are. Investments by governments or businesses in infrastructure or the costs of providing tourism services are not tourism expenditures. Thus, the costs of cruise ship construction or employee salaries at a visitor and convention bureau are outside the definition of tourism. Visitors do pay for these activities, but only indirectly. The costs of building and operating tourism facilities are "upstream" costs and represent part of the economic impact of tourism, but they are not part of the output of tourism any more than the cost of fuel is part of the output of the airline industry.

Second, the definition refers to "usual environment." In the context of international travel, this is defined as the crossing of an international border. The actual length of the journey is not relevant. On a conceptual basis, one might debate if "usual environment" could not include both sides of an international boundary. For example, Niagara Falls, Canada, and Niagara Falls, USA, are separated by a bridge a few hundred meters long over the Niagara River. Residents of either city frequently travel to the other to visit friends and to shop, forming a cross-border social action space. The emphasis on national borders as a defining characteristic of international travel is also problematic in the European Union where border-crossing formalities have disappeared for residents of the EU. This is more than just a technical problem; it reflects the conceptual challenge of understanding the meaning of borders in multi-jurisdictional regions and even the nature of what it means to be a nation.

The definition does not specify a minimum length of stay. Same-day trips are tourism trips, as are multi-month tours, as long as they last less than a year. This is somewhat arbitrary but has precedents in issues related to legal matters such as residence for the purposes of income tax liability and entitlement to certain governmental or workplace benefits. In addition to defining tourism, the Ottawa conference reached consensus on the labels used to describe persons involved in tourism as consumers (WTO 1994).

Visitor	Anyone involved in tourism as a consumer
Tourist	A visitor who stays overnight
Same-day visitor	A visitor who does not stay overnight

They also defined a *tourism commodity*: *A tourism commodity is any good or service for which a significant portion of demand comes from persons engaged in tourism as consumers.* (This is sometimes referred to as a "tourism characteristic product.")

Many consumer commodities are purchased by persons engaged in tourism. However, only a small number of commodities account for the bulk of tourism spending. Identifying the portion of demand for a commodity that can be directly attributable to tourism is a substantial hurdle and requires significant data resources for both tourism supply and demand. Consider, for example, the case of meals from food and beverage services in Canada. The estimation of tourism's share of total demand requires examining a number of sources, particularly Statistics Canada's business surveys of restaurants, to obtain an estimate of total revenues, the Canadian Travel Survey and International Travel Survey to obtain estimates of total spending by persons engaged in tourism, and the Family Expenditure Survey that provides data on spending at restaurants both in the home community and on a trip. From these and other sources, Statistics Canada estimated the tourism ratio for meals from food and beverage services at 26 percent (Lapierre and Hayes 1994). A similar process was used for the other commodities identified as candidates for "tourism commodities."

Some "non-tourism commodities" will, in certain locations and at certain times of the year, receive a high percentage of demand from visitors. For example, a bathing suit boutique (which belongs to the "women's apparel industry") in a resort community will see the majority of demand for its products come from visitors. However, TSAs are usually constructed for a national economy, so national averages guide the selection of commodities. The identity of tourism commodities will, however, vary among nations. Crafts, textiles, agricultural products, and fisheries products may receive a significant portion of their demand from visitors in some nations but not in others.

While tourism is not an industry in the conventional sense, one can still speak of "tourism industries." So, *tourism industries* is also a core concept: *A tourism industry is any industry that produces a tourism commodity.* In other words, a tourism industry is one that would greatly diminish in size or even disappear in the absence of tourism.

This definition is not as simple as it might appear. For example, the hotel industry not only produces hotel accommodation, but also provides food and beverage services and possibly guided tours (tourism commodities) as well as dry-cleaning services and telecommunications services (non-tourism commodities). Some department stores (a non-tourism industry) offer restaurant meals, rental cars, and travel agency services (tourism commodities). Some of the challenges in measuring the magnitude of tourism can thus be summed as four dilemmas:

1 Visitors consume both tourism and non-tourism commodities.
2 Non-visitors consume tourism and non-tourism commodities.
3 Tourism industries produce tourism and non-tourism commodities.
4 Non-tourism industries produce tourism and non-tourism commodities.

This is where TSAs come in. TSAs involve looking at the complex patterns of demand of tourism and non-tourism commodities produced by tourism and non-tourism industries and pulling out only those portions that are directly attributable to persons involved in tourism. Accumulating these data, balancing supply and demand (to be sure that production equals consumption), and identifying tourism's share of the complex flow of production and consumption of commodities by tourism and non-tourism industries lays the foundation for the credible and comparable measures of tourism as a component of national economies.

Extensions to TSAs

The development of TSAs is a major step forward in understanding the magnitude of global tourism. However, much remains to be done. TSAs are being extended in numerous ways. Among these extensions are:

Labor market modules. These are designed to measure the number of jobs, both specific positions as well as full-time equivalents (the statistical aggregation of seasonal and part-time work into permanent full-time equivalents). Such measures are being developed for tourism industries as well as all tourism-supported employment (jobs in tourism industries plus jobs in non-tourism industries generated by tourism revenues to those industries).

Consumer durables. Expenditures on consumer durables such as boats or camping equipment require special attention because, while these expenditures are clearly associated with tourism, their purchase is not tied to a specific trip. Efforts are underway in several countries to develop methods for estimating total expenditures made by consumers on such items and for expanding the framework of TSAs to permit reporting these expenditures in a way that does not inflate estimates of trip-specific spending.

Purchases of cottages. Unlike the purchase of boats or camping equipment, which are personal expenditures, investment in real estate is a capital purchase – an investment in productive capacity. SNAs make a clear distinction between consumer purchases and investment in productive capacity, so TSAs also have to make that distinction. However, the use of second homes as a tourism accommodation does provide a service with economic value to the owner; that value is implicit because the owner does not have to pay rent to himself, but it is real. Efforts are underway to develop methods for imputing the rent value of use of private second homes by owners that could be added, as a separate module, to a TSA.

Regional TSAs. TSAs typically are developed for national economies. The concepts and methods of TSAs can, in principle, be applied to sub-national levels if adequate data are available. Regional TSAs can provide a more detailed understanding of regional variations in the magnitude of tourism within a nation – information that has significant planning value.

Challenges

There are a number of practical and conceptual challenges associated with TSAs and related concepts. One of the practical challenges is that TSAs are "data greedy." They require substantial amounts of high-quality data on both supply and demand. Many nations do not yet have adequate statistical infrastructures in place to support TSA development, nor do they have the money and expertise to develop the infrastructure. Even those nations that have a good statistical system do not necessarily have all the data they would like to have. For example, the extensions described above typically require new data sources.

While there is agreement on the conceptual definitions of tourism industry and tourism commodity, work is still required in developing more useful lists of industries and commodities that are meaningful for tourism. The UN's ISIC, Rev. 3.1 is a comprehensive list of industries that form the basis for SNA guidelines. However, these do not necessarily represent industry categories that are optimal for TSAs. For example, ISIC 6010, railway transport, does not distinguish between passenger and freight transportation. As a result, the WTO is working on developing a list of industry codes that is more relevant to tourism, as a subset of ISIC. This list is know as "SICTA" (Standard Industrial Classification of Tourism Activities). Similar work is being done to refine the CPC system that provides a standard system for categorizing all commodities for general SNA purposes to make it more useful for TSAs.

Finally, other international bodies have yet to incorporate the WTO definition of tourism and related concepts into their views of tourism. For example, the World Trade Organization identifies only four "sub-sectors" of commodities it consider to be tourism: "hotels and restaurants" (CPC 641–643), "travel agencies and tour operator services" (CPC 7471), "tourist guide services" (CPC 7472), and a vague, undifferentiated category of "other." Transportation services, recreation services, sport services, and cultural services are excluded from tourism (World Trade Organization 1998). This is an important issue because as international negotiations continue on GATS (General Agreement on Trade in Services), the definition of what is in and what is out of tourism can profoundly affect the global liberalization of tourism services as well as the development of international standards of quality and even the drive to promote sustainable tourism development.

Conclusion

The measurement of the magnitude of global tourism has challenged industry, governments, and analysts for over 50 years. Progress has been made in developing a consensus on definitions and concepts among tourism statisticians. This work led to the creation of Tourism Satellite Accounts (TSAs), a revolution in the measurement of tourism in nation's economies. For the first time, tourism statisticians have a tool for the credible comparison of tourism to other industries and between nations. This work provides scholars with a well-reasoned, coherent, and rigorous set of concepts that allow tourism to be examined in the context of other forms of economic behavior. The ideas presented in this chapter are still unfamiliar to many tourism researchers but they will, as nations reshape their measurement systems to conform to new global agreements on tourism statistics, become a fundamental part of tourism education and research.

The definitions of tourism, tourism commodities, and tourism industries are already beginning to have an impact on how organizations such as the World Trade Organization view tourism and how tourism will be dealt with in trade negotiations. The importance of tourism in the context of trade liberalization under the World Trade Organization can be inferred from the fact that the level of commitments to liberalizing trade in tourism services is far greater than any other sector (114 out of 134 members have made such commitments). In response to this fact, an unpublished communication from the European Communities (2000) to the Council for Trade in Services suggested "the tourism sector... is a strong candidate for full liberalization by all WTO members." A sound definition of the "tourism sector" clearly is essential before such sweeping negotiations can proceed.

The full impact of TSAs on our understanding of global tourism will take years to be realized. Eventually TSAs will not only provide insights into the magnitude of tourism, they will lead to a better understanding of the structure and evolution of global tourism, and the underlying concepts will help pave the way for long-term improvements in liberalizing global tourism. The field of global tourism statistics is at the same point that astronomy was at when Galileo turned his first telescope to the heavens. We do not yet know everything we will learn, but exciting discoveries are waiting for us.

REFERENCES

Boorstin, D. (1962). From traveller to tourist. In D. Boorstin, *The Image* (pp. 77–117). New York: Atheneum.

Boskin, M. J. (1996). National satellite accounting for travel and tourism: A cold review of the WTTC/WEFA Group research. *Tourism Economics* 2, 3–11.

Chatwin, B. (1988). *The Songlines*. London: Pan.

Cohen, E. (1974). Who is a tourist? *Sociological Review* 22, 527–55.

European Communities (2000). Reaction to the communication from the Dominican Republic, El Salvador, and Honduras on the need for an annex on tourism. Unpublished communication, 28 September. Council for Trade in Services document S/CSS/W/5.

Jafari, J. (1977). Editorial. *Annals of Tourism Research* 5, 6–11.

Jafari, J. (1992). The scientification of tourism. In S. A. El-Wahababd and N. El-Roby (eds), *Scientific Tourism* (pp. 43–75). Cairo: Egyptian Society of Scientific Experts on Tourism.

Lapierre, J. (1991). *A Proposal for a Satellite Account and Information System for Tourism*. Discussion paper delivered to the International Conference on Travel and Tourism Statistics. Ottawa: Statistics Canada.

Lapierre, J., and D. Hayes (1994). The tourism satellite account. *National Income and Expenditure Accounts, Quarterly Estimates, Second Quarter, 1994*, pp. xxxiii–lvii.

Leiper, N. (1979) The framework of tourism: Towards a definition of tourism, tourist, and the tourist industry. *Annals of Tourism Research* 6, 390–407.

Leiper, N. (1983). An etymology of "tourism." *Annals of Tourism Research* 10, 277–81.

Leiper, N. (1990). *Tourism Systems: An Interdisciplinary Perspective*. Palmerston North, New Zealand: Department of Management Systems, Massey University.

National Task Force on Tourism Data (1987). *Tourism Satellite Account*. Working Paper 3. Ottawa: Statistics Canada.

National Task Force on Tourism Data (1989). *National Task Force on Tourism Data Final Report*. Ottawa, Canada: Ministry of Supply and Services Canada.

OECD (Organization for Economic Co-operation and Development) (1973). *Tourism Policy and International Tourism in OECD Member Countries*. Paris: OECD Tourism Committee.

OECD, Statistical Office of the European Communities, United Nations, and World Tourism Organization (2001). *Tourism Satellite Account: Recommended Methodological Framework*. Madrid: WTO.

OED (*Oxford English Dictionary*) (1971). Compact edn. New York: Oxford University Press.

OED (1994). On-line edn. <http://www.lib.uwaterloo.ca/cgi-bin/uwonly/weboed1/> (accessed October 15, 2002).

Pearce, D. (1979). Towards a geography of tourism. *Annals of Tourism Research* 6, 245–72.

Sebbar, H. (2001). The tourism satellite account: A new approach or extension to input–output tables. In *Enzo Paci Papers on Measuring the Economic Significance of Tourism*, vol. 1 (pp. 139–53). Madrid: WTO.

Smith, S. L. J. (1988). Defining tourism: A view from the supply side. *Annals of Tourism Research* 15, 179–90.

Smith, S. L. J. (2000). New developments in measuring tourism as an area of economic activity. In W. C. Gartner and D. W. Lime (eds), *Trends in Outdoor Recreation, Leisure, and Tourism* (pp. 225–34). Oxon., UK: CABI Publishing.

Smith, S. L. J., and Wilton, D. (1997). TSAs and the WTTC/WEFA methodology: Different satellites or different planets? *Tourism Economics* 3, 249–64.

UN Statistics Division (1990). *International Standard Industrial Classification of all economic activities (ISIC), Revision 3*. New York: United Nations.

WTO (World Tourism Organization) (1983). Determination of the importance of tourism as an economic activity within the framework of the National Accounting System (Addendum B.5.2.1 to the report of the Secretary-General). Madrid: WTO.

WTO (1994). *Recommendations on Tourism Statistics*. Madrid: WTO.

WTO (1999). *Tourism Satellite Account: The Conceptual Framework*. Madrid: WTO.

WTO (2001). *The Tourism Satellite Accounts as an Ongoing Process: Past, Present, and Future Developments*. Madrid: WTO.

World Trade Organization (1998). *Tourism Services: Background Note by the Secretariat* (Council for Trade in Services). Geneva: World Trade Organization.

Chapter 3

Tourist Flows and the Spatial Distribution of Tourists

Bob McKercher and Alan A. Lew

Introduction

Tourism involves the movement of people through time and space, either between their home and destinations, or within destination areas. Somewhat surprisingly, the study of tourist flows has been the subject of relatively little academic enquiry. Yet understanding tourist movements and the factors that influence the time/space relationships that tourists have with destinations has profound implications for infrastructure and transport development, tourism product development, the commercial viability of the tourism industry, and the management of social, environmental, and cultural impacts of tourism. An understanding of tourist flows, and the spatial patterns of tourist movements between destinations and within a destination, can help tourism policy-makers, transport geographers, and the tourism industry itself provide better services and facilities to cater for the needs of tourists. Further, an understanding of the factors that affect tourist movement, such as distance decay, market access, time availability, and socio-demographic characteristics, can help the industry to determine the optimum location of tourism attractions.

This chapter examines the temporal-spatial relationship that exists between tourism-generating areas and destinations. The first part of the chapter compares a number of itinerary models that have been developed to predict the spatial movement of tourists. The balance of the chapter then identifies a number of intervening factors that exert a moderating effect on tourism movements.

Modeling the Movement of Tourists

Little empirical or conceptual work has been conducted examining and modeling tourism itineraries, in spite of the long understood need to study this phenomenon (Pearce 1989; Dietvorst 1995; Fennell 1996). One of the reasons for this lack of research is that the study of itineraries presents significant practical problems in gathering data (Lew and McKercher 2002). Maps of routes taken and lists of planned destinations and stopovers are the two most commonly used methods, but each has its own weaknesses. Mapping techniques, by necessity, rely on small-scale maps, resulting in loss of fine detail. Listing destinations and stopovers assumes the most direct route is taken between points, when no such assumption can be made. In addition, any researcher who has tried to document itineraries comes to appreciate very quickly how complicated this task is. What on the surface appears to be a relatively simple task of mapping travel from point A to point B, in reality becomes the extremely complicated task of documenting and then attempting to make sense of hundreds or thousands of individual travel routes, some going directly from A to B, some using different routes to make the trip, and others stopping at C, D, or E. Finally, the research tool used complicates sampling issues. Space limitations, arbitrary decisions, and questionnaire wording can all influence the type and quality of information gathered.

Yet in spite of these difficulties a small number of scholars have attempted to model tourist itineraries. The following discussion introduces the reader to the most influential publications.

Mings and McHugh (1992) identified four types of touring routes taken by domestic American tourists who visited Yellowstone National Park. Three of the itinerary models involved automobile travel exclusively, while the fourth involved a combination of air and automobile transport. Respondents who displayed a "direct route" itinerary took the most direct path to and from Yellowstone National Park and followed exactly the same route in both directions. The "partial orbit" itinerary consisted of taking the most direct route to a large destination area, such as the Rocky Mountains, then embarking on a touring loop in the area. The return trip follows the original outward-bound transit route. These types of itineraries are typified by a significant transit journey followed by an extensive tour visiting the key attractions and staying in different destinations in an area some distance from home. By contrast, the "full orbit" tour itinerary involves visiting a number of destinations with no overlap in the tour route. The "fly-drive" itinerary is similar to the partial orbit itinerary except that the mode of transport used to reach the touring area is different. Instead of driving to the regional destination, tourists fly, and then embark on an orbit tour.

Lue, Crompton, and Fesenmaier (1993) focused their research on multi-destination trips. However, in doing so, they recognized that individuals could also embark on single-destination, direct-route trips. Four types of multi-destination itineraries were described. The "en-route" itinerary recognizes that individuals may make a number of short stops on their way to or from a main destination. The travel pattern is similar to that of the direct route itinerary in that the tourist follows the same route to and from the main destination, with possible detours to nearby destinations. The "base camp" model represents a further elaboration of the single-destination model. Conceptually, it resembles a hub and spoke. Tourists base themselves in one main destination and then venture out from that destination in a series of short day tours to nearby attractions and destinations. In the "regional tour," tourists travel to a destination region, but rather than basing themselves in one locale, they stop overnight in a number of places in a sequential pattern before returning home. The "trip-changing" pattern involves a multi-focus touring trip visiting a number of destinations without overlapping any leg of the trip.

Oppermann (1995), focusing on international travel, identified seven possible itinerary types. In addition to the five previously mentioned by Mings and McHugh (1992) and Lue, Crompton, and Fesenmaier (1993), he added two more possible itineraries that are particularly relevant to long-haul air travel. The "open jaw loop" model applies to tourists who enter a country through one gateway and leave through another. In between, they embark on a linear tour connecting the two gateways. For example, a European visiting the United States may arrive in New York, travel overland to San Francisco and then return home from there. The "multiple-destination areas loop" itinerary model is the most complex. This type of itinerary recognizes that some long-haul tourists will visit many countries or regions within large countries and tour extensively through these different destinations. The person may engage in different travel patterns at any given stop. Thus, Oppermann recognizes that within an extended trip, a person could participate in any or all of he "single-destination stopover," "base camp tours," "full tours," or "open jaw tours" at different destinations.

Flognfeldt (1999), building on ideas first developed by Campbell (1966, as cited by Flognfeldt), identified four modes of recreation and vacation travel. The "resort trip" (direct travel, single destination), "base holiday," and "round trip" are similar to other itinerary models discussed previously. In addition, he identifies "recreational day trips" from the individual's home community as a fourth travel type. While technically not a tourism trip because no overnight stay is involved, day trips must certainly be considered when examining the full of range of touring options.

Finally, *Lew and McKercher* (2002) examined itineraries from the perspective of the destination. Their research showed that a destination could serve up to five roles simultaneously depending on tourism volume. It could be seen as a single, main destination by some tourists. It could be the gateway destination, or the access point for an extended touring trip. It could be the egress point or the point of embarkation back to the individual's home at the end of the trip. It may also function as a touring, or stopover destination between main destinations. Finally, it could serve as a hub destination for day trips into the hinterland, or as an air hub for more extensive overnight trips to other destinations.

Commonalties and Key Features of Proposed Itinerary Models

A total of 26 different itinerary types are identified in the papers reviewed. Yet, on closer inspection, the distinction between some of the different models appears rather forced and arbitrary. Mode of transport, distance, and domestic versus international travel are used to delineate different models, when the overall patterns described are largely similar. Indeed, as figure 3.1 illustrates, the 26 models proposed can be classified into four broad themes. The simplest itinerary type involves a single-destination, there-and-back trip that may or may not include side trips to other places along the way. A second type of itinerary involves a transit leg to the destination area, followed by a circle tour within the destination, stopping overnight at different places. A third type involves a circle tour with or without multiple access and egress points. Lastly, hub-and-spoke itineraries may be evident where tourists base themselves in a destination area and take side trips to other destinations.

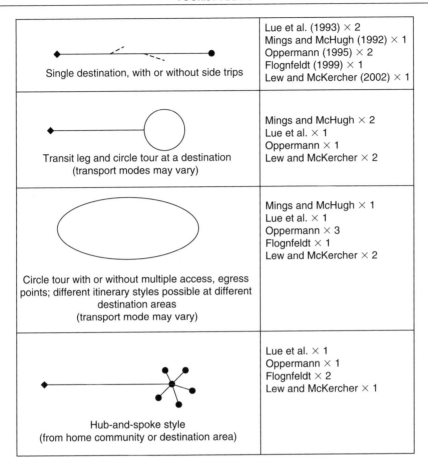

 Single destination, with or without side trips	Lue et al. (1993) × 2 Mings and McHugh (1992) × 1 Oppermann (1995) × 2 Flognfeldt (1999) × 1 Lew and McKercher (2002) × 1
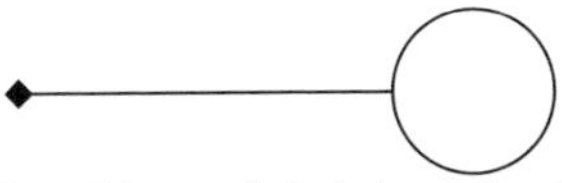 Transit leg and circle tour at a destination (transport modes may vary)	Mings and McHugh × 2 Lue et al. × 1 Oppermann × 1 Lew and McKercher × 2
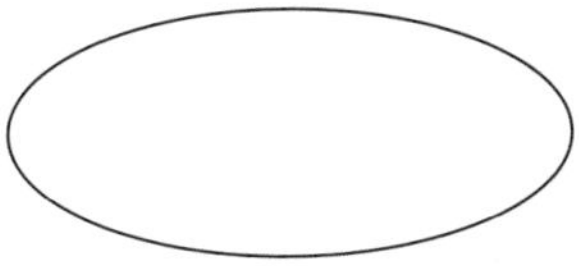 Circle tour with or without multiple access, egress points; different itinerary styles possible at different destination areas (transport mode may vary)	Mings and McHugh × 1 Lue et al. × 1 Oppermann × 3 Flognfeldt × 1 Lew and McKercher × 2
 Hub-and-spoke style (from home community or destination area)	Lue et al. × 1 Oppermann × 1 Flognfeldt × 2 Lew and McKercher × 1

Figure 3.1 Itinerary types

Indeed, any examination of the movement of tourists involves two elements: a transit component and a destination touring component. The different types are shown in figure 3.2. The various tour combinations identified result from different mixing and matching of transit and touring elements. An outbound and inbound transit leg following the same route is implied in the single-destination, base camp, stopover/en-route and the regional tour/partial orbit or destination area loop models. Multiple transit legs are needed for the various loop tours identified. In rare instances, tourists may embark on a single transit leg and then have an extended return tour home. (An example is a bicycle tourist who rides from his/her home to a destination and then takes a train or plane to return home.)

The same or different modes of transport may be used for the transit and touring elements depending on the individual's budget, time availability, and the location of the destination area. Some tourists may choose to drive to the destination, while others may choose to take various forms of public transport. Multiple transport modes are also possible for the transit legs of a journey. Tourists may fly to a destination, hire a car for a touring trip, and return home by train or ship. The

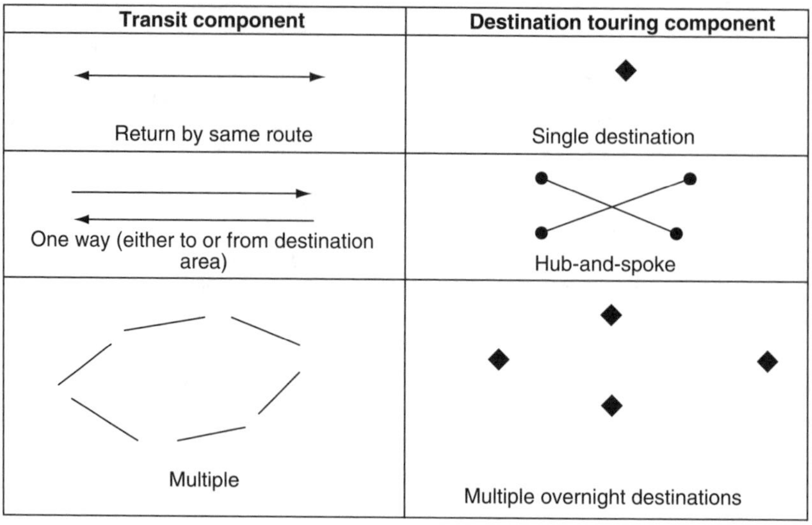

Figure 3.2 Different transit and destination touring components of itineraries

only impact mode of transport has is on the ability of intervening destinations to capture a share of through traffic.

Intervening factors

The spatial distribution of tourists, either on a macro scale across destinations, or on a micro scale within a destination, is influenced by an number of factors, including distance decay, market access, time and budget availability, trip characteristics, and sociocultural or demographic characteristics. Understanding the moderating effect each has on tourism helps explain tourism flows further.

Distance decay

Distance decay plays such an important role in understanding spatial interactions that it has been identified as one of the key laws of geography (Eldridge and Jones 1991). The concept suggests that demand for activities varies inversely with the distance traveled or with increased time, money, or effort (Bull 1991). Distance decay is predicated on the assumption that most people are rational consumers who will seek the more proximate option between two similar experiences, unless there is some compelling reason to travel further. Thus, as figure 3.3 shows, tourism demand should decline exponentially as distance increases. Most distance decay models suggest that demand decays immediately, but tourism models recognize that people must travel a minimum distance before they feel sufficiently removed from their home environment to make a journey worthwhile (Greer and Wall 1979). As such, demand peaks some relatively short distance from home, before beginning to decline.

Distance decay has been the subject of academic inquiry by geographers since at least the late 1960s (Beaman 1974) and has been used to examine behavior in such activities as crime (Rengert, Piquero, and Jones 1999), retail shopping, and com-

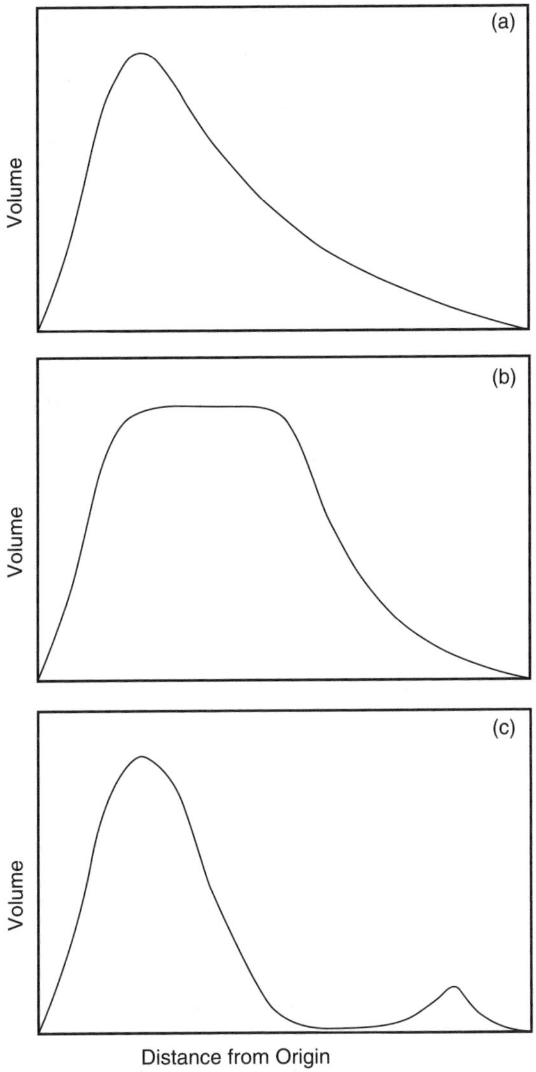

Figure 3.3 Variations in distance decay
Source: Based on McKercher and Lew 2004.

muting (Beaman 1974; Truong and Hensher 1985; Drezner and Drezner 1996). It has also been applied widely in recreation research (Baxter 1979; Greer and Wall 1979; Hanson 1980; Paul and Rimmawi 1992; McKean, Johnson and Walsh 1995; Hanink and White 1999; Zhang et al. 1999).

It was popular in tourism research in the 1960s and early 1970s, when it was used as a proxy to forecast demand. However, as more sophisticated demand-modeling techniques were developed, distance decay fell into disuse. Today, distance decay is largely forgotten in the tourism literature, with few academics examining its effect on tourist flows (McKercher 1998a). However, it should receive more attention than it does, for the underlying assumption of decaying demand over time still holds true. Empirical studies indicate that both domestic and international tourist flows exhibit a frictional effect over time and space. Understanding rates of decay can provide insights into the types of tourism products and services that certain markets will desire.

The shape of the standard curve is based on a flawed assumption that the supply of tourism opportunities is distributed uniformly over space, resulting in the absolute quantum of opportunities increasing geometrically with distance. In reality, tourism opportunities are not distributed evenly, nor does the supply of appealing destinations for international tourists necessarily increase geometrically. Thus the supply curve would never be smooth and upward-sloping for all cases. Instead, it would be distorted by areas having more or fewer attractions/products, which in turn would lead to distortions in identified demand.

As a result, empirical studies rarely support the standard distance decay curve portrayed in figure 3.3a. Instead, actual decay rates are more likely to reflect those presented in figures 3.3b and 3.3c. Figure 3.3b shows that demand can plateau for some distance before declining, as a result of a finite number of destination options and accommodation supply along a linear touring route (McKercher 1998a). Figure 3.3c shows a decay curve with a tail on the end. This pattern is produced by two interacting factors. First, some distant destinations may have such drawing power that their appeal can overcome normal expected rates of decay, producing secondary peaks at extreme distances (Baxter 1974; Fotheringham 1981; Hanink and White 1999). Second, the supply of potential tourism destinations is not equal over space. The presence and proximity of Effective Tourism Exclusions Zones (ETEZ), areas where little or no tourism activity occurs, can accentuate the peak and accelerate the rate of decay leading up to the ETEZ, while at the same time producing strong secondary peaks after the exclusion zone has been crossed (McKercher and Lew 2004).

Distance decay affects tourist behavior. Clearly, as one would expect, total time availability exerts a significant impact on destination choice – the more time one has, the further one is likely to travel, or the more intervening destinations one is likely to visit (McKercher 1998b; Walsh, Sanders and McKean 1990; Paul and Rimmawi 1992). Likewise, a relationship exists between distance, time, and the percent of the total trip spent at the main destination. Up to a certain distance threshold, virtually all of the trip except transit time is spent at the main destination. Beyond that threshold, a greater proportion of the trip is devoted to touring and a subsequently lower percent is spent at the main destination. The threshold point varies with mode of transport used.

Destination choice, travel party type, and distance also seem to be linked (McKercher 1998b). The presence of young children will accelerate the rate of decay. Families with young children show a strong preference for short trips, regardless of the travel time available. Families with older children and people with longer time budgets, on the other hand, show the greatest propensity to travel long distances and to engage in touring vacations. Couples with no children on limited time budgets prefer proximate destinations, but show a greater tendency for multi-destination touring trips when on higher time budgets.

Market access

Market access is a concept that builds on the idea of distance decay. It argues that the number of intervening destinations offering similar experiences has a greater effect on demand than absolute distance alone. In theory, proximate destinations should have a competitive advantage over less proximate ones (Pearce 1989). The main difference between market access and distance decay is that distance decay adopts a consumer orientation (How far do I want to travel?) while market access adopts a destination orientation (How many similar destinations must the prospective visitor pass before reaching this one?). The key element of market access, therefore, is the need to compare the destinations offering similar experiences. For example, residents of the subtropical city of Brisbane, Australia, have the choice of literally dozens of beaches within a 150 km radius of the city, but must travel more than 2,000 km to access Australia's nearest downhill ski resort, Falls Creek. As a result, a beach located 100 km away may be deemed to have poor market access, while a ski resort located 2,000 km away might enjoy strong market access.

Again, destination choice is felt to be influenced by convenience and that, given a choice between similar destinations, the tourist will tend to choose the more convenient one. Market access can be measured by the relative difference in the time, cost, distance, or effort involved in accessing different destinations (Pearce 1989). At a functional level, it can be measured by the number of destinations a visitor must pass before arriving at the main destination of the trip. Few studies have examined this issue explicitly.

Market access has a profound effect on destination choice, both in terms of its influence on visitor flows and in terms of influencing the market mix of competing destinations. In theory, destinations with strong market access should enjoy two significant competitive advantages over similar destinations with poorer market access. On the one hand, they are attractive to people who want to minimize travel time and maximize time spent at a destination. In addition, destinations with strong market access have the potential to capture a share of the passing traffic of people heading to more distant destinations, creating secondary destination opportunities.

While the theory suggests that market access influences destination competitiveness, the only empirical study conducted on this issue (McKercher 1998b) suggests this is not necessarily the case. Instead, market access exerts an influence on the type of visitor attracted to different destinations. Areas with strong market access did not necessarily attract more visitors or more visitor nights. But, they did attract short-break vacationers, through travelers, and international tourists seeking a short escape from gateway cities. Destinations with poor market access tend to attract repeat visitors and those who stay for long periods. Families traveling with children seek places with strong market access for short-break vacations. On the other hand, families who have more time to travel seek destinations with poor market access. Couples with no children choose to vacation at destinations with modest market access, bypassing the most proximate destinations.

Time

Ultimately, it can be argued that all tourist flows are influenced by the time budget available to tourists and how they choose to spend that time. Indeed, time has a profound effect on the spatial movement of tourists to and through destinations (Chavas, Stoll, and Sellar, 1989; Walsh, Sanders, and McKean 1990; McKean, Johnson, and Walsh 1995). Time exerts both an absolute and a relative impact on tourist behavior. It is the only absolute most tourists must deal with. Vacation time budgets are usually fixed, with limited scope to expand time availability. A family must fit the entire trip from departure to return within the allotted number of days to ensure that the parents can return to work or children return to school by a specified date. Most business travel is similarly constrained, either by predetermined flight schedules or the pressing need to return to the office to do other business. Indeed, few tourists have much flexibility in their total time budgets. The exceptions are backpackers or retired people for whom trip duration is influenced more by financial means than time.

How they spend their time, however, is not fixed. Some will choose to allocate a greater percentage to transit by trading off time spent at the final destination. Others will choose to maximize the time spent at a destination by minimizing travel time. Transport mode choice and affordability can result in more or less use of travel time. Similarly, different tourists will spend their time budgets differently within destinations. Again, some people will choose to do and see as much as possible, while others will do fewer things, but spend more time doing them.

Indeed, time can be perceived differently by different types of tourists. One school of thought argues that time has a resource value. This line of thinking argues that travel time (unlike travel cost) cannot be saved in the sense of being stored and accumulated for future use. It can only be transferred from one activity to another. It represents an opportunity cost that must be traded off, usually for a shorter stay at a destination (Truong and Henscher 1985). An alternative school of thought argues that travel time has a positive commodity value if the act of traveling itself is viewed positively (Chavas, Stoll, and Sellar, 1989; Walsh, Sanders, and McKean 1990).

McKean, Johnson, and Walsh (1995) postulate that time rationing rather than time pricing may be the most important factor in the travel cost equation. Thus a positive commodity value associated with the act of traveling, or simply greater time availability (and the subsequent need to ration time less stringently), may explain why tourists on longer motoring trips spend relatively more time touring and relatively less time at the destination. Travelers with limited time, or who enjoy the act of traveling less, will tend to transit directly to the destination.

Trip characteristics

Trip characteristics, such as length of stay, whether it is the person's first visit to a destination, and whether the destination is the main destination or a stopover destination will also have an effect on tourist behavior. Oppermann (1997a), for example, studied the impact of the length of stay on the spatial distribution of tourists in New Zealand. He found a strong correlation between trip duration and destination choice. An increased trip duration meant that people could visit more places, instead of spending more time at any one place. He also found that there was a hierarchy of destinations, and that the longer people traveled the more likely they were to visit lower-order destinations.

Others (Fakeye and Crompton 1991; Oppermann 1997b) found substantial differences between how first-time and repeat visitors perceive and consume destinations. First-time visitors are interested in exploring widely throughout a destination and have a strong desire to discover an area's cultural and natural amenities. Repeat visitors, on the other hand, are more interested in social experiences, entertainment, shopping, and dining. As a result, first-time visitors tend to be much more active tourists than repeat visitors, participating in more activities and visiting more places. They are also more likely to visit primary built attractions than repeat visitors.

Similarly, people identifying an area as the main destination demonstrate quite different tourist behavior than those seeing it as a secondary or stopover destination (McKercher 2001). In part, this is to be expected since main-destination visitors stay longer than through travelers. However, length of stay only explains part of the difference noted. Main-destination visitors are much more likely to use the destination as a base for exploratory trips into hinterland areas and are also more likely to seek secondary or tertiary attractions. Convenience dictates the behavior of through travelers. Apart from seeing icon attractions, few through travelers are willing to stray from transport corridors or tourism nodes.

Finally, trip purpose may also have an effect on the spatial distribution of tourists. Pleasure travelers are far more likely to explore a destination than business travelers. VFR travelers, by virtue of visiting residents of the destination, demonstrate different spatial patterns and other tourists. They tend to do less, while spending more time with family. When they travel, they may go to areas not predominantly identified as tourism nodes. However, it is not possible to assume all pleasure travelers display similar behavior, for tourists will demonstrate different behaviors depending on their reasons for visiting (Fennell 1996). Special-interest tourists will tend to confine their actions to activities that relate to the specialized reason for visiting, while the generalist sightseeing tourist will tend to travel more widely with no clearly evident pattern.

Sociocultural differences

Finally, a growing body of knowledge recognizes that tourist behavior is influenced by the sociocultural background of tourists. Yan (2004), studying tourist flows in China, for example, found that spatial patterns of international tourists are influenced, in part, by cross-cultural differences, geographic origin, nationality, and cultural background. Likewise, tourists from cultures generally seen as being more extroverted are likely to display more adventuresome behavior than those traveling from more introverted countries (Pizam and Sussmann 1995). Cultural distance may also affect behavior, with tourists from culturally proximate source markets seeing different attractions and traveling to different areas within a destination than those from culturally distance source markets (Lew 1987; Flognfeldt 1999; McKercher and Chow 2001).

Conclusions

An intricate relationship exists among time, space, and tourism movements. Over the years, a variety of models have been developed to portray the movement of tourists from their homes to destination areas or between destination areas. These models recognize that tourism movement involves two components: a destination component and a transit component, which may or may not be integrated into the destination component. The movement of tourists is moderated by a number of factors, including the frictional effect of distance on demand, the number of intervening opportunities available, tourists' total time budget and how they choose to spend that time, trip variables, and the sociocultural make-up of the tourist.

Yet, in spite of the fact that the spatial movement of tourists affects tourism development, policy, and transport planning, this subject has received relatively little attention in the tourism literature. Practical methodological and operationalization challenges explain some of the lack of inquisitiveness, but the study of tourism flows also seems to have fallen out of favor over the past 20 years. Perhaps the emergence of GIS and other more sophisticated transport modeling software packages can help address the methodological issues. Perhaps, too, a renewed interest in this topic by geographers can help address the latter issue.

The discipline of geography has played a central role in the evolution of tourism as a field of study. The desire to understand the spatial interactions of tourists with a destination and the movement of tourists between destinations has played a critical role in developing investigation of the phenomenon of tourism. The geography of tourism seems to have become relatively less important over the last 20 years as other disciplines have discovered tourism; yet an appreciation of spatial relationships forms one of the foundations of tourism on which any study, regardless of discipline, is based. Many exciting research opportunities exist to build on the existing knowledge base or to reexamine other tourism concepts from a temporal/spatial perspective.

REFERENCES

Baxter, M. J. (1979). The interpretation of the distance and attractiveness components in models of recreational trips. *Geographical Analysis* 11(3), 311–15.

Beaman, J. (1974). Distance and the reaction to distance as a function of distance. *Journal of Leisure Research* 6 (Summer), 220–31.

Bull, A. (1991). *The Economics of Travel and Tourism*. Melbourne: Pitman.

Chavas, J. P., Stoll, J., and Sellar, C. (1989). On the commodity value of travel time in recreational activities. *Applied Economics* 21, 711–22.

Dietvorst, Adri G. J. (1995). Tourist behavior and the importance of time-space analysis. In G. J. Ashworth and A. G. J. Dietvorst (eds), *Tourism and Spatial Transformations: Implications for Policy and Planning* (pp. 163–81). Wallingford: CAB International.

Drezner, T., and Drezner, Z. (1996). Competitive facilities: Market share and location with random utility. *Journal of Regional Science* 36(1), 1–15.

Eldridge, D., and Jones, J. P. (1991). Warped space: A geography of distance decay. *Professional Geographer* 43(4), 500–11.

Fakeye, P. C., and Crompton, L. (1991). Image differences between prospective, first-time, and repeat visitors to the lower Rio Grande Valley. *Journal of Travel Research* 30(2), 10–16.

Fennell, D. (1996). A tourist space-time budget in the Shetland Islands. *Annals of Tourism Research* 23(4), 811–29.

Flognfeldt, T. (1999). Traveler geographic origin and market segmentation: The multi trips destination case. *Journal of Travel and Tourism Marketing* 8(1), 111.

Fotheringham, A. S. (1981). Spatial structure and distance decay parameters. *Annals of the American Association of Geographers* 71(3), 425–36.

Greer, T., and Wall, G. (1979). Recreational hinterlands: A theoretical and empirical analysis. In G. Wall (ed.), *Recreational Land Use on Southern Ontario* (pp. 227–46). Department of Geography Publication series 14. Waterloo, Canada: Waterloo University.

Hanink, D. M., and White, K. (1999). Distance effects in the demand for wildland recreational services: The case of national parks in the United States. *Environmental and Planning Annals* 31, 477–92.

Hanson, S. (1980). Spatial diversification and multipurpose travel: Implications for choice theory. *Geographical Analysis* 12(3), 245–57.

Lew, A. A. (1987). The English-speaking tourist and the attractions of Singapore. *Journal of Tropical Geography* 8(1), 44–59.

Lew, A. A., and McKercher, B. (2002). Trip destinations, gateways and itineraries: The example of Hong Kong. *Tourism Management* 23(6), 609–21.

Lue, C. C., Crompton, J. L., and Fesenmaier, D. R. (1993). Conceptualization of multi-destination pleasure trips. *Annals of Tourism Research* 20, 289–301.

McKean, J., Johnson, D., and Walsh, R. (1995). Valuing time in travel cost demand analysis: An empirical investigation. *Land Economics* 71(1), 96–105.

McKercher, B. (1998a). The effect of market access on destination choice. *Journal of Travel Research* 37 (August), 39–47.

McKercher, B. (1998b). The effect of distance decay on visitor mix at coastal destinations. *Pacific Tourism Review* 2(3/4), 215–24.

McKercher, B. (2001). A comparison of main destination and through travelers at a dual purpose destination. *Journal of Travel Research* 39 (May), 433–41.

McKercher, B., and Chow, B. (2001). Cultural distance and cultural tourism participation. *Pacific Tourism Review* 5(1/2), 21–30.

McKercher, B., and Lew, A. A. (2004). Distance decay and the impact of "effective tourism exclusion zones" on international travel flows. *Journal of Travel Research*.

McKercher, B., Lew, A., and Hui, L. L. (2004). Distance decay in international air travel. *Journal of Travel Research*.

Mings, R. C., and McHugh, K. E. (1992). The spatial configuration of travel to Yellowstone National Park. *Journal of Travel Research* 30 (Spring), 38–46.

Oppermann, M. (1995). A model of travel itineraries. *Journal of Travel Research* 33(4), 57–61.

Oppermann, M. (1997a). Length of stay and travel patterns. In R. Bushell (ed.), *Tourism Research: Building a Better Industry* (pp. 471–80). Canberra: CAUTHE, BTR.

Oppermann, M. (1997b). First-time and repeat visitors to New Zealand. *Tourism Management* 18(3), 177–81.

Paul, B. K., and Rimmawi, H. S. (1992). Tourism in Saudi Arabia: Asir National Park. *Annals of Tourism Research* 19, 501–15.

Pearce, D. (1989). *Tourist Development*, 2nd edn. Harlow: Longman.

Pizam, A., and Sussmann, S. (1995). Does nationality affect tourist behavior? *Annals of Tourism Research* 22(4), 901–17.

Rengert, G. F., Piquero, A. R., and Jones, P. R. (1999). Distance decay re-examined. *Criminology* 37(2), 427–45.

Truong, T., and Hensher, D. (1985). Measurement of travel time values and opportunity cost model from a discrete-choice model. *The Economic Journal* 95 (June), 438–51.

Walsh, R., Sanders, L., and McKean, J. (1990). The consumptive value of travel time. *Journal of Travel Research* Summer, 17–24.

Yan, L. J. (2004). A cross-cultural study of international tourist flows in China's tourism regions. *Tourism Geographies.*

Zhang, J., Wall, G., Du, J. K., Gan, M. Y., and Nie, X. (1999). The travel patterns and travel distance of tourists to national parks in China. *Asia Pacific Journal of Tourism Research* 4(2), 27–34.

Chapter 4

Behavioral Approaches in Tourism Research

D. Jim Walmsley

Introduction

Tourism is in many ways an activity that is emblematic of the twenty-first century. It is also something that involves millions of people worldwide, creating major employment opportunities and having significant impacts, both positive and negative. It is important therefore that the behavior of tourists be understood. Herein lies a challenge. On the face of it, "behavior" seems an unproblematic term. In fact, intuitively, a term like "the behavior of tourists" appears to have an obvious meaning. Reality is more complex and there exist many different ways in which behavior can be studied. The field of tourism research therefore faces an intellectual challenge in teasing out the different behavioral approaches that can be adopted. This chapter looks at how this intellectual challenge can be met before examining two topics that are the focus of contemporary behavioral research in tourism studies and illustrative of the intellectual challenge.

The Intellectual Challenge

Behavior has to be conceptualized in order that it can be studied. This intellectual challenge is best met in a series of binary distinctions. One of the most obvious ways of looking at behavior distinguishes *obligatory* from *discretionary* activity. The former represents things that an individual is obliged to do (e.g. eating, sleeping, working), whereas the latter covers activities that can be indulged in at the discretion of the individual concerned (e.g. leisure, recreation). In reality, this first binary distinction is simplistic. For example, there is a degree of discretion involved in obligatory behavior, as when individuals choose how much to eat, sleep, or work. Conversely, it may be that individuals are obliged to undertake some leisure-time activities if they are to maintain acceptable levels of well-being and life satisfaction. Despite this blurring of the distinction between "obligatory" and "discretionary," it is true to say that tourism is at the discretionary end of the obligatory–discretionary spectrum. In other words, there is a major element of voluntarism in much tourist behavior. The corollary to this is that tourist behavior is likely to be diverse in character because it reflects the whims and choices of the individuals involved. This presents a challenge in terms of capturing the variety of experience while at the same time seeing the general in the particular (Ryan 1997).

A second binary distinction is helpful in understanding how the challenge of describing both the particular and the general can be met. This distinction is between studying *behavior in space* and analyzing *spatial behavior* (Walmsley and Lewis 1994). This might seem like a play on words but the distinction is an important one. An emphasis on "behavior in space" involves description of the context in which the behavior in question occurs and the relating of behavior to that specific context. In simple terms, researchers putting the emphasis on "behavior in space" tend to answer the question "who does what where?", sometimes adding the questions "when, why and with what effect?" Such studies tend to be very descriptive. Examples are to be seen in descriptive accounts of who uses which tourist facilities in a particular holiday area. In contrast, advocates of the study of "spatial behavior" focus on trying to find the general in the particular in the sense of distilling the rules, principles, and laws that describe behavior independently of the context in which it occurs. In other words, with "spatial behavior," the search is for general principles of people–environment interaction and for understanding of how humans as a whole behave in certain types of settings (e.g. shopping centers, theme parks) rather than with particular contexts (e.g. Oxford Street, London; Disneyland). Examples are to be seen in studies of the way in which the likelihood of an individual visiting a specific tourist attraction diminishes the further the individual is from the attraction, a phenomenon that results from the so-called "friction of distance." Because studies of "behavior in space" are heavily descriptive, they tend to be non-cumulative in the sense that they do not add to understanding of tourist behavior in general. They are in fact often market research exercises that are geared to the promotion of particular enterprises. Therefore, what is learned about behavior in one context can rarely be extrapolated to different contexts. There are no such problems with the study of "spatial behavior" because the emphasis is on discovering that which is general to a number of contexts. Because of its applicability beyond the particular, the study of spatial behavior is where most emphasis has been placed in human geography and in social science generally. Of course, this is not to say that extrapolation knows no bounds. Culture is obviously critical and seeing the general in the particular is usually limited to extrapolations within one culture or at least between very similar cultures. Thus there exist different levels of generality. Some forms of behavior might be characteristic of humans as a species. More commonly, behavior is influenced by culture, and generalization is only possible within the bounds of a given cultural context.

Notwithstanding the attractiveness of studying "spatial behavior," a third binary distinction needs to be made in order to give full understanding of the range of behavioral approaches that are available within studies of "spatial behavior." This distinction is between approaches that focus on *behavior in the aggregate* and approaches that focus on *the behavior of individual tourists*. With studies of behavior in the aggregate, the goal is to identify regularities in overall patterns. Thus, it is recognized that not all people will behave in an identical manner but it is felt that individual differences in behavior can be thought of as more or less random variations around an average form of behavior. There is in fact a whole family of "spatial interaction models" that describe such average behavior, perhaps best exemplified by so-called gravity models which describe how the amount of interaction between two places increases with the size of the places but decreases the further apart the places are.

The underlying principle in the study of aggregate behavior is that there are behavioral characteristics that are observable irrespective of the individuals under study. Advocates of this approach argue that spatial behavior is so complex as to be extremely difficult to study at the individual level. According to this view, studies of individual behavior are inefficient and time-consuming because what is important can be seen in aggregate patterns. This is a contentious view. Critics of this approach take a different line. According to them, studies of aggregate behavior have little predictive power because no causal links are established between the environment and human actions. Therefore, it is unclear whether a change in contextual conditions would lead to a change in behavioral outcomes. For example, a new facility, or a different advertising strategy for an existing facility, might well produce a different pattern of aggregate behavior. Moreover, the approach ignores things like cognition and values which are undoubtedly important in human affairs but which cannot be measured at an aggregate scale. To give a specific example, the level of patronage of a tourist attraction might reflect almost subconscious cultural bonds such as the iconic status of national landmarks like Buckingham Palace and the White House. According to many researchers, what seems to be needed in order to remedy these shortcomings in aggregate-scale study is an approach which is focused on the individual and which recognizes that individuals have a modicum of free will and a degree of latitude in interpreting and ascribing meaning to the environment. In other words, researchers need to recognize that humans are reflexive actors who reflect upon, and think about, their behavior. At the same time, the approach should take stock of the fact that much human behavior is constrained and that behavioral outcomes are the product of both reflexive human agency and the structures within which humans operate. Studies of spatial behavior at the individual level attempt to do just this. Primacy is afforded to decision-making units (usually individuals but sometimes larger units such as families) and consideration is given to acted-out or measurable behavior as well as to what goes on in the mind of the individual, all within the context of constraints of one sort or another.

These approaches are sometimes known as micro-scale behavioral approaches or, more commonly, actor-oriented approaches. In essence, micro-scale behavioral approaches have their origins in models of micro-economic behavior which assume that individuals are rational economic actors. Such an approach is normative in intent in that it specifies what will happen, in terms of behavioral outcomes, in any given situation. This is possible because individuals are hypothesized to be omniscient, fully rational actors who seek to maximize economic gain. Such a view is of course overly deterministic because it allows for only one logical behavioral outcome (the one with the highest economic value) in a given situation. It is also unrealistic because humans are complex beings who are motivated by much more than economic gain. Some attempts to model behavior from an actor-oriented perspective seek to remedy this situation by hypothesizing "bounded rationality" (the fact that individuals do not know everything) and "satisficing" (the fact that individuals settle for satisfactory rather than optimal solutions when confronted with the need to make decisions about what to do and where to go) (Simon 1957; Um and Compton 1999). It is, however, more common to recognize that a variety of antecedent conditions (attitudes, preferences, values, beliefs, perception, cognition) influence behavior (see Ross 1998). The rationale behind this view is simple: "if we can understand *how* human minds process information from external environments and if we can determine *what* they process and use, then we can investigate how and why choices concerning those environments are made" (Golledge and Rushton 1976: viii). In short, the emphasis in actor-oriented behavioral approaches is usually on how information is filtered from the environment as a result of personality, cultural forces, and cognitive factors and how that information is used to arrive at decisions about what facilities to patronize. There are many different models of decision-making, some of them mathematical in nature (Golledge and Stimson 1997; Pizam and Mansfield 1999).

The underlying philosophy behind actor-oriented behavioral approaches is transactional constructivism (Moore and Golledge 1976). According to this, individuals construct their own notion of "reality" in their minds while they are engaged in interaction with the environment. As a result, behavior can only be understood if due attention is paid to the way in which people experience the environment. Underpinning the approach, in other words, is a non-normative stance that emphasizes the world as it is rather than as it should be under certain theoretical assumptions (like perfect knowledge). In this respect, behavioral approaches that focus on individual spatial behavior reject the idea of sovereign decision-makers. Rather, there is awareness of the way in which decision-making is constrained, often significantly so (Hudson and Gilbert 2000). According to Desbarats (1983), constraints can be conceptualized as involving a progressive reduction in the number of options open to individual decision-making units: extrapolating to the field of tourism research, institutional and accessibility constraints on the supply of facilities (deriving from the way in which the tourism industry is organized and located) produce an *objective choice set* from which individual tourists have to make a selection; information constraints (deriving from different advertising and marketing strategies) reduce the number of options to an *effective choice set*; socially constructed preferences (arising from what is considered appropriate and "fashionable" behavior) then constrain the range of options to a *destination choice set*; and finally, situational constraints (involving things like time and money) can limit *actual choice*.

Actor-oriented behavioral approaches have much to recommend them. Nevertheless, they are not an end in themselves because they complement rather than supplant other approaches to the study of tourism. Moreover, although actor-oriented behavioral approaches can be applied, in principle, to any decision-maker within the tourist arena (e.g. the providers of tourism facilities), they have been used primarily to understand the behavior of visitors rather than hosts. In many ways, actor-oriented behavioral approaches should be thought of as a point of view rather than a rigorous paradigm because there is no one approach. Indeed, a further binary distinction can be used to illustrate the variety of techniques used within the general field of actor-oriented approaches. This binary distinction contrasts *positivist approaches* with *humanistic approaches* (Walmsley 1988). The term "positivism" is a strange one. Basically, it refers to what many regard as mainstream social science. It is an approach that focuses on scientific rigor and on the recording of facts in as objective a fashion as possible, usually within the context of statistical analysis and hypothesis-testing. This is very different from humanistic approaches. These do not attempt to *explain* behavior in the sense of identifying cause-and-effect relationships. Instead, the goal is *understanding*. This is achieved by researchers trying to imagine themselves in the shoes of the individual whose behavior is under consideration and trying to see the world through that person's eyes. So, rather than seeking replicable and verifiable measurement (as would researchers of a positivist persuasion), advocates of a humanistic approach try to empathize with their subjects in order to understand why they behave as they do. Very often the focus is on what might be termed "the taken-for-granted world" because it is often the things that are embedded in culture, and taken for granted in an unselfconscious way, which have a major bearing on behavior (Walmsley and Lewis 1994: 121–2). Illustrations are to be seen in notions of what forms of behavior are appropriate in the sorts of public spaces that are important in tourism (e.g. parks, cathedrals). One particular form of the taken-for-granted world that is especially important in tourism is landscape. Landscape is, after all, something that is all around, something that is being continually changed, and something that is imbued with cultural meaning (Punter 1982). How Australians think of the outback and how the English view rural villages is a reflection of the culture of both places. Adopting a humanistic approach is not easy. It demands a different set of research tools from those adopted in mainstream social science (see Riley and Love 2000). In particular, humanistic researchers commonly use unstructured and semi-structured interviews, focus groups, and participant observation (Decrop 1999). These techniques can be very challenging, especially when used in a cross-cultural context. In particular, it is difficult for a researcher to know when he or she has managed to fully understand the behavior of another individual. There are no tests of statistical significance. Rather, the researcher is usually forced into a strategy of triangulation whereby the views of different actors (usually three, hence the term) are investigated to get a depth of understanding that might be missing from a single perspective.

Over the years, there has been a good deal of conflict between positivistic and humanistic researchers, with both sides attempting to denigrate the other. This is now mostly a thing of the past because there has been some melding of the two approaches as researchers come to recognize the importance of contextual and non-quantifiable issues in human behavior (Aitken 1991). Part of the reason for the coming together of positivist and humanist approaches possibly stems from the fact that theorists in social science are increasingly wrestling with the issue of how to relate behavior to the structure or context within which it occurs and this struggle has made researchers less partisan in advocacy of specific approaches, despite ongoing concern in some quarters about the need for epistemological purity and the dangers of combining approaches with different epistemological underpinnings (Johnston 1983). One illustration of the willingness to consider new approaches, in a somewhat different vein from the debate about positivism and humanism, is heightened interest in the notion of *structuration* put forward by Giddens (1987). Giddens' argument is simple but profound: spatial structures (the way we organize the physical environment) and social structures (the way society is organized) are inextricably linked. The corollary to this is that spatial structures are not just containers within which social forces are acted out; rather, they are a means by which social forces are actually constituted. Put simply, society does not exist independently of human activity nor as a product of human activity. The two are linked in a recursive manner so that a change in one triggers a change in the other. This has important implications in tourism research, in so far as the way society is organized (e.g. the amount of leisure time available) and the way tourism is organized (the location of attractions) both influence each other and, ultimately, the day-to-day behavior of tourists.

The increasing breadth that ideas like structuration bring to behavioral research is significant. After all, such approaches emphasize the importance of context and therefore resonate with the distinction between behavior in space and spatial behavior. They also highlight the intellectual challenges which have been at the center of attention in this section and which need to be addressed prior to embarking on any behavioral research in the field of tourism studies. The enduring issues are: (1) how to relate individual human behavior to the context within which it takes place so as to capture the general without losing sight of the particular, thereby making the results meaningful in terms of the social scientific goal of explaining behavior, as well as useful, through the identification of aggregate patterns, to planners and policy-makers; and (2) how to tease out the degree to which behavior results from a trade-off between choice and constraint, both of which may operate at an almost subconscious level. There have been attempts to grapple with these issues in a wide variety of contexts, but two research emphases stand out.

Research Emphases

Cognition and images

It is widely recognized that, in the contemporary world, people suffer from information overload. The real world is too big and too complex for people to understand it in its entirety. People cope with this situation of overload by building up, in their minds, simplified versions of reality and then acting out their lives in relation to the "perceived world" rather than the "real world" (Boulding 1956). In other words, a useful distinction can be made between the "objective environment" that can be characterized in a map and the "behavioral environment" which is the simplified version of reality that individuals carry around in their heads. An individual's behavioral environment is often thought of as the "mental map" that guides their behavior. The map can have holes in it for places that the individual does not know. As well as being partial, the mental map is invariably distorted, in terms of distance and direction, and idiosyncratic in the sense of being unique to the individual in question. Some researchers have claimed that the influence of the mental map is so strong that the dictum "seeing is believing" can be reversed to suggest that "believing is seeing." That is to say, individuals see in the environment that which they expect to see (Walmsley and Lewis 1994).

The importance of mental maps in everyday life is well established (Walmsley 1988). Of course, if the everyday world with which people are familiar is too complex to be understood, it must be very much more difficult for tourists, as short-term visitors, to come to terms with the unfamiliar areas that they visit. It is not surprising, therefore, that researchers in the tourism arena are interested in the way in which visitors develop mental maps of tourist regions. The term "mental map" is, in this sense, a metaphor because it is not at all clear whether the image of the environment that people hold in their minds is in the form of the spatial coordinates normally associated with maps. It is therefore more common, as well as more correct, to speak of *cognitive images*. That said, it has to be acknowledged that relatively little is known about the way in which tourists develop images of the places they visit. Predictably, visitors seem to have limited knowledge and very simplified images. There is also evidence of learning occurring to the extent that the images become more sophisticated the longer a visitor is in the area in question. These findings were confirmed by Walmsley and Jenkins (1992) in relation to the image that tourists have of a popular Australian holiday coast. The authors found that an ability to draw sketch map images of the area develops very quickly so that comprehensible maps are evident within three days of a new visitor arriving in the area. The content of the map (in the sense of the number of items it contains) improves the longer a visitor stays. Lifestyle is also significant in that metropolitan dwellers compile more complex maps than do rural dwellers and car drivers draw more complex maps than do passengers. Different market segments, in other words, seem to interpret tourist areas differently. The sketch maps of campers and caravanners are more complex than the maps of those tourists who are staying with friends and relatives and these, in turn, are much more complex that the maps of those visitors who stay in relatively exclusive resorts (Jenkins and Walmsley 1993). Perhaps hiding away in a resort is a reflection of personality. Certainly there is evidence of different personality types cognizing the tourist environment in different ways. In terms of activity, individuals who are "space searchers" have more detailed and complex images than visitors who are "space sitters." Likewise, in terms of the personality trait usually labeled locus of control, individuals who see themselves as in control of their own fate possess more complex images than individuals who see themselves as controlled by outside forces (Walmsley and Jenkins 1991). Similar overall observations have been made about the images developed by visitors interested in nature-based tourism: environmental knowledge is influenced by length of stay, return visitation, mode of travel, visitor origin, age, and gender (Young 1999).

If research attention is diverted away from overall images and to specific elements of the images, such as distance, similar findings emerge. Cognitive distance is almost always exaggerated relative to "real" distance, more so for car travelers than for bus travelers. However, the accuracy of distance estimates improves with age and with the length of time that visitors spend in an area. There are also differences between residents and visitors in terms of how they view distance. For example, in the Australian context, tourists tend to be better at estimating long distances (>160 km) than are residents, while the opposite is the case for short distances (<160 km) (Walmsley and Jenkins 1999). This might be indicative of the upper limit of day trips for residents and reflective of the fact that Australian holiday-makers often travel great distances. It remains to be seen if these figures also obtain in other countries. It also needs to be remembered that the images that have been described so far are what are termed "designative images" in that they represent attempts by tourists to designate what is where. Such images can be captured in sketch maps, but these tell the researchers very little about how places are evaluated (except in the sense that a place that is omitted from a sketch map might be deemed to be unimportant). To study evaluations of places, attention needs to turn to "appraisive images" (Walmsley and Lewis 1994). Characteristically, these have involved fitting contour lines to people's preferences to show peaks at places that are popular and troughs at places that are disliked. Walmsley and Jenkins (1993) tried to go beyond this. Using personal construct theory, they attempted to identify the constructs by which places are evaluated vis-à-vis each other. Six constructs were suggested as important: commercialized–not commercialized; appealing/attractive–unappealing/unattractive; quiet–busy; trendy–not trendy; boring–interesting; and relaxed pace of life–fast pace of life. Subsequently, Walmsley and Young (1998) suggested that these constructs can be reduced to a 2×2 matrix where the discriminating axes are arousing–sleepy and unpleasant–pleasant. This is an interesting finding because it fits comfortably with the evaluative schema that are used in a wide variety of fields, especially in social and environmental psychology (Russell 1980; Russell and Lanius 1984). There is, however, still a great deal of work to be done to further understanding of cognitive imagery in tourism and many of the issues to be faced relate to the intellectual challenges outlined above. There is, for instance, a need to probe the meaning that places have for people in a subjective, experiential sense that recognizes the importance of cultural bias, ideology, and power. It is also important to remember that images are intensely personal phenomena and that attempts to build composite images obviously lose a great deal of actor-oriented specific information.

The changing nature of society and the regional impact of tourism

Behavioral approaches in social science are sometimes criticized for focusing on behavior as it is rather than on how behavior might be changed to improve human well-being. In this sense, behavioral approaches can be seen as supportive of the status quo. This is as true of tourism studies as of the rest of social science. It is important, therefore, that one of the emphases in tourism research be on the behavioral underpinnings of societal change and on what this might mean for regional development in areas reliant on tourism. Of importance in this connection is the notion that advanced Western society might be moving into a new era. Very often the term "postmodern" is used to describe this new era (Rojek 2000). The noun "postmodernism" is, however, a very confused term (Hollinshead 2002). It can be used to describe style (what comes after modernism in fields like architecture and painting), to describe method (notably the deconstruction of texts to uncover the way in which meaning very often reflects power), and to describe an epoch (approximately the 1980s onwards) (Dear 1986). The essential message to be drawn from postmodernism, as far as behavioral studies in tourism are concerned, is that there is no overarching theory of how society works, because how society works varies from place to place. Postmodernism celebrates this variety and variability. In some senses, this views harks back to the distinction between "behavior in space" and "spatial behavior" because it reflects a growing recognition that place matters. Geographical patterns should not be seen merely as reflections of social processes (Soja 1989). One corollary of this is that researchers need to look at how places and spaces are invested with meaning. However, researchers need to do this at a level beyond the realm of actor-based experience. A distinction needs to be made between place *per se*, space as a contextual given, and socially based spatiality, that is the created space imbued with social meaning through processes at work in society as a whole (Ryan 2000).

One of the key issues to be confronted is the changing role of leisure in advanced Western societies. This concerns the way in which leisure is viewed in society as a whole. Centuries ago, leisure was the preserve of the rich who were wealthy enough not to need to work. Today, some writers believe that leisure has been extended from "the rich" to encompass "the retired" and "the redundant." To some, work might be changing from the curse of the masses to the preserve of the well-educated (at least in the sense of stimulating and rewarding work) (Jones 1997). Other writers have talked of "the leisure shock" brought on by technological change which increases the productivity of labor and so means that the volume of work that needs to be done can be undertaken by a smaller labor force than was the case in the past. This has prompted some writers to talk of "the end of work" (at least as we have known it) (see Walmsley 2001). The result of these changes is often predicted to be a large increase in the amount of attention devoted to leisure, recreation, and tourism. Despite these predictions, there is little sign of the Western world's commitment to work and to materialism diminishing (Schor 1992). This may, however, change, and one of the challenges that researchers face in tourism studies is that of assessing whether the centrality of wealth creation will continue to be an overarching aim of Western society or whether leisure lifestyles (incorporating tourism) will emerge. There is certainly evidence of a shift from production to consumption occurring in society, and this will bring with it the opportunity for the development of tourism (Walmsley 2003). However, not all places will be "winners." People might well use leisure lifestyles rather than class as a basis for projecting an image of who they are, but there are likely to be major differences in the extent to which different places are able to meet the demand for leisure lifestyle. In this regard, behavioral researchers need to pay special attention to the emergence of leisure subcultures and, especially, to the notions of threshold and range. The former describes the volume of demand that is necessary for a service to be provided effectively (usually commercially) whereas the latter describes the distance that tourists are prepared to travel in order to access and use a service (something that depends very much on the notion of cognitive distance described above). It is easy to speculate on what changes might be occurring in society. It is, however, vitally important to go beyond speculation and into the realm of behavioral research to assess whether the hypothesized changes are actually taking place. After all, tourism is not just about the attractions that are available at different destinations; it is also very much about filling psychological needs for self-actualization and social interaction (Waitt 1997). The interface between the individual and society therefore needs continued research.

Conclusion

Behavioral research is an integral part of tourism research generally. It is also an intellectually challenging undertaking. There are many different approaches to the study of tourist behavior and the strengths and weaknesses of each of these need to be appreciated fully. The extent to which the general can be seen in the particular should be a critical consideration in all tourism research. Studies of cognitive imagery and of the behavioral bases for the changing nature of tourism serve to illustrate the work that is currently being undertaken. However, more needs to be done in these and other fields. Micro-scale behavioral approaches have advanced the understanding of tourist behavior greatly, especially in relation to an appreciation of the way information is used to develop perceptions and images that serve as important inputs to tourist decision-making. There are nevertheless gaps in the level of understanding, and researchers need to tackle these issues. For example, despite acceptance of the role of constraints in tourist behavior, there is still a widespread and often implicit research emphasis on consumer sovereignty, that is to say, the perspective that tourists make and act upon their own decisions. This perspective needs to be tempered with the realization that tourist experience is very much socially constructed, often in an unselfconscious way, rather than the outcome of individual volition. The research agenda needs to take stock of the information providers (the tourism promoters) as well as the information consumers (the tourists) and of their role in the social construction of tourism. Much more also needs to be known about tourism from an experiential perspective, particularly the way in which experience can differ markedly between different segments of the tourism market. The need for this research is urgent, given the changing nature of tourism demonstrated in this chapter. In this regard, it is important to note that advances in the understanding of tourist behavior will undoubtedly inform general theories of people–environment interaction. Studies of tourist behavior are not a field where existing knowledge is simply applied; rather, they are an area of activity that is at the cutting edge of social science generally and human geography in particular.

REFERENCES

Aitken, S. C. (1991). Person–environment theories in contemporary perceptual and behavioural geography I: personality, attitudinal and spatial choice theories. *Progress in Human Geography* 15, 179–93.

Boulding, K. E. (1956). *The Image*. Ann Arbor: University of Michigan Press.

Dear, M. J. (1986). Postmodernism and planning. *Environment and Planning D: Society and Space* 4, 367–84.

Decrop, A. (1999). Tourists' decision-making and behavior processes. In A. Pizam and Y. Mansfield (eds), *Consumer Behavior in Travel and Tourism* (pp. 103–33). New York: Haworth Hospitality Press.

Desbarats, J. (1983). Spatial choice and constraints on behavior. *Annals of the Association of American Geographers* 73, 340–57.

Giddens, A. (1987). *Social Theory and Modern Society.* Oxford: Blackwell.

Golledge, R. G., and Rushton, G. (1976). Introduction. In R. G. Golledge and G. Rushton (eds), *Spatial Choice and Spatial Behavior* (pp. 1–2). Columbus: Ohio State University Press.

Golledge, R. G., and Stimson, R. J. (1997). *Spatial Behavior.* New York: Guilford Press.

Hollinshead, K. (2002). Playing with the past: Heritage tourism under the tyrannies of postmodern discourse. In C. Ryan (ed.), *The Tourist Experience*, 2nd edn. (pp. 1–26). London: Continuum.

Hudson, S., and Gilbert, D. (2000). Tourism constraints: The neglected dimension of consumer behaviour research. In A. G. Woodside (ed.), *Consumer Psychology of Tourism, Hospitality and Leisure* (pp. 137–54). New York: CABI Publishing.

Jenkins, J. M., and Walmsley, D. J. (1993). Mental maps of tourists: A study of Coffs Harbour, NSW. *GeoJournal* 29, 233–41.

Johnston, R. J. (1983). *Philosophy and Human Geography.* London: Arnold.

Jones, B. (1997). *Sleepers, Wake!* 3rd edn. Oxford: Oxford University Press.

Moore, G. T., and Golledge, R. G. (1976). Environmental knowing: Concepts and theories. In G. T. Moore and R. G. Golledge (eds), *Environmental Knowing* (pp. 3–24). Stroudsburg: Dowden, Hutchinson & Ross.

Pizam, A., and Mansfield, Y. (eds) (1999). *Consumer Behavior in Travel and Tourism.* New York: Haworth Hospitality Press.

Punter, J. V. (1982). Landscape aesthetics: A synthesis and critique. In J. Gold and J. Burgess (eds), *Valued Environments* (pp. 100–23). London: Allen & Unwin.

Riley, R. W., and Love, L. L. (2000). The state of qualitative tourism research. *Annals of Tourism Research* 27, 164–87.

Rojek, C. (2000). *Leisure and Culture.* Basingstoke: Palgrave.

Ross, G. F. (1998). *The Psychology of Tourism*, 2nd edn. Melbourne: Hospitality Press.

Russell, J. A. (1980). A circumplex model of affect. *Journal of Personality and Social Psychology* 39, 1161–78.

Russell, J. A., and Lanius, U. F. (1984). Adaptation level and affective appraisal of environments. *Journal of Environmental Psychology* 4, 119–35.

Ryan, C. (1997). Similar motivations – diverse behaviours. In C. Ryan (ed.), *The Tourist Experience* (pp. 25–47). New York: Cassell.

Ryan, C. (2000). Stages, gazes and constructions of tourism. In C. Ryan (ed.), *The Tourist Experience*, 2nd edn. (pp. 1–26). London: Continuum.

Schor, J. (1992). *The Overworked American.* New York: Basic Books.

Simon, H. A. (1957). *Models of Man.* New York: Wiley.

Soja, E. W. (1989). *Postmodern Geographies.* London: Verso.

Um, S., and Crompton, J. L. (1999). The role of images and perceived constraints at different stages in the tourist's destination decision process. In A. Pizam and Y. Mansfield (eds), *Consumer Behavior in Travel and Tourism* (pp. 81–102). New York: Haworth Hospitality Press.

Waitt, G. (1997). Selling paradise and adventure: Representations of landscape in the tourist advertising of Australia. *Australian Geographical Studies* 35, 47–60.

Walmsley, D. J. (1988). *Urban Living.* London: Longman.

Walmsley, D. J. (2001). The "consumption society" and the changing nature of leisure. In P. Holland, F. Stephenson, and A. Wearing (eds), *Geography: A Spatial Odyssey.* Proceedings of the Third Joint Conference of the New Zealand Geographical Society and the Institute of Australian Geographers (pp. 432–8). Hamilton: New Zealand Geographical Society.

Walmsley, D. J. (2003). Rural tourism – a case of lifestyle-led opportunities. *Australian Geographer* 34(1), 61–72.

Walmsley, D. J., and Jenkins, J. M. (1991). Mental maps, locus of control, and activity: A study of business tourists in Coffs Harbour. *Journal of Tourism Studies* 2, 36–42.

Walmsley, D. J., and Jenkins, J. M. (1992). Tourism cognitive mapping on unfamiliar environments. *Annals of Tourism Research* 19, 268–86.

Walmsley, D. J., and Jenkins J. M. (1993). Appraisive images of tourist areas: Application of personal constructs. *Australian Geographer* 24, 1–213.
Walmsley, D. J., and Jenkins, J. M. (1999). Cognitive distance: A neglected issue in travel behavior. In A. Pizam and Y. Mansfield (eds), *Consumer Behavior in Travel and Tourism* (pp. 287–303). New York: Haworth Hospitality Press.
Walmsley, D. J., and Lewis, G. J. (1994). *People and Environment*. London: Longman.
Walmsley, D. J., and Young, M. (1998). Evaluative images and tourism: The use of personal constructs to describe the structure of destination images. *Journal of Travel Research* 36, 65–9.
Young, M. (1999). The social construction of tourist places. *Australian Geographer* 30, 373–89.

Chapter 5

Toward a Political Economy of Tourism

Allan M. Williams

Introduction

Political economy embraces different perspectives on the production and distribution of wealth, and the role of the state in these, but it has become particularly associated with neo-Marxism in recent decades. Marxism, of course, is also constituted of diverse theoretical strands, but only some of these can be considered within this short chapter. Tourism studies have grappled tentatively and selectively with political economy perspectives of any hue.

This is not to deny a critical tradition in tourism studies, as epitomized by de Kadt's (1979) seminal volume, *Tourism: Passport to Development?* Subsequently, critical writing in tourism, and concerns about distributional questions, crystallized around sustainable tourism issues. However, as Williams and Montanari (1999) argued, the sustainable tourism literature has been strong on morality, advocacy, and prescription, but weak in analyzing the structures and relationships inherent in tourism production and distribution. Large swaths of the subject seem to have sidestepped political economy, which may in part reflect its strong roots in the different theoretical traditions of management and recreational studies.

The most significant exception to the above assessment is research on development and dependency (see Bianchi 2002; Telfer 2002). Dependency theory emerged as a critique of modernization, focusing on wider international relations as the main cause of lack of development, as summarized by Bianchi (2002: 270): "tourism contributed directly toward an extension of metropolitan dominance over weaker destination peripheries and ultimately leads to a loss of self-reliance." In tourism, research on dependency has focused on the roles of transnational companies (Britton 1982; Lea 1988). Britton, in particular, elaborated on the unequal relationships between international capital and different fractions of domestic capital, which he encapsulated in a model of hierarchical firm relations. The other thread of dependency theory – unequal exchange (in the terms of trade) – has received less attention in tourism, although research on multipliers and price elasticities provide empirical insights into the tourism trade relations between less and more developed economies. More recently, research on the role of the state in tourism development (see Dieke 2000 on Africa) has emphasized that the political is necessarily interrelated with the economic in political economy.

While there have been some significant strands of research on the political economy of tourism in less developed economies, the more developed economies have been largely ignored, except for critiques of place marketing, set within the context of urban studies. Britton's (1991) paper represented a clarion call drawing on the work of Harvey and others on the changing nature of production and consumption in capitalist economies. He outlined a vision of political economy which was culturally- and place-sensitive, and historically specific (see Telfer 2002). Despite the frequent citation of Britton's paper, fruitful theoretical developments in political economy have largely bypassed tourism in the intervening years. Therefore, this chapter is as much a review of gaps in research as of research undertaken. The chapter is necessarily selective, and focuses on three main theoretical issues: commodification, the labor process, and regulation theory.

Tourism Commodification and Market Relationships

Commodification is the starting point for understanding how tourism is constituted in modern societies, at least in terms of economic relationships. Nigel Thrift, in *The Dictionary of Human Geography* (Johnston et al. 2000: 56), writes that "commodification reaches into every nook and cranny of modern life... Practically every human activity in Western countries either relies on or has certain commodities associated with it, from births to weddings to funerals, at work or in the home, in peace or in war." Commodification refers to the system of market exchange of goods, services, and experiences (Watson and Kopachevsky 1994). It has profound implications, not only for tourists, but for host communities (for example, the commodification of traditional domestic production for souvenirs, or of festivals) as well as nature (which may be "gated," or transformed in the interests of tourism production and consumption).

The commodification of tourism is based as much on the "sign value" of tourism, as it is on the labor, capital, and natural resources used in production. MacCannell (1976) emphasizes "the semiotics of capitalist production," whereby tourism commodities become forms of cultural capital, and indicators of lifestyle and taste. This partial detachment of exchange value from material production conditions results in tourism commodities becoming "fetishised" (Watson and Kopachevsky 1994), as "sacred" objects or experiences. Examples include the very high prices charged by highly esteemed hotels and restaurants. The process of signification is socially contested. In part, this is class-based – as witnessed by the hegemony of the aristocracy in the Grand Tour, and of the new middle class in rural and heritage tourism (Urry 1990). But the advertising industry is also important in signposting and, while embedded in material relations, has its own dynamic, including a strong element of human agency.

While commodification has touched "every nook and cranny" of tourism, there are limits. It is often difficult to exert property rights over tourism experiences. The casual visitor to a village festival can no more be excluded from experiencing this than can the urban *flâneur* from experiencing city life. Moreover, some tourism services are provided outside of market exchange relationships, most obviously the accommodation, catering, and guiding services provided by hosts to visiting family and friends.

Therefore, it is necessary to recognize four possibilities with respect to commodification (Shaw and Williams 2004). First, direct commodification, for example charging for access to a theme park or a beach. Secondly, indirect commodification, or the market exchange of hospitality and other services which support the direct tourism experience. Thirdly, part commodification, whereby exchange relationships are intertwined with non-commodification, as in self-catering (where labor is provided by tourists). And, fourthly, non-commodification, such as hill walking (although transport and walking equipment may be used which are commodified). A particular place is likely to be the site of all four types of commodification, but they are combined in ways that reflect national political economic conditions, the tourism attraction, the local economic and cultural environment, and consumer characteristics. Hence commodification is variable across space and time. Direct commodification may be strongly evident at a theme park while part commodification and non-commodification may be more evident in visiting friends and family tourism in rural areas.

There are two important features to note. First, that the precise combination of commodification forms largely determines the characteristics of tourism's economic systems. The organization of production and consumption, levels of tourism expenditures and income, and their social distribution – all central political economy concerns – are determined by the extent, and the forms, of tourism commodification. In turn, this means that – in so far as place characteristics are rooted in material relations (which is contested) – they are also shaped by the complex interweaving of commodification forms. Secondly, the commodification of tourism has generally increased over time, particularly in recent decades (Britton 1991). Commodification encompasses not only the holiday period but also to the pre- and post-tourism experiences. Guide books and equipment (from skis to power boats) are purchased before the holiday, while the tourism experience may influence subsequent consumption (from a taste for "tapas" bars to Tuscan ceramics).

Despite the centrality of commodification to modern economic systems, there has been remarkably little research on this, at least in respect of material relations. In contrast, there has been considerable research on the commodification of culture, typified by Greenwood's (1977) classic study, but this lies beyond the bounds of this discussion. However, transition processes in emerging market economies and the commodification of souvenir production provide two important research nodes.

At first sight, the transition to market economies would be expected to result in tourism experiences being mediated by exchange relationships, in place of central planning and collective consumption. Market relationships were introduced in the transition economies of central and eastern Europe, as Williams and Balaz (2000, 2002) indicate in a case study of the former Czechoslovakia. There was price liberalization, privatization of tourism facilities, and increased scope for international holidays. Weak market institutions and regulation created high levels of risk and uncertainty for both tourists and tourism firms, whilst corruption and deception were widespread in the commodification process (Williams and Balaz 2000). Nevertheless, market exchange relationships were introduced, with mixed and partly unexpected implications for tourism consumption (Williams and Balaz 2001). There was growth of commodified consumption, especially in the international and short-break domestic market segments. But given the depression and polarization of wages, there was also survival – and even increased relative importance – of non-commodified tourism (visiting friends and relatives), and collective consumption (subsidized holidays provided by employers and labor organizations). Therefore, as in Western societies, the tourism production system was constituted of particular, and shifting, forms of commodification.

The commodification of domestic and small-scale craft work to provide tourism souvenirs has also attracted research attention (Hitchcock and Teague 2000). Souvenir production can be non-commodified – for example, where tourists collect fossils or plants directly from nature – but most material souvenir production constitutes indirect commodification, with visitors purchasing objects at or near tourist attractions. In many instances – for example, miniature Eiffel Towers and Taj Mahals – these are obviously mass-produced goods. However, the association of souvenirs with "traditional" or highly localized craft work in some settings lends them a patina of "authenticity," and they may become fetishized commodities. Whether the outcome of such commodification is loss of authenticity (MacCannell 1973) or support for their survival (Cohen 1988) is contested. But of greater significance here is the need to study how commodification has influenced tourism production, and the distribution of income. Markwick's (2001) study of lace and glass souvenirs in Malta is particularly instructive. Lace production remains household-based, but tourism access is controlled by a class of intermediaries. In contrast, glass production is a relatively new form of "craft" work introduced by small-scale immigrant capitalists, who exercise greater control over market access, and the goods they produce.

These examples remind us that commodification takes diverse forms over time and space, reflecting differences in economic and cultural systems. However, this should not detract from the central argument that tourism production has become increasingly commodified within capitalist societies. An array of tourism services and experiences are directly mediated by market relationships. Even where they are apparently non-commodified – such as staying with friends and relatives, or hill walking – the experiences are produced within capitalist societies. As a minimum, transport will have been used (whether a car or a bicycle) and food consumed, which will have involved market relationships. And, more fundamentally, the free time to enjoy these tourism experiences, and the landscapes to be visited and gazed on, will have been shaped by capitalist relationships. In this sense, commodification really does extend into every "nook and cranny" of tourism in modern societies.

The Tourism Firm: The Labor Process

The wage relationship between capital and labor is central to capitalist production. Labor is a commodity that is bought and sold, and class relations are constructed around this relationship, although these are intertwined with gender, nationality/ethnicity, and age, for example, in complex ways. Tourism studies have largely neglected these relationships, with very few exceptions (see Ireland 1993 on gender and class, and Urry 1995 on the "new middle class"). Simplistic analyses of the conflict between capital and labor are generally rejected because labor is a distinctive commodity: workers are reflexive and *actively* engage in tourism production.

Tourism researchers have shown greater interest in the role of labor in tourism production (see Riley, chapter 11 this volume) than in class issues. Neo-Marxists understand the labor process as the organization of work, involving both the objects worked on and the instruments used in production. In capitalist societies, the labor process is characterized by attempts to subsume labor to capital (Storper and Walker 1989). One of the key concepts is the division of labor, which is manifested in how home is separated from the workplace, social divisions between workers in terms of socially constructed skills hierarchies, and across space, including the international division of labor (see Massey 1995).

In so far as tourism researchers have grappled with these larger issues, their focus has been the contested shift between two forms of labor process organization: Fordism and neo-Fordism (discussed later in more detail, but see also Debbage and Ioannides, chapter 8 this volume). These studies have been undertaken against recognition that tourism is a "fragmented industry" with largely undifferentiated products and no firm being in a position to dominate markets (Knowles, Diamantis, and El-Mourhabi 2001: 128). Moreover, the space-time fixity of tourism consumption (Urry 1987) means that tourism firms face variable and polarized demand, which requires considerable flexibility in the production of tourism experiences.

Labor process adjustment is crucial to firm survival – and the reproduction of tourism capital – in the face of these conditions. This is not to argue that the labor process is predetermined in any economic system; rather, it is negotiated between capital, labor (individually and through collective organizations), and the state (through its regulatory role). Moreover, even if capital seeks to subordinate labor in the labor process, the latter is not a passive participant. Instead, as Baldacchino (1997: 92) argues, "workers cannot be forced to work without a modicum of consent on their part; nor do workers agree to sell an exact quantity of labor." Capital has to negotiate with workers about how much work they do, and how they do it. This is critical in an industry where the quality of the tourism experience depends in large part on the interaction between tourist and tourism worker.

The key question for firms is how to obtain the quantity and quality of labor they require, at prices that will yield surplus value and guarantee their survival. Riley, Ladkin, and Szivas (2002), in an overview of the causes of relatively low wages in tourism, identified three main sets of factors: job attributes, psychological issues, and industrial structure and economic factors. All three are undoubtedly important, but political economy studies would focus more on the last. Fluctuations in demand lead to greater emphasis on employment flexibility, while the small scale of most tourism enterprises means there are weak divisions of labor.

Employers focus on the ratio of capital to labor within the labor process. While generally low in most branches of tourism, it is increasing, with implications for worker recruitment and working practices. The outcomes are variable. On the one hand, Milne and Pohlmann (1998: 188) argue that increased use of IT in hotels raised the overall skill profile, because it reduced the number of unskilled workers while increasing the number of "front-line" workers with technological and customer skills. On the other hand, new technology facilitates the replacement of craft production by Fordist production, where work is routinized, repetitive, deskilled and specialized; for example, the deskilling of cooking in McDonalds's and other fast food chains (Ritzer 1998). However, capital–labor shifts in the restaurant business can also eliminate unskilled *and* skilled jobs, as Bagguley (1987) demonstrates in respect of automatic dishwashers and cook-chill technology. Political economy studies emphasize that there is no inevitability in how capital and labor are combined. Instead, this is highly contingent, and has to be teased out through case studies set within a broad theoretical framework.

Another major concern for firms is to ensure that labor is sufficiently flexible to meet variable tourism demand conditions. There is a vast literature on flexibility, much of which centers on Atkinson's (1984) conceptual distinction between numerical and functional flexibility: that is, changes in employment levels, and in the movement of workers between tasks within the firm, respectively, in response to variations in demand. Several researchers have examined this perspective in tourism studies, both conceptually and empirically (Lockwood and Guerrier 1989; Urry 1990; Milne and Pohlmann 1998; Shaw and Williams 2002). Wood's (1997: 172–3) comprehensive review concludes that numerical flexibility is prevalent, but there is little evidence of functional flexibility. In both cases, however, political economy draws attention to the role of labor market segmentation in the attempts by capital to reconcile flexibility, reducing labor costs, and maintaining the quality of labor inputs.

Labor market segmentation, rooted in wider social differentiation, allows employers to reduce labor costs through the creation of social divisions of labor. The segmentation of workers (for example, by race, age, or gender) with unequal power is exploited both as a basis for paying differential wages for jobs done by particular social groups, and for depressing overall wage levels. Some jobs are constructed as "unskilled work" *because* they are undertaken by particular social groups (typically by women, by migrants, by young people) not because of their specific skill content. Workers are not passive in the labor process. They help create such divisions, as well as contesting them (perhaps individually through the courts, or through collective labor action). Political economy emphasizes that the social divisions people bring with them into the labor force are structurally embedded (Hudson 2001: 200).

There is only room here to consider the most widespread social division, that is gender. This is manifested in different ways. There are contingently gendered jobs, undertaken by women because they are low-waged, or because they are part-time (many women have dual roles in both waged labor and the home). There are also jobs, such as that of air hostess, that commodify perceived female characteristics such as glamor or sex appeal (Jordan 1997). In addition, the domestic division of labor – where women's role has been constructed around notions of care, and domestic duties – is carried over into the labor market in jobs such as cleaning and making beds (Crompton and Sanderson 1990). Gender is of course intertwined with class (and other axes of social differentiation) in the social division of labor. There are different theoretical perspectives on this, depending on whether patriarchy or class is emphasized. The dual systems approach considers both are important: whereas capitalism creates the hierarchical structure of jobs, access to these is determined by patriarchal relations (Sinclair 1997: 7). Inevitably, when moving from abstraction to concrete analysis, the class-gender structuring of tourism employment is worked out differently in different places.

While this chapter has thus far emphasized labor costs, real unit costs rather than nominal wages matter to employers. Employers have to take into account not only the full costs of training workers, but also the motivation and skills required to deliver quality tourism experiences. Employers have to take into account the need to retain or attract workers with experience and skills in order to ensure continuity in work practices. In reality, jobs involving direct contact with customers are more complex than this because of the importance of the emotional content of such transactions. This is epitomized by the notion that particular attributes are embodied in labor performance. In jobs such as those of airline steward, beach attendant, or hotel receptionist, employers have expectations of how employees should look and act (in terms of their voice or their bodily movements). Crang's (1994) study of waiters in themed restaurants provides a detailed case study of performance in the hospitality industry. Customers expect certain performances from waiters and waitresses, and they interact to co-produce these performances. This means not only that the labor process can not be predetermined by managers, but also that managers need to attract and retain staff with valued embodied skills.

The above examples urge caution in not reducing the labor content of the labor process merely to hours worked, the intensity of work, and costs. Equally, however, studies of tourism employment as performance should not be detached from material relations. Employers seek to minimize real unit costs, and even if they cannot entirely control labor performance, they try to manage it. Most obviously, they may try to routinize the tourist–employee encounter, through training the latter to use stock phrases such as "have a nice day." Performance may be encouraged by managers, but only within the parameters established by material relations (of costs versus income), even if performance contributes to defining these parameters; for example, restaurants with reputations for entertaining performances from employees may be able to charge higher prices to customers. Above all, Wood (1997) reminds us not to romanticize tourism employment by exaggerating performance, so that we lose sight of the drudgery which is the reality of the labor process for many workers. That drudgery needs to be comprehended in context of the labor process.

Tourism and Regulation Theory

Individual firms are unable to guarantee their own survival; for example, they are unable to invest in the collective provision of education and the infrastructure essential to their operations. This leads to the question of how capitalist societies seek to guarantee their reproduction, which brings the *political* element of political economy more into focus. Regulation theory provides one of the more coherent theoretical frameworks for analyzing societal reproduction. Essentially, societies are characterized as having a regime of accumulation and a mode of regulation. The former is a systematic organization of production, consumption, circulation, and income distribution, while the latter is a nationally specific set of institutional forms (involving formal regulatory bodies, notably the state, as well as norms and customs) which stabilize and coordinate economic activity (Dunford 1990: 305–6). The regulatory system mediates and normalizes crisis tendencies inherent in capitalist accumulation (Tickell and Peck 1992). At any one time, and in any one country, there tends to be a hegemonic (dominant) structure, which is the dominant political, economic, and institutional strategy. There have been two main hegemonic structures, in the last century, in capitalist societies: Fordism/Keynesianism and neo-Fordism/neoliberalism. As the Fordism/Keynesianism model became exhausted, and no longer able to contain recurring crises (evident in declining profits, falling investment, and labor unrest), it was supplanted by neo-Fordism/neoliberalism. This argument is, however, theoretically and empirically contested (Hudson 2001).

Regulation theory provides a useful level of abstraction about production and consumption, and their regulation. It is not a deterministic theory, but directs attention to national differences. It provides a useful framework for a holistic approach, but has received relatively little attention from tourism researchers – even if several authors comment on its value (Ateljevic 2000; Shaw and Williams 2004). In general, the regime of accumulation (the system of production–consumption) has received more attention than the mode of regulation.

Ioannides and Debbage (1998) review the prevalence of Fordist and post-Fordist regimes in tourism. Focusing on the regime of accumulation, they consider three main types:

- *Pre-Fordist* artisanal and craft production is typical of many small-scale and independently owned souvenir shops, small restaurants, and lodging houses. They often survive through long hours, self- and family exploitation, and flexible working practices.
- *Fordist* mass consumption and production is typical of large hotels, airlines, tour companies, and cruise ships, characterized by economies of scale, industrial concentration, and horizontal and vertical integration.
- *Neo-Fordism* is increasingly evident in new niche market tourism, displaying increased flexibility.

Perhaps inevitably, the authors conclude that "a polyglot of coexisting multiple incarnations has evolved, displaying varying traits of flexibility" (Ioannides and Debbage 1998: 108). The tourism industry landscape, in other words, is characterized by varying combinations of regimes of accumulation. But this does not preclude a generalized tendency for a Fordist to neo-Fordist shift (Urry 1995), although the extent of this is contested by Shaw and Williams (2002: 239–43), who argue that mass production may have been transformed into new forms of high-volume production.

Tourism studies – in common with research on other economic sectors – have paid even less attention to the mode of regulation than the regime of accumulation. They have focused on how the state specifically intervenes in the tourism sector (Hall 2000), thereby ignoring how tourism is shaped by the wider regulatory framework. Regulation theory argues that the national is the key site of regulation, and there are a number of ways in which national states influence tourism:

- Mediating relations with the global economy, through exercising control over the mobility of people, goods, and capital.
- Providing a legal framework for production, which includes health and safety laws, requirements for company reporting, the application of competition law, environmental protection, and consumer protection.

- Shaping production and consumption through national macroeconomic policies.
- Intervening in local and regional development, although this is increasingly likely to be the preserve of subnational bodies.
- Contributing to the reproduction of the labor force, especially through the collective consumption of education, health, and housing.
- Social investment in response to the perceived inability of private capital to ensure its own reproduction, e.g. in waterfront redevelopment, or roads.
- Providing a climate of security and stability for tourism.

Regulation encompasses more than the roles of the state, noted above. It also involves institutions, customs, and habits. In terms of consumption, for example, this includes the deeply institutionalized custom in developed countries of taking holidays. While the state plays a role in this – for example, through legislation guaranteeing workers minimum paid holiday entitlements – it is also based on the social value that is attached to tourism, and to deeply ingrained social routines.

The hegemony of Fordism in the middle decades of the twentieth century was assured by the Keynesian mode of regulation, whereby national states sought to manage economic crises through macroeconomic instruments, welfare states, and territorial (urban, regional, and local) policies. Although there were national differences, this mode of regulation did contribute to prolonged economic growth after ca. 1950, facilitating international mass tourism. In the longer term, the Keynesian mode of regulation was undermined by globalization, increased competition, and economic liberalization pressures. States have become increasingly powerless in the face of globalization, especially of capital and finance. The frontiers of the state have also been rolled back, as states have slashed their budgets, reduced welfare programs, and privatized. Tourism has been directly affected by some of these measures, with states seeking to shift responsibility for tourism promotion to private capital, and state-owned assets – such as the Paradores hotel chain in Spain – being privatized. Tourism has, however, generally continued to expand despite the climate of increased economic uncertainty after the mid-1970s. In truth, the evidence for a change in the mode of regulation is highly contested (Tickell and Peck 1992), and much of the Keynesian mode of regulation remains in place, even if in reduced form – although, as ever, this is nationally differentiated.

Tourism is both shaped by and contributes to the mode of regulation. Holidays – as a source of relaxation and renewal – support the reproduction of the labor force. Developed countries have a long tradition of "work outings" for this purpose and, in some ways, this represented the origins of modern working-class tourism in the second half of the nineteenth century. Expenditure on tourism – as a highly valued product – also contributes to the generalized incentive system for workers in capitalist societies, as well as helping to maintain the balance between production and consumption.

Regulation theory provides a framework for a more holistic understanding of tourism, by setting tourism production and consumption in a broader societal context. It is not a rigid theoretical framework to be applied mechanically in concrete analyses, but an overall analytical framework. The focus on the national state has been questioned in the light of globalization tendencies, but claims that it has become outmoded seem overstated in the light of significant differences in the power of different states and how this is used to pursue national policies (Held 2000). However, case studies undertaken within a regulation theory perspective increasingly need to focus on global–local and global–national relationships, as well as national–local ones.

Conclusions

There are rich theoretical seams of political economy to be investigated in tourism studies. This chapter has highlighted three of these: commodification, the labor process, and regulation theory. This chapter should not be read, however, as advocating a one-way theoretical street, with tourism studies drawing down debates developed in other social sciences. Instead, the particularities of tourism commodification, the specificities of flexibility and performance in the tourism labor process, and the contribution of tourism to the mode of regulation all signify the need for a (two-way) theoretical and empirical dialogue. This agenda can be advanced in several ways, including studies of place and production–consumption interrelationships.

First, in political economy, places are viewed in context of material relationships but are not reducible to these. Rather, they are complex mixes of material objects, companies, workers, local civil societies, the state, and all kinds of practices, values, and multiple identities (Massey 1995). As Hudson (2001: 5) argues, places are "created by socialized human beings with a wider agenda than simply profitable production," albeit these need to be understood in context of material relationships. Turning to tourism, Gordon and Goodall (2000: 292), echo Massey's views that "Tourism places are shaped by the sequence of roles which each has played in the spatial division both of tourism and of other economic activities." For them, tourism interacts with place characteristics, and is both place-shaped and -shaping. This represents a call for studies of how past and present investment, cultural practices, state interventions, etc. in both tourism and non-tourism have shaped places. This would help strengthen the bridge between tourism studies and other social science research.

Secondly, Britton's (1991) seminal paper needs to be seen in context of what has become known as the "cultural turn" in economic geography (Lee and Wills 1997). In essence, this recognizes that economic relationships are infused with culturally symbolic processes, which are expressed differently in different cultural systems. One of the themes of the "cultural turn" is the need to look at the interplay of production and consumption (Gregson 1995). Ateljevic (2000: 371) echoes these views, arguing that tourism should be conceptualized "as a nexus of circuits operating within production–consumption dialects enabled by the processes of negotiated (re)production." Consumers – in this case, tourists – are not just passive objects; rather, they explore and experience sites of consumption. More explicitly, tourists contribute to tourism experiences; they actively create these for themselves and for other tourists: the atmosphere of a tourism site, and the experiences of tourists, are often dependent on the co-presence of other tourists. These relationships are perhaps most evident in respect of tourist attractions such as shopping malls and theme parks, which Ritzer (1999: 8) sees as "cathedrals of consumption" that increasingly appear to offer fantastic, and enchanted settings. Consumption in these and other settings informs production, as much as production shapes consumption. Tourism studies has only just begun to study such phenomena, and a political economy perspective would ensure that the underlying material relations are not lost sight of.

Finally, political economy studies provide not only a way of advancing understanding of tourism, but also a necessary contribution to the development of critical tourism studies. This is particularly important in a discipline where many researchers have often been closely allied with the needs of a narrow range of research users – the tourism industry and government. Only in this way can the broader issues of equity be addressed. Sustainable tourism has at least brought some of these issues on to the research agenda, but, as argued earlier, much of the resulting literature has been strong on advocacy, but lacking the deeper understanding that is offered by a political economy perspective.

REFERENCES

Ateljevic, I. (2000). Circuits of tourism: Stepping beyond the "production/consumption dichotomy." *Tourism Geographies* 2(4), 369–88.

Atkinson, J. (1984). *Flexibility, Uncertainty and Manpower Management.* Brighton: Institute of Manpower Studies, University of Sussex, Report 89.

Bagguley, P. (1987). *Flexibility, Restructuring and Gender: Employment in Britain's Hotels.* Lancaster: Lancaster Regionalism Group, Working Paper 24, University of Lancaster.

Baldacchino, G. (1997). *Global Tourism and Informal Labour Relations: The Small-Scale Syndrome at Work.* London: Mansell.

Bianchi, R. V. (2002). Towards a new political economy of global tourism. In R. Sharpley and D. J. Telfer (eds), *Tourism and Development: Concepts and Issues* (pp. 265–99). Clevedon: Channel View Publications.

Britton, S. G. (1982). The political economy of tourism in the Third World. *Annals of Tourism Research* 9(3), 331–58.

Britton, S. (1991). Tourism, capital and place: Towards a critical geography of tourism. *Environment and Planning D: Society and Space* 9, 452–78.

Cohen, E. (1988). Authenticity and commoditization in tourism. *Annals of Tourism Research* 15, 371–87.

Crang, P. (1994). It's showtime: On the workplace geographies of display in a restaurant in south east England. *Environment and Planning D: Society and Space* 12, 675–704.

Crompton, R., and Sanderson, K. (1990). *Gendered Jobs and Social Change.* London: Unwin Hyman.

de Kadt, E. (1979). *Tourism: Passport to Development? Perspectives on the Social and Cultural Effects of Tourism in Developing Countries.* New York: Oxford University Press.

Dieke, P. U. C. (ed.) (2000). *The Political Economy of Tourism Development in Africa.* New York: Cognizant Communication Corporation.

Dunford, M. (1990). Theories of regulation. *Environment and Planning D: Society and Space* 8, 297–321.

Gordon, I., and Goodall, B. (2000). Localities and tourism. *Tourism Geographies* 2(3), 290–311.

Greenwood, D. J. (1977). Culture by the pound: An anthropological perspective on tourism as cultural commoditization. In V. Smith (ed.), *Host and Guests: The Anthropology of Tourism* (pp. 129–39). Oxford: Blackwell.

Gregson, N. (1995). And now it's all consumption. *Progress in Human Geography* 19, 135–41.
Hall, C. M. (2000). *Tourism Planning: Policies, Processes and Relationships*. Harlow: Pearson.
Held, D. (2000). Introduction. In D. Held (ed.), *A Globalizing World? Culture, Economics, Politics* (pp. 1–12). London: Routledge.
Hitchcock, M., and Teague, K. (2000). *Souvenirs: The Material Culture of Tourism*. Aldershot: Ashgate.
Hudson, R. (2001). *Producing Places*. New York: Guilford Press.
Ioannides, D., and Debbage, K. (1998). Neo-Fordism and flexible specialization in the travel industry: Dissecting the polyglot. In D. Ioannides and K. Debbage (eds), *The Economic Geography of the Tourist Industry: A Supply-Side Analysis* (pp. 99–122). London: Routledge.
Ireland, M. (1993). Gender and class relations in tourism employment. *Annals of Tourism Research* 20(4), 666–84.
Johnston, R. J., Gregory, D., Pratt, G., and Watts, M. (eds) (2000). *The Dictionary of Human Geography*, 4th edn. Oxford: Blackwell.
Jordan, F. (1997). An occupational hazard? Sex segregation in tourism employment. *Tourism Management* 18(8), 525–34.
Knowles, T., Diamantis, D., and El-Mourahbi, J. B. (2001). *The Globalization of Tourism and Hospitality: A Strategic Perspective*. London: Continuum.
Lea, J. (1988). *Tourism and Development in the Third World*. London: Routledge.
Lee, R., and Wills, J. (eds) (1997). *Geographies of Economies*. London: Arnold.
Lockwood, A., and Guerrier, Y. (1989). Flexible working in the hospitality industry: Current strategies and future potential. *Journal of Contemporary Hospitality Management* 1, 11–16.
MacCannell, D. (1973). Staged authenticity: Arrangement of social space in tourist settings. *American Journal of Sociology* 79(3), 589–603.
MacCannell, D. (1976). *The Tourist: A New Theory of the Leisure Class*. New York: Schocken Books.
Markwick, M. C. (2001). Tourism and the development of handicraft production in the Maltese islands. *Tourism Geographies: An International Journal of Tourism Space, Place and the Environment* 3(1), 29–51.
Massey, D. (1995). *Spatial Divisions of Labour: Social Structures and the Geography of Production*, 2nd edn. London: Macmillan.
Milne, S., and Pohlmann, C. (1998). Continuity and change in the hotel sector: Some evidence from Montreal. In D. Ioannides and K. G. Debbage (eds), *The Economic Geography of the Tourist Industry: A Supply-Side Analysis* (pp. 180–94). London: Routledge.
Riley, M., Ladkin, A., and Szivas, E. (2002). *Tourism Employment: Analysis and Planning*. Clevedon: Channel View Publications.
Ritzer, G. (1998). *The McDonaldization Thesis*. London: Sage.
Ritzer, G. (1999). *Enchanting a Disenchanted World: Revolutionizing the Means of Consumption*. Thousand Oaks, CA: Pine Forge Press.
Shaw, G., and Williams, A. M. (2002). *Critical Issues in Tourism: A Geographical Perspective*, 2nd edn. Oxford: Blackwell.
Shaw, G., and Williams, A. M. (2004). *Tourism and Tourism Places*. London: Sage.
Sinclair, M. T. (1997). Issues and theories of gender and work in tourism. In M. T. Sinclair (ed.), *Gender, Work and Tourism*. London: Routledge.
Storper, M., and Walker, R. A. (1989). *The Capitalist Imperative*. Oxford: Blackwell.
Telfer, D. J. (2002). The evolution of tourism and development theory. In R. Sharpley and D. J. Telfer (eds), *Tourism and Development: Concepts and Issues* (pp. 35–78). Clevedon: Channel View Publications.

Tickell, A., and Peck, J. (1992). Accumulation, regulation and the geographies of post-Fordism: Missing links in regulationist research. *Progress in Human Geography* 16(2), 190–218.

Urry, J. (1987). Some social and spatial aspects of services. *Environment and Planning D: Society and Space* 5, 5–26.

Urry, J. (1990). *The Tourist Gaze: Leisure and Travel in Contemporary Societies*. London: Sage.

Urry, J. (1995). *Consuming Places*. London: Routledge.

Watson, G. L., and Kopachevsky, J. P. (1994). Interpretations of tourism as commodity. *Annals of Tourism Research* 21, 643– 60.

Williams, A. M., and Balaz, V. (2000). *Tourism in Transition: Economic Change in Central Europe*. London: I. B. Tauris.

Williams, A. M., and Balaz, V. (2001). From collective provision to commodification of tourism? *Annals of Tourism Research* 28(1), 27–49.

Williams, A. M., and Balaz, V. (2002). The Czech and Slovak republics: Conceptual issues in the economic analysis of tourism in transition. *Tourism Management* 23, 37–45.

Williams, A. M., and Montanari, A. (1999). Sustainability and self-regulation: Critical perspectives. *Tourism Geographies: International Journal of Place, Space and the Environment*, 1(1), 26–40.

Wood, R. C. (1997). *Working in Hotels and Catering*, 2nd edn. London: International Thomson Business Press.

Chapter 6

Cultural Geographies of Tourism

Mike Crang

Introduction

Cultural geography, with its traditions of studying regional cultures, has tended to position "tourism" as a problem, as something that homogenizes local cultures towards one undifferentiated aggregate – an "erosion thesis" where change is seen only as diminishing original cultures and reducing global differences (Hannerz 1996). However, recent work has tried to open up this grim account in two main directions: first, examining tourism not simply as consuming places but also as a dynamic force creating them – which still leaves room for conflict, exploitation, and resistance, but takes a more neutral start-point; second, looking at the cultures of tourists and seeing how these evolve historically. So rather than dismissing tourism as just "a logical extension of the general principle of industrial capitalism to the realm of leisure" (Böröcz in Koshar 1998: 325), treating it as a modern culture in and of itself. Tourism mobilizes powerful social dreams and desires as the currency in which it trades, by offering dream holidays, romance, paradise on earth and so on (Krippendorf 1987). These are social imaginaries, maps of what people believe and hope for – but they are rarely examined as such. As Inglis notes: "The dreams are powerful and beautiful. Of course, dedicated dreambusters in their big boots will, correctly, point out the horrors and boredom of actually existing tightly packaged trips, the mutual exploitation of tourist and native" (Inglis 2000: 5). In this chapter, then, I want to sketch how tourist cultures develop rather than engage in the "dreambusting" that tends to characterize academic work which so often exemplifies distaste, treating tourists almost as another species – "turistas vulgaris" (Löfgren 1999: 264), who travel in "herds," "stampede" onto beaches, "flock" to see places, and "swarm" around "honey-pots."

Analyses of how tourism shapes places can become locked into a "coercive conceptual schema" of tourism "impacting" on local cultures which sees a local culture pitted against a global industry where "cultural changes arising from tourism are produced by the intrusion of a superior sociocultural system in a supposedly weaker receiving milieu" (Picard 1996: 104, 110). This risks portraying the "hosts" as a bounded, static, undivided, and happy culture prior to tourism. Now this is a dubious characterization of even island destinations – as Picard (below) shows in terms of Bali – but seems cock-eyed when we think of places like Las Vegas, Blackpool, or Benidorm, or the city tourist centres of London, New York, or Hong Kong. Thus it seems more productive to use

> a more culturally complex rendering of tourism's "consumption" of places, one that sees not merely a globalizing force bearing down upon a once-isolated community, but also the dynamic ways local cultural meanings – which are themselves a product of a dialogue between local and extra-local cultural systems – wrap the tourism experience in an envelope of local meaning. (Oakes 1999: 124)

I want to start by thinking about what cultural geography can say about the shaping of destinations, about tourism as inventing, making, and remaking places.

Tourism as Geography Writ Large

Tourism is an active agent in the creative destruction of places in what can be a violent, contested, unequal, but sometimes welcomed, transformative and productive process. The process is one of co-construction where the destination is fashioned between different actors. This does not necessarily mean in an equal or harmonious fashion, but it is important not to start by denying locals or tourists any agency in the process, since that leads not only to a negative view of tourism, but to a pessimism about the possibilities for people to shape it. Tourism is part of a reflexive process where all the actors learn from experiences (good, bad, and indifferent). Thus the industry adapts and develops, tourists respond with changing tastes and preferences, and locals rework their identities and strategies in changing conditions. So Picard's (1996) account of Balinese tourism describes a small culture that has experienced large-scale tourist development bringing with it economic and cultural changes. At one level Balinese culture is being "replaced" by touristic culture with local rituals repackaged for tourists. At this level we can see the commodification of a culture turned into a bankable asset and given a new value in terms of its earning potential rather than any "intrinsic" value. But looking at this slightly differently we can see a more intricate set of developments. For a start, touristic interest and marketing of Balinese culture has intersected with a Hindu caste system, whose preservation has enabled powerful Hindus to counter possible Islamic growth on the island as "un-Balinese." Indeed there has been a "Balinization" of Bali, and the aesthetic interest of tourists has prompted locals to reinvigorate cultural activities and celebrate their roles as cultural artists. So that, far from eroding traditional forms, a new vitality and interest have developed in them. Picard suggests this might be called "cultural involution," since:

> The Balinese . . . aspire to become modern while at the same time seeking to maintain their cultural traditions, and to do so, they need money; the tourists, who are the bearers of modernisation, are drawn to Bali essentially by the wealth of its traditions; consequently, for reasons of both cultural conservation and economic necessity, the Balinese cultivate their traditions with a view to procuring the necessary means for their modernisation.

> Thanks to this process of cultural involution, the modernisation of Balinese society may be based not on industrial production, whose destructive effects on traditional social structures is well known, but on cultural productions, thus permitting the establishment of a post-industrial society based on tourism services. (1996: 111)

The implication is that tourism is premised upon and sustained by difference over space, and indeed it may well increase some kinds of differentiation.

Tourism takes dreams and myths and inscribes them on to places; in other words, it spatializes social meanings (Hughes 1998). Tourism could be seen as a semiotic process creating meanings through signs and symbols in a communicative environment (Dann 1996a: 25). Using the analogy of texts and language to look at how tourism inscribes meanings on to the landscape it seems a very literal sort of "geography" with its direct translation as "writing the earth." In doing this it works upon and amplifies associations already existing about places as part of a reflexive developing process – where, for instance, the northern wilderness of Canada was scripted in adventure stories as an arena for masculine endeavor (Phillips 1996) – a reputation as an environment for adventure which tourism has perpetuated and traded upon (Shields 1991). The scripting may also rework the actual histories and geographies of places, as where the carefully maintained and managed deer-shooting ranges of Scotland are marketed in terms of "wilderness" and "natural" scenery (Lorimer 2000). As Jane Desmond notes, "tourism is not just an aggregate of merely commercial activities; it is also an ideological framing of history, nature and tradition; a framing that has the power to reshape culture and nature to its own needs" (1999: xii). With deliberate hyperbole, the architects MVRDV thus predict a Norway turned from a forest to a super-village, the Alps becoming a park with hotel cities, France changing into a "'Guide du Routard' landscape, in which the agricultural products became the instrument for a gastronomically oriented zone penetrated by hotels and restaurants according to special nostalgic rules," and Tuscany as an "international villa park" where "gigantic private gardens are maintained by the former farmers" (MVRDV 2000: 57). Meanwhile other areas become associated with "ludic" activities – spaces where play is not only allowed but, in many cases, demanded. MVRDV suggest there is a single linear city spreading along the Iberian coast, and "[i]t is a space that has become the most effective substitute for the time of the breaking-up party, that countryside festival that industrialization eliminated from the calendar of Europeans" (MVRDV 2000: 109). Tourism forms a "territorialized hedonism" (Löfgren 1999: 269). We might think of these as liminal zones with social rituals where normal rules of conduct are suspended, in times and spaces apart from the everyday (Shields 1991). Spaces become scripted with particular rules of behavior: for instance, on many European beaches women are happy to go topless – but would feel it necessary, in the company of the same people, to put on a top to leave the beach and go for lunch even just across the street – or alternatively may feel pressured to go topless on some beaches. Shields illustrates the long history of beach resorts as places of sexual license and intrigue, or how Niagara Falls became associated with honeymoons to the extent that it became a cliché. Various destinations become coded with a sexualized appeal since "tourism is about desire – desire for change, but also a more sensuous desire to become intimate with the unfamiliar," and so the depicted and marketed "exotic other is most often female. Gender joins race on the manipulated bottom line of tourism" with seduction and adventure both "embodied as male goals in female flesh" (Lippard 1999: 51). This analysis sees language as not only telling or showing but creating and doing (Kirshenblatt-Gimblett 1998: 6). An example is the attempts to transform the everyday into the exceptional through, for instance, literary references, as in south Tyneside becoming "Catherine Cookson country," the North Yorkshire moors "Herriott country," Hampshire becoming "Austen country," and so on (for discussions see Pocock 1992; Dann 1996a; Crang 2002). This process has been likened to one of "sacralization," marking out special and "exceptional" sites.

We thus need to pay attention to the texts of tourism, which may be novels but are more often guidebooks, postcards, travel books, brochures, adverts, and the like. These help shape notions of the destination and can be seen as "linguistic agents of touristic social control" (Dann 1999: 163). This is because guidebooks do not just describe places but set normative agendas of, in the words of Murray's 1858 guide, "what ought to be seen" (Koshar 1998). A semiotic analysis of these materials can tell us something of how a place is being shaped, by examining what or who is depicted (and what and who are not chosen to be included). Dann's (1996b) study of Cyprus package tour marketing showed the hotel is in 68.2 percent of pictures, the pool or beach in 14.1 percent, but that only 17.7 percent depicted the actual locality, suggesting levels of priorities. Meanwhile Chang has argued that cultural marketers may work to simplify or "tame" the associations of specific places. Thus Singapore's "New Asia" campaign involved zoning the ethnically marked "historic" districts of the central city (into the civic quarter, Chinatown, Little India, and Kampung Glam). While this has meant the physical preservation of these areas in the face of massive property development, "by prescribing themes to places, planners inadvertently freeze their identities and stultify their potential to evolve organically, effacing their myriad histories on the one hand while confining their future to a pre-ordained narrative on the other" (Chang 2000: 35).

Tourist discourses create sights to be seen, they etch significance onto the landscape and direct our attention. The ironic plaque on a house in Grasmere (in the Lake District in England) stating that "this house has absolutely nothing to do with Wordsworth" suggests a pertinent truth. Looking at any of the houses that do claim connections, it is the markers and signs that lend lustre, not the building's intrinsic qualities. So, sacralization often depends on texts and stories that circulate elsewhere or around the site so that our sense of having visited somewhere special is premised upon other signs and texts. As Barbara Kirshenblatt-Gimblett put it, there is a phantom landscape of associations underlying the one we see, where "the production of hereness in the absence of actualities depends increasingly on virtualities" so that we travel to actual destinations to experience virtual places (1998: 169, 171).

This, we might say, chimes closely with the aesthetic appreciation encouraged in tourism. An example of vision shaping and sacralizing a site comes from the novel *White Noise* by Don DeLillo:

> Murray asked me about a tourist attraction known as the most photographed barn in America... We counted five signs before we reached the site. There were forty cars and a tour bus in the makeshift lot. We walked along a cowpath to the slightly elevated spot set aside

for viewing and photographing. All the people had cameras...A man in a booth sold postcards and slides – pictures of the barn taken from the elevated spot. We stood near a grove of trees and watched the photographers. Murray maintained a prolonged silence, occasionally scrawling some notes in a little book.

"No one sees the barn," he said finally. "Once you've seen the signs about the barn, it becomes impossible to see the barn...We're not here to capture an image, we're here to maintain one. Every photograph reinforces the aura...They are taking pictures of taking pictures...We can't get outside the aura." (cited in Crang 1996: 438)

The markers, far from being secondary, are actually creating the site. Perhaps an extreme example is that of the small town of Wall's drugstore in South Dakota. In a town of 800 residents, a small drugstore opened in 1931 whose only especial feature was the sale of iced water. It was then a 24 × 60 foot structure. By the 1950s there were some 28,000 signs to "Wall Drug" – and American servicemen and visitors continued to plant them in Korea, Vietnam, Pakistan, Europe, and elsewhere. What is famous about the store is its celebrity – on the back of which it grew to a 55,000 square foot emporium with chapel, art gallery, memorabilia store, and a vast array of kitsch (Meltzer 2002). Markers may be more important than the sites themselves:

The proliferation of markers frames something as a sight for tourists; the proliferation of reproductions is what makes something an original, the real thing: the original of which the souvenirs, postcards, statues, etc. are reproductions. The existence of reproductions is what makes something original, or authentic, and by surrounding ourselves with markers and reproductions we represent to ourselves...the possibility of authentic experiences in other times and other places. (Culler 1981: 132)

The process is bound up with a specific type of vision – where the practice of photography sacralizes the site with tourism as a specific way of seeing, or what John Urry (1990), drawing upon Foucault, called the tourist gaze. We do, though, need to remember the plural influences and multiple motivations people have both individually, when between different holidays or within the same one they may have different priorities and interests at different moments, and for the majority of tourists traveling in (maybe, family) groups, that this is multiplied by the competing and collective desires of different members, rather than simply being a matter of deterministic meanings about destinations. So one of the key ideas is that destinations are shaped, but also that they are shaped ready for a particular sort of reception and particular tourist practices. It is to these tourist practices that I now want to turn.

Being a Tourist, Doing Tourism

It is not just the destinations that are scripted, but also the practices that comprise being a tourist. So if we take the example of the beach resort, the norms and expectations of behavior have clearly evolved through history and it has taken centuries for the seashore to be colonized as the pre-eminent site for recreational visiting, and to be transformed into a theatre of pleasure (Lencek and Bosker 1998: 6), while the practices associated with beaches have marked changing notions of social propriety and cultures of the body. Tourism is a set of learned competences and skills, and most definitely not something natural or innate. Even the apparently obvious sun, sea, and sand tourism comprises a host of specific cultural practices. When MVDRV asked what people actually do at Benidorm, their surveys suggested wandering around town comprises four hours and 14 km per day, with being on the beach taking only three and a half hours, which suggests "tourists surveyed in Benidorm are notable for their passion for the streets... incited by its charms, which they find unending, moved by surprise, encouraged by the possibility of meeting and recognizing and urged on by the fleeting nature of their stays" (2000: 112). We would not suggest that all visitors to Benidorm have a passion for the street, but the point is that neither should we ignore the fact that many do. To illustrate the different norms and practices we might contrast the practices and norms of solitary, undeveloped "edenic" beaches and coves of Menorca or Cornwall with:

> The carefully curated resorts of the French and Italian Riviera [which] parcel out the beach with the precision of Mondrian painting. [Where] in tiny plots staked out by private clubs and hotels, paying guests recline on color-coded chairs laid out with graph-paper rectilinearity in front of brilliantly painted cabanas. The beach fairly sizzles with the erotic voltage of bare-breasted, bare-buttocked beauties and virile stalwarts, but strict decorum, the sensual stew at a steady, socially acceptable simmer. (Lencek and Bosker 1998: xxiii)

Other apparently obvious and banal practices of tourism also reward closer attention. Recently Löfgren has looked at how nineteenth-century nationalists promoted rambling in the Swedish countryside as a way of coming into contact with "real folk" which would enable you to "walk yourself Swedish" (1999: 50). Likewise Edensor has looked to modern British countryside walking to unpack a series of cultivated ideologies of taste and value about independence, a notion of organic peace and contrasts with urban life (2000: 81). The values and habits of even walking thus vary between groups and over time. For some the adventurous and arduous is the aim, for others this implies a reduction in scenic appreciation, while for others the clothing and accouterments offer avenues for pleasure and displaying social identities.

However, we also need to inject some dynamism here – the tourist is not just someone who has a particular cultural baggage or who responds to a given culture of a destination. These two elements are mutually constitutive, and from this it follows that both place and person may change, and change the other. For instance, rumors help shape expectations of visitors (Hutnyk 1996; O'Hara 2001), circulating, not just in a one-way street from marketers to audience, but among tourists, as in Hutnyk's description of "the endless flow of indo-babble" (1996: 145) about stories told about going to India, having been to India, and so forth. Moreover, one of the effects (and sometimes aims) of travel is not to just experience a destination but to change our "self" – in some forms of tourism, as part of a more or less explicit project of "self-creation." We might see "vacationing as a cultural laboratory where people have been able to experiment with new aspects of their identities, their social relations, or their interaction with nature and also to use important cultural skills of daydreaming and mind-travelling. Here is an arena in which fantasy becomes an important social practice" (Löfgren 1999: 7).

So we could examine how tourism fits into, reinforces, challenges, and changes our stories about ourselves. So the flip-side of thinking about "liminal spaces" is to think about the role they play in our lives. It may be that they are experienced cyclically – an annual escape to somewhere we can "be ourselves," or just let our hair down. On the other hand, they might figure as part of an unfolding self-narrative of personal development. Anthropological work links liminal places with rites of passage, where people travel as part of social rituals that mark changing social status and position. So we might take "backpackers" or independent travelers as examples. In Britain there is a strong class and age association where a "gap year" out is taken between school and going to university, whereas in New Zealand the "Big OE" (Overseas Experience) tends to be longer and associated with a post-university stage (Bell 2002; Mason 2002), but in both cases they form rites of passage. Such episodes may be part of the reflexive construction of autobiographies, by linking interior narratives of personhood with exterior experiences and practices, and as moments when we take time out to "find ourselves" and offer answers to questions we ask about "who we are" at key junctures in our lives (Desforges 2000: 936). We bring our backgrounds and desires, but tourism also impacts upon our senses of self. Even for the antithesis of the backpacker – the Club Med "party" holiday – the definition of self through hedonistic consumption can feed back into senses of identity. "The full process of the anticipation of holidays, the act of travel, and the narration of holiday stories on return are all tied into an imagination and performance which enables tourists to think of themselves as particular sorts of person" (Desforges 2000: 930). Tourism both sustains and is sustained by stories that define ourselves. The telling of these stories is as important as actual events where "the journey becomes a spatial and temporal frame to be filled with identity narratives" (Elsrud 2001: 605). This may be by differentiating ourselves from others – as in backpackers who deride the collective travel of Japanese tourists, and who thus form "imagined ghosts upon which to build difference narratives" (Elsrud 2001: 607) and instead define their own holiday in terms of adventure, solitariness, and indeed the thrill of stories of hardship and danger.

These stories are exchanged in a variety of locales such as hostels, particular cafés, and so forth with specific topics and norms of conversation (Hutnyk 1996; Murphy 2001). Information about specific places is exchanged as people plan itineraries and stories get exchanged. However, these conversations also spill out into circulating narratives, as where it is becoming common for "experienced" backpackers to distance themselves from newcomers by calling the latter "FNGs" – an abbreviation for "fucking new guys" used by US soldiers in Vietnam, and popularized by Alex Garland's novel about backpacking, *The Beach* (Elsrud 2001: 610). The experience becomes one of the resources we mobilize and recount when we are called upon to define ourselves. Using Pierre Bourdieu's terms we could see trips as a means of accumulating "cultural capital" (Bourdieu 1984, 1991) where, just as economic resources can be accumulated, so too can cultural "wealth" be stockpiled. The value of particular experiences is going to change according to time and taste – and also social group. So different holiday experiences will have different values to different tourists. This highlights a dynamic field where as one site becomes popular it loses or gains cachet with different groups of people according to the various canons of taste that apply within and between groups. *The Beach* exemplifies this, being structured around the quest for the unspoilt beach, as yet untramped by other tourists – even backpackers – hidden in a national park:

> "travellers try to find new islands beyond Ko Pha-Ngan because Ko Pha-Ngan is now the same as Ko Samui."
> "The same?"
> "Spoiled. Too many tourists. But look this book is three years old. Now maybe some travellers feels these islands past Ko Pha-Ngan are also spoiled. So they find a completely new island, in the national park."
> "But they aren't allowed in the national park"
> Étienne raised his eyes to the ceiling. "Exactly! This is why they go there. Because there will be no other tourists."...
> Set up in Bali, Ko Pha-Ngan, Ko Tao, Borocay, and the hordes are bound to follow. There's no way you can keep it out of the Lonely Planet, and once that happens it's countdown to Doomsday. (Garland 1996: 25, 139)

Here the protagonists' cultural capital comes from avoiding the "hordes," from the abilities that allow them to find an untouched beach. This is not a literal example of how tourists think; rather, it resonates with an audience because it does evoke some of the feelings about tourism and because we have seen that this novel is one of the discourses circulating with tourists and shaping their practices. Many studies suggest there is something of a continuum of cultural values – for upper- and middle-class Western tourists – that privileges first the explorer, then the traveler, and judges them in distinction to the déclassé mass tourist. More scrupulous accounts also point out that academic sympathies with travelers and against tourism tend to suggest commonalities of cultural values and practices between academics and elite tourists.

One upshot of seeing tourist practices as ways of narrating ourselves is that we have to look at tourist itineraries as not just beginning and ending with the trip but also extending into the whole life course. For instance, people take still or video pictures in part to provide evidence of a trip, of experience accumulated and places visited to be shown upon their return (Neumann 1988: 23; Crang 1997). More strategically this might be linked with notions of sights that "must be seen" or the way people "do" Italy to suggest that a key element of tourism is not going to places, or being at places but rather attaining the status of "having been" somewhere (Kelly 1986). Thus if we look at iconic sites like the Taj Mahal that are often a non-negotiable, "must-see" element in tours to India, tourists may only spend about an hour there – but it is an "essential" hour since such "symbolic sites are foci around which the mnemonic devices of travel narratives and photography are structured" (Edensor 1998: 107, 141). We might therefore see many tourist itineraries as ways of picking up sites, ticking off activities that are required in order to have a "successful" holiday. There are holidays that market directly to this practice – for instance literary tours, where tourists pay often substantial prices to be guided around key sites in an author's life and writings (Crang 2002). Here there may be "serious leisure" with dedicated "collectors" building up complete sets of sites over several vacations. As we noted above, the cachet offered by different activities or their "cultural capital" will vary, and may well change over the life course of an individual. These changes may be due to changes in the "value" of a destination, as somewhere becomes more well known it may lose the distinctiveness it held when visited; or it may be that social groups change, so what was admired by one's 18-year-old friends as mature and sophisticated appears less so when one is 30; or it may be that through our lives we move through different social circles which value things differently.

This notion of self-development can also apply to apparently "non-cultural" practices. Thus if we look at beach tourism, there is often a great investment in the body – in honing it, tanning it, and displaying it. Not only coming back from holiday with a body bearing the physical imprint of a sunny climate, not only deliberately and possibly dangerously exposing it to the sun, but exercising before the holiday, going to tanning salons in advance. It is not just the bodies and cultures of locals that are shaped through tourism. As Picard notes, the bare breasts of Bali were used in illustrations as part of campaigns to make Bali a (male) paradise of Western fantasies, but ironically, "today it is the Balinese, dressed from head to foot, who come to contemplate the generously exposed breasts of the foreign women" (1996: 80). This points to a whole range of corporeal practices and investments bound up in tourism. Beach tourism's sun worship is so obvious it is easy to overlook, but as we have seen there are also bodily performances of walking holidays, and we might add a range of sports and adventure tourism. In the latter the mode of perceiving the landscape and our bodily relationship may well change, as where we think of a shift from the physical exertion of slowly climbing a peak to the stomach-churning thrill of hurtling from a bridge on a bungee line – from an appreciation of the individual and sublime nature we have an accelerated body and an inverted sublime (Bell and Lyall 2002) or a body pitted against the rocks and rapids in whitewater rafting (Cloke and Perkins 1998). Indeed we might look at the whole constitution of body–nature relationships, where some speak to notions of conquest, or the body transcending nature, while others may speak to the sense of loss of self (Fullagar 2001).

Conclusions

I have attempted to show that destination and tourist cultures are both transformed and produced through tourism. We started with notions of tourism "scripting" and shaping the landscape and then addressed how tourists too are scripted by these preshaped destinations. I hope I have suggested that both of these processes are massively overdetermined in a recursive and reflexive system that creates a multitude of opportunities and unplanned outcomes. Throughout I have tried to emphasize a language of scripts (where language shapes action) rather than images and representation (where reality is more or less distorted). Places are made, done, and performed, and through making, doing, and performing them tourists become, well, tourists. In other words both places and tourists are processual. The implications of all these examples, then, are that tourists do not have pre-given identities; rather, there are identities formed through processes of identification and self-creation. One of the tendencies is to see this self-definition as operating against a foil of localized and bounded local cultures – destinations which are visited. But we need caution, since the meaning of places is constructed through actors and discourses that are both local and distant, and when we think of "locals" and "tourists," we should recall that many of us are both (mostly at different times and places, as our homes too may well be someone else's destination, but we may even switch roles in one place, for instance as we take out guests to visit particular sites).

This sense of instability is not meant to imply that outcomes are always surprising, and certainly not that they are always happy, but that there are opportunities here, for change, contestation, and even struggle. The cultural geography of tourism is not about a fixed map of destinations and peoples who are more or less neatly packaged or accurately represented, but rather about a set of practices that constitute notions of what "over there," and thus "over here," is like and what constellations of practices and performances that recursively produce destinations and visitors. These two categories are produced as active creations and accomplishments which require work from many parties and vary over and space. Moreover, not only do the cultures of tourism vary, they represent the active spatialization of identities through the scripting of places, most surely, but also as people structure their performances through the division of space into home/destination/transit, through their mobilization of travel stories and experiences in various situations.

REFERENCES

Bell, C. (2002). The Big "OE." *Tourist Studies* 2(2), 143–58.

Bell, C., and Lyall, J. (2002). The accelerated sublime: Thrill-seeking adventure heroes in the commodified landscape. In S. Coleman and M. Crang (eds), *Tourism: Between Place and Performance* (pp. 21–37). Oxford: Berghahn Books.

Bourdieu, P. (1984). *Distinction: A Social Critique of the Judgement of Taste*. London: Routledge.

Bourdieu, P. (1991). *Language and Symbolic Power*. Cambridge: Polity.

Chang, T. C. (2000). Theming cities, taming places: Insights from Singapore. *Geografiska Annaler B* (1), 35–54.

Cloke, P., and Perkins, H. C. (1998). Cracking the canyon with the Awesome Foursome: Representations of adventure tourism in New Zealand. *Environment and Planning D: Society and Space* 16(2), 185–218.

Crang, M. (1996). Envisioning urban histories: Bristol as palimpsest, postcards, and snapshots. *Environment and Planning A* 28(3), 429–52.

Crang, M. (1997). Picturing practices: Research through the tourist gaze. *Progress in Human Geography* 21(3), 359–74.

Crang, M. (2002). Placing Jane Austen, displacing England: Between book, history and nation. In S. Pucci and J. Thompson (eds), *Jane Austen and Co.: Remaking the Past in Contemporary Culture* (pp. 111–32). New York: SUNY Press.

Culler, J. (1981). Semiotics of tourism. *American Journal of Semiotics* 1, 127–40.

Dann, G. (1996a). *The Language of Tourism: A Sociolinguistic Interpretation*. Wallingford, Oxon.: CAB International.

Dann, G. (1996b). The people of tourist brochures. In T. Selwyn (ed.), *The Tourist Image: Myths and Myth Making in Modern Tourism* (pp. 61–82). Chichester: Wiley.

Dann, G. (1999). Writing out the tourist in space and time. *Annals of Tourism Research* 26(1), 159–87.

Desforges, L. (2000). Traveling the world: Identity and travel biography. *Annals of Tourism Research* 27(4), 926–45.

Desmond, J. (1999). *Staging Tourism: Bodies on Display from Waikiki to Sea World*. Chicago: University of Chicago Press.

Edensor, T. (1998). *Tourists at the Taj: Performance and Meaning at a Symbolic Site*. London: Routledge.

Edensor, T. (2000). Walking in the British countryside: Reflexivity, embodied practices and ways to escape. *Body & Society* 6(3–4), 81–106.
Elsrud, T. (2001). Risk creation in traveling: Backpacker adventure narration. *Annals of Tourism Research* 28(3), 597–617.
Fullagar, S. (2001). Encountering otherness: Embodied affect in Alphonso Lingis' travel writing. *Tourist Studies* 1(2), 171–84.
Garland, A. (1996). *The Beach*. London: Penguin.
Hannerz, U. (1996). *Transnational Connections: Culture, People, Places*. London: Routledge.
Hughes, G. (1998). Tourism and the semiological realization of space. In G. Ringer (ed.), *Destinations: Cultural Landscapes of Tourism* (pp. 17–32). London: Routledge.
Hutnyk, J. (1996). *The Rumour of Calcutta: Tourism, Charity and the Poverty of Representation*. London: Zone Books.
Inglis, F. (2000). *The Delicious History of the Holiday*. London: Routledge.
Kelly, R. (1986). *International Tourism: Pilgrimage in the Technological Age*. The American Marketing Association's International Marketing Conference, Singapore.
Kirshenblatt-Gimblett, B. (1998). *Destination Culture: Tourism, Museums, and Heritage*. Berkeley: University of California Press.
Koshar, R. (1998). "What ought to be seen": Tourists' guidebooks and national identities in modern Germany and Europe. *Journal of Contemporary History* 33(3), 323–40.
Krippendorf, J. (1987). *The Holiday Makers: Understanding the Impact of Leisure and Travel*. Oxford: Heinemann.
Lencek, L. and Bosker, G. (1998). *The Beach: The History of Paradise on Earth*. London: Secker & Warburg.
Lippard, L. (1999). *On the Beaten Track: Tourism, Art and Place*. New York: The New Press.
Löfgren, O. (1999). *On Holiday: A History of Vacationing*. Berkeley: University of California Press.
Lorimer, H. (2000). Guns, game and the grandee: The cultural politics of deerstalking in the Scottish highlands. *Ecumene* 7(4), 403–31.
Mason, P. (2002) The Big OE: New Zealander's travel experiences in Britain. In C. M. Hall and A. M. Williams (eds), *Tourism and Migration* (pp. 87–102). Dordrecht: Kluwer.
Meltzer, E. (2002). Performing place: A hyperbolic drugstore in Wall, South Dakota. In S. Coleman and M. Crang (eds), *Tourism: Between Place and Performance* (pp. 160–75). Oxford: Berghahn Books.
Murphy, L. (2001). Exploring social interactions of backpackers. *Annals of Tourism Research* 28(1), 50–67.
MVRDV (2000). *Costa Iberica*. Barcelona: Actar.
Neumann, M. (1988). Wandering through the museum: Experience and identity in a spectator culture. *Border/lines* (Summer), 19–27.
Oakes, T. (1999). Eating the food of the ancestors: Place, tradition and tourism in a Chinese frontier river town. *Ecumene* 6(2), 123–45.
O'Hara, C. (2001). Passing through Pantnirtung: Rumour, practice and perceptions of place. *Tourist Studies* 1(2), 149–70.
Phillips, R. (1996). *Mapping Men and Empire: A Geography of Empire*. London: Routledge.
Picard, M. (1996). *Bali: Cultural Tourism and Touristic Culture*. Singapore: Archipelago Press.
Pocock, D. (1992). Catherine Cookson country: Tourist expectation and experience. *Geography* 77, 236–43.
Shields, R. (1991). *Places on the Margin: Alternative Geographies of Modernity*. London: Routledge.
Urry, J. (1990). *The Tourist Gaze: Leisure and Travel in Contemporary Societies*. London: Sage.

Chapter 7

Tourist Practices and Performances

David Crouch

Introduction

Why talk practices and performances? During recent years debates in tourism have turned increasingly to a consideration of the tourist, the consumer, as a subjective individual who actively constructs and constitutes his and her value of the tourism, or tourist, experience. Ideas of practice and performance provide fresh ground for a robust development in understanding tourism. Key conceptual areas through which this shift to the tourist has occurred include cultural and social geography, social anthropology, studies of material and visual culture, performance studies, sociology, and social psychology. These areas are not dealt with equally in this chapter, and cultural geography is used as an organizing discipline. This discipline now contributes to the debates in these other disciplines through its articulation of space, and thereby to issues of tourism in terms of contemporary culture and identity. The particular emphasis explored here is the bodily character of the ways in which individuals encounter tourism experiences, events, and spaces and their potential connections with the figuring of their own lives. The developing notion in cultural geography of the active relation between the individual, space, and life-contexts is germane to making sense of tourism, including the idea that tourists make sense of space themselves. It is through this reorientation as tourist studies that tourism becomes the focus of increasing multi- and interdisciplinary interest.

These conceptual debates inform a number of more familiar areas of tourism analysis. Making better sense of what the consumer does in tourism informs further the role of tourism in contemporary society and culture and the ways in which these relationships work. Understanding places of tourism as more than the product of an industry and its marketing unsettles the view of the industry and its cultural mediators as main players in tourism, and in tourism space-making. More broadly the tourist and tourism operators and producers and their relationships become problematic. The working of tourism consumption becomes more complex. Similarly issues of heritage and the critique of authenticity, and the position of the tourist as the object of management and regulation are raised in new ways. The anticipation of tourism changes and, for example, niche markets turns on a more sophisticated interpretation of what the tourist is doing. The role and mode of policy in tourism may, similarly, need to be rethought. There is a strong professional interest in understanding how people make sense of their experiences, and of places and events. Imagination and creativity are essential in this unstable and changing market. The panoply of work on tourist behavior and motivations has tended to come from the producer's perspective, presumes rationality in the tourist, and seeks to discover how to situate what the tourist does within the framework of formal production, management, and policy. In this chapter I argue the value of new discussions and their orienting theoretical arenas that are contributing to the fuller understanding of contemporary tourism.

Indeed the word "doing" usefully mobilizes the discussion of practice and performance. "Practice" refers to the encounters tourists have with their surrounding material space, metaphor, and imagination and a complexity of contexts. "Performance," as used in this chapter, concerns the tourist-in-action rather than the staged events and displays that resemble the tableaux of representations familiar in terms of brochures and televisual and filmic contexts through which places may be experienced *by* the tourist. Of course all of these contextual components are important in the experience of the tourist, and these are engaged later in the chapter. The key issue is that they are not adequate in delivering an understanding of that experience. Nor does working only from these contexts to the character and content of what the tourist does, in familiar linear form, provide this understanding. It is in the articulation between what the tourist does, the industry, and wider culture, as contexts, that a clearer comprehension of tourist activity is likely to emerge.

The tourist experience is only partly, incompletely, prefigured in the contexts and representations of the tourism "producers." Tourism locations are often poorly considered in terms of the word "product"; they may frequently serve as somebody else's church, mosque, shopping street, beach, river, or mountain. Similarly the familiar positivist polarization between tourism business, policy, investors, even hosts, on the one side as producers, and tourists on the other as consumers is no longer sustainable. Tourists emerge from this critical reflection on practice and performance as both consumers and, themselves, producers. Tourism is a process rather than merely a product. Tourism is something that people do (Crouch 1999).

This chapter is organized as follows. In the first section the key ideas of practice and of performance are discussed, drawing upon key theorists, and exemplified through a consideration of tourist examples in the literature. In the subsequent section practice and performance are discussed in terms of how they influence the sense that individuals make of what they do, as knowledge, explored through the notion of lay geographical knowledge, in tourism. From this a discussion is developed that takes these debates back to some of the orienting arguments of what tourism is and why tourists do tourism, and in particular the affect and effect of contexts. This section considers the work of, for example, Cohen and Taylor and Rojek and their idea of escape; Urry's position on tourism as significantly understood through the gaze; MacCannell's argument for understanding tourism as a search for deep significance, and the more recent work on identity by Luke Desforges, and on material and visual culture (Cohen and Taylor 1993; Rojek 1993; Miller 1998; MacCannell 1999; Desforges 2000; Urry 2002; Crouch and Lubbren

2003). From this a reflection is made on the working of contexts in tourism, and questions of their renewed engagement with tourist practices and performance are raised. Of course there are limits to the focus on practice and performance, and the intention of this chapter is not to reify the individual but to return tourism to its significant subjective character, and to explain how this works and may be understood.

Thinking Practice and Performance

The particular focus of "practice" developed in this chapter is "embodied practice." "Practice" is a widely used term in social sciences, for example in the work of Pierre Bourdieu. His work on practices argued that they are socially constructed and situated ways of living that produce and reproduce, especially, class distinction (Bourdieu 1984). His empirical research in France evidenced practice as structured process in even the most everyday activities and actions of individuals, from the material objects used to decorate a room to the way they eat fish. Tourism choices would supply another example of this mode of practices. However, an increasingly critical debate developed from this notion of practice through the post-structuralist focus on the subjectivities and flexibilities of individuals as they negotiate and adjust their lives (Fiske 1989; Willis 1990; Miller 1998; Crouch 1999). Focus on embodied practice comes from the developments across the social sciences and humanities called "non-representational" theory. Its emphasis is on the individual as a mind/body construction, not merely thinking but simultaneously engaged in the world bodily. The individual not only thinks but also does, moves and engages the body practically and thereby imaginatively, and in relation to material objects, spaces, and other people. Such aspects may inform the character of reflexivity, as noted further below. The individual is surrounded by spaces rather than acting as an onlooker. The key informing ideas of non-representational work emerge from recent reworking of the ideas of French philosopher Merleau-Ponty (1962).

Merleau-Ponty built on extensive empirical research to argue that the individual is engulfed by space and encounters that space both multi-sensually and multi-dimensionally and is thereby likely to be similarly informed. Touch, a feeling of surrounding space, sight, smell, hearing, and taste are worked interactively. All the senses are involved. However, this mode of embodied practice does not operate as a gathering device but is worked through the way the individual uses her or his body expressively – it turns, touches, feels, moves on, dwells. Rather than set aside, the individual is engulfed by the space around him or her. Paul Cloke and Harvey Perkins have explored the possibilities of the individual acting bodily in a discussion of whitewater rafting (1998). Through what the individual as embodied human being does, he or she engages the world through feeling; as connector as well as receiver. Things, artifacts, views, and surrounding spaces become signified through how the individual feels, and how he or she feels about them.

Furthermore the character of the surrounding world is not merely gathered in data but is engaged, and constituted expressively. Radley points to the significance of expressivity in the way individuals do things, and thereby the way in which performance is felt in a relationship with others, objects, and spaces, and things are given significance (1995). There is a power of being poetic through which places, events, and things are given value. Soile Veijola and Eva Jokinen explored the enactment of the bodily sense through a discourse on the body and the beach. Their work is formulated not merely through the appearance of the body as inscribed with conventions, expectations, and projected desire, but in terms of the bodily practice of the beach by sensuous, and sensual, and poetic beings (Veijola and Jokinen 1994). Individuals can overflow the boundaries of the rational and the objective and be playful, imaginative, and go beyond what is evidently "there" in an outward, rational sense. This capture of space may be described as a poetics of practice, as Birkeland explored in her discussion of the experience of the North Cape in Norway (de Certeau 1984; Birkeland 1999).

Furthermore what is done is frequently done in relation to other people, i.e. inter-subjectively, and therefore the character of events, experiences, and sites is additionally attributed through what people do in relation to others (Crossley 1995). For tourists this may include both other tourists and people who are at that moment not tourists, who may be locals and so on (Crouch 2001). The social anthropologist Tim Ingold has used ideas of embodied practice in thinking through how individuals may thereby relate to the world through the practical things they do and how they do them, that Harre terms "the feeling of doing" (Harre 1993; Ingold 2000). Ingold develops his notion of doing in terms of "dwelling" (Ingold 2000). He distinguishes between ideas for things, space, and so on, as prefigured and determinate, and the motor of "dwelling" – of the mix of the everyday and of other influences – that sustains the present and future, from which contemplation and new possibilities of reconfiguring the world, in tensions and flows, can occur.

Before going on to consider how these embodied practices may be worked in constructing and constituting value, character, and geographical knowledge, recent developments in terms of performance are outlined. Like embodied practice, performance is profoundly bodily; expressive, potentially poetic, and inter-subjective (Tulloch 2000). Both acknowledge the often illusory character of body-performance (Radley 1995; Dewesbury 2000). Performance concerns the enaction of life through protocols of engagement, surrounded by ritualized practice, working to pre-given codes, habitually repeated, conservative, working to cultural givens. Yet it can also be potentially disruptive and unsettling, or at least have the potential of openness in refiguring space and the self in relation to those protocols (Carlsen 1996). Tourism experience may, then, be sought and used in ways that both reassure and pursue risk, in different proportions. The general discourse on performance, informed by performance studies, understands the individual's actions to be done in relation to the self or to others, "performed for," including self-regulation and negotiation inter-subjectively.

This potentially unsettling character of performance is called performativity. This awkward term seeks to identify the potential of ordinary life actions, incidental, not focused around intentions and competences. These are components of how individuals can move their life forward, discover new potential in things and in what they do, as "becoming," the possibility of making something different from life's apparently prefigured and mundane protocols. "Becoming" tends to be considered in terms of profound rearrangement of the self, and as niches and nuances in getting along with life, that may or may not make life more enjoyable or bearable, and may consist of numerous momentary acts that may themselves be significant (Dewesbury

2000). Yet individuals do not only seek to move life forward, and individuals have the potential to both secure where they are in life and what things mean to them, and to change it: "holding on" and "going further," becoming something new. The expressive character in performativity is especially significant in "becoming." Dance has been considered in terms of its potential for opening up possibilities in the individual through what he or she does (Radley 1995; Thrift 1997; Malbon 1999). Dance can combine choreography and deviation from it; dance is a significant constituent of the tourism experience, and Malbon's work on clubbing in London bears comparison with that on Ibiza and Rio tourism.

The reconfiguring, or reconstitutive potential, of performance is increasingly cited in terms of performativity, as modulating life and discovering the new, the unexpected, in ways that may reconfigure the self, in a process of "what life (duration, memory, consciousness) brings to the world: the new, the movement of actualization of the virtual, expansiveness, opening up": enabling the unexpected (Grosz 1999: 25). Immediately the potential of such a perspective for understanding tourism is considerable, given the ways in which tourism can be presented and contextualized in terms of its potential for breaking free, and the exotic. Edensor has explored the performance of tourism (2001). In his work on the Taj Mahal he has identified the diverse ways in which different groups of visitors make their way around the site, amble and queue and make sense of their experience and the spaces they occupy (1998).

But tourism can also be used to regulate the self, to sustain or achieve security in life, to "hold on" to life-references. Even in the apparently extreme tourism of white water rafting there is considerable effort to achieve security in the way things are done, and dance can be enacted with repetition in the maintenance of life identity rather than in "going further." The care that tourists may give to identifying the minutiae of their travel, of knowing what to expect, in advance, and the frequent repeated visits they may make, points to tourism as "holding on" as well as "going further." To investigate the ways in which these different elements may be negotiated by the tourist offers a rich potential for better understanding the tourist consumer, and the partial character of the messages offered in tourism representations, brochures, and staged events, to which this chapter will return. Discourses on embodied practice focus on the potential of the individual to develop their own significance in events, places, and things. The work on performance, and in particular so-called performativities, points in particular toward the negotiative work the individual may do in opening up new possibilities in their life. Practice and performance color the character of consumption. In consequence working through the circuits of consumption may also color the character of production as producers respond to their consumers' practice.

In the following sections the value of embodied practice and the performative are considered further in terms of their informing an understanding of tourists "making sense" of what they do. Consequently it is suggested that such a perspective may also enlighten the possibilities and limits of refiguring identity through the process of tourism, and the ways in which these may be achieved and give character to tourism spaces. Working from a perspective that engages (but does not privilege) practice augurs for a consideration of geographical knowledge as informed by embodied practices and performativities. Embodied practices – multi-sensual, multi-dimensional, expressive, inter-subjective, and poetic – and the unevenness and negotiative possibility of performativities take the formal frames of reference of life further, and can be incorporated in the ways in which we understand individuals making sense of what they encounter. Thus individuals may consume spaces and constitute spaces in their own experience.

As Shotter argues, from a social constructionist perspective in his exploration of knowing and feelings, the individual works the practice of everyday life ontologically, making sense through what is done and the ways in which it is done (Shotter 1993). Burkitt (1999) has engaged the embodied character of this process of practical ontology and its emergent ontological knowledge and its potential role in refiguring the self and negotiating identity. Embodied practice is engaged in the flow of reflexive thinking that individuals make (Lash and Urry 1994) to constitute the character of their knowledge. In part at least individuals produce their own geographical knowledge through what they do and think (Crouch 2001), not in detachment from contexts and representations, but in relation to them. The mechanism of this process will be returned to in the following section.

Rethinking Tourism

In this section the ideas of embodied practice and performance are considered in relation to some of the key debates on tourism and the tourist. A discussion on embodied practices and performativities introduces an emphasis on what the tourist does and how the "doing" may inform their experience of tourism, of tourist sites, places, and events. This section sometimes uses the present tense in an effort to capture the immediacy of tourist consumption.

First, it is absolutely important to stress that the shift of focus to the individual and the idea of the embodied does not turn away from the importance of contexts, of representations of events, activities, or places, and the role of mediators in their construction. Instead it delivers these in new dimensions and perspectives. Cultural contexts work in relation to the individual *and* vice versa, and in a way that incorporates the bodily and mental character of the individual (Crossley 1995; Nash 2000; Tulloch 2000). The individual operates in relation to the cultures in which she or he lives and finds him- or herself in, for example, tourism. Equally, however, in order to make sense of the working of contexts in tourism it is not appropriate to consider them in isolation from the individuals who, amongst other things, enact them.

Furthermore Ann Game argues, through her own reflections on being a visitor to Bondi Beach and to the English Pennines, that the individual constructs his or her own "material semiotics" of places through their bodily encounters (1991). Acknowledging the significance of body-practices it is appropriate to argue that these become *embodied semiotics* (Crouch 2001). A reading of the signs of tourism needs to be reconfigured in terms of this practical ontology. The power of contexts in the tourist experience is thereby informed. The tourist may stand and stare at prepared sites/sights, but engages them as a complex individual in the round and with an expressive character, extending character of his or her own to the site as well as using it as informing data. The arrival at the site may conclude a long trek that is exciting but also tiring. Moreover the "visit" is a moment in a whole series of events, actions, arrangements and waitings, and emotions.

The relative power of particular site-visits in the flow of tourist activity may be more complex than guide-book privileging may imply. Tourism analysis, whether in terms of the power of individual sites/sights or the power of the individual in gazing upon them, has tended to extract particular moments of experience, and to work with one line of inquiry (MacCannell 1999; Urry 2002). Instead of such overarching perspectives the complexity of tourism needs to be unpacked. The tourist can refigure the significance attached to particular sites. Why do tourists tend to set up their cameras where they are directed? Is this merely an expression of the pre-programmed tourist? It may be because these points are convenient and practical or mark an achievement. Yet the value given to the photographs they take may be contextualized just as much from their own feelings at the time, their company, and so on (Crang 1997, 1999). Recent work in material culture studies has argued that objects can be given new significance through the ways in which they are consumed. Consumption is taken to be an active process whereby objects, products, places, and things can be made to *matter*; they are made to matter through the way individuals consume them (Miller 1998). The programmed visual culture of tourism can be similarly refigured, as in the diverse versions of London Bridge in Arizona (Jewesbury 2003). Sites, destinations, and particular locations are constantly being refigured. To practice and to perform are components of the flow of contemporary culture. Meanings change and are changed.

Tourism undoubtedly has components of seeking escape (Rojek 1993; Cohen and Taylor 1993). The arguments of performativity support this potential in what individuals may achieve, however momentarily, possibly with longer-term significance. However, it is in the complex tensions of going further and holding on that the individual tourist may make some resolution of what can be achieved. The awareness, or feeling, of being able to change one's life, however temporarily, in the practices of being a tourist may be significant in the tourist's frequent desire to return and to experience this again.

In changing destinations the individual may seek to continue the possibility of change, however frustrated their desire may be. In any of these cases, people negotiate what they are doing, how they feel, and cope with, or reject, staged performances and visual or aural tableaux that precede and follow, and may seek to reconstruct memory in the present. Memory is constantly refigured in practice and performance through what individuals do. As things are done, other "events" are remembered and re-placed into the present. Memory is temporalized and can reinvigorate what one is doing "now"; it is also reinvigorated and can be rerouted in the "now," but not in an exact rerun of the past (Crang 2001). Performing time/spacing appears to be more than a linear "moving on" from ideas, and memory is operated as an active character of performativity. As Bachelard argues, we have "only retained the memory of events that have created us at the decisive instants of our pasts" (2000: 57). These are drawn into a focus through the character of performativity, in nodes and knots of significance. When individuals speak of what and how they "do" they compile events reduced to an instant. Although we "may retain no trace of the temporal dynamic of the flow of time" (Bachelard 2000:

57), moments of performance when and through which things are remembered as significant can be revealed.

In the doing, moments of memory are recalled, reactivated in what is done, and thus, while memory may be drawn upon to signify, it is made anew, drawn through performance, and thus flows in time with the other components of performance. It is less that memory is performed than it is "in performance." Thus memory and the immediate are performed as complexities of time. Individuals do not simply remember by picking the memory up momentarily, they return to it through performance and re-form it. Time, too, is performed again and again, differently, and embodied thereby, grasped from clock or other time and wound up in body-performance. At the same time representations of tourism events and sites do not act on a tabula rasa. Most individuals have experienced a tourist site or event, or find it resonant in other parts of their own lives. Individual places and objects too, are remembered as significant because of the ways in which they were encountered (Radley 1990). The significance of places and artifacts is not merely constituted through significance that is pre-given and projected, but also gained in the practice and in combinations of the two, and through reflection.

"Modern" societies seek to separate and regularize social practices, and tourism is one manifestation of the fracturing of work and leisure (Urry 1990: 2). Tourist places and services are "consumed" because they provide pleasurable experiences that are different from those encountered in everyday life. It is because of this difference from the normal environment that Urry claims modern tourism can be interpreted as a "gaze."

> The tourist gaze is directed to features of landscape and townscape which separate them off from everyday experience. Such aspects are viewed because they are taken to be in some sense out of the ordinary. The viewing of such tourist sights often involves different forms of social patterning, with a much greater sensitivity to visual elements of landscape or townscape than is normally found in everyday life. People linger over such a gaze which is then normally visually objectified or captured through photographs, postcards, films, models and so on. These enable the gaze to be endlessly reproduced or recaptured. (Urry: 1990: 1)

The tourist "gaze" is an important component of a deeper, wider practice (Urry 2002). Looking is complex too. There is an engaging, connecting, caring content and character of looking, rather than merely a detached, observing, exploitative one. Of course these different elements work together, or may figure more prominently at certain moments than others. Yet it is insufficient to argue that the presentation of a sight for sightseeing necessarily enforces the detached gaze. The achievement of regulation is complicated through the diversities of consumption. The diversities, partly through social distinctions, of tourism enable individuals in contemporary culture to experience something different from their world outside being a tourist (Urry 2002). Yet rather than comprehend the tourist acting in a tourist bubble there is increasing evidence that tourism overflows the boundaries of its apparently tight contexts and is rather a component of ongoing life (Crouch, Aronsson, and Wahlstroem 2001). Moreover the individual may use tourism to discover, reaffirm or to change his or her identity. Desforges (2000) argues that individuals backpacking along the Andes may use this activity in an active negotiation of their identity. They may enact this through their bodily practice in particular places, in cultural contexts, and in ways in which the individual makes sense of the experience. Along the way they may enact adjustments, negotiations, and also tensions in their lives, relationships, and identities. Tourism emerges from this discussion as a less stable component of contemporary culture, less easily controlled and managed in terms of contemporary society.

From a perspective of practice tourism is an encounter. An encounter between people, people and space, amongst people, bodily, and in a way that engages expectations, desire, contexts and representations, imagination, and feeling. Such an encounter occurs in particular spaces, events, and activities. Thus meaning and value in tourism are constructed and constituted in a complex way. The embeddedness of the everyday practice and meaning of the use of space for tourist consumption, its "lay" geographic knowledge, may be described as

> a process in which the subject actively plays an imaginative, reflexive role, not detached but semi-attached, socialised, crowded with contexts. This includes the gaze, and much more. The resulting knowledge resembles a patina and kaleidoscope rather than a perspective with horizon, a series of mutually inflected and fluid images rather than a map...the subject bends, turns, lifts and moves in often awkward ways that do not participate in a framing of space, but in a complexity of multi-sensual surfaces that the embodied subject reaches or finds in proximity and makes sense of imaginatively. This combination contains meanings of landscapes, fragments, spaces, whole and abstract places, abstractions of the city and the country, street, nation, gender, ethnicity, class, valley, arena and field, through which human feelings, love, care and their opposites may be refracted. The subject mixes this with recalled spaces of different temporality. (Crouch 1999: 12)

Further relevance of this discourse on embodied practice and performance for making sense of tourism emerges in the form of a reworking of the notions of host and guest. The relation has frequently been polarized, and considered in terms of one-way exploitation. Of course there is a possibility of exploitation both ways (Hitchcock, Stanley, and Siu 1997). Moreover, the complexities and flows in an increasing number of host cultures mean that both host and guest operate in a situation of change, flux (Clifford 1997). Furthermore, both performative and embodied practice offer means through which to comprehend the more intimate character of the ways in which individuals as tourists may encounter and value a place and its culture, that may disrupt contextual characterization and merge with everyday performances of locals (Crouch, Aronsson, and Wahlstroem 2001). For example, being a tourist may offer more grounds for the enactment of caring, engaging visuality than the detached component of the gaze may assert. This is not to argue naive utopianism but to engage the complexity of what is happening, from which more reasoned responses may be achievable.

Conclusions

The discourses of embodied practice and performativity concern the individual and thereby seek to comprehend more completely what, for example, the tourist does, and the sense he or she makes of what he or she does. These interpretations offer new components for research methods too. In-depth and ethnographic work, including visual methods and participant observation, are some of the key mechanics that provide insight into practice and performance and demand reflexivity of the researchers (Crouch 2001). Heritage, sustainable culture and environments, and indeed the notion of authenticity, are enabled to address new grounds through which tourism generates significance and value. The power of tourism in the contemporary world may also need to be refigured through the discourse on practice and performance. While the power of investment and global capital movements, of major redevelopment and the erasure of local cultures and environments, need not be rehearsed (Meethan 2001), the cumulative, and diverse, consequences of tourism need to be comprehended from an awareness of the tourist's competences in refiguring the world. There is considerable potential in engaging the insights of practice and performance in relation to the diverse contexts of tourism brochures and other visual culture, and what individuals do at home. Thus, while the idea of embodied practice may appear ephemeral, practice constantly informs knowledge, holds on, reshapes, and refigures. The two approaches considered in this chapter enhance the understanding of tourism consumption.

REFERENCES

Bachelard, G. (2000). *The Dialectics of Duration.* Manchester: Clinamen Press.

Birkeland, I. (1999). The mytho-poetic in northern travel. In D. Crouch (ed.), *Leisure/Tourism Geographies* (pp. 17–33). London Routledge.

Bourdieu, P. (1984). *Distinction: A Critique of the Social Judgement of Taste.* London: Routledge.

Burkitt, I. (1999). *Bodies of Thought: Embodiment, Identity and Modernity.* London: Sage.

Carlsen, M. (1996). *Performance: A Critical Introduction.* London: Routledge.

Clifford, J. (1997). *Routes: Travel and Translation in Late Twentieth-Century Travel.* Cambridge, MA: Harvard Press.

Cloke, P., and Perkins, H. S. (1998). Cracking the canyon with the Awesome Foursome. *Environment and Planning D: Society and Space* 16, 185–218.

Cohen, S., and Taylor, L. (1993). *Escape Attempts*, 2nd edn. London: Routledge.

Crang, M. (1997) Picturing practices: Research through the tourist gaze. *Progress in Human Geography* 21(3), 359–73.

Crang, M. (1999). Knowing, tourism and practices of vision. In D. Crouch (ed.), *Leisure/Tourism Geographies* (pp. 238–56). London: Routledge.

Crang, M. (2001). Rhythms of the city: Temporalised space and motion. In J. May and N. Thrift (eds), *Time/Space: Geographies of Temporality* (pp. 187–207). London: Routledge.

Crossley, N. (1995). Merleau-Ponty, the elusive body and carnal sociology. *Body and Society* 1, 43–61.

Crouch, D. (1999). The intimacy and expansion of space. In D. Crouch (ed.), *Leisure/Tourism Geographies* (pp. 257–76). London: Routledge.

Crouch, D. (2001) Spatialities and the feeling of doing. *Social and Cultural Geography* 2(1), 61–75.

Crouch, D., Aronsson, L., and Wahlstroem, L. (2001). Tourist encounters. *Tourist Studies* 1(3), 253–70.

Crouch, D., and Lubbren, N. (eds) (2003). *Visual Culture and Tourism.* Oxford: Berg.

De Certeau, M. (1984). *The Practice of Everyday Life.* Berkeley: University of California Press.
Desforges, L. (2000). Traveling the world: Identity and travel biography. *Annals of Tourism Research* 27(4), 926–45.
Dewesbury, J.-D. (2000). Performativity and the event. *Environment and Planning D: Society and Space* 18, 473–96.
Edensor, T. (1998). *Tourists at the Taj.* London: Routledge.
Edensor, T. (2001). Performing tourism, staging tourism: (Re)producing tourist space and practice. *Tourist Studies* 1(1), 59–82.
Fiske, J. (1989). *Understanding Popular Culture.* London: Routledge.
Game, A. (1991). *Undoing the Social: Towards a Deconstructive Sociology.* Buckingham: Open University Press.
Grosz, E. (1999). Thinking the new: Of futures yet unthought. In E. Grosz (ed.), *Becomings: Explorations in Time, Memory and Futures* (pp. 15–28). Ithaca, NY: Cornell University Press.
Harre, R. (1993). *The Discursive Mind.* Cambridge: Polity.
Hitchcock, M., Stanley, N., and Siu, K. (1997). The South-East Asian "living museum" and its antecedents. In S. Abram, J. Waldren, and D. Macleod (eds), *Tourists and Tourism: Identifying with People and Places* (pp. 197–221). London: Berg.
Ingold, T. (2000). *The Perception of the Environment: Essays in Livelihood, Dwelling and Skill.* London: Routledge.
Jewesbury, D. (2003). London Bridge in Arizona. In D. Crouch and N. Lubbren (eds), *Visual Culture and Tourism* (pp. 223–40). Oxford: Berg.
Lash, S., and Urry, J. (1994). *The Economies of Signs and Space.* London: Sage.
MacCannell, D. (1999). *The Tourist: A New Theory of the Leisure Class.* London: Macmillan.
Malbon, B. (1999). *Clubbing: Dancing, Ecstasy, Vitality.* London: Routledge.
Meethan, K. (2001) *Tourism in Global Society: Place, Culture, Consumption.* Basingstoke: Palgrave.
Merleau-Ponty, M. (1962). *The Phenomenology of Perception.* London: Routledge.
Miller, D. (ed.) (1998). *Material Culture: Why Some Things Matter.* London: Routledge.
Nash, C. (2000). Performativity in practice: Some recent work in cultural geography. *Progress in Human Geography* 24(4), 653–64.
Radley, A. (1990). Artefacts, memory and a sense of the past. In D. Middleton and D. Edwards (eds), *Collective Remembering.* London: Sage.
Radley, A. (1995). The elusory body and social constructionist theory. *Body and Society* 1(2), 3–23.
Rojek, C. (1993). *Ways of Escape.* London: Routledge.
Shotter, J. (1993). *The Politics of Everyday Life.* Cambridge: Polity.
Thrift, N. (1997). The still point: Resistance, expressive embodiment and dance. In S. Pile and M. Keith (eds), *Geographies of Resistance* (pp. 124–54). London: Routledge.
Tulloch, J. (2000). *Performing Culture.* London: Sage.
Urry, J. (1990). *The Tourist Gaze.* London: Sage.
Urry, J. (1999). Sensing leisure spaces. In D. Crouch (ed.), *Leisure/Tourism Geographies* (pp. 34–45). London: Routledge.
Urry, J. (2002). *The Tourist Gaze,* 2nd edn. London: Sage.
Veijola, S., and Jokinen, E. (1994). The body in tourism. *Theory and Society* 11(3), 125–51.
Willis, P. (1990). *Common Cultures.* Buckingham: Open University Press.

Part III Producing Tourism and Tourism Spaces

Chapter 8

The Cultural Turn? Toward a More Critical Economic Geography of Tourism

Keith G. Debbage and Dimitri Ioannides

Introduction

With hindsight it would appear that the untimely death of tourism geographer Stephen Britton in June 1991 was a major blow for more than just his immediate circle of family and friends. Just before his death, Britton (1991) published what has become one of the academic classics in tourism geography and an intellectual benchmark in the development of our understanding of how the tourist industry produces tourism and manipulates tourism spaces. Britton powerfully argued that tourism is a sophisticated production system that explicitly markets and packages places and, therefore, is implicated in many of the economic, political, and cultural issues of current concern to geographers. These issues include the ongoing debates about the globalization of capital; the creation of new "postmodern" landscapes; the transformation and rapid emergence of the cultural product industries; broader processes of industrial and regional restructuring; the changing role of cities as places of consumption as well as production; labor and entrepreneurial issues; and place commodification and its connections to symbolic and cultural capital. Britton provided an enduring and provocative road-map for tourism geographers to follow and we honor his 1991 publication "Tourism, capital and place: Towards a critical geography of tourism" by incorporating some of his language in the title of this chapter.

Partly based on the momentum generated by Britton's paper – although even today many tourism geographers are relatively unaware of much of his work – some tourism geographers have taken up Britton's charge to identify more explicitly the capitalistic nature of tourism and better integrate their work into contemporary debates in geography. The purpose of this chapter is to review some of these crucial recent developments, particularly as they relate to broader theoretical issues focused on the economic geography of tourism. More specifically, we intend to follow up on our own call for tourism geographers to embrace a supply-side orientation (Ioannides and Debbage 1998).

The study of tourism has been handicapped by inattention to the supply side, and we have long argued that comprehending tourism requires improved understanding of how the tourism production system manipulates and shapes tourist places and destinations (Debbage 1990, 2000, 2002; Ioannides 1995; Debbage and Daniels 1998; Ioannides and Debbage 1997, 1998). Consequently, this chapter highlights specific works that have made an explicit attempt to dovetail tourism supply-side issues with the broader body of work in economic geography. We also argue that the recent "cultural turn" in economic geography (Thrift and Olds 1996; Crang 1997; Barnes 2001) offers numerous opportunities for tourism geographers interested in exploring the broader economic-cultural manifestations of the tourist industry.

Some Definitional Issues: The Tourist Industry – Fact or Fiction?

Tourism's status as an industry remains a hotly debated issue. Unlike many other economic activities, there is no universally accepted definition of tourism. Part of the difficulty rests with the amorphous nature of tourism and the conceptual and methodological complexity characterizing terms like tourism, travel, and tourist. The lack of consensus on what these terms mean has resulted in conceptual fuzziness that has triggered an ongoing debate between geographers, and other social scientists, about the validity of treating tourism as an industry (Tucker and Sandberg 1988; Leiper 1990; Smith 1994, 1998; Tremblay 1998; Wilson 1998).

Tourism is a fundamentally different type of industry from other forms of commodity production. According to Debbage and Daniels (1998: 23), "tourism is no simple product but, rather, a wide range of products and services that interact to provide an opportunity to fulfill a tourist experience that comprises both tangible parts (e.g., hotel, restaurant, or airline) and intangible parts (e.g., sunset, scenery, mood)." For many tourists, the actual purchase and consumption/production of tourist services (e.g., the airline seat, the meal, the admission ticket) may be incidental to "non-market" activities such as independent sightseeing, hiking, sunbathing, or photography. Leiper (1990) coined the phrase "partial industrialization" to capture the notion that tourism has significant non-industrialized component parts, while Urry (1990) utilized the idea of the "tourist gaze" to demonstrate the wider context of the social relations that shape the production and consumption of the tourist experience – a point to which we shall return in our later discussion of the "cultural turn" in economic geography.

More recently, Daniels and Bryson (2002) have argued that the ongoing transformation of advanced economies has yielded increasingly complicated production chains that frequently blur the boundaries between the service sector and manufacturing.

They suggest that we should just forget about artificial terms like "services" and "manufacturing" and instead think about production chains and information flows within and between companies. Daniels and Bryson also argue that intangible assets or non-physical factors such as exotic holiday destinations (i.e., symbolic goods) are increasingly determining economic value, and that the ways in which services are "manufactured" is a much-neglected avenue of research. Such an approach might be useful to tourism geographers since the production of the tourist experience has both manufactured and service component parts.

Fortunately, the commodification of the tourist experience has received substantial attention in recent years and the work of Smith (1994, 1998) has been central to our heightened understanding of the tourism production system. Smith articulated a complex production process for tourism that begins with a series of primary inputs or factors of production (e.g., land, labor, and capital). These primary inputs are then converted into intermediate inputs or tourist facilities (e.g., restaurants, airlines, hotels) that are further refined by various intermediate outputs or tourist services (e.g., room service, and the serving of meals and drinks). The end result is a final output or tourist experience irrespective of the motivation of the individual tourist (e.g., for pleasure, business, or visiting friends or relatives). A central element in this sort of conceptualization of the tourism product is what Urry (1990) termed the "spatial fixity" of tourist services where part of what is consumed is, in effect, the *place* in which the product is located and produced.

According to Daniels and Bryson (2002), the notion that both producer and user must be "co-present" in time and place may be one of the unique or distinctive features of several service industries, including health care, education, and tourism. Certainly, tourism services require the active involvement of consumers in their production. For example, certain tourism products do not strictly exist until the consumer arrives at the point of production or destination and consumes the tourist experience (e.g., the experience of spending a night in a luxury hotel or of gazing on a famous painting in an art gallery). In this sense, tourism is an "experience good," and thus is implicated in the raging debates in economic and cultural geography about symbolic and cultural capital. Center-stage in this debate is how the creation and marketing of experiences through the nascent cultural products industry – and the related place commodification it entails (e.g., theme parks, festival marketplaces, and conference centers) – can shape the economic geography of production in both urban and rural areas.

Although it is now well understood that the tourism production system is inherently heterogeneous and complex, involving both manufacturing and service inputs, many of the conventional geographical models of tourism have continued to fail to incorporate all the complexities of the supply-side of tourism into the spatial context. However, the tourist industry (e.g., airlines, travel agents, tour operators, and hotel chains) can heavily influence the geography of origin–destination tourist flows. We now highlight some of the more recent works in tourism geography that have attempted to more fully integrate supply-side issues in developing a more critical economic geography of tourism production.

Toward a More Critical Economic Geography of Tourism Production

In previous work, Ioannides and Debbage (1998) have suggested several new research directions for a more informed economic geography of the tourist industry. Their recommendations include: the development of a more rigorous and flexible conceptualization of what comprises the tourism production chain; a better appreciation for how the larger competitive environment shapes the geography of tourism production; and a heightened awareness of the ongoing place and cultural commodification processes at play in the contemporary economy, especially as they relate to the tourism production chain.

We have already touched on some of these issues relating to the tourism production chain, but we also strongly recommend that better understanding of the tourism production system be grounded in the logic of industrial classification. Roehl (1998: 75, 76) argued that the relatively new North American Industrial Classification System or NAICS "will create the opportunity for the improved study of tourism geography" and "may also help to reintegrate tourism geography into the mainstream of economic geography." Prior to 1997, the Standard Industrial Classification System or SIC was the primary manner in which US economic activity was classified by government. Roehl (1998) argued that many economic activities that were part of the tourism production system could not be identified using the SIC system. He suggested that the more refined and disaggregated NAICS has provided tourism geographers with a more detailed and sophisticated level of analysis for studying supply-side issues. For example, Roehl stated that, while data on sightseeing services were not recoverable in the SIC system, it is possible to analyze scenic and sightseeing transportation under the new NAICS. He also suggested that one advantage of using NAICS is that it encourages multiple definitions of tourism depending on the context, and that it will facilitate cross-national studies of tourism in all three NAFTA countries – the USA, Mexico, and Canada. However, despite the richness of the data available since the introduction of the NAICS in 1997, we have been unable to find a single tourism geography research publication that has extensively utilized this database. While we confess we may have missed some of the more contemporary NAICS-based research being undertaken, we nevertheless encourage tourism geographers to better exploit this under-utilized resource.

One related area where there has been some progress in terms of defining and measuring tourism as an industry from an empirical standpoint has been the development of the tourism satellite accounts (TSAs) approach, a system that derives from a country's national accounts (Smith 1998). A number of countries, including the US and Canada, have now adopted TSAs in order to measure tourism's impact on various economic sectors (Kass and Okubo 2000). Smith (1998: 49) makes it clear that a TSA "is not a definition of tourism... [instead]... it is a tool for measuring and describing economic activity directly attributable to tourism." Nevertheless, even though the TSA can be described as a powerful methodological tool for calculating the tourist industry's magnitude in any given economy, most tourism geographers have thus far shied away from making use of it in their recent work, and there is no evidence that economic geographers on the whole are familiar with the concept. Obviously, this may have something to do with the fact that the concept is fairly novel but, again, we urge tourism and economic geographers to make use of TSAs when attempting to measure tourism's economic impact on different sectors.

By contrast, greater progress has been made in our understanding of how the tourism production system is shaped by the larger competitive environment. Some of the most recent and most theoretically stimulating work in this field has been carried out by Agarwal et al. (2000), Agarwal (2002), Torres (2002) and Hjalager (2000). Agarwal et al. (2000) echoed the concerns of Ioannides and Debbage (1998) when they argued that the overall understanding of the economic geography of tourism production is theoretically isolated and threadbare. In an analysis of tourism development in the UK, they found that changes in tourists' consumption patterns, changes in the scale and ownership of production through strategic alliances, and changes in the geographical organization of production are all leading to new supply-side structures. Agarwal et al. (2000) also suggested that the most promising work on the geography of tourism production has focused on the role of globalization, labor markets, small businesses and entrepreneurship, information technology, and economic restructuring processes. They also articulated a research agenda for tourism production by suggesting that tourism geographers should focus more attention on developing typologies of small businesses in tourism to assist in our understanding of the spatial variation of small tourism businesses like bed and breakfast inns and farm tourism. Finally, they persuasively argued for the need to provide more empirical work investigating the social and spatial division of labor in tourism companies, and also a better handle on how the forces of globalization and commodification have shaped the geography of tourism production.

Agarwal (2002) followed up on her earlier work by linking Butler's (1980) resort cycle model to broader economic and social changes in the geography of production. She argued that greater attention to restructuring processes can help explain the spatial variation in economic performance among localities and tourist destinations. In an analysis of three declining English seaside resorts – Minehead, Weymouth, and Scarborough – Agarwal found that, in response to increasingly discerning markets, all three resorts sought to introduce more flexible production methods targeting a variety of niche markets.

It was less clear whether this change in production strategy was explicitly connected to the ongoing, contested debate about Fordist/post-Fordist shifts in the geography of production (Ioannides and Debbage 1997). For those readers unfamiliar with this debate, Fordism describes the dominant industrial production method for much of the last century (i.e., economies of scale and standardized production) and derives its name from Henry Ford's automated assembly-line production methods. By contrast, post-Fordism refers to the relatively recent shift to economies of scope and high levels of product differentiation and the sophisticated customization of the product.

Agarwal (2002) argued that declining market shares in the English seaside resorts reflected a "general weariness" with the product, although it may have less to do with the Fordist/post-Fordist dialectic and more to do with the plummeting symbolic capital of seaside resort holidays in the UK domestic market. No matter how much effort has been made to improve the competitiveness of the product in places like Minehead, Weymouth, and Scarborough, they can no longer compete with the cachet attached to an overseas trip to the continent of Europe, America, or the South Pacific. The manner in which shifts in consumer tastes and consumption preferences can dramatically reconfigure the geography of production is an under-researched area worthy of more attention from tourism geographers. For example, it remains unclear if production-based relationships in the tourism industry are significantly culturally defined, even though the nature of consumption is crucially important in tourism since its services are produced and consumed in the same location (i.e., spatial fixity).

Torres (2002) has partially corrected this imbalance by providing some insight into how the consumption preferences of tourists might influence the tourism production system. Her research is notable because it is one of the first empirically grounded Fordist analyses of the tourism production chain. Torres conducted a survey of 615 visitors to the Yucatan Peninsula and 60 Cancún hotels to provide a contextual application of the Fordist/post-Fordist theoretic. She argued that, while

Cancún appeared to be the archetype of a Fordist, mass tourism destination, a closer examination revealed a more heterogeneous tourist space that offered more flexible, customized forms of mass tourism. Torres suggested that interpreting the Fordist/post-Fordist dialectic as binary logic underplays the complex spectrum of Fordist and post-Fordist influences that can simultaneously act upon the larger tourism production system (i.e., neo-Fordism) (see Ioannides and Debbage 1998). Based on her empirical work, Torres argued that the predominantly Fordist modes of production and consumption in Cancún have evolved to provide greater access to offbeat destinations and to cater to more specialized niche markets in order to meet changing consumer demand for alternative products to "sun and sand" (e.g., archeological and eco-tourism tours). She concluded by suggesting that tourism development processes in resorts like Cancún are not static or trapped in a predetermined evolutionary path of mass tourism as suggested by Butler's (1980) resort cycle model. Instead, resorts are shaped by the larger competitive environment where capitalistic systems of production are embedded in the wider context of the social relations of consumption at a global scale, resulting in a complex and continuously changing tourism landscape.

Another formidable area of research long neglected by tourism geographers is that of industrial districts and agglomeration economies. Economic geographers have long studied why specific clusters of interrelated firms that agglomerate in specific metropolitan regions are more successful than others, particularly with regard to high-tech industrial districts such as Silicon Chip Valley, California, and Route 128 in Boston. However, Hjalager (2000) questioned why economic activities that are connected to tourism and resorts have not yet been included in this powerful analytical framework. Hjalager argued that many of the essential features of an industrial district are directly applicable to tourism destinations. These key features included: an interdependence of firms oftentimes triggered by a division of labor and subcontractual relationships; flexible firm boundaries in terms of numerical and temporal flexibility (e.g., seasonal variations in the number of employees); cooperative competition such as joint marketing schemes or the development of strategic alliance networks between competitors (e.g., airlines and hotels); the maintenance of trust through sustained collaboration; and a community culture with supportive public policies, particularly in regard to the provision of physical infrastructure and land-use planning. While Hjalager (2000) accepts that elements of the industrial district literature do not facilitate a direct comparison with tourism resorts, she questions why tourism researchers have largely ignored the industrial district literature. Other researchers such as the Harvard Business School's Michael Porter and Princeton economist Paul Krugman have successfully embraced the agglomeration/industrial district literature to great effect and much acclaim (Krugman 1995; Porter 1980, 1990, 2000) although little of their work focuses on tourism production systems.

Hjalager concludes by posing a number of intriguing research questions concerning the manner in which the tourism production system shapes and manipulates tourism spaces. Some of the more explicitly spatial research questions included: What is the relationship between local/global collaboration and a firm's economic performance? and How does geographic proximity stimulate the development of new tourist products and production methods?

It is our hope that tourism geographers will rise to Hjalager's call and develop a research agenda in this area over the next few years. One recent example of such a response is Jackson and Murphy's (2002) extension of Hjalager's work in an analysis of tourism clusters in Albury-Wodonga, Australia, and Victoria, Canada. They applied Porter's (1980, 1990, 2000) logic of competitive advantage and utilized some of his work on industrial clusters in their own examination of the internal structure of tourism destinations. More importantly, Jackson and Murphy (2002) utilized those features of industrial districts first identified by Hjalager as most useful in any tourism analysis as a comparative reference point for their own work. They argued that the industrial district literature cited by Hjalager generally refers to the clustering of firms that make varied products at different points in the value chain, albeit within the same generic industry (e.g., automobile industry or high-tech sector). By contrast, Porter's cluster theory is better designed to accommodate an extremely heterogeneous product, and thus more suited to tourism analysis, especially given the complex mix of supplier arrangements in most tourism destinations. The value of the work of both Hjalager (2000) and Jackson and Murphy (2002) is that it demonstrates to tourism geographers that they can tap into the industrial district literature and play a key role in situating the competitive strategies of the tourist industry in a broader theoretical context. Such work is important not just in an academic sense but also in terms of providing useful policy guidance from a management perspective.

The "Cultural Turn" in Economic Geography: Implications for Tourism Geographers

According to Scott (2001: 16), "one of the more remarkable attributes of the post-Fordist production system . . . is the rising significance of [the] cultural products industries in national output and employment." By some accounts, the cultural products industry comprises about 3 percent of the US labor force and is disproportionately represented in large cities. For example, over 50 percent of the 3 million plus workers employed in the cultural products sector in the US were located in metropolitan areas with a population of 1 million or more (Scott 2001). Most definitions of the cultural products industry include the media and entertainment sectors (e.g., film, television, music, and publishing), fashion-intensive consumer goods such as high-end clothing and jewelry, plus advertising and tourist facilities or places of entertainment. Of course, large cities are major centers of both production and consumption and it is no accident that the recently redeveloped Times Square district is both a major tourist attraction and host to some of the world's largest news media and entertainment conglomerates (Gladstone and Fainstein 2001). Although most researchers acknowledge the important role of the tourist industry in cultural products complexes like Times Square, a universal definition of the culture industry remains elusive and highly contested.

The rapid growth of the culture products milieu has been partially triggered by the ongoing commodification of culture and experience which has in turn seen the emergence of what some have called symbolic or cultural capital (Bourdieu 1984; Featherstone 1991; Zukin 1998). We return full circle to the Britton (1991) article for a fuller explanation of what all this means for tourism geographers. According to

Britton (1991: 465), places are increasingly marketed as desirable products for tourists "not necessarily as ends in themselves, but because visits to them, and the seeking of anticipated signs and symbols, are a vehicle for experiences which are to be collected, consumed and compared." Based on Britton's interpretation, we would argue that tourism is inherently a social construction with an explicit spatial dimension (e.g., origin–destination flows and spatial fixity).

Tourism is thus heavily implicated in what Barnes (2001: 558) and others (Crang 1997; Lee and Wills 1997) have called the "new economic geography" or the "cultural turn" in economic geography that "emphasizes above all the social and especially the cultural character of the economy." Urry (1987, 1990, 1995) has long noted the social-cultural dimension of the tourist industry. He has argued that touristic experiences cannot be left to chance since such experiences are frequently socially constructed and organized and are, thus, not in any sense "natural." Tourists frequently consume goods and services that are in some sense unnecessary and "out of the ordinary" where the viewing of tourist sites and places can generate a "much greater sensitivity to visual elements of landscape or townscape than is normally found in everyday life" (Urry 1990: 3). Urry has also argued that tourists essentially learn to have such experiences, and thus, they require clear markers that any given tourist site is an appropriate venue for such an experience. Based on all this, tourism necessarily involves complex production processes when producing tourism spaces so that regular, predictable, and profitable touristic experiences can be generated. It is in this sense that tourism is at the vanguard of the cultural products industry, where it is less about the material goods an individual possesses, and more about the experiences or "tourist gazes" you have purchased and accumulated over time.

In our view, tourism geographers can play a substantive role in better understanding how these larger processes of cultural transformation manipulate and shape the contemporary economy. In the tourist industry, a focal point has been the growing emphasis on the creation and marketing of tourist experiences through place commodification (Squire 1994). Prototypes of these landscapes include: amusement and theme parks, casinos, spectacle events such as the Olympics, and festival marketplaces like Boston's Faneuil Hall, London's Covent Garden, and Baltimore's Inner Harbor. Even previously dilapidated industrial sites are now commonly promoted as tourism products, such as the Tate Modern gallery in London, where a formerly obsolescent power plant has been transformed into a culture tourism spectacle.

Although many economic geographers are actively engaged in developing a thoroughgoing economic geography of cultural forms, the dialogue with tourism geographers and tourism research is relatively muted. One exception is the recent work by Kneafsey (2001), who analyzed the processes of cultural commodification in the rural tourism economy of Brittany, France. She found that the culture economy was clearly evident through the commodification of the landscape in terms of the production of an "idealized countryside" and "vernacular buildings." Kneafsey also suggested that more empirical research was required to better understand the social relations that shape traditional knowledge and culture in Brittany.

Conclusion

All of these theoretical developments in both tourism geography and economic geography suggest to us that the analysis of how the tourist industry produces tourism spaces can contribute substantially to any critical discourse focused on the geography of production and the cultural economy. It is our contention that tourism geographers can substantively shape the theoretical evolution of this "new economic geography" by more actively engaging the economic geography literature. We remain impressed by and excited about the recent efforts of many tourism geographers, but more work needs to be done.

We believe tourism geographers need to more actively engage the industrial cluster or agglomerative district literature and explore more research questions that explicitly reference the "cultural turn" in economic geography. For example, a key concern in contemporary economic geography remains sorting out the complex causal connections that link consumption and production within diverse agglomerative systems. The tourist industry is a major force in many of these urban agglomerations, yet our understanding of the cultural commodification processes that shape urban tourism remains primitive. Tourism would seem to be an ideal laboratory for investigating such issues especially in "fantasy cities" like Las Vegas, Orlando, and Atlantic City, where the distinction between "reality" and "illusion" is blurred. Tourism geographers need to do a better job of understanding how spaces of tourist consumption connect back to the production of tourist space. Such issues are becoming vitally important as tourism entrepreneurs seem to be increasingly developing themed and controlled environments in spatially constrained tourist districts or "tourist bubbles" (Judd 1999) featuring fantasy experiences and gigantic-sized edifices (e.g., Nike towns, Virgin megastores, ESPN sports zones, and IMAX theatres) in places like Orlando, Times Square, and Los Angeles.

In our introductory comments we honored Britton (1991) for his vision and critical thinking and we believe he anticipated much of the discussion in this chapter. We implore tourism geographers to embrace Britton's call for a more critical examination of the tourism production process, particularly with regard to the manner in which the industry manufactures the social construction of place. By doing so, we believe tourism geographers can inform the larger geographical community about the key role the tourist industry plays in shaping the emerging cultural products industry.

REFERENCES

Agarwal, S. (2002). Restructuring seaside tourism: The resort lifecycle. *Annals of Tourism Research* 29(1), 25–55.

Agarwal, S., Ball, R., Shaw, G., and Williams, A. M. (2000). The geography of tourism production: Uneven disciplinary development? *Tourism Geographies* 2(3), 241–63.

Barnes, T. J. (2001). Retheorizing economic geography: From the quantitative revolution to the "cultural turn." *Annals of the Association of American Geographers* 91(3), 546–65.

Bourdieu, P. (1984). *Distinction: A Social Critique of the Judgement of Taste*. Andover, Hants.: Routledge & Kegan Paul.

Britton, S. G. (1991). Tourism, capital, and place: Towards a critical geography of tourism. *Environment and Planning D: Society and Space* 9(4), 451–78.

Butler, R. W. (1980). The conception of a tourist area cycle of evolution: Implications for management of resources. *Canadian Geographer* 24(1), 5–12.

Crang, P. (1997). Cultural turns and the (re)constitution of economic geography: Introduction to Section One. In R. Lee and J. Wills (eds), *Geographies of Economies* (pp. 3–15). London: Arnold.

Daniels, P. W., and Bryson, J. R. (2002). Manufacturing services and servicing manufacturing: Knowledge-based cities and changing forms of production. *Urban Studies* 39(5/6), 977–91.

Debbage, K. (1990). Oligopoly and the resort cycle in the Bahamas. *Annals of Tourism Research* 17(4), 513–27.

Debbage, K. (2000). Air transportation and international tourism: The regulatory and infrastructural constraints of aviation bilaterals and airport landing slots. In M. Robinson et al. (eds), *Reflections on International Tourism: Management, Marketing and the Political Economy of Travel and Tourism* (pp. 67–83). Gateshead: Business Education Publishers.

Debbage, K. (2002). Airport runway slots: Limits to growth. *Annals of Tourism Research* 29(4), 933–51.

Debbage, K., and Daniels, P. (1998). The tourist industry and economic geography: Missed opportunities. In D. Ioannides and K. G. Debbage (eds), *The Economic Geography of the Tourist Industry: A Supply-Side Analysis* (pp. 17–30). New York: Routledge.

Featherstone, M. (1991). *Consumer Culture and Postmodernism*. London: Sage.

Gladstone, D. L., and Fainstein, S. S. (2001). Tourism in US global cities: A comparison of New York and Los Angeles. *Journal of Urban Affairs* 23(1), 23–40.

Hjalager, A. M. (2000). Tourism destinations and the concept of industrial districts. *Tourism and Hospitality Research* 2(3), 199–213.

Ioannides, D. (1995). Strengthening the ties between tourism and economic geography: Theoretical agenda. *Professional Geographer* 47(1), 49–60.

Ioannides, D., and Debbage, K. G. (1997). Post-Fordism and flexibility: The travel industry polyglot. *Tourism Management* 18(4), 229–41.

Ioannides, D., and Debbage, K. G. (eds) (1998). *The Economic Geography of the Tourist Industry: A Supply-Side Analysis*. New York: Routledge.

Jackson, J., and Murphy, P. (2002). Tourism destinations as clusters: Analytical experiences from the New World. *Tourism and Hospitality Research* 4(1), 36–52.

Judd, D. (1999). Constructing the tourist bubble. In D. Judd and S. Fainstein (eds), *The Tourist City* (pp. 35–53). New Haven: Yale University Press.

Kass, D. I., and Okubo, S. (2000). U.S. travel and tourism satellite accounts for 1996 and 1997. *Survey of Current Business* 80 (July), 8–24.

Kneafsey, M. (2001). Rural cultural economy: Tourism and social relations. *Annals of Tourism Research* 28(3), 762–83.

Krugman, P. (1995). *Development, Geography and Economic Theory*. Cambridge, MA: MIT Press.

Lee, R., and Wills, J. (eds) (1997). *Geographies of Economies*. London: Arnold.

Leiper, N. (1990). Partial industrialization of tourism systems. *Annals of Tourism Research* 17, 600–5.

Porter, M. E. (1980). *Competitive Strategies*. New York: Free Press.

Porter, M. E. (1990). *The Competitive Advantage of Nations*. New York: Macmillan.

Porter, M. E. (2000). Location, competition, and economic development: Local clusters in a global economy. *Economic Development Quarterly* 14(1), 15–34.

Roehl, W. (1998). The tourism production system: The logic of industrial classification. In D. Ioannides and K. G. Debbage (eds), *The Economic Geography of the Tourist Industry: A Supply-Side Analysis* (pp. 53–76). New York: Routledge.

Scott, A. J. (2001). Capitalism, cities, and the production of symbolic forms. *Transactions of the Institute of British Geographers* 26, 11–23.

Smith, S. L. J. (1994). The tourism product. *Annals of Tourism Research* 21(3), 582–95.

Smith, S. L. J. (1998). Tourism as an industry: Debates and concepts. In D. Ioannides and K. G. Debbage (eds), *The Economic Geography of the Tourist Industry: A Supply-Side Analysis* (pp. 31–52). London: Routledge.

Squire, S. J. (1994). Accounting for cultural meanings: The interface between geography and tourism studies re-examined. *Progress in Human Geography* 18(1), 1–16.

Thrift, N. J., and Olds, K. (1996). Refiguring the economic in economic geography. *Progress in Human Geography* 20, 31–7.

Torres, R. (2002). Cancún's tourism development from a Fordist spectrum of analysis. *Tourist Studies* 2(1), 87– 116.

Tremblay, P. (1998). The economic organization of tourism. *Annals of Tourism Research* 25(4), 837–59.

Tucker, K., and Sandberg, M. (1988). *International Trade in Services*. London: Routledge.

Urry, J. (1987). Some social and spatial aspects of services. *Environment and Planning D* 5(1), 5–26.

Urry, J. (1990). *The Tourist Gaze: Leisure and Travel in Contemporary Societies*. London: Sage.

Urry, J. (1995). *Consuming Places*. London: Routledge.

Wilson, K. (1998). Market/industry confusion in tourism economic analyses. *Annals of Tourism Research* 25(4), 803–17.

Zukin, M. (ed.) (1998). *Variations on a Theme Park*. New York: Hill & Wang.

Chapter 9

Transnational Corporations, Globalization, and Tourism

Kevin Meethan

Introduction: Globalization

Globalization is rapidly becoming one of those portmanteau terms that has, over the past decade or so, become part of everyday language. We can find analyses in the mass media, as much as in academia, describing globalization as something to be feared and to be protested about, or something to be welcomed and celebrated as an opportunity. Often there is confusion over whether or not it is the cause of change or the consequence of change (Jones 1995: 199). In short, the arguments over what globalization is, and what it is leading toward, are far from being resolved (Held et al. 1999) even if there is some degree of consensus about what globalization involves. Because of the complexities of these issues, a detailed examination of the overall debates is beyond both the scope and remit of this chapter; rather, my approach toward globalization will be restricted to an examination of a number of economic and institutional changes.

In its most abstract form we can refer to globalization as an expansion and deepening of economic interdependence that is also reshaping, or compressing, the constraints of space and time (Harvey 1989). In this sense, globalization differs from earlier forms of transnational trade and economic ordering on a number of counts, and Hoogvelt (2001) provides a useful summary of the main issues. First, she argues that it is important to distinguish between the existence of a global marketplace and the principle of global markets, with the latter referring to the notion of the global as a shared phenomenal world, so that although our lives are on the one hand circumscribed by localities, on the other hand both social and economic relations can be organized regardless of spatial constraints. For Albrow (1996: 130–2) too, the difference between earlier forms of transnationalism and contemporary globalization is not simply one of degree, and is more than just a culmination of international links. Instead, globalization involves a different level of organization that, among other things, cuts across the established parameters of the nation-state. It is this last point – the apparent erosion of the autonomy of the nation-state – that distinguishes globalization from its earlier predecessor, internationalization.

In turn, the developments described above would not have been possible without global financial deregulation, and in particular the almost universal adoption of neoliberal economic policies from the early 1980s onwards. The easing of financial regulation was coupled with reductions in state funding and ownership across a number of economic sectors, resulting in a restructuring of relations between the state and capital in both the developed and developing economies in favor of private enterprise (Van der Hoeven and Sziracki 1997; Bornschier and Chase-Dunn 1999; Held et al. 1999). On the surface, it may appear that the economic, to say nothing of the political, role of the state has been significantly undermined by globalization. However, this is far from being the case. Rather, what is occurring, as Sassen and Roost (1999) point out, is a transfer of power from the public to the private sector, which relies on different forms of regulation. However, it must also be recognized that in some regions, such as Africa, the tourism sector, as Poirier (2000) notes, is dominated by multinational corporations (MNCs) while Carroll and Fennema (2002: 415) also record that, despite this, international corporate governance is still embedded in national and regional structures (see also the different readings of global–national relationships in Ohmae 1990, 1995; Hirst and Thompson 1996).

The next factor to account for is the role of information technologies (Castells 1996). Most obvious is the speed at which both information and financial transactions can occur and, arguably, these factors have contributed most to the increasing interconnectivity of the world. Industrial sectors such as manufacturing, banking insurance and finance are no longer as constrained by delays in communication imposed by spatial and temporal boundaries, so that both financial transactions and the flow of information takes place in real time.

The fourth factor relates to changes to the organization of many companies and businesses which can generally be described as post-Fordist. Here, labor force flexibility (see Scholte 2000: 222–4) is coupled with the decentralization and geographical dispersal of functions, and the development of global marketing strategies. Although most applicable to forms of mass commodity production, the service sector is not immune to such developments; indeed, one of the consequences of globalization has been a breakdown of the previously established division of economic activities into primary, secondary, tertiary, and quaternary (Dicken 1998: 391–421). However, as Ioannides and Debbage (1998) point out, the shift to post-Fordism within the travel industry is not as clear-cut as may be imagined, and what we see is more accurately described as a "complex and inchoate polyglot" (1998: 119), in which the Fordist and the post-Fordist exist side by side with the pre-Fordist.

Tourism and the Service Sector

One of the issues that needs to be addressed is whether or not tourism can be considered a distinct area of economic activity, or an industry in its own right (see Hall et al., chapter 1; Smith, chapter 2). As Knowles, Diamantis, and El-Mourahbi (2001: 177) point out, the globalization literature has tended to rely on models drawn from the manufacturing sector, whereas the response of the service sector has been rather different. In part this is because the production-consumption chains of services differ in many ways from those involved in commodity production, as this involves an "economy of ideas and knowledge," whereas the relations between production and consumption are of a different order (Aharoni 2000: 13). I would also argue that this applies all the more in the case of tourism; perhaps the term "tourism industry" itself is, as Smith (1998: 32) comments, really "a convenient way of referring to the large and fragmented collection of firms producing commodities that support the activities of people temporarily away from their usual environment." The caveat to be added here is that this also includes a wide range of services, some of which are consumed in the act of travel, and some at the point of destination.

Although tourism also clearly cuts across what are often considered to be sectoral boundaries, it is better conceptualized as part of the service sector, involving as it does financial, insurance, transportation, accommodation, restaurant, and recreational services (for a typology see Dicken 1998: 388). Unlike other forms of production, service providers rely on the more intangible elements of interpersonal skills (DuGay and Pryke 2002: 3) and, as such, the quality of services is judged by their delivery, which cannot easily be separated from the management functions of the provider (Dicken 1998: 388). In terms of tourism this is most evident when we consider the role that hospitality management plays (Go and Pine 1995). What all this adds up to is that, within tourism, the elements of production and consumption are inextricably intertwined at a number of levels, cannot easily be separated out into supply and demand issues, and are better considered as existing in dialectical relationship to each other (Ateljevic 2000; DuGay and Pryke 2002).

As figure 9.1 illustrates, the circuit of production and consumption involved in tourism comprises a bundle of both services and commodities that are purchased and consumed across space and time. At the point of origin these include the purchase of tickets, accommodation, foreign exchange, travel and medical insurance, perhaps also visas and inoculations, to say nothing of the consumer paraphernalia that goes into the tourist's baggage, while in transit and on arrival, tourists also consume a variety of both services and commodities (see also Wheatcroft 1998: 160; Knowles et al. 2001: 156). The availability of such services and facilities is also evidence of the growing spread of accepted minimum standards of service provision within tourism. As Hoogvelt (2001: 133) points out, the corollary of global competition is that goods and services, even if produced for consumption for domestic markets, will now be judged on global standards of quality so that global convergence is at the level of product and service delivery, a fact acknowledged by the World Tourism Organization, which states that "there should be common, irrevoc-

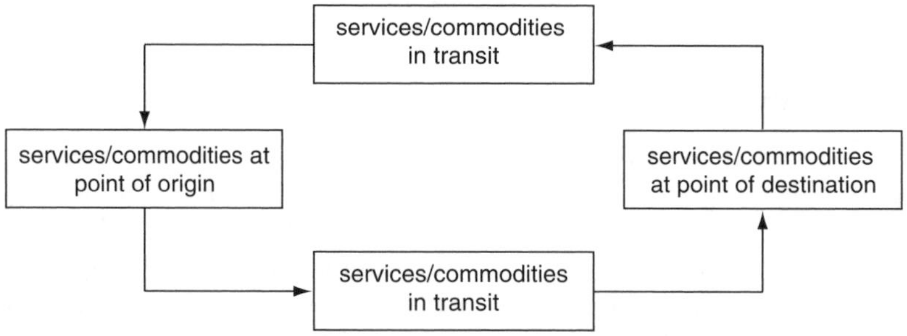

Figure 9.1 Circuit of tourism production and consumption

able criteria of quality which are vital for the consumer independently of category or class of the product, establishment, facility or service sophistication" (World Tourism Organization 2002: unpaginated).

Despite the mobility of commodities, and the production chains that they involve, no activity can really be said to be "placeless" (see e.g. Hoogvelt 2001: 131). For tourism, the specificity of the material and natural environment, of localities and destinations (Meethan 2001; Urry 2002) is a crucial factor. Unlike other economic sectors, tourism destinations cannot simply relocate to take advantage of global cost differentials, even if that may be a factor in the purchasing behavior of some tourists, or in the corporate strategies of the hotel chains and other associated subsectors.

Tourists must travel to consume the destination as product, or rather the product mix which links together a number of different elements. It is these linkages across a number of apparently disparate sectors that also lead to the diversity or fragmentation that Smith (1998) refers to. In part this is also due to the involvement of both large-scale MNCs, as can be found in the airline and hotel subsectors, in addition to the high number of small and medium-sized enterprises (SMEs) which may range in both size and scope from independent hotel and accommodation providers, to bus and taxi operators, to souvenir retailers and producers (see e.g. Xu 1999: 185–9), to caterers, to tour guides and other cultural intermediaries. Finally, we also need to bear in mind that socioeconomic and political elements may also enter into the equation. In terms of tourism production, the state may pursue policies that are designed to impart a particular ideological message and justification of the state (Hall and Jenkins 1995) while national, regional, and local labor market conditions may also influence the nature and development of the tourism product on offer. On the consumption side, we also have to consider that the right to travel, the right to be a tourist, is not in itself a universal phenomenon, even if it may be a universal aspiration (see Bauman 1998; Ghimire 2001). The movement of people for leisure purposes, then, may also be compromised by economic status, as well as the bilateral and multilateral agreements that govern the issuing of visas, currency controls, and other national or regional policies (Xu 1999; Nyaruwata 2000; Teye 2000; Williams and Baláz 2002). Each of these may interact at any stage in the tourism production and consumption circuit, and they are thus bound together in complex arrangements of interdependence. While tourism is therefore rooted in the specific nature of particular destinations, at the same time it is one of the most globalized of activities that cuts across a variety of different sectors and in which, like other service sector industries, the processes of production cannot easily be separated out from those of consumption. Such cross-sector linkages are partly a consequence of changes and developments within information technology (IT).

Information Technology

Leaving aside the simplistic notion that the spread of IT will result in some form of electronic "global village," there is no denying that there is a clear synergy between recent advances in IT and globalization. Hoogvelt (2001: 131) argues that one of the consequences of this is a breakdown of economic activities into those that are undertaken in "real time," where distance and location are no longer significant determinants, and those that are constrained by "material" determinants where location is important. I also argued above that, in the case of tourism, what we actually see is a combination of both elements. Even taking this into account, there are also some areas within the circuit of tourism production and consumption where the introduction of new technologies, the real-time part of the equation, has had a significant impact. In terms of the overall pattern of tourism, this is most evident in the use of computer reservation systems (CRS) by airlines, holiday agents, and hotels, from the late 1970s onwards (Poon 1993). Prior to the introduction of large-scale CRS systems, the booking of airline tickets, and indeed other forms of service such as accommodation, was a labor-intensive activity. Typically this would involve a travel or booking agent searching printed guides for information, then confirming the availability and making a booking by telephone. The introduction of remote networked terminals also resulted in many of the functions being passed on from the service providers to intermediaries such as travel agents (Milne and Gill 1998: 124–5).

In addition, the development of such systems creates the capacity for more than one service, or even a combination of services, to be provided at one point of contact. For example, airline alliances (see below) have developed a system of code-sharing by which onward and connecting flights, even if with a different airline, are booked and ticketed as a single flight. Code-sharing schemes can be bilateral, as well as involving larger alliances, as in the code-sharing systems operated by British Airways (British Airways 2002) and Star Alliance (Star Alliance 2002). The use of such systems can also extend to the selling of services in other subsectors,. For example, Singapore Airlines can also offer hotel accommodation with its tickets at discount rates, and the French railway company SNCF teamed up with the hotel chain Accor so that room reservations could be made at the same time that a train ticket is purchased, with discounts acting as an extra incentive (Accor Hotels 2002).

In these cases, the benefits to the service providers are twofold. By easing the process of booking flights, economies of scale can be achieved through "farming out" the booking function to a wider spread of intermediaries and other service providers while also cutting costs by removing the more labor-intensive elements from the process. The benefits to the consumer are that the one-stop system provides greater ease of access to a number of different services on a global basis. At the more individualized level of consumption, another important factor in the use of IT has been the global spread of both credit and debit banking facilities. As banks are now linked into world-wide and real-time systems, cash can be withdrawn in local currency, and payments made in local currency, through the use of debit and credit cards. However, like all aspects of globalization, the spread and reach of IT are uneven, so that some areas of the world, and particular localities, may not be accessible.

Many of the developments outlined above, such as the use of new technologies and the creation of global alliances, are options only for those who are in a position to afford the necessary investment. As one example, Milne and Pohlman (1998) note that although computer management is influencing the operations of certain SMEs, in this case the hotel trade, the high cost of computerized systems favors larger organizations. However, IT technology changes rapidly, and the advent of cheaper and more powerful desktop computers not only provides capacity for accounting and other management systems, but also allows relatively cheap access to markets through the use of the internet (although resources are required for the constant updating of software and hardware).

For those who have easy access, the internet also has the capacity to make the tourism process much more immediate for individual consumers (Knowles et al. 2001: 88). Not only is information easily accessed, but itineraries can be arranged, and bookings and payments made for a variety of goods and services, which can even extend to the issuing of tourist visas, as is the case with Australia, without the need for intermediaries (see <http://www.cheapflights.com> and <http://www.asia-hotels.com>). The relatively low cost of website provision also makes the internet an attractive proposition to small and medium-sized enterprises, as even the smaller operators can now advertise themselves globally, even if this is subsumed under national and regional branding. An example is provided by Accommodate Scotland, which "promotes Country Houses Hotels, Guest Houses, Bed and Breakfast and Self-Catering Accommodation (Vacation Rentals), as well as Camping and Caravanning holiday sites on the Internet" (Accommodate Scotland 2002).

Overall, the role of IT has followed a trend from the use of large in-house systems, to the development of decentralized systems, to the spread of information and marketing provision through individual home-based internet access. The use of IT systems also extends to the realm of tourism marketing (Vanhove 2001). With IT, consumer spending habits and preferences can easily be logged and stored. The amount of electronic information now in circulation then becomes a tradeable commodity in itself (Aharoni 2000), giving rise to the development of more focused database marketing opportunities (Go and Pine 1995). Developments in IT clearly have an impact at all levels within the circuit of tourism production and consumption. Another important development is that they also create the conditions in which collaboration between different organizations is easier and more effective (Eaton 1996: 37–8).

Alliances and Franchises

In most sectors there is an overall trend toward fewer and larger MNCs at a global level, even if the use of IT allows SMEs to enter into a more globalized market. One example connected to tourism is that of Travelex, which began as a Bureau de Change in London in 1976. Through a process of acquisitions and mergers, most recently the purchase of Thomas Cook's financial services division, it is now the world's largest retail foreign exchange network (Travelex 2000). Another important trend has been an increase in strategic alliances and franchising agreements between MNCs, with those in the airline and hotel sectors being of particular importance for tourism. Since the early 1990s the airline industry has seen a significant growth in the number of strategic alliances. According to Evans (2001), the number of alliances within the airline sector has risen from 280 in 1994 to 513 in 1999 (see also Eaton 1996; Seristo 2000; Sinha 2001). Formed in 1997, the Star Alliance brings together 14 airlines serving over 700 destinations in 124 countries (Star Alliance 2002). The development of these alliances is, in part, driven by technological developments, but also by the deregulation of air travel, and its consequent exposure to a more open market (Wheatcroft 1998). Yet, as Evans (2001) notes, even with the global trend for deregulation and privatization, there are often controls over the ownership of equity. For example, the major shareholder in Malaysian Airlines is still the Malaysian government, while other restraining factors include the number of bilateral and multilateral agreements in force (Sinha 2001).

In addition to formal alliances of this kind, some airlines have developed franchising agreements, such as those operated by Air France (Air France 2002) and British Airways (British Airways 2002). Under these agreements, subsidiary carriers offer a level of service comparable to larger carriers, while the latter benefit from an expansion of routes and destinations under their own brand without the need to create new subsidiaries. According to Evans, this latter factor is also favored by airline customers, who still tend to prefer their country's national carrier (2001: 230). A similar situation also applies to the hotel sector (Jones and Pizam 1993; Go and Pine 1995: 342; Milne and Pohlman 1998). In the case of hotels, alliances offer the ability to exploit local or regional advantages while, at the same time, catering for the needs of an increasingly globalized market (Go and Pine 1995; Aung 2000) from which consumers are also demanding global standards.

Alliances, however, are not the preserve of MNCs and the private sector. (Fayos-Solà and Bueno 2001). As one example, Nyaruwata (2000) describes the development of the Regional Tourism Organization of Southern Africa (RETOSA), a public–private and cross-border alliance which seeks to develop and market the tourism potential of its 14 member states. The problems that RETOSA faces are as much to do with political issues, such as the need for regional policies that coordinate the movement of people across borders, and the need for coordination in terms of investment and development across the region. As Teye (2000) comments, one of the advantages of such developments is the capacity to develop cross-sectoral linkages which, as we have already seen, is a particular characteristic of tourism.

Broadening Services across Sectors

The examples of alliances and franchises cited above are clear evidence of the widening and deepening of economic ties that is characteristic of globalization. What is clear is that the notion of distinct economic sectors is also being challenged by these developments. Service sector MNCs often make strategic decisions not only to expand their core business on a global scale, but also to diversify the nature of the products on offer. Dicken (1998: 410–11) notes how financial services, for example, are diversifying and offering not just one service, but a "package" of different goods/services. Earlier it was stressed that one of the characteristics of tourism was the way in which it ties together, in a circuit of production and consumption, a variety of goods and services from what may otherwise be considered to be different sectors. As Jones (1993: 18) comments, "The future lies with firms who can use the new two-way channels of communication to create customer based relationships, reaching across a whole range of travel, leisure and financial services products" (cited in Go and Pine 1995: 87). For example, the use of air miles schemes, loyalty cards, and frequent flyer programs, and the issuing of credit cards, are developments shared with the retail sector. Accor offer an Asia Pacific Advantage Plus Card (Accor 2002) and Singapore Airlines also offers its own credit and discount card, in alliance with American Express (Singapore Airlines 2002)

Club Med provides another example of expansion and diversification. From its beginnings in France, Club Med has expanded into a global operation which is run as a number of semi-autonomous companies within national borders. In this sense the expansion of Club Med follows the decentralized organizational pattern, and spatial distribution of functions characteristic of globalization. Currently the company runs 120 sea and mountain villages, villas, and cruise ships in approximately 40 countries around the world, and is also diversifying and expanding the nature of its business portfolio. As the latest annual report records: "the Group is expanding its business base to become a services provider specialized in recreational and leisure activities in a broader sense, with a range of businesses developed under the Club Med brand" (Club Med 2001).

This also includes expansion into Southeast Asia, where the market is seen as regional rather than global (see also Ghimire 2001). This also fits the pattern described by Go and Pine (1995: 272), who point out that many hotel chains use different brands under a global marketing strategy in order to serve different and more localized markets and, as Dicken (1998: 411) observes, in many cases localization may be a marketing advantage.

In addition to both geographical spread and the creation of global markets, we can also see the extension of commercial operations outside of what may once have been considered "traditional" sectoral constraints. Globalization then appears to pull in two ways, both toward the creation of MNCs by the extension of operations through take-overs, the formation of strategic alliances or franchising agreements, and, in terms of consumption, toward more localized or regional "branding" and niche marketing. In addition, we also see that the extension of services cuts across "traditional" sectoral boundaries, so that convergence at one level is complemented by divergence at another.

Conclusion

At a base level, globalization refers to a number of convergent trends which, taken together, suggest we are moving toward – if we have not already arrived at – a radically new way of organizing economic and social relations that extends across time and space. Although there is considerable debate as to the nature and extent of global change, there are also several factors that are seen to be the main drivers. Within the tourism industry, broadly defined here to encompass a range of travel and hospitality services, there are a number of MNCs whose organizational characteristics and structure are clearly tied up with the processes of globalization as described above. It is also clear that the processes of globalization appear to favor the larger organizations that can take advantage of global economies of scale in order to expand their operations into new markets.

However, there are also a number of important qualifications to be made at this point, about globalization in general and tourism in particular. First, globalization is not a monolithic entity in itself, but rather a term used to describe a number of converging developments that are technological, economic, political, and also social and cultural. Secondly, these developments are far from being evenly distributed in terms of either economic benefits or disbenefits, and in terms of the new kinds of working practices and organizational forms that follow as a consequence. Thirdly, although these developments are also clearly linked to information technologies, globalization is not technologically determined. Fourthly, we need to be wary about collapsing the complexities of the new globalized economy into a simplistic global–local dichotomy (Dicken 1998; Held et al. 1999), thus ignoring the issue of regional factors, while at the same time there is a need to account for the very localized and specific nature of tourism destinations. These changes operate at a variety of spatial scales. While national boundaries are certainly less constraining than they have been in the past, so that it appears that the drivers of globalization are beyond the control of the national state (Knowles et al. 2001: 176), neither global cultural convergence (Meethan 2001) nor global economic convergence are necessarily foregone conclusions (Rhodes and Higgot 2000).

Although in some areas of activity we can point to increasing globalization, it is also apparent that there are a number of constraining factors at work. This in itself should make us wary of producing grand or universal claims concerning the impacts or effects of globalization, as if it had a single trajectory. The specific nature of tourism – which, as noted above, relies on both real-time and material elements tied together as packages of services, including those provided by global MNCs and more localized SMEs – also has to be taken into account, and as such it is much more diverse than other economic sectors. IT clearly plays an important role in these processes, from the on-time booking systems operated by the airline and hotel conglomerates to the development of home computing and the internet, which allows even smaller providers relatively cheap access to what is, in effect, a globalized market. However, what is unknown is whether or not for such SMEs this potential access translates into increased sales from beyond the national and regional markets they had previously relied on. However, this also offers the opportunity for niche marketing.

The implications for the future are quite clear. Globalization involves more than the large MNCs which appear to play on the global stage, especially given the impacts that the actions of these organizations must have at regional and more localized levels. In addition, standards in hospitality management and the hotel sector are now judged by global comparisons, even at the more localized level of SMEs. Globalization, though, is not entirely about supply-side issues, but also affects patterns of consumption. What marks tourism as a distinct area of activity are the facts that, on the one hand, it is arguably the most globalized of social activities, while on the other it is irreducibly bound to the specificity of locales, and that both these elements are connected through the cycle of production and consumption of commodities, services, and places.

REFERENCES

Accommodate Scotland (2002). Accommodate Scotland bids you a warm welcome from an ancient land! <http://www.scotland2000.com/accom/> (accessed July 3, 2002).

Accor Hotels (2002). *Corporate Information.* <http://www.accorhotels.com/>

Aharoni, Y. (2000). Introduction: Setting the scene. In Y. Aharoni and L. Machum (eds), *Globalization of Services: Some Implications for Theory and Practice* (pp. 1–22). London: Routledge.

Air France (2002). Partners. <http://www.airfrance.com> (accessed July 3, 2002).

Albrow, M. (1996). *The Global Age: State and Society beyond Modernity.* Cambridge: Polity.

Ateljevic, I. (2000). Circuits of tourism: Stepping beyond the "production/consumption dichotomy." *Tourism Geographies* 2(4), 369–88.

Aung, M. (2000). The Accor multinational hotel chain in an emerging market: Through the lens of the core competency concept. *The Service Industries Journal* 20(3), 43–60.

Bauman, Z. (1998). *Globalization: The Human Consequences.* Cambridge: Polity.

Bornschier, V., and Chase-Dunn, C. (1999). Technological change, globalisation and hegemonic rivalry. In V. Bornschier and C. Chase-Dunn (eds), *The Future of Global Conflict* (pp. 285–302). London: Sage.

British Airways (2002). Fact Book 2002. <http://www.bashares.com/content/factbook.shtml> (accessed July 3, 2002).

Carroll, W. K., and Fennema, M. (2002). Is there a transnational business community? *International Sociology* 17(3), 393–419.

Castells, M. (1996). *The Rise of the Network Society.* Oxford: Blackwell.

Club Med (2001). Annual Report 2001. <http://www.clubmed.co.il/corporate/photos/presentations/engann2001.pdf>.

Dicken, P. (1998). *Global Shift: Transforming the World Economy*, 3rd edn. London: Paul Chapman.

Du Gay, P., and Pryke, M. (eds) (2002). *Cultural Economy: Cultural Analysis and Commercial Life.* London: Sage.

Eaton, M. J. (1996). *Globalization and Human Resource Management in the Airline Industry.* Aldershot: Avebury Aviation.

Evans, N. (2001). Collaborative strategy: An analysis of the changing world of international airline alliances. *Tourism Management* 22(3), 229–43.

Fayos-Solà, E., and Bueno, A. P. (2001). Globalization, national tourism policy and international organizations. In S. Wahab and C. Cooper (eds.), *Tourism in the Age of Globalisation* (pp. 45–56). London: Routledge.

Ghimire, K. (ed.) (2001). *The Native Tourist: Mass Tourism within Developing Countries.* London: Earthscan.

Go, F. M., and Pine, R. (1995). *Globalization Strategy in the Hotel Industry.* London: Routledge.

Hall, C. M., and Jenkins, J. M. (1995). *Tourism and Public Policy.* London: Routledge.

Harvey, D. (1989). *The Condition of Postmodernity.* Oxford: Blackwell.

Held, D., McGrew, A., Goldblatt, D., and Perraton, J. (1999). *Global Transformations: Politics, Economics and Culture.* Oxford: Blackwell.

Hirst, P., and Thompson, G. (1996). *Globalization in Question: The International Economy and the Possibility of Governance.* Cambridge: Polity.

Hoogvelt, A. (2001). *Globalization and the Postcolonial World: The New Political Economy of Development*, 2nd edn. Basingstoke: Palgrave.

Ioannides, D., and Debbage, K. (eds) (1998). *The Economic Geography of the Tourist Industry: A Supply-Side Analysis.* London: Routledge.

Jones, C. B. (1993). *Applications of Database Marketing in the Tourism Industry.* PATA Occasional Papers 1. San Francisco: Pacific Asia Travel Association.

Jones, P., and Pizam, A. (eds) (1993). *The International Hospitality Industry: Organizational and Operational Issues.* London: Pitman.

Jones, R. J. B. (1995). *Globalisation and Interdependence in the International Political Economy.* London: Pinter.

Knowles, T., Diamantis, D., and El-Mourahbi, J. B. (2001). *The Globalization of Tourism and Hospitality: A Strategic Perspective*. London: Continuum.

Meethan, K. (2001). *Tourism in Global Society: Place, Culture, Consumption*. Basingstoke: Palgrave.

Milne, S., and Gill, K. (1998). Distribution technologies and destination development. In D. Ioannides and K. Debbage (eds), *The Economic Geography of the Tourist Industry: A Supply-Side Analysis* (pp. 123–38). London: Routledge.

Milne, S., and Pohlman, C. (1998). Continuity and change in the hotel sector. In D. Ioannides and K. Debbage (eds), *The Economic Geography of the Tourist Industry: A Supply-Side Analysis* (pp. 180–96). London: Routledge.

Nyaruwata, S. (2000). RETOSA and tourism development cooperation in Southern Africa. In P. U. C. Dieke (ed.), *The Political Economy of Tourism Development in Africa* (pp. 285–311). New York: Cognizant Communication Corporation.

Ohmae, K. (1990). *The Borderless World: Power and Strategy in the Interlinked Economy*. New York: Harper Business.

Ohmae, K. (1995). *The End of the Nation State: The Rise of Regional Economies*. New York: The Free Press.

Poirier, R. A. (2000). Tourism in the African economic milieu: A future of mixed blessings. In P. U. C. Dieke (ed.), *The Political Economy of Tourism Development in Africa* (pp. 32–48). New York: Cognizant Communication Corporation.

Poon, A. (1993). *Tourism, Technology and Competitive Strategies*. Wallingford, Oxon.: CAB International.

Rhodes, M., and Higgot, R. (2000). Introduction: Asian crises and the myth of capitalist "convergence." *The Pacific Review* 13(1), 1–20.

Sassen, S., and Roost, F. (1999). The city: Strategic site for the global entertainment industry. In D. R. Judd and S. S. Fainstein (eds), *The Tourist City*. New Haven: Yale University Press.

Scholte, J. A. (2000). *Globalization: A Critical Introduction*. Basingstoke: Palgrave.

Seristo, H. (2000). International alliances in service industry: The case of the airline industry. In Y. Aharoni and L. Machum (eds), *Globalization of Services: Some Implications for Theory and Practice* (pp. 258–83). London: Routledge.

Singapore Airlines (2002) About SIA. <http://www.singaporeair.com/saa/app/saa> (accessed July 18, 2002).

Sinha, D. (2001). *Deregulation and Liberalisation of the Airline Industry: Asia, Europe, North America and Oceania*. Aldershot: Avebury.

Smith, S. L. J. (1998). Tourism as an industry: Debates and concepts. In D. Ioannides and K. Debbage (eds), *The Economic Geography of the Tourist Industry: A Supply-Side Analysis* (pp. 31–52). London: Routledge.

Star Alliance (2002). Member Airlines. <http://www.star-pr.com/web/press_room/indexhtm> (accessed July 3, 2002).

Teye, V. B. (2000). Regional cooperation and tourism development in Africa. In P. U. C. Dieke (ed.), *The Political Economy of Tourism Development in Africa* (pp. 259–84). New York: Cognizant Communication Corporation.

Travelex (2000). Travelex Annual Report and Accounts 2000. <http://www.travelex.com/companyprofile/annualreport.asp> (accessed July 3, 2002).

Urry, J. (2002). *The Tourist Gaze*, 2nd edn. London: Sage.

Van der Hoeven, R., and Sziraczki, G. (eds) (1997). *Lessons from Privatization: Labour Issues in Developing and Transitional Countries*. Geneva: International Labour Organization.

Vanhove, N. (2001). Globalisation of tourism demand, global distribution systems and marketing. In S. Wahab and C. Cooper (eds), *Tourism in the Age of Globalisation* (pp. 123–56). London: Routledge.

Wheatcroft, S. (1998). The airline industry and tourism. In D. Ioannides and K. Debbage (eds), *The Economic Geography of the Tourist Industry: A Supply-Side Analysis* (pp. 159–79). London: Routledge.

Williams, A. M., and Baláz, V. (2002). The Czech and Slovak republics: Conceptual issues in the economic analysis of tourism in transition. *Tourism Management* 23(1), 37–45.

World Tourism Organization (2002). Quality in tourism: A conceptual framework. <http://www.world-tourism.org/frameset/frame_quality.html> (accessed June 14, 2002).

Xu, G. (1999). *Tourism and Local Economic Development in China: Case Studies of Guilin, Suzhou and Beidaihe*. Richmond: Curzon.

Chapter 10

Entrepreneurial Cultures and Small Business Enterprises in Tourism

Gareth Shaw

Entrepreneurship and Tourism: A Widening Research Agenda

During the last 20 years there has been a growing recognition of the importance of entrepreneurship within the tourism industry. Early interest focused on rather general perspectives on the role of transnational enterprises in developing economies. In this context, Rodenburg (1980) examined the dichotomy between locally owned small businesses and larger organizations based on inward investment. This research served to highlight the need for some form of coordinated coexistence between such development pathways, but it also stressed the polarized nature of the tourism industry. In most tourism economies the growth of large organizations, and their increased market share, stands in contrast to the numerical importance of small enterprises. The latter became a growing focus of interest in the 1980s, following a series of case studies concerned with the role of small businesses, particularly in the economy of British coastal resorts (Stallinbrass 1980; Shaw and Williams 1987).

These limited case studies were expanded upon from the late 1980s as entrepreneurship within the small business sector became more closely researched in tourism studies (Williams et al. 1989; Shaw and Williams 1990, 1998; Wanhill 1996; Buhalis and Cooper 1998). The debate has increasingly centered on what Ateljevic and Doorne (2000) termed lifestyle entrepreneurship, with its emphasis on serving the niche markets created by the demand for specialized tourism products. These and other related studies have substantially widened the research agenda around the small tourism enterprise, expanding investigation into different tourism environments. As Dahles (1999a) shows, this has led to an increased interest in microbusinesses within developing countries focused around economic dualism, with an emphasis on the informal economy, and increasingly in the context of sustainable tourism strategies. More significantly, research has increasingly attempted to fully engage with generalized perspectives of small firms in non-tourism studies. This, in turn, has led to greater awareness of the importance of business networks and network theory (Tinsley and Lynch 2001) and the potential importance of e-commerce in one of the few comparative studies to include tourism (Tiessen, Wright, and Turner 2001).

In spite of such developments, Page, Forer, and Lawton (1999) claimed that small businesses and entrepreneurship in tourism was still "*Terra incognita*." This may be a deliberately exaggerated view, but in some senses the widening research agenda is still fragmented and partial, with substantial gaps. Such shortcomings have been raised by a number of authors, some of whom have attempted a partial synthesis (Morrison, Rimmington, and Williams 1999; Page et al. 1999). Nevertheless, problems still exist, and the failure to establish a dialogue with researchers working within the mainstream of research on small firms and entrepreneurship remains a key issue. In large part, this is due to the tourism "blind spot" of most economists and economic geographers, whose focus has been on the small firm within manufacturing, information technology, and financial services, to the detriment of the tourism sector.

The aim of this chapter is to examine tourism entrepreneurship, especially in terms of the small firm, within a broader research context by highlighting a number of key issues. These include entrepreneurial cultures, the growth of the small firm, and the role of small firm networks within tourism destinations. The chapter starts with a short discussion of entrepreneurship and its position within studies of small firms.

Entrepreneurship and the Small Firm

At the outset there are definitional problems associated with both what constitutes an entrepreneur and the boundaries of a small firm. Early studies within tourism tended to ignore such problems, but as the research agenda has widened, definitions have become more debated. In both cases, there are problems of locating precise definitions that are widely acceptable.

The general notions of entrepreneurship within tourism have been reviewed by Morrison et al. (1999), who settled on identifying types of entrepreneurship within specific contexts. In this they made a broad distinction between entrepreneurship, intrapreneurship, and team entrepreneurship. It is the first of these that relates to the small firm situation, as intrapreneurship relates to processes within corporations and team entrepreneurship tends to be found mainly in larger organizations. Entrepreneurs have traditionally been seen as "innovators" in terms of the Schumpeterian perspective (Schumpeter 1934) or exploiters of profitable opportunities by Kirzner (1973). Such views stress the "heroic" nature of entrepreneurs as business pioneers driven by strong profit-making motives. However, few small-scale entrepreneurs within tourism share these characteristics and, at best, they may be described as "reproducers" of standard formats rather than business innovators. More socially led perspectives on the entrepreneur have modified these views and stressed that it is possible to recognize a range of entrepreneurial types. These have been identified by different terminologies including: "classical entrepreneur," "artisan entrepreneur," interested in employment satisfaction and independence, and the "managerial" type, who emphasizes the recognition of management skills. Within tourism, increasing attention has been given to the artisan type, although, as will be seen later, this can be deconstructed into a range of entrepreneurial cultures.

Definitions of small business are equally variable, with Ateljevic (2002) claiming to have identified more than 70 in his international review. There are also sectorial differences in such definitions, although academic perspectives have attempted to identify common features. Furthermore, the term SMEs (small and medium-sized enterprises) is increasingly used, especially within the EU (Wanhill 2000). This is also problematic, for its EU definition encompasses medium-sized enterprises of between 100 and 499 employees, small enterprises employing 10–99 people, and micro-enterprises of fewer than 10 employees. General surveys across SMEs in the UK show that such divisions do mark significant differences in firm behavior (Morgan, Mayes, and Smith 2002). Evidence from a range of studies within tourism suggests that the majority of firms under this definition would be so-called micro-enterprises. A range of other definitions have been presented, based on the number of employees and, as Thomas (1998) shows, the only common agreement is on micro-enterprises (those with fewer than 10 employees). Within the UK, for example, in the hospitality sector the percentage of enterprises in each of the three categories in 2001 was: medium-sized 0.5 percent; small 12.2 percent; and micro 87.2 percent (Morgan et al. 2002). In this chapter, particular emphasis is given to those businesses with fewer than 10 employees, which form the majority of tourism enterprises. Few definitions have been applied in developing economies, although Doswell (2000) has identified micro-tourism enterprises and medium-sized tourism enterprises (those employing 30 or more) in an African context.

Entrepreneurial Cultures in Tourism: The Small-Scale Enterprise

The majority of work on tourism entrepreneurship has focused on the small firm and its operating characteristics, especially those relating to the owner-manager. Early work utilized Goffee and Scase's (1983) model of organizational structures and entrepreneurial characteristics (Shaw and Williams 1990). This basic model identifies four main types of firm, ranging from the self-employed through to owner-directors. Within the tourism sector, studies emphasized the relatively large numbers of self-employed and small employers who comprise much of the holiday accommodation sector. At present, research on entrepreneurial cultures is strongly divided between developed and developing economies, with relatively few points of comparison. Nevertheless, there are some obvious common features, including the relative ease of entry and strong elements of economic marginality in both environments, although even in this context it is possible to explore differences in marginality. In the context of tourism in Africa, Dieke (2000: 310) claims that, for many small businesses, "life is a daily struggle, with many of them operating at the margin of survival." This is also illustrated by Sindiga's (1999) research on tourism in Kenya, which showed that many Africans were unable to raise sufficient start-up capital for micro-businesses selling souvenirs to tourists. In practice, small-scale African entrepreneurs were forced into temporary, unlicensed kiosks, while the main souvenir shops became dominated by Asians. Certainly, early studies in the UK highlighted the low levels of capitalization and skills needed to enter the tourism industry. Similar characteristics are found in developing countries, although in some instances, as in Indonesia, more complex situations exist mediated by patronage and brokerage (Dahles 1999b).

These small and often economically marginal enterprises are characterized by entrepreneurs with a diverse range of motives for entering the tourism industry and very different employment experiences. Studies in south-west England showed an important route into tourism entrepreneurship was taken by ex-employees without any directly relevant management experience. Furthermore, these entrepreneurs relied heavily on informal sources of capital, with more than half being mainly dependent on personal and family savings. Similar figures have been recorded for small tourism firms in New Zealand, with 67 percent of businesses using personal funds (Page et al. 1999: 450). A final major defining characteristic of these small business entrepreneurs is a complex combination of motives and aspirations. Many entrepreneurs have strong lifestyle aspirations concerned with wanting to live and work in an attractive environment. Williams, Shaw, and Greenwood (1989) saw in the case of Cornwall in England a blurring of the boundaries between production and consumption, since many of the entrepreneurs were former tourists who had made repeated visits to the destination before opting to run a small business there. Similarly, in North America, Snepenger, Johnson, and Rasker (1995) have identified this process as "travel-stimulated entrepreneurial migration," only in this case they examined the role of tourism in attracting entrepreneurs in all types of economic sectors. In all cases, such entrepreneurs were attracted to the Yellowstone National Park area because of quality-of-life variables. Significantly, almost one-third of small business owners were motivated by non-economic factors in the Cornish case study. More recent work based in Australia has highlighted these lifestyle motives alongside strong family-related goals (Getz and Carlson 2000). This work identified two distinct motivational types, namely "family first," which accounted for 66 percent of enterprises – many of which were termed "copreneurs" (to describe married couples operating a business), and "business first," although even within this group half the owners had no formal business goals. The role of the household in such business operations is clearly an important factor, but one requiring further analysis, especially in terms of negotiations within the family over how resources are utilized. Within the context of developing economies, Gartner (1999) has shown in the case of Ghana that small tourism businesses are very much run around the extended family. His research demonstrated that, for most small entrepreneurs, a major factor was to develop the business in order to employ more family and friends as part of the workforce. This led to high levels of reinvestment as profits were ploughed back into the business.

Another important characteristic of entrepreneurs within tourism concerns their role as cultural brokers within host communities. They can act as important bridges between the world of the tourist and that of the local community, since they may be members of both (Jafari 1989). Viewed in this way, tourism entrepreneurs are important in the cultural exchanges within tourism and are strongly embedded in these processes. Increasingly, this dual role of entrepreneurship is being recognized in terms of the small-scale enterprise within sustainable tourism (Horobin and Horobin 1996).

The importance of such lifestyle motives within tourism entrepreneurship is a significant feature of small firms in this economic sector. In this context, Ateljevic and Doorne (2000) have argued for a refocusing of tourism entrepreneurship around such non-economic strands. This follows the ideas of Dewhurst and Horobin (1998) which stressed non-economic motives in tourism entrepreneurship and the difficulty in applying economic models to many of the small enterprises within the hospitality industry. In a similar way Morrison et al. (1999) discuss the notion of entrepreneurship in tourism within a range of contexts, including the importance of lifestyle motives. Upadhya and Rutten (1997) go further, and argue that entrepreneurial culture should be positioned within structural power relations, with a perspective that combines economic, political, and cultural contexts.

As a starting point, it is important to recognize that there is a series of entrepreneurial cultures within tourism that range from a strong preoccupation with economic motives through to those concerned more with non-economic ones. In this sense, the concept and definition of the entrepreneur is more complex and reflects the need to adopt different forms (Swedberg 2000). As previously recognized, economic perspectives of the entrepreneur stress the notions of creativity, innovation, risk-taking and, above all, the pursuit of economic growth. In contrast, sociological and psychological perspectives highlight the knowledge, background characteristics, and personality traits of the entrepreneur. As various authors have argued, there is increasing evidence to show that lifestyle factors and non-economic motives are significant, and that the definition of the entrepreneur needs to be more inclusive of these ideas. For some entrepreneurs, as Dewhurst and Horobin (1998: 30) explain, "success might best be measured in terms of a continuing ability to perpetuate their chosen lifestyle."

This refocusing of entrepreneurship is significant and, as Ateljevic and Doorne (2000: 381) point out, the "rejection of an overtly profit-driven orientation does not necessarily result in financial suicide or developmental stagnation, but rather provides opportunities to engage with 'niche' market consumers." They go further, and claim that such lifestyle-motivated entrepreneurs can be important in the creation of new tourism products. Such views are based on their research into adventure tourism enterprises and other small businesses in New Zealand. To many of the entrepreneurs within their survey, lifestyle values were important, not only in themselves for the individual, but also because they represented the rejection of a mass, homogenized tourism product. These entrepreneurs operate within an ideological fence that encloses their value systems which, in turn, conditions their management styles and organizational practices. Research in Austria has also distinguished between "life-style enterprises, established to provide their owners with an acceptable standard of living, within a preferred level of activity, and entrepreneurial small businesses" driven mainly by growth motives (Buhalis and Paraskevas 2002).

The growth of such entrepreneurs is a relatively recent phenomenon and appears to be a direct response to the niche markets provided by the changes in tourism consumption associated with postmodernism, and the growth of the experience economy. Such trends have seen the growth of ecotourism, homestay, adventure tourism, and the backpacker market, for example, and provide new business opportunities. These range from backpacker hostels to specialized travel agents marketing ecotourism holidays on the internet. It would be wrong to assume, however, that all such enterprises are motivated by lifestyle/ethical motives, as many of the tourism dot.com businesses embrace a number of the features of traditional entrepreneurship, including risk-taking and innovation, behaving more like Schumpeterian-type entrepreneurs. As yet, we know little about the detailed motives and background characteristics of these entrepreneurs.

On the basis of current research, it is possible to identify a number of different types of small-scale tourism entrepreneur, including:

- So-called lifestyle entrepreneurs who are motivated less by profit and more by non-economic factors. Early work by Shaw and Williams (1998) identified two subgroups: (1) those termed "non-entrepreneurs" who had usually taken early retirement to a tourism destination and had little desire to develop their business. They were motivated by a certain type of lifestyle that fitted their semi-retirement status. Many were also characterized by low levels of managerial skills and expertise. (2) more ethically bounded lifestyle entrepreneurs of the type identified by Ateljevic and Doorne (2000), who were interested in developing certain types of niche tourism products and had strong interests in environmental issues. These tend to be younger people and may also share some of the characteristics of the "constrained" entrepreneurs recognized by Shaw and Williams. Constraints may either be based on a lack of capital for expansion, or an unwillingness to develop and compromise lifestyle goals, i.e. people who want to stay within ethical, usually environmental, boundaries.
- Business-oriented entrepreneurs whose motives are mainly economic. Here it is possible to recognize entrepreneurs in the Schumpeterian sense, who are capable of growing their businesses and those whose development may be constrained by various financial barriers. It seems likely that these comprise the majority of small business operators within the tourism industry, certainly with the accommodation sector. Clearly, these entrepreneurial types are based on developed economies and, as yet, our knowledge in other environments remains limited.

Entrepreneurship and Models of Small-Firm Growth

One of the significant limitations of research on small business operators in tourism is its rather static perspective. The majority of studies have paid only scant attention to firm growth, and the dynamics of such businesses are usually only considered in terms of dates of foundation and rates of failure – that is, the classic births and deaths of firms literature (Hjalager 1999). This stands in contrast to the mainstream literature on small businesses which has placed increasing emphasis on the pathways of firm development. Morrison et al. (1999) provide a brief overview of some of the models of small business growth, including the work of Churchill and Lewis (1983). This postulates five main stages through which firms can pass in their move from "existence" (stage 1) to "resource maturity" (stage 5) (figure 10.1). Each of the five stages is characterized by specific managerial styles, organizational structures, and key problems. For example, the "existence" stage is represented by firms with informal management systems and a strong reliance on start-up capital. As studies in tourism have shown, such capital is very often informally sourced, using family or personal savings. The second stage is that of "survival" and characterized by viable businesses, but management systems are still minimal, in that the owner/entrepreneur is still synonymous with the business. As figure 10.1 suggests, a large number of tourism businesses never progress beyond this stage, whether for the lifestyle reasons

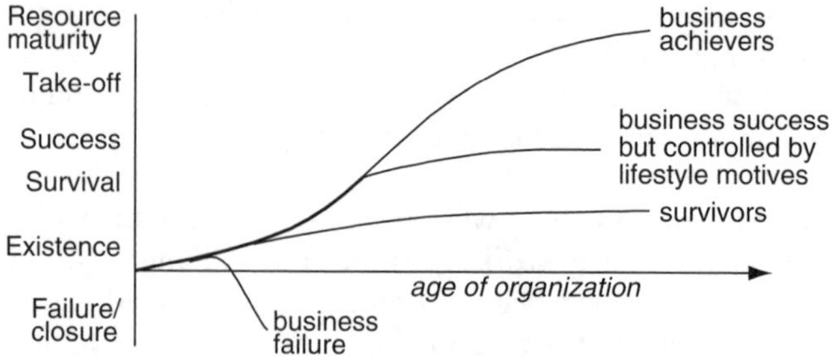

Figure 10.1 Stages of small business development over time
Source: Morrison et al. 1999.

or because they are constrained in some other way. Evidence suggests that the majority of tourism businesses may well fall within the survivor category.

For many entrepreneurs of small businesses it is stage 3, "success," which is most critical. Churchill and Lewis (1983) suggest that at this stage the entrepreneur is faced with two options:

- Stability, in which the owner adapts only to survive. This may be a forced option because of various constraints or, as studies have suggested, a lifestyle choice.
- Growth, which requires developing new management structures and, more significantly, the ability to resource expansion, either from within the firm, through external borrowing or, more likely, a combination of both. Studies by Shaw and Williams (1987, 1997) demonstrate that many small-scale operators become "constrained entrepreneurs" at this critical stage as formal capital is hard to come by, or management expertise is inadequate. Similarly, research in New Zealand suggests that as many as 50 percent of small businesses in tourism used only personal savings to establish themselves. Although for some this may have been a matter of choice, some 20 percent of the sample who had applied for a bank loan claim they had been turned down (Page et al. 1999).

If growth is an option and proves possible, the model suggests businesses enter a take-off stage before reaching resource maturity. The usefulness of this model has been questioned in that some researchers claim to have found no conclusive evidence of firms passing through recognizable stages of growth (Birley and Westhead 1990), while more significantly O'Farrell and Hitchens (1988) argue that such stages are symptoms of growth rather than underlying processes. In contrast, others, such as Burns (1989), have suggested alternative models, while Eggers, Leahy, and Churchill (1994) have attempted to update the work of Churchill and Lewis, arguing that there may be very different pathways of growth which they term "management phases."

From these perspectives two key interrelated ideas appear important. The first concerns the timing of change or growth, while the second is associated with the main distinguishing features between "survival" firms and "growth" firms. In terms of the former, Churchill and Lewis (1983) suggest that a number of major

Table 10.1 Changing features of small-firms growth and development

Feature	Increases in
Financial resources	Cashflow and borrowing power
System resources	Degree of planning and control systems
Personnel resources	Numbers and range of staff
Business resources	Emphasis on customer relations and marketing
Owner's abilities	Management skills, structures, and strategic planning

Source: Modified from Churchill and Lewis 1983.

factors change as the small business develops. As table 10.1 shows, these may be the critical indicators of entrepreneurial growth. Similarly, MacRae (1990), researching small business development in Scotland, has attempted to test those variables thought to distinguish low-growth firms from high-growth ones. He concluded that the key factors were entrepreneurial learning and experience. In this context Hannon (1998) argues that growth is largely contingent on the entrepreneur's ability to adapt to new situations and learn from past experiences. These "learning opportunity environments" are characterized by strong transactional relationships between the entrepreneur and others that create what Hannon terms "experiential learning."

Evidence from the tourism sector is partial on a number of these issues, although we do know that for many tourism entrepreneurs experiences are limited and motives extremely varied. Certainly, many small businesses in both developed and developing economies are poorly connected to other parts of the business community. Equally, evidence suggests that many small-scale entrepreneurs have only limited managerial skills and even more limited planning horizons. For example, in New Zealand, even where small firms had formulated business plans, they were mostly over a one-year time-frame or less, while only 18 percent of businesses took a more strategic view. In general studies of small firms, Ackelsberg and Arlow (1985) suggest that most planning is restricted to the formative, or "existence," stage. We have, therefore, only partial knowledge of some areas and for others we know even less. For example, there have been virtually no detailed studies of successfully growing small firms within tourism, as most emphasis has been directed at the stable or survivor group. As Ateljevic (2002: 54) concludes, the "available literature offers no clear understanding as to whether STF [small tourism firm] owners formalize their activities during establishment."

Entrepreneurial Networks and Destination Areas

Small-scale enterprises operate within specific tourism destinations and, as several studies have shown, they tend to dominate the industrial structures of such areas. As such, they are a key component in determining the development of tourism destinations. This was recognized early in the tourism literature via Butler's (1980) life-cycle model, which Din (1992) and Shaw and Williams (1998) have expanded as they explored the links between entrepreneurs and destination development. Similarly, Dahles (1999a: 4) argues that "the activities of small-scale tourism entrepreneurs do not unfold in a vacuum." Such perspectives remain sketchy and general, with Tinsley and Lynch (2001) arguing that the tourism production system within destinations continues to be an under-researched theme.

Recent research, however, is providing significant insights into this theme. First, in terms of the recognition that tourism producers also need to be viewed as being socially constructed (Huang and Stewart 1996), and second through the growing interest in entrepreneurial networks (Tinsley and Lynch 2001). Both are strongly related as they inform each other, certainly within tourism where, according to Tinsley and Lynch (2001: 374), "the role of networks has to be teased out from . . . the tourism system." Within tourism destinations, only scant regard has been paid to the collective operation of small firms. The main exception to this is the substantial research on inter-firm networks and partnerships in the area of food and wine tourism (Hall et al. 2000; Hall et al. 2003). In this context, a range of studies have demonstrated the significance of business networks, not only in terms of small firms, but also for specific destinations (Telfer 2000). In such environments, competition and cooperation sit side by side. For example, while accommodation establishments compete for tourists, they often cooperate to help market their destination and may even form business networks to aid this process. Such networks can take a variety of forms, but the main features usually include the daily operations of firms, inter-firm networks, and localized or regional public–private interfaces. All are important in tourism destinations, but for many small businesses the third feature is becoming increasingly significant. The degree of "institutional thickness," representing the quality and quantity of support organizations, has become a key factor in many destination areas through local community groups and, more especially, government agencies charged with supporting small firms.

Within these business networks, important informal and formal flows of information and support can be identified. These untraded dependencies are both a cause and an effect of increased collaboration. In terms of such networks, research on small firms has drawn attention to so-called "entrepreneurial networks," created from the personal contacts of entrepreneurs (Johannisson 2000). Such personal contacts are especially important in the start-up stage of small businesses, as many of these firms, certainly within tourism, tend to rely on informal flows of information. The networks may be with friends or family members who provide some form of "collective" experience or social capital. Within the small-family tourism firm such personal networks are important in both developed and developing economies, and can often produce a blurring of business and social life. In terms of firm growth, these informal networks can be constraining, in that experience may be limited and may increase the tendency for a survivor rather than a growth strategy.

Within tourism research we know little about how such entrepreneurial networks evolve, or indeed how they vary across sub-sectors of the industry. It seems likely, however, that such networks are characterized by diversity relating to locational (i.e., destination) and structural characteristics. This, in turn, is important in understanding how small firms communicate within destination areas. Furthermore, the increasing complexity of the tourism sector, and the high levels of competition between destinations, place greater importance on the role of networks and the need to understand them. The strength of individual destinations is based on the tourism product and its marketability. In both cases, business networks and the notion of collaboration become significant.

Conclusion

The increased interest in tourism entrepreneurship has not only produced a broader research agenda, but also highlighted some key characteristics of the small-firm economy. A wider range of case studies has confirmed the economic marginality of many small enterprises and the different motives for operating such businesses. The recognition of an increased number of more ethically driven entrepreneurs concerned with certain lifestyle values has also highlighted a type of entrepreneurial culture which is associated with the shifting consumption patterns of postmodernism. Such enterprises would also appear to fit more closely with the increasing demands for more sustainable forms of tourism production based on community-level needs – although this needs to be viewed critically. This adds to a complex typology of the entrepreneurial cultures that are being identified within the tourism sector.

While such lifestyle motives are clearly important, it should be remembered that in many other cases it is more profit-driven motives that are driving forward small businesses. In this context, we still know little about how small enterprises grow and achieve economic maturity. One recent area of growth has been the impact of the "dot.com revolution" on certain types of specialized travel agency: as yet, the growth of this form of tourism entrepreneurship remains a significantly under-researched theme.

Finally, this chapter has attempted to position studies of tourism entrepreneurship more firmly within more general research on the small-scale entrepreneur. In doing so, it has highlighted the importance of understanding the complexity of the entrepreneur, the nature of small-firm growth, and, more especially, the increasing significance being given to business networks of all types.

REFERENCES

Ackelsberg, R., and Arlow, P. (1985). Small businesses do plan and it pays off. *Long Range Planning* 18(5), 61–7.

Ateljevic, I. (2002). Survival of small tourism firms: Owners, environment and management practices in the Centre Stage Region. Unpublished Ph.D. thesis, Victoria, University of Wellington.

Ateljevic, I., and Doorne, S. (2000). Staying within the fence: Lifestyle entrepreneurship in tourism. *Journal of Sustainable Tourism* 8(5), 378–92.

Birley, S., and Westhead, P. (1990). Growth and performance contrasts between "types" of small firms. *Management Journal* 11(3), 535–57.

Buhalis, D., and Cooper, C. (1998). Competition or co-operation: Small and medium sized tourism enterprises at the destination. In E. Laws (ed.), *Embracing and Managing Change in Tourism* (pp. 45–56). London: Thompson Business Press.

Buhalis, D., and Paraskevas, A. (2002). Conference report: Entrepreneurship in tourism and the contexts of the experience economy, University of Lapland, Rouaniemi, Finland. *Tourism Management* 23, 427–8.

Burns, P. (1989). Strategies for success and routes to failure. In P. Burns and J. Dewhirst (eds), *Small-Business and Entrepreneurship* (pp. 32–67). Basingstoke: Macmillan.

Butler, R. (1980). The concept of a tourist area cycle of evolution: Implications for management of resources. *Canadian Geographer* 24(1), 5–12.

Churchill, N. C., and Lewis, V. L. (1983). The five stages of small business growth. *Harvard Business Review* 6(3), 30–50.

Dahles, H. (1999a). Tourism and small entrepreneurs in developing countries: A theoretical perspective. In H. Dahles and K. Bras (eds), *Tourism and Small Entrepreneurs. Development, National Policy and Entrepreneurial Culture: Indonesian Cases* (pp. 1–19). New York: Cognizant Communications.

Dahles, H. (1999b). Small businesses in the Indonesian tourism industry: Entrepreneurship or employment? In H. Dahles and K. Bras (eds), *Tourism and Small Entrepreneurs. Development, National Policy and Entrepreneurial Culture: Indonesian Cases* (pp. 20–34). New York: Cognizant Communications.

Dewhurst, P., and Horobin, H. (1998). Small business owners. In R. Thomas (ed.), *The Management of Small Tourism and Hospitality Firms* (pp. 19–39). London: Cassell.

Dieke, P. U. C. (2000). Tourism and Africa's long term development dynamics. In P. U. C. Dieke (ed.), *The Political Economy of Tourism Development in Africa* (pp. 301–12). New York: Cognizant Communications Corporation.

Din, K.M. (1992). The "Involvement Stage" in the evolution of a tourist destination', *Tourism Recreational Research* 17(1), 10–20.

Doswell, R. (2000) African tourism training and education hits and misses. In P. U. C. Dieke (ed.), *The Political Economy of Tourism Development in Africa* (pp. 247–59). New York: Cognizant Communications Corporation.

Eggers, J. H., Leahy, K. T., and Churchill, N. C. (1994). Stages of small business growth revisited: Insights into growth path and leadership/management skills in low- and high-growth companies. In *Proceedings of the Babson Entrepreneurship Research Conference* (pp. 131–44). Wellesley, MA.

Gartner, W. C. (1999) Small-scale enterprises in the tourism industry in Ghana's central region. In D. W. G. Pearce and R. Butler (eds), *Contemporary Issues in Tourism Development* (pp. 78–89). London: Routledge.

Getz, D., and Carlson, J. (2000). Characteristics and goals of family and owner-operated businesses in rural tourism and hospitality sectors. *Tourism Management* 21(6), 547–60.

Goffee, R., and Scase, R. (1983). Class entrepreneurship and the service sector: Towards a conceptual clarification. *Services Industries Journal* 3(2), 146–60.

Hall, C. M., Sharples, E., Cambourne, B., and Macionis, N. (2000). *Wine Tourism Around the World: Development, Management and Markets*. Oxford: Butterworth-Heinemann.

Hall, C. M., Sharples, L., Mitchell, R., Cambourne, B., and Macionis, N. (2003). *Food Tourism Around the World: Development, Management and Markets*. Oxford: Butterworth-Heinemann.

Hannon, P. (1998). *Who are the Real Educators and Learners? Exploring Learning Needs within Small Firms: Stakeholder Transactional Relationships*. London: Routledge.

Hjalager, A.-M. (1999). The ecology of organisations in Danish tourism: A regional labour perspective. *Tourism Geographies* 1(2), 164–82.

Horobin, H., and Horobin, L. J. (1996). Sustainable tourism: The role of the small firm. *International Journal of Contemporary Hospitality Management* 8(5), 16–19.

Huang, Y., and Stewart, W. (1996). Rural tourism development: Shifting basis of community solidarity. *Journal of Tourism Research* 34(4), 26–9.

Jafari, J. (1989). Sociocultural dimensions of tourism in an English language literature review. In J. Bustrzanowski (ed.), *Tourism as a Factor of Change: A Sociocultural Study* (pp. 17–60).

Vienna: Economic Coordination Centre for Research and Documentation in Social Sciences.
Johannisson, B. (2000). Networking and entrepreneurial growth. In D. L. Sexton and H. Landström (eds), *The Blackwell Handbook of Entrepreneurship*. Oxford: Blackwell.
Kirzner, I. (1973). *Perception, Opportunity and Profit: Studies in the Theory of Entrepreneurship*. Chicago: Chicago University Press.
MacRae, D. (1990). *The Scottish Development Survey*. Edinburgh: University of Edinburgh.
Morgan, A., Mayes, S., and Smith, E. (2002). *The Age of Business, its Potential to Learn and Need for Support*. Report to Small Business Service: Business Research. Newcastle: Trend.
Morrison, A., Rimmington, M., and Williams, C. (1999). *Entrepreneurship in Hospitality, Tourism and Leisure Industries*. London: Butterworth-Heinemann.
O'Farrell, P. N., and Hitchens, D. (1988). Alternative theories of small-firm growth: A critical review. *Environment and Planning A* 20(9), 1365–83.
Page, S. J., Forer, P., and Lawton, G. R. (1999). Small business development and tourism: *Terra incognita? Tourism Management* 20(4), 435–49.
Rodenburg, E. (1980). The effects of scale on economic development in tourism in Bali. *Annals of Tourism Research* 7(1), 177–96.
Schumpeter, J. A. (1934). *The Theory of Economic Development*. Cambridge, MA: Harvard University Press.
Shaw, G., and Williams, A. M. (1987). Firm formation and operating characteristics in the Cornish tourism industry. *Tourism Management* 8(3), 344–8.
Shaw, G., and Williams, A. M. (1990). Tourism, economic development and the role of entrepreneurial activity. In C. P. Cooper (ed.), *Progress in Tourism, Recreation and Hospitality Management* (vol. 2, pp. 67–81). London: Belhaven Press.
Shaw, G., and Williams, A. M. (1997). The private sector: Tourism entrepreneurship – a constraint or resource? In G. Shaw and A. M. Williams (eds), *The Rise and Fall of British Coastal Resorts* (pp. 117–37). London: Cassell.
Shaw, G., and Williams, A. M. (1998). Entrepreneurship, small business culture and tourism development. In D. Ioannides and K. D. Debbage (eds), *The Economic Geography of the Tourism Industry* (pp. 235–55). London: Routledge.
Sindiga, I. (1999). *Tourism and African Development: Change and Challenge of Tourism in Kenya*. Aldershot: Ashgate.
Snepenger, D. J., Johnson, J. D., and Rasker, R. (1995). Travel-stimulated entrepreneurial migration. *Journal of Travel Research* 34, 40–4
Stallinbrass, C. (1980). Seaside resorts and the hotel accommodation industry. *Progress in Planning* 13(2), 103–74.
Swedberg, R. (ed.) (2000). *Entrepreneurship: The Social Science View*. Oxford: Blackwell.
Telfer, D. J. (2000). Tastes of Niagara: Building strategic alliances between tourism and agriculture. *International Journal of Hospitality and Tourism Administration* 1, 71–88.
Thomas, R. (1998). An introduction to the study of small tourism and hospitality firms. In R. Thomas (ed.), *The Management of Small Tourism and Hospitality Firms* (pp. 1–16). London: Cassell.
Tiessen, J. H., Wright, R. W., and Turner, I. (2001). A model of e-commerce use by internationalising SMEs. *Journal of International Management* 7(3), 211–33.
Tinsley, R., and Lynch, P. (2001). Small tourism business networks and destination development. *International Journal of Hospitality Management* 20(4), 367–78.
Upadhya, C., and Rutten, M. (1997). In search of a comparative framework: Small-scale entrepreneurs in Asia and Europe. In M. Rutten and C. Upadhya (eds), *Small Business Entrepreneurs in Asia and Europe: Towards a Comparative Perspective*. London: Cassell.

Wanhill, S. (1996). Local enterprise and development in tourism. *Tourism Management* 17(1), 35–42.

Wanhill, S. (2000). Small and medium tourism enterprises. *Annals of Tourism Research* 27(1), 132–47.

Williams, A. M., Shaw, G., and Greenwood, J. (1989). From tourist to tourism entrepreneur, from consumption to production: Evidence from Cornwall, England. *Environment and Planning A* 21(6), 1639–53.

Chapter 11

Labor Mobility and Market Structure in Tourism

Michael Riley

Introduction

A simplistic way to view labor mobility would be that it is about the movement of people from one job to another and about the motives that engender such movement. Furthermore, as this necessarily involves change, the study of labor mobility must therefore involve understanding of this transition and its causes and effects. The basic components of most mobility studies are movement, motives, and effects, and these can be applied at all levels of abstraction in relation to the phenomenon. In this respect the literature uses a range of frameworks that runs from, at the macro level, trans-national migration through to, at the micro level, individual job change, while taking in inter-sector, geographical, inter-organizational, and occupational mobility. It is worth noting that tourism employment, somewhat unusually, involves significant mobility in all these categories. From a macro perspective, labor mobility in tourism is significant in relation to the general case of mobility as a social phenomenon. This significance comes, firstly, from the fact that tourism is an international business and, secondly, because the ease with which it can be accessed for employment makes it important in the larger picture of national employment/unemployment, migration, and illegal immigration.

The causes of labor mobility are normally sought through studies of patterns of movement and attendant motives. In a sense, these approaches are not too dissimilar to other studies of movement, such as those of tourism destination studies, in which the concern is for both the characteristics of the present location and those of the intended destination, whether a country, an organization, a set of skills, or a job. The attendant motives, however, are attributed, in a structural sense, to economic and knowledge/skill differentials and, in a psychological sense, to individual drives, which can be either of a self-advancing or of a deprivation avoidance character. In other words, perceived differentials, whether they be greater earnings, more knowledge, or better life chances, can evoke a positive need for self-enhancement or a negative one to avoid the consequences of being deprived by the differential (Mueller 1982).

The effects of labor mobility in tourism surface in diverse areas of the literature and at different levels of abstraction; for example, tourism jobs are commonly implicated in migration issues, often in the context of illegal immigration (Stalker 1994: 96; King 1995). More damagingly for the industry, in many instances the general reputation of tourism employment is done a disservice by its reputation for high levels of mobility, which, to outsiders, implies career and job instability. Ironically, to insiders such mobility is seen as a positive platform for development and a definite advantage. At a more pragmatic level, vociferous complaints can be heard in the hospitality literature about the managerial "hassle" of coping with high labor turnover (Johnson 1981, 1985; Denvir and McMahon 1992; Lashley and Chaplain 1999). The fact that labor mobility appears so often on the surface as a "problem" in tourism but later, and at a deeper level, as a "solution" means that a holistic approach to analysis is required which is concerned with all the functions of mobility. This functionalist approach is led by economics, where, on a more analytical level, labor mobility constitutes "proof" that the labor market is functioning and efficient. Markets are supposed to distribute skills to where they are needed and therefore mobility patterns can be used to reflect upon market functioning. Studies of inter-sector mobility into tourism show that it is supplied from a wide range of other labor market segments, which informs us not just about tourism but also about those other sectors (Szivas and Riley 1999; Szivas, Riley, and Airey 2003). However, in order to obtain a more complete analysis, labor mobility in tourism has to be seen alongside the associated concepts of pay, employment level, and skill – mobility has effects on, and is affected by, all three. This is why the heart of understanding labor mobility lies in analysis of the structural forces that shape, form, and motivate people in the market to move (Hachen 1992).

In general terms, labor turnover follows economic cycles (Cazes and Nesporova 2001). However, in some industries it has a life of its own, driven by structural and psychological propellants – tourism is one such. Perhaps the best way to place labor mobility in the context of tourism as a whole is to depict it as an industrial dynamic – a common, if not universal, phenomenon that has knock-on effects: positive and negative. These penetrate the economics of the industry, the quality of its products, the energy of its management, and its reputation in the wider economic/political field.

Structure and Labor Mobility

An understanding of labor mobility and labor market dynamics in tourism requires the appreciation of three major features of the industry: that consumer demand is variable in the short term; that the industry structure is, for the most part and irrespective of ownership, fragmented into small units; and that, relatively speaking, the skills of the industry can be easily acquired.

It is a conspicuous feature of consumer demand in tourism that it fluctuates and does so across all sectors. At the macro level there is a business cycle that follows the general business cycle while "seasonality" is an accepted part of tourism life, but equally, at the micro level, it is part of the daily life of hotels, restaurants, attractions, and museums. While there are differences in the pattern of seasonality between destinations, the microscopic variations are endemic to all patterns. Both, however, are subject to the sudden shifts of fortune caused by political upheaval, war, and terrorism. Notwithstanding such seismic changes Riley (1999) goes so far as to suggest that it is the nature of demand that arbitrates the labor productivity of the industry. In simple terms, the consequence of this fluctuation is that all units in every sector have to adjust labor supply to demand in the short run. It is this need to push and pull people in and out of the organization, and in and out of the market, that creates the fundamental dynamic on which labor mobility is built. This dynamic has a well-known form in that rates of recruitment and labor turnover follow each other with only a small time lag. This means that when the industry is expanding labor mobility increases, vacancies rise and are filled by the swelled secondary labor market, and the processes also work in reverse (Hyman 1976). The inevitable manipulations of labor supply by management in response to constant demand shifts is well documented and was, in many respects, a forerunner of the modern theme of flexibility (Alpert 1986; Riley 1990). These standard practices by management are fine as long as the adjustment is reasonably small in scale. The serious question arises when management is confronted with a substantial labor shortage. Notwithstanding the fact that turnover velocity can obscure the real market situation, there is sometimes a case of a real shortage. At this point, considerations of importing labor and mass migration come to the fore, although these flows can be generated at different inter- and intra-national scales.

This responsiveness between supply and demand, on whatever scale, would be impossible if the required skills necessitated long periods of training. Tourism does contain many occupations that, in any reasonable judgment, would be described as skilled occupations, but the majority of jobs, even those that require a degree of skill, contain skills and knowledge that can be easily acquired either by short periods of training or by experience. This fact alone places tourism employment firmly in what economists call secondary markets, which are more unstable than the primary markets filled with secure jobs built on developed and educated human capital. The very nature of the secondary market acts to encourage mobility – where there is diversity of opportunity and accessibility, irrespective of level of pay, then there is increased mobility (Greve 1994). Indeed the very fact that mobility is possible is part of the attractiveness of the industry in the first place, so structure and motive go hand in hand. The push to be mobile comes from the fact that, on the one hand, many tourism skills are unique to the industry but have utility across many sectors of the industry – a cook can operate on a cruise ship, a hotel, at an airport, etc. Of course there are differentials in the market, but these come up against transferable skills. Furthermore, what is interesting here is that within the industry there is one conspicuously important differential, namely, the difference between jobs with unsocial hours and those with working hours shared with the majority of the population. This differential promotes mobility, especially in the absence of compensating remuneration for unsocial hours. On the other hand, within the secondary labor market, tourism jobs share a great deal of commonality with jobs in other sectors and therefore mobility to those sectors is facilitated – a hotel receptionist can become a dentist's receptionist with relative ease (Riley, Ladkin, and Szivas 2002). The important structural feature of tourism labor markets is that their dynamic movement allows, even encourages, access – like getting on a carousel. Ease of access is, in a way, an invitation. The debate about the role of tourism jobs in employment/unemployment studies and migration studies, particularly in illegal immigration, is based on the premise of easy access. Similarly, the literature on labor turnover "as a problem" points to the fact that, for the most part, it is not dissatisfaction that spurs mobility. Indeed, the industry appears to have high levels of satisfaction. In part this satisfaction is built around the task variety embodied in dealing with people, lack of close supervision, a sense of "not factory," and on the work–social group fusion which tends to culminate in occupational communities. This last phenomenon is encouraged by unsocial working hours. However, it is the simple fact that other jobs are always available that explains mobility (Brown and McIntosh 2000).

The acceptance of basic instability in the labor market does not, however, fully explain labor mobility patterns in tourism. What has to be taken into consideration is the small-unit structure of the industry. In some respects, it could be argued that small work groups have the effect of lowering labor turnover, but this generalization is unsafe in the case of tourism. Tourism operating units, irrespective of size, exhibit a dual character in that, within each unit, there is a stable population as well as a mobile one (Simms 1987). Furthermore, if the relationship between units is structured in a hierarchical form, based on such criteria as prestige, standards, and skill levels, then the very existence of such a structure encourages mobility between units based on both ambition and the need to learn higher skills. Mobility channels are created by industrial structure (Maillat 1984).This is the basis of Riley's model of skill accumulation through mobility, which he applies to the hotel sector (Riley 1991). The principle, he argues, is relevant to any sector with a competitive market where there are differentials of knowledge between organizations and where any level of skill can be acquired relatively easily. This is a positive perspective on labor mobility, and one which emphasizes its learning function – it is reflected in the structure of careers.

The Mobile Career Structure

This notion of using labor mobility as an instrument of learning is reflected in the way careers are managed. A number of studies of careers show a central role for the labor market and for vocational education. Ladkin and Riley (1996) suggest that the conventional bureaucratic model of careers does not fit the pattern for hotel managers. While not denying that careers, and particularly managerial careers, are, to an extent, a function of organizational hierarchy and size, they argue for a hybrid model in which movement upwards within hierarchies and across organizational variance in size is through inter-organizational mobility rather than intra-organizational mobility. Gunz (1998) devised a typology of managerial orientations toward careers. The three orientations are:

- where managers construct deliberate sequences of jobs in which they accumulate human capital;
- where managers take the same role but with ever-increasing amounts of responsibility and prestige; and
- where managers do not change jobs but alter the scope of their role.

On what evidence exists, careers in hotel management, for example, appear to follow the first orientation in the early years and then, encouraged by the unit structure, pursue greater responsibility later (Ladkin and Juwaheer 2000). A key aspect of the picture that emerges particularly, but not exclusively, from hotels is that there exists a culture of mobility (Iverson and Deery 1997). Mobility becomes a way of life. Perhaps the most conspicuous aspect of tourism labor is the international mobility of its managers and skilled workers.

Some Effects of Mobility

Given that tourism has developed a reputation for being a future provider of jobs (International Labor Office 2001), it is essential to examine the effects of labor mobility on employment levels and pay. Ease of access itself means that tourism is an area of opportunity, added to which it is also attractive to many people who are drawn to its glamor and lack of routine, but these supply-side characteristics bring their own problems, particularly in respect of pay.

Whether at national or regional level, there is always a concern for the effect of inward migration of labor upon the indigenous population. At the forefront of this concern is the displacement of local workers by newcomers and consequent unemployment. Given that the motive for the recruitment of outsiders is normally a perceived shortage of labor, we need to consider the effects not only on employment but also on pay levels. The two issues are inexorably linked and, unfortunately, the empirical evidence here tells a slightly ambiguous story. For skilled indigenous labor the effects of imported skilled labor appear to be beneficial both in terms of extending job opportunities and increasing pay. Both were presumably caused by the labor shortage that motivated migration in the first place. However, the evidence of similar positive effects is somewhat less strong for unskilled workers (Pedace 1988). Here the argument is that, on the one hand, imported skilled labor reduces the opportunities for development of unskilled workers but, on the other, and more importantly, where unskilled labor is imported to fill a shortage, the effect is to deflate existing pay levels. At the moment, the evidence for the latter remains conceptual and circumstantial but is, nevertheless, strong.

Riley, Ladkin, and Szivas (2002: 39–60) outline a conceptual framework for the determination of pay in tourism. The framework uses the economic, structural, and psychological features of the industry to show how managers will adopt any strategy to deal with labor shortages other than increasing pay, and that workers within the industry, for the most part, understand and accept, as an "industrial norm," the rationale that lies behind the managerial approach. In other words, there is a deflationary process embedded in the life of the industry that is always at work irrespective of the performance of the labor market. The framework is constructed from a focus on the assumptions that guide the decision-making of both managers and workers in respect of pay. At the heart of the framework is a set of managerial assumptions, which are:

- that the external labor market will always provide labor;
- that there is no economic reason to reward job tenure;

- that there will always be a need to match labor supply to short-term demand fluctuations; and
- that there is a tolerance of low pay in the workforce.

The framework is based on two broad theoretical propositions: firstly, on Rosen's notion of the virtual wage, which represents a sum that employers would theoretically pay for a fully trained worker but choose not to pay because of the ease with which skills can be acquired on the job without substantive loss (Rosen 1972); secondly, on the notion that economic decisions are embedded in social structures, and here the social structure is the industry rather than the organization (Granovetter 1973). In this argument the fragmented structure of the tourism industry is brought together by a set of industrial norms about relative levels of skill, the value of differentials, and, above all, how the labor market works and that low pay is an inevitable consequence of that. Inter-organizational mobility helps to maintain these industrial norms and helps them to prevail against institutional mechanisms.

Labor mobility contributes to wage deflation through three processes. Firstly, it tends to ensure that the unskilled labor market is always over-supplied and thus reinforces the managerial assumption that the market will always provide. As if to reinforce this assumption, markets are becoming more global even for unskilled workers (Choi, Woods, and Murrmann 2000). Reitz (1998) argues that the very existence of deregulated unstable markets makes them a magnet for migrant unskilled workers. Biachi (2000), in a study of mobility in the Mediterranean region, suggests that migrants who fail to find economic success even on the margins of regulated markets of northern European cities head southward toward the more deregulated markets of holiday resorts. Secondly, mobility reinforces the managerial assumption that there is no reason to reward job tenure. If there were tangible benefits in maintaining people in the same job, then seniority awards and job evaluation devices would be used and would have the effect of lowering rates of labor turnover. Strong internal labor markets are, for the most part, conspicuous by their absence in tourism (Simms, Riley, and Hales 1988). Against this background, and given the priority of controlling wage costs, it is not too surprising to find that sometimes in a recession imported unskilled labor fares better than the indigenous population (Ng and Grace 1998). Thirdly, mobility also contributes to the acceptance of industrial pay norms in that, as skills are transferable within sectors of the industry, they represent a commonality, which is the basis of the formation of social norms. That mobility is a consequence of that commonality is due to the information-spreading functions that are part of movement itself – knowing what it is like elsewhere is important information that tips the market toward "perfection" (Krackhardt and Porter 1986).

One of the constant findings of mobility studies of any type is that personal attributes and opportunities count. It is interesting that, at any level of analysis, the case of individual differences and differential propensities applies. Certain people are more likely to move than others, whether that is through ambition or a lower tolerance of their present position. Szivas and Riley (1999) sought to find the orientations to work in tourism of those moving from other sectors. Basically they found five orientations:

- an instrumental utility whereby the industry was an easy and convenient place to earn;
- an entrepreneurial outlook for developing small business with a desirable lifestyle;
- a positive orientation to enjoy the intrinsic merits of tourism jobs;
- a refugee mentality whereby tourism was a useful port in a storm; and
- an uncommitted wanderer orientation.

These empirical studies reaffirm the notion of an industry that is easy to enter. No evidence, however, was offered as to successful performance. That people entered tourism for "lifestyle" motivations, often associated with the desire for an absence of boundaries between life and work, has been clearly identified but not as yet fully explored. This question does raise some important issues as to the quality of the tourism product. Commitment rooted in dual objectives does not automatically confer dedication or professionalism.

Having drawn a picture of the market as "deregulated" and dynamic, it is probably time to consider institutionalist, global, and "big" organizational perspectives. Tourism is global, and it does have powerful corporations with strategic objectives – but the problem is that, putting aside for the moment the global market in managers and skilled technical staff, it is the small local dimension that really counts (Baldacchino 1997). At the sharp end even big companies "go native" in that they go along with the dynamics in the local market. There is often friction between corporate strategies and local conditions but, in the long run, the local market usually wins. Large organizations can cream off the more skilled workers in a market through offering opportunity without necessarily being the pay leader (Evans and Leighton 1989; Barth 1994). Indeed, for the most part, large organizations behave exactly like small ones in the market. This is not to say that institutional effects do not influence industrial relations and pay strategies; they do. However, the tourism industry has very low rates of union density that tend to occur only in legally regulated industrial relations systems (e.g., Canada, Australia, Italy) and only then in high employment concentrations (e.g., big-city hotels, airlines). Even here small businesses are often excluded from such regulation. But even when workers are managed in a bureaucratic mode, as for example in the airline industry or unionized hotel companies, agreements are made on flexibility that guarantee that the economic imperative of matching supply to demand is not threatened (Riley 1992a; Hanlon 1996). One of the characteristics of tourism organizations is that they tend to combine higher-level institutional structures with very loose market-orientated structures at the customer interface. Although the customer might be aware of "brand" there is very little sense of "big company" in the daily life of a tour representative, a cruise ship purser, or the landlord of a pub chain.

In a sense, branding and standardizing a tourism product while going along with the caprice of the local labor market is *the* dilemma of tourism quality. The one serious benefit of less mobility is a better quality of tourism product based on more professional staff (Hjalager and Anderson 2001). On the assumption that, in most cases, having a stable workforce allows customer service to be more consistent, there is a genuine desire in the management literature to encourage organizational commitment (Paxton 1993). However, the familiar dilemma is never far away. All service operations, because economically they are dependent upon throughput, generate short-term fluctuation and are required to vary labor supply while maintaining some continuity of service. Tourism organizations, like most other types of organization, want commitment and flexibility – it is a challenging problem for human resource management (Riley, Gore, and Kelliher 2000). Despite the evidence that much mobility is market-engendered, the school of thought that labels labor turnover as pathological has a point. Given all the positive skill-enhancing, career-advancing mobility, there is still a case to answer in terms of mobility caused by simple poor working conditions and unsatisfactory labor–management relations. At one level this is a management/human relations problem and the terrain of management psychology and industrial relations, but, at another level, it is also a labor market issue. If the market is unstable, can any single employer operate a stable unit? In fact the market is becoming more unstable as modern transactional cost economics kick in, with the result that operations are being subdivided and work subcontracted. Against this is the argument that secondary labor markets can become more stable if dominant players in the market decide to manage their employees in a bureaucratic mode. If the benefits showered on those in primary markets are reproduced for the unskilled, then it is suggested that mobility slows (Edwards 1979). There is an uncomfortable irony here: if large corporations really started to impose their enhanced conditions of employment on the labor market, by, metaphorically speaking, bullying the smaller operator, there might be unintended benefits for all. In other words, when the big players offer employment packages that encourage stability, eventually the market itself stabilizes to the benefit of all the employers. The rationale for employers to do this has to be rooted in a desire for quality that takes precedence over economic contingencies. History suggests that on this point we should not hold our breath. Functional flexibility, whereby traditional roles and working practices are remodeled to create more malleable role boundaries and multi-skilled workers, is a kind of rope bridge between the two positions. However, its advocates may have won the argument, but they have not won support (Riley 1992b).

Discussion

It has been suggested that tourism labor markets are largely unregulated and that, even when they are, they manage to maintain a dynamic mobility. At the macro level, this character could be interpreted as a reflection of a friction that exists between the forces that are globalizing taste and those that are trying to differentiate destinations – international versus national. In these circumstances, skills follow demand but are pulled in a number of directions simultaneously (for a discussion of how this applies to culinary skill, see Wood 2000). This is just one of the reasons that vocational curricula, despite their taken-for-granted good performance in the market, are so insecure. Another is that in general, despite welcoming the skills that vocational education provides, the industry does not recruit and promote on qualifications. In other words, credentials are respected but are not a form of differentiation. All this makes vocational education an easy target and one that is difficult to defend – having a complex labor market that does not operate on credentials is no help at all. At the micro level, work is becoming more specialized and deskilled. High technology, on the other hand, has entered the industry as a major augmentation of its services but without substantially replacing its existing skill base. This too is a problem for vocational education, which has to distribute its resources between its continuing skill base and business related technology.

Finally, one of the problems which constantly confronts the analysis of tourism is the lack of comprehensive statistical data – this is especially true of labor. Often researchers use hotel workers as proxy for the rest of the industry – which is clearly unsatisfactory. This lack of data does not disable the arguments. It does, however, make some of the debates that exist within the industry, such as those on employment, pay, and education, that much more difficult. But, in truth, it is not simply the lack of statistics that causes this; the real culprit is the complexity and velocity of the labor market, which makes argument based on evidence hard to sustain. Hence opinion and reputation play a rather large part in the industrial and educational debates on policy-making. Furthermore, the dynamics of the labor market bequeath problems to forecasting and planning, which cannot rely on credentials or wage rates to accurately navigate around the market to produce employment forecasts. In modern economic thinking, labor market flexibility is seen as desirable, but the devil is in the detail and it is legitimate to ask in the context of tourism the same question that has been asked in the case of economic transition: how much is too much?

This question leads toward a research agenda that must take as its starting point that labor markets in tourism are inherently dynamic and *naturally* unregulated. In such circumstances the study of labor turnover has run its course simply because its findings are consistent and suggest a phenomenon that is labeled as a problem worth tolerating. Given the character of tourism employment, the key question appears to be: what role does it play in general labor market functioning? The argument that it is a refuge is convincing but not complete. While we know something about mobility into tourism we know almost nothing about mobility out of tourism and into other industries. Furthermore, in this context there is the issue of how the industry contributes to ethnic marginality. Is tourism employment some form of economic rite of passage toward primary labor markets? If so, how does this occur and why are some ethnic minorities content to form enclave markets which sustain identities at the expense of greater prosperity? It is possible to suggest that one way into these issues is to understand pay determination processes within the industry, particularly its role in engendering mobility and tensions that exist between labor market dynamics and institutional priorities.

REFERENCES

Alpert, W. T. (1986). *The Minimum Wage in the Restaurant Industry.* London: Praeger.

Baldacchino, G. (1997). *Global Tourism and Informal Labour Relations: The Small-Scale Syndrome at Work.* London: Mansell.

Barth, E. (1994). Wages and organizational factors: Why do some establishments pay more? *Sociologica* 37(3), 253–68.

Biachi, R. V. (2000). Migrant tourist-worker: The "contact zones" of post-industrial tourism. *Current Issues in Tourism* 3(2), 107–87.

Brown, D., and McIntosh, S. (2000). Job satisfaction and labour turnover in the retail and hotel sectors. In W. Salverda, C. Lucifora, and B. Nolan (eds), *Policy Measures for Low-Wage Employment in Europe* (pp. 218–37). Cheltenham: Edward Elgar.

Cazes, S., and Nesporova, A. (2001). Labour market flexibility in the transition countries: How much is too much international? *Labour Review* 140(3), 293–325.

Choi, J.-G., Woods, R. H., and Murrmann, S. K. (2000). International labor markets and the migration of labor forces as an alternative solution for labor shortages in the hospitality industry. *International Journal of Contemporary Hospitality Management* 12(1), 61–6.

Denvir, A., and McMahon, F. (1992). Labour turnover in London hotels and the cost effectiveness of preventative measures. *International Journal of Hospitality Management* 11(2), 143–54.

Edwards, R. (1979). *Contested Terrain: The Transformation of the Workplace in the Twentieth Century.* London: Heinemann.

Evans, D. S., and Leighton, L. S. (1989). Why do small firms pay less? *Journal of Human Resources* 24(2), 299–318.

Granovetter, M. (1973). The strength of weak ties. *American Journal of Sociology* 78(6), 1360–80.

Greve, H. R. (1994). Industry diversity effects on job mobility. *Acta Sociologica* 37(2), 119–39.

Gunz, H. (1998). Organizational logics of managerial careers. *Organization Studies* 9(4), 529–54.

Hachen, D. S. (1992). Industrial characteristics and job mobility. *American Sociological Review* 57(1), 39–45.

Hanlon, P. (1996). *Global Airlines.* Oxford: Butterworth-Heinemann.

Hjalager, A. M., and Anderson, S. (2001). Tourism employment: Contingent work or professional career? *Employee Relations* 23(2), 115–29.

Hyman, R. (1976). Economic motivation and labour stability. In D. J. Bartholomew (ed.), *Manpower Planning* (pp. 162–89). Harmondsworth, UK: Penguin.

International Labor Office (2001). Human resources development, employment and globalization in the hotel, catering and tourism sector. Report for discussion at the Tripartite Meeting on Human Resources Development, Employment And Globalization in the Hotel, Catering and Tourism Sector, Geneva: International Labour Office, TMHCT/2001.

Iverson, R. D., and Deery, M. (1997). Turnover culture in the hospitality industry. *Human Resource Management Journal* 17(4), 71–82.

Johnson, K. (1981). Towards an understanding of labour turnover. *The Service Industries Journal* 1(1), 4–17.

Johnson, K. (1985). Labour turnover in hotels – revisited. *The Service Industries Journal* 5(2), 135–51.

King, R. (1995). Tourism, labour and international migration. In A. Montanari and A. M. Williams (eds), *European Tourism: Regions, Spaces and Restructuring* (pp. 177–90). Chichester: Wiley.

Krackhardt, D., and Porter, L. (1986). The snowball effect: Turnover embedded in communication networks. *Journal of Applied Psychology* 71(1), 51–5.

Ladkin, A., and Juwaheer, T. D. (2000). The career paths of hotel managers in Mauritius. *International Journal of Contemporary Hospitality Management* 12(2), 119–25.

Ladkin, A., and Riley, M. (1996). Mobility and structure in the career paths of UK hotel managers: A labour market hybrid of the bureaucratic model? *Tourism Management* 17(6), 443–52.

Lashley, C., and Chaplain, A. (1999). Labour turnover: Hidden problem, hidden cost. *Hospitality Review* 1(1), 49–54.

Maillat, D. (1984). Mobility channels: An instrument for analysis and regulating local labour markets. *International Labour Review* 130(3), 349–62.

Mueller, C. F. (1982). *The Economics of Labor Migration: A Behavioural Analysis*. London: Academic Press.

Ng, S.-H., and Grace, O. M. L. (1998). Hong Kong labor market in the aftermath of the crisis: Implications for foreign workers. *Asian and Pacific Migration Journal* 7(2–3), 171–86.

Paxton, M. C. (1993). A review of the organizational commitment literature as applied to hospitality organizations. In C. Cooper and A. Lockwood (eds), *Progress in Tourism, Recreation and Hospitality Management* (vol. 5, pp. 211–28). London: Belhaven Press.

Pedace, R. (1988). The impact of immigration on the labor market for native-born workers: Incorporating the dynamics of internal migration. *Eastern Economic Journal* 24(4), 446–62.

Reitz, J. G. (1998) *Warmth of Welcome: The Social Causes of Economic Success for Immigrants in Different Nations and Cities*, Boulder, CO: Westview Press.

Riley, M. (1990). The labour retention strategies of UK hotel managers. *The Service Industries Journal* 10(3), 116–19.

Riley, M. (1991). An analysis of hotel labour markets. In C. Cooper (ed.), *Progress in Tourism, Recreation and Hospitality Management*, vol. 3 (pp. 232–46). London: Belhaven Press.

Riley, M. (1992a). Functional flexibility in hotels – is it feasible? *Tourism Management* 13(4), 363–7.

Riley, M. (1992b). Labour utilization and collective agreements: An international comparison. *International Journal of Contemporary Hospitality Management* 4(4), 21–3.

Riley, M. (1999). Redefining the debate on hospitality productivity. *Tourism and Hospitality Research* 1(2), 182– 6.

Riley, M., Gore, J., and Kelliher, C. (2000). Economic determinism and human resource management practice in the hospitality and tourism industry. *Tourism and Hospitality Research* 2(2), 118–28.

Riley, M., Ladkin, A., and Szivas, E. (2002). *Tourism Employment: Analysis and Planning*. Clevedon: UK Channel View Publications.

Rosen, S. (1972). Learning and experience in the labor market. *Journal of Human Resources* 7(4), 326–42.

Simms, J. (1987). A study of the extent and nature of labour turnover in hotels. Unpublished M.Phil. thesis, University of Surrey, UK.

Simms, J., Riley, M., and Hales, C. (1988). Examination of the concept of internal labour markets in UK hotels. *International Journal of Tourism Management* 9(3), 3–12.

Stalker, P. (1994). *The Work of Strangers: A Survey of International Labour Migration*. Geneva: International Labour Office.

Szivas, E., and Riley, M. (1999). Tourism employment in conditions of economic transition; The case of Hungary. *Annals of Tourism Research* 26(4), 747–71.

Szivas, E., Riley, M., and Airey, D. (2003). Labor mobility into tourism: Attraction and satisfaction. *Annals of Tourism Research* 30(1), 64–76.

Wood, R. C. (2000). *Strategic Questions in Food and Beverage Management*. Oxford: Butterworth-Heinemann.

Chapter 12

Transport and Tourism

Stephen Page

Introduction

Transport is a fundamental requirement for tourism to occur. It is the pivotal element which connects the tourist with the destination, unifying the origin-destination elements and thereby is a dynamic element in the tourism system. The relationship between transport and tourism has largely been researched by geographers who have used the concepts developed by spatial scientists to understand the interactions and locational aspects of transport systems as they impact and depend upon recreation and tourism activities. One of the weaknesses in transport geography is the continued absence of geographers who research transport and its relationship with tourism. Reviews of progress in transport research, such as Knowles (1993), are notable for their lack of any substantive research efforts in this area. In some respects, transport tends to be viewed as a passive element by geographers in the tourism context rather than as an integral part of tourism activity. In fact there has been comparatively little progress made by researchers in this area of study since the influential studies undertaken in the 1960s and 1970s by geographers (e.g., Wall 1971; Patmore 1983).

While useful syntheses such as Halsall (1992) provide bibliographies of past studies, few of the studies reviewed by Halsall (1992) were written by geographers in the 1980s and 1990s to explicitly develop an understanding of the way in which transport facilitates and in some cases conditions the type of recreational and tourism activity which occurs. Much of the research activity that has been published in the *Journal of Transport Geography* and *Journal of Air Transport Management* has been preoccupied with air travel (Chou 1993; Shaw 1993; Feiler and Goodovitch 1993). Other studies have examined the impact of congestion on tourist travel (Shailes, Senior, and Andrew 2001), with Page (1999) the only existing study which explicitly focuses on the tourism–transport interface.

Recent texts such as Tolley and Turton (1995) and Hoyle and Knowles (1999) do at least highlight the need to consider recreation and tourism in the context of transport geography. Yet even Tolley and Turton (1995) do not devote much space to the topic, and few other studies have sought to place transport for recreation and tourism on the research agenda beyond the notable occasional studies by the Transport Study Group of the Institute of British Geographers (Tolley and Turton 1987; Halsall 1982). Where previous studies exist (e.g., Halsall 1992), the emphasis has been on modal forms of recreational and tourist travel (e.g., land-based transport and the use of trails, waterborne transport and heritage transport for nostalgic travel – see Page 1993, 1994a). This does not adequately develop the contribution that geographers can make to the management, planning, and development of transport for recreational and tourist travel (Page 1994b).

An important starting point for any analysis of the transport–tourism interface is what Hall and Page (1999: 181) describe as four spatially expressed roles: "linking the source market with the host destination; providing mobility and access within a destination area/region/country; providing mobility and access within an actual tourism attraction and facilitating travel along a recreational route which is itself the tourism experience." Yet what is also notable is the apparent disregard of the situation in less developed countries where transport may be an instrument or symbol of inequality. What Hall and Page (1999) observed was that, where the local population is excluded from international tourist transport (e.g., air-conditioned transport) and a two-tier system of transportation exists, this may compound feelings of relative deprivation.

This chapter commences with a discussion of the relationship between transport and tourism to explore some of the conceptual, semantic, and practical issues associated with establishing the role of transport in this context. This is followed by a discussion of two contrasting examples: the role of the car and cycling as a sustainable form of tourist transport and the problems and prospects for tourism. The chapter then provides a review of a number of key research issues which are currently affecting the tourist–transport agenda. Many studies of tourism and transport have been conceived in the logical positivist tradition, as a preliminary analysis of papers published in a disparate range of journals such as the *Journal of Transport Geography*, the *Journal of Air Transport Management* and *Tourism Management* suggests. In some specific cases there has been a greater interest in political economy perspectives of tourism and transport from a regulation standpoint (i.e., the impact of deregulation on the air transport industry) (Debbage and Ioannides 1998).

The Relationship between Transport, Recreation, and Tourism

Within the growing literature on tourism there is a debate which recognizes that tourism activities are a subset of leisure. This implies that leisure activities are discretionary because they occur in juxtaposition to work and other household functions. In other words, these activities occur in three contexts: "time not required for work or basic functions such as eating and sleeping, of activities, or recreation within leisure time, and an attitude of mind based upon a perception of pleasure and enjoyment, recognizing that there may be blurring within and between these areas" (Patmore 1983: 5–6, cited in Halsall 1992: 155). A further complication in seeking to understand the relationship between leisure, recreation, and tourism is that in the immediate post-war period in developed countries, the amount of leisure time has increased as the hours of work have decreased. But for certain social groups such as women, and housewives in particular, leisure may actually mean work. So while leisure time has become a firmly ingrained element in the routine of many people, often defined as non-work time, the growth in daily, weekly, and annual leisure time has not been distributed evenly in social and spatial terms. For example, Williams (1995) highlights the relationship in urban recreational patterns in British cities where residents in the most affluent neighborhoods have relatively easy access to recreational and leisure resources. This is not only reflected in the spatial distribution of such resources but also through the increased levels of car ownership in such neighborhoods compared to residents in poorer districts. Although certain researchers see recreation as dependent upon a range of facilitating factors in social and economic contexts (i.e., the availability of time and financial resources to capitalize on leisure opportunities), the distinction between leisure and recreation activities has remained increasingly fuzzy and open to differing interpretations.

Conventional definitions of recreation tend to emphasize the outdoor context and non-home-based nature of such activities, yet when one attempts to distinguish between the use of transport for leisure and for recreation it becomes increasingly difficult. For example, on a rail journey through a national park, the train may be carrying local passengers who are enjoying a passive use of their leisure time by sightseeing and it may also be carrying fell walkers who are using the train as a mode of transport into the national park to reach the starting point for their walk and thereby participate in outdoor recreation. The train may also be carrying non-residents journeying from point A to point B. These may be domestic tourists who are staying away from home for more than 24 hours or international tourists who are on holiday. Herein lies the complexity of disentangling the complex relationship between leisure, recreation, and tourism and the fact that tourists also undertake recreational activities at their destination area. How, therefore, does one define tourism in this context?

While the previous discussion introduced the functional definition of tourists, who are distinguished by their journeys and stay at destinations for temporary leisure periods away from their normal place of residence, the domestic and international nature of such journeys creates a complex array of spatial patterns. Only a limited number of geographers have modeled and analyzed these patterns on the domestic, intra-regional, and international scale (see Pearce 1995). More socially constructed definitions of tourism (e.g., Urry 1990) are useful in understanding the separate and regulated spheres of work and leisure time and in showing how individuals do not necessarily distinguish between leisure, recreation, and tourism, as has been observed by various researchers (e.g., Shaw and Williams 1994). In spatial and social terms, differentiating between leisure, recreation, and tourism remains a semantic and somewhat tautological issue since no clear boundary exists between each, and there is a significant interaction between each form of activity since "recreational environments . . . are important tourism destinations" (Smith and Godbey 1991: 97). Nevertheless, Halsall (1982) identified the fundamental relationship between transport and leisure time which geographers have neglected to develop further in the late 1980s and early 1990s:

> Transport is an integral part of much recreational behaviour, both as an aid to access to recreational opportunities, and as a recreational activity in its own right . . . Progressive

reductions in the relative costs of travel, and in the frictional effects of distance have dramatically increased the demand for recreational trips. In particular, the growth of car ownership has extended both the distances travelled and the range of recreational foci. (Halsall 1982: ii)

What Halsall (1982) fails to acknowledge in this context, however, are the implications for international tourism, even though, as Pearce (1995) acknowledges, the volume of domestic tourism is up to ten times greater than that of international tourism on a global scale. Nevertheless, tourism has also been a major beneficiary of these changes in accessibility, with people being encouraged to travel further afield as package holidays and charter flights have widened access to international travel. But recreational trips and domestic tourism remain the dominant form of activity in terms of the volume of traffic. As table 12.1 shows, the growth in international tourism since 1950 which involves crossing an international border, and therefore some form of travel involving tourist transport, indicates the scale of international tourism growth. In a European context, air travel between EU countries in 1999 illustrates the scale of intra-EU passenger traffic (i.e., travel amongst EU citizens) which highlights one example of the volume of tourist travel (table 12.2) with the main generating markets being the UK, Germany, and France among the top five flows. This highlights the dominance of the charter holiday markets for the top two flows and a mixture of the business and "visiting friends and relatives" (VFR) markets for the remaining flows, highlighting the complexity of disaggregating the type of travel driving certain traffic flows.

Table 12.1 The growth of international tourist travel since 1950

Year	Thousands of arrivals
1950	25,282
1960	69,320
1970	165,787
1980	285,997
1990	458,229
2000	697,000
2001	692,000

Source: WTO 2003.

Table 12.2 Main intra-EU country flows in 1999

Flow	Volume of departures (millions)
UK–Spain/Spain–UK	23.86
Germany–Spain/Spain–Germany	18.54
UK–Ireland/Ireland–UK	8.81
UK–Germany/Germany–UK	8.07
France–UK/UK–France	7.71

Source: Eurostat 2003.

One of the important ways in which the geographer has attempted to explain the relationship between transport, recreation, and tourism is in terms of the development of models; Johnston (1991) examines the development of models in geography in the logical positivist tradition. Although such models do not adequately accommodate the role of the individual traveler and their behavioral traits, such models do provide an insight into the transport–recreation–tourism interface.

The Car and Recreational Travel

In the post-war period, the growth of car ownership has not only made the impact of recreational and tourist travel more flexible, it has induced over-use at accessible sites. This ease of access, fueled by a growth in road-building and the upgrading of minor roads in many developed countries, has been a self-reinforcing process leading to over-use and a greater dominance in passive recreational activities. Probably the most influential study of car usage among recreationalists was Wall's (1972) study of Kingston upon Hull in 1969. Wall (1972) identified the two principal types of study used to analyze recreational activity, namely site studies (of particular facilities or areas) and national studies, such as the widely cited Pilot National Recreation Survey (British Travel Association and University of Keele 1967, 1969). Wall (1972) supplemented data from the national survey with a regional sample of 500 Hull car-owners in 1969. While the results are now very dated, it highlighted the importance of seasonality and timing of pleasure trips by car and the dominance of the car as a mode of transport for urban dwellers. It also highlighted the role of the journey by car as a form of recreation in itself as well as the importance of the destination. Such results emphasized the importance of the car as more than just a means of transport. In fact the study also has a degree of similarity with other studies that followed, such as Coppock and Duffield's (1975) survey of recreation and the countryside. This focused on patterns and processes of recreational activity in Scotland and mapped and described patterns of recreational travel, especially those of caravanners. At the same time, the study noted the tendency for many recreationalists not to venture far from their car at the destination, a point reiterated by Glyptis's (1981) innovative and seminal study of recreationalists using participant observation in Hull. Wall (1971) also found that the majority of pleasure trips were day trips less than 100 km away from Hull, being spatially concentrated in a limited number of resorts along the Yorkshire coast and southerly part of the region. Other research (Burton 1966; Wager 1967) highlighted the versatility of the car and its use to venture into the reaches of the North Yorks Moors national park. Other researchers' findings (e.g., Burton 1966) explained the attraction of the car to recreationalists as allowing them to enjoy the countryside and observe its visual characteristics rather have than physical contact.

More recent research by Eaton and Holding (1996) identified the growing number of such visits to the countryside by recreationalists in cars. In 1991, 103 million visits were made to national parks in the UK (Countryside Commission 1992), the most popular places being the Lake District and Peak District national parks. In terms of car usage, it was estimated that car traffic would have grown by 267 percent by 2025 from the levels current in 1992 (Countryside Commission 1992). This was further emphasized by more recent statistics which show that, in 1998, 1.4 billion leisure trips were made to the countryside (including national parks) of which 85 percent were made by car in the UK and a mere 1 percent by train or bus. The growing dependence on car usage internationally is shown in table 12.3 for a number of industrialized countries. The greatest pressures of rising car usage have been the decline in public transport usage for recreational trips, and many national parks seem unlikely to be able to cope with the levels of usage predicted for 2025 given their urban catchments and relative accessibility by motorways and A roads. A recent draft transport strategy produced for Scotland's first national park in 2002 recognized these key issues in relation to "people movement" within the park area. Here the emphasis was placed on developing transport initiatives within the park area requiring measures to address the problems of car use, as the following extract suggests:

Vision – Sustainable Movement
The National Park will be a place where, although the car is expected to remain as the principal means of transport, more sustainable alternatives will be available to travel to and move around the Park. More extensive and integrated public and shared transport systems on roads and lochs will be put in place in conjunction with measures to manage private car access where this is damaging sensitive areas. There will also be an increasing range of safe opportunities for non-motorized transport.

This reiterates many of the concerns of Eaton and Holding (1996), who review the absence of effective policies to meet the practical problems of congestion facing many sites in the countryside in Britain. While schemes such as the Sherpa bus routes in Snowdonia national park, which replace car usage with bus usage, exist (Mulligan 1979), these have not been incorporated into any wider policy objectives for transport. This combines with a failure to design public transport to suit the needs and perceptions of users to achieve reductions and solutions to congestion in national parks. Thus it is clear that the car poses a major problem not only for urban areas

Table 12.3 Percentage of passenger transport which is car-based in selected countries in 1999

Country	%
Belgium	79.6
Denmark	74.6
Germany	80.1
France	83.7
Ireland	75.4
The Netherlands	79.9
Austria	72.6
Portugal	79.5
Spain	74.4
UK	84.6
USA	*80.4
EU average	80.8

* for 1998
Source: Eurostat 2003.

and their use by commuters and recreationalists but also in terms of the sheer growth in volume in areas not designed for large numbers of car-users. This problem is especially marked when spatially concentrated at "honeypots" (locations which attract large numbers to congregate in a confined area) in national parks.

The UK Tourism Society's response to the Government task force on tourism and the environment (English Tourist Board/Employment Department 1991) highlighted the impact of the car by commenting that

> no analysis of the relationship between tourism and the environment can ignore transportation. Tourism is inconceivable without it. Throughout Europe some 40 per cent of leisure time away from home is spent travelling, and the vast majority of this is by car... Approaching 30 per cent of the UK's energy requirements go on transportation... [and] the impact of traffic congestion, noise and air pollution... [will] diminish the quality of the experience for visitors.

Various management solutions exist, such as encouraging urban areas to develop "intervening opportunities" in the urban fringe through networks of country parks in the UK (see Harrison 1991) which are capable of absorbing large numbers of visitors seeking a countryside experience. Such parks are able to fulfill the need for local recreational demand and to reduce the need for recreationalists to seek out countryside sites, thereby reducing the impact of transport on other sites. Other options include a modal switching to public transport, but in many countries this has proved difficult as the car has become ingrained in the culture of tourist consumption, where its flexibility and ease of use make public modes of transport less attractive (see Page 2002). However, one area where some progress has been made is in the use of the bicycle as a mode of tourist transport.

Cycling as a Sustainable Form of Recreational and Tourist Transport

Sustainability has become a fashionable term during the 1990s and the early years of the twenty-first century (see chapter 40). However, in the context of tourist transport, such a concern has not led to any dramatic changes in the operation and management of transport systems, but in many cases merely some readjustment to accommodate green issues. In fact some researchers might argue that it is impossible to talk about sustainability in the context of recreation and tourism without a fundamental re-evaluation of the concept of pleasure travel and its necessity. Wood and House (1991) argue that, while transport operators need to pursue good environmental practices, the onus should be placed on tourists, who need to audit their trip on the basis of such questions as:

- Why go on holiday? Consider your motivations and whether you need to travel.
- How can you choose the right type of holiday to meet your needs?
- Have you thought about traveling out of season to less well-known destinations?
- How can you choose the right tour operator? For example, ask environmentally related questions to ascertain what the company is doing to minimize tourism's environmental impact.
- Are using public transport, or cycling or walking, options as opposed to hiring a car?

It is the last point which raises the issue of using sustainable and low-impact forms of transport at the destination, particularly the use of cycling. This is now a highly topical issue which many EU countries are promoting to act as a counterweight to the overdependence on the car for leisure travel.

Cycling, Tourism, and Leisure Travel

According to Lumsdon (1996), the market for recreational cycling activities can range from day or part-day casual usage through to long-distance touring holidays. In fact cycling can present tourists and recreationalists with unique views of rural areas and it is particularly appealing to free independent travelers. There are a limited number of studies of cycle tourism (Schieven 1988; Beoiley 1996; Lumsdon 1996; SUSTRANS 1997; Ritchie 1998) and many of these have not been widely disseminated in the transport literature beyond the seminal study by Tolley (1990). In the UK, cycle tourism generates approximately £535 million a year, derived from leisure day trips, domestic holidays, and overseas trips (Beoiley 1996). Cycling can also make a major contribution to environmental management where it offers a pollution-free form of recreation. For example, the Scottish Tourist Board (1991) developed a strategy to enhance cycle tourism, and the Broads Authority initiated a "Broads Bike Hire" network in 1996 supplemented by the development of a series of short circular routes which avoid main roads and sensitive areas for wildlife. Each route in the Broads begins and ends at a cycle hire shop. In The Netherlands, such schemes are even more highly developed, as Tolley and Turton (1995) show in the case of Delft, where cycles are segregated from motorized traffic to reduce the risk of conflict and accidents. This can enhance the use of cycles for recreational and other uses. In fact the Dutch National Environmental Policy Plan has also improved cycle parking at stations to aid commuters, and inter-modal transfer to assist in promoting sustainable transport options.

In New Zealand, the central Otago region on South Island has followed the lead of several other countries, converting former rail routes into linear cycle routes for recreational and tourist traffic. The Central Otago Rail Trail (Ritchie 1997) is the only one of its kind in South Island and complements the growing interest in long-distance cycling by tourists, who tend to use secondary routes (B-grade roads in the UK). While the majority of cycle tourists interviewed by Ritchie (1997) were experienced cyclists, they conformed to an international profile of cyclists, tending to be 20–34 years of age, predominantly male, and traveling with a partner or alone. While issues such as signposting, quality of roads, and safety are rated highly, participating in tourist activities seemed of less importance. What emerges from Ritchie's (1997) study has important implications for the spatial distribution and planning of sustainable transport modes such as cycling, which is that countries seeking to promote this form of recreational and tourist travel need to develop a national strategy or cycle network. Such networks, as the experience in the Netherlands suggests, need to be safe and able to provide opportunities for rural tourism development by providing opportunities for cyclists to stop. The national cycling strategy in the UK was expected by SUSTRANS (1997) to generate growth in cycling by the year 2000 through the stimulation of demand through the national cycling network. In fact by 2002 this had grown to 6,750 miles of cycle routes, with 97.2

million trips and a 20 percent growth in patronage since the network was opened in 2000 as a non-polluting and less intrusive form of transport. What this illustrates is that cycling can expand the opportunities for recreationalists, and can fulfill a wide range of recreational and tourism needs. Recent research examining leisure cycling undertaken at the University of Stirling (Edgar 2002), in conjunction with SUSTRANS, has illustrated a number of key achievements and challenges for this form of leisure transport. First, existing policy and strategy on sustainable transport have illustrated that many cycle-users are forced to drive to near-urban cycle routes to access them before commencing their leisure activities, contributing to increased car usage. This raises issues in relation to developing feeder routes from major conurbations to make cycle routes more accessible. Second, there is growing evidence from Edgar (2002) and SUSTRANS that the profile of cycle-users is extremely broad; the activity is not socially exclusive, aside from the necessary initial investment in buying or hiring a bicycle. There is also a growing debate on how such adaptations in leisure and tourist use of rural areas are seeking more sustainable activities such as cycling to reduce impacts on fragile resource bases, while cycle routes have sought to reuse redundant rail routes and former routeways as a means of fostering sustainable development. This may very well indicate a new stage in the life cycle of tourist travel and its dependence on the car as the main mode of sedentary travel in countryside areas, as local authorities and SUSTRANS promote the objectives of sustainable development and Agenda 21 through cycling. In this respect, a step change in consumer behavior may signal a new phase in tourist transport within, and travel to, destinations. Although much of the experience is necessarily UK-based, reflecting the considerable research efforts being devoted to this area of study, it is likely that similar experiences are being mirrored across the EU.

Emerging Research Issues for Tourism and Transport

While this chapter has not reviewed the full modal range of tourist transport options (e.g., air travel, rail, coach, car, and other land- and sea-based transport modes), it is apparent that air travel is one of the principal modes of transport used by international travelers. Among the key issues facing researchers in the twenty-first century are: gender concerns about access to travel (i.e., are certain groups still prohibited from travel due to race and gender constraints?); the extent to which air travel will move from being based on a national system of regulation to being based on a global system of regulation, leading to a complete overhaul of existing post-war agreements; and the likely effect of new technology (i.e., larger aircraft such as the new generation of large passenger carriers in planning/production by major aircraft manufacturers). Yet among many of the criticisms of existing research in tourism and transport is the lack of detachment among researchers from the actual experiences of the tourist themselves while traveling. Here much of the interdisciplinary research agenda has been dominated by psychologists to the detriment of geographers, who have addressed macro issues to the detriment of personal issues for the tourist. For example, access for the disabled is now a real issue as EU legislation on removing barriers to access for such groups affects many countries. For this reason, it is useful to focus on some of the current issues and themes emerging in the research literature which affect tourists' experience and their willingness to travel by air.

Within the specialized area of research known as travel medicine, there is a growing concern about the role of situational anxiety and physical health problems associated with air travel on short-haul and long-haul flights. This problem has been accentuated following the 11 September 2001 terrorist attacks in the USA. Among the stresses facing travelers are the growing delays at airports (pre-flight and in transit) which may exacerbate cardiac problems and account for a significant proportion of in-flight emergencies. In-flight problems commonly reported included ear problems, headaches, swollen ankles, and stuffy nose. Anxiety levels increase at the most hazardous parts of the journey (take-off and landing), although flight delays and baggage delays are also proven to be stressful. In the last two years there has also been a major growth in awareness of a medical condition associated with being cramped on long-haul flights – deep vein thrombosis. Again the stress of long-haul travel has been raised, and has led to a number of class actions against airlines for failing to alert passengers to the dangers of this potential hazard (Page 2002).

In-flight injuries associated with turbulence have also attracted interest within the US air sector (Page 2002). In the USA turbulence accounted for 62 percent of all US air carrier accidents, which cost the aviation industry US$100 million a year. Many of these injuries affect cabin crew who are not seated, although passenger injuries are also recorded in the statistics. There was also an upward trend in such accidents, making the case for forward turbulence systems, given that this is a significant safety issue in the aviation industry and the availability of products to reduce the impact of these weather-related events. At the same time, airlines are being expected to make additional safety investments for staff and flight crew so that terrorist hijacking on the scale of 11 September is minimized, and to reassure tourists about in-flight safety. This renewed interest in tourist safety is certainly a major agenda for transport operators of both land- and air-based systems (Page 2002). It will remain an important research agenda and focus for the traveling public for a number of years to come.

Conclusion

Halsall's (1992: 175) comment that "transport provision is a permissive factor in much tourist/recreation development, itself a product of increasing mobility, leisure time and affluence" remains a valid assessment of the relationship between transport and tourism a decade later. The continued neglect of this relationship by researchers has meant they have failed to raise the issue more prominently on the research agenda, although there is growing evidence that the sustainability debate and the growth in special interest tourism (Weiler and Hall 1992) are stimulating a renewed interest in this area of research, especially in the case of cycling. Yet there has been a paucity of research which is longitudinal and able to follow up on earlier studies such as that by Wall (1972) to assess the degree of change in urban dwellers' use of transport for tourism. Such longitudinal studies are necessary to establish how cultural and environmental factors are shaping the use of transport for recreation and tourism. To date, much of the dated literature offers few modern insights into the real significance of transport in the overall social construction of holidaymaking and day trips by urban and rural populations in the developed and less developed world. A number of recent studies which adopt a highly theoretical perspective (e.g., Halsall 1992) have sought to pursue this research, but there is considerable scope for a renewed interest in how integral transport is in facilitating and stimulating tourism activity and development. Tourism continues to grow at a significant rate in most developed countries and finding new and diverse opportunities for such activities may mean a greater concern for the economic use of existing forms of transport for tourism. It may also require the development of innovative schemes to manage the volume and spatial distribution of visitors in sensitive natural environments.

REFERENCES

Beoiley, S. (1996). On yer bike – cycling and tourism. *INSIGHTS*, September, B17–31.

British Travel Association and the University of Keele (1967). *Pilot National Recreation Survey.* Keele: BTA/University of Keele.

British Travel Association and the University of Keele (1969). *Pilot National Recreation Survey.* Keele: BTA/University of Keele.

Broads Authority (1997). *Broads Plan.* Norwich: Broads Authority.

Burton, T. (1966). A day in the country: A survey of leisure activity at Box Hill in Surrey. *Journal of the Royal Institute of Chartered Surveyors* 98, 378–80.

Chou, Y. (1993). Airline deregulation and nodal accessibility. *Journal of Transport Geography* 1(1), 36–46.

Coppock, J. T., and Duffield, B. (1975). *Recreation in the Countryside.* London: Macmillan.

Countryside Commission (1992). *Trends in Transport and the Countryside.* Cheltenham: Countryside Commission.

Debbage, K., and Ioannides, D. (eds) (1998). *The Economic Geography of Tourism.* London: Routledge.

Eaton, B., and Holding, D. (1996). The evaluation of public transport alternatives to the car in British national parks. *Journal of Transport Geography* 4(1), 55–65.

Edgar, G. (2002). Working towards sustainable transport in Scotland: The contribution of leisure cycling. Unpublished dissertation submitted in partial fulfilment of the M.Sc. in Environmental Management, University of Stirling

English Tourist Board/Employment Department (1991). *Tourism and the Environment: Maintaining the Balance.* London: English Tourist Board.

Eurostat (2003). <http://www.europa.eu.int/comm/dgs/energy_transport/index_en.html> (accessed January 4, 2003).

Feiler, G., and Goodovitch, T. (1993). Decline and growth, privatisation and protectionism in the Middle East airline industry. *Journal of Transport Geography* 2(1), 55–64.

Glyptis, S. (1981). People at play in the countryside. *Geography* 66(4), 277–85.

Hall, C. M., and Page, S. J. (1999). *Geography of Recreation and Tourism: Place and Space.* London: Routledge.

Halsall, D. (ed.) (1982). *Transport for Recreation.* Lancaster: IBG Transport Geography Study Group.

Halsall, D. (1992). Transport for tourism and recreation. In B. Hoyle and R. Knowles (eds), *Modern Transport Geography* (pp. 155–77). London: Belhaven.

Harrison, C. (1991). *Countryside Recreation in a Changing Society.* London: TML Partnership.

Hoyle, B., and Knowles, R. (eds) (1992). *Modern Transport Geography.* London: Belhaven.

Hurst, M. (ed.) (1974). *Transportation Geography: Comments and Readings.* London: McGraw Hill.

Johnston, R. J. (1991). *Geography and Geographers*. London: Edward Arnold.
Knowles, R. (1993). Research agendas for transport geography in the 1990s. *Journal of Transport Geography* 1(1), 3–11.
Lumsdon, L. (1996). Future for cycle tourism in Britain. *INSIGHTS*, March, D27–32.
Moseley, M. (1979). *Accessibility: The Rural Challenge*. London: Methuen.
Mulligan, C. (1979). The Snowdon sherpa: Public transport and national park management experiment. In D. Halsall and B. Turton (eds), *Rural Transport Problems in Britain: Papers and Discussion* (pp. 45–55). Keele: IBG Transport Geography Study Group.
Page, S. (1993). European rail travel. *Travel and Tourism Analyst* 1, 5–30.
Page, S. (1994a). European coach travel. *Travel and Tourism Analyst* 1, 4–18.
Page, S. (1994b). *Transport for Tourism*. London: Routledge.
Page, S. (1999). *Transport and Tourism*, 2nd edn. London: Addison Wesley Longman.
Page, S. (2002). Tourist health and safety. *Travel and Tourism Analyst* 5, 1–31.
Patmore, J. (1983). *Recreation and Resources*. Oxford: Blackwell.
Pearce, D. (1995). *Tourism Today: A Geographical Analysis*. London: Longman.
Ritchie, B. (1997). Cycle tourism in the South Island of New Zealand: Infrastructure considerations for the twenty first century. In *Trails in the Third Millennium Conference*, Cromwell, New Zealand, 2–5 December (pp. 325–34). Dunedin: Centre for Tourism, University of Otago.
Ritchie, B. (1998). Bicycle tourism in the South Island of New Zealand: Planning and management issues. *Tourism Management* 19(6), 567–82.
Schaeffer, K., and Sclar, E. (1975). *Access for All: Transportation and Urban Growth*. London: Penguin.
Schieven, A. (1988). A study of cycle tourists on Prince Edward Island, unpublished master's thesis, University of Waterloo, Canada.
Scottish Tourist Board (1991). *Tourism Potential of Cycling and Cycle Routes in Scotland*. Edinburgh: Scottish Tourist Board.
Shailes, A., Senior, M. L., and Andrew, B. P. (2001). Tourists' travel behaviour in response to congestion: The case of car trips to Cornwall, United Kingdom. *Journal of Transport Geography* 9(1), 49–60.
Shaw, G., and Williams, A. (1994). *Critical Issues in Tourism: Geographical Perspectives*. Oxford: Blackwell.
Shaw, S. (1993). Hub structures of major US airlines. *Journal of Transport Geography* 1(1), 47–58.
Smith, S. L. J. (1983). *Recreation Geography*. London: Longman.
Smith, S. L. J., and Godbey, G. (1991). Leisure, recreation and tourism. *Annals of Tourism Research* 18, 85–100.
SUSTRANS (1997). *The Tourism Potential of National Cycle Routes*. London: Tourism Society.
Tolley, R. (1990). *The Greening of Urban Transport: Planning for Walking and Cycling in Western Cities*. London: Belhaven.
Tolley, R., and Turton, B. (eds) (1987). *Short Sea Crossings and the Channel Tunnel*. Lancaster: Transport Geography Study Group.
Tolley, R., and Turton, B. (1995). *Transport Systems, Policy and Planning: A Geographical Approach*. London: Longman.
Ullman, M. (1974[1954]). Geography as spatial interactions. In M. Eliot-Hurst (ed.), *Transportation Geography: Comments and Readings* (pp. 27–40). New York: McGraw Hill.
Urry, J. (1990). *The Tourist Gaze: Leisure and Travel in Contemporary Societies*. London: Sage.
Wager, J. (1967). Outdoor recreation on common land. *Journal of the Town Planning Institute* 53, 398–403.

Wall, G. (1971). Car-owners and holiday activities. In P. Lavery (ed.), *Recreational Geography*. Newton Abbot: David & Charles.

Wall, G. (1972). Socioeconomic variations in pleasure trip patterns: The case of Hull car owners. *Transactions of the Institute of British Geographers* 57, 45–58.

Weiler, B., and Hall, C. M. (eds) (1992). *Special Interest Tourism*. London: Belhaven.

Williams, S. (1995). *Urban Recreation*. London: Routledge.

Wood, K., and House, S. (1991). *The Good Tourist*. London: Mandarin.

World Tourism Organization (WTO) (2003). <http://www.world-tourism.org/press releases> (accessed January 4, 2003).

Chapter 13

The Tourism Area Life Cycle in the Twenty-First Century

Richard Butler

Introduction

It is now almost a quarter of a century since the original article (Butler 1980) presenting the Tourism Area Life Cycle (TALC) model was first published (figure 13.1). Its appearance in *The Canadian Geographer* was somewhat fortuitous (resulting as it did from a paper presented at an annual meeting of the Canadian

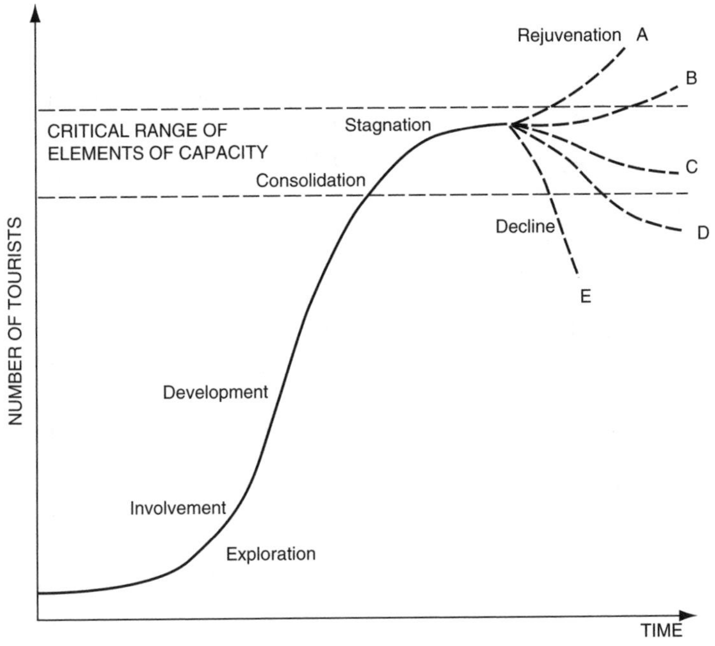

Figure 13.1 A tourism area cycle of evolution
Source: Butler 1980.

Association of Geographers, subsequently accepted for the only (at that time) special edition of the journal) and its continued popularity and application totally unexpected. The origins of the TALC have been discussed in some detail elsewhere (Butler 2004a, 2004b) and a paper which is contemporary and futuristic is not the place to look backwards to any great degree. It would be inappropriate, however, not to provide a brief comment on the origins of the model and its linkages with the then contemporary research in tourism, because without such a reflection, some of the comments on its current and future application might appear rather surprising.

The real origins of the TALC lie in a now rather obscure and unpublished paper presented at a meeting in Ottawa in 1972 (Butler and Brougham 1972). This paper hypothesized what might happen to tourist destinations as they developed and reached their limits in terms of carrying capacity. It was focused more on the spatial implications of the growth and development of tourist destinations than on the specific pattern and process of development in specific destinations. One of the hypotheses was that, as destinations began to suffer from a loss of quality because of excessive levels of development and use, new destinations would be developed, and that this new development might be modeled in both space and time (figure 13.2). Over the intervening years attention shifted more to what was observed to be happening within destinations in terms of the process of development, rather than the development of patterns of destinations. The published

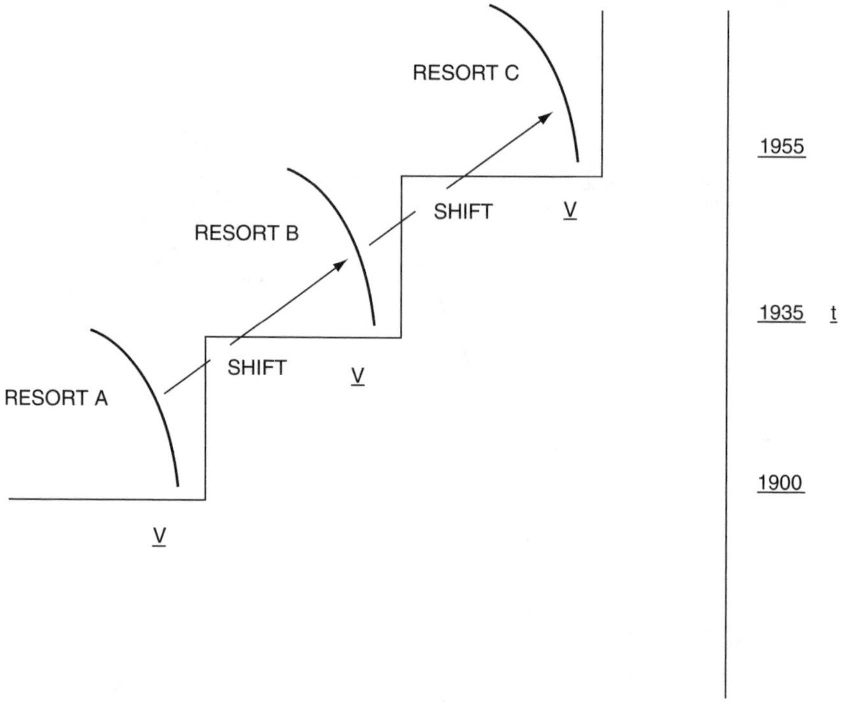

Figure 13.2 Destination shift in resort development over time
Source: Butler and Brougham 1972.

form of the model saw the proposed stages of resort development given much greater prominence than in the earlier version and the theoretical links of the model were focused more on growth than dispersion. As Hall (2004) and Coles (2004) have pointed out, the geographical concepts at the heart of the TALC were clear in the 1980 version, but in reality the original form was much more spatial in its orientation.

The response to the model and its subsequent application has been generally positive, although a number of pertinent and highly appropriate criticisms have been made. These began with Wall (1983) and Haywood (1986), and have continued fairly regularly since then, including most recently articles by Johnson (2001a, 2001b). Reviews of many of the applications and critiques (Lagiewski 2004; Haywood 2004a, 2004b), and a large collection of invited papers on applications, modifications, and alternative viewpoints about the TALC are due to appear in two specific volumes on the TALC in the near future (Butler 2004a, 2004b). The focus of this chapter, therefore, is to discuss the relevance of the TALC more than two decades after its appearance and the potential applications of the model in the future.

Contemporary Relevance

One is tempted to argue simply that, as versions and adaptations of the model are still appearing in contemporary publications, it is clear that the model continues to have relevance in the current tourism scene. Such an argument would be both too brief and too naive. In an earlier revisit of the TALC (Butler 2000), the emphasis was placed on what were argued to be key elements of the model that were still relevant at the present time. These were identified as *dynamism*, *process*, *carrying capacity*, *management*, and the *spatial component*. To these might be added, with the power of hindsight, *exogenous forces* and *triggers of change*. None of these, it can be argued, is any less significant in the early twenty-first century than it was in the last quarter of the twentieth century. While tourism has great inbuilt inertia, caused in part by people's reluctance to change habits and patterns, and in part by institutional arrangements and capital investment, it is, nevertheless, an industry which thrives on innovation and change in certain aspects. Tourism, much more than leisure and recreation perhaps, is a fashion industry, subject to whims, fancies, and promotions. While individual forms of leisure such as music and entertainment change in popularity more frequently than most things in life, it is mostly the superficial elements which change, the activities (e.g., listening to music) themselves remaining constant. In tourism, not only such elements but also the patterns of activities change, as do the places in which they take place. Few destinations remain constant and unchanging, and those that do are most likely to be perceived as out of date and unattractive. While there may be fascination and appeal in staying at a century-old hotel, if the interior and accommodations are not up to contemporary standards, the appeal quickly disappears. Thus destinations inevitably change, if only to bring themselves up to date, but more likely to keep abreast of market preferences and remain competitive. Thus both the dynamism and the process by which change occurs should still be of interest and concern to those involved in destination development and operation.

As a greater variety of destinations have appeared, the nature and scale of developments have become less regular and predictable, but destinations are still products, and as such subject to the "laws" of product cycles and marketability. They are created, packaged, and sold now to a degree not anticipated even 30 years ago, but the fashion element in tourism, perhaps combined with the human fascination with the new, the different, and the unknown (if not too unknown and different), has meant that demand for new products (destinations) is apparently endless. Coupled with this is of course the entrepreneurial nature of individuals, corporations, and even municipalities which see economic returns from tourism. Apparently endless competition ensures that few destinations can remain unchanged if they are to retain their market share. While none can match Las Vegas in the sense of that town's ability not only to reinvent itself but to do so in an even more outrageous form on a regular basis, most other destinations realize that they have to replace and add attractions and facilities to have any chance of competing with newer destinations. There is thus the inevitability of change, and it would appear, in more cases than not, something approaching the TALC curve is the result.

The element of limits to growth, or carrying capacity, was at the heart of the original model and there is little reason to change this approach. While in some destinations the key issue may not be absolute numbers, some relationship between numbers, amount of development and the nature and attractiveness of the destination would appear to exist. The realities of economies of scale almost inevitably drive many destinations to expand. Individual elements still tend to be more economically efficient if they are larger rather than smaller, and there is a normally repetitive cycle of growth, sometimes of demand followed by supply, and sometimes of supply, hopefully followed by demand. In the latter case one would witness an expansion of infrastructure which would require a growth in markets or market share to guarantee a return on investment, which in turn ultimately requires additional infrastructure development as visitor numbers increase, and so on *ad infinitum*. At some point in this cycle the amount of development is likely to exceed its level of appropriateness, or the balance point between economic efficiency and attractivity, in other words, the carrying capacity of the destination. The most likely result is a decline in visitation, followed by a decline in investment, resulting in reduced attractivity and further declines in visitation, the downward side of the positive cycle noted above. Despite this fairly obvious and oft-repeated pattern, which has been visible in resorts for well over half a century, few have examined the links between the over-use and over-development of destinations and the literature on inappropriate and excessive resource use (Healy 1994), particularly the exploitation of common resources, so eloquently discussed by Hardin (1968).

The original article (Butler 1980) had as part of its title, "implications for management," although this aspect of the model has often been ignored in favor of discussion of the process of change and how well the model fits the specific case study being examined. The original article was seen by its author as a commentary on the inevitability of loss of quality by destinations in the absence of management, not, as sometimes has been implied, the inevitability of decline regardless of intervention. The TALC, from its inception, was, and remains, a call for the acceptance of reality, namely, that virtually all destinations will ultimately face greater and greater challenges to remain competitive and attractive, especially in a world which is becoming ever more globalized (if there is such a concept). Skillful planning from the beginning, appropriate management, including the identification of limits to growth, the setting of realistic targets, appropriate change in response to and in anticipation of market shifts, and good fortune are all essential to ensure a destination a long and successful life. While management of publicly owned destinations such as national parks is possible, even that is difficult and many parks are under considerable threat from tourism, despite tourism often being their greatest ally in securing funds for conservation (Butler and Boyd 2000). In the case of communities, where individual elements are privately and independently owned and often in competition with one another, and where several groups of residents may have very different goals for, and views on, tourism, creating and maintaining such a developmental, operational, and marketing plan and strategy is near impossible. The inevitability of the TALC process is akin to the inevitability of over-use of the commons which is at the heart of Hardin's argument. The only apparent way to prevent both processes reaching their "normal" end is regulation and responsibility, allied with management, and the crucial realization that some element of managed change is almost always inevitable for survival in tourism.

This is not to say that all original features and attractions need to be sacrificed on the altar of modernity and passing fancy. Heritage and nostalgic features such as piers, old buildings, and infrastructure can all remain viable and attractive to tourists, but in virtually all cases they only retain their attractiveness with investment, planning, and management. "Old" resorts can still be competitive and attractive to a modern market if they are well managed and appropriately marketed. Examples as varied as lake resorts in Canada (Butler and Hinch 1996) or St. Moritz in Switzerland are proof of this. In most of these cases the careful renovation and maintenance of historic properties has been matched with appropriate new development and a deliberate limitation on the amount of additional development. This allows such destinations to continue to offer not only a relatively individualistic experience to the visitor, with elements of nostalgia and heritage, but also high-quality facilities. If successful, the result is a market that is both sympathetic to the destination and its ambience and high spending, the dream of an increasing number of destinations around the world.

The idea of rejuvenation of destinations, one of the alternative stages at the end of the cycle, has been discussed by Agarwal (1997, 2002) in particular, and it is clear that such a process does not and cannot occur by accident. It can only be the result of planning, consultation, and the application of specific strategies. Whether rejuvenation implies permanent or long-term shifts away from decline remains to be seen and is almost certainly location-specific in the form which it takes. Where rejuvenation is not successful, the future would appear to be a decline period that may be excessively drawn out, or the adoption of a deliberate exit strategy from tourism (Baum 1998). Tourist destinations in general are like old soldiers and academics: in some cases they refuse to go away and remain as increasingly unattractive reminders of times and tastes of previous generations that are no longer marketable. Only in a few cases, and perhaps Atlantic City is the flagship, have destinations that appear to have truly reached the end of their cycle been able to be rejuvenated in a complete manner. Even in the case of Atlantic City, spectacular though its rebirth has been, specific problems remain unresolved (Stansfield 2004). Few destinations can ever hope to emulate the scale at which rejuvenation has taken place there, and most can only hope for readjustment of their functions to ones more in tune with contemporary market preferences. As Strapp (1988) has noted, movement from conventional tourism into related areas such as retirement is much more common and is more likely to represent the future for resorts which have difficulty generating capital or innovative ideas for major regeneration. In a few cases, especially in the United Kingdom, old resorts such as Margate have become bases for the temporary housing of asylum-seekers, utilizing their considerable and often under-used accommodation capacity. In general, most parties appear to hope that such a regeneration strategy, often imposed from outside, is not a permanent feature for the destinations concerned.

It is not hard to draw the links between the sentiments expressed above about the necessity for regulation and limitation on growth and the late twentieth-century concept of sustainability. Whether sustainable development is really applicable to any economic sector such as tourism is debatable, but nevertheless the influence of the concept on tourism has been significant (see Weaver, chapter 41 this volume). While it has been applied much more on paper than in reality, the concept has attracted a great deal of attention, and one of the upshots is the appearance of sustainable tourism (see e.g., Wahab and Pigram 1997; Hall and Lew 1998; Mowforth and Munt 1998). The principles at the heart of sustainability are similarly implicit in the TALC (taking a long-term view, keeping development within environmental and social limits, an emphasis on the community, a respect for the environment, and the need for regulation and responsibility), although the elements of inter- and intra-generational equity, a major feature of sustainable development, were not discussed or implied in the TALC. The spatial component of the TALC, as noted earlier, dealt with the pattern of the relocation of capital and the development of new destinations once the original site had begun to reveal signs of over-use or unsustainable development. The crux of the argument was that, without limits on development and growth, the destination would exceed its carrying capacity, thus becoming unsustainable (before the term was in use in its modern context) and new development would take place at another site. That pattern of development is clearly unsustainable and, as Plog (1973) argued, the supply of new destinations is not limitless. Put simply, it is necessary to treat current destinations in a more sustainable manner.

The TALC and the Future

The ideas expressed in the TALC were not particularly original. Wolfe (1952) had commented much earlier on the process of change in tourist destinations, remarking on "The divorce from the geographical environment." He was later (1982) to suggest an alternative curve of destination development (which he labeled the "Ellis Curve"), which had axes of economic and environmental quality with positive and negative components (figure 13.3). A typical trajectory for a destination, he argued, was from a situation of tourism being positive for both elements through a stage where only the economic aspect was positive, to a point at which both elements were negative, as tourism began to affect the environment in a negative way and failed to generate sufficient return on investment. The conclusions Wolfe reached are not radically different from those implied in the original TALC article, even though the shape of the two curves is not very similar.

The appeal of the TALC perhaps lies in its apparent universality, combined with the relative absence of alternative models of destination development. The global tourism system has changed considerably since 1980, and it is reasonable to argue that the nature of destination development has changed also. Intuitively and anecdotally it would appear that destinations are proceeding through their life cycle at a faster rate than a century or even half a century ago. New destinations are being developed at a greater rate, the tourist market is growing and becoming both more sophisticated and more demanding, and also less loyal in terms of returning regularly to the same location. The ability to travel more speedily to a far greater variety of destinations increases the level of competitiveness that destinations face as

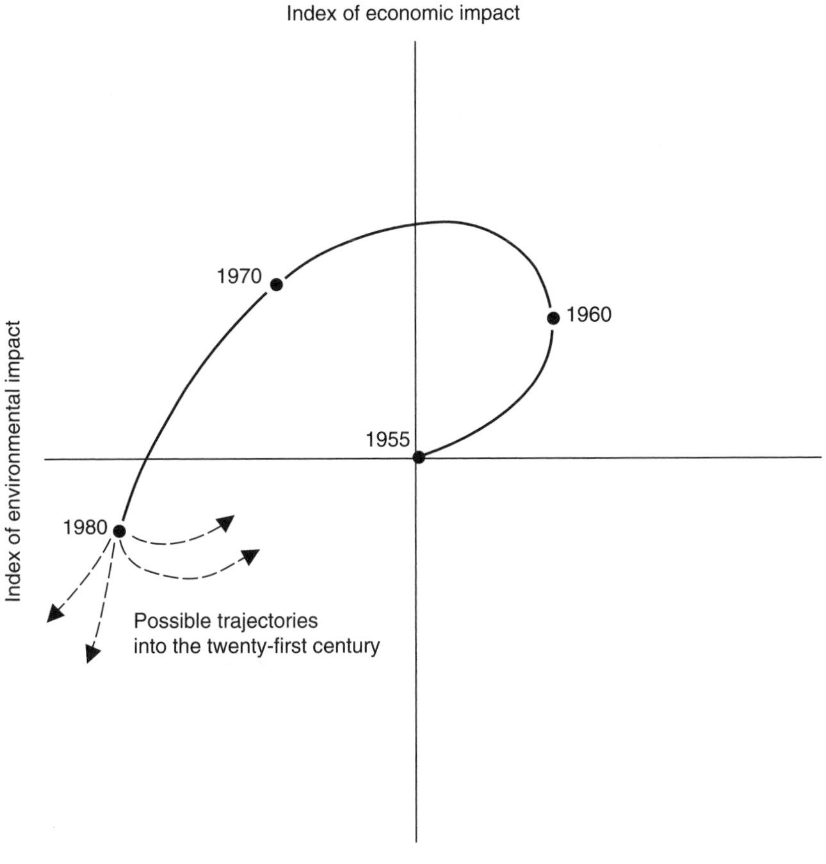

Figure 13.3 Wolfe's "Ellis Curve" of the economic and environmental impacts in the development progression of a tourist destination
Source: Wolfe 1982: 109, 115. Note: *Ontario Geography* no longer exists. The publisher was the Department of Geography University of Western Ontario, London, Ontario, Canada.

The matrix

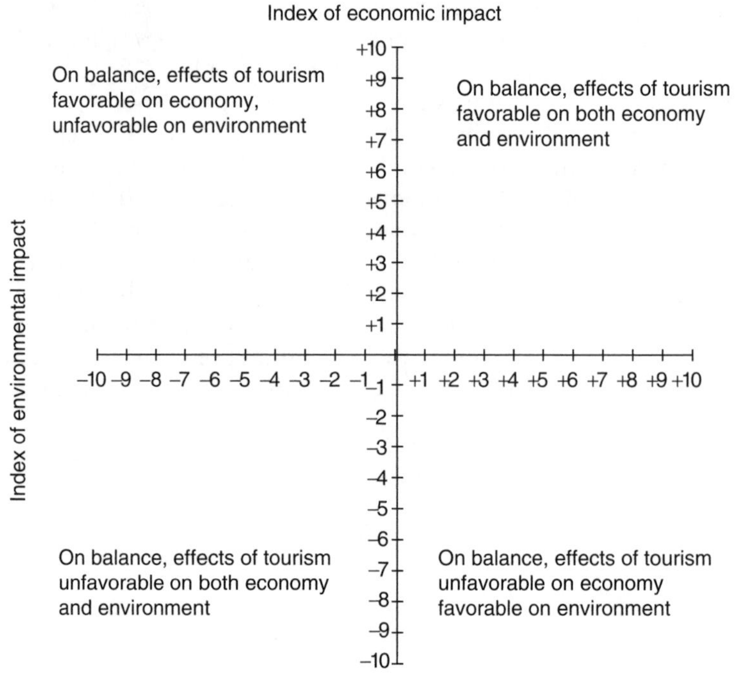

Putative current examples

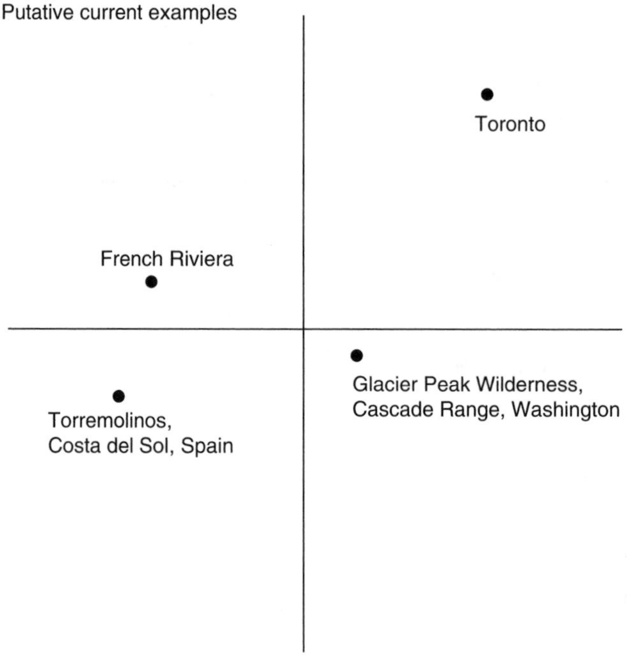

Figure 13.3 *(Continued)*

consumer choice has been dramatically enhanced. Thus people can combine a scuba diving holiday on the Red Sea and visit most of the key sites in Egypt (and even some in Jordan and Israel), all during a ten-day package to a resort. In such situations it is not surprising that specific market segments appear to have run through their cycle at such resorts within a ten-year period. These changes do not invalidate the basic process or essential arguments that underlie the TALC. As the world suggests that it is somewhat more serious about environmental quality, sustainability, and heritage (including cultures and societies) conservation than it has been in the past (even if implementation still has far to go to catch up on rhetoric), then the application of the TALC has even more relevance than at the time of its creation.

One of the issues with the TALC was whether it had predictive capability or was simply a descriptive model that relied on looking backwards to provide explanations of process. It has certainly been used in efforts relating to the "revisioning" of resorts (Butler 2004a, 2004b), and there is now evidence (Butler 2004a, 2004b) that in fact the TALC can be used in a predictive manner, that indicators of change can be identified and that the stages can be anticipated. This is clearly an aspect that warrants further application and exploration and would provide additional support for the continued relevance of the TALC into the future. In a recent (May 2003) journal article (Moss, Ryan, and Wagoner 2003) the model was used to forecast casino winnings, suggesting that there are also other elements which have not been fully explored and which perhaps bear further examination. Earlier mention was made of exogenous forces and triggers of change. The work of Russell and Faulkner (1998) in particular on entrepreneurs and the TALC, and also the application of chaos theory to destination development, are two such areas relating to these elements. Another area that warrants study is that of the relationship of movement of a destination from one stage to another and the issue of control over development. Keller (1987) argued that an overlooked element, and one which could be related strongly to the stages of development, was control over development and sources of investment, and the same issue of control was raised in a different context by Debbage (1990). Not unrelated to this was the research already mentioned by Strapp (1988), who incorporated the TALC into the process of conversion of second home destinations from conventional tourist places into retirement havens, a process which is taking place in many established tourist areas with potentially serious implications, one of which is control over the nature of the destinations concerned (Butler 2004a, 2004b).

It is not surprising that the TALC does not always fit reality. Any generalized simplistic model is unlikely to match the pattern of development at every destination. It is perhaps more appropriate to consider whether it still has validity in the twenty-first century rather than whether it totally explains all examples of destination development. Researchers are still using the TALC to describe and interpret destination development in varying locations, and thus the conclusion may be that in academic terms it is still relevant. To this writer that is somewhat satisfying. On the other hand, the nature of much contemporary destination development (along with an apparent absence of management and control) would suggest that lessons have not been learned from some of the failures of the past, and therefore the TALC is still highly relevant in the applied sense, which is rather more disappointing.

REFERENCES

Agarwal, S. (1997). The resort cycle and seaside tourism: An assessment of its applicability and validity. *Tourism Management* 18(3), 65–73.

Agarwal, S. (2002). Restructuring seaside tourism: The resort life-cycle. *Annals of Tourism Research* 29(1), 25–55.

Baum, T. (1998). Taking the exit route: Extending the tourism area life cycle model. *Current Issues in Tourism* 1(2), 167–75.

Butler, R. W. (1980). The concept of a tourist area cycle of evolution: Implications for management of resources. *The Canadian Geographer* 24(1), 5–12.

Butler, R. W. (2000). The resort cycle two decades on. In B. Faulkner, E. Laws, and G. Moscardo (eds), *Tourism in the 21st Century: Reflections on Experience* (pp. 284–99). London: Cassell.

Butler, R. W. (2004a). *The TALC: Applications and Modifications.* Clevedon: Channel View Press.

Butler, R. W. (2004b). *The TALC: Conceptual and Theoretical Issues.* Clevedon: Channel View Press.

Butler, R. W., and Boyd, S. W. (2000). *Tourism and National Parks Issues and Implications.* Chichester: John Wiley.

Butler, R. W., and Brougham, J. E. (1972). The applicability of the asymptotic curve to the forecasting of tourism development. Paper presented to the Research Workshop, Travel Research Association Conference, Quebec City, June 1972.

Butler, R. W., and Hinch, T. (1996). *Tourism and Indigenous Peoples.* London: Thompson Business Press.

Coles, T. E. (2004). Enigma variations? The TALC, marketing models and the descendants of the product life cycle. In R. W. Butler (ed.), *The TALC: Conceptual and Theoretical Issues.* Clevedon: Channel View Press.

Debbage, K. G. (1990). Oligopoly and the resort cycle in the Bahamas. *Annals of Tourism Research* 18(2), 251–68.

Hall, C. M. (2004). Space-time accessibility and the TALC: The role of geographies of spatial interaction and mobility in contributing to an improved understanding of tourism. In R. W. Butler (ed.), *The TALC: Conceptual and Theoretical Issues.* Clevedon: Channel View Press.

Hall, C. M., and Lew, A. A. (1998). *Sustainable Tourism: A Geographical Perspective.* London: Addison Wesley Longman.

Hardin, G. (1968). The tragedy of the commons. *Science* 162, 1243–8.

Haywood, K. M. (1986). Can the tourist area life-cycle be made operational? *Tourism Management* 7(3), 154–67.

Haywood, K. M. (2004a). Evolution of tourism areas and the tourism industry. In R. W. Butler (ed.), *The TALC: Applications and Modifications.* Clevedon: Channel View Press.

Haywood, K. M. (2004b). Legitimizing the tourism area lifecycle as a theory of development and change. In R. W. Butler (ed.), *The TALC: Conceptual and Theoretical Issues.* Clevedon: Channel View Press.

Healy, R. G. (1994). The "Common Pool" problem in tourism landscapes. *Annals of Tourism Research* 19(4), 596–611.

Johnston, C. S. (2001a). Shoring the foundations of the destination life cycle model, part 1: A case study of Kona, Hawaii. *Tourism Geographies* 3(1), 2–28.

Johnston, C. S. (2001b). Shoring the foundations of the destination life cycle model, part 2: Ontological and epistemological considerations. *Tourism Geographies* 3(1), 135–64.

Keller, C. P. (1987). Stages of peripheral tourism development: Canada's North West Territories. *Tourism Management* 8, 20–32.

Lagiewski, R. M. (2004). The application of the TALC model: A literature survey. In R. W. Butler (ed.), *The TALC: Applications and Modifications*. Clevedon: Channel View Press.

Moss, S. E., Ryan, C., and Wagoner, C. B. (2003). An empirical test of Butler's resort product life cycle: Forecasting casino winnings. *Journal of Travel Research* 41(4), 393–9.

Mowforth, M., and Munt, I. (1998). *Tourism and Sustainability: New Tourism in the Third World*. London: Routledge.

Plog, S. C. (1973). Why destination areas rise and fall in popularity. *Cornell Hotel, Restaurant and Administration Quarterly* 15, 13–16.

Russell, R., and Faulkner, B. (1998). Reliving the destination life cycle in Coolangatta. In E. Laws, B. Faulkner, and G. Moscardo (eds), *Embracing and Managing Changes in Tourism: International Case Studies* (pp. 95–115). London: Routledge.

Stansfield, C. A. (2004). The rejuvenation of Atlantic City: The resort cycle recycles. In R. W. Butler (ed.), *The TALC: Applications and Modifications*. Clevedon: Channel View Press.

Strapp, J. D. (1988). The resort cycle and second homes. *Annals of Tourism Research* 15(4), 504–16.

Wahab, S., and Pigram, J. (1997). *Tourism, Sustainability and Growth*. London: Routledge.

Wall, G. (1983). Cycles and capacity: A contradiction in terms. *Annals of Tourism Research* 10, 268–70.

Wolfe, R. I. (1952). Wasaga Beach: The divorce from the geographic environment. *The Canadian Geographer* 2, 57–66.

Wolfe, R. I. (1982). Recreational travel: The new migration, revisited. *Ontario Geography* 19, 103–22.

Part IV Globalization and Contested Places

Chapter 14

Problematizing Place Promotion

Nigel Morgan

Introduction

Human beings have been representing landscape for at least nine thousand years, and today places are represented in a myriad visual and written texts, as well as in spoken language. Indeed, landscapes, like the places of which they are composed, are so bound up with representation that "to be a landscape at all, to be an integral part of a sensuously qualified place-world, is already to have entered the encompassing embrace of the representational enterprise" (Casey 2002: xv). This is a chapter about place promotion rather than representation, but it is concerned with place representation since, by definition, tourists tour, consume, and represent landscapes, places, and cultures that have been produced, presented, and represented through tourism marketing. While the concept of landscape is ambiguous, it is important in this context for its focus on the way the visible materiality of a place expresses the emotional attachments of its residents and visitors, as well as the means by which it is imagined, produced, consumed, and contested. Residents, visitors, and the wider tourism industry all participate in the continuous social construction of tourism landscapes and their places. Recent discourses in tourism have begun to emphasize the interplay between tourism, landscape, representation, and social structures, experiences, and identities (e.g., Ashworth and Dietvorst 1995; Ringer 1998; Crouch 1999; Aitchison, MacLeod, and Shaw 2000). Yet, despite this work, the conceptual power of destinations continues to be "treated in cavalier fashion" (Saarinen 1998: 155) by theoretical constructs which fail to tie it to space, history, or identity.

In this chapter I will be problematizing the promotion of tourism destinations and tourism places, arguing for a more critical and historical approach to its study and exploring it as a complex, culturally contested, and ideologically laden act. As part and parcel of the process of contemporary destination management, place promotion could be regarded as a deceptively shallow, if multifaceted, marketing activity. Here I want to explore how place promotion contributes to the cultural production and consumption of landscapes, spaces, and places for different people at different times. Today we see place – unlike the Cartesian concept of space (as objective, physical surface) – as a site which we not only inhabit, but which we all, differentially empowered and socially positioned, actively construct and invest with meaning (Mitchell 2000). Geographers have often regarded tourism as an academic backwater and yet, paradoxically, tourism is arguably the prime contemporary determinant of space. Most landscapes and places "have become subject to strategies of 'theming', 'designation', 're-visioning', 're-imaging' and the comprehensive application of marketing techniques... the familiar repertoire of place marketing" (Hughes 1998: 19). Thus, despite its neglect by academia, the tourism industry has a culturally powerful role that challenges and complements (though the use of literary and cinematic connections in place promotion) literature and film in representing and differentiating place. Destination taglines such as "Two hours and a million miles away" (Wales), "Passion for life" (Spain), "Live a different life" (Ireland), and "Come as you are. Leave different" (Louisiana), are not mere marketing ephemera but promoters and endorsers of powerful place myths and identities.

Place promotion occurs through a variety of spheres – most obviously in advertising, on websites, and in brochures – but also through place marketers' cooperation with tourist trails, travel journalists, and cinema commissioning agencies. Moreover, place promotion, defined as "the conscious use of publicity and marketing to communicate selective images of specific geographic localities or areas to a target audience" (Ward and Gold 1994: 2), not only involves advertising and publicity but also encompasses "flagship" developments and "spotlight" events in the arts, media, leisure, heritage, retailing, or sports industries (Ward 1998). It has a clear business function and marketing rationale, yet the discourse of place promotion – its preferred panoramas and privileged tourism stories – also reveals the underlying narratives of place. Place promotion is essentially a scopic process that not only furnishes the potential traveler with an imaginary place archive but also elevates the primacy of the viewer through its ocular centrism. Place promotional appeals based on "natural," mountainous landscapes or palm-tree-fringed tropical beaches are not simply advertisements but are complex, multi-dimensional social constructs, reflecting deep-seated cultural influences. Yet, as consumers, producers, and reproducers of such texts, we use, reuse and recycle the narratives of place promotion with hardly a thought to their origins or meanings. When we gaze on a vista of snow-capped mountains in an advertisement for Canada, subconsciously we are not only engaging with echoes of "wilderness," but also reconnecting with the notions of Nature that underpinned European Romanticism.

This is the essence of place promotion. It immobilizes our dynamic world, changing it to spectacle and straitjacketing it in cliché and stereotype; as Osborne (2000: 115) writes, its "representations suck the historical matter out of things, the better to embalm them in myth." It is this aspect of place promotion that concerns this chapter and in it I will suggest that semiotics and discourse analysis offer much to tourism scholars interested in unpicking these constructed mythologies of tourism places. The chapter concludes with a discussion of the opportunities offered to tourism study by a theorization of place and its marketing which engages with space *and* time, with the visual *and* the linguistic, and with identity *and* the body. First, however, we need to contextualize this problematization of place promotion by briefly examining how the tourism academy has studied the praxis of place promotion in terms of public policy and marketing.

Researching the Praxis of Place Promotion

The place promotional literature has been synthesized into three approaches: the "marketing approach," the "public policy approach" and the "critical approach" (Ward 1998). The first is concerned with the business of place promotion and there is now a sizeable industry-focused literature covering issues from stakeholder involvement (Buhalis 2000) to destination marketing management (Kotler, Haider, and Rein 1994; Ritchie and Crouch 2000) and destination branding (Morgan, Pritchard, and Pride 2002). The public policy approach is concerned with the use of place promotion to stimulate economic development (e.g., Ashworth and Goodall 1990; Ashworth and Voogd 1990), especially in relation to urban tourism (Law 1993; Page 1995) and the hosting of mega-events (Hall 1994; Getz 1997; Smith 2002). Perhaps the greatest volume of this policy- and marketing-related work discusses the management and formation of place image, and many authors (e.g., Gunn 1988; Chon 1990; Gold and Ward 1994) have discussed image-related issues in destination marketing (see Selby 2000; Smith 2002). Much of this research has relied heavily on behavioral geography and the psychological premises on which it is based, both for conceptual ideas and methodological approaches (e.g., Mayo and Jarvis 1981). A considerable amount of the work has attempted to conceptualize the components of destination image (see Um and Crompton 1990; Echtner and Ritchie 1991; Gartner 1996; Walmsley and Young 1998). In addition, many authors have investigated the image-formation process, beginning with Gunn's (1988) work on induced and organic images. In particular, they have examined the three main influences on destination image formation, namely promotional material, secondary experiences (e.g., the opinions of others) and the media (Gartner 1993, 1996; Ross 1994; Font 1996). Of particular interest here is work that has discussed the role of films in shaping place identity (Butler 1990; Riley, Baker, and Van Doren 1998; Busby and Klug 2001). The assumption of much of this destination image-formation literature is that these three key influences combine with personal or individual factors (Ashworth and Voogd 1990) to produce a destination image (Font 1996; Baloglu and McClearly 1999). Yet, as outlined above, place promotion can be seen not merely as a marketing response to consumer behavior but also as a cultural process; I will now turn to the critical approach to place promotion.

Contesting Place Promotion

The "cultural turn" in the social sciences has been reflected in tourism in the conceptualization of tourism places, spaces, and sites as political and contested sociocultural constructions, although not to the same degree as in cognate fields. Cultural and feminist geographers have argued for some time that there are no politically neutral spaces, focusing on the ways in which places are heterosexualized (Valentine 1993; Ashworth and Dietvorst 1995; Bell and Valentine 1995; Duncan 1996; Aitchison 1999a) and racialized (Segal 1990; Anderson 1996). Likewise, they have noted that landscapes are often gendered in that they are portrayed and represented in feminine and sexualized terms. Indeed, Lewes (2000) has highlighted the ancient notion that women and land are analogous and researchers, such as Rose (1993), have argued that representations of landscapes are grounded in wider gendered power relationships that oppose masculinized Culture and feminized Nature. In this way, both women and Nature are burdened with men's meaning and interpreted by masculinist discourse.

As a result of such scholarship, today we see landscapes not as fixed, objective artifacts, but as symbolic, mutable, and culturally constructed mixtures of representation and physical form. They mean different things to different people at different times and represent, reinforce, idealize, and naturalize sociocultural power relations. The new cultural geography thus "demonstrates that space, place and landscape – including landscapes of leisure and tourism – are not fixed but are in a constant state of transition as a result of continuous, dialectical struggles of power and resistance among and between the diversity of landscape providers, users and mediators" (Aitchison 1999a: 29). The "meanings" of any landscape – from the intimate places of home to the public spaces of shopping malls, parks, and tourism resorts – draw on the cultural codes of the society that constructed it. These meanings (which have evolved over time and are not only to be understood in terms of contemporary societies) are thus embedded in and permeated by a society's social and cultural norms and symbols. This theme in tourism research particularly gathered pace during the 1990s and scholars explored how space, place, and landscape are sites where dominant discourses and wider hegemonic sociocultural relations are resisted, contested, or affirmed (Ringer 1998; Crouch 1999; Aitchison, MacLeod, and Shaw 2000). Much of this work explored how tourism landscapes and places have gendered and sexualized identities. For instance, Valentine (1993) and Pritchard and Morgan (2000a, 2000b) demonstrated that leisure space is masculinized and heterosexually dominated, while Edensor and Kothari (1994) and Aitchison (1999b) critiqued the role of gendered heritage representations in the creation of gendered places in cultural tourism.

If we are to build on these critical approaches to tourism promotion and further theorize place promotion, we must contextualize the industry in global sociocultural, economic, and political systems. It is essential, therefore, that analyses of place promotion incorporate discussions of the relationship between tourism marketing and ideology. To date this has received little attention, resulting in an incomplete analysis of what is a powerful political and cultural phenomenon. Hall's (1994: 11) comment that, despite its importance, "discussions of the ideological dimensions of tourism have been virtually non-existent" remains pertinent. There is thus an imperative to re-examine the interplay between ideas, culture, and history if we are to recognize the configurations of power that underpin contemporary tourism processes. Place promotion scholars need to confront these configurations in concert with the notion that places change in form and nature according to how people construct them – they have no objective reality, only intersubjective ones. These intersubjective realities inherently express social divisions and, in the same way as cultural forms have been divided into "high" and "low" spaces, can be mapped as "systems of 'centres and peripheries'" (Shields 1991: 3). This hierarchical ordering of places is particularly strong in the field of place promotion, with its dependence on ideologically laden dichotomies – so that places are marketed as timeless or modern, natural or technological, and sensuous or civilized. Such labels are significant for the places and peoples whose stories are told by place promoters as they reinforce the dominant configurations of power.

Place promotion presents the world as image, inviting the viewer to become an imaginary traveler to an imagined place. In place promotion we see the mediation of visitor–place relationships and reflections of travelers' perceptions of the Other across space and time – just as in travel photography. The photograph's ability to induce reverie and metaphor also applies to place promotion and "the reveries of tourists are likely to be the reveries determined by tourism and its imagery...the freedom to dream is the freedom to dream on tourism's terms" (Osborne 2000: 27). In this undeniably ideological dialectic, the echoes of tourism's colonial antecedents are palpable – endorsing Lévi-Strauss's (2001) famous description of tourism as the child of imperialism. Colonialism's ghostly footprints continue to be visible, through the touristic Othering of places and cultures. Witness the contemporary place promotion of Egypt, which echoes its representation in the West since the eighteenth century. As Osborne (2000: 22) comments, by this date "Egypt was...Egypticity – the signifier of mythical values, already a sign of itself...already representation... Egypt was less a contemporaneous political entity than a stone theatre of frozen time arranged to instigate reverie and wonder." In the discourses of colonialism, travel, photography, and tourism, Egypt has been for ever trapped in its past, "seized in the amber of European iconising" (Osborne 2000: 24). Such iconizing remains strong in contemporary place promotion of destinations as diverse as the Caribbean (Silver 1993; Cohen 1995), the Pacific (Goss 1993; Hall 1998), and the Far East (Morgan and Pritchard 1998). Yet for many this influence of the Western eye remains uncontested and rarely problematical, neglected by industry-driven tourism marketing studies.

Applying Critical Approaches

Scholars seeking to theorize the discourse of place promotion are doubly challenged. Not only is the study of place promotion dominated by an industry perspective, it is also primarily concerned with the visual. It is well documented, however, that the written word is the dominant mode of research and representation in the social sciences while visual research is frequently misunderstood and rarely appreciated (Pink 2001). As a result, although social researchers constantly encounter images, they are disinclined to incorporate the visual into their scholarship (Banks 2001). In place promotion studies the visual is frequently paramount and the analysis usually takes one of three forms: focusing on "what's in an image" (its content), "the image as object" (whether postcard, brochure, advertisement, etc.) and "the image in context." As social researchers, therefore, we can look at, look through, or look behind the visual representation (Wright 1999) of places and peoples.

Which approach the place promotion researcher will favor will depend on his or her epistemological perspective. Content analysts will undertake a survey of images in "an attempt to apply conventional, and indeed positivist, notions of rigour to the unruly and ostensibly subjective field of cultural meaning" (Slater 1998: 234–5). In contrast, semioticians argue that place promotional communications are best understood through an analysis of how signs interact to produce meaning. They are primarily concerned with a fine-grained, inward-looking interpretation of texts, rarely venturing into outward generalizations. Having said this, some authors (in the spirit of interdisciplinary collaboration) have suggested that both these approaches can be combined to produce rich, insightful analyses of texts (Slater 1998). The third key approach to textual analysis is discourse analysis. Although sharing some affinity with semioticians, discourse analysts focus on the meaning of the image in context, examining the social as opposed to the individual construction of meaning. Recognizing the need to read both the internal and external narratives of the visual, discourse analysts explore how texts are "forms of *discourse* which help to create and reproduce systems of social meaning" (Tonkiss 1998: 245).

While research on the contestation of places and images is gathering momentum, these approaches to visual analysis remain marginal in tourism studies. Of the three, content analysis has the strongest presence and underpins several recent papers on place promotion (see Morgan and Pritchard 1999). In contrast, studies of destination image have rarely used semiotics (Echtner 1999), although such analyses have been applied to other spheres, including advertising, photography, popular culture, and fashion (Fiske 1994). Urry (2001) is the best-known researcher to address sign systems in the formation of the tourist gaze, although there are others, including Culler (1981), Thurot and Thurot (1983), and Selwyn (1993). While, at the beginning of the twenty-first century, the semiological differentiation of tourism destinations has become "a highly self-conscious, self-reflective process" (Hughes 1998: 20), academic interest has been muted and semiotics is an under-utilized approach. This remains the case, despite MacCannell's (1989: 3) suggestion that "there is a privileged relationship between tourism and semiotics" and Dann's (1996: 6) comment that "nowhere . . . is a semiotic perspective considered more appropriate than in the analysis of tourism advertising with its culture coded covert connotations, in the study of tourism imagery and in the treatment of tourism communication as a discourse of myth."

If semiotics offers rich opportunities for place promotion analysis, even fewer studies have used discourse analysis to explore how these texts reflect and reproduce systems of social meaning, shaping both social and place identities. As a result, the mosaic of tourism place promotion often appears as an orderly, unchanging, unchallenging environment, "a celebration of things as they are, a beautiful pacification" (Osborne 2000: 91). This is particularly unhelpful because, as Hall (1998: 141) suggests: "Any meaningful understanding of the creation of the destination . . . [should involve] situating the artfully constructed representation of that destination within the context of place consumption and production and more particularly, the manner by which places are incorporated into the global capital system."

Systems of representation do not merely *convey* meaning, but also contribute to the production of knowledge – which is closely related to social practices, enabling some in society to have more power to speak than others. This is the essence of discursive approaches, which are concerned less with the poetics and more with the politics of representation, and incorporate knowledge, power, and historical specificity into their analyses of meaning (Foucault 1980). In contrast to semioticians, discourse analysts not only examine the production of meaning but also how such meanings are linked with social knowledge and power, recognizing that knowledge "defines the way certain things are represented, thought about, practised and studied" (Hall 1997: 6). The production of knowledge, therefore "'rules in' certain ways of talking about a topic . . . so also by definition, it 'rules out,' limits and restricts other ways of talking, of conducting ourselves in relation to the topic or constructing knowledge about it (Hall 1997: 44).

Concluding Thoughts

This chapter has argued that place promotion plays a key role in the social construction of place myths. Place promotion contributes to the cultural production and consumption of landscapes, spaces, and places for different people at different times and its texts are redolent of gendered, sexual, race, and class messages, myths, and ideologies. Such place promotional texts are cultural texts, representations of ethnographic knowledge and sites of cultural production – the culmination of both social interaction and individual experiences (Pink 2001). As such, we need to understand the discourses that govern place promotion, and yet the discourses of production remain largely hidden from view and resistant to academic investigation (Nixon 1997). We can, of course, read their scripts and look at, through, and behind their texts – applying and enhancing approaches developed by cultural historians. Place promotional texts can be investigated as cultural artifacts and subjected to explorations that reveal the systems of production and signification that give rise to them and from which they derive their meanings (Ashplant and Smyth 2001). We can interrogate their systems of production – concerned with their authorship, their mode of publication, and their contemporary, historical and cultural contexts. Similarly, we can focus on their systems of signification – highlighting the conventions within which these cultural texts are produced (e.g., their language and their performative dimensions). We should also add examinations of the *reception* of these cultural artifacts to our research agenda – how contemporaries and those who come later interact with them is an underexplored area. We also need to research the influence of the actions, motivations, and values of local participants on the social construction of tourism places.

The way in which people understand and engage with tourism landscapes will depend upon the specific time and place and historical conditions. Such landscapes are never inert, immutable objects – local stakeholders and tourists (differentially engaged and differentially empowered) appropriate and contest them, and such acts are part of the way identities are created and disputed, at the individual, group, or nation-state level. Here I have sought to problematize the promotion of tourism destinations, places, and sites, arguing for more critical and historical approaches and more explorations that treat place promotion as a complex, culturally contested, and ideologically laden act. Tourism as an academic field remains peripheral to most disciplines and this has had the effect of hiding both the landscapes of tourism and the texts of place promotion from theoretically informed analysis. These culturally powerful texts remain too removed from investigations that connect with historical, cultural, media, or postcolonial studies. The discipline of history has largely ignored tourism and its promotion (Morgan 1997; Walton 2000), visual ethnography and anthropology continue to marginalize tourism texts, and scholars in linguistic studies are only now turning their attention to the topic (e.g., Thurlow and Jaworski 2002). And yet there are many opportunities in a theorization of place that engages with a range of epistemologies, approaches, and methodologies, especially semiotic, discourse, visual, and linguistic approaches.

The time is long overdue for a theorization of the cultural discourse of place promotion that engages with space and time, with the visual and the linguistic, and with identity and the body. Above all, in pursuit of this critical conceptualization, we must not consider the content of mind and language at the expense of embodying the tourism landscape. Work elsewhere (see Pritchard, chapter 25 this volume) is construing the body as the ultimate site of social, cultural, and political power and of place experience and yet place promotion studies have rarely engaged critically with questions of race, gender, and the body. Tourism places, like all landscapes, exist at the convergence of history and politics, social relations and cultural perceptions. If we are, therefore, to unpick the wider significances of how these places are promoted, scholars engaged across all these fields must turn their gaze to the tourism vista.

REFERENCES

Aitchison, C. (1999a). New cultural geographies: The spatiality of leisure, gender and sexuality. *Leisure Studies* 18(1), 19–39.

Aitchison, C. (1999b). Heritage and nationalism: Gender and the performance of power. In D. Crouch (ed.), *Leisure/Tourism Geographies: Practices and Geographical Knowledge* (pp. 59–73). London: Routledge.

Aitchison, C., MacLeod, N. E., and Shaw, J. (2000). *Leisure and Tourism Landscapes: Social and Cultural Geographies*. London: Routledge.

Anderson, K. (1996). Engendering race research: Unsettling the self–other dichotomy. In N. Duncan (ed.), *Bodyspace: Destabilizing Geographies of Gender and Sexuality* (pp. 197–211). London: Routledge.

Ashplant, T. G., and Smyth, G. (2001). In search of cultural history. In T. G. Ashplant and G. Smyth (eds), *Explorations in Cultural History* (pp. 3–43). London: Pluto Press.

Ashworth, G., and Dietvorst, A. (eds) (1995). *Tourism and Spatial Transformations*. Oxford: CAB International.

Ashworth, G. J., and Goodall, B. (eds) (1990). *Marketing Tourism Places*. London: Routledge.

Ashworth, G. J., and Voogd, H. (1990). *Selling the City*. London: Belhaven.

Baloglu, S., and McClearly, K. W. (1999). A model of destination image formation. *Annals of Tourism Research* 26(4), 868–97.

Banks, M. (2001). *Visual Methods in Social Research*. London: Sage.

Bell, D., and Valentine, G. (eds) (1995). *Mapping Desire: Geographies of Sexualities*. London: Routledge.

Buhalis, D. (2000). Marketing the competitive destination of the future. *Tourism Management* 21(1), 97–116.

Busby, G., and Klug, J. (2001). Movie-induced tourism: The challenge of measurement and other issues. *Journal of Vacation Marketing* 7(4), 316–32.

Butler, R. W. (1990). The influence of the media in shaping international tourist patterns. *Tourism Recreation Research* 15(2), 46–53.

Casey, E. S. (2002). *Representing Place: Landscape Painting and Maps*. Minnesota: University of Minnesota Press.

Chon, K. S. (1990). The role of destination image in tourism: A review and discussion. *Tourist Review* 45(2), 2–9.
Cohen, C. (1995). Marketing paradise, making nation. *Annals of Tourism Research* 22(2), 404–21.
Crouch, D. (ed.) (1999). *Leisure/Tourism Geographies: Practices and Geographical Knowledge*. London: Routledge.
Culler, J. (1981). Semiotics of tourism. *American Journal of Semiotics* 1(2), 127–40.
Dann, G. (1996). The people of tourism brochures. In T. Selwyn (ed.), *The Tourist Image* (pp. 61–82). Chichester: John Wiley.
Duncan, N. (1996). Sexuality in public and private spaces. In N. Duncan (ed.), *Bodyspace: Destabilising Geographies of Gender and Sexuality* (pp. 127–45). London: Routledge.
Echtner, C. M. (1999). The semiotic paradigm: Implications for tourism research. *Tourism Management* 20(3), 47–57.
Echtner, C. M., and Ritchie, J. R. B. (1991). The meaning and measurement of tourism destination image. *Journal of Tourism Studies* 2(2), 2–12.
Edensor, T., and Kothari, U. (1994). The masculinisation of Stirling's heritage in tourism: A gender analysis. In V. Kinnaird and D. Hall (eds), *Tourism: A Gender Analysis* (pp. 164–87). Chichester: John Wiley.
Fiske, J. (1994). *Understanding Popular Culture*. London: Routledge.
Font, X. (1996). Managing the tourist destination image. *Journal of Vacation Marketing* 3(2), 123–31.
Foucault, M. (1980). *Power/Knowledge*. Brighton: Harvester.
Gartner, W. (1993). Image formation process. *Journal of Travel Research* 28(2), 16–20.
Gartner, W. (1996). *Tourism Development: Principles, Processes and Policies*. New York: Van Nostrand Reinhold.
Getz, D. (1997). *Event Management and Event Tourism*. New York: Cognizant Communications Corporation.
Gold, R., and Ward, S. V. (eds) (1994). *Place Promotion: The Use of Publicity and Marketing to Sell Towns and Regions*. Chichester: John Wiley.
Goss, J. D. (1993). Placing the market and marketing place. *Environment and Planning D: Society and Space* 11(2), 663–88.
Gunn, C. (1988). *Tourism Planning*. New York: Taylor & Francis.
Hall, C. M. (1994). *Tourism and Politics: Policy, Power and Place*. Chichester: John Wiley.
Hall, C. M. (1998). Making the Pacific: Globalization, modernity and myth. In G. Ringer (ed.), *Destinations: Cultural Landscapes of Tourism* (pp. 140–53). London: Routledge.
Hall, S. (1997). Introduction. In S. Hall (ed.). *Representation: Cultural Representations and Signifying Practices* (pp. 1–13). London: Sage/Open University.
Hughes, C. G. (1998). Tourism and the semiological realisation of space. In G. Ringer (ed.), *Destinations: Cultural Landscapes of Tourism* (pp. 17–32). London: Routledge.
Kotler, P., Haider, D. M., and Rein, I. (1994). *Marketing Places: Attracting Investment, Industry and Tourism to Cities, States, and Nations*. New York: The Free Press.
Law, C. M. (1993). *Urban Tourism: Attracting Visitors to Large Cities*. London: Mansell.
Lévi-Strauss, C. (2001) *Myth and Meaning*. London: Routledge.
Lewes, D. (2000). *Nudes from Nowhere: Utopian Sexual Landscapes*. Maryland: Rowman & Littlefield.
MacCannell, D. (1989). Introduction to special issue on the Semiotics of Tourism. *Annals of Tourism Research* 16(1), 1–16.
Mayo, E. J., and Jarvis, L. P. (1981). *The Psychology of Leisure Travel: Effective Marketing and Selling of Travel Services*. Boston: CBI.
Mitchell, D. (2000). *Cultural Geography: A Critical Introduction*. Oxford: Blackwell.

Morgan, N. J. (1997). Seaside resort strategies: The case of inter-war Torquay. In S. Fisher (ed.), *Recreation and the Sea* (pp. 84–100). Exeter: Exeter University Press.

Morgan, N. J., and Pritchard, A. (1998). *Tourism Promotion and Power: Creating Images, Creating Identities*. Chichester: John Wiley.

Morgan, N. J., and Pritchard, A. (1999). Editorial, special issue of the *Journal of Vacation Marketing on Branding. Travel and Tourism* 5(3), 213–14.

Morgan, N. J., Pritchard, A., and Pride, R. (eds) (2002). *Destination Branding: Creating the Unique Destination Proposition*. Oxford: Butterworth-Heinemann.

Nixon, S. (1997). Circulating culture. In P. Du Gay (ed.), *The Production of Culture/Cultures of Production* (pp. 179–234). London: Sage.

Osborne, P. D. (2000). *Travelling Light: Photography, Travel and Visual Culture*. Manchester: Manchester University Press.

Page, S. (1995). *Urban Tourism*. London: Routledge.

Pink, S. (2001). *Doing Visual Ethnography: Images, Media and Representation in Research*. London: Sage.

Pritchard, A., and Morgan, N. J. (2000a). Privileging the male gaze: Gendered tourism landscapes. *Annals of Tourism Research* 27(3), 884–905.

Pritchard, A., and Morgan, N. J. (2000b). Constructing tourism landscapes: Gender, sexuality and space. *Tourism Geographies* 2(2), 115–39.

Riley, R., Baker, D., and Van Doren, C. S. (1998). Movie-induced tourism. *Annals of Tourism Research* 25(4), 919–35.

Ringer, G. (ed.) (1998). *Destinations: Cultural Landscapes of Tourism*. London: Routledge.

Ritchie, B. J. R., and Crouch, G. I. (2000). The competitive destination: A sustainable perspective. *Tourism Management* 21(1), 1–7.

Rose, G. (1993). *Feminism and Geography: The Limits of Geographical Knowledge*. Cambridge: Polity.

Ross, G. F. (1994). *The Psychology of Tourism*. Melbourne: Hospitality Press.

Saarinen, J. (1998). The social constructions of tourist destinations: The process of transformation of the Saariselka tourism region in Finnish Lapland. In G. Ringer (ed.), *Destinations: Cultural Landscapes of Tourism* (pp. 154–73). London: Routledge.

Segal, L. (1990). *Slow Motion: Changing Masculinities, Changing Men*. London: Virago.

Selby, M. (2000). People, place and consumption: Conceptualising and researching urban tourist experience, with particular reference to Cardiff, Wales. Unpublished Ph.D. thesis, University of Wales Institute, Cardiff.

Selwyn, T. (1993). Peter Pan in South-East Asia: Views from the brochures. In M. Hitchcock, V. King, and M. Parnwell (eds), *Tourism in South-East Asia* (pp. 117–37). London: Routledge.

Shields, R. (1991). *Places on the Margins: Alternative Geographies of Modernity*. London: Sage.

Silver, I. (1993). Marketing authenticity in third world countries. *Annals of Tourism Research* 20(2), 302–18.

Slater, D. (1998). Analysing cultural objects: Content analysis and semiotics. In C. Seale (ed.), *Researching Society and Culture* (pp. 233–44). London: Sage.

Smith, A. (2002). Reimaging the city: The impact of sport initiatives on tourists' images of urban destinations. Unpublished Ph.D. thesis, Sheffield Hallam University, Sheffield.

Thurlow, C., and Jaworski, A. (2002). Communicating a global reach: In-flight magazines and globalising genres in tourism. Paper presented at Tourism Research 2002: An interdisciplinary conference in Cardiff, Wales, September.

Thurot, J., and Thurot, G. (1983). The ideology of class and tourism: Confronting the discourse of advertising. *Annals of Tourism Research* 10(1), 173–89.

Tonkiss, F. (1998). Analysing discourse. In C. Seale (ed.), *Researching Society and Culture* (pp. 245–60). London: Sage.

Um, S., and Crompton, J. L. (1990). Attitude determinants in tourism destination choice. *Annals of Tourism Research* 17(2), 432–48.

Urry, J. (2001). *The Tourist Gaze: Leisure and Travel in Contemporary Societies*, 2nd edn. London: Sage.

Valentine, G. (1993). Hetero(sexing) space: Lesbian perceptions and experiences of everyday spaces. *Society and Space* 11(2), 395–413.

Walmsley, D. J., and Young, M. (1998). Evaluative images and tourism: The use of personal constructs to describe the structure of destination images. *Journal of Travel Research* 36(3), 65–9.

Walton, J. K. (2000). *The British Seaside: Holidays and Resorts in the Twentieth Century.* Manchester: Manchester University Press.

Ward, S. V. (1998). *Selling Places: The Marketing and Promotion of Towns and Cities, 1850–2000.* London: E. and F. N. Spon.

Ward, S. V., and Gold, J. R. (1994). Introduction. In J. R. Gold and S. V. Ward (eds), *Place Promotion: The Use of Publicity and Marketing to Sell Towns and Regions* (pp. 1–17). Chichester: Wiley.

Wright, T. (1999). *The Photography Handbook.* London: Routledge.

Chapter 15

Tourism, Information Technology, and Development: Revolution or Reinforcement?

Simon Milne, David Mason, and Julia Hasse

Introduction

The links between tourism, information and communication technology (ICT), and development have captured researchers' attention for many decades (Poon 1993; Buhalis 2000). Since the mid-1990s this interest has grown with the advent of the internet and the need to better understand the role that digital technologies play in shaping industry structure, performance, and impacts.

In this chapter we review some of the major themes that have emerged from academic discourse on the role that ICT plays in influencing the shape and nature of tourism and its associated development outcomes. There is little doubt that ICT has influenced the structure and economic performance of the tourism industry greatly (Sheldon 1997; Cooper and Lewis 2001). Our focus here is on the degree to which ICT is actually enhancing the ability of the tourism industry to meet the broader objectives that are increasingly being set out in tourism strategies around the world, particularly the desire to achieve higher economic yield and more sustainable development outcomes.

The key questions that underlie our discussion are whether ICT can bring about a revolution in the ability of the industry to create and sustain an improved quality of life for communities, regions, and nations, or whether technology will simply reinforce past trends. There is a great rush among tourism destinations to be part of the network age, and high hopes are held that digital technologies will lead to increased knowledge, more productive livelihoods, and greater participation in tourism planning. Yet many commentators argue that these technologies may be of little use to marginalized populations – and may actually widen the inequalities between rich and poor unless appropriate policy instruments are developed (UNDP 2001).

Tourism, ICT, and Development: A Review

ICT has had a major impact on the business of tourism. Studies of the intra-firm benefits of new technologies have been paralleled by broader analyses of ICT ability to alter distribution networks and industry structures (Sheldon 1997; Laws and Buhalis 2001). Some commentators have even suggested that ICT changes the very rules of tourism – with industry leaders adopting new managerial and strategic "best practice" (Poon 1993).

The pace and extent of change have increased with the explosion of the internet as a tool for business (Lawrence et al. 2002). Online resources are proliferating and many tourism businesses can not afford being invisible in cyberspace. Many governments are implementing policies to foster ICT adoption by the tourism industry (Nodder et al. 2003), and tourists everywhere are exploring the potential for new technologies to improve their travel planning and experiences (Morgan and Pritchard 2000).

The literature focuses on a number of ways in which the structure, performance, and impacts of the tourism industry are being influenced by the adoption and development of ICT, and particularly the internet (see Buhalis and Schertler 1999: v):

- *Information management and flows.* In addition to reducing communication and transaction costs the internet is also changing the nature of traditional tourism distribution channels (Buhalis 2001). Inclusion on these channels is vital for business survival (Milne and Gill 1998).
- *Shaping consumer behavior.* While it is difficult to quantify the internet's ability to shape consumer perceptions and decision-making processes it is clear that the internet is already a force to be reckoned with (Beirne and Curry 1999).
- *New product development.* ICT offers the industry improved possibilities for price differentiation and also enables greater networking between disparate elements of the industry. ICT can improve the ability of the tourism industry to provide a flexible array of product choices (Poon 1993; Buhalis and Cooper 1998).
- *Small and medium tourism enterprises (SMTE).* Many argue ICT can "level the playing field" for smaller businesses that have difficulty accessing traditional tourist distribution channels, but only if the correct skills, resources, and infrastructure are in place (Hull and Milne 2001; Braun 2002).
- *Disintermediation.* There is a growing interest in the impact of the internet on elements of the tourism industry that have previously acted as intermediaries (especially travel agents). The job losses and restructuring that occur can have important impacts on urban labor markets (Garkavenko, Bremner, and Milne 2003).
- *Labor security, training, and skills* are being shaped and altered by new technologies. Recent writers have emphasized service quality and training issues and the role of workers as active participants in shaping tourism development outcomes (Tufts 2000; Milne and Ateljevic 2001a).
- *Planning and participation.* ICT can potentially create opportunities for new and more appropriate forms of public participation in the development planning process, including tourism planning (Hasse 2002; see also Kenny 2002).

While there is plenty of "hype" about what ICT can do for various elements of the tourism industry and their links to development, comprehensive accounts of the impacts associated with the adoption of technologies remain relatively rare. Some commentators argue that the very technologies heralded as providing the basis for a resurgence of small firms and peripheral regions may, instead, simply reinforce existing power structures and inequalities (see Castells 2000) and lead to social discord, individual isolation, and limited economic opportunity (Rochlin 1997; Swarbrooke 2001). It is also easy to get caught up in the hype and forget that the bulk of the world's population, and many of its travel destinations and real/potential tourist market, still remain unwired and outside these new networks (UNDP 2001; Coleman and Gotze 2002). We now review some of the areas where ICT has been identified as playing a particularly important role in influencing the development outcomes associated with tourism: (1) distribution channels and marketing, (2) SMTE, and (3) policy, participation, and control.

Distribution channels

ICT has had a major influence on the ability of tourism operators to reach the marketplace, and perhaps circumvent the intermediaries that lie between their product and the consumer. One tool that has historically dominated the way in which travel professionals gather and pass on information about destinations is the Computer Reservation System (CRS) or Global Distribution System (GDS). Essentially all travel agencies (online or offline) use one of the "big four" CRS (Sabre, Galileo/Apollo, Amadeus, or Worldspan). The CRS connect these intermediaries to airlines and other suppliers and also link the suppliers to each other. As the oligopolistic repositories of data about travelers, CRS have the same central role and importance for travel data that credit bureaus have for financial data (Milne and Gill 1998; Buhalis 2001).

These powerful travel distribution systems have been seen by many commentators to offer significant opportunities for companies to improve customer service and increase the efficiency and flexibility of product delivery. Poon (1993) argues that such systems enable destinations, businesses, and communities to create more flexible tourism products that can be customized to meet different demands and which can also enhance local economic development opportunities.

CRS are also now increasingly using the web as an interface with travel agents and consumers. Each of the "big four" systems has set up a website that serves as a gateway from the internet to their database of travel records. Whether web-based or not, CRS remain difficult to access for many smaller operators. CRS can be prohibitively expensive and have difficulty in serving, and integrating with, small enterprises (Swarbrooke 2001). As Milne and Nowsielski (1996) argue in the context of the South Pacific, larger, often foreign-owned, concerns are likely to reap the competitive rewards associated with access to CRS.

Advertising

If large, overseas-owned operations dominate the marketing of a destination they are likely to steer the bulk of visitor revenue flows their way, while small-scale operators are relegated to the backwaters of the industry (Britton 1981). Marketing campaigns and the structure of the global tourism distribution system also shape visitor perceptions of the host population and can play a role in shaping inequalities and reinforcing pre-existing colonial economic structures and dependency (Hall 1996; Harrison 2001).

The internet offers the potential to break out of the "cycle" of tourism marketing and development outlined by Britton and others. By enabling clients to circumvent traditional travel distribution channels, the internet cuts costs and facilitates the direct creation and management of websites. Websites also offer more comprehensive information, through internal content and links.

Websites can be particularly important in improving the match between tourism and the surrounding economy. A local hotel website can, for example, be a portal to nearby suppliers and surrounding community interests. An online dinner menu can be linked to the local producers that supply food. Other links can be created to handicrafts or community events. This type of information and depth of knowledge increases the likelihood that visitors are aware of spending opportunities before they arrive, and begins to build goodwill between tourism operations and the surrounding community (Mason and Milne 2002). It is this type of networking that can begin to enhance yield and also improve SMTE performance.

SMTE and the Internet

The internet has several features that make it an important alternative to traditional marketing approaches (Loader, Hague, and Eagle 2000; Lawrence et al. 2002):

- websites are flexible, their content can be changed easily;
- internet sites provide an international presence;
- the internet can make customer relations easier and more individualized;
- the net decentralizes and democratizes access to the customer;
- customers can make easier decisions with more precise product information and book online;
- there are cost savings in distribution, service, marketing, and promotion;
- numbers of internet users are growing rapidly; their socioeconomic profile is important to communities seeking to attract high-yield, low-impact visitors;
- partnerships between tourism agencies can be nurtured more easily;
- websites have the potential to facilitate networks.

Networks, knowledge, and relationships have become crucial assets to SMTE survival in the new economy (Braun 2002). The association of growth in regions and of industries with conspicuous networking activity has encouraged suggestions that successful regional economies in the world economic system must be "intelligent regions," network economies or learning regions (Clark, Feldman, and Gurtler 2000). Likewise the notion of "smart" or "intelligent" tourism regions and strategies is now beginning to come to the fore (Nodder et al. 2003).

The lack of uptake and ineffective use of ICT have been identified in the literature as a significant weakness in the development of SMTE (Buhalis and Cooper 1998; Buhalis 2000). Small-business owners are often intimidated by the "hidden costs" of ICT adoption, such as training and upgrading software. They are also wary of time commitments and the problems of relying on external expertise. The initial cost is in website design, which requires some technical expertise that is often hard to find in peripheral developing nations (UNDP 2001). However, with increased educational opportunities and improved ICT infrastructure, such skills are becoming more prevalent in the developing world and rural settings (Mitchell 1999).

Unfortunately a number of less positive issues must also be addressed. Many websites are developed and maintained by people who live far away from the localities and businesses that rely on them and have limited knowledge of tourism industry issues. Indeed it is the lack of understanding between web-developers and tourism operators that has been shown to be a factor in poor website performance in some settings (Milne and Mason 2001).

This state of affairs leads to a continued dependence on external expertise, and also tends to remove the ability for the developer to interact on a face-to-face basis with the community of businesses that they are working with. Thus there is a need to not just provide web access, but also the tools to use it to its full potential (Hargittai 2002). Unfortunately, many countries, especially in the developing world, also do not currently possess the framework of policies and tools to assist SMTE to overcome these hurdles (Nodder et al. 2003).

Even if resources are provided, relatively few SMTE make use of the true potential of the internet. Most websites remain as little more than "virtual brochures," with limited interactivity and e-commerce, and few links to other elements of the local tourism product.

Perhaps the main conclusion to be drawn from the literature is that ICT can only do so much to minimize the difficulties associated with small size, isolation, and limited budgets. While the internet can, and will, enhance the ability of small destinations and operators to reach the elusive tourist, they will still have to rely on a mixed array of tools, both traditional and new, and on the continued willingness of consumers to embrace the internet as a travel-shopping and information-gathering tool (Morgan and Pritchard 2000).

Public Participation

If the tourism industry is to perform effectively for communities it must not only generate long-term economic benefits, it must also mesh with the needs and desires of local people (Mowforth and Munt 1998; Timothy 2002). Key elements of sustainable development include: broad-based local participation in policy forums, developing consensus around national and local government initiatives, communicating new initiatives to the public, and encouraging a sense of individual responsibility for action (Bramwell and Lane 2000; OECD 2001).

An emerging role for ICT?

Just as ICT has had profound effects upon ways that the tourism industry performs and is structured so it offers the opportunity to establish new channels to connect residents, tourism operators, planners, and other stakeholders. ICT has the potential to open up a greater array of channels of engagement through email, news groups, chatrooms, and linear/threaded asynchronous bulletin boards (Coleman and Gotze 2002).

These "technologies of connection" allow people to communicate, give feedback, ask questions, complain, exchange information, and build relationships (White 2001). Some argue that this approach can facilitate a better understanding of how different stakeholders perceive shared resources and, in turn, influence the performance of tourism development at the local scale (Hasse 2002). Two approaches which are now beginning to be applied to tourism development issues are community informatics (CI) and public participation geographic information systems (PPGIS).

Community informatics

CI is a discipline that focuses on the design and delivery of technological applications to enhance community development, and improve the lives of residents (Gurstein 2000). The CI literature focuses on five key areas in which ICT can enhance community quality of life (O'Neil 2002):

- the promotion of strong democracy and participation in planning processes;
- the development of social capital;
- the empowerment of individuals, especially marginalized groups;
- the strengthening of community and "sense of place";
- the creation of sustainable community economic development opportunities.

Gurstein (2000) has shown that CI projects, including the introduction of community "telecenters," will not be successful unless there is a clear link to local economic activity through sectors such as tourism. He identifies three strategies for using CI as an enabler of community development: as a marketing tool for local business; as a mechanism to bring together a range of "linked" resources of value to improving quality of life; and as a distributed network that can assist the creation of new relationships and economic linkages (O'Neil 2002).

Thus the core themes of CI research match closely with the linkage creation, stakeholder communication, and small business/community marketing that we argue underpin the ability to enhance tourism's role in the development process. We now outline an example of a CI method called "web-raising" that has the potential to create an internet presence capable of strengthening these relationships.

Web-raising is the digital equivalent to a barn-raising – a community working together to create a collective asset. While it may take several forms, web-raising generally brings residents and local businesses together to share experience and skills and empower one another in the creation of web documents (Milne and Mason 2001). While an effective and unique website is developed, the building process itself allows different groups to learn more about each other, in the same way that barn-raising helped to forge important notions of communal trust and reciprocity in the American west during the twentieth century (Rheingold 2000).

The focus is on empowering communities to build effective tourism marketing and development tools that will advertise the region, handle inquiries, take bookings for local tourist facilities, and allow businesses to actively pursue appropriate market segments. The website is a foundation, rather than an end in itself, aimed at creating the nucleus of a self-sustaining and appropriate industry that is owned and operated by local people (Mason and Milne 2002). Such a website creates a platform for other forms of information on sectors related to tourism (organic farming, arts and crafts) and can provide the basis for local participation in the planning process. In effect the site becomes a resource for the local community as well as visitors, and offers the ability to create a more balanced web-model – one that is technically competent and also effective in facilitating local network development and relationship building and management. In a sense tourism therefore becomes a catalyst to enhance levels of community participation at a broader level.

PPGIS

There is a growing body of literature on the use and applications of GIS in the tourism arena (Bahaire and Elliott-White 1999; Hasse 2002). In addition to the conventional mapping of tourist flows and spatial analysis of destinations, GIS use has expanded to address issues of access and public participation – PPGIS or GIS/2 (McAdam 1999). Much of this research seeks to develop a GIS that will be adaptable to input from people and communities (Obermeyer 1998). A key concern of this literature is the need to have a deeper understanding and representation of multiple realities of space and environment in a GIS (Jankowski and Nyerges 2001).

Traditional use of GIS usually focuses on capturing versions of reality, which are biased toward scientific and "expert" approaches to data-driven planning. The system can struggle to include generally qualitative forms of knowledge such as sketch maps, cognitive and mental maps, and narrative and oral histories. Indeed, Harris and Weiner (1998) argue that GIS is a contradictory technology that simultaneously marginalizes and empowers people and communities. The effects of a GIS are contingent upon a particular localized mix of historical, socioeconomic, political, and technological conditions.

A "community-integrated GIS" may broaden the use of digital data-handling technologies, and increase the number and diversity of people participating in spatial decision-making. The potential then exists to provide this information on a community developed and run website. This enhances the ability of community voices to be heard through mental maps and images and begins to form the basis for a community controlled and driven decision support system (Kingston et al. 2000; Ghose 2001).

Some Problems and Pitfalls

While community informatics and PPGIS offer the potential to enhance public input in the planning and development process they are not without their difficulties. Castells (2000) argues that traditional sources of exclusion are duplicated on the internet. The challenge, therefore, becomes one of ensuring equality of access while at the same time tackling the consequences of marginalization and underdevelopment. Access to the internet is unevenly biased in favor of developed countries and, within these, the middle and upper classes of largely urban centers (UNDP 2001). Thus those who are already marginalized are becoming even more so because they are unable to access the new technologies available to wealthier communities (MacGillivray and Boyle 2001).

Building a toolkit for online engagement over tourism and other issues requires an understanding of how technology can help and hinder community-building (Coleman and Gotze 2002). It is also important to bear in mind that, while technology does not itself determine social process, it can be seen as a mediating factor in the complex interactions between social structures, social actors, and their socially constructed tools.

Castells (2000) argues that the electronic world does not exist in a vacuum and that it requires some reference to the physical and social worlds of its participants. Glogoff (2001) states that online communication is not as "rich" as face-to-face communication, nor is it as personal, trusting, or friendly. While the internet changes the quantity of information that is available and the capacity to access it, Bimber (1998: 138) asserts that "it is not yet clear that it will also change motivation and interest, let alone cognitive capacity." On the internet, just as in traditional communities, citizens must be motivated if they are to participate.

Conclusions

ICT has the potential to alleviate some of the traditional problems associated with tourism and its impacts on the development process. Nevertheless, we have shown that many of the factors that reduce tourism's potential developmental benefits, including limited economies of scale, isolation, dependency, and lack of capital, will continue to persist regardless of the introduction of new technologies.

It is not yet apparent whether the internet will "level the playing field" and improve the access of peripheral destinations and/or small firms to the elusive tourist, or simply exacerbate the dominance of large, well-connected firms and destinations. It is equally unclear what ICT, and particularly the internet, mean for citizens wanting to engage more fully in tourism development at the beginning of the twenty-first century. How, for example, will the tourism industry, and those who are influenced by it, deal with the democratization of information and technology occurring on a broader scale in many societies around the world (Coleman and Gotze 2002)?

While there are no clear answers about whether ICT is creating a revolution in tourism's relationship with the development process or merely reinforcing existing patterns, it is clear that tourism researchers ignore these issues at their peril. If we are to better understand the ability of the local to survive and thrive in the era of globalization we must grapple with ICT impacts on the perception, consumption, and construction of tourism spaces, and the final development outcomes of the industry (Milne and Ateljevic 2001b).

Most importantly it is time for tourism researchers to begin to embrace the broader context within which rapid technological change occurs. We follow Nardi and O'Day (1999) in arguing that social understanding, values, and practices are integral aspects of ICT, and must be accounted for if we are to understand its impacts. If ICT is to enable a revolution in tourism's development outcomes, there needs to be responsible, informed engagement with technology in local settings. We need to begin to view and understand tourism, and its development outcomes, as being part of an "information ecology" of people, practices, values, *and* technologies.

REFERENCES

Bahaire, T., and Elliott-White, M. (1999). The application of GIS in sustainable tourism planning: A review. *Journal of Sustainable Tourism* 7(2), 159–74.

Beirne, E., and Curry, P. (1999). The impact of the internet on the information search process and tourism decision making. In D. Buhalis and W. Schertler (eds), *Information and Communication Technologies in Tourism* (ENTER) (pp. 88–97). New York: Springer Wein.

Bimber, B. (1998). The internet and political transformation: Populism, community and accelerated pluralism. *Polity* 31(1), 133–60.

Bramwell, B., and Lane, B. (2000). Collaborative tourism planning: Issues and future directions. In B. Bramwell and B. Lane (eds), *Tourism Collaboration and Partnerships: Politics, Practice and Sustainability* (pp. 333–41). Clevedon: Channel View Publications.

Braun, P. (2002). Networking tourism SMEs: E-commerce and e-marketing issues in regional Australia. *Information Technology and Tourism* 5(1), 13–23.

Britton, S. (1981). *Tourism, Dependency and Development: A Mode of Analysis*. Canberra: ANU Press.

Buhalis, D. (2000). Tourism and information technologies: Past, present and future. *Tourism Recreation Research* 25(1) 41– 58.

Buhalis, D. (2001). Tourism distribution channels: Practices and processes. In D. Buhalis and E. Laws (eds), *Tourism Distribution Channels: Practices, Issues and Transformations* (pp. 7–32). London: Continuum.

Buhalis, D., and Cooper, C. (1998). Competition or cooperation: Small and medium-sized tourism enterprises at the destination. In E. Laws, B. Faulkner, and G. Moscardo (eds), *Embracing and Managing Change in Tourism* (pp. 324–46). London: Routledge.

Buhalis, D., and Schertler, W. (1999). Preface. In D. Buhalis and W. Schertler (eds), *Information and Communication Technologies in Tourism* (ENTER) (pp. v–vi). New York: Springer Wein.

Castells, M. (2000). *The Rise of the Network Society*, 2nd edn. Oxford: Blackwell.

Clark, G. L., Feldman, M. P., and Gertler, M. S. (2000). Economic geography: Transition and growth. In G. L. Clark, M. P. Feldman, and M. S. Gertler (eds), *The Oxford Handbook of Economic Geography* (pp. 3–17). Oxford: Oxford University Press.

Coleman, S., and Gotze, J. (2002). *Bowling Together: Online Public Engagement in Policy Deliberation*. London: Hansard Society, London School of Economics. <www.hansardsociety.org.uk>

Cooper, C., and Lewis, J. (2001). Transformation and trends in the tourism industry: Implications for distribution channels. In D. Buhalis and E. Laws (eds), *Tourism Distribution Channels: Practices, Issues and Transformations* (pp. 315–31). London: Continuum.

Garkavenko, V., Bremner, H., and Milne, S. (2003). Travel agents in the "Information Age": New Zealand experiences of disintermediation. In A. Frew, M. Hitz, and P. O'Connor (eds), *Information and Communication Technologies in Tourism* (ENTER). New York: Springer Wein.

Ghose, R. (2001). Use of information technology for community empowerment: Transforming GIS into community information systems. *Transactions in GIS* 5(2), 141–63.

Glogoff, S. (2001). Virtual connections: Community bonding on the internet. *First Monday* 6(3). Available at <http://firstmonday.org/issues/issue63/glogoff/index.html> (accessed September 28, 2003).

Gurstein, M. (2000). Community informatics: Enabling community uses of information and communications technology. In M. Gurstein (ed.), *Community Informatics: Enabling Community Uses of Information and Communications Technologies* (pp. 1–31). London: Idea Group.

Hall, C. M. (1996). Political effects of tourism in the Pacific. In C. M. Hall and S. J. Page (eds), *Tourism in the Pacific: Issues and Cases* (pp. 81–90). London: International Thomson Business Press.

Hargittai, E. (2002). Second-level digital divide: differences in people's online skills. *First Monday* 7(4), <http://www.firstmonday.dk/issues/issue7_4/hargittai/> (accessed July 19, 2003).

Harris, T. M., and Weiner, D. (1998). Empowerment, marginalization and "community integrated" GIS. *Cartography and GIS* 25(2), 67–76.

Harrison, D. (2001). Islands, image and tourism. *Tourism Recreation Research* 26(3), 7–12.

Hasse, J. (2002). Stakeholder perceptions of tourism development in Marahau, New Zealand: A role for participatory approaches and GIS. Unpublished Ph.D. thesis, Victoria University of Wellington.

Hull, J., and Milne, S. (2001). From nets to the net: Marketing tourism on Quebec's Lower North Shore. In J. O. Baerenholdt and N. Aarsaether (eds), *The Reflexive North* (pp. 159–79). Copenhagen: Nordic Council of Ministers.

Jankowski, P., and Nyerges, T. (2001). *Geographic Information Systems for Group Decision Making: Towards a Participatory Geographic Information Science*. London: Taylor & Francis.

Kenny, C. (2002). Information and communication technologies for direct poverty alleviation. *Development Policy Review* 20(2), 141–57.

Kingston, R., Carver, S., Evans, A., and Turton, I. (2000). Web-based public participation geographical information systems: An aid to local environmental decision making. *Computers, Environment and Urban Systems* 24(2), 109–25.

Lawrence, E., Newton, S., Corbitt, B., Braithwaite, R., and Parker, C. (2002). *Technology of Internet Business*. Sydney: Wiley.

Laws, E., and Buhalis, D. (2001). Tourism distribution channels: Agendas for future research. In D. Buhalis and E. Laws (eds), *Tourism Distribution Channels: Practices, Issues and Transformations* (pp. 371–6). London: Continuum.

Loader, B. D., Hague, B., and Eagle, D. (2000). Embedding the net: Community empowerment in the age of information. In M. Gurstein (ed.), *Community Informatics: Enabling Community Uses of Information and Communications Technology* (pp. 81–103). Hershy, PA: Idea Group Publishing.

MacGillivray, A., and Boyle, D. (2001). Sink or surf? Social inclusion in the digital age. In J. Wilsdon (ed.), *Digital Futures: Living in a Networked World* (pp. 118–38). London: Earthscan.

Mason, D., and Milne, S. (2002). E-commerce and community tourism. In P. C. Palvia, S. C. Palvia, and E. M. Roche (eds), *Global Information Technology and Electronic Commerce: Issues for the New Millennium* (pp. 294–310). Marietta, GA: Ivy League Publishing.

McAdam, D. (1999). The value and scope of GIS in tourism management. *Journal of Sustainable Tourism* 7(1), 77–92.

Milne, S., and Ateljevic, J. (2001a). Technology and service quality in the tourism and hospitality industry. In J. Kandampully, C. Mok, and B. Sparks (eds), *Service Quality Management in Hospitality, Tourism and Leisure* (pp. 281–95). New York: Howarth Press.

Milne, S., and Ateljevic, I. (2001b). Tourism, economic development and the global–local nexus: Theory embracing complexity. *Tourism Geographies* 3(4), 369–93.

Milne, S., and Gill, K. (1998). Distribution technologies and destination development: Myths and realities. In D. Ioannides and K. Debbage (eds), *The Economic Geography of the Tourism Industry: A Supply-Side Analysis* (pp. 123–38). London: Routledge.

Milne S., and Mason, D. (2001). Tourism, web-raising and community development. In P. J. Sheldon, K. W. Wober, and D. Fesenmaier (eds), *Information and Communication Technologies in Tourism (ENTER)* (pp. 283–94). New York: Springer Wein.

Milne, S., and Nowosielski, L. (1996). Travel distribution technologies and sustainable tourism development: The case of South Pacific microstates. *Journal of Sustainable Tourism* 4, 131–50.

Mitchell, W. J. (1999). *E-topia: Urban life, Jim – But Not As We Know It*. Cambridge, MA: MIT Press.

Morgan, N., and Pritchard, A. (2000). *Advertising in Tourism and Leisure*. Oxford: Butterworth-Heinemann.

Mowforth, M., and Munt, I. (1998). *Tourism and Sustainability: New Tourism in the Third World*. London: Routledge.

Nardi, B. A., and O'Day, V. L. (1999). *Information Ecologies: Using Technology with Heart*. Cambridge, MA: MIT Press.

Nodder, C., Mason, D., Ateljevic, J., and Milne, S. (2003). ICT adoption and use in New Zealand's small and medium tourism enterprises: A cross sectoral perspective. In A. Frew, M. Hitz, and P. O'Connor (eds), *Information and Communication Technologies in Tourism (ENTER)*. New York: Springer Wein.

Obermeyer, N. J. (1998). The evolution of public participation: GIS. *Cartography and GIS* 25(2), 65–6.

OECD (2001). *Citizens as Partners: Information, Consultation and Public Participation in Policy Making*. Paris: OECD.

O'Neil, D. (2002). Assessing community informatics: A review of methodological approaches for evaluating community networks and community technology centers. *Internet Research: Electronic Networking Applications And Policy* 12(1), 76–102.

Poon, A. (1993). *Tourism, Technology, and Competitive Strategies*. Wallingford: CAB International.

Rheingold, H. (2000). *The Virtual Community: Homesteading on the Electronic Frontier*. Boston: MIT Press.

Rochlin, G. I. (1997). *Trapped in the Net: The Unanticipated Consequences of Computerization*. Princeton: Princeton University Press.

Sheldon, P. (1997). *Tourism Information Technology*. Wallingford: CAB International.

Surman, M., and Wershler-Henry, D. (2001). *Commonspace: Beyond Virtual Community*. London: FT.com (Financial Times/Pearson).

Swarbrooke, J. (2001). Distribution channels: Ethics and sustainability. In D. Buhalis and E. Laws (eds), *Tourism Distribution Channels: Practices, Issues and Transformations* (pp. 87–118). London: Continuum.

Timothy, D. (2002). Tourism and community development issues. In R. Sharpley and D. J. Telfer (eds), *Tourism and Development: Concepts and Issues* (pp. 149–64). Clevedon: Channel View Publications.

Tufts, S. (2000). "We make it work": Competing tourism development narratives in the making of a hospitality workforce. Paper presented at the 96th Annual Meeting of the American Association of Geographers, April, Pittsburgh, PA.

UNDP (2001). *Human Development Report 2001: Making New Technologies Work for Human Development*. New York: Oxford University Press.

White, N. (2001). Facilitating and hosting a virtual community. Online publication at <http://www.fullcirc.com/community/communityfacilitation.htm> (accessed July 19, 2003).

Chapter 16

Theming, Tourism, and Fantasy City

Thomas W. Paradis

Themed environments are predominantly designed to appeal to tourists and visitors. These are *other-directed* places (Jackson 1970; Hoelscher 1998) such as restaurants, gas stations, motels, airports, historic business districts, city parks, casinos, theme parks, shopping malls, resort communities, and even local festivals. In the US, the emergence of themes in the built environment has coincided with the growth of tourism as a major form of economic development in the 1960s and 1970s (Lew 1989). In this chapter I provide an overview of theme development, including its characteristics, manifestations in the human landscape, and scholarly explanations for the proliferation of theming. While the focus is primarily on the United States, a global perspective is emphasized throughout, given that theme development is clearly a global phenomenon rather than exclusively an American one. Further, this chapter highlights a representative sample of multi-disciplinary literature featuring a variety of research methodologies and theoretical perspectives to determine the status of current research with respect to themed environments. To close the chapter I provide some general direction for future investigation.

Not surprisingly, much of the literature focused on theming is directed toward touristed landscapes. This is nowhere more evident than in John Hannigan's (1998) book *Fantasy City*, in which Hannigan explores how large cities in America are transformed into destinations for entertainment. In metropolitan settings, corporate-sponsored *urban entertainment destinations* (UEDs) are transforming previously tired downtown cores into new, postmodern centers of entertainment and leisure. Large cities worldwide are responding to an emerging post-industrial economy by rooting their economic base less in traditional secondary manufacturing and more in the realm of tertiary tourism, sports, culture, and entertainment. Of the six primary characteristics of Fantasy City discussed by Hannigan (1998: 3), the first is its "theme-o-centric" qualities, whereby "everything from individual entertainment venues to the image of the city itself conforms to a scripted theme, normally drawn from sports, history or popular entertainment." The king of fantasy cities in the US is Las Vegas, arguably the urban tourism capital of North America, with its landscape comprising a veritable museum of themed environments. Once known as an epicenter for social vices such as gambling, sex, and alcohol, Las Vegas casinos have moved toward becoming a family-oriented entertainment destination, collectively focused around a dazzling variety of scripted themes and images centered on its casino complexes (Gottdiener 1997; see also Gottdiener, Collins, and Dickens 1999; Hannigan 1998).

Few cities have so intensely themed such a major portion of their urban landscape to the degree of Las Vegas. However, virtually every "modern" city has developed various forms of thematic commercial districts. In the US, these themed retail centers are found in both large metropolitan areas and small rural communities. Within the urban realm, the intensification of theming is best understood in the context of larger global processes. Theming is one component of urban tourism, which, in turn, has emerged with newer post-industrial and postmodern urban forms. Cities today are being restructured and reorganized as centers of consumption, where "consumer goods and media images play a major role in the everyday life of urbanites" (Page and Hall 2003: 34). In the postmodern metropolis, hierarchies of taste, or niche markets, have increasingly replaced the mass consumption of goods, and places themselves are being designed for consumption, particularly through the use of visual images and scripted themes. The production of themes and all the symbolic imagery they entail has therefore occurred in conjunction with a massive global restructuring. Mansfield (1999: 330, cited in Page and Hall 2003: 32) highlighted the dominant characteristics of postmodernism that influence today's world metropolises. Paraphrased here in part, these include a focus on difference, diversity, discontinuity, and fragmentation as opposed to the modernist ideals of sameness and universalism; an emphasis on the consumption and reproduction of images, whereby social identity is formed in relation to the sphere of consumption (e.g. leisure) rather than production (e.g. work); and an increasing acceptance (and encouragement) of pastiche, collage, spectacle, and the associated promotion of commodities designed specifically for differentiated markets.

Translated to the urban cultural landscape, these postmodern conditions are revealed in cities around the world that are now more defined by their multinodal, consumption-driven, and rather disorganized geographic spaces that have proven inherently difficult to model (Page and Hall 2003). For a growing number of scholars, it is the Los Angeles experience that describes (if not models) the direction of postmodern urban development occurring around the world. Dear (2000: 111) argued as much with his nearly frustrated description of postmodern Los Angeles:

> This polycentric, polarized, polyglot metropolis long ago tore up its social contract, and is without even a draft of a replacement. There is no longer a single civic will nor a clear collective intentionality behind LA's urbanism; and the obsolete land-use planning machinery is powerless to influence the city's burgeoning social heterodoxy. This is the insistent message of postmodern Los Angeles: that all urban place-making bets are off; we are engaged, knowingly or otherwise, in the search for new ways of creating cities.

All bets may indeed be off, though Page and Hall (2003) recognize that this postmodern diversity and uncertainty translates directly into the domain of tourism, given that employment lost through deindustrialization has encouraged tourism to become a fundamental element of urban economies. Postmodern tourism and leisure development now characterize cities worldwide, and the role of capital is central to the emergence of what Page and Hall refer to as "the new urban tourism." That is, most contemporary cities exhibit an urban tourism landscape characterized by "the homogenized symbols and presence of the multinational hotel chain (e.g. Quality Inn, Sheraton, Radisson), global hospitality brands (e.g. KFC, McDonalds, Pizza Hut, Starbucks and other franchises) juxtaposed with the heterogeneous examples of the locally or regionally distinctive products for consumption" (Page and Hall 2003: 39). As detailed below, the proliferation of themed environments is central to the success of urban tourism, focused as they are on the consumption of products and places – regardless of their local or global origins.

Mullins (1991) recognized the close relationship of consumption with tourism and leisure in the world's postmodern cities, where the pursuit of pleasure is often the central focus. Through his examples of the Australian urban scene, Mullins described the emergence of "tourism urbanization," whereby the process of urbanization occurs specifically through the sale and consumption of pleasure. Building on Mullins's tourism urbanization thesis, Gladstone (1998) examined similar concepts with respect to the United States. He identified two basic types of urbanization, namely the sun, sea, and sand resort and the capital-intensive, attraction-based city. Through his further classification of *Tourist Metropolises* (Atlantic City, Las Vegas, Orlando, and Reno) and *Leisure Cities* (nine other US cities) based primarily on employment in the tourism-related sector, Gladstone broadened the scope of Mullins's initial work on tourism urbanization and thereby emphasized the growing specialization of tourism and leisure functions in the postmodern city.

The rural countryside and its inclusive smaller communities are mirroring their metropolitan counterparts in their promotion of tourism through the use of themes. If Las Vegas is the veritable poster child of themed cities, its small-town equivalent in the US may be found in New Glarus, Wisconsin. In what is probably the most thorough academic study of non-metropolitan theming to date, Steven Hoelscher's book, *Heritage on Stage: The Invention of Ethnic Place in America's Little Switzerland* describes this Midwestern village as "A Place More Swiss than Switzerland" (Hoelscher 1998: 3). Prior to the 1960s, New Glarus regularly celebrated its Swiss heritage through various cultural displays and festivals, oriented primarily to its own residents. This inward-focused ethnic identity became increasingly commodified and directed to outsiders until the 1960s, when the town's cultural heritage became its own economic lifeblood. Through the production of what Hoelscher refers to as "Swisscapes," the community adjusted to the emerging post-industrial economy by consciously transforming its ethnic past into a tourist attraction, heavily themed for the enjoyment of visitors as well as locals.

This self-conscious display of ethnicity reflects rapidly growing interest in ethnic heritage nationwide, and the experience of New Glarus represents a "fundamental shift" in what it means to be "ethnic" and "American" (Hoelscher 1998: 17). The place further represents a more fundamental shift in America's rural economy, away from place-based extractive industries, agriculture and manufacturing to one dependent more than ever on leisure, tourism, recreation, and retirement services (Galston and Baehler 1995). The town's production of commodified "Swisscapes" accelerated following the closure of its most significant employer, the Pet Milk condensery in 1962. Since then, the community's main industry has been ethnic tourism.

New Glarus is not alone. The relatively few studies of "theme towns" do not adequately represent the ever-growing multitude of smaller communities that have reinvented their identities to attract visitors and their habits of consumption. In the Pacific Northwest, for instance, the number of communities that transformed their older retail districts into themed tourist attractions jumped from only five in 1960 to more than 50 by 1983 (Lew 1989). Scripted themes and identities have since become a typical component of America's small-town and metropolitan "tourism business districts," as Donald Getz (1993) refers to traditional downtowns that have reoriented themselves to visitors and entertainment functions.

Authenticity and Community Values

Whether urban or rural, themed spaces elicit a wide variety of responses from their viewers and participants. Themes are social constructions, contrived and applied to the landscape by certain individuals with their own unique perspectives. Thus, a specific identity imparted to a place will invariably hold different meanings for different people (DeLyser 1999; Gottdiener 2001). In turn, individuals hold unique value judgments regarding themed environments and can ultimately form strong opinions about such places. This is true for scholars and laypeople alike. In the scholarly realm, the recurrent issue of authenticity in tourist landscapes also applies to themed environments. This makes inherent sense, given that themed environments and tourist landscapes are often one and the same, designed to be gazed upon by others. This point was made clear by Gottdiener (2001: 151), who observed, "When we enter any themed environment, we become very much like a tourist. Malls, theme parks, casinos, and themed restaurants are all engineered to produce a special effect that stimulates our desire to spend money."

Like tourist venues, then, themed landscapes are sometimes lamented by scholars for not representing some kind of "authentic" character. Prior to Hannigan's *Fantasy City*, Sorkin (1992: xiv) described urban touristed space as a "city of simulations, television city, the city as theme park," and even likened them to urban renewal: "Here is urban renewal with a sinister twist, an architecture of deception which, in its happy-face familiarity, constantly distances itself from the most fundamental realities." For MacCannell (1992), the idea of reality is associated with a place's *natural* development. Authenticity is therefore merely staged and packaged for the benefit of tourist consumption, doing little to accurately represent the natural, or organic, production of a place.

More recent authors have tackled this conundrum by treating authenticity "as a social construction the meaning of which varies with different people, at different times, and in different places" (DeLyser 1999: 604) and which, moreover, is negotiable. The ambiguous nature of authenticity is recognized by Hoelscher (1998), who acknowledged various negative implications of contrived theming in New Glarus, Wisconsin. However, he emphasized that the complete story of the authenticity debate surrounding New Glarus and places like it is complex. "Authenticity, like tradition and ethnic identity," Hoelscher argued, "is far from an either/or proposition. Sentiments toward authenticity – so critical to other-directed places – are a matter of status discrimination and, as a corollary, a matter of power" (1998: 185). Importantly, however, redirecting the scholarly focus on authenticity should not refute aforementioned critical opinions toward places perceived as contrived, but instead should acknowledge these sentiments as one type of possible reaction toward themed environments. We do not have to like these places – and, for various well-argued reasons, many scholars do not.

Segments of local and regional communities have also opposed theming at times and to varying degrees. On a large scale the issue of theming has become embedded within the economic process of globalization, in that organized protests against perceived "Disneyfication" (Gottdiener 2001) and "McDonaldization" (Ritzer 1993) of culturally distinct locales are growing in number worldwide. For instance, a recent proposal to refurbish an old clothing store in the centuries-old square of Oaxaca, Mexico into a McDonald's restaurant has infuriated the local community there. Local artists and activists held a protest picnic for 4,000 people featuring the unique cuisine of the area, which was perceived to be threatened by the proposed global intrusion (Borden 2002).

Even Americans have their limits when it comes to theming. In 1994 the Disney Corporation reluctantly withdrew its ambitious plan for a $650 million history theme park called "Disney's America" about 35 miles west of Washington, DC (Gottdiener 2001). The reason for Disney's retreat was a surprise to those involved in the project: a mounting environmental protest and deeply felt public animosity toward the Disneyfied simulation of the nation's heritage. Numerous preservation and environmental interest groups banded together at the grassroots level to stop the project.

Smaller towns and cities have also been the scene of local contestation of the transformation of historic business districts into miniature theme parks. Community conflict pertaining to issues of authenticity and the associated inconveniences of mass tourism are particularly acute in such places. In Leavenworth, Washington, for example, the near total "Bavarianization" of its main street (which started in the 1960s) irritated the community to the point where two-thirds of nearby rural residents were opposed to any further theme development by 1980 (Frenkel and Walton 2000). The influx of thousands of visitors a day into the heart of Leavenworth had alienated much of the community from its own downtown, making them wonder whether they still "owned" their community.

In the Southwestern ranching town of Roswell, New Mexico, long-time residents decried the image makeover of the old Plains Theatre into the International UFO Museum and Research Center in 1996 (Paradis 2002). Promoted by the Roswell Main Street Program and other growth interests, the downtown has become a sort of "alien zone," with numerous businesses adopting the UFO/alien theme in various guises. One consequence has been a mild rift in the community between those who enjoy the town's new space-age identity and others who are embarrassed by the phenomenon. Though organized protests against their town's unique theme have yet to materialize, one only need turn to the opinion pages of the *Roswell Daily Record* during the city's annual "Encounter" festival to find a divided community.

It appears that grassroots concerns related to tourism in general and theming in particular are often one and the same. Still, scholars have only begun to investigate the various implications of theming in any type of setting. Instead, research has predominantly focused on the explanatory realm – and perhaps rightly so, given the relatively recent emergence of themed environments. The bulk of contemporary literature primarily describes the diversity of themed landscapes and provides various explanations for their development.

Consuming Places

While authors typically present their own unique approaches for understanding themes materialized in the landscape, one overarching concept predominates – that of consumption. The most fundamental explanation for the proliferation of themed environments during the past few decades has been fairly straightforward and well accepted. That is, themes are attached to otherwise mundane products and places as a competitive strategy to enhance the generation of profits. In a market economy based increasingly on consumption rather than production, contrived meanings and identities become all the more important to create perceived differences in products that are in actuality quite similar. In short, themes are designed specifically to promote the virtual and experiential consumption of places.

Scholars in various disciplines have recognized this economic rationale for some time. Even without the guidance of contemporary theoretical approaches, J. B. Jackson observed in the 1950s how roadside architecture was already being designed with the consumer in mind. "We must accustom ourselves," instructed Jackson, "to the fact that the basic motive in the design of these establishments – whether motels or drive-in movies or nightclubs – is a desire to please and attract the passerby" (1970: 62). He further suggested that "almost every retail business," no matter its location, is dependent on eye-appeal of some kind. Jackson was witnessing the emergence of themed environments along America's roadside. Banham (1971) observed similar trends in the Los Angeles metro area during the 1970s. In trying to explain why standardized buildings owned by retail-oriented businesses were being plastered with enormous signs, colorful façades and other symbolic motifs, Banham (1971: 101) understood that it "makes financial sense to put up relatively simple single-story boxes, and then make them tall enough to attract attention by piling up symbols and graphic art on top." He further observed that this practice "has become more apparent as the years have passed" and that the coinciding emergence of symbolic motifs with the "hard-nosed rationalism of the market economy" was recognized by scholars and learned by businesses decades, if not centuries, ago (Banham 1971: 100).

Although contemporary literature is generally more sophisticated and theoretically driven, the basic rationale behind the imagined façade has remained the same: the drive for profit. As one might expect, however, the reality beyond this profit-driven explanation is significantly more complex. This fact has become apparent within one of the most in-depth works on themed environments to date, Mark Gottdiener's two-edition set of *The Theming of America* (1997 and 2001). The basis of his argument centers around the concept of the *realization of capital*. This is the transfer of value from a specific commodity produced to its realization in sales. Though apparently a simple and assumed dynamic within the realm of capitalism, economic analysts, including Karl Marx himself, often neglected this side of the capitalist system. For business owners to realize the extra value in a commodity, it becomes imperative that they sell what is produced for the marketplace. Only then can companies hope to achieve a profit and, in turn, reinvest those earnings back into further production. Marx identified this cycle of capital, whereby money (M) is invested in the production of a specific commodity (C), which then translates into more money (M') after its sale (Gottdiener 1997, 2001).

Early economists focused more on the M to C aspect of capitalism and typically neglected the complex dynamics of the C to M' process. This latter transition, of course, represents the act of consumption, as goods and services are produced and then consumed – their extra value hopefully realized as profits for reinvestment. The bottom line is that if C to M' doesn't happen (i.e., if people do not consume the goods that companies produce) the entire cycle of capitalism theoretically collapses. Consequently, building on the work of Jean Baudrillard (1973), Gottdiener (1997: 47) argued that "the critical dynamics of capitalist development hinges on the ability to realize capital once commodities are produced." With consumption now the critical focus rather than production, the attachment of symbolic themes to ordinary products and places has become a necessary mechanism for stimulating demand and promoting ever more consumption. "A nation of consumers must be fed by appeals to consume even when the goods they are offered have dubious use-values" (Gottdiener 1997: 48). These appeals constitute all the signs, symbols, and imagery that collectively make up a themed environment and have the power to encourage the realization of capital (C to M').

If Gottdiener succeeds with spelling out the intricate theoretical connections between the dynamics of capitalism and themed environments, Hannigan (1998) provides an additional, more practical explanation of how themes are strategically used by the corporate world. Sparking the growth of Fantasy City and its inclusive themed environments is the building of "synergies," or tie-ins, often pursued by the world's entertainment giants. Designed primarily to add value to existing merchandise and entertainment, synergies are typically created in several ways (Hannigan 1998). The first is the distribution of existing "properties" in new formats, such as when the Disney Corporation reworks its animated movies and turns them into theatrical stage productions. Other companies convert popular video games into movies, and movies become the basis for theme park rides. Synergies can also be created through the forging of cross-business opportunities, exemplified by Disney naming its professional hockey team the "Mighty Ducks," taking advantage of its popular movies of the same name. The creation of entirely new businesses can also provide synergistic opportunities, such as Dreamworks SKG, producing TV shows, movies, recordings, and an entire chain of super-arcades.

Hannigan points out, however, that theming found within Fantasy City is further about adding value. Basically, the value of the whole ensemble of themes is worth more than its individual parts. In turn, Hannigan notes, "this aggressively themed, value-added component of Fantasy City" materializes through the strategic convergence and overlap of four specific "consumer activity systems," including shopping, dining, entertainment and education, and culture (Hannigan 1998: 89). The three main hybrids of these activity systems are referred to within the retail industry as shopertainment, eatertainment, and edutainment. In short, the typically ordinary activities of shopping, eating, and education have been purposely fused with entertainment opportunities for consumers. In various themed restaurants such as the Hard Rock Café, the entertainment experience may actually overshadow the food itself. Hannigan (1998: 94) describes these places as "a combination of amusement park, diner, souvenir stand and museum," representing the epitome of adding value through the creation of synergistic opportunities – the exemplar of a themed commercial space designed to promote consumption of less than extraordinary products.

Together, the works of Gottdiener (1997, 2001) and Hannigan (1998) provide a powerful economic rationale for the existence and proliferation of themed environments. A number of detailed empirical case studies only substantiate these authors' general claims regarding the role of political economy in theme development, whether their focus is on shopping malls (Crawford 1992; Goss 1999), commercial architecture of the American roadside (Liebs 1985; Jakle and Sculle 1994), urban historic districts (Frieden and Sagalyn 1989; Boyer 1992), or small towns and cities (Engler 1994; Frenkel and Walton 2000; Paradis 2002). The problem of understanding the emergence of themed environments has apparently been solved. Or has it? What of the cultural realm in the context of themed environments?

Culture, Identity, and Semiotics

Aforementioned consumption- and market-oriented factors have certainly helped encourage the production of themed environments in recent decades. But who, or what, actually decides *which* themes will be used in specific circumstances, and for what purposes? Specifically, how do culture and ideology play a role in such decisions that, in turn, will materialize in the built environment? In a sense, business-minded individuals intent on generating profits through the creation of symbolic spaces must somehow decide which symbols will assist them with selling their products and constructed spaces. One case in point is offered by Kevin Blake (1999), who invokes the cultural landscape approach to understand why small towns scattered throughout the San Juan mountains of Colorado consistently demonstrate the use of mountain-related imagery and themes throughout their communities. While certain images are designed with the goal of separating tourists from their money, Blake (1999: 29) observed the mountains themselves have become symbolic landscapes, "forming the bedrock of how some cultures perceive themselves and their relationship with their environment." Various images of mountain scenes are used, for example, as logos for local newspaper mastheads, chamber of commerce materials, public library signs, government seals, welcome signs, and heritage sites. Arguably, many of these images are created not just in the pursuit of dollars, but more in celebration of community pride and local history. The San Juans have therefore become "cultural landscapes with multiple themes of meaning, including scenic landmarks of home, mining heritage, recreation activities, spiritual renewal, and hallowed ground" (Blake 1999: 52). Theming thus contributes to local sense of place and community identity – attributes not readily quantifiable with dollar values.

Further, culturally-based aspects of authenticity, trends in popular culture, and social status must also contribute to how and why theming occurs in certain places. Individual perception of authenticity engenders local discussions regarding the appropriateness of specific themes for representing their own collective identity. In "Bavarian" Leavenworth, Washington, the complete absence of a local German heritage did not prevent city leaders and boosters from reimagining the entire business district as an *authentic* alpine village. Bavarian authenticity was based in this case on the "quality of the copy" (Frenkel and Walton 2000: 569). Avid boosters even sought to control the types of merchandise sold in stores, pushed for the adoption of an "authentic" dress code, and encouraged merchants to "act the part" of their scripted Bavarian culture ways.

One should question whether or not these extreme measures were actually pursued primarily with the *realization of capital* in mind. Apparently, tourists were coming to Leavenworth regardless of what merchants were wearing or what specific types of merchandise were being sold in the shops. While Leavenworth's makeover was certainly aimed to revive the local economy through the creation of "fantasy shopping landscapes" (Frenkel and Walton 2000: 576), there appear to be more complicated dynamics at work. The role of local agency, or individuals and groups pushing their agendas for change, was paramount. From one perspective, it could be argued that it was their own cultural values and personal meanings of "authenticity" that drove the production of specific themes and images within the town's landscape, festivals, and behaviors. Explaining Leavenworth, therefore, necessarily becomes much more complex than relying entirely on the realization of capital argument.

Semiotics, or the study of signs and sign systems, provides one avenue for exploring various cultural creations, including themed environments. Culture can be conceived as both a mediator and a medium of social interaction. Consequently, cultural creations may be interpreted *semiotically*, as a collection of signs and texts (Hopkins 1998). The subject of semiotics concerns itself with the production and consumption of meanings as a function of social processes (Gottdiener 1997). For this reason, argued Gottdiener (1997), the concepts of semiotics can be useful for the analysis of symbols that appear throughout a society's themed environments. In short, the basic unit of semiotics is the *sign*, most commonly defined as "something that stands for something else," such as any written words representing an object, idea, or meaning (Sebeok 1986, cited in Hopkins 1998). Each sign consists of a *signifier* (usually a word or object) and a corresponding cultural meaning, known as a *signified* (Gottdiener 1997). For example, one can attach the word "computer" as a signifier to the idea of a "computer," an electronic device enabled by the circuit chip to quickly process and manipulate large quantities of data.

Importantly, every signifier maintains both a *denotative* and *connotative* level of meaning, a fact that allows semiotics to be extremely useful for interpreting themes and themed environments. When a signifier conveys rather simple information, often functional in nature, we *denote* meaning (Gottdiener 1997). The word "computer" can denote data manipulation, software, and hardware. On a connotative level, however, the word "computer" can convey meanings derived from some social or cultural context that may differ from one person, or one society, to another. A computer can connote a variety of associated meanings, such as a fast-paced, professional lifestyle, freedom to communicate inexpensively around the world, frustration with advanced technology, or social status and economic success, among many others. This dual nature of signs (operating at both denotative and connotative levels of meaning) makes them necessarily ambiguous and open for multiple interpretations. Thus, various social forces can work to constrain or encourage the use of words or images to a specific "universe of meaning" (Gottdiener 1997: 10). "Powerful interests in society, such as corporate business leaders or officials of government, accomplish the task of manipulating the public towards their desired ends by constraining the normally wide range of meanings in social discourse" (Gottdiener 1997: 10).

The advertising industry constantly structures the universe of meaning by attaching a limited set of connotative meanings to their products. Thus, we learn through creative advertising that a new automobile signifies social status, sex appeal, speed, freedom, and even patriotism – well beyond the automobile's denotative meaning of "transportation." For its own part, the tourism industry "may be said to operate with a sign system that facilitates its own ideology of consumption by attempting to manipulate the leisure and recreational decisions of people for the purposes of selling commodities: tourist places" (Hopkins 1998: 198).

An empirical study of place-image marketing by Jeffrey Hopkins (1998) demonstrates how the semiotics approach can be applied to understand the creation of identities and themes. Hopkins analyzed the meanings of advertisements as they applied to the marketing of various *place-myths*, "the connoted, embellished identities attributed to places" (Hopkins 1998: 193) used to promote the rural countryside of southwestern Ontario, Canada. Through a content analysis of 210 pieces of advertising material (signifiers), Hopkins identified and analyzed 85 slogans and 74 logos used to establish images and identities in the minds of urban and suburban consumers. Emerging from this study was a series of dominant place-myths used to promote the rural countryside, the most dominant of which included: (1) the natural environment and its associated outdoor experiences and amenities; (2) community, represented by a sense of innocence, safety, friendship, and family values; and (3) local heritage, as expressed through historic sites, experiences, and crafted goods. In its totality, "Lake Huron's countryside has taken on mythical qualities of a special place with unique characteristics that distinguish it from the city," concluded Hopkins (1998: 208). Specific connotative meanings had been promoted to commodify Ontario's rural countryside, ultimately creating an entirely constructed cultural identity with questionable levels of authenticity. That two studies of rural Britain (Cloke 1993; Urry 1995) found similar promotional themes prompted Hopkins (1998: 208) to question, "how many nature/heritage/community themed tourist places does it take before market-saturation occurs in the countryside?" Such a narrowly defined and homogenized set of place-myths therefore calls into question the sustainability of rural areas promoted as visitor attractions.

When integrated with the realization of capital argument, the semiotics approach promises a more thorough understanding of *why* the process of theming occurs, *which* themes are used in particular circumstances, and – perhaps most importantly – *why* various themes and their respective identities can be widely contested at local or regional levels. Granted, the promotion of rural myths in southwestern Ontario is ultimately aimed to benefit the profit margins of business entrepreneurs in rural communities. It is the semiotic approach, however, that focuses more on the cultural content of meanings and identities themselves – identities that are not necessarily used exclusively in the process of commodifying places. This recognition of the need to integrate both economic and cultural rationales to comprehend themed environments is arguably the primary strength of Gottdiener's (1997 and 2001) two-edition set of *The Theming of America*.

Conclusions

I will close this chapter with some personal observations of theming in my hometown of Flagstaff, Arizona (population 57,000), primarily to focus on some general directions for future research. In contrast to the scripted and relatively unified themes found in Leavenworth, New Glarus, and Roswell, the recent transformation of Flagstaff's downtown into a tourism business district has produced a wide variety of local and regional symbols and images connoting an eclectic array of cultural meanings. It is more a confusing jumble of unassociated images than it is a scripted and unified "theme town." Its postmodern quality is materialized through a seemingly unorganized concoction of themes, images, architecture, and symbols pointing to a seemingly unconnected variety of historical periods, social processes, and local identities. For instance, one can find throughout the small urban park of Heritage Square images and relics associated with the railroad industry, geologic strata of the Grand Canyon, recreations of Southwestern Indian pictographs, and a "flag staff" carved from ponderosa pine symbolizing the town's beginnings. Outside of Heritage Square, the theme of sports reveals itself during summer months with banners announcing the arrival of the Arizona Cardinals NFL football team for summer camp, creating an identity with big-city sports entertainment. In addition to the expanding array of statues, artifacts, buildings, banners, and signage reminding one of the railroad and logging industries in Flagstaff, the presence of old US Route 66 provides another important identity for the downtown area.

The downtown's postmodern character is enhanced with a host of environmental themes and images, including that of the San Francisco Peaks, visible to the north of town. In many ways, the variety of mountain-related images found here resembles those found in Kevin Blake's (1999) small towns of the San Juans. Further, various ethnic/cultural, mountain/environment, and, to a lesser extent, Grand Canyon identities are popular with local retailers and restaurants. While the mountain theme was used in 2002 more than any other for business names, other names collectively invoked a wide range of environmental imagery: snow, pine, desert, sage, painted desert, aspen, creek, monsoons, rain, Mogollon, and plateau. Combined with the mountain theme, these distinct environmental identities constituted the bulk of connotative symbols adopted by downtown businesses.

I argue that both cultural and political-economic forces are at work here. Business owners are most likely to associate themselves with the natural environment due to its strong connotations with outdoor recreation, fun, and leisure. Flagstaff's tourism industry is directly related to outdoor activities, reflecting the region's natural amenities, and Flagstaff boosters promote the town as a sort of environmental "paradise" to the Phoenix metropolitan area located 140 miles to the south. Certain businesses are likely promoting the consumption of their products or services by promoting connotative meanings with Flagstaff's natural environment.

What can be viewed downtown, then, are themes and images that perhaps reflect two coexisting values, each materialized somewhat differently in the landscape. On the one hand, the economic-related value of *consumption* commands top priority for local businesses attempting to capitalize on the local tourist trade. What might be overlooked through an economic perspective, however, is an equally dominant cultural-based value of local *heritage*, for which images of the railroad, logging industry, Route 66, and restored historic buildings serve well. Consequently, two dominant modes of theming are exhibited downtown, each reflecting either primarily economic or cultural values. Kevin Robins' (1999) distinction between *heritage culture* and *enterprise culture* in explaining trends of localization and globalization, respectively, is instructive. A similar distinction between *heritage theming* and *enterprise theming* may be useful to understand Flagstaff's divergent trends in theme production. While enterprise themes are those generated predominantly by businesses striving for the realization of capital, heritage themes are those produced for the celebration of some perceived local history, often steeped in nostalgia and rooted in Anglo-American, and male-oriented, perspectives

In this case, Flagstaff's various enterprise and heritage themes revealed distinct contrasts in the material landscape. Scripted themes invented and created by municipal planning and civic groups are focused on local heritage, particularly signifying the nostalgia of the Santa Fe railroad, Route 66, and regional logging traditions. Conversely, locally owned businesses adopted enterprise themes that promoted environmental place-myths related to northern Arizona's diverse natural landscape. This observation gives rise to the question of why local business interests did not adopt the scripted themes of heritage, industry, and transportation. Does this apparent distinction between enterprise and heritage themes exist within other touristed public spaces across the United States, or within other countries and societies? Or is Flagstaff an anomaly? In other places and venues, heritage (localizing) and enterprise (globalizing) themes may converge, as they apparently do within privately controlled spaces such as shopping malls, casinos, and theme parks. One direction for future research consequently involves how theme development coincides with the *global–local nexus*. In what ways does theming in both private and public sectors reflect the influence of globalization, while simultaneously promoting distinct local and regional identities in the face of a homogenizing society?

Further, to what extent are the tourist spaces of Flagstaff and places like it becoming postmodern? Does theming contribute to a place's postmodern character, and if so, in what ways? Regardless of country or region, urban cores or business districts have always consisted of a dizzying array of functions, specialties, images, and identities. Does an eclectic assortment of themes and images therefore necessarily add to the postmodernity of such places? Research that focuses more specifically on the relationships between postmodernism and themed environments might prove immensely beneficial in determining the role that theme development plays in the new postmodern, urban condition. Specifically, for whom are themed environments primarily designed, and how do they influence trends toward social polarization between various socioeconomic groups?

Continuing in this postmodernist vein, what are the various hegemonic implications, regarding those who control the resources to create the "universe of meaning," or the ideologies that various themes are meant to connote? What are the various gender, political, and power relationships regarding theme development, especially with respect to cultural dominance, and the control of heritage production?

The imagery that dominates Flagstaff's downtown landscape, for instance, is certainly controlled and invented predominantly by Anglo-American white males. If one trait of postmodernism is the acceptance and encouragement of "multiple voices and perspectives," then can downtown Flagstaff truly be considered a postmodern landscape? At what point can it be considered as such? I imagine that members of Flagstaff's sizeable American-Indian, African-American, or Hispanic communities may not relate similarly to the various heritage and environmental themes found downtown, simply because they had little if anything to do with the creation and choices of images. In short, whose Flagstaff is being celebrated, and what implications may exist for this apparent "hegemony of theme development"?

Some authors have touched upon these issues, especially as they pertain to the process of globalization and the perceived "Westernization" of world culture, but much research remains to be done, especially in the local realm of community contestation. As acknowledged in the study of semiotics, signs and sign systems are necessarily ambiguous; a theme that may connote "fun" for one person (e.g., Roswell's UFO/alien imagery) may connote sacrilegious and offensive meanings to another. To what extent, therefore, can themes encourage community divisiveness and polarization, or even ethnic tensions? Conversely, how might unified and themed community identities serve to strengthen social and community ties, both in urban neighborhoods and rural places? The process of theming has been shown to pull certain communities together toward self-improvement and economic rebirth, and to instill pride in local heritage through an enhanced sense of place.

Generally speaking, what are the positive and negative implications of theme development, and how are these implications similar or different with respect to contrasting geographical settings: public versus private spaces, shopping malls versus business districts; metropolitan cores versus small-town main streets; Southeast Asia versus Western Europe? As this chapter reveals, scholarly research has predominantly focused on the descriptive and explanatory realms of theme development – that is, describing themes that have materialized in various built environments around the world, and explaining their existence through a combination of cultural, political, and economic perspectives. While more research is warranted within these realms, it may be appropriate to shift the focus to implications rather than explanations. In this way important lessons might be learned and subsequently shared with societies and communities worldwide.

What is clear is that trends of globalization, postmodern urbanism, and tourism development will only increase in intensity. The human race is becoming an increasingly urban one, oriented more to global consumption patterns and with more leisure time and expendable income than ever before. The creation of themed environments of all kinds and scales is therefore likely to continue unabated. We are only at the beginning stages of this trend. What is unclear is how societies, communities, and individuals will react to such environments over time and help to shape the future of these places. Perhaps a more targeted research agenda that focuses directly on the social relationships between themed environments and the people who consume them can assist communities with shaping their futures, even in very modest ways, for the better.

REFERENCES

Banham, R. (1971). *Los Angeles: The Architecture of Four Ecologies*. Berkeley: University of California Press.

Baudrillard, J. (1973). *The Mirror of Production*. St. Louis: Telos.

Blake, K. (1999). Peaks of identity in Colorado's San Juan mountains. *Journal of Cultural Geography* 18(2), 29–55.

Borden, T. (2002). Plan to put McDonald's in Oaxaca Square fought. *The Arizona Republic* (Phoenix, AZ), 24 August.

Boyer, M. (1992). Cities for sale: Merchandising history at South Street seaport. In Michael Sorkin (ed.), *Variations on a Theme Park* (pp. 181–204). New York: Hill & Wang.

Cloke, P. (1993). The countryside as commodity: New rural spaces for leisure. In Sue Glyptis (ed.), *Leisure and the Environment* (pp. 53–67). London: Belhaven Press.

Crawford, M. (1992). The world in a shopping mall. In Michael Sorkin (ed.), *Variations on a Theme Park* (pp. 3–30). New York: Hill & Wang.

Dear, M. (2000). *The Postmodern Urban Condition*. Oxford: Blackwell.

DeLyser, D. (1999). Authenticity on the ground: Engaging the past in a California ghost town. *Annals of the Association of American Geographers* 89(4), 602–32.

Engler, M. (1994). Theme towns: The pitfalls and alternatives of image making. *Small Town*, January–February, 14–23.

Frenkel, S., and Walton, J. (2000). Bavarian Leavenworth and the symbolic economy of a theme town. *The Geographical Review* 90(4), 559–84.

Frieden, B., and Sagalyn, L. (1989). *Downtown Inc.: How America Rebuilds Cities*. Cambridge, MA: MIT Press.

Galston, W., and Baehler, K. (1995). *Rural Development in the United States: Connecting Theory, Practice, and Possibilities*. Washington, DC: Island Press.

Getz, D. (1993). Planning for tourism business districts. *Annals of Tourism Research* 20, 583–600.

Gladstone, D. (1998). Tourism urbanization in the United States. *Urban Affairs Review* 34(1), 3–27.

Goss, J. (1999). Once-upon-a-time in the commodity world: An unofficial guide to Mall of America. *Annals of the Association of American Geographers* 89(1), 45–75.

Gottdiener, M. (1997). *The Theming of America: Dreams, Visions, and Commercial Spaces*. Boulder, CO: Westview Press.

Gottdiener, M. (2001). *The Theming of America: American Dreams, Media Fantasies, and Themed Environments*, 2nd edn. Boulder, CO: Westview Press.

Gottdiener, M., Collins, C., and Dickens, D. (1999). *Las Vegas: The Social Production of an All-American City*. Malden, MA: Blackwell.

Hannigan, J. (1998). *Fantasy City: Pleasure and Profit in the Postmodern Metropolis*. London: Routledge.

Hoelscher, S. (1998). *Heritage on Stage: The Invention of Ethnic Place in America's Little Switzerland*. Madison: University of Wisconsin Press.

Hopkins, J. (1998). Commodifying the countryside: Marketing myths of rurality. In R. Butler, C. Hall, and J. Jenkins (eds), *Tourism and Recreation in Rural Areas* (pp. 193–213). Chichester: John Wiley.

Jackson, J. (1970). Other-directed houses. In Ervin Zube (ed.), *Landscapes: Selected Writings of J. B. Jackson* (pp. 55–72). Amherst: University of Massachusetts Press.

Jakle, J., and Sculle, K. (1994). *The Gas Station in America*. Baltimore: Johns Hopkins University Press.

Lew, A. (1989). Authenticity and sense of place in the tourism development experience of older retail districts. *Journal of Travel Research* Spring, 15–22.
Liebs, C. (1995). *Main Street to Miracle Mile*. Baltimore: Johns Hopkins University Press.
MacCannell, D. (1992). *Empty Meeting Grounds: The Tourist Papers*. London: Routledge.
Mansfield, J. (1999). Consuming spaces. In R. Le Heron, L. Murphy, P. Forer, and M. Goldstone (eds), *Explorations in Human Geography: Encountering Place* (pp. 318–43). Oxford: Oxford University Press.
Mullins, P. (1991). Tourism urbanization. *International Journal of Urban and Regional Research* 15, 326–43.
Page, S., and Hall, C. (2003). *Managing Urban Tourism*. Harlow, UK: Prentice Hall.
Paradis, T. (2002). The political economy of theme development in small urban places: The case of Roswell, New Mexico. *Tourism Geographies* 4(1), 22–43.
Ritzer, G. (1993). *The McDonaldization of America*. Newbury Park, CA: Pine Forge.
Robins, K. (1999). Tradition and translation: National culture in its global context. In David Boswell and Jessica Evans (eds), *Representing the Nation: A Reader* (pp. 15–32). London: Routledge.
Sebeok, T. (ed.) (1986). *Encyclopedic Dictionary of Semiotics*. Berlin: Mouton de Gruyter.
Sorkin, M. (1992). Introduction: Variations on a theme park. In Michael Sorkin (ed.), *Variations on a Theme Park* (pp. xi–xv). New York: Hill & Wang.
Urry, J. (1995). *Consuming Places*. New York: Routledge.

Chapter 17

Whose Tourist-Historic City? Localizing the Global and Globalizing the Local

Gregory J. Ashworth and John E. Tunbridge

The original model of the tourist-historic city (Ashworth and Tunbridge 1990) was conceived largely as an attempt to understand the role of historic city tourism within the urban mosaic of forms and functions and to consider the impacts of the spending and behavior of such tourists upon the cities they visited. It was seen as a contribution to the planning and management of cities, typified by the examples used, such as Norwich, Heidelberg, Colmar, Groningen, Quebec City, and Boston. However, it fairly rapidly became evident that the tourist-historic city model and its many derivatives and potential implications was not an ideologically neutral instrument of urban planning. It was both a reflection of how cities were viewed and a vehicle for creating particular visions of the city. It was not, however, until the idea became broadened out from its original application in western European medium-sized historic cities that it found a political and cultural dimension beyond the original assumptions. Once the idea itself had been globalized (Ashworth and Tunbridge 1990, 2000; Alsayyad 2001), it became increasingly obvious that the contemporary tourist-historic city was a source of major dualities and dichotomies, not unfortunate by-products but centrally inherent in the idea.

It is the purpose of this chapter to examine three pairs of such dualities, all of which focus on the way the valuation and thus conservation and use of the historic built environment have been contested. In particular, the tourist-historic city has played, and continues to play, different roles within the economic and social globalization to which tourism itself is central.

Localism versus Globalism

The case for localism

There is a widely influential assumption that if all places on earth and their inhabitants have a past, and if this past related through history is necessarily unique to a specific place and people, then its transformation into heritage should produce a unique product reflecting and promoting a unique place or group identity. Small wonder that the tourist-historic city has frequently been seen as not merely a local phenomenon but one which could be used as an assertion of localism, the belief in and expression of the unique character of localities.

The development and spread of the idea of the tourist-historic city coincided with and was an integral part of a number of wider contexts. Perhaps the most important of these was place marketing, which largely shared a trajectory of development and local application with the tourist-historic city (Ashworth and Voogd 1990, 1994). Place marketing was seen as a welcome planning instrument by city managers attempting to come to terms with the impacts and opportunities manifest in the increasing consumer demands being made upon cities, not least by heritage tourism. Simultaneously, those exploring the potential of place-marketing techniques saw tourism, and especially heritage tourism, as an opportunity to apply appropriate market management methods and the tourist-historic city as a useful source of examples of place products. This intimate relationship of heritage tourism and place marketing had at least three implications.

The first and most obvious of these was that the growth in heritage tourism led not only to an increase in consumer demands but equally to a sharp increase in the supply of cities attempting to cater for and profit from such demand expansion. Heritage was used to endow places with what the tourism industry called a product's "unique selling point." Secondly, related to this and also an assertion of localism, is a concept drawn from marketing science called "city branding." As in the production of any marketable commodity, there is a need to differentiate clearly your product in the mind of consumers from that of competitors, even if most of the attributes of the product are barely distinguishable from each other. Much of the supply of tourism facilities is, for various reasons of economy of production and customer preference, broadly homogeneous. Heritage, however, could provide the additional product attribute that facilitated a marketable differentiation among cities. Place-specific tourism, where the character of the spatial location of the tourism activity is an inherent aspect of the product, frequently depends upon the presence and recognition of a major heritage component. One noteworthy illustration of using a heritage element to brand a city could be termed the "Gaudi gambit," after the most successful use in Barcelona of the work of the highly distinctive designer/architect. Here the place is inseparably associated with the memorable and idiosyncratic architectural style or design of an individual, or possibly a school of individuals. Examples that currently spring to mind are Macintosh's Glasgow, Sullivan's Chicago, Dudok's Hilversum (Koenders 2001), or even Owen's Southsea (Riley 1972).

Thirdly, the city itself was not just a passive spatial arena where these events took place. It was inhabited, used, and owned by local people. Although much early place promotion was directed at attracting new exogenous investment or new customers, it quickly became apparent that places needed to be "sold" in the first instance to their existing inhabitants and users. A local pride or "civic consciousness" was seen as not only desirable in itself, but also as a precondition for successful external marketing. This became evident at a time when in many countries there was a noticeable decline in the economic power and political authority of the local state, due in part to a trend toward national centralization as well as globalization. This rendered an identification of the local people with localities more necessary. The tourist-historic city was an important vehicle for such self-marketing and also a highly visible symbol of its operation. The local inhabitant was daily confronted with an observable public good evident in the buildings and spaces of the tourist-historic city that at the very least indicated that something was happening, so that the citizen could proudly declare, as did Paul of Tarsus, that he was "a citizen of no mean city" (Acts 21: 39).

National governments have also recognized that heritage may be expressly used to encourage and strengthen an identification of people with localities. The attempt to use local identity as part of a national reaction to internationalism is well exemplified by the Dutch "Belvedere" program launched in 1999 by a joint initiative of four government departments. The national government has found it desirable to act through a major long-term policy to encourage, coordinate, and subsidize consortia of local governments, private organizations, and commercial firms established to promote local identity through the conservation of places. This is not a nationalist reaction; there is no attempt to discover and sacralize a specifically Dutch image of place to support an idea of Dutch nationhood. It is a national attempt to foster localism through land and cityscapes. Some 70 "landscapes," accounting for a third of the national land area, and some 105 towns and cities, have already been designated as possessing "potential local character" that should be recognized, preserved, and propagated though planning actions. The object is clearly stated to be the enhancement of local place identities as a countervailing force to a feared cultural and social homogenization viewed as an unavoidable by-product of globalization. Culture and history are seen as the elements that operate upon places to foster diversity, which in turn is regarded as essential if people are to identify with localities. Some commentators have argued that the programme is fundamentally misconceived because no such single local identity exists; society is now anyway so pluriform that the simple identification of local communities with a specific land or townscape is unlikely (Ashworth and Kuipers 2001, 2002). Nevertheless, the most far-reaching conservation programme in The Netherlands is now underway as a result of a belief by governments that localism can be evoked to mitigate less welcome effects of an inexorable, and accepted, globalization.

The case for globalism

There are thus many arguments that heritage, with the tourist-historic city as its major vehicle, is local and supportive of localism. However, the contrary argument must now be made, namely that heritage development was, and still is, itself an international phenomenon and part of the very globalization which it is now being called upon to counter. "Heritagization" is the process through which heritage is created from the attributes of the past, whether these are relict artifacts, memories, or recorded histories. It is intrinsically a global process and will be reflected in a global tourist-historic city.

Most of the reasons argued above for the adoption of heritage in local policies were part of trends in Western societies and economies that transcended the local. It might be expected therefore that local reactions to a similar perception of similar problems resulted in similar solutions. Thus cities were searching to express their unique individuality for reasons, and using instruments, that were broadly comparable and aimed at comparable goals. The tourist-historic city in particular was created by the cooperative actions of numerous individual and corporate actors in a coalition of interests. Many of these were local but equally many were not, and the argument here is that almost all such actors, regardless of their local connection, had a strong motive for global networking. In addition, tourism is quite obviously a global phenomenon in its demands and facility supply.

The creation of the tourist-historic city, or more modestly its heritage attractions, can be viewed as an economic risk where public or private venture capital is invested in expectation of a return at least as high as alternative possibilities. Unsurprisingly, such investors seek to minimize risk in various ways, notably replication of previous success. Such security-seeking imitative behavior will not be confined to investors but is similarly apparent in project development. This applies to the choice of consumer markets being targeted, the mix of functions to be included, the uses of historicity to add atmosphere, and the balance of new and conserved old forms and structures. Such timidity is not only a feature of the private sector but is also evident among public sector policy-makers. Architects and designers, town planners, and local politicians, all have an interest in minimizing risk, whether financial, professional, or political, through global networking, interaction, and ultimately standardization.

In the tourist-historic city this has frequently resulted in a replication complete to the detailing of materials, signage, and street furniture. This can be caricatured as an "off-the-peg" heritage. This is typified in the cities of western Europe and eastern North America by cobblestones, and "period" litter bins and traffic bollards, while in Mediterranean cities it is potted palms, red pantiles, and light color-washed stucco façades. Such "catalogue heritage" is, however, only a visible indication of a much deeper standardization of practice. The point is merely that there will be an inherent tendency for investors to reuse previously profitable financial structures, developers to imitate previously successful plans, local planners and politicians to approve what has already been approved, and even architects and urban designers to replicate previously lauded forms and designs, albeit at a cost to local identity.

Consider some of the more globally evident types of what can be termed cliché heritage in urban development. The Boston Quincy Market/Faneuil Hall marketplace is now seen as the archetype of festival market/waterfront leisure retailing and commercial redevelopment, coupled with a central heritage conservation component. It has been praised for its impact upon area regeneration and has spawned numerous imitators around the world since its completion in 1976. Specifically, its Baltimore Harborplace derivative, less constrained by existing structures, has become a stereotype of planning practice with notable cases in all six continents (Hoyle, Pinder, and Husain 1988). Subsequent US criticism of it as "Rousification" (after originator James Rouse) prompted some waterfront alternatives but did not end its global diffusion, as 1990s Cape Town and most recently Portsmouth's Gunwharf attest.

There are many other planning and design clichés associated with the tourist-historic city. In all of these, pioneer projects of originality and uniqueness have been globally replicated, for the reasons advanced above, to the point where they no longer express the sense of a locally distinctive identity that was the intention of their creators. Such clichés can be easily identified in urban heritage developments worldwide and are worth listing.

- The use of now redundant quayside buildings and piers for leisure services, often creating a linear waterside recreation strip incorporating historic buildings and associations, commonly with greater or lesser festival marketplace affinities or components (Fisherman's Wharf, San Francisco; Privateers' Wharf in Historic Properties, Halifax; Queen's Quay, Toronto) (Hall 1993).

- The pedestrianized and heritagized shopping street typified by appropriate street furniture, shop-type design and function and often conserved buildings. Known in Britain as the "Laura Ashleyization" of the high street after a well-known chain, among the oldest archetypes are Elm Hill, Norwich, the "Shambles," York, and Bottscherstrasse, Bremen.
- The "plaza mayor" phenomenon, most noticeable in Spanish cities (Ford 1985). It is a combination of architecturally imposing façades, enclosing an open-air dining room with "happening" space. It is not confined to Spanish and Italian cities but has been self-consciously imported into a climatically less sympathetic northern Europe (e.g., Grote Markt, Groningen; "Brink," Tilburg; Marktplatz, Bremen). To this could often be added the "Ramblas," a linear pedestrian boulevard combining some aspects of the park with "happening" space for commercial leisure and entertainment activities.
- The Mediterranean "fishing harbor" with its quayside promenade, lined with fish restaurants, and boats as décor accessory and tourism facility, preferably enhanced by some heritage harbor structure of castle, customs house, mole, or lighthouse. Kyrenia (Girne), North Cyprus is probably the most perfect case, but it is replicated not only around the Mediterranean but also in self-consciously "Mediterranean" Cornwall (Looe/Polperro) and even in Sydney Harbour and South Africa's Cape Peninsula.
- The "artist colony" is the deliberate use of a previous, and often long vanished, association of a place with creative artists. It becomes merged into a general arts and crafts concept used as a saleable product but also a means of shaping a distinctive atmosphere. Perhaps the oldest archetype is Montmartre, Paris, but examples are found as widely as St. Ives, Cornwall, Taos, New Mexico, and numerous small communities across Canada (Bunting and Mitchell 2001). Indeed, the local shaping of this identity acts as a magnet for global attraction of artists exemplified by Chemainus, British Columbia, which has created a tourist identity around its mural paintings, itself now a globally replicated idea.
- The "landmark museum," and public cultural buildings such as opera houses or theatres, have been used to restore local self-confidence and promote a new externally marketable image in cities needing economic or social renewal. They are generally intended to act not only as a catalyst for revitalization of the local areas in which they are set but more widely as a new "signature of the city" as a place of culture, heritage, and creativity. Although the structures themselves are usually new and often designed to be deliberately and shockingly anti-historicist, they are often used as part of heritage districts and as statements of the importance of culture to the place concerned. Bilbao and Groningen exemplify such museums, while the Sydney Opera House may be the best-known urban cultural signature.

This inventory could continue, and further such elements are constantly being added to the repertoire of the heritage planner. However, all that needs to be argued here, somewhat cynically, is that the contemporary tourist-historic city is a pastiche assembled through a selection of one or more of these "off-the-shelf" elements, seasoned with only a minimal addition of local historical or cultural flavor through local events, artifacts, or place associations.

In this discussion of the globalization of heritage, it is worth mentioning the ambivalent role of the world agencies officially charged with the definition, recognition, designation, and protection of global heritage. The agencies of UNESCO (especially the World Heritage Center and its expert advisory groups such as the International Council on Monuments and Sites) seem to make a hesitant and ambiguous contribution to the local/global arguments pursued here. On the one hand their much sought-after WHS designations might seem to encourage the establishment of a set of heritage sites around the world displaying similar characteristics. The trend toward the homogeneous would be favored by the stimulation and transfer of "best practice" and the internationalization of expert knowledge, frequently coupled with UNESCO-approved site management plans. On the other hand UNESCO remains a forum for national representation rather than world governance. This is demonstrated especially clearly in the national conflicts, agreements, and compromises that govern World Heritage Site selection. The sites designated therefore represent those national choices and priorities that have successfully been lobbied for, rather than any international standard (Graham, Ashworth, and Tunbridge 2000).

National versus Vernacular

Related to the global/local dichotomy, but differently expressed and focused, is what can be termed the national/vernacular.

The case for the national

The argument for labeling the tourist-historic city as a national creation and product of the political ideology of nationalism is easy to make but expressed largely in the past tense. The legal structures, institutional agencies, and management and financing systems that allowed the creation of heritage were, and still are in most countries, usually established by national governments and their agencies as an integral part of official national government policies. What was selected for preservation and memorialization, how this was expressed through interpretation, and the propagation of this to specific markets was accepted as a public function of the nation-state. Thus the foundation of heritage as it exists today was powered by the nation-state for the purpose of discovering and delimiting the idea of the nation and legitimating its right to rule. The obvious corollary of this argument is that the tourist-historic city was part of this process of a nationalization of the past and often an especially potent vehicle for the expression of national identity.

Evidence for these assertions can be sought in three arguments. First, and most directly, the dominant role of national governments in heritage-related activities, arts, and indeed in culture in general, can be demonstrated through a description of the regulatory roles of official bodies and agencies, statistics on public finance, and summaries of policy documents and statements (Evans 2001). Other public and private actors are involved, but the multiplicity of points of contact between national governments and heritage is clear.

Secondly, there should therefore be recognizably national schools or styles of tourist-historic city planning and design that suppress or incorporate the local into a national archetype. Reference could be made here to, for example, the self-styled "Polish school" of conservation (Milobedski 1995), or to the Dutch "Vermeer" style (a country-wide replication of seventeenth-century Delft, sometimes derisively called the "Anton Piek effect" after a well-known artist of medieval scenes). Similarly, elements of the local vernacular can be appropriated to serve as national design symbols. For example, Rothenburg ob der Tauber became an iconic expression of German identity, as did Amsterdam "within the 'grachten'" for the Netherlands, despite the reality that in these, and similar cases, the actual design features iconized in this way were regional rather than national.

Thirdly, some national governments have deliberately created a tourist-historic city to serve as a visible symbol of their existence and function. This is likely to be especially evident in the capital cities of settler societies with a perceived need to create a unity from a culturally diverse immigrant population and a postcolonial national identity. In Canada, for example, the transformation of the small lumber settlement of Bytown into the federal capital of Ottawa has been in process for almost 150 years and long pre-dates the establishment of an official body, the National Capital Commission, specifically charged with this task (Taylor 1986). What is especially interesting in this case, as Tunbridge (2002) has narrated, is that the tourist-historic city as national symbol is not static but has evolved in response to changes in the perception of such national identity. However, the province of Quebec competes on a different scale, especially through the creation of Quebec City as symbol of a Québécois national identity (Graham, Ashworth, and Tunbridge 2000). Most symbolic showcase capitals of newly created nations are not yet historic in our sense but, like Ottawa and Washington, will acquire a historic patina (see Taylor, Lengell, and Andrew 1993).

The case for the vernacular

Counter to these arguments for a national dominance, or perhaps in reaction to their strength, is a countervailing tendency in the rise of vernacularism. If "national heritage" is characterized by being official, standardized, and regulated by superior institutional authorities, then "vernacular heritage" is characterized by being unofficial, diverse, and an expression of the local and individual. It is strongly linked to the concept of "folk," i.e. the idea of the "common people," the "ordinary" leading "everyday lives." In architecture, Hubke (1993) contrasted the official architecture built by and for an elite, with "just folks building." To this could be added the idea of "craft," which asserts an opposition not only to industrialized production but also to "art" produced by a self-consciously elitist caste. Craftwork is endowed with moral values, self-evidently superior to those conveyed by modern industrial processes.

As a political and artistic movement, vernacularism parallels the rise of nationalism and national identity and can be viewed as a reaction to it. The economic, social, and political changes that produced the modern industrial world also encouraged a conservative nostalgia for a vanishing or even imagined idealized pre-modern society. This resulted in the explicitly vernacular folk museum movement associated with Hazelius and the first eponymous "Skansen" (1891) or open-air folk museum collection of vernacular buildings, artifacts and, not uncommonly, craftsmen (Oliver

2001). The tourist-historic city also adopted many vernacular elements. It is a short step from the deliberately assembled museum town, such as the archetypal "Gamle By," Aarhus, and its numerous imitators (Àrebro; Szentendre, Budapest; Singelton, Sussex; St. Fagan's, Cardiff; Sturbridge, Massachusetts; Morriston, Ontario, and many more), to the vernacular museumification of existing towns and districts. Sherbrooke, Nova Scotia, is perhaps the intermediate case where part of an existing town is fenced off for visitors and "animated" by period-costumed "real" residents, blurring the distinction between town and museum. More conventionally Lunenburg, Nova Scotia, a World Heritage Site, is more than just an assemblage of mid-nineteenth-century urban morphology: it is explicitly vernacular in the memorialization of the fast-vanishing craft of fishing, its tools, artifacts, and techniques, and especially the everyday lives of the simple but physically and morally robust fisherfolk who conducted it.

National and vernacular may, however, merge. Soane (1994) has argued for the case of Germany that post-war urban rebuilding used international modernist architectural styles. Although this may be largely explained by the practical constraints of the rapid post-war reconstruction of German cities, there remains also a semiotic element. Post-war Germany was rejecting a nationalist past in favor of integration into a global economic and political community. Soane then traces a steadily growing reaction to this international style as part of an emerging national economic and political self-confidence and reassertion of a German national identity. This is expressed through a vernacularization of the built environment, reintroducing stylistic design elements that refer back to a more local, and specifically German, traditional style.

The vernacularization of modernist international architecture may be explained by such a defensive reassertion of national, regional, or local identities. However, equally it may be little more than a fashionable eclecticism reacting to more than 50 years of austere functional modernism in design. The paradox is, of course, as with the tourist-historic city more generally, that such vernacular design elements first introduced to express local difference become widely imitated and diffused, for the same reasons as those outlined above in relation to tourist-historic city development. They thus may become part of a new recognizable global style, composed of imported elements divorced from the localities and societies that originated them.

Residents versus Tourists

It has become conventional wisdom to contrast visitors and residents in terms of their characteristics, behavior, expectations, and vision of the city. If the tourist's "gaze" is not different from that of the resident then why distinguish it? From the definition of the tourist as a voluntary pleasure-seeking non-resident, however, a number of differences can be deduced in time-space budgets, action space, local knowledge and cultural familiarity, and, especially relevant here, attitudes toward heritage and the characteristics of its consumption.

The case for the resident

The resident's tourist-historic city is frequently contrasted to that of the tourist in terms of heritage that is "real," authentic, profound, and meaningful, compared with its tourism antithesis, "artificial," inauthentic, superficial, and devoid of significance. From these distinctions assumptions are made about values and priorities which can, in turn, be used to underlie, implicitly or explicitly, policy toward the management of the tourist-historic city and its users. In short, residents are often accorded primacy over visitors in their claim upon heritage. This is most clearly evident in those tourist-historic cities where the demands of visitors are perceived to be so large as to either threaten the continued existence of the heritage resource itself or to crowd out other, and by implication more worthy, users from the tourist-historic city. These assumptions are usually subtly incorporated into policies dependent upon a concept of an idealized local community and its primacy of interest and even empowerment.

The two cases most often referred to in discussions of this issue, and which fulfill an admonitory function as nightmare scenarios awaiting other tourist-historic cities, are those of Bruges (see, among others, Jansen-Verbeke 1990) and Venice (van der Borg 1998). In both, heritage tourism has grown rapidly, now dominates the local economy, and has become a near mono-functional use of much of the central city. In both cities there has been a reaction that amounts to an atmosphere of permanent crisis, leading to policies aimed at taming what are seen as the voracious demands of the tourist and the reassertion of the place of residents in their own heritage cities. Such polemics conveniently forget that the architectural form of central Bruges, as it exists today, was largely a creation of a "medieval" vision of nineteenth-century visitors and that most of the residents of the lagoon city of Venice have themselves long departed for the mainland, for reasons not directly related to the growth in heritage tourism. Such cities may indeed have particular problems as a consequence of their success and thus require particular management strategies. But such particularity should not be generalized to apply universally to tourist-historic cities, to the model of which Bruges and Venice are exceptional, nor should solutions be sought in an assumed and self-evident prioritization of users of the city.

The case for the tourist

To accord local residents primacy in the claim to the tourist-historic city is to accept a number of assumptions as the basis of heritage management policy. These include the propositions that local residents' heritage has a higher intrinsic aesthetic or historical value than tourist heritage, that local claims upon the past are self-evidently more legitimate, and even that local elites are more acceptable and effective guardians of heritage resources and sites than are national or international ones. The logic of such thinking is that local communities should possess a veto on selection, presentation, access, and even the continued preservation of the heritage. This of course in the worst cases could be "the road to Bamyan" (Ashworth and van der Aa 2002), where the primacy of a local valuation of heritage led to its deliberate destruction. However, more usually it is just that the tourist is reduced to a somewhat grudgingly accepted marginal user. None of these assumptions is easy to justify, nor do they necessarily produce management policies that optimize the uses of the tourist-historic city.

Two counter-arguments can be advanced. First, it can no longer be assumed that visitors are inevitably less knowledgeable about local heritage, or more superficial in their appreciation of it, than are local residents. It can certainly be demonstrated in many instances that a rich and varied local heritage is selected, simplified, and sanitized for rapid and easy tourist consumption, the scenario of our tourist-historic city model and its historic city-led expansion (Ashworth and Tunbridge 2000). Equally, however, it is often the tourists, or the tourism industry, that can be credited with the widening of the tourism product, the "discovery" of more saleable aspects of "local" heritage, and the celebration and promotion of local cultures. Indeed, tourism's need to continually expand its product line in response to its increasingly sophisticated and fickle markets renders this likely. In many parts of the world it has been the visitor and the local identities projected onto visitors that have ultimately been adopted by local residents as their identity. The local identity as projected globally to visitors may in turn become the local self-image, as Arreola (1995) argues has occurred in some Hispanic cities in the United States, and Overton (1980, 1996) argues has happened in the island of Newfoundland as a whole.

Secondly, the sharp dichotomy between tourists and residents may be diminishing. The growing importance of what has been termed "special-interest tourism," which is strongly represented among visitors to the attractions of the tourist-historic city, is in essence only tourists pursuing on holiday activities and interests they also pursue at home. The tourist thus becomes the resident on holiday and the resident just the tourist between trips. The distinctions of knowledge, experience, and behavior, notably of heritage, have become blurred. All that needs to be argued here is that the distinction between the tourist-historic city of the resident and that of the tourist is not immutable but that the two interact over time and even frequently exchange the roles of active initiator and passive reactor.

The Rise of a Concept of Non-Place-Bound Heritage

The response of the tourist-historic city to these sets of contradictory trends is not surprisingly also contradictory and can be summarized as the search for distinctiveness, balance, and universality.

First, competition amongst cities leads to a continuous embellishment, expansion, and differentiation of the heritage product, rapidly consumed by tourists and residents alike. Such a process is ultimately self-defeating, as each city attempts to increase the distinctiveness of its heritage in similar ways among the limited range of possibilities. For example, one of the most popular optional "add-ons" to the tourist-historic city is the ethnic district to the extent that it is now almost obligatory in the North American city to discover and promote a "Chinatown" or "Little Italy," if not yet a "Little Chechnya." The mainly ethnic festival calendar is emerging as a related repetitive "add-on." Even the globally diffusing "Open Doors" initiative may showcase local heritage through ethnic lenses (Nasmith 2002).

Secondly, there has been an evident attempt in many countries to construct a more representative heritage and thus a tourist-historic city that includes a wider selection from the diversifying composition of society. This can be seen as a response to the demands of tourism for more product variety and the requirement that tourists, themselves socially varied, can identify with their own heritage presented abroad. It is also a response to the political and social demands within host societies for a heritage that represents the currently un- or under-represented. The instrumental role of heritage within pluriform societies is a much wider topic than can be tackled here, but suffice it to note that the growing appreciation of such roles has led to the search for a "balanced" tourist-historic city. This may be a chimera, as "balance" is at best changing and at worst undefinable but it cannot be ignored. The case of Singapore is interesting in this respect (see Chang and Huang, chapter 18 this volume).

Finally, not only is the planning of the tourist-historic city becoming more clichéd, but the detailing of the heritage itself is becoming meaningless, to the extent that it conveys no heritage meaning other than a simple idea of antiquity. This is not specifically related to any historical period, artistic style, political message, or locality. It is just instantly recognizable as heritage, a property in itself, rather than a vehicle for conveying any further message. It is not difficult to illustrate the universalization of artifacts and design features. There are numerous magazines and even retailing chains devoted to supplying "period" fixtures, designs, and objects on demand (e.g., *Period House*, Past Times). Consider such indicators of a universal heritage as the Mississippi paddle-boat, most usually turned into a restaurant, generally without an appropriate cuisine, now found on historic waterfronts throughout the world. It conveys no geographical, historical, or ideological associations but merely indicates that this is a heritage waterfront. Similarly, the Victorian cast-iron street lamp, the carriage lamp exterior door light, granite paving setts, even the use of a pseudo-Gothic script on signage, have all become near-ubiquitous non-place-bound codes conveying a generalized historicity, in Western-dominated cities at least.

This is not necessarily to be deplored. Much has been written on the conflicts inherent in heritage messages and the sometimes serious consequences of such conflicts (see Tunbridge and Ashworth 1996). A generic heritage is, at least, relatively free of dissonance and unlikely to provoke social friction. The tourist-historic city, then, becomes a near-universal icon, symbolizing just "old" or "traditional," without reference to any particular age or local tradition. As such it evokes almost universal feelings of continuity, familiarity, well-being, or reliability. The tourist-historic city becomes a stage for the display of a placeless vernacularism. The local becomes globally accessible as all can experience it everywhere, anywhere, through a localism that is now divorced from locality. Similarly, localities can express themselves through universal rather than place- or time-specific symbols. This prospect may be viewed as a deplorable nightmare of sterile uniformity or a highly desirable conflict-free, all-accessible utopia.

The dualities discussed here are, as noted at the outset, three among others which we expect to power the continuing elucidation of the tourist-historic city. Among these, issues of marketing cultural depth versus breadth in socially pluralizing tourist-historic cities, and their intersection with the issues discussed above, are centrally positioned in the future research agenda.

REFERENCES

Alsayyad, N. (ed.) (2001). *Consuming Tradition, Manufacturing Heritage: Global Norms and Urban Forms in the Age of Tourism*. London: Routledge.

Arreola, D. D. (1995). Urban ethnic landscape identity. *Geographical Review* 85(4), 518–34.

Ashworth, G. J. (1996). Jewish culture and Holocaust tourism: The case of Kraków–Kazimierz. In M. Robinson (ed.), *Tourism and Cultural Change* (pp. 1–12). Newcastle: University of Northumbria.

Ashworth, G. J., and Kuipers, M. J. (2001). Conservation and identity: A new vision of pasts and futures in the Netherlands. *European Spatial Research and Policy* 8(2), 55–65.

Ashworth, G. J., and Kuipers, M. J. (2002). Identiteit in een multiculturele samenleving. *Agora* 18(1), 25–8.

Ashworth, G. J., and Tunbridge, J. E. (1990). *The Tourist-Historic City.* London: Belhaven.

Ashworth, G. J., and Tunbridge, J. E. (2000). *The Tourist-Historic City: Retrospect and Prospect of Managing the Heritage City.* London: Elsevier.

Ashworth, G. J., and van der Aa, B. (2002). Bamyan: Whose heritage was it and what should we do about it? *Current Issues in Tourism* 5(5), 447–57.

Ashworth, G. J., and Voogd, H. (1990). *Selling the City: Marketing Approaches in Public Sector Urban Planning.* London: Belhaven.

Ashworth, G. J., and Voogd, H. (1994). What are we doing when we sell places for tourism? *Journal of Consumer Marketing* 6(3/4), 5–19.

Borg, J. van der (1998). Tourism management in Venice, or how to deal with success. In D. Tyler, Y. Guerrier, and M. Robertson (eds), *Managing Tourism in Cities.* London: John Wiley.

Bunting, T. E., and Mitchell, C. J. A. (2001). Artists in rural locales: Market access, landscape appeal and economic exigency. *Canadian Geographer* 45(2), 268–84.

Evans, G. (2001). *Cultural Planning: Towards an Urban Renaissance.* London: Routledge.

Ford, L. R. (1985). Urban morphology and preservation in Spain. *Geographical Review* 75, 265–99.

Graham, B. J., Ashworth, G. J., and Tunbridge, J. E. (2000). *A Geography of Heritage: Power, Culture and Economy.* London: Arnold.

Hall, P. (1993). Waterfronts: A new urban frontier. In R. Bruttomesso (ed.), *Waterfronts: A New Frontier for Cities on Water* (pp. 12–20). Venice: International Centre Cities on Water, Venice.

Hoyle, B. S., Pinder, D., and Husain, M. S. (eds) (1988). *Revitalising the Waterfront: International Dimensions of Dockland Redevelopment.* London: Belhaven.

Hubke, T. C. (1993). Just folks designing: Vernacular designers and the generation of form. In M. Bogdani-Czeptia (ed.), *Heritage Landscape.* Kraków: International Cultural Centre.

Jansen-Verbeke, M. (1990). Toerism in de binnenstad van Brugge: Een planologische visie. *Nijmegse Planologische Cahiers* Ä 35. K.U.Nijmegen.

Koenders, A. (2001). *Hilversum: Architecture en stedebouw 1850–1940.* Zwolle: Waanders Uitgevers.

Milobedski, A. (1995). *The Polish School of Conservation.* Kraków: International Cultural Centre.

Nasmith, C. (2002). Doors open spreads from Europe to Toronto: Catch the bug, start a program in your community. *Heritage* 5(1), 26–8.

Oliver, P. (2001). Re-presenting and representing the vernacular: The open air museum. In N. Alsayyad (ed.), *Consuming Tradition, Manufacturing Heritage: Global Norms and Urban Forms in the Age of Tourism* (pp. 191–210). London: Routledge.

Overton, J. (1980). Promoting the real Newfoundland: Culture as tourist commodity. *Studies in Political Economy* 4, 115–37.

Overton, J. (1996). *Making a World of a Difference: Essays on Tourism, Culture and Development in Newfoundland.* St. John's: Memorial University of Newfoundland.

Riley, R. C. (1972). *The Growth of Southsea as Naval Satellite and Victorian Resort.* Portsmouth Papers 16.

Soane, J. (1994). The renaissance of cultural vernacularism in Germany. In G. J. Ashworth and P. J. Larkham (eds), *Building a New Heritage: Tourism, Culture and Identity in the New Europe* (pp. 159–77). London: Routledge.

Taylor, J. (1986). *Ottawa: An Illustrated History.* Toronto: James Lorimer/Canadian Museum of Civilisation.

Taylor, J., Lengell, J., and Andrew, C. (eds) (1993). *Capital Cities: International Perspectives.* Ottawa: Carleton University Press.

Tunbridge, J. E. (2002). Whose heritage? The shaping of Ottawa as a multicultural tourist-historic city. Paper presented at the international conference on the tourist-historic city, Bruges, March.

Tunbridge, J. E., and Ashworth, G. J. (1996). *Dissonant Heritage: The Management of the Past as a Resource in Conflict.* Chichester: Wiley.

Chapter 18

Urban Tourism: Between the Global and the Local

T. C. Chang and Shirlena Huang

Introduction

The city is home to at least two apparently contradictory geographic scales. The city may be regarded on a global plane, as a connecting node that links a locality to the world at large through networks of capital, people, and commodity and information flows. The city may also be regarded at a local level, as a home for millions and a locale for the meaningful transactions of social, political, and economic lives. Like the city, tourism is simultaneously global and local. Tourism is global as its very nature entails the crossing of borders, often at a transnational scale, by millions of people and billions of dollars. Yet tourism is inherently local since tourists are lured by distinctive cultures and sceneries, and tourism development is often an exercise in accentuating the local uniqueness of a destination site.

This coincidence of tourism and the city with the geographic scales of the "global" and "local" constitutes the thrust of this chapter. Specifically, we review relevant urban tourism research from a global-local perspective, with three goals in mind. First, to establish thematic links between what may appear to be disparate studies on urban tourism; second, to chart a sense of direction for comparative research; and third, to link the largely empirical research to critical discourses in geographic thought on urban change and tourism development. The chapter is divided in three sections: (1) identifying the need for an integrative framework in urban tourism research and proposing a global-local perspective as a possible tool that allows for multi-scale research; (2) a review of the relevant literature, interpreting it through a global-local lens; and (3) a case study of Singapore, demonstrating the value of a multi-scale perspective to empirical work.

Urban Tourism Research: The Search for a Focus

The increase in urban tourism research particularly since the late 1980s is tied to two real-world phenomena: escalating demands by tourists for urban historic sights and heritage cities, and concerted efforts of policy-makers to focus on the role of tourism in revitalizing urban areas and economies (Pearce 2001). The growing literature, however, belies the dearth of a distinctive structure or conceptual focus on what some regard as the "emerging field" of urban tourism. Beyond questioning the existence and definition of "urban tourism" and what it encompasses (cf. Ashworth 1992; Page 1995), recent work has highlighted the lack of a "coherent corpus of work, pursuing common goals and carrying out comparable studies" (Pearce 2001: 928), a result of poor synthesis of urban tourism materials within theories of development, location, and spatial transformation (Hughes 1997). Hence, while many conceptual and thematic clusters exist within the literature, they are researched and discussed in isolation from one another.

Despite attempts to classify the various existing approaches in urban tourism research, most studies of urban tourism have tended to be descriptive and "individualistic in their choice of subject matter, research design and areas of application" (Ashworth 1989: 50). This has further contributed to the lassitude in developing overarching "paradigms of urban tourism" (Hughes 1997: 180). For example, more than a decade ago Ashworth (1989) identified four broad categories of research in urban tourism: "facility approaches" concerned with locational analyses of tourism facilities; "ecological approaches" focusing on urban morphological models; "user approaches" examining the profile, impacts, and perceptions of visitors; and "policy approaches" looking at urban management policies and marketing efforts. To date, little has been done to synthesize these approaches, regardless of intensified calls throughout the 1990s for a more integrative approach. This lack of integration parallels wider concerns in the geography of tourism, often criticized as having its own narrow concerns and "unique problems" (de Kadt 1979, cited in Shaw and Williams 1994: 16).

Thus Britton (1991: 466) has called for a "critical geography of tourism" that more directly engages in ongoing discussions of socio-spatial transformations wrought by global capitalist shifts as a means of rescuing tourism geography from its theoretical isolation. This call applies equally to the field of urban tourism. Indeed, we would argue that urban tourism provides the ideal ground for developing paradigms that engage with broader theories because it is in cities that global capitalism, economic restructuring, and social change coalesce. And as Ashworth (1989: 35) has noted, it is "the very integration of tourism activities in the city, in both a functional and morphological sense" that makes it particularly suited to synthetic (rather than systematic) approaches.

Pearce's (2001) proposal of an integrative framework for urban tourism research (figure 18.1) goes some way to meeting the challenge meted out by Britton. Pearce proposes a matrix comprising two axes: *urban themes* and *spatial scales*. Linkages across themes and scales suggest possibilities of research areas crossing different domains simultaneously on the one hand, while being easily pigeonholed into discrete matrices on the other. This enables existing works to be systematically placed within a broader context to allow for comparisons, identification of literature gaps, and even collaboration at the planning level. More specifically, Pearce identifies two directions for research in urban tourism that contribute to a more "critical geography." The first calls for a multi-scale examination of urban themes. Urban "marketing," for example, can be analyzed on many scales simultaneously: at the city level (how the city is represented in publicity campaigns) and at a district or site

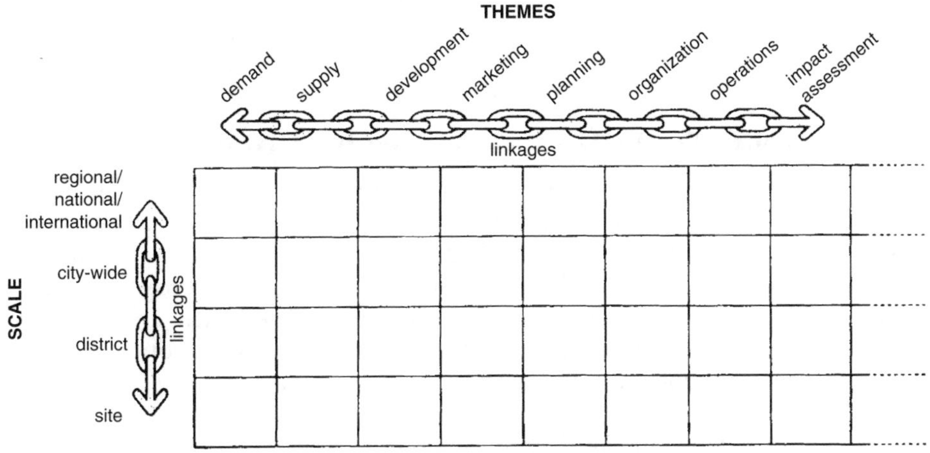

Figure 18.1 Pearce's integrative framework for urban tourism research
Source: Pearce 2001: 929.

level (how specific areas within cities are highlighted or downplayed as attractions). Local-level research can be complemented by insights from wider processes such as regional competition between cities (regional level), nation-building goals (national level), and global trends and events (international level). A multi-scale analysis allows for a comprehensive perspective on the forces driving cities, and encourages us to consider the connections and contradictions between scales. A second dimension focuses on the linkages and causal influences between scales, which can be done by linking the micro with the macro. While existing work has employed theories and concepts such as "inter-organizational analysis," the "globalization-localization nexus," and "tourism gateways and hubs," more effort is needed to understand how micro-level events (i.e. occurring within a city) are influenced by, and in turn influence, macro-level processes (i.e. occurring beyond the city).

In this chapter we argue that the globalization-localization relationship is a useful integrative tool for tourism geographers to contribute knowledge beyond narrow urban confines while engaging in theorizations on globalization-localization. The globalization-localization relationship has long been debated in geographic research. It is generally accepted that the "global" often implicates the "local" and vice versa, and that the two scales are relational rather than oppositional. Increasing global flows of capital, people, and information reflect "a deepening enmeshment of the local and global such that the impact of distant events is magnified while even the most local developments may come to have enormous global consequences" (Held et al. 1999: 15). By investigating specific case sites within larger geographic, economic, and political canvases, the city is presented as a meeting point for global/regional processes and local-site forces. As one of the authors' own works has shown, contextualizing tourism in individual cities within the framework of broader forces will become progressively more vital as globalization transforms the meanings of borders and creates increased competition among cities (see Chang 1999; see also Chang et al. 1996). In the next section, using Pearce's framework as a broad guide, we adopt a scalar perspective (global-local) to review pertinent literature on urban tourism to demonstrate its usefulness in better understanding the urban tourism phenomenon, and contributing to a critical geography of tourism.

A "Global-Local" Perspective on Urban Tourism Literature

Our review is structured according to three select and intertwined themes focused on the intersections of the "global" with the "local": (1) the impacts of global tourist trends on local urban landscape; (2) how cities, as the meeting ground of global and local forces, are more generally shaped by the interaction of these forces; and (3) the "selling" of local uniqueness in a global tourist market. These three areas not only afford insights into the workings of globalism–localism, they constitute the main literature where the global-local nexus has been addressed.

Global tourism demand and local urban impacts

A popular area of research relates to global demand for urban attractions and the redevelopment strategies by cities to cater to these demands. Radical transformations in the global economy, demography, society, and culture since the early 1970s have given rise to postmodernism, post-Fordist economic practices, and a post-industrial society. Such wide-ranging changes have translated into changing trends in travel, with the emergence of a "new tourism" (Poon 1989, 1990; Mowforth and Munt 1998) and "post-tourists" (Urry 1990, 1995). An important tenet here is the focus on touristic "differentiation" and increasing segmentation of the tourism market, with emphasis given to visitor fulfillment and self-enlightenment.

Perhaps the most persuasive work focusing on changing global trends in tourist demand and their effects on and implications for cities is Urry's (1990, 1995) notion of the "tourist gaze." Urry argues that touristic consumption (demand) is interpreted not only in the form of actual purchases (of hotel rooms, souvenir goods, and the like), but also in the form of visual consumption, that is, to look upon a place, product, or object. The "gaze" is a socially constructed exercise that is influenced by media, marketers, and other mediators. Local "places" are instrumental in visual consumption: "Places are chosen to be gazed upon because there is an anticipation, especially through day-dreaming and fantasy... The gaze is directed to features of landscape and townscape which separate them off from everyday and routine experiences" (Urry 1995: 132).

Cities capitalize on the tourist gaze in revamping themselves as destination sites. Urry substantiates this argument with a case of industrial Lancashire and the city of Lancaster, the sites of England's first industrial revolution and the birth of the mass holiday resort. Then changing market preferences led to a fall in the popularity of seaside resorts, Lancashire was given a new lease of life in terms of the region's industrial past. Other cities throughout the 1980s also began reconstructing their economies and landscapes to create their own "heritage industry" (Hewison 1987; De Bres 1994); the working past has taken on a nostalgic patina of the exotic, and industrial cities have been revalorized, at least in the eyes of the post-tourist, as quaint sites of leisure and heritage experiences. The re-emergence of the city as a tourist lure, including ostensibly "unattractive" and "problematic" sites – industrial cities, ghost towns, and inaccessible villages – is thus explained as part of the sea-change in consumer demand at a global level (Buckley and Witt 1985, 1989; Cameron 1991). Ironically, as Thorns (1997) points out, although they impact the way local landscapes and economies are redeveloped, visitors on the tourist circuit rarely have time or opportunity to directly engage with the local, unfiltered by the commentary of their tour guide. As such, how much of the "local" tourists actually bring home with them, and how the "local" impacts the "global," are questions worthy of further scrutiny.

Other authors, while not explicitly addressing the global-local nexus, extend the theme of changing global demands and local urban effects. Page (1995) details general trends in touristic demand, and notes an escalating propensity for special interests such as pilgrimage tourism and arts tourism. The implications for cities are tremendous, leading to, in the case of arts tourism, the gentrification of urban quarters as cultural and arts districts in places like Manchester and Glasgow. Ashworth and Tunbridge's (1990) work on the "tourist historic city" also highlights recognition of "new" urban forms emerging from, *inter alia*, growing consumer interest in heritage, arts, museum visits, nostalgia, and lifestyle. Whereas in the past the historic city and the tourist district were separate (because business visitors and leisure seekers tend to have distinct interests), increasingly the overlapping of space and urban function reflects changing motivations and mindsets of consumers. As Ashworth and Tunbridge maintain, the contemporary tourist is "multi-motivated" and tourist cities are becoming in turn "multi-functional" and "multi-dimensional."

It is important, however, for more work in urban tourism to go beyond simply examining the critical role that wider global forces have in the development of local urban forms, but also to explicitly question how local urban landscapes and processes help to shape global tourist trends. This would not only acknowledge the important role that local urban resources play in mediating the growing global tourism industry, but also add to a better understanding of global-local interactions and their impacts at various geographical scales.

The city as a meeting ground for the global and the local

A second and closely related research area focuses on the city as a meeting ground for the interaction of global processes and local forces, and the variety of urban outcomes – ranging from the loss of local distinctiveness and identity as places become alike, to a (re)assertion of local difference – that this interaction is argued to produce.

One popular school of thought argues for a global convergence of tourism cities. Mullins (1990, 1991), for example, conceptualizes "tourism urbanization" as a process of dominant economic processes shaping cities toward a common end. In such "postmodern tourist cities," characteristics include the predominance of a service economy, a rise in consumption and a consumer class, intensification of inter-city competition based on "image," and local authorities taking on a boosterist or entrepreneurial role. Mullins's thesis is applied to various Australian cities, and he contends that local differences tend to give way to a singular model of global urban tourism.

The literature is rich with other empirical cases exemplifying urban tourism's homogenizing fiat. The urban geography literature on "theme cities" in America (Sorkin 1992; Gottdiener 1997), festive urban waterfronts (Goss 1996), and public entertainment spaces (Cybriwsky 1999) substantiates this viewpoint. In the planning of urban festive landscapes, for example, what has come to be known as the "Rousification" and "Faneuilization" of spaces (after James Rouse, whose redevelopment projects in Boston, including Faneuil Hall, and Baltimore in the 1970s are said to have inspired the retail-entertainment renaissance in American downtowns and waterfronts; Hannigan 1998: 117), also underlines the pervasive role of transnational property companies in shaping urban landscapes for a leisure class. For example, Hannigan (1998: 72) highlights a discernible drift in the development of cities toward fantasy themes, spectacles, theme parks, and entertainment zones; the planning philosophy is to provide "safe, reassuring and predictable" environments where the requirements of quotidian living are replaced by the spectacle of the tourist class.

As counterpoint to the homogeneity thesis, others have argued for the mediating role of local factors. Chang et al.'s (1996) analysis of Montreal and Singapore, for example, argues that global and local forces are equally important in shaping places. Thus, cities may look and operate like each other (because of globalization's homogenizing tendencies), but they are also unique and distinctive (because of site-specific influences). On the one hand, homogeneity results from "urban heritage tourism" being adopted as a means of rejuvenating Montreal's and Singapore's inner cities and their economies, with downtown heritage quarters such as festive waterfronts and ethnic districts being developed to cater to tourists and lifestyle services. On the other hand, "geography also matters," as exemplified by the cities' different historical trajectories and heritages, be it Montreal's industrial experience or Singapore's colonial and multicultural heritage. The public–private sector involvement in urban planning and heritage conservation is also different, reflecting variation in urban governance. Local communities' reactions to urban enhancement also vary widely, resulting in different social impacts.

Comparative analyses of cities also show the insistence on the local in the face of globalization. Craig-Smith and Fagence's (1995) edited volume reveals that, while the "best practice" of urban waterfronts has been adopted by cities around the world, failures are inevitable. The specific agenda for waterfront enhancement, the architectural heritage in cities, landscape themes adopted by planners and approved by local constituents, the political and fiscal climate under which development takes place all mean that global prototypes take on a local complexion, resulting in the "unique attributes" and "distinctive ambience" of cities (Craig-Smith and Fagence 1995: 145). In a study of eight European sites, van der Borg and van der Meer (1995) similarly conclude that, although cities may converge in their philosophy on culture and heritage planning, universal success is never guaranteed. The domestic/international visitor mix, the urban "image," the imprint of historical legacies, and investment in "new" attractions such as theme parks and monumental museums pull cities apart rather than together in their competitive bid to be regional hubs (see Ashworth and Larkham 1994).

In recognizing that the meanings and identities of places are often the negotiated results of the local with larger-scale forces (and vice versa), work in urban tourism can contribute to keeping geographers' attention on the fact that, despite the apparently all-encompassing forces of globalization (often analogous to Westernization), geographical difference is not only expressed, but "also matters," at all levels from the city to the national and the global, and everywhere in between. Such an emphasis is necessary to dismantle prevalent systems of investigating tourist cities through neocolonial lenses (or Eurocentric frameworks of analysis), and the assumption that Western policies and practices are best for the development of the city as a tourist site.

Marketing and management: selling local uniqueness in a global village

The manner in which tourist cities are marketed and managed yields a third example of employing the global-local nexus as an analytical framework. Urban tourism marketing refers to the promotional and imaging strategies by cities to project an attractive image to visitors and tourism investments, while urban tourism management is a process of planning and controlling tourism development to meet the needs of visitors and residents (Murphy 1997). The marketing and management of tourist cities is an exercise in balancing the global with the local, complementing images of local allure with global appeal on the one hand, while striking a balance between the needs of residential constituents and external interests on the other. This balancing act has been more successful in some cities than others.

Cities are often marketed as a blend of cosmopolitan connections and local charm. As tourism gateways, urban centers are necessarily worldly as they are the staging point for international visitors arriving at and sojourning in a country. At the same time, these cities are also portrayed as beguilingly homely and distinctive enough to attract visitors. These global-local connectivities (and conflicts) are often the focus of academic discourse. In a study of Christchurch, New Zealand, for example, Schollmann, Perkins, and Moore (2000) interpret global marketing influences as reaching across space and time. Christchurch is marketed in tourism brochures and campaigns as a city with intimate connections to its British colonial past. As a "garden city," Christchurch caters to visitors seeking a slice of the colonial British charm while also broadening its appeal as a historic city. To maintain a more contemporary global edge, the city also promotes itself as a trendy place with cafés, pubs, nightlife, and lifestyle outlets, and a home to cosmopolitan youth cultures. On the local front, Christchurch highlights its attributes as a gateway to New Zealand's South Island, an adventure capital, and its proximity to the country's diverse rural and pastoral attractions. These global/local images – colonial, lifestyle, sports, and ecological – are clearly at odds with one another but explain the city's multifaceted appeal (see also Thorns' (1997) paper on Auckland, Wellington, and Christchurch).

Global and local agendas also influence the marketing of tourist cities. Nijman's (1999) account of Amsterdam, Cartier's (2001) case of Melaka, Waitt's (1999) paper on Sydney, and Chang's (1997) analysis of Singapore all reveal how urban destinations benefit from processes of global imaging and local identity-formation. However, we must also be cognizant that global images need not always be in tune with local realities of place. For example, while Sydney was marketed to the world through the 2000 Olympics, cultural, ecological, and political tensions in the city contradicted many marketing claims; thus, while the Olympic spectacle provides a vehicle through which the city is imaged favorably at a global level, it also contradicts, defuses, and renders invisible the local realities of postcolonial racism and environmental degradation (Waitt 1999). The case of Singapore presents a slightly different global-local scenario. Singapore's image as "Instant Asia" in the 1960s and

1970s was prompted by global/economic needs (to market Singapore to the global market as exotic) and local/political agendas (the multicultural image was aimed at national identity and nation-building in this multiracial state). Thus, unlike Sydney, a single place theme is conveyed through tourism marketing; this image, however, is directed at multiple markets (tourists and residents) for different purposes (economic and sociopolitical). The global-local nexus in both cases shows that tourism marketing is never simply a case of selling a city; local agendas are also often fulfilled in implicit and ideological ways.

Because of this and the fact that tourism cities are simultaneously places of work, residence, and leisure, an important aspect of tourism management is the ability to juggle competing demands (such as global versus local needs and interests) and come up with reconciliatory policies that will help create a "saleable tourism product" and an "environment for living and working" (Burtenshaw, Bateman, and Ashworth 1991: 218; see also Murphy 1997: 3). To ensure that urban attractions cater to foreign visitors and local people alike, questions of resource sustainability, conflict resolution, and management of tourist–local tensions are important considerations. For example, Tyler, Guerrier, and Robinson (1998: 234) show that the most common problem in tourist cities is competition for and "ownership of spaces" by tourists and locals, new and old residents, foreign and domestic visitors. Whether the "local" or the "tourist" is prioritized, and the extent to which the public is involved in localized planning, depends on the contributions of tourism to the urban economy (Akehurst 1998; Hall 1998).

Urban management is a highly political exercise where the imperatives of global economics and the demands of local cultural politics often collide, and "success" is not a given if the management of internal/local issues is not appropriately addressed. Ultimately, such research on tourist cities is particularly instructive in illuminating that what constitute "global" or "local" management issues – and hence, what constitutes the "global" and the "local" – can be interpreted in different ways. Are global forces necessarily "external" mega-events (the Olympics for example), international arts and cultural festivals, and world-scale organizations (like UNESCO)? And does the "local" necessarily refer to "internal" factors such as grassroots agencies, the rights of indigenous people, and the politics of community heritage (Murphy 1997)? Indeed, the "global" and "local" are relative terms, and "neither can exist without the other" (Schollmann, Perkins, and Moore 2000: 73).

Singapore: Global City, Local Landscapes

We conclude our chapter by examining how a scalar perspective may be profitably deployed to analyze tourism development in the city-state of Singapore. In its bid to make Singapore a world-class destination, the Singapore government has often looked to "global" success stories to provide a way for the local tourist industry to revamp itself. For example, recommendations of the Tourism Task Force (formed in 1984 to devise ways to attract more tourists to Singapore) included the redevelopment of the Singapore River "along the lines of the 'Latin Quarter' on the left bank of River Seine in Paris" (MTI 1984: 28); the Christmas light-up in Orchard Road modeled after the "gaily-decorated Regent/Oxford Street in London" (1984: 31);

and the introduction of a festival of the arts on the scale of the Hong Kong Arts Festival and the Edinburgh Festival. Global models do, at times, take on local variations. The success of the Orchard Road Christmas light-up, for example, has spawned similar celebrations for all major ethnic festivals in Singapore's historic districts of Chinatown, Little India, and Arab Street. Since the 1990s, the quest for global recognition – with implications for local society and space – has remained unabated through Singapore's "tourism capital" goal. The Singapore Tourism Board (STB) envisions the tourism product to be revamped in line with Singapore's tourism hub status. Towards this end, eleven "place-themes" have been suggested, including enhancing the ethnic historic districts, creating new night spots along the Singapore River, and repositioning suburban residential areas as tourist attractions. Such a massive reconfiguration of local places for global tourism is not without problems. Much has been written about the vociferous tensions generated by tourism. For example, how local residents are displaced and marginalized by developments that essentially target tourists (Teo and Huang 1996), or how local places are becoming theme parks and losing their traditional activities (Yeoh and Lau 1995; Chang 2000). Such academic insights are regularly buttressed by public forums and letters to the press where grassroots objections to the STB's plans are aggressively aired. Expressed in global-local terms, a fundamental disjuncture between the government's vision of global-city development and local receptivity appears to be emerging.

The global-local nexus, however, need not always be a case of development models imposed unwillingly upon the local community. Tourism development can also be "bottom-up" as local initiatives are devised as part of grassroots attempts at remaking Singapore. Our own research on the Singapore River – the birthplace of modern Singapore where early immigrants first worked and resided, and today a popular heritage and culinary site where major hotels, and cultural and dining amenities may be found – exemplifies this.

On the one hand, the Singapore River has been planned with global models in mind – the Urban Redevelopment Authority (URA) has Paris's Seine and San Antonio's Paseo del Río as prototypes in its draft development plan. On the other hand the river has also been proudly proclaimed a "model river" that other cities can emulate in their waterfront development. According to URA officials, visiting teams of planners from other countries are usually brought to the river to showcase how urban planning in Singapore has "paid off" (Fun 2002). The river is also often lauded as a Singapore success story for reconciling many of the contradictions of contemporary urban life: the blending of urban development with a clean/green environment, and the juxtaposition of historic buildings alongside modern infrastructure and facilities.

The STB is currently in the process of developing the Singapore River Interpretative Center, emulating an idea popularized by waterfronts at San Francisco and Boston where museums of historical tableaux and artifacts are displayed. However, in a novel twist to this concept, the STB has proposed an open-air interpretative center comprising a network of sculptures depicting various aspects of local life sited along the riverbanks. The sculptures depict people who lived and worked along the river, such as the *samsui* women (female construction workers), river boatmen, children who used to swim in the river, and others. Feedback from interviews and public forums with Singaporeans provided the basis upon which these "river people" were identified. Prominent Singaporean sculptors have also been commissioned to produce the works, and the first was installed in 2001. This project is a clear departure from earlier schemes, where sculptures were individually commissioned by private enterprises, and depicted abstract modernist themes by international artists such as Fernando Botero, Salvador Dali, and Henry Moore. By ensuring that local historic personalities and sculptors are represented at the river, it is hoped that a world-class waterfront might develop with a distinctive Singaporean identity.

Conclusion

By focusing a global-local lens on three specific themes in urban tourism, we have demonstrated that such a perspective permits richer empirical analyses and theoretical contributions by allowing for comparative research on urban change and tourism development. More specifically, we argued that this could happen in three ways. First, adopting a global-local analytical framework for urban tourism research enables a more critical geographical investigation because it focuses investigations not exclusively on either the local or the global, but on multiple scales of analysis. Such a perspective helps correct the misconception that interaction between the local and the global is a one-way process, directing our focus on how the local might also possibly impact the global. Second, by showing that geographical difference at all scales matters, urban tourist research can contribute alternatives to Eurocentric frameworks of analysis and ideologies more suitable for site-specific situations. Finally, a global-local perspective will contribute to discussions of what constitutes the "global" and the "local." For our discussion, we adopted a simple division of the global as "beyond the nation" relative to the local as specific to an urban area. We acknowledge, however, that the terms "global" and "local" are not unproblematic (although often used unproblematically). For example, are forces arising from within an urban area necessarily "local"? At what point beyond the city limits do we see the "local" as ending, and the "regional" or the "global" beginning? At the other extreme, we need to ask what constitutes the "global" – forces that originate from beyond national borders? If so, would it not mean, then, that the idea of "local" should refer to forces from within the nation? How does this gel with the idea of "local" as a more confined arena, especially in large countries with large urban systems? What of scales in between? And how about city-states where the city and nation are essentially one?

In contributing answers to questions like these which emphasize the relativity of urban development and management with wider social-spatial processes, investigations of tourism in/of urban areas from a multi-scalar perspective can play a more critical role in geography. In this way, urban tourism research can begin to challenge, dismantle, and transform existing geographical concepts and approaches, as well as play a role in social and political change. Ultimately, we argue that thinking about geographical differences from the local to the global scale will be a vital key in bringing down the current boundaries that isolate work in (urban) tourism from wider academic research.

REFERENCES

Akehurst, G. (1998). Community-oriented tourism strategy development: Kalisz, Poland. In D. Tyler, Y. Guerrier and M. Robertson (eds), *Managing Tourism in Cities: Policy, Process and Practice* (pp. 25–44). New York: Wiley.

Ashworth, G. J. (1989). Urban tourism: An imbalance in attention. In C. Cooper (ed.), *Progress in Tourism, Recreation and Hospitality Management* (vol. 1, pp. 33–54). London: Belhaven Press.

Ashworth, G. J., and Larkham, P. J. (eds) (1994). *Building a New Heritage: Tourism, Culture and Identity in the New Europe*. London and New York: Routledge.

Ashworth, G. J., and Tunbridge, J. E. (1990). *The Tourist Historic City*. London and New York: Belhaven Press.

Britton, S. (1991). Tourism, capital, and place: Towards a critical geography of tourism. *Environment and Planning D: Society and Space*. 9(4), 451–78.

Buckley, P., and Witt, S. (1985). Tourism in difficult areas: Case studies of Bradford, Bristol, Glasgow and Hamm. *Tourism Management* 6(3), 205–13.

Buckley, P., and Witt, S. (1989). Tourism in difficult areas II: Case studies of Calderdale, Leeds, Manchester and Scunthorpe. *Tourism Management* 10(2), 138–52.

Burtenshaw, D., Bateman, M., and Ashworth, G. J. (eds) (1991). *The European City: A Western Perspective*. London: David Fulton.

Cameron, C. (1991). Cultural tourism and urban revitalisation. In T. Singh, V. Smith, M. Fish, and L. Richter (eds), *Tourism Environment: Nature, Culture, Economy* (pp. 161–71). New Delhi: Inter-Indian Publications.

Cartier, C. (2001). Imaging Melaka's global heritage. In P. Teo, T. C. Chang, and K. C. Ho (eds), *Interconnected Worlds: Tourism in Southeast Asia* (pp. 193–212). Oxford: Elsevier Science.

Chang, T. C. (1997). From "instant Asia" to "multi-faceted jewel": Urban imaging strategy and tourism development in Singapore. *Urban Geography* 18, 542–62.

Chang, T. C. (1999). Local uniqueness in a global village: Heritage tourism in Singapore. *The Professional Geographer* 51, 91–103.

Chang, T. C. (2000). Theming cities, taming places: Insights from Singapore. *Geografiska Annaler* 82B(1), 35–54.

Chang, T. C., Milne, S., Fallon, D., and Pohlmann, C. (1996). Urban heritage tourism: The global–local nexus, *Annals of Tourism Research* 23, 284–305.

Craig-Smith, S., and Fagence, M. (eds) (1995). *Recreation and Tourism as a Catalyst for Urban Waterfront Redevelopment: An International Survey*. Westport: Praeger.

Cybriwsky, R. (1999). Changing patterns of urban public space: Observations and assessments from the Tokyo and New York metropolitan areas. *Cities* 16(4), 223–31.

De Bres, K. (1994). Cowtowns or cathedral precincts? Two models for contemporary urban tourism. *Area* 26(1), 57–67.

Fun, Siew Leng (2002). Deputy Director of Urban Design and Development, Conservation and Urban Design Division, Urban Redevelopment Authority (URA), Singapore, personal communication, 5 June.

Goss, J. (1996). Disquiet on the waterfront: Reflections of nostalgia and utopia in the urban archetypes of festival marketplaces. *Urban Geography* 17, 221–47.

Gottdiener, M. (1997). *The Theming of America: Dreams, Visions, and Commercial Spaces*. Boulder, CO: Westview Press.

Hall, C. M. (1998). The politics of decision making and top-down planning: Darling Harbour, Sydney. In D. Tyler, Y. Guerrier, and M. Robertson (eds), *Managing Tourism in Cities: Policy, Process and Practice* (pp. 9–24). New York: Wiley.

Hannigan, J. (1998). *Fantasy City: Pleasure and Profit in the Postmodern Metropolis.* London and New York: Routledge.

Held, D., McGrew, A., Goldblatt, D., and Perraton, J. (1999). *Global Transformations: Politics, Economics and Culture.* Cambridge: Polity.

Hewison, R. (1987). *The Heritage Industry: Britain in a Climate of Decline.* London: Methuen.

Hughes, H. (1997). Review of C. Law (ed.), *Tourism in Major Cities. Journal of Vacation Marketing* 3(2), 180.

Mowforth, M., and Munt, I. (1998). *Tourism and Sustainability: New Tourism in the Third World.* London and New York: Routledge.

MTI (1984). *Report of the Tourism Task Force.* Singapore: Ministry of Trade and Industry.

Mullins, P. (1990). Tourist cities as new cities: Australia's Gold Coast and Sunshine Coast. *Australian Planner* 28(3), 37–41.

Mullins, P. (1991). Tourism urbanisation. *International Journal of Urban and Regional Research* 15, 326–42.

Murphy, P. (ed.) (1997). *Quality Management in Urban Tourism.* Chichester: John Wiley.

Nijman, J. (1999). Cultural globalization and the identity of place: The reconstruction of Amsterdam. *Ecumene* 6(2), 146–64.

Page, S. (1995). *Urban Tourism.* London: Routledge.

Pearce, D. (2001). An integrative framework for urban tourism research. *Annals of Tourism Research* 28(4), 926–46.

Poon, A. (1989). Competitive strategies for a "new tourism." In C. P. Cooper (ed.), *Progress in Tourism, Recreation and Hospitality Management* (vol. 1, pp. 91–102). London: Belhaven Press.

Poon, A. (1990). Flexible specialization and small size: The case of Caribbean tourism. *World Development* 18(1), 109–23.

Schollmann, A., Perkins, H., and Moore, K. (2000). Intersecting global and local influences in urban place promotion: The case of Christchurch, New Zealand. *Environment and Planning A* 32, 55–76.

Shaw, B., and Williams, S. (1994). *Critical Issues in Tourism: A Geographic Perspective.* Oxford: Blackwell.

Sorkin, M. (ed.) (1992). *Variations on a Theme Park.* New York: Noonday Press.

Teo, P., and Huang, S. (1996). Tourism and heritage conservation in Singapore. *Annals of Tourism Research* 22(3), 589–615.

Thorns, D. C. (1997). The global meets the local: Tourism and the representation of the New Zealand city. *Urban Affairs Review* 33(2), 189–208.

Tyler, D., Guerrier, Y., and Robertson, M. (eds) (1998). *Managing Tourism in Cities: Policy, Process and Practice.* New York: John Wiley.

Urry, J. (1990). *The Tourist Gaze: Leisure and Travel in Contemporary Societies.* London: Sage Publications.

Urry, J. (1995). *Consuming Places.* London: Routledge.

van der Borg, J., and van der Meer, J. (1995). *Urban Tourism: Performance and Strategies in Eight European Cities.* Brookfield: Ashgate.

Waitt, G. (1999). Playing games with Sydney: Marketing Sydney for the 2000 Olympics. *Urban Studies* 36(7), 1055–77.

Yeoh, B. S. A., and Lau, W. P. (1995). Historic district, contemporary meanings: Urban conservation and the creation and consumption of landscape spectacle in Tanjong Pagar. In B. S. A. Yeoh and L. Kong (eds), *Portraits of Places: History, Community and Identity in Singapore* (pp. 46–67). Singapore: Times Edition.

Chapter 19

Postcolonialism, Colonialism, and Tourism

Anne-Marie d'Hauteserre

This chapter demonstrates how theories used in postcolonial studies can be applied to tourism. The study of tourism is most fruitful when different modes of analysis are brought together. Postcolonialism is but one perspective on tourism, testimony to the dissolution of traditional boundaries in academic research and the increasing importance of a global and multidisciplinary approach. Postmodern critique has enfeebled paradigms of positivist objective metanarratives of explanation and postcolonialism has adopted the "interpretive" cultural turn, embracing discursive understandings of social, economic, and cultural developments, particularly in non-Western areas. The means may differ but scientific search remains the basis of inquiry.

Defining Postcolonialism and Colonialism

The concept of postcolonialism was crystallized as a general theory and field of study in Edward Said's book *Orientalism* (1978). However, there is little consensus as to the methods and goals of postcolonial studies, and even definitions of the term "postcolonial" are hotly contested (Hall 1996; Slemon 1996). Most authors contend that postcolonialism offers a critique of Western structures of knowledge and power. It is defined as reflexive Western thought, interrogating and rethinking the very terms by which it has constructed knowledge through the duality of colonizer and colonized. As a general category of intellectual critique, postcolonialism includes an incredibly disparate array of phenomena (e.g., literary, cultural, economic, and political) linked in some way to colonialism (McClintock 1992; Rattansi 1997).

It is "post"colonial both in historical and chronological terms, and in its conscious self-awareness of the dualism that Western thought has created. Homi Bhabha argued that "post" can be taken as meaning "beyond," that is, "on the borderlines of the present" (Bhabha 1994: 1), and Hall (1996) confirmed that, while "postcolonial" does not describe a periodization, it still represents a metaphoric time "after" colonization, even though decolonization is still incomplete. McClintock pointed out, though, that "the singularity of the term [postcolonialism] effects a recentering of global history around the single rubric of European time" (1992: 86). Postcolonialism remains complicit with colonialism, due, in great part, to its origin in the Western intellectual tradition (Castle 2001).

European colonization has had lasting and inequitable results, extending well beyond the independence of the colonized, who remain "condemned only to use a telephone, never to invent it, fixed in zones of dependency and peripherality, stigmatised as ... underdeveloped ... ruled by a superior, developed or metropolitan coloniser" (Said 2000: 295). Western discourses have often successfully obfuscated the bias in the construction of the colonized/colonizer duality. This has been done through colonizer control over representations of both the colonizer and the colonized. Such representations are an ideological vehicle of power, which is not readily relinquished. They have led to weakened resistance to capitalist models of modernization. At the same time, the continued use of European forms of education, government, and popular culture in former colonial societies leads one to question whether postcolonialism is really just a new phase of colonialism.

Colonialism was also experienced in the colonizer's homeland, from a distance and through representations, especially literary ones (Phillips 1999: 280). Colonialism fostered a vast growth of knowledge about subjugation, which shaped power relationships in a similar manner both in the colonizer core and the colonized periphery. Rattansi (1997: 485), for example, argued that "strategies of containment [were] being learnt and mutually transferred between the two widely separated territories of governance" to reduce the threat of internal others such as the urban working class, as well as "external Other threatening subalterns." These led to the colonization of not just territories and peoples outside its borders but also of "others" within, such as women, the proletariat, and immigrants.

Colonialism was indeed a set of processes that shaped the project of Westernization and modernity throughout the world. The "becoming-West of Europe and the becoming-modern of the world [were] conjoined processes," which Venn named "occidentalism" (2000: 74).

Dirlik (1994: 353) argues that "post-coloniality represents a response to a genuine need, the need to overcome a crisis of understanding produced by the inability of old categories to account for the world." Most scholars, however, take a more dim view of postcolonial discourses, which, they argue, direct attention away from the present political and economic inequities structured by global capitalism (Mongia 2000). These critics charge that postcolonialism has subsumed all oppositional discourses, flattening the diversity of colonialism's impacts, while its oppositional stance to colonialism wavers as it becomes increasingly institutionalized. Khaira (1998) adds that postcolonialism tends to "'steal' the voice of the postcolonial subject in its very bid to re-assess it." As a cultural descriptor for most of the world, postcolonialism erases the complexity and specificities of peripheral area geographies as they are generalized under the rubric "Third World."

Nawal El Saadawi (2000: 1335) commented that First World academicians' "postmodern vision and thinking fragmented us into a colourful mosaic ... But the other was not of great weight, not of real value in the future of the world." Postcolonialism's geographic and linguistic limitations, for example, keep it essentially silent about indigenous liberation struggles. The "other" as interlocutor is already disenfranchised in the very mechanisms of its nondiscrete subjectivity – it only exists as a reflection of the subject. For example, Venn noted that "in the discourse of Western philosophy, the hyphen linking Judaism and Christianity silently erases Islam from Semitic thought, casting the Islamic world into invisibility when it comes to a genealogy of modernity" (2000: 79). For postcolonialism to have more universal significance, the Eurocentric time-space colonial must be displaced as its point of reference, along with the romanticized nostalgia of a pristine precolonial period. We need to weave a more complex narrative of continuity and change, otherwise the obsession with colonialism may reinscribe the racism which a post-colonial critique should subvert.

Tourism in Colonialism and Postcolonialism

The relationship between post/colonial theories and tourism is largely centered on the "exoticism" that many tourists seek in former colonies. Exoticism itself is deeply rooted in colonialism and tourist experiences of "exotic" landscapes are a thin parody of the colonial experience. Landscapes of the colonized world have been used as cultural manuscripts on which meanings have been inscribed, erased, and overwritten in the broad geopolitics of Western superiority (Ashcroft, Griffiths, and Tiffin 1995). The choices about what is included and what is excluded, as well as how to depict what has been retained, are not haphazard. Erasing and obscuring are fundamental to the collective process of social memory. "Indian rubber works well for rubbing out anything" Milne (1958) tells us, to which Das Nuffa Dat asks in reply, "isn't this a trope for repression, and specifically for repression of what 'trade' with Southeast Asia was actually like?" (2001: 87).

Tourism, like postcolonialism, has its roots in colonialism, both as a theoretical construct and as a perceptual mechanism (cf. Temple 2002). Tourism development, through its approach to Third World destinations (in the form of, for example, resort enclaves and "international standard" hotels), perpetuates colonial forms of interaction that treat the exotic as inferior. Exotic places are controlled by being familiarized and domesticated through a language that locates them in a "universal" (meaning Western) system of reference that visitors recognize and can communicate about. Tourist representations draw heavily upon cultural memories produced elsewhere, even though the destination is layered with indigenous cultural inscriptions. As Appiah reminded us, "we do need to be clear when we travel in the cosmopolitan spirit, the spirit that celebrates and respects difference, that sometimes, the ease with which we find ourselves taking pleasure in that difference – the cosmopolite's *jouissance* – reflects the fact that it has been produced in forms we have learned *chez nous*" (Appiah 2001: 207).

Postcolonialism and tourism both perpetuate the myths of the colonial exotic. This *imaginaire* is now consumed as a pleasure/leisure destination, and not just as a fantasy or an escape reserved for the elite. Colonial and, today, tourist narratives have strategically functioned to produce geopolitical myths about destinations. The emphasis is on a particular set of illusions that conflate weather and social climate, transforming them into paradise. Claims that the sun always shines on tourism destinations means that darker geographies have been displaced. The tourists' gaze seeks to familiarize the landscape and naturalize their presence in it. The meaning of tourism landscapes as texts is located in the tourist activity of reading (through touring and visiting): their meaning is in what it does to their readers. Thus Amirou (1995: 94–5) could assert that "space, in geographical terms, disappears from the tourist *imaginaire* to allow for 'readings' of a space (scape) strewn with words."

Today the geographies of destinations are imaginary ones based on images and representations that purport to describe potential sites of leisure/pleasure, but are actually part of an economic system whose reach is global but whose articulation remains colonial. Postcolonialism connects remarkably little with conventional developmental agendas (Simon 1998), of which tourism is often a part, even though tourism very clearly participates in the articulation and perpetuation of uneven development and of unequal territorial and cultural relationships, both between countries, and within them. Dharwadker (2001: 10) noted that "the dirty work, in fact, is done not so much on generalized national maps as on the detailed inset maps of particular cities and countrysides . . . where raw materials, labor, economic production, distribution networks, infrastructure and consumers can be quantifiably located and exploited."

The production of tourism destinations responds to the interests of the metropolitan center. Just as past colonial projects were presented with an acceptable or even exciting face so they would be supported at home (e.g., Defoe's *Robinson Crusoe*), promotional representations and images of tourism today do not just describe destinations, they construct and authorize them, thereby controlling tourism development. Tourism in developing countries is eagerly organized for the Western traveler even as it becomes a locus of contradictions, juxtapositions, and intersections, and even as the new global cultural economy is increasingly a complex, disjunctive order, which cannot really be understood in terms of a simple center–periphery model (Appadurai 2000). Furthermore, deterritorialization has engendered movements of money and persons such that many travel agencies thrive on the need of diasporas for contact with their homelands. In this highly structuralist view, the tourist is not a free subject of thought or action, and nor is the host (Said 1993).

Decolonization has not meant an end either to unequal relationships or to imperialism (Hardt and Negri 2000). Indigenization of the production of destinations (which Din 1997 called "indigenising modernity"), on the other hand, could become a mimic "whose mimicry is neither a real understanding of Western culture nor a form of resistance against Western hegemony, but rather a half-conscious attempt to belong to a 'civilized' world which promotes and feeds on this misguided desire for its own profit" (Al-Nowaihi 2000: 297). Alison Johnston (2000: 95) finds that, although tourism can be a powerful tool in indigenous peoples' fights for their rights, "existing regimes for land rights and intellectual property rights promote the privatization and globalization by industry players of indigenous marketable resources." When indigenization has been successful, it has caused a backlash of accusations against practices detrimental to the area and the exalting of "lucky" circumstances rather than a recognition of visionary management by the tribal group (d'Hauteserre 2000, 2001).

Postcolonial theorization should open up a space to question the categories and epistemologies that have supported these Western constructions of travel and tourism. Tourism thus demands a contested and subverted response through narratives of subalterns, women, and other groups that are marginalized and even expunged by neocolonial relationships and structures. Only in this way can these groups begin to develop a metonymic rapport with visitors, and resist their erasure from the tourist imagination, and especially from networks of capital accumulation. Contestations of colonial narratives force us to remember differences and variations that had been there all the time. They also demonstrate how past colonial discourses are still manifested in the postcolonial present (see Mowforth and Munt 1998).

Other Sites of Tourism

"As capitalism is central to civilization, desire is central to capitalism and becomes its most resilient and captivating export," asserts Ashcroft (2001: 78). Desire is generally translated as sexual desire and sexuality has been used as a driver of consumption, even in tourism, through, for example, the advertising tropes of destinations as receptive females (Kinnaird and Hall 1994; Opperman and McKinley 1997; Morgan and Pritchard 1998). Even though such advertising is seldom actually encouraging men to travel to specifically purchase sexual services (Enloe 1989), the line between leisure and play, and sexuality, is often not clearly demarcated. Women too pursue sexual favors through tourism, for example in the way Jamaica is visited by women in quest of romance (as described in *Newsweek* 2002: 63). But, as Pruitt and Lafont (1995) have indicated, neither partner in the "romantic" exchanges perceives them to be prostitution.

Much of this power struggle is engendered by narratives in which the mind is privileged while the "unruly" and "disruptive" body must be tamed by masculine reason (Grosz 1994; Gatens 1996), in much the same way as masculine imperialism led to the "feminization" (and associated inferiorization) of the colonized male (Sinha 1995). The natural sexual expressiveness that was "reported" by early explorers, a sort of exotic eroticization, was a source of both fascination and attraction, as well as fear and repulsion, especially since "that which appears alluringly feminine is not always, or necessarily, female" (Boone 2000: 965). Colonizing males desired control not only over their relations with others but also over their own potential internal fragmentation. Boone thus asserts that "both straight and non-straight travellers are implicated in a colonizing enterprise that often 'others' the homosexually inscribed Arab male . . . whether that 'other' is perceived with dread or with desire" (2000: 963). This transcultural fascination is reflected by the attraction of gay parades (as tourist destinations), which become a contact zone for testing one's constructed heterosexuality (L. Johnston 1998).

Different myths have evolved over the centuries on which much tourism marketing is still based. The "island paradise," created by males for male readers, is an imagined world where island women merely await Western men's attentions and affections. The destination in the mind of the Western tourist is a feminized static place to conquer, "removed from the light of self-conscious history and forever wrapped in the dark mantle of European night" (Hegel 1975: 174). Indigenous women are rejected if too "savage"; and they are rejected if they become too modern. Women must "protect tradition" to remain exotically captivating (Faessel 1995). An idyllic encounter with such others is without risk for the European visitor since he is just passing through, and discrimination insures that he will never bring an indigenous person back home (though rare exceptions do exist).

The exotic "other" can only provide a happy interlude for the Western visitor who searches not for a real person but for what she represents, the essence of her "exotic culture" that the visitor believes they can harmonize with even though it is an impossibility (Lyotard 1988). According to Lyotard the identities of "others" are not just an inchoate opposite; they are radically inaccessible. They are different, unrepresentable. And although the discussion here has focused on the colonizing male domination of the colonized female, as we have seen above, similar paradigms centered on the romantic forays of Western females into the sun, sand, and sex of the tropical exotic are also present, if not as well researched by academics.

Travel writing is still a lively industry despite earlier predictions of its demise because of "a sense of exhaustion of the planet and exhaustion of the forms we use to write about it" (Russell 2000: 9). Authors such as Theroux, Mayle, Lanchester, and Temple have displayed a postmodern sensibility of the complex evolution of our world as they have written about their travels and experiences. Such imaginative geographies, which script practices and performances, are still produced, even though the post-tourist, according to Feifer (1986: 271), is "resolutely 'realistic'; he [*sic*!] cannot evade his condition of outsider." Nineteenth-century writing colonized the landscape and its indigenous population through its "monarch of all I survey" (Pratt 1992) recounting of explorations and its almost obsessive ocularcentrism. But the "realism" of the post-tourist does not reduce his or her colonizing voyeurism. Tourist spaces continue to be claimed through discursive power while the "sense of exhaustion" has led travelers to seek challenges beyond the forbidden frontiers in Asia (Danziger 1987). Russell introduces the postcolonial concept of hybridity in travel writing when she underlines that many of these postmodern texts "direct us to examine the ways they are constructed and shaped by the world and its social practices" (2000: 15).

Many "post"-theorists have investigated travel writing by women to understand how they have negotiated or "resisted" colonial inscriptions, and how they have attempted to inscribe their itinerary through space. Rattansi (1997: 488) commented that "there is a sense in which the worst fears of the white colonial male were realized in the person of that curious creature, the white woman traveller, who would commit the even greater transgression of writing about her 'experiences.'" Simone de Beauvoir (1948) described how the tourist myths, clichés, and images of North America served as reference points for the traveler. She refused, however, to confirm these myths, and opted to describe how the country revealed itself to her from day to day. Where traveling often results in annexing a new object to one's experience/knowledge, de Beauvoir was looking for "a world filled to the brim, so rich and so unpredictable that [she] will experience the extraordinary adventure of becoming another" (1948: 12).

Morin (1999) concluded that, as white women explored and contested powerful inscriptions of roles, they may well have reconstituted hegemonic ideologies, and constructions of racialized difference (Blunt 1994). These travel narratives, despite "geometrics of difference and contradiction" (Haraway 1991: 170), provided a forum for these women to "consolidate their positions as members of the ruling classes ... making themselves good imperialists more than anything else" (Morin 1999: 510–11). However, though their narrations incorporated imperial assumptions they also represent counter-discourses potentially destabilizing or subverting the colonized/colonizer binary (Mills 1994) or masculine authority (Wheeler 1996). The feminist contribution to postcolonialism has introduced vital thinking "about the intersection of race, gender, sexuality, and class in the representations of other places and people" (Blunt and Rose 1994: 8).

Tourism's Postcolonial Relations(hips)

Other postmodern intersections between the colonial past and the tourism present occur in the form of recent demands by tourists to penetrate the farther peripheries of tourist space, in parallel with their quest to affirm their own identities through the existential "other." Can we speak of transcultural or postcolonial relationships in this tourist-oriented contact zone? One can question whether the penetration of the periphery is but a continued conquest (even if only at the individual level) rather than a true search for a personal identity through interactive appreciation. At the same time, is the "other" a true interlocutor, as postcolonial discourses would have us believe? Can this host truly demand interaction so as to extract recognition through active encounters, rather than being merely gazed at? Both sides should become co-implicated and mutually constituted through these very struggles. Gregory (1998: 53) has promoted the pursuit of transgressive and multidimensional narratives "which disclose complex, foliated spaces of transculturation" so we may hear the voice of the subaltern which the colonial or tourist hegemonic discourses have not succeeded in totally disarticulating (Parry 1987).

Westernized natives are increasingly seen by tourists as "mere inventors of themselves, as false representatives of their [authentic, primitive] cultures" (Friedman 1998). As the worldwide popularity of indigenous peoples' arts and cultures grows, in the form of tourist destinations and souvenirs, the ability of indigenous peoples to interpret their own cultures, to defend the integrity of their cultures, and to receive compensation for the use and enjoyment of their cultural manifestations by tourists becomes increasingly challenged. Battiste and Henderson (2001: 59) noted that "To be effective, the protection of indigenous peoples' heritage should be based broadly on the principle of self-determination, which includes the right and the duty of indigenous peoples to develop their own cultures and knowledge systems, and forms of social organisation."

However, existing legal systems (and society at large) rely on an ideological structure that still relegates indigenous peoples to a category incapable of ingenuity and creativity, and on a system of individual ownership of property (including land, ideas, and things), which is alien to most indigenous groups. Hall (1996: 252–3) observed that

> Colonisation so refigured the terrain that, ever since, the very idea of a world of separate identities, of isolated or separable and self-sufficient cultures and economies, has been obliged to yield to a variety of paradigms designed to capture these different but related forms of relationship, interconnection and discontinuity.

One form of evasion of a true dialogue between tourists and native hosts is that of describing the "authentic African" as one not yet spoilt by Western knowledge (Achebe 2000: 1798). Jahn (in Achebe 2000: 1799) points out the ethnocentric domination implicit in this image: "Only the most highly cultivated person counts as a 'real European.' A 'real African,' on the other hand, lives in the bush ... goes naked ... and tells fairy stories about the crocodile and the elephant. The more primitive, the more really African." The essential primitive only exists within Western constructs of race relations, whatever the geographical location. Contemporary Africans, for example, are erased from images of African "wilderness" and safari destinations in the same way as they have been consistently dehumanized and deterritorialized over the past 400 years. They are continually erased from tourism projects (Akama 1999). Some ecotourism operators maintain the traditional conception of "other lands" as *terra nullius* (Wheat 2002), so tourists can follow A. A. Milne's lead in *Pooh*: "There is nobody else in the world and the world was made for me" (in Crews 2001: 85).

Researchers have long recognized that economic, cultural, and other forces originating from global metropolitan centers become indigenized as rapidly as they are brought into new societies (Hannerz 1987; Yoshimoto 1989), while heterogeneity and hybridity increasingly occupy and challenge the metropolitan cores (Goldberg 2000). There has been continuity in both the core and the periphery, despite colonialism's and tourism's onslaughts, due to the capacity of people to integrate diverse experiences into coherent forms. Durix adds that "the cultures of the world are now intertwined, involved ... in an accelerated process of hybridisation [which] ... may lead to a new form of cultural colonisation ... But it also contains the seeds of cross-fertilisation" (1998: 3). Nabudere (in Simon 1998) has advocated the use of post-traditionalism to promote a new people-centered and indigenously generated alternative to the colonial one evoked by tourism: to create a "rich tapestry of crosscutting continuity and change; of old, new, and hybrid identities ... of the preservation versus the transcendence of categories" (Simon 1998: 238).

Hybridity brings with it ambiguity, and thereby threatens the orderliness of the schematized reality of tourists. Hybridity is redolent of miscegenation, which was one of the greatest fears of most self-respecting travelers. The French had an even stronger discursive aversion to "going native," as expressed in the term *s'encanaquer* (to become Kanak). Hybridized identities are sometimes said to have lost authenticity, and thus authority, while primitivism is exalted as a means of redressing past indigenous marginalization and the only "authentic" form of culture for tourist consumption. There is no primitively "pure" or "authentic" native tradition to commodify for tourists. The point, however, is not to preclude the past. The narrative of the present must remain open to its heritage and roots (Gilroy 1993), while remembering that the past does not wait around like an object to be recuperated. What one seeks to reclaim is a representation that is structured and conditioned by prevailing ideological models, then and now (Lowenthal 1985). The present and the past mutually condition each other, and they relate to the future through the possibility of different visions issued from new syntheses.

Conclusion

To make it more comprehensible for their consumption, tourists reorder the world through the manipulation of images, words, and practices, in the same way that colonialism codified colonial people to better impose its institutions and policies.

Representations are never far removed from economic or political implications. We thus learn from postcolonial studies that there has always been a profoundly symbiotic relationship between the discursive and the material practices of domination, whether they be imperialistic or capitalist, the latter of which tourism is an integral part. Relationships with visited "others" are difficult to enact because of a continued fear of pollution or contamination, as expressed in the concept of hybridity. Resistance would be for "hosts" to return the gaze in an effort to redress asymmetric ignorance. The difficulties of the postcolonial present do not, however, concern relations just between the Western world and the Third World. Contemporary globalization masks unequal relations within the First World through occlusions and mystifications inherent in most attractions, including, for example, heritage sites. Tourism studies could follow postcolonialism in unveiling oppression not just of Third World hosts, even though decolonization has been heralded, but also of those who serve visitors in the First World, i.e. outside traditionally colonized spaces.

REFERENCES

Achebe, C. (2000). Viewpoint. In D. Brydon (ed.), *Postcolonialism* (pp. 1796–1800). New York: Routledge.

Akama, J. (1999). Marginalization of the Maasai in Kenya. *Annals of Tourism Research* 26, 716–18.

Al-Nowaihi, M. (2000). The "Middle East"? Or... Arabic literature and the postcolonial predicament. In H. Schwarz and S. Ray (eds), *A Companion to Postcolonial Studies* (pp. 282–303). Oxford: Blackwell.

Amirou, R. (1995). *Imaginaire touristique et sociabilités du voyage*. Paris: PUF.

Appadurai, A. (2000). Disjuncture and difference in the global cultural economy. In D. Brydon (ed.), *Postcolonialism: Critical Concepts* (vol. 5, pp. 1801–23). London: Routledge.

Appiah, A. K. (2001). Cosmopolitan reading. In V. Dharwadker (ed.), *Cosmopolitan Geographies*. London: Routledge.

Ashcroft, B. (2001). *On Postcolonial Futures*. New York: Continuum.

Ashcroft, B., Griffiths, G., and Tiffin, H. (1995). *The Empire Writes Back*. London: Routledge.

Battiste, M., and Henderson, J. Y. (2001). *Protecting Indigenous Knowledge and Heritage*. Saskatoon, Canada: Purich.

Beauvoir, S. de (1948). *L'Amérique au jour le jour*. Paris: Gallimard.

Bhabha, H. K. (1994). *The Location of Culture*. London: Routledge.

Blunt, A. (1994). Mapping authorship and authority: Reading Mary Kingsley's landscape descriptions. In A. Blunt and G. Rose (eds), *Writing Women and Space: Colonial and Postcolonial Geographies* (pp. 51–72). New York: Guilford Press.

Blunt, A., and Rose, G. (1994). Introduction. In A. Blunt and G. Rose (eds), *Writing Women and Space: Colonial and Postcolonial Geographies*. New York: Guilford Press.

Boone, J. (2000). Vacation cruises; or, the homoerotics of orientalism. In D. Brydon (ed.), *Postcolonialism* (pp. 961–87). New York: Routledge.

Castle, G. (2001). Editor's introduction: Resistance and complicity in postcolonial studies. In G. Castle (ed.), *Postcolonial Discourses*. Oxford: Blackwell.

Crews, F. (ed.) (2001). *Postmodern Pooh*. New York: North Point Press.

Danziger, N. (1987). *Danziger's Travels: Beyond Forbidden Frontiers*. New York: Vintage.

Dat, Das Nuffa. (2001). Resident aliens. In F. Crews (ed.), *Postmodern Pooh* (pp. 81–96). New York: North Point Press.

Dharwadker, V. (2001). Introduction. In V. Dharwadker (ed.), *Cosmopolitan Geographies*. London: Routledge.

d'Hauteserre, A.-M. (2000). Lessons in managed destination competitiveness: The case of Foxwoods Casino Resort. *Tourism Management* 21(1), 23–32.

d'Hauteserre, A.-M. (2001). Representations of rurality: Is Foxwoods Casino Resort threatening the quality of life in southeastern Connecticut? *Tourism Geographies* 3(4), 405–30.

Din, K. (1997). Indigenization of tourism development: Some constraints and possibilities. In M. Opperman (ed.), *Pacific Rim Tourism* (pp. 76–81). London: CAB.

Dirlik, A. (1994). The postcolonial aura: Third World criticism in the age of global capitalism. *Critical Inquiry* 20, 328–56.

Durix, J.-P. (1998). *Mimesis, Genres and Post-Colonial Discourse*. New York: St. Martin's.

El Saadawi, N. (2000). Why keep asking me about my identity? In D. Brydon (ed.), *Postcolonialism* (pp. 1328–43). New York: Routledge.

Enloe, C. (1989). *Bananas, Beaches and Bases: Making Feminist Sense of International Politics*. Berkeley: University of California Press.

Faessel, S. (1995). La Femme dans l'idylle polynésienne. In S. Faessel (ed.), *La Femme entre tradition et modernité dans le Pacifique Sud*. Paris: l'Harmattan.

Feifer, M. (1986). *Tourism in History*. New York: Stern & Day.

Friedman, J. (1998). Knowing Oceania or Oceanian knowing: Identifying actors and activating identities in turbulent times. In J. Wassmann (ed.), *Pacific Answers to Western Hegemony* (pp. 37–66). New York: Berg.

Gatens, M. (1996). *Imaginary Bodies: Ethics, Power and Corporeality*. London: Routledge.

Gilroy, P. (1993). *The Black Atlantic: Modernity and Double Consciousness*. London: Verso.

Goldberg, D. T. (2000). Heterogeneity and hybridity. In H. Schwarz and S. Ray (eds), *A Companion to Postcolonial Studies* (pp. 72–86). Oxford: Blackwell.

Gregory, D. (1998). Power, knowledge, geography. *Geographische Zeitschrift* 86(2), 50–73.

Grosz, E. (1994). *Volatile Bodies: Towards a Corporeal Feminism*. Bloomington: Indiana University Press.

Hall, S. (1996). When was the postcolonial? In I. Chambers and L. Curti (eds), *The Postcolonial Question*. London: Routledge.

Hannerz, U. (1987). The world in creolisation. *Africa* 57(4), 546–59.

Haraway, D. (1991). *Simians, Cyborgs, and Women: The Reinvention of Nature*. London: Free Association Books.

Hardt, M., and Negri, A. (2000). *Empire*. Cambridge, MA: Harvard University Press.

Hegel, G. W. F. (1975). *Lectures on the Philosophy of World History*, trans. H. B. Nisbet with an introduction by D. Forbes. Cambridge: Cambridge University Press.

Johnston, A. (2000). Indigenous peoples and ecotourism: Bringing indigenous knowledge and rights into the sustainability equation. *Tourism Recreation Research* 25(2), 89–96.

Johnston, L. (1998). Body tourism in queered streets: Geographies of gay pride parades. Ph.D. thesis, University of Waikato, Hamilton.

Khaira, H. (1998). Postcolonial theory: A discussion of directions and tensions with special reference to the work of Frida Kahlo. *Kunapipi* 20(2), 41–51.

Kinnaird, V., and Hall, D. (eds) (1994). *Tourism: A Gender Analysis*. New York: John Wiley.

Lanchester, J. (2002). *Fragrant Harbour*. London: Faber & Faber.

Lowenthal, D. (1985). *The Past is a Foreign Country*. New York: Cambridge University Press.

Lyotard, J.-F. (1988). *The Différend: Phrases in Dispute*, trans. G. van den Abbeele. Minneapolis: University of Minnesota Press.

McClintock, A. (1992). The angel of progress: Pitfalls of the term "postcolonialism." *Social Text* 31/2, 82– 8.
Mills, S. (1994). Knowledge, gender, and empire. In A. Blunt and G. Rose (eds), *Writing Women and Space: Colonial and Postcolonial Geographies* (pp. 29–50). New York: Guilford Press.
Milne, A. A. (1958). *Winnie-the-Pooh*. London: Methuen.
Mongia, P. (2000). Introduction. In P. Mongia (ed.), *Contemporary Postcolonial Theory: A Reader.* New Delhi: Oxford University Press.
Morgan, N., and Pritchard, A. (1998). *Tourism Promotion and Power.* New York: John Wiley.
Morin, K. (1999). Peak practices: Englishwomen's "heroic" adventures in the nineteenth century American West. *Annals of the Association of American Geographers* 89(3), 489–514.
Mowforth, M., and Munt, I. (1998). *Tourism and Sustainability.* London: Routledge.
Newsweek (2002). *Sex on the Beach* by Sana Butler, July 22–9, 63.
Opperman, M., and McKinley, S. (1997). Sexual imagery in the marketing of Pacific tourism destinations. In M. Opperman (ed.), *Pacific Rim Tourism* (pp. 117–27). New York: CAB International.
Parry, B. (1987). Current problems in the study of colonial discourse. *Oxford Literary Review* 91/2, 34–40.
Phillips, R. (1999). Colonialism and postcolonialism. In P. Cloke, P. Crang, and M. Goodwin (eds), *Introducing Human Geography* (pp. 277–86). New York: Arnold.
Pratt, M.-L. (1992). *Imperial Eyes: Travel Writing and Transculturation.* New York: Routledge.
Pruitt, D., and Lafont, S. (1995). For love and money romance: Tourism in Jamaica. *Annals of Tourism Research* 22(2), 422–40.
Rattansi, A. (1997). Postcolonialism and its discontents. *Economy and Society* 26(4), 480–500.
Robertson, R. (1992). *Globalisation: Social Theory and Global Culture.* London: Sage.
Russell, A. (2000). *Crossing Boundaries: Postmodern Travel Literature.* New York: Palgrave.
Said, E. (1978). *Orientalism.* Harmondsworth: Penguin.
Said, E. (1993). *Culture and Imperialism.* London: Chatto & Windus.
Said, E. (2000). *Reflections on Exile.* London: Granta.
Simon, D. (1998). Rethinking (post)modernism, postcolonialism, and posttraditionalism. *Environment and Planning D: Society and Space* 16, 219–45.
Sinha, M. (1995). *Colonial Masculinity.* Manchester: Manchester University Press.
Slemon, S. (1996). Postcolonial critical theories. In B. King (ed.), *New National and Post-Colonial Literatures: An Introduction.* Oxford: Clarendon Press.
Temple, P. (2002). *The Last True Explorer.* London: Godwit.
Venn, C. (2000). *Occidentalism, Modernity and Subjectivity.* Thousand Oaks, CA: Sage.
Wheat, S. (2002). Visiting disaster. *Guardian Weekly,* June 20–6, 8.
Wheeler, S. (1996). *Terra Incognita: Travels in Antarctica.* New York: Random.
Yoshimoto, M. (1989). The postmodern and mass images in Japan. *Public Culture* 1(2), 8–25.

Chapter 20

Indigenous People and Tourism

Tom D. Hinch

"The nexus between land and culture defines sustainable tourism for indigenous peoples"

(Zeppel 1998a: 65)

Introduction

The world of indigenous people represents an intriguing frontier for both tourists and geographers. It offers spaces where few non-indigenous people have visited and it encourages travel to many peripheral areas in the world. Destinations associated with the culture of indigenous people tend to be unique places, which can enrich the way tourists understand the world. The complex interplay of cultures and the unique relationship that indigenous people have with the land present intriguing environmental insights for tourists and geographers alike. Indigenous tourism is also rife with issues inherent in cross-cultural activities. This chapter is an examination of the key challenges associated with indigenous people and tourism.

As a starting point for this discussion, it is helpful to define the terms "indigenous people" and "indigenous tourism." In general, most indigenous people would prefer to be identified specifically by their tribe, band, clan, or nation (Waitt 1999). However, the phrase "indigenous people" is increasingly used in reference to communities, peoples, and nations that have historical continuity with pre-invasion and precolonial societies. It generally refers to people who:

> consider themselves distinct from other sectors of societies now prevailing in those territories, or parts of them. They form at present non-dominant sectors of society and are determined to preserve, develop, and transmit to future generations their ancestral territories, and their ethnic identity, as the basis of their continued existence as peoples, in accordance with their own cultural patterns, social institutions and legal systems. (United Nations Development Programme, n.d.)

Indigenous tourism refers to tourism activity in which indigenous people are directly involved either through control and/or by having their culture serve as the essence of the attraction (Hinch and Butler 1996: 9). This chapter focuses on indigenous themed tourism, with the question of control, or the ability of indigenous people to influence tourism development, featuring prominently throughout.

The past decade has been characterized by dramatic growth in both the demand for indigenous tourism experiences and the supply of these experiences (e.g., Zeppel 1998b). One of the reasons for this surge in demand is that, as society has become more complex and hectic, tourists have sought escape to simpler times and places. Robinson (1999) describes this in terms of a search for the fading link between nature and culture in an increasingly urban landscape. In response, tourists are pursuing the "other" and in many cases they are actively searching for the "primitive" as a way to develop an understanding of their own place in the world (Waitt 1999). Many indigenous people are catering to this demand as part of their strategy for cultural survival. Their motivations include economic objectives designed to overcome poverty, political objectives associated with bolstering land claim arguments, environmental objectives such as the promotion of non-consumptive uses of resources, and sociocultural goals aimed at fostering cultural identity and pride (Hinch 2001). Many other indigenous people are passive or even unwilling participants in this activity as they and their communities are presented as significant attractions in the tourism landscape by external stakeholders.

While a variety of geographic questions can be asked about indigenous tourism, a fundamental line of inquiry is whether it represents a sustainable form of development or not. This question is complicated by concerns about the sustainability of indigenous cultures themselves and by the complex interrelationship between culture and the indigenous tourism environment. Advocates suggest that indigenous tourism development can be sustainable and may even serve to save or rejuvenate indigenous communities. For example, based on her study of tourism and indigenous communities in the Peruvian Amazon, Ingles (2002: 59) concludes that "[t]ourist entertainment not only brings in much needed income, but also offers an opportunity for locals to embrace, and showcase, their own cultural identity that may be threatened in a changing world." A more conservative view is that, while indigenous tourism has the potential to be sustainable, a significant level of planned intervention by all affected stakeholders is required. Moreover, even carefully planned indigenous tourism will be characterized by trade-offs in terms of the costs and benefits of this activity (Butler and Hinch 1996).

Writers who argue that indigenous tourism is not likely to be sustainable include Waitt (1999), who concludes that, as presently practiced in Australia, indigenous tourism creates a publicly constructed view of aboriginality that is inferior to non-aboriginal culture and, therefore, unsustainable. Johnston (2000: 89–90) shares this pessimism in her statement that tourism "is not only a pronounced form of consumerism, but also a flagship for the lifestyle of consumer society. As such, it can rapidly accelerate the cycles of cultural loss, poverty, and environmental degradation caused by any existing market integration." Indigenous people are particularly susceptible to these impacts to the extent that they are seldom privileged as power-holders in emerging tourism economies or in the broader social-political economy in which they exist.

The remainder of this chapter examines the sustainability of indigenous tourism by considering issues related to indigenous territories, the commodification of indigenous cultures, and the intellectual property rights of indigenous peoples. The principle of self-determination is then addressed, with further consideration given to strategies designed to operationalize this principle in the context of indigenous tourism.

Indigenous Territories

The unique relationship that indigenous people have with the land is one of the greatest attractions of indigenous tourism as well as one of the greatest challenges (Zeppel 1998a; Hinch 2001; Petterson 2001). Indigenous territories represent "many of the best – and often the last – remaining places of rich wilderness and biological diversity" (Stevens 1997: 1). There are at least three possible explanations for this. First, indigenous people have historically immigrated or been forcibly relocated to peripheral areas that were not originally felt to offer strong development opportunities to colonizing cultures. Often these lands were only weakly integrated into the evolving forms of capitalist economies established by the original colonizers. Second, indigenous peoples have tended to live in ways that have left the lands that they inhabit with much biodiversity. Finally, in many cases, the indigenous peoples have been successful in warding off outside threats to the integrity of their lands.

Yet the attraction of indigenous territories goes beyond the simple fact that these lands represent a high proportion of increasingly rare ecosystems. The fact is that indigenous peoples often have a unique cultural relationship to the land. In a traditional context, indigenous people consider that they belong to the Earth rather than the land belonging to them (Hollinshead 1992; Ryan 1997). While not universal, the concept of the land as the "mother" on whom survival depends is a recurring one among indigenous peoples. As a result, indigenous people have drawn much of their self-identity from the land of which they are a part. To many, the land is the essence of their life. A further distinction between the way indigenous and non-indigenous people relate to the land is the holistic perspective of indigenous people. Indigenous people have traditionally been "one with the land." Whereas non-indigenous peoples tend to separate their lives into "economic" and "cultural" domains, "for indigenous peoples they are aspects of the same phenomenon, where time, space, resource use, management and conservation are all part of the same complex, linking identity to production and reproduction" (Gray 1991: 22). It is, of course, dangerous to extend this generalization too far. Indigenous communities are not homogeneous. They are influenced by various external factors in contemporary society. Basic values that are reflected in the way that indigenous people related to the land in the past are being modified as indigenous people increasingly engage in entrepreneurship and the global economy (Wuttunee 1992).

Even in the context of contemporary indigenous communities, there is a unique bond between indigenous people and the land. Two implications of this bond are particularly important in the context of tourism. First, because indigenous people tend not to see the land as a possession, they are very wary of treating it as a commodity, even in the purportedly benign context of alternative or environmentally sensitive tourism. Secondly, because of their deep attachment to the land, indigenous people see the landscape differently. They attach unique and often complex meanings to place that go beyond its physical properties. Often, these complex meanings include a spiritual dimension (Hollinshead 1996). Indigenous peoples may choose not to share spiritual insights with visitors, or they may choose to restrict visitors' access to certain sacred places within this landscape. For example, the Sa people of Vanuatu have imposed strict regulations on where and how tourists can observe the *gol* – a cultural ritual that includes a dramatic 70-foot land dive by Sa men whose fall is broken just before impact by vines attached to their ankles (de Burlo 1996).

There is, however, growing pressure for indigenous people to capitalize on the resources inherent in their lands. Despite their reluctance to treat the land as a commodity, indigenous peoples are increasingly open to non-traditional uses of the land (McCullum and McCullum 1975). To the extent that indigenous peoples still see themselves as caretakers of the land, they are continually trying to find ways of protecting it while surviving as indigenous cultures in a changing world. Tourism is one of the new activities that have been introduced to these traditional lands as a way of seeking a balance between conservation and the financial rewards of development. Underlying this search for appropriate land use in indigenous territories is the maintenance and reaffirmation of indigenous control.

"Indigenous peoples have reiterated time and time again that land title is inextinguishable and that land rights are an absolute prerequisite for sustainable tourism" (Johnston 2000: 92). However, tourism is just one consideration in the complex process of settling these land claims. In fact, it is only relatively recently that the notion of legitimate land tenure rights for indigenous peoples gained widespread legal recognition. Early claims by indigenous people related to "aboriginal title" were generally rejected in North America under the doctrine of *terra nullius* (empty land), which asserts that "lands occupied by foraging peoples at the time of settlement by Europeans became the sole property of the 'original [European] discoverers' because native people were deemed to be even more primitive than others encountered in European expansion" (Wilmsen 1989: 2). A similar rationale was often presented to justify the displacement of indigenous peoples in other regions of the world, including Australia, until very recently (e.g., Waitt 1999).

In those instances where a sovereign state has recognized specific indigenous land titles in law, there are legal obligations associated with tourism operations on these lands. However, by judging these claims on the basis of Western legal concepts and institutions, non-Western societies have been at a definite disadvantage. The majority of indigenous territories remain under dispute. Increasingly, however, the tide has been changing. A landmark point in this change occurred in 1957 with the passing of Article 11 of the International Labour Organization Convention 107 which affirms in international law: "The right of ownership, collective or individual, of members of the populations concerned over the lands which these populations traditionally occupy" (Colchester 1994: 7). Of particular importance under this Article was the establishment of land rights based on the historic occupation of such lands and the recognition of the legitimacy of "collective" as well as "individual" land rights (McCullum and McCullum 1975). Legal rights and settlements are increasingly being awarded to indigenous peoples throughout the world, as state governments face both internal and external political pressure to resolve these land claims.

Commodification of Indigenous Culture

Tourism is characterized by its commercial nature. It is not surprising, therefore, that the tourism industry has responded to the demand for culture by packaging it into marketable products. Robinson (1999: 383) has suggested that the "tourism industry largely understands culture(s) in two ways: either as an inconsequential, and value-neutral, backdrop, or/and a product/commodity which can be packaged for the tourist." The connotation of this statement and similar views dominating much of the academic literature on the subject is that the commodification of indigenous culture is destructive and ultimately unsustainable (e.g., Whitford, Bell, and Watkins 2001). It is often argued that the commodification of culture destroys its meaning and significance. Alternatively, it may be argued that the packaging of indigenous culture for tourism is not necessarily destructive in and of itself. Even under the latter view, it is clear that the commodification of culture raises significant issues. Questions of authenticity and cultural evolution dominate these concerns.

At its most basic, authenticity refers to whether something is real or not. But, as Wong's recent (1999) review of this concept has demonstrated, there are many different perspectives on the meaning of this term in a tourism context. There is, however, widespread criticism aimed at blatantly false representations of indigenous people such as the Sami in Finland, where pseudo-ceremonies have been invented to construct marketable touristic images (Müller and Petterson 2001). Yet in the majority of cases the concerns about authenticity are less dramatic but perhaps more insidious. These concerns relate to the gradual erosion of the cultural practices and activities of indigenous peoples as they are transformed into demonstrations, souvenirs, and experiences for the consumption of visitors. Throughout this process, cultural meanings are transformed as concessions are made to accommodate restricted travel schedules, to emphasize the colorful over the mundane, and to meet the sensitivities of the visitors and the hosts. In the last instance, indigenous hosts are increasingly exercising their right to keep certain aspects of their culture private whether it is the location of sacred lands or the interpretation of activities that have particular spiritual significance. Similarly, visitors may want some exposure to indigenous cultures but they may not be looking for in-depth exposure. For example, Fagence (2000: 83) suggests that the

> interest of the tourists may not extend to profound levels of understanding the behavior, beliefs and lifestyles of these groups; rather, the interest may be superficial, focused on the token evidence of difference in such matters as the dress code, the trappings of the domestic environment, and the produce of the labor and skill of the people.

One of the ways that this type of demand has been managed in an attempt to mitigate many of the negative impacts of cultural commodification is by consciously packaging culture as a form of staged authenticity or entertainment (Ingles 2002).

Beyond the marketed product, authenticity has also emerged as an issue in terms of the business culture of indigenous tourism enterprises. In northern Canada, indigenous tourism operations have been criticized by patrons for what could be interpreted as operating practices that reflect indigenous values (e.g., less emphasis on mechanical time and more on the natural rhythms of the environment) (Notzke 1999). Such business practices often clash with the operating expectations and requirements of foreign tour operators. The level of compromise between these operating environments has a direct bearing on authenticity through the evolution of indigenous culture.

Indigenous tourism promotions (Zeppel 1998b) and activities (Petterson 2001) tend to emphasize traditional over contemporary aspects of culture. While this may be an attempt to respond to perceived demand, it creates a false and often romanticized impression of indigenous culture. Viken (1998: 46–7) provides a good illustration of the conundrum that this has created for the Sami of Scandinavia:

> There is an expectation that the Sami hosts shall perform in a traditional way. This is the image known from books and marketing materials. To satisfy their customers the Sami hosts try to fulfill these expectations and perform much more traditionally than they would usually. For example, they wear traditional clothing, use tents, and use reindeer transportation. At the same time they feel that their activities are counter-productive with regards to another important aim: to become a respected and integrated part of the world.

In this instance, the demand for traditional indigenous tourism products encourages a static culture that is consistent with existing stereotypes of the "noble savage" of the past. In reality, such stereotypes have often been romanticized to the point that they have very little basis in reality. Moreover, they ignore the fact that culture is dynamic and that authenticity is time-specific. On the other hand, the presence of growing numbers of non-indigenous visitors to the peripheral territories of indigenous peoples, along with the increased contact between indigenous tourism operators and their non-indigenous partners have in themselves become significant forces for change. These activities combine with a broad range of other globalization forces, many of which are actively pursued for their perceived benefits, to accelerate the transition from traditional to contemporary practices. It has been suggested that these conflicting trends create a paradox whereby the very process of succeeding at indigenous tourism based on the packaging of tradition leads to modernity (Ryan 1997).

The goal of sustainability is clouded by the question of what culture, or stage of a culture, to sustain given its inherent dynamic nature. Passionate efforts of the tourism industry to "protect" traditional culture may hide a form of romantic "elitism" which is actually attempting to "freeze" these cultures for the benefit of the tourists and the tourism industry rather than for the benefit of the indigenous hosts themselves. Robinson (1999) has suggested that it is not so much the dynamic nature of these cultures that should be suppressed but that indigenous hosts should exert considerable control over the nature and pace of this change. The concept of "glocalization" is used to describe the complementary heterogenizing process of affirming and reaffirming local cultural identities in the face of global forces. Indigenous peoples have the opportunity to use tourism as one of the ways in which they can exert control over this process. A good example of this approach is the way that the local indigenous people in Potosi, Bolivia are able to present their own narratives, which emphasize the tragedy of the Spanish conquest (Pretes 2002). Rather than losing their voice in the face of the dominant social group, or in the face of globalization, they have maintained it through community-based tourism.

The preservation of indigenous culture is a fundamental requirement if indigenous tourism is to be sustained. It logically and ethically becomes the prerogative and responsibility of local hosts to make decisions on the authenticity of their culture, the balance that they would like to have between traditional and contemporary representations of their culture, and ultimately whether they would like to commodify their culture. This must be attempted, however, in a complex tourism environment where the locus of control or power tends to be external to indigenous communities. Yet even external power-brokers ultimately depend on the goodwill and hospitality of local indigenous hosts if tourism activity associated with these communities is to be sustainable.

Intellectual Property Rights

There are numerous examples of indigenous images being used to promote destinations, including: Maori images in New Zealand (Ryan 1997), Sami images in Norway, Sweden, and Finland (Müller and Petterson 2001), Aboriginal images in Australia (Zeppel 1998b), and Inuit and Dene images in northern Canada (Notzke 1999). This list could be extended to almost every destination that is home to an indigenous group. Along with unique physical landscape found in a region, the cultural landscapes associated with these indigenous peoples distinguish one destination from another. Unfortunately, the tourism industry has seldom asked for permission to use these images, nor has it sought the advice of indigenous peoples on the most appropriate way to incorporate this type of information into their promotions. As a result, indigenous peoples have often been misrepresented, and they have become increasingly resentful of this practice (Waitt 1999).

The appropriation of indigenous images by the tourism industry is part of a broader issue related to intellectual property rights. This term refers to "rights asserted in the products of the mind" (Simons 2000: 412) and is inclusive of indigenous art, traditional knowledge, and many other aspects of indigenous culture. While the industry has benefited from this practice through increased visitation and expenditure, these benefits have seldom been passed along to the indigenous hosts.

In the case of Australia, Waitt (1999) argues that these practices have reinforced historic hegemonic practices of exclusion and control. The powerlessness of Aboriginal people is reinforced by the appropriation of their culture for tourism. By using these images abroad, Waitt suggests that the Australian government creates an "imagined geography" of Australia and an "imagined community" which falsely presents Aboriginal people as contented but secondary citizens in Australian society. Ryan (1997) identifies two additional issues relating to intellectual property rights in the context of tourism and the Maori in New Zealand. The first issue involves the exploitation of *taonga* (property or treasure) through fake reproduction. This exploitation involves the mass production of machine-carved souvenirs or their production with inappropriate materials. In either case, the cultural meaning of these reproductions is diminished for the indigenous hosts. The second issue is the threat to ownership and control of *taonga*. Maori claim not only ethical but also constitutional ownership over their culture. They see this ownership extending beyond relatively tangible treasures such as those housed in museums to certain types of traditional knowledge that they possess. While this latter view in particular is contested by *pakeha* (New Zealanders of European extraction), the traditional practices of cultural appropriation by the broader New Zealand tourism industry are increasingly being challenged.

Progress is being made in relation to intellectual property rights. The broader tourism industry is becoming more sensitive to the concerns of indigenous people in this regard. This increased sensitivity is the result of legal challenges and a growing appreciation that the support of indigenous peoples is needed if indigenous activities and themes are to succeed in a tourism context. Indigenous peoples have initiated trademark programs to provide evidence of authenticity, and they are increasingly seeking legal recourse for infringements of their ownership. The Maori of Aotearoa (New Zealand) are leaders in this struggle for intellectual property rights, as highlighted by their efforts to control the use of *pounamu*-greenstone and the more general appropriation of Maori heritage by tourism marketers (Hall 1996). At the same time, intellectual property rights have been receiving increased attention in non-indigenous societies as efforts are made to protect private business and artistic interests. Despite these trends, defenders of indigenous interests, such as Johnston (2000), argue that, in a legal context, it is difficult for indigenous people to win redress for infringements of their intellectual property through the legal system. One reason for this is that these rights have been developed as a Western concept (Simons 2000). They therefore emphasize the rights of the individual. In the cultural context of many indigenous peoples, the communal or collective interest is much more important. This collective interest needs to be reflected in new intellectual property right legislation if indigenous people are to enjoy more success in the courts.

The Principle of Self-Determination

Self-determination appears to be the key for sustainable indigenous tourism. This means that indigenous peoples should "set the terms for visitation to their traditional territories, as well as other third party uses of their collective cultural property" (Johnston 2000: 91). Support for this principle is inherent within the concept of community-based tourism. Zeppel (1998b: 73) arrived at a similar conclusion, as reflected in her view that the perquisites for sustainable indigenous tourism include: "land ownership, community control of tourism, government support for tourism development, restricted access to indigenous homelands and reclaiming natural or cultural resources utilized for tourism."

The challenge is to translate these objectives into practice. Litigation has been presented as one potential strategy for indigenous people to gain control. Unfortunately, this approach can be frustratingly slow and may, in fact, be counterproductive in terms of working constructively within the broader tourism industry. Two other strategies include tourism policy development and industry-based partnerships.

At a national level, tourism policy has had limited success as a strategy to operationalize the principle of self-determination of indigenous peoples in tourism. Whitford, Bell, and Watkins's assessment (2001) of indigenous tourism development in Australia suggested that most of these policies are published on an ad hoc basis; that they tend to be dominated by economic concerns, which inevitably encourage the further commodification of indigenous cultures for tourism; and that they reflect a fundamentally economic-rationalist ideology. While these policies may have strengthened Australia's position as an international tourism destination, Whitford, Bell, and Watkins conclude that they have not enhanced the level of self-determination from the perspective of the Aboriginal people. This assessment is consistent with Robinson's (1999: 385) observation that, as tourism policies emanate from the dominant social paradigm, they will tend to reflect "first world values of materialism, consumerism, and scientific rationalism." More fundamentally, they are characterized "by a paternalism and although able to shift resources, they are not equipped to deal with the transfer of power." The intransigence of existing tourism power-brokers with regard to relinquishing a significant level of control of indigenous tourism is a major obstacle facing indigenous tourism. Industry-based partnerships represent an even more direct way for indigenous people to determine the nature of their development in tourism. While it may seem like a contradiction to suggest that entering a partnership may lead to more independence, partnerships with other players in the tourism industry are essential for destination operators if they are to function effectively within the broader tourism system.

One of the fundamental constraints on these partnerships is that indigenous people tend to have different world-views than non-indigenous people (Hinch 1998). The values which guide their decisions may therefore be quite distinct from those that guide decisions of non-indigenous tourism stakeholders, one example being the communal values of indigenous people versus the individualistic perspective of non-indigenous people. Just as in the case of indigenous tourism policy, the major challenge to the real empowerment of indigenous peoples in a tourism context is that the stakeholders who currently hold power tend to be very reluctant to give it up. Robinson (1999: 193) warns:

> The operations of power between the culture of dominant paradigms within joint management arrangements and indigenous cultures that have historic claims to the land, can mean that hegemonic constructions of the indigenous culture can position it as the "other," and hence, inferior to the dominant park (tourism) management regime.

Successful partnerships require the mutual respect of each party. Indigenous people should not be viewed as intruders into the tourism business but rather as imaginative contributors whose culture is engaging and dynamic. The prerequisites for such partnerships include informed consent, a readiness to negotiate, culturally appropriate methods and timelines, and respect for traditional indigenous knowledge (Johnston 2000; Bramwell, chapter 43 this volume).

A more equitable share of power between indigenous peoples and non-indigenous tourism managers is likely to promote sustainable tourism, but it is unlikely to do so without some serious growing pains. Robinson (1999: 392) notes a fundamental challenge based on the differing world-views held by indigenous people. He raises the possibility that their decisions "may produce outcomes which do not conform to the sustainable criteria and the environmental standards developed nations expect." Such discrepancies are sure to be controversial, but they are a necessary condition of a partnership that respects indigenous viewpoints. Another example of a growing pain associated with increased indigenous control is potential conflict between tourist expectations and indigenous interests. A good illustration of this has occurred in the context of visitor behavior at Uluru (Ayers Rock) in central Australia. While Aboriginal people have initiated an educational campaign discouraging visitors from climbing this sacred site, visitors have been slow to change this practice (Brown 1999). Patience will be required for this type of strategy to work. Despite these challenges, it is clear that sustainable indigenous tourism depends upon the establishment of effective working partnerships. Hall (2000: 69) emphasized the necessity of these relationships for national park partners by arguing that "national parks are a cultural landscape and in order for the environmental processes which create that landscape to be effectively maintained, it is vital that the cultural component through the contribution of Aboriginal peoples become a living element of contemporary park management."

Conclusion

This chapter has explored the question of sustainability in the context of indigenous tourism with special attention given to indigenous territory, the commodification of culture, and the protection of intellectual property rights. Significant challenges were identified in all of these areas, but it is also clear that there has been progress for indigenous people especially in terms of the recognition of legal title over traditional lands. Legal title provides more opportunity for self-determination. Resolutions to the challenges in the realms of the commodification of culture and the protection of intellectual property rights are also closely related to the principle of self-determination. Self-determination is not enough, however. Decision-makers need to have an accurate understanding of the dynamics of tourism development if they are to plot the most preferable course for indigenous people in terms of tourism development.

One of the challenges facing researchers in this area is the multifaceted nature of indigenous communities. Although reference was made to this complexity earlier in this chapter, much more attention is merited. Indigenous communities are dynamic and they are heterogeneous. Smith's (1989) seminal writing in this area highlighted the fact that early tourism entrepreneurs of indigenous descent were often marginalized in their communities as they tried to straddle cultures. Similarly, indigenous communities have traditionally valued the wisdom of their elders, and while this generally remains true, schisms have emerged between indigenous youth and community elders. The extent to which these divisions parallel the "generation gaps" found in other societies or represents a fundamental shift in indigenous values needs additional consideration. In a similar vein, the cross-cultural issues raised in this chapter are themselves complicated by the globalization of world economies and societies. The implication of this for tourism researchers is that indigenous tourism is a moving target. Research in this area needs to recognize and account for this dynamic in relation to the research questions that are raised, the way that they are addressed, and the way that the findings are interpreted.

Much work therefore remains to be done in the study of indigenous people and tourism. One of the ironies of the existing literature in this area is that it is dominated by non-indigenous voices. The power imbalance between indigenous and non-indigenous decision-makers in terms of the practice of tourism is therefore paralleled in the realm of study and research associated with this topic. Indigenous voices are therefore needed to provide a more complete range of cultural perspectives. From a disciplinary perspective, geographers are in a privileged position to provide research insights into the dynamics of tourism as it relates to indigenous peoples. Research that relates to space, place, and the environment can make a major contribution to the pursuit of sustainable indigenous tourism as it addresses the nexus between land and culture.

REFERENCES

Brown, T. J. (1999). Antecedents of culturally significant tourist behavior. *Annals of Tourism Research* 26(3), 676–700.

Butler, R. W., and Hinch, T. D. (eds) (1996). *Tourism and Indigenous Peoples*. London: International Thomson Business Press.

Colchester, M. (1994). Salvaging nature: indigenous peoples, protected areas and biodiversity conservation. Discussion paper. Geneva: United Nations Research Institute for Social Development.

de Burlo, C. (1996). Cultural resistance and ethnic tourism on South Pentecost, Vanuatu. In R.W. Butler and T. D. Hinch (eds), *Tourism and Indigenous Peoples* (pp. 255–76). London: International Thomson Business Press.

Fagence, M. (2000). Ethnic tourism in developed countries: Special interest or specialized mass tourism? *Tourism Recreation Research* 25(2), 77–87.

Gray, A. (1991). Between the spice of life and the melting pot: Biodiversity conservation and its impact on indigenous peoples. IWGIA Document no. 70. Copenhagen: International Work Group on International Affairs.

Hall, C. M. (1996). Tourism and the Maori of Aotearoa, New Zealand. In R.W. Butler and T. D. Hinch (eds), *Tourism and Indigenous Peoples* (pp. 155–75). London: International Thomson Business Press.

Hall, C. M. (2000). Tourism, national parks and Aboriginal peoples. In R.W. Butler and S. W. Boyd (eds), *Tourism and National Parks* (pp. 57–72). Chichester: John Wiley.

Hinch, T. D. (1998). Ecotourists and indigenous hosts: Diverging views on their relationship with nature. *Current Issues in Tourism* 1(1), 120–3.

Hinch, T. D. (2001). Indigenous territories. In D. B. Weaver (ed.), *The Encyclopedia of Ecotourism* (pp. 345–58). Wallingford: CAB International.

Hinch, T. D., and Butler, R. W. (1996). Indigenous tourism: A common ground for discussion. In R. W. Butler and T. D. Hinch (eds), *Tourism and Indigenous Peoples* (pp. 3–19). London: International Thomson Business Press.

Hollinshead, K. (1992). "White" gaze, "red" people. Shadow visions: The disidentification of "Indians" in cultural tourism. *Leisure Studies* 11, 43–64.

Hollinshead, K. (1996). Marketing and metaphysical realism: The disidentification of Aboriginal life and traditions through tourism. In R.W. Butler and T. D. Hinch (eds), *Tourism and Indigenous Peoples* (pp. 308–48). London: International Thomson Business Press.

Ingles, P. (2002). Welcome to my village: Hosting tourists in the Peruvian Amazon. *Tourism Recreation Research* 27(1), 53–60.

Johnston, A. (2000). Indigenous peoples and ecotourism: Bringing indigenous knowledge and rights into the sustainability equation. *Tourism Recreation Research* 25(2), 89–96.

McCullum, H., and McCullum, K. (1975). *This Land is Not For Sale*. Toronto: Anglican Book Centre.

Müller, D. K., and Petterson, R. (2001). Access to Sami tourism in Northern Sweden. *Scandinavian Journal of Hospitality and Tourism* 1, 5–18.

Notzke, D. (1999). Indigenous tourism development in the Arctic. *Annals of Tourism Research* 26, 55–76.

Petterson, R. (2001) Sami tourism: Supply and demand. Ostersund and Umeå: European Tourism Research Institute and Department of Social and Economic Geography, University of Umea.

Pretes, M. (2002). Touring mines and mining tourists. *Annals of Tourism Research* 29(2), 439–56.

Robinson, M. (1999). Collaboration and cultural consent: Refocusing sustainable tourism. *Journal of Sustainable Tourism* 7(3/4), 379–97.

Ryan, C. (1997). Maori and tourism: A relationship of history, constitutions and rites. *Journal of Sustainable Tourism* 5(4), 257–78.

Simons, M. S. (2000). Aboriginal heritage art and moral rights. *Annals of Tourism Research* 27(2), 412–31.

Smith, V. (ed.) (1989). *Hosts and Guests: The Anthropology of Tourism*, 2nd edn. Philadelphia: University of Pennsylvania Press.

Stevens, S. (1997). Introduction. In S. Stevens (ed.), *Conservation Through Cultural Survival: Indigenous Peoples and Protected Areas* (pp. 1–8). Washington, DC: Island Press.

United Nations Development Programme (UNDP) (n.d.). Indigenous peoples. <www.undp.org/csopp/CSO/NewFiles/ipaboutfaqs.html> (accessed February 6, 2003).

Viken, A. (1998). Ethnic tourism: which ethnicity? In M. E. Johnston, G. D. Twynam, and W. Haider (eds), *Shaping Tomorrow's North: The Role of Tourism and Recreation* (pp. 37–53). Northern and Regional Studies Series no. 7. Thunder Bay: Lakehead University.

Waitt, G. (1999). Naturalizing the "primitive": a critique of marketing Australia's indigenous peoples as "hunter-gatherers." *Tourism Geographies* 1(2), 142–63.

Whitford, M., Bell, B., and Watkins, M. (2001). Indigenous tourism policy in Australia: 25 years of rhetoric and economic rationalism. *Current Issues in Tourism* 4(2/4), 151–81.

Wilmsen, E. N. (1989). *We Are Here: Politics and Aboriginal Land Tenure*. Berkeley: University of California Press.

Wong, N. (1999). Rethinking authenticity in tourism experience. *Annals of Tourism Research* 26(2), 349–70.

Wuttunee, W. A. (1992). *In Business For Ourselves*. Montreal and Kingston: McGill-Queens University Press.

Zeppel, H. (1998a). Land and culture: Sustainable tourism and indigenous peoples. In C. M. Hall and A. A. Lew (eds), *Sustainable Tourism: A Geographical Perspective* (pp. 60–74). New York: Longman.

Zeppel, H. (1998b). "Come share our culture": Marketing Aboriginal tourism in Australia. *Pacific Tourism Review* 2(1), 67–81.

Part V Tourists, Values, and Practices

Chapter 21

Tourist Motivation and Typologies

Richard Prentice

A Hotchpotch for a Legacy

Motivation is about the causes of personal action, in tourism and in other activities. Our understanding of tourists' motivations is surprisingly limited in view of the potential importance of motivations in framing appropriate product design and marketing. A little harshly perhaps, the legacy of motivational discourse in tourism can be described as a hotchpotch. It is a multiple legacy, and these different legacies structure the present chapter. In so doing, the present discussion ignores the frequent structural distinction between "push" factors as individual factors and "pull" factors as destination or attraction factors likely to meet motives for travel. In a mass consumption world, this distinction is essentially irrelevant as tourism is mediated (Ooi 2002), overtly through package tours and advertising, or more covertly through television, magazines, guide books, attraction interpretation or internet sites and the like. What the individual is seeking is in part what she or he has been led to believe is desirable in personal identity formation: she or he is varyingly versatile within the mediated structure experienced. Further, given that needs as motivators are potentially innumerable in variety, in the practical sense of destination promotion, it is often more useful to start from the product base of the destination, and the motivations this product base can meet.

Motivations are simultaneously inferred and potentially plural, the former either by those actually undertaking the action or by others. Even seemingly "obvious" motivations for behavior may be incomplete. For example, female tourists seeking sex with beach boys have been described as actually seeking romance, rather than sex with as many partners as possible (Herold, Garcia, and DeMoya 2001). These women are described as seekers of flattery, physical contact, and the opportunity to buy gifts for their "lover." Similarly, tourists who can be classed as ecotourists by their visiting patterns often have motivations that are far from straightforward. For example, most tourists to a Thai national park have been found to be "highlights" tourists: tourists visiting iconic sites with no further ecotourism intentions, and arguably not ecotourists at all (Hvengaard and Dearden 1998).

That the "obvious" interpretation of behavior may be wrong is not the only hazard in considering tourists' motivations and groupings. The very limited cross-cultural research that is available demonstrates substantial differences between even globally contiguous cultures. For example, Moscardo et al. (2001) considered three types of beach tourism: eco-coastal tourists, active beach tourists, and passive beach tourists. In a three-country comparison, the first group was found to be most common in Germany, the second in The Netherlands, and the third in the United Kingdom. Similarly, tourists to New Zealand's national parks have been found to vary by national group in terms of the "purity" of the wilderness perception sought (Higham 1998): Australian and British tourists were found to be much more demanding of a "pure" experience, and Japanese and Israeli tourists much more demanding of a "non-purist" experience. And yet cross-cultural comparisons are comparatively few! Nor should we assume that tourists necessarily rationalize their motivations in advance of their actions (or at any time, unless asked), and act accordingly. Concerns about tourists' inability to reflect on, or reveal, their true motives are hardly new (Pearce and Caltabiano 1983), but tend to have been ignored in tourism. In contrast, some consumer behavioralists and leisure scientists have instead tried to predict behavior not from motivation, but from behavioral, normative, and control beliefs (Ajzen and Driver 1991). Oh and Hsu (2001) have recently used such an approach in tourism. Kim and Littrell (2001) have also used beliefs to predict North Americans' holiday souvenir purchases. They used interest in other cultures, consumer ethnocentrism, and open-mindedness as predictors. However, studies such as these are comparatively unusual. As such, when motivation is explicitly considered in tourism, it is usually subject to post priori rationalization and interpretation by those motivated, by businesses and organizations seeking to motivate people to become tourists at their destination, and by academics. Potentially it is a hotly contested area of tourism research, but strangely one that in practice has lacked dialogue or dialectic. Instead, it has left a substantially uncontested mix of models and paradigms on the one hand, and, on the other, case studies, many of which are practical studies, some unrelated to academic paradigms. Of the former, the legacy of models is essentially psychological in origin, dealing with individuals; that of paradigms is generally sociological, dealing with tourists as groups. Both models and paradigms have offered, or have been used, as grand theories purporting to explain *the* universal essential of motivation in tourism. On the other hand, we are proffered a multitude of site-specific studies of destinations and attractions, often lacking both generality and prospect for change or substitution. It is as if in one context we collectively think all tourists are essentially the same in terms of motivation (or can be easily segmented into a few universal groups or described by key motivations), and in another, that all destinations and attractions are essentially different in their motivational profile. This paradox is only partly explained by different commentators or researchers working in different traditions, and not comparing traditions; equally it flows from the different audiences the work is intended for.

Other theoretical limitations also abound in this mixed legacy. In the extreme, motivations to visit destinations have sometimes been defined in case studies simply as the desire to visit a castle, a museum, a beach, a pub, etc. In other words, motivations have been defined as propensities to undertake activities, without thought to the differing benefits tourists might gain from doing so. Further, both leisure and tourism and work and tourism have often been thought of as conceptually distinctive: indeed, that tourism is the opposite to work. Such assumptions further oversimplify our thinking. Often, tourism is implicitly divorced from lifestyle by the assumptions made by many writers. This matters, for a stance of looking to identify the benefits people are seeking in the sequence of personally meaningful leisure and work experiences they themselves evolve, and then relating these to tourism choices about destinations and activities, has not been a dominant tradition. This is despite lifestyle being increasingly recognized by academics as a primary driver to personal identity in affluent Western societies (Edensor 2002), and holidaying being integral to contemporary lifestyles for many. It is also despite contemporary practice, with *VisitScotland*, for example, in 2002 suggesting that we "*Live it*" by visiting Scotland for a holiday. As such, this chapter is as much about the need for a new approach as it is about consolidating existing knowledge.

The Legacy of Dominant Models and Paradigms

The paradox of silence in motivational debate by academics in large part flows from the largely uncritical acceptance in the 1980s and 1990s of particular models and paradigms describing tourism consumption. Ten years ago, Pearce (1993) reviewed the leading three psychological models. That his review still stands today as a comprehensive and current discussion of issues in itself indicates some lack of conceptual progress since then. Pearce identified three theoretical approaches to motivational psychology in tourism: *psychocentric-allocentric*, the *travel career ladder*, and *intrinsic motivation-optimal arousal*. As these models appear frequently in general introductory tourism texts their substantial elaboration is unnecessary here.

The psychocentric-allocentric model was developed by Plog in the 1970s to explain destination choice by airline passengers, psychocentrics being non-adventuresome and inhibited, allocentrics being adventurous and variety-seeking. It is a unidimensional model (reducing all motivation for airline travel to a single dimension of personality), but was still the subject of active debate in the 1990s (Smith 1990; Nickerson and Ellis 1991; Griffith and Albanese 1996).

The second model develops from Maslow's general motivational theory of the 1950s, with a hierarchy of needs, and is thus part of a much broader theoretical application. The ladder model postulates an ascending hierarchy of needs from relaxation/bodily needs, through stimulation needs, relationship needs, and self-esteem needs, to fulfillment needs, through which a tourist will progress through experience. The laddering model was debated in the 1990s (Loker-Murphy 1996; Kim 1997; Ryan 1997, 1998), but is limited in its fundamental assumption that all tourists tend to progress through the same succession of motivations as a career. It also ignores socialization as a substitute for experience. It further ignores the complexity of needs felt, as illustrated by the mix of holiday types taken by tourists, or the mix of activities they may undertake when on holiday.

The intrinsic motivational model defines depth of motivation, beginning with the superficial reasons given in leisure participation surveys. These progress in terms of depth through perceived freedom and competence, needs for optimal arousal, to biological, socialization, and personality factors. Both the latter models therefore impel selective orderings of motivations. The intrinsic motivation-optimal arousal model flows from the work of Iso-Ahola (1982), and is of particular importance in reminding us of how difficult it can be to understand the real motivations of tourists, and the need to be cautious of the summary methodologies frequently used to elicit so-called motivations. Most of the motivations solicited in this way are best described as "reasons" for making a trip, rather than motivations.

The legacy of sociological paradigms is one that describes the purposes of tourism in terms of consumption. The first is the *romantic* paradigm (figure 21.1) in which the use of tourism is primarily for personal enlightenment, with motivations to consume the extraordinary as a means to self-education and spirituality. This is essentially a pre-mass tourism form of consumption, enjoyed by the European elite of the eighteenth and nineteenth centuries. The second paradigm (figure 21.2) concerns *mass tourism*, for which escape from the everyday tedium of work into a dream world is seen as the principal motivator. This leads to the proffering and consumption of both inauthenticity and triviality, in a vicious circle of mindlessness. It is difficult to break out of this paradigm, as inauthenticity is consumed because that is all that is available. The consumption of inauthenticity occurs either intentionally (to escape the harsh realities of authenticity) or because there was little else offered as a tourism experience through standardization in commodification, even if authenticity was in fact sought. Both paradigms emphasize the visual as sensory enjoyment. In particular, MacCannell's (1976) and Urry's (1990, 1995) work fed these paradigms. MacCannell's work was particularly important in setting North American research agendas in tourism, and Urry's in northern Europe, particularly in Britain, where tourism research expanded enormously in volume in the 1990s. The motivationally reductionalist intent implicit in MacCannell's work – a reduction

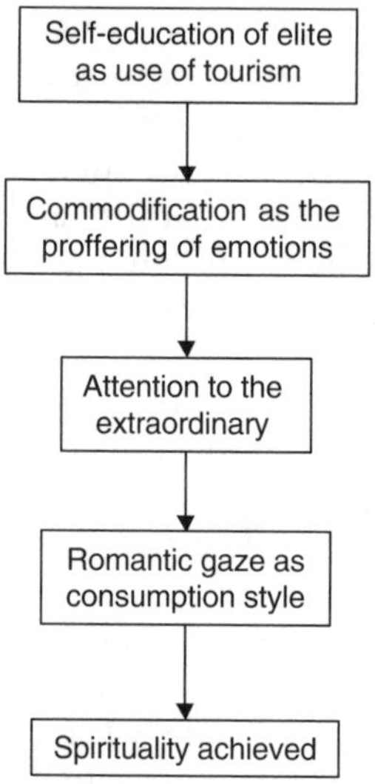

Figure 21.1 The romantic paradigm

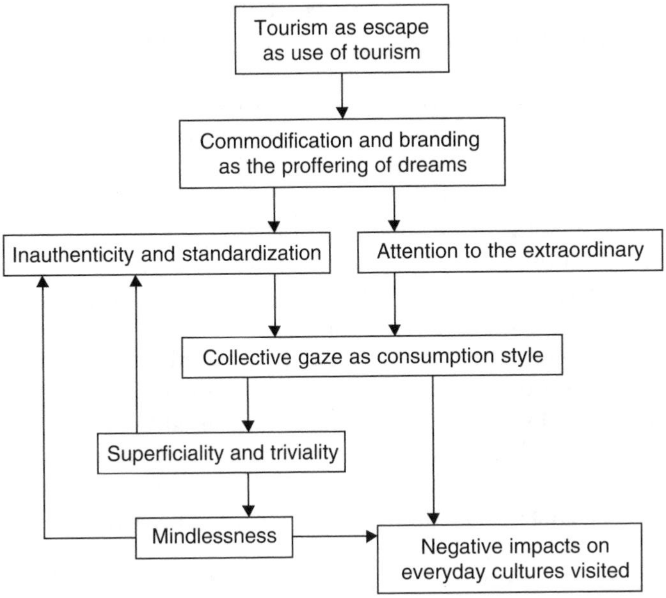

Figure 21.2 The mass tourism paradigm

to the futile search for authenticity – can be seen in the title of his book, "*The* Tourist" (as if there was only one, or one sort of, tourist). Urry's attempt also to develop a postmodern gaze was essentially aesthetic in focus, with aesthetic judgments made about places by tourists, and their semiotic skills in the interpretation of mediated tourism.

The mass tourism paradigm was largely useful in explaining motivations for beach and poolside tourism, clubbing and like gregarious tourism, casual sightseeing, and also the superficiality of international travel to consume essentially visual imagery of distant (often tribal or peasant) cultures. But it assumes a general mindlessness on the part of tourists, passivity, and the dominance of the visual. Not all tourists are mindless, nor are all primarily motivated by escape and the desire to consume unreal dreams as a form of self-delusion. Nor are all passive or accepting only of essentially visual experiences. Experiential learning has been frequently found as a motivator for tourists visiting heritage attractions, with processes of reflection prompted by spotting items familiar from a tourist's past or prompting conscience (Prentice 1993a; Prentice, Witt, and Hamer 1998; McIntosh and Prentice 1999; Herbert 2001). What might be thought surprising in the extent to which the mass tourism paradigm affected thinking about tourism motivation, is that, in the 1970s, Cohen (1979) identified a phenomenology of tourism experiences which included mindful as well as mindless forms of contemporary tourism.

The Legacy of Case Studies

Case studies, particularly those derived from practitioner surveys, have long been commented on in respect of their limitations of varying definitions and lack of sophistication (Prentice 1989). One legacy of the many case studies looking at motivation is a plethora of "reasons" for visiting; another is a range of tourist typologies, many of which are not in fact based upon motivation. Some present formidable batteries of motivational scaling. For example, Murphy and Williams's (1999) respondents were asked to rate their motivations on 80 specific trip motivational scales and nearly 40 general motivational scales. A vast bulk of empirical studies exists, which is of potential use to researchers as a resource to be dipped into to inform more systematic arguments. Also, what is obvious to practitioners from commonsense reflection on their daily routine of servicing tourists may not be obvious to academics. As such, practitioner studies can inadvertently challenge established discourses by providing evidence about motivation which does not fit established paradigms. For example, attention to mindfulness through tourism owes its prominence today in part to practitioner studies and practitioner-funded studies, which repeatedly showed the importance of insight-gaining motivations and experiences among sizeable proportions of visitors to heritage attractions (Herbert, Prentice, and Thomas 1989; Prentice 1993a). Unfortunately, many practitioner case studies remain restricted in availability, and are often unknown to the wider research community.

From the mass of case studies, those which have developed motivational typologies of tourists are of particular interest. Only a few can be mentioned here to indicate the potential resource that exists. Those selected for presentation here are largely from academics as they are accessible internationally to readers of this chapter. These studies also more readily offer challenges to established ideas about motivations.

- Tourists interested in Australian aboriginals have been grouped into seven types (Ryan and Huyton 2000): iconic sightseers, reluctant engagers, campervanners, intellectual comfort seekers, active information seekers, nature-orientated tourists, and those visiting friends or relatives.
- Tourists visiting Australian wilderness have been grouped into five types (Ryan and Sterling 2001): day visitors to easily accessible sites, hedonists, generalists, four-wheel drive enthusiasts, and information seekers.
- Tourists interested in Maori culture have been grouped into six segments (McIntosh, Smith, and Ingram 2000): cultural tourists, organized tour participants, cultural experientialists, once in a lifetimers, family fun lovers, and general sightseers.
- Short break tourists in England have been likewise grouped into six segments (MEW Research 1994): cities and culture, brogues (tourists wearing strong walking shoes) and National Trust, kids rule OK, out for good time, sport and interests, and rural relaxation.
- Autumn visitors to US national parks have been similarly grouped into six segments (Spotts and Mahoney 1993): inactives, active recreationists/non-hunters, campers, passive recreationists, strictly autumn colors viewers, and active recreationists/hunters.
- Snow mobiler tourists in Wyoming have been grouped into five segments (May et al. 2001): nature lovers seeking to be alone, avid snow mobilers wanting to "experience it all," those wanting to be alone but not too excited, nature lovers

not wanting to be too excited, and nature lovers wanting to be with family and friends.

- Summer tourists to North Carolina have also been grouped into six sorts by benefits sought (Loker and Perdue 1992): naturalists, non-differentiators, family/friend-orientated, excitement/escape, pure excitement seekers, and escapists.

There is nothing magical or "natural" in the recurrence of a similar number of groups. Researchers try to balance group homogeneity with a need to have only a manageable number of groups to consider. However, as there are an infinite number of attributes to use to differentiate groups, and destinations differ in how they meet needs, there is an infinite array of potential groupings. The need for theoretical reference is obvious if some reduction to more generic types of groups across like destinations is to be obtained.

Alternative Conceptualizations

Even during the 1990s when the paradigm of figure 21.2 was enthusiastically embraced by many academics in tourism studies, alternative motivational interpretations had developed in leisure and tourism, often with long antecedents. These recognized the importance of multiple motivation. Among others, these alternative interpretations involved the work of Crompton, Stebbins, Driver and Brown, and Prentice. In the 1970s, Crompton (1979) had postulated a system of leisure motives in tourism: novelty, socialization/kinship, prestige, relaxation, education/knowledge, and regression. This system was tested and developed in the 1990s, for example in the context of cultural tourism (Crompton and McKay 1997; Andersen, Prentice, and Watanabe 2000). Stebbins' work had likewise originated from the 1970s (Stebbins 1979), but was incorporated into tourism discourse more in the 1990s. It too was incorporated for its contribution to the understanding of cultural tourism (Stebbins 1996, 1997a, 1997b). Stebbins has argued that some cultural tourists are career-like in their commitment. They are motivated by perseverance, attaining stages of achievement, the acquisition of specialist knowledge, membership of a specialist world, identity formation and the desire for long-term benefits. Stebbins has termed this *serious leisure*. The multiple benefits he identified include: self-actualization, self-enrichment, self-expression, self-gratification, and image enhancement. The notion of "serious leisure" has subsequently been applied to other areas, notably special interest tourism. For example, Crang (1996) described much the same. Driver and Brown developed the *Benefit Chain of Causality* conceptualization in leisure science during the 1980s (Manning 1986; Driver, Brown, and Peterson 1991). It focused motivational attention on what tourists seek as multiple benefits from their activities and experiences (Prentice and Light 1994). Finally, in the 1990s as a basis for heritage interpretation at attractions, Prentice was interested in the multiple benefits tourists sought and gained from visiting cultural attractions (Prentice 1993b; Beeho and Prentice 1996; Prentice, Davies, and Beeho 1997). The benefits sought included a general insight into what was being visited. Taken together, these authors – along with others not mentioned here – implicitly and explicitly challenged the dominant paradigm of mass tourism.

Back to Basics in Conceptualization

If tourism is in fact both multi-motivational and made up of multiple groups of tourists, many of whom are experienced as tourists and versatile in their use of tourism, and some of whom demand more than superficiality, a conceptual rethink is needed. For example, once we accept that many tourists are experienced in being tourists, critical, and often socialized into tourism, our potential inability to understand their deep motivations through asking them to rationalize their motivations is less important. As a proxy, we can ask about what they found meaningful in their present or past tourism experiences, and assume that their descriptions imply signposts to motivation. We can use these signposts to ask *why* each tourist found her or his experience meaningful, and *why* this was important. This is an application of the *Means–End Chain* linking behavior with values (Gutman 1982; Klenosky, Gengler, and Mulvey 1993). In other words, we can use the experiences of experienced tourists and others as a way into deeper motivations. The diary extract included as table 21.1 is an example of this frequently overlooked approach. It is from a professional informant in a service sector (destinations and actual activities being removed to ensure confidentiality). Tourists can also be asked what sort of person by interest they might think would enjoy the destination they themselves have experienced (Irish Marketing Surveys Ltd. 1995). Or we can ask tourists to compare their rating of their last destination with their expectations of their next (Shoemaker 1994).

A conceptual rethink is also required if tourism is no longer an exceptional part of people's lives. That leisure, work, and tourism are fully distinctive aspects of human existence defies common observation in postmodern society. In an extreme form, holidaying in Europe has been found to be a means of career advancement for some Japanese (Andersen, Prentice, and Watanabe 2000). More generally, *neo tribes* have been commented on (Maffesoli 1996), as impermanent collectives of individuals seeking everyday meaning through a multitude of individual acts of self-identification. This is the celebration of lived experience, with identity found in the everyday mix of experiences (Edensor 2002). In Britain, the blending of work and leisure can be seen in the offices, galleries, bars, and cafés of London, Edinburgh, Newcastle, Glasgow, Cardiff, and other cities. The mobile phone and laptop have put the office into the café and bar. The internet has brought a virtual world of personal exploration and imagining into the office. The spatial form of cities shows the same mixing, with bank and exchange buildings becoming bars, former warehouses becoming galleries, and residential and office uses blended together to create the 24-hour city. Those parts of cities now used for recreation have also developed tourism uses, as cities become destinations in their own right. Tourists are attracted from one city to another to experience varieties of the same, differentiated by a sense of place, if only by remnants of earlier architectural styles or regional cuisine, or by the language spoken or the accent in which the same language is spoken. This has been termed "globalization from below" (Henry, McEwen, and Pollard 2002), with cities mobilizing their cultural diversity to reinvent themselves as variants of a similar cultural mixing sought by consumers.

That service sector workers tend increasingly to do the same in leisure time in their home areas as when they are on holiday is being picked up in surveys of leisure

Table 21.1 Extracts from an informant's reflexive motivational diary

Day	Principal activity	Duration	Type of activity	Type of time	Location	Why undertaken?	Why is this important to you?
week 1/day 4 Wednesday	Writing	Morning	Employment	Holiday	Home	To meet deadline	Pride in meeting deadlines; integral part of job
	Shopping	Afternoon	Domestic work	Holiday	Home city	To assemble items	Items needed for home
	Watching film	Evening	Leisure	Own time	Home	Entertainment	Imaginative relaxation
1/6 Friday	Preparation for trip and travel to Other Country 2	All day	Employment	Paid work	Home city, Other Country 1 (en route) and Other Country 2	Networking for business links	Integral part of job
				Own time (evening)			
1/7 Saturday	Ethnic shopping	Morning	Leisure	Own time	Other Country 2	To find souvenirs authentic to the country	As items to treasure and to recall the trip
	Museum visit	Afternoon	Professional development	Own time	Other Country 2	To inform myself professionally and to understand country visited	To continue to learn through engagement with new subject matter
	Dined out	Evening	Leisure	Own time	Other Country 2	To spend time with spouse	To be together

Cont'd

Table 21.1 *Cont'd*

Day	Principal activity	Duration	Type of activity	Type of time	Location	Why undertaken?	Why is this important to you?
week 2/day 1 Sunday	Ethnic shopping	Morning	Leisure	Own time	Other Country 2	To help spouse in secondary business and to find souvenirs authentic to the country	To help each other and to acquire items to treasure and to recall the trip
	Travel within Other Country 2	Afternoon	Employment	Own time	Other Country 2	Networking for business links	Integral part of job
	Meeting	Evening	Employment	Own time	Other Country 2	Networking for business links	Integral part of job
2/2 Monday	Meetings	Morning	Employment	Paid work	Other Country 2	Networking for business links	Integral part of job
	Site visits	Afternoon	Employment	Paid work	Other Country 2	To inform presentation for tomorrow	Integral part of job
	Meeting	Evening	Employment	Own time	Other Country 2	Networking for business links	Integral part of job
2/4 Wednesday	Meetings	Morning	Employment	Paid work	Other Country 2	Networking for business links	Integral part of job
	Site visit	Afternoon	Professional development	Paid work	Other Country 2	To inform myself professionally	To continue to learn through engagement with new subject matter
	Meetings	Evening	Employment	Own time	Other Country 2	Networking for business links	Integral part of job

2/5 Thursday	Writing report on trip	Early hours	Employment	Own time	Other Country 2	Networking for business links	Integral part of job
	Drafting proposal	Morning	Employment	Own time	Other Country 2	Business development	Integral part of job
	Travelling within Other Country 2	Morning	Employment	Paid work	Other Country 2	Networking for business links	Integral part of job
	Met with spouse	Afternoon	Leisure	Own time	Other Country 2	To spend time with spouse	To be together (spouse also on a business trip)
	Travelling back home	Afternoon and evening	Employment	Paid work and own time	Other Country 2 and home city	Networking for business links	Integral part of job
2/6 Friday	Writing proposal	Morning	Employment	Paid work	Home	Business development	Integral part of job
	Travel to Other Country 3	Afternoon and evening	Employment	Paid work and own time	Home city and Other Country 3	To lead a training summer school for young professionals	Contribution to professional development of others; integral part of job
2/7 Saturday	Travel within Other Country 3	Early hours	Employment	Own time	Other Country 3	To lead a training summer school for young professionals	Contribution to professional development of others
	Site visit	Morning and afternoon	Professional development	Own time	Other Country 3	To inform myself professionally and to enjoy the works displayed	To continue to learn through engagement with new subject matter

Cont'd

Table 21.1 *Cont'd*

Day	Principal activity	Duration	Type of activity	Type of time	Location	Why undertaken?	Why is this important to you?
week 3/day 1 Sunday	Site visits	Morning	Professional development	Own time	Other Country 3	To inform myself professionally and to understand country visited	To continue to learn through engagement with new subject matter
	Museum visits with colleagues from Other Country 3	Afternoon	Employment	Own time	Other Country 3	To inform presentation for tomorrow	Contribution to professional development of others
	Dinner meeting	Evening	Employment	Own time	Other Country 3	To help young professionals	Contribution to professional development of others
3/3 Tuesday	Ethnic shopping	Morning	Leisure	Own time	Other Country 3	To find souvenirs and gifts authentic to the country	As items to treasure and to recall the trip
	Shopping	Morning	Professional development	Own time	Other Country 3	To locate and buy professional literature pertinent to country visited	Development of personal professional expertise

	Presentation and review of those of others	Afternoon	Employment	Paid work	Other Country 3	To help young professionals	Contribution to professional development of others
	Dinner party	Evening	Leisure	Own time	Other Country 3	To socialize with new colleague	To be hospitable and to gain insight into country visited; integral part of job
	Writing	Evening	Employment	Own time	Other Country 3	To meet deadline	Pride in meeting deadlines; integral part of job
3/7 Saturday	Transporting and setting up displays	Morning	Domestic work	Own time	Home city	To help spouse in secondary business	To help each other
	Museum visit	Afternoon	Leisure	Own time	Home country	Relaxation	Rejuvenation

activities. For example, Aitchison (2002) has recently found the recurrence of "holiday" activities among an affluent middle-class sample in their "leisure" activities, including going away for the weekend. Walking, visits to parks and to countryside, visits to historic sites and villages, visits to museums and theatres, were equally frequent leisure pursuits as holiday pursuits among her sample. A similar intermixing is apparent from the diary extract included as table 21.1. The intermixing is not only at the level of activities, but also at that of the purposes for which the activities were undertaken. Leisure, work, and tourism intertwine in these extracts. Likewise, young city clubbers tend to enjoy clubbing as leisure or tourism, or as an adjutant to work. With low-cost airline travel, the nightlife of the cities of Europe is increasingly accessible to young British adults, enabling the hedonistic enjoyment of clubbing Europe-wide: where shall we party this weekend? Much the same has been written about *échangisme* in France, married couples clubbing or holidaying to have sex with strangers, and so-called "swinging" in Britain (Wee 2003). Indeed, interpretations of *échangisme* show the difficulties of inferring motivation. Do 30-something Parisians using a *club échangiste* do so merely for entertainment, or are they seeking to preserve otherwise failing marriages? More generally, do these clubs threaten or preserve the marriage and couple structure, and are they antidotes to or agents of social repression and conservatism?

A conceptual rethink is also needed if familiarity is sought through tourism. Holidaying in table 21.1 concerns the familiar as much as it does the extraordinary: for example, the informant does much the same as a business tourist in both places, and likewise at home. Motivation to consume the familiar is in fact by no means unusual. Summarily, this can be inferred through simple profiling of visitors in several ways: as visiting the same place, being a tourist within one's own country, visiting countries with similar cultures, or doing the same things in different places. For example, in 2001, over three-quarters of all tourists to the island of Bornholm were repeat visitors (Hartl and Rassing 2002). Of the repeat tourists, four out of ten had made in excess of ten previous visits to the island. Of all tourists to this Danish island in the Baltic, two-thirds were visitors from elsewhere within Denmark. Most other visitors were from neighboring countries: a fifth were from Germany and a tenth from Sweden. Compared to the situation five years previously the consumption of the familiar would seem to have *increased* for those visiting Bornholm (Rassing and Hartl-Nielsen 1997). In terms of doing much the same thing in different places, it has been known for at least two decades that heritage site visitors frequently include substantial proportions of recent visitors to other similar heritage attractions (Prentice 1989). Of the tourists among these visitors, many have been found to have made leisure trips from home to a range of heritage attractions (Prentice 1993a). It has also been found that familiarity with a place is a key influence both on the way a place is imagined and the propensity to visit it (Prentice and Andersen 2000). The theoretical underpinning to an interest in the familiar comes from work on the construction of identity through everyday experience, rather than through exotic experience (Edensor 2002). The practical consequence in marketing is to evoke familiarity.

If familiarity is in fact as important as the exotic as a tourism motivator, how is it developed, and how should it be investigated? The process is essentially informal (Prentice and Light 1994). It is also affective. Gyimóthy (2000) had tourists to

Bornholm describe their holidays to her in their own words. Her study in effect operationalized the logic of looking at the experience of the experienced to understand their deeper motivations. The attraction of the island, and therefore why people visited and returned, was its perceived purity and calmness, the nostalgia for a past Denmark which their visit prompted, the island's Scandinavianness in neither compelling interaction with locals nor denying it, and its difference from contemporary, busy urban Denmark. It was felt to be a cosy place, reassuring, amiable, and keeping vital traditions alive: in essence visitors were consuming their own or an allied ethnicity, and returning to do so. Repeat visitors were building their cultural capital through becoming more familiar with the destination, in effect, getting beyond superficialities to more nuanced understandings. As such, every visit was progressive and a different version of the same as familiarity was built up.

This reconceptualization leads to a third paradigm, that of *lifestyle formation* (figure 21.3). Central to this paradigm is becoming rather than being through tourism, and, on the one hand, the motivational objectives of mindfulness and cultural capital accumulation to achieve this, and on the other, hedonism. In this paradigm tourism is a purposive and expressive activity. Quite literally, journeys are made for experiences (Prentice 2001). This is the paradigm allied to the *VisitScotland* slogan mentioned earlier, "*Live it.*" As such, paradigm and practice are in this case beginning to concur. It is a paradigm in which tourists construct their own itineraries, blending aspects of mass tourism with those of more particular interest: in essence buying components from multiple suppliers to "live" one's holiday (Sørensen 1999; Ooi 2002). Similar to shopping for clothes in a department store,

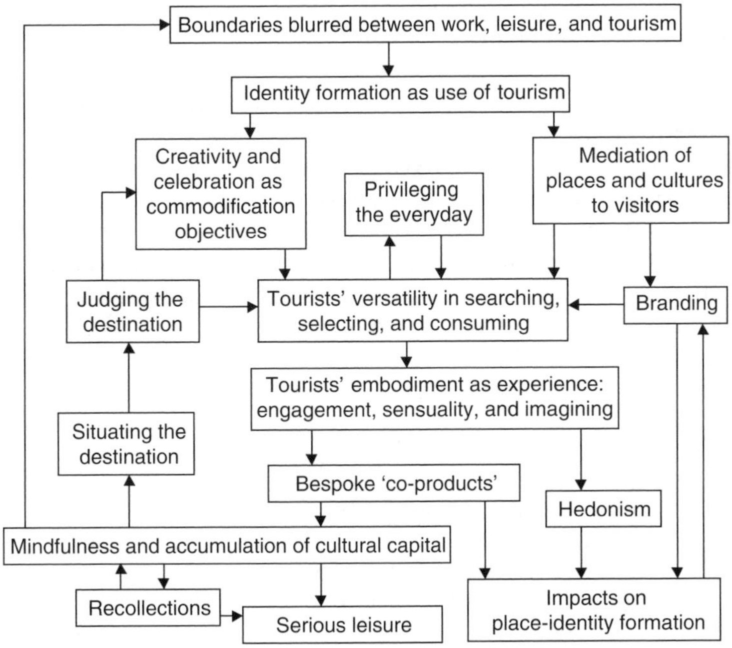

Figure 21.3 The lifestyle formation paradigm

tourists "mix and match" aspects of their holidays to produce a bespoke product out of standardized component parts. It is also a paradigm with many feedback links into destination management, enabling diversity and differentiation in product development.

Conclusion

The arguments in this chapter have been necessarily brief. But the uncontested must become contested and a dialogue needs to develop if motivational research in tourism is to embrace diversity as mainstream. Change will depend on the willingness of academics in tourism not only to question what have become implicitly established ways of thinking about tourism motivation, but also to seek to integrate perspectives. No single paradigm or model is likely to explain all tourism behavior. No single typology is likely to have more than specific relevance. We cannot really expect similar motivations to drive genealogist tourists as beach tourists, or thrills tourists to be similarly motivated as art museum-goers. Sensual and cognitive diversity needs to be embraced. Equally, we cannot expect people to self-cast themselves only as one type of tourist: people may move between types and destinations depending on opportunities and multiple needs for expression, attainment, or escape. This chapter will have made its point if a more critical approach to motivation develops in tourism studies.

Greater attention to cultural variations in holiday motivations is required. At present this literature is dominated by academics working essentially to, on the one hand North American, and on the other Australian/New Zealand/British discourses. Many studies of Asian holiday motivations, for example, derive from these competing discourses, especially the former. The motivations of many South American, Arab, African, Indian, or non-English-speaking Europeans are hardly known at all internationally. Even within Europe, English-speaking paradigms have tended to dominate discourse, despite the range of identities that Europe represents. Cultural diversity needs to be embraced. Surprisingly, the role of tourism in national identity formation and change has yet to be studied. The creation of a common research agenda is an immediate necessity, recognizing the need for bottom-up studies to challenge existing paradigms or models rather than to implicitly accept them. This discourse needs to interact with practice, and if it is to contribute to more appropriate forms of tourism which are simultaneously sustainable, meaningful, and respectful of cultural diversity, to offer a usable lead to practice.

REFERENCES

Aitchison, C. (2002). *Cotswold Cultural Strategy Consultation Final Report*. Cheltenham: Leisure and Sport Research Unit, University of Gloucestershire.

Ajzen, I., and Driver, B. L. (1991). Prediction of leisure participation from behavioral, normative and control beliefs. *Leisure Science* 13(3), 185–204.

Andersen, V. A., Prentice, R. C., and Watanabe, K. (2000). Journeys for experiences: Japanese independent travelers in Scotland. *Journal of Travel and Tourism Marketing* 9(1/2), 129–51.

Beeho, A. J., and Prentice, R. C. (1996). Understanding visitor experiences as a basis for product development: ASEB Grid Analysis and the Black Country Museum in the West Midlands of England. In L. C. Harrison and W. Husbands (eds), *Practising Responsible Tourism* (pp. 472–94). New York: John Wiley.

Cohen, E. (1979). A phenomenology of tourist experiences. *Sociology* 13(2), 179–201.

Crang, M. (1996). Magic kingdom or a quixotic quest for authenticity? *Annals of Tourism Research* 23(2), 415–31.

Crompton, J. (1979). Motivations for pleasure vacation. *Annals of Tourism Research* 6(4), 408–24.

Crompton, J. L., and McKay, S. L. (1997). Motives of visitors attending festival events. *Annals of Tourism Research* 24(2), 425–39.

Driver, B. L., Brown, P. J., and Peterson, G. L. (eds) (1991). *Benefits of Leisure*. State College: Venture.

Edensor, T. (2002). *National Identity, Popular Culture and Everyday Life*. Oxford: Berg.

Griffith, D. A., and Albanese, P. J. (1996). An examination of Plog's psychographic travel model within a student population. *Journal of Travel Research* 34(4), 47–51.

Gutman, J. (1982). A means–end chain model based on consumer categorisation processes. *Journal of Marketing* 46(2), 60–72.

Gyimóthy, S. (2000). *The Quality of Visitor Experience*. Nexø, Bornholm: Research Centre of Bornholm, Report 17/ 2000.

Hartl, A., and Rassing, C. R. (2002). *Survey of Visitors to Bornholm January–December 2001*. Nexø, Bornholm: Working Paper 13, Center for Regional og Turismeforskning.

Henry, N., McEwan, C., and Pollard, J. S. (2002). Globalization from below. *Area* 34(2), 117–27.

Herbert, D. T. (2001). Literary places, tourism and the heritage experience. *Annals of Tourism Research* 28(2), 312–33.

Herbert, D. T., Prentice, R. C., and Thomas, C. J. (eds) (1989). *Heritage Sites: Strategies for Marketing and Development*. Aldershot: Avebury.

Herold, E., Garcia, R., and DeMoya, T. (2001). Female tourists and beach boys. Romance or sex tourism? *Annals of Tourism Research* 28(4), 978–97.

Higham, J. (1998). Sustaining the physical and social dimensions of wildnerness tourism. *Journal of Sustainable Tourism* 6(1), 26–51.

Hvengaard, G. T., and Dearden, P. (1998). Ecotourism versus tourism in a Thai National Park. *Annals of Tourism Research* 25(3), 700–20.

Irish Marketing Surveys Ltd. (1995). *Visitor Attitudes Survey 1995*. Dublin: Bord Failte.

Iso-Ahola, S. (1982). Toward a social psychological theory of tourism motivation. *Annals of Tourism Research* 9(2), 256–62.

Kim, E. Y. (1997). Korean outbound tourism. *Journal of Travel and Tourism Marketing* 6(1), 11–19.

Kim, S., and Littrell, M. A. (2001). Souvenir-buying intentions for self versus others. *Annals of Tourism Research* 28(3), 638–57.

Klenosky, D. B., Gengler, C. E., and Mulvey, M. S. (1993). Understanding the factors influencing ski destination choice. *Journal of Leisure Research* 25(4), 363–79.

Loker, L. E., and Purdue, R. R. (1992). A benefit-based segmentation of a nonresident summer travel market. *Journal of Travel Research* 31(1), 30–5.

Loker-Murphy, L. (1996). Backpackers in Australia. *Journal of Travel and Tourism Marketing* 5(4), 23–45.

MacCannell, D. (1976). *The Tourist: A New Theory of the Leisure Class*. London: Macmillan.

Maffesoli, M. (1996). *The Time of the Tribes*. London: Sage.

Manning, R. E. (1986). *Studies in Outdoor Recreation.* Corvallis: Oregon State University Press.

May, J. A., Bastian, C. T., Taylor, D. T., and Whipple, G. D. (2001). Market segmentation of Wyoming snow mobilers. *Journal of Travel Research* 39(3), 292–9.

McIntosh, A. J., and Prentice, R. C. (1999). Affirming authenticity: Consuming cultural heritage. *Annals of Tourism Research* 26(3), 589–612.

McIntosh, A., Smith, A., and Ingram, T. (2000). *Tourist Experiences of Maori Culture in Aotearoa, New Zealand.* Dunedin: Centre for Tourism Research Paper 8, University of Otago.

MEW Research (1994). Short break destination choice. *Insights* 5(A), A77–A94.

Moscardo, G., Pearce, P., Green, D., and O'Leary, J. T. (2001). Understanding coastal and marine tourism demand from three European markets. *Journal of Sustainable Tourism* 9(3), 212–27.

Murphy, A., and Williams, P. W. (1999). Attracting Japanese tourists into the rural hinterland. *Tourism Management* 20(4), 487–99.

Nickerson, N. P., and Ellis, G. D. (1991). Traveler types and activation theory. *Journal of Travel Research* 29(3), 26–31.

Oh, H., and Hsu, C. H. C. (2001). Volitional degrees of gambling behaviors. *Annals of Tourism Research* 28(3), 618–637.

Ooi, C.-S. (2002). *Cultural Tourism and Tourism Cultures.* Copenhagen: Copenhagen Business School Press.

Pearce, P. L. (1993). Fundamentals of tourist motivation. In D. G. Pearce and R. W. Butler (eds), *Tourism Research: Critiques and Challenges* (pp. 113–34). London: Routledge.

Pearce, P. L., and Caltabiano, J. (1983). Inferring travel motivation from travelers' experiences. *Journal of Travel Research* 22(1), 16–20.

Prentice, R. C. (1989). Visitors to heritage sites. In D. T. Herbert, R. C. Prentice, and C. J. Thomas (eds), *Heritage Sites: Strategies for Marketing and Development* (pp. 15–61). Aldershot: Avebury.

Prentice, R. C. (1993a). *Tourism and Heritage Attractions.* London: Routledge.

Prentice, R. C. (1993b). Motivations of the heritage consumer in the leisure market: An application of the Manning–Haas demand hierarchy. *Leisure Sciences* 15(4), 273–90.

Prentice, R. C. (2001). Journeys for experiences. In P. Keller and T. Bieger (eds), *Tourism Growth and Global Competition* (pp. 263–76). St. Gallen: International Association of Scientific Experts in Tourism.

Prentice, R. C., and Andersen, V. A. (2000). Evoking Ireland: Modelling tourist propensity. *Annals of Tourism Research* 27(2), 490–516.

Prentice, R. C., Davies, A. J., and Beeho, A. J. (1997). Seeking generic motivations for visiting and not visiting museums and like cultural attractions. *Museum Management and Curatorship* 16(1), 45–70.

Prentice, R. C., and Light, D. F. (1994). Current issues in interpretative provision at heritage sites. In A. V. Seaton (ed.), *Tourism: The State of the Art* (pp. 204–21). Chichester: John Wiley.

Prentice, R. C., Witt, S. F., and Hamer, C. (1998). Tourism as experience: The case of heritage parks. *Annals of Tourism Research* 25(1), 1–24.

Prentice, R. C., Witt, S. F., and Wydenbach, E. G. (1994). The endearment behaviour of tourists through their interaction with the host community. *Tourism Management*, 15(2), 117–25.

Rassing, C. R., and Hartl-Nielsen, A. (1997). *Survey of Visitors to Bornholm January 1996–December 1996.* Nexø, Bornholm: Research Centre of Bornholm.

Ryan, C. (ed.) (1997). *The Tourist Experience.* London: Cassell.

Ryan, C. (1998). The travel career ladder. *Annals of Tourism Research* 25(4), 936–57.

Ryan, C., and Huyton, J. (2000). Who is interested in aboriginal tourism in the Northern Territory, Australia? *Journal of Sustainable Tourism* 8(1), 53–88.

Ryan, C., and Sterling, L. (2001). Visitors to Litchfield National Park, Australia. *Journal of Sustainable Tourism* 9(1), 61–75.

Shoemaker, S. (1994). Segmenting the US travel market according to benefits realized. *Journal of Travel Research* 32(3), 8–21.

Smith, S. L. J. (1990). A test of Plog's allocentric/psychocentric model. *Journal of Travel Research* 28(4), 40–3.

Sørensen, A. (1999). *Travellers in the Periphery.* Nexø, Bornholm: Report 16/1999, Research Centre of Bornholm.

Spotts, D. M., and Mahoney, E. M. (1993). Understanding the fall tourism market. *Journal of Travel Research* 32(2), 3–15.

Stebbins, R. A. (1979). *Amateurs: On the Margin Between Work and Leisure.* Beverly Hills: Sage.

Stebbins, R. A. (1996). Cultural tourism as serious leisure. *Annals of Tourism Research* 23(4), 948–50.

Stebbins, R. A. (1997a). Casual leisure: A conceptual statement. *Leisure Studies* 16(1), 17–25.

Stebbins, R. A. (1997b). Identity and cultural tourism. *Annals of Tourism Research* 24(2), 450–2.

Urry, J. (1990). *The Tourist Gaze.* London: Sage.

Urry, J. (1995). *Consuming Places.* London: Routledge.

Wee, E. (2003). French exchange. *The Scotsman* 49(742), S1–S2.

Chapter 22

Tourism, Modernity, and Postmodernity

Tim Oakes and Claudio Minca

Introduction

In this brief chapter we focus on the ways that tourism is mobilized by theorists as a particularly revealing lens through which to view and make sense of modernity and postmodernity. However, one's view of the relationship between tourism and post/modernity depends greatly upon how modernity and postmodernity are themselves conceived. This is of crucial importance, because there exist diverging views of post/modernity that cannot be conceptually unified, and tourism's relationship with post/modernity cannot be given a coherent interpretation unless a particular view of post/modernity is assumed. Consider the debate over the tourist as the emblematic modern subject, for example (cf. MacCannell 1989; Kaplan 1996). We have noticed that this debate tells us much more about the divergent perspectives on, and critiques of, modernity than it does about tourism itself. Interpretations of the relationship between tourism and modernity, then, can illustrate differing philosophical and sociological conceptions of modernity, or they can focus more on how tourism illustrates the structural transformations of capitalism from modern "Fordist" to postmodern "post-Fordist" modes of production. Interpretations might *also* focus more on the tourism industry itself as a distinctly post/modern phenomenon, reflecting within its changing dynamics the broader social changes associated with industrialization and deindustrialization, shifting modes of production, and the increasing power of consumption in conditioning contemporary cultural production. Tourism is both a product of modernity and a unique microcosm of the whole post/modern experience. As such, tourism tends to reflect whatever perspective one might have on that experience. It is thus a useful vehicle for sorting out some of the complexities of the debates surrounding post/modernity, while at the same time theories about post/modernity offer important insights into the nature of tourism and tourist subjectivities.

Our approach has been to examine the ways tourism captures modernity's paradoxical qualities with particular poignancy and richness. We therefore begin by summarizing our understanding of modernity, postmodernity, and the relationship between these terms. Modernity is conceptualized in a way that makes the question of modern subjectivity particularly problematic, and in addressing this question we find tourism a rich resource for making sense of the debates over modern subjectivity. In making our way through this debate, we draw upon the distinction between cognitive and aesthetic reflexivity to discuss how tourism helps reveal the post/modern experience as one in which the tensions and contradictions between these forms of reflexivity are negotiated and acted upon in the process of subject formation.

Modernity and Postmodernity

We begin our approach to modernity by focusing on its discursive constructions and observing that modernity is commonly expressed through fundamental dualisms such as subject – object, mind – body, culture – nature, progress – tradition, reason – experience, and masculine – feminine, among many others.[1] Modernity has often been thought to denote one side of these dualisms, but we will argue that it is the dualisms themselves that best capture modernity in all its paradoxical (in)completeness. Thus, modernity does not simply represent a privileging of reason over experience, or a celebration of progress over the death of tradition, but also conveys the ambivalence between reason and experience, and the sense of loss and nostalgia that progress entails. Modernity is less an order than an incomplete process of ordering (Hetherington 1997). We might, then, speak of the modernity of Enlightenment, of what Ning Wang (2000: 28) has identified as "logos modernity," and what Scott Lash (1999) has called the "first modernity." This is the cognitive modernity of reason and progress. But, in addition to this, we must also speak of "another modernity," one that is more self-critical, less celebratory, and more reflexive in spirit.

Enlightenment modernity's trend toward increasingly alienating forms of social rationalization in the name of abstract notions of progress has generated a profound history of criticism and, indeed, revolution. Critiques by Rousseau, Marx, Weber, Marcuse, Adorno, Foucault, Lefebvre, and many others have both inspired and been inspired by major social upheavals since the eighteenth century. At the same time, however, the critique of modernity includes not only the political-economy critique of capitalism's contradictions and the social critique of alienation and rationality, but also the existential critique of identity, being, authenticity, and associated romantic, subaltern, and anarchic movements as well. These have also generated an enormous amount of creative and artistic production, only some of which would be identified as "modernist." Yet, the modernity of reason has shown remarkable resilience in the face of its diverse critics. This is seen with particular clarity when considering capitalism's ability to transform itself as social and political contradictions generated by new relations of production are coopted and readjusted. Capitalism seemingly commodifies all obstacles in its path, and thus, for many, the triumph of rational modernity is most succinctly expressed in the power of the global corporation and the increasing trend toward worldwide standardization of not just production, but also consumption (identified by some as "McDonaldization," see Ritzer 1996).

An extension of this idea – of the triumph of the modernity of reason – recognizes the profound critical and creative challenges to modernity but argues that modernity has found ways to channel its self-critical impulses into approved zones or spaces, thus releasing their explosive power into a world of sanctioned marginality (Marcuse 1955; Lefebvre 1991; Shields 1991). Modernity thus results in the structural and institutional separation of rational (logos) modernity from non-rational needs and desires (eros) (Wang 2000: 39). Tourism, then, can be interpreted as one of the institutional manifestations of this separation. Tourism promises an escape from the world of logos into that of eros, a satisfaction of all those needs and desires repressed by logos modernity. But, from this point of view, tourism ultimately remains an embodiment of the triumph of rational modernity; it promises escape, but such escape is in fact standardized and delusional (Rojek 1993). Tourists escape into a world of fantasy and simulacra, a carefully controlled simulation of eros which maintains the profoundly ordered world of rational modernity.

Rather than taking this perspective in which the primary contemporary social dialectic is between "modernity" and "modernity's critics," however, we seek a more holistic approach to modernity in which the critical and creative impulses driven by so-called logos modernity are viewed as equally "modern" as the phenomena they see themselves opposing. Rather than divide modernity into its logos and eros components, then, we focus instead on the reflexive nature of modernity, and in particular on the tension between cognitive and aesthetic reflexivity. This allows us to conceive of that which is more commonly referred to as the "postmodern" as simply "another modernity" (Lash 1999: 138). Heller (1999: 4) has described this other modernity as that which we more familiarly know as the postmodern, or modernity's "self-reflexive conscience." "It is a kind of modernity," she argues, "that knows itself in a Socratic way. For it (also) knows that it knows very little, if anything at all." We approach postmodernity, then, as an "other" which has shadowed modernity throughout modern history itself; it is modernity in its aesthetic reflexive mode. Thus our use of the term "post/modernity" instead of "modernity and postmodernity."

On one level, these two modernities remain encased within dualisms: where cognitive modernity celebrates reason, aesthetic "postmodernity" is reflexive, experiential, and hermeneutic. Where the former is concerned primarily with epistemological questions, the latter develops a critical stance toward knowledge and concerns itself more with ontology. On another level, however, Heller's comment suggests that, while the cognitive modernity of Enlightenment is busy building dualisms through which to know the world, the other modernity of aesthetic reflexivity is busy trying to escape these dualisms altogether (see Olsson 2001). Yet this pursuit is fraught with ambivalence, for the ontological questions broached have no clear answers; they merely confirm that modernity "knows that it knows very little, if anything at all." As Lash has argued, cognitive "reflexive monitoring" of the modern experience yields little reassurance as to the actual truth of things. Unlike Giddens (1990, 1991), who relies upon cognitive reflexivity to provide a sense of "ontological security" in the face of modernity's ever-changing, even chaotic, knowledge of the world (see also Beck 1992), Lash (1993) suggests that the experience of modernity is too contradictory and paradoxical for cognitive reflection to get any kind of handle on. Instead, we develop a kind of aesthetic reflexivity that allows us to "live with contingency." Thus, while the modernity of Enlightenment creates a world in which knowledge is dynamic and continuously updated, Lash's "other modernity" assumes an ambivalent ontology, recognizing that there are few absolute answers to the questions generated through cognitive reflexivity. Enlightenment modernity, then, is recognized as a paradox by its shadowy other. Heller (1999: 15) echoes this idea when she states that, "Reflected postmodern consciousness *thinks this paradox*; it does not lose it from sight, it lives with it."

Accordingly, our focus shifts away from the tourist's deluded search for escape from the alienation and rationality of logos modernity. We find such an approach overly structural and unable to conceive of subjectivity in anything but a passive-response way. Instead, we focus more explicitly on the paradoxes of modern subject formation and find that a concern with subjectivity yields a much more complicated picture of tourism than that which simply finds it filling a social safety-valve role for the contradictions of Enlightenment modernity. Tourists are not simply deluded by the simulacra of escape but, as agents of aesthetic reflexivity, embody the paradoxes of post/modernity themselves.

The Traveling Modern Subject

There are several ways in which one might approach the relationship between tourism and modern subjectivity. At a most basic level, modern subjectivity has in many ways been characterized by mobility. This approach has presumed a critique of received notions of subjectivity as essentially sedentary. Traditional notions of civilization have been associated with agriculture over pastoralism, settlement over nomadism; movements of people were typically associated with abnormal events such as war or famine. "Subjectivity," writes Wang (2000: 1), "is presumably sedentary and excludes mobility." The mobile subjectivity of modernity, then, heightens its critical and iconoclastic stance toward "traditional society." Like Goethe's Faust and Mephistopheles, the modern subject was a traveler, a stranger, a highwayman, a disrupter of traditional place-based norms (Berman 1982: 38–60).

On another level, however, the modern subject as traveler has also presumed a critique of modernity itself. In these terms, travel has been linked to the alienation and placelessness of modernity. For Bauman (1991), the modern subject was an ambivalent stranger, an exile, pilgrim, someone out of place yet longing for a place, obsessed with anguish and fear yet seeking a sense of control and a unifying gaze upon the world. For Simmel (1950), it was the exiled foreigner who most cogently expressed this kind of ambivalence toward the world (see also Touraine 1995: 202). And it was noted by Bradbury (1976) that a great body of modern Western literature was written by writers experiencing some form of exile (cf. Wilson 1956). The displacement of exile and the chaos of uprooting enforced an oxymoronic, if not paradoxical, *experience of detachment*. Exile in fact cultivated this kind of modernist experience while releasing a tremendous amount of creative energy directed toward understanding that which exile had relinquished: the "eternal and immutable," the home from which one had been uprooted (Baudelaire 1995). Thus, the exile metaphor also highlights another important modernist experience: nostalgic melancholia (Kaplan 1996: 15).

Perhaps the most emphatic image of the ambivalent and aloof modern traveling subject, however, comes from Benjamin's (1973) characterization of the *flâneur* (see also Tester 1994). The *flâneur* was an ambivalent consumer of images, a man of leisure who was at once alienated by and drawn to the urban maelstrom that defined nineteenth-century modernity. Benjamin wrote of the *flâneur* in the context of his work on those glass-covered commodity gauntlets, the Paris arcades. Here, the pedestrian *flâneur* strolled the passageways, dismissive of the commodity fetishism that swirled around him, yet at the same time drawn to the images conveyed by the commodity form like a window-shopper. "The *flâneur* still stood at the margin, of the great city as of the bourgeois class. Neither of them had yet overwhelmed him. In neither of them was he at home. He sought his asylum in the crowd. The crowd was the veil from behind which the familiar city as phantasmagoria beckoned to the *flâneur*" (Benjamin 1973: 170). Both detached viewer and drawn by subjective engagement, the *flâneur* articulates the paradox of modern subjectivity: a reinforcing of the subject–object dualism even as one desires to *transcend and escape* that dualism.

This paradox of subjectivity comes about, following Foucault (1990) and Butler (1997), as a result of subject formation being an *articulation of self to others*. As Berger and Pullberg (1965: 199–200) argued, human subjectivity must continuously "objectivate" itself; it is a necessary human condition to know the self by establishing a subject – object dualism. We all "objectivate" our world, they claim. Objectivation is a process "whereby human subjectivity embodies itself in products that are available to oneself and one's fellow men [*sic*] as elements of a common world." Further, "the moment in the process of objectivation in which man [*sic*] established distance from his producing and its product, such that he can take cognizance of it and make it an object of his consciousness" is called objectification. These are necessary means by which post/modern subject formation occurs, and because of them, humans are continuously "making their world" as they act to modify the given, structuring it into a meaningful totality (a process that is never complete). The object-world, in other words, must be made and remade over and over again. "The world remains real, in the sense of subjective plausibility and consistency, only as it is confirmed and re-confirmed" (Berger and Pullberg 1965: 201). Furthermore, such making and remaking is necessarily an intersubjective process; the object-world (and thus the subject) must be continuously reconfirmed by others.

Yet, if subject formation depends on the certainty and security of a distinction between subject and object, closer examination reveals that such a distinction cannot be sustained. This is the problem of representation. Being of the phenomenal world, we cannot claim *a priori* knowledge of the object-world, and so must rely on representations to *see* the truth of things. And, as Giddens (1990: 40) points out, being aware that such representations are constantly subject to cognitive readjustment and revision creates "anxieties which press in on everyone." This anxiety is that which Heller (1999: 15) attributes to an aesthetics of living the paradox of modernity. To be post/modern, then, is less to express a scientific certainty about the world than to regard our knowledge of the world with some suspicion. Cognitive reflexivity, as a result, strives for ever more reliable forms of representation, while aesthetic reflexivity regards all forms of representation with suspicion.

If post/modernity, in other words, constitutes a state of anxiety over the awareness that our representations of the object-world are not reliable, then the cognitive response to this reflexive anxiety has been to turn to the visual as the most comfortingly reliable form of representation. Exhibiting the world for visual consumption objectifies it in a way that calms the demons of post/modern anxiety. Indeed, in industrializing Europe, for instance, such cognitive reflexivity resulted in a greater emphasis on representation itself than on "reality," as Timothy Mitchell (1988) has argued. Europeans of the nineteenth century, Mitchell observed, were inclined to see their world as an "exhibit" of something. This was most clearly illustrated in the prominence of the "great exhibitions" of this period, offering elaborate displays that sought to replicate as faithfully as possible the far-flung places of empire. The "authenticity" of these replicas was insured not only by the exquisite craftsmanship and original materials used for the construction of model buildings and streets, but also by displaying actual people from the places represented. The presence of "natives" reinforced the theme of social evolution while at the same time enhancing the authenticity of the replicas exhibited. Indeed, the presence of actual humans confused the distinction between the real (original) and the fake (replica), creating the sensation of a "living display" which was promoted as a key attraction of London's Great Exhibition of 1851 (Briggs 1979: 398). According to Mitchell (1988: 12), the world itself was for nineteenth-century European metropolitans a kind of exhibition, objectified and displayed before them to gaze upon:

> Outside the world exhibition . . . one encountered not the real world but only further models and representations of the real. Beyond the exhibition and the department store . . . the theatre and the zoo, the countryside encountered typically in the form of a model farm exhibiting new machinery and cultivation methods, the very streets of the modern city with their deliberate façades, even the Alps once the funicular was built . . . Everything seemed to be set up before one as if it were a model or the picture of something.

What this speaks to is the possibility that the great exhibitions drew upon a deeper need, a modern longing not so much for the real thing itself as for a particular kind of *representation of the original*, one which faithfully met certain expectations or needs. The object-world, in other words, was propped up by a kind of mimetic authenticity of representation. To the extent that post/modern subject formation relies on the continuous remaking of a reliable object-world, such subjectivity is necessarily problematic and even paradoxical. The tourist, we argue, both embodies and negotiates this paradox.

The Traveling Subject is a Man! And a Creepy One At That!

It must be acknowledged that much of the ambivalence and anxiety associated with cognitive reflexivity – ambivalence and anxiety which generates the detached, strolling *flâneur* – is highly gendered. Feminist critiques of the traveling subject and, in particular, the *flâneur*, have been developed by Wolff (1985), Wilson (1992), and Kaplan (1996), among others. We are clearly reminded of this, for instance, when considering Berman's (1982: 58–9) interpretation of Goethe's Faust and Mephistopheles, who, "bursting with money, sexuality and ideas," are classic "outside agitators," seducing the village girl, Gretchen, and precipitating the destruction of her "cellular world." Their modernity is clearly marked by their maleness just as Gretchen's tradition is marked by her femaleness. And yet Bauman, Benjamin, Bradbury, and Simmel all behave as if their travelers embody *universal* qualities of all modern subjects.

Wilson (1992: 109) argues that a feminist reading of Benjamin's *flâneur* finds a subjectivity constituted not by a confident male gaze but rather by the *attenuation* of male power. The commodified spaces through which the *flâneur* ambivalently strolled were a labyrinth in which male sexual drive was visually stimulated yet actually deferred, such that impotency became the sexual mark of the *flâneur*. "The *flâneur* himself never really existed, being but an embodiment of the special blend of excitement, tedium and horror aroused by many in the new metropolis, and the disintegrative effect of this on the masculine identity." Along related lines, Jokinen and Veijola (1997) take Bauman to task for masking the gendered qualities of his ambivalent post/modern figures: the stroller, the vagabond, the tourist, the player. Arguing that these figures should be recognized for the gendered subjectivity they in fact embody, Jokinen and Veijola suggest substituting the paparazzi, homeless drunk, sex tourist, and womanizer for Bauman's more deliberately ambiguous terminology. Looking for alternatives, they find Braidotti's (1994) reworking of Deleuzian nomadism useful for expressing a kind of critical consciousness that resists socially coded behavioral conventions and thought (see Deleuze and Guattari 1987: 351–423).

We would suggest that Jokinen and Veijola's use of Braidotti assigns a role to aesthetic reflexivity as an alternative to the gendered ideologies that infuse Bauman's more cognitive reflexive subjects. Such reflexivity is also suggested by Lynda Johnston's (2001) focus on the tourist's body as a means of moving beyond a universalized modernist dualism of mind and body to achieving a more gender-specific and bodily rendering of the tourism experience (see also Veijola and Jokinen 1994). We are moving, in other words, away from the disembodied and ideologically gendered traveler of cognitive reflexivity and toward an embodied, contradictory, and contingent tourist seeking experience and negotiating post/modernity's paradoxes through aesthetic reflexivity.

The Tourist as Post/modern Subject

If the aloof and ambivalent traveler and *flâneur* are considered highly problematic emblems of modern subjectivity, then what of the tourist? In some ways, the tourist may simply be regarded as an equivalent, twentieth-century version of the nineteenth-century *flâneur*. As Urry (1990: 138) comments, "The strolling *flâneur* was a forerunner of the twentieth century tourist." If "acting like a tourist is one of the defining characteristics of being modern," then the tourist might be regarded as an updated version of the *flâneur*, marking the structural transformations in capitalist relations of production and consumption that characterized the rise of so-called "Fordist" production systems (Urry 1990: 2–3). The tourist was the "mass-produced" traveler. But, along with repeating the gendered ideology underlying the *flâneur*, this interpretation risks losing sight of subject formation as a critical concern of our understanding of post/modernity. A great deal of work has argued that the behavior of tourists reveals the underlying structures of capitalist modernity (MacCannell 1989; Urry 1990; Britton 1991). Yet when one actually considers the motivations of tourists themselves one finds a bewildering array of complex and contradictory issues to explain why people travel (Ryan 1997). Tourism needs to be interpreted in the context of reflexivity to help make sense of this.

In terms of cognitive reflexivity, tourists might be understood to seek escape from the hyper-rationality of logos modernity, to rest and relax, have a holiday, a break from the everyday world of production (work) and reproduction (home). Such vacations, however, have themselves been highly standardized and rationalized. Or, as MacCannell has suggested, tourists might be cognitively responding to logos modernity by seeking "real life," unbounded by such rational strictures, in other places and peoples. MacCannell has argued that such pursuits inevitably lead the tourist to the "staged authenticity" of touristic space. In the end, the tourist never really escapes, and the implication is that she or he probably does not really want to anyway. From this perspective, the tourist ultimately confirms the rationalizing power of Enlightenment modernity. This remains, in our view, a rather attenuated version of modern subjectivity, one in which reflexivity is limited to the "self-monitoring" of cognition (the need for a vacation, the desire for authenticity). Yet this does not begin to approach the paradoxical nature of post/modern subjectivity itself, and we suggest that tourists can also be understood in these terms as well. This implies more specific attention to "aesthetic reflexivity" in tourism (see also Urry 1995).

Thus, it has been noted that even as tourists seek to escape the rationality of Enlightenment modernity, many of them remain ever-restless in this quest, finding their initial escape itself too confining and rationalized. Ryan notes the paradox of escape in that even as tourists seek to escape the everyday, they are always inventing new ways to escape tourism itself (Ryan 1997: 1–5). This is perhaps indicative of another level of reflexivity. This can mean an escape *back into* the world of the everyday (see Hodge et al. 2003), but with an awareness that *problematizes the assumed distinction between the worlds of work and play, travel and home, displacement and place, logos and eros*. Along these lines, Rojek and Urry (1997) observe that tourism and post/modern culture are seen to increasingly overlap in contemporary societies. On the one hand, society is increasingly characterized by an economy of signs and experiences, along with a general commercialization of culture (Lash and Urry 1994; Zukin 1995). On the other hand, tourism has itself become increasingly "culturalized," indicating perhaps the industry's adjustment to the aesthetic reflexivity of tourists themselves. At the same time, tourism theorists increasingly recognize that the tourist's consumption of culture is highly complex and very difficult to decode.

If, following Hetherington (1997), we think of modernity as a process of ordering – rather than an order – we might try to locate the constitution of the tourist as post/modern subject in some space between cognitive and aesthetic reflexivity – a space that is, by definition, rational and utopian at the same time, a space of ambivalence and of endless possibilities. We might argue, therefore, that the tourist is in eternal search of some "external" (dis)order to put "right," to order. Yet the disorder that (s)he seeks is obviously constitutive of the very order that modern cognitive epistemologies try to pursue. Indeed, if we conceive post/modernity as the outcome of the dialectic between cognitive and aesthetic reflexivity, the tourist experience can also be described as an unreachable "space of possibilities," as the fruit of this impossible striving. In other words, the so-called tourist anxiety derives from the fact that post/modernity is an unfinished project, producing an endless series of unfinished experiences: the tourist has to construct her/his subjectivity facing an infinite range of possibilities of experiencing post/modernity through space and place, tempered by the equally pressing need for a finite order that can allow her/him to conceptualize and control these possibilities. This infinite interplay of control and freedom, of cognitive closure and aesthetic opening, is genuinely post/modern and represents a constitutive element in the construction of the tourist subject. From the tourist village to the explorations of the global drifter, the tourist faces a revealing search for spaces that offer different "cocktails" of freedom and control.

Desperately striving to touch the horizon – trying to expand the space of her/his aesthetic reflexivity "out there" – the tourist wanders around the world in search of completion, of ordering, while trying at the same time to "get along" with her/his cognitive reflexivity. Yet, paradoxically enough, she/he is quite aware that the horizon for which she/he reaches keeps moving away just as she/he appears to get closer, remaining always at the same (cognitive and aesthetic) distance. For this reason, we could envision the constitution of the tourist subject as a way of facing this challenge, or better, as an attempt to overcome the contradictions embodied by such a position, as a way of displacing its most unsustainable tenets. The tourist's interpretative framework therefore necessitates an endless process of translation for every new encounter – with places or other modern subjectivities; it calls for a process of ordering the aestheticized "disorder" that fatally attracts her/his gaze. The encounter with an aestheticized "other" is obviously a moment of self-definition that occurs through negation. But it is not just a potentially new form of (cognitive) colonization of otherness; it is a hybrid space of encounter where different subjects redefine themselves through the other's presence and interaction (see Oakes 2004; Minca forthcoming).

Conclusion

In the spirit of this chapter, a definitive conclusion remains "just beyond the horizon." But we *will* say that a post/modern approach to tourism is fundamentally an attempt to codify and/or overcome the ambivalence and the dialectic between cognitive and aesthetic reflexivity in place. While we have said almost nothing about actual places in this chapter, we believe that the most revealing quality of tourism in its expression of post/modern subject formation and the dialectic between cognitive and aesthetic reflexivity is that it must occur in actual places. There is nothing abstract about tourism, and neither should we be satisfied to consider the question of post/modern subject formation an abstract textual exercise. Tourist places and landscapes are rich resources for understanding how post/modern subject formation takes actual material form and achieves tactile expression. Here, we are thinking of examples such as Herzfeld's (1991) study of Rethymnos, Adams's (1996) work on Lhasa, Macdonald's (1997) study of Aros on the Isle of Skye, Edensor's (1998) study of the Taj Mahal, Hodge et al.'s *Exeter Mis-guide* (2003), and the case studies presented in Minca and Oakes (forthcoming). Tourism, we are suggesting, offers a nearly inexhaustible set of "field sites" for taking the study of post/modern subjectivity out of its textual home and "onto the streets" where it ultimately belongs.

NOTE

1. This should not be taken as a definition of modernity *per se*. For a basic definition, Charles Taylor (2002: 91) offers the following: "that historically unprecedented amalgam of new practices and institutional forms (science, technology, industrial production, urbanization), of new ways of living (individualism, secularization, instrumental rationality), and of new forms of malaise (alienation, meaninglessness, a sense of impending social dissolution)."

REFERENCES

Adams, V. (1996). Karaoke in modern Lhasa, Tibet: Western encounters with cultural politics. *Cultural Anthropology* 11(4), 510–46.

Baudelaire, C. (1995). *The Painter of Modern Life and Other Essays*, trans. and ed. J. Mayne. London: Phaidon.

Bauman, Z. (1991). *Modernity and Ambivalence.* Ithaca, NY: Cornell University Press.

Beck, U. (1992). *The Risk Society: Towards Another Modernity.* London: Sage.

Benjamin, W. (1973). *Charles Baudelaire: A Lyric Poet in the Era of High Capitalism*, trans. H. Zohn. New York: New Left Books.

Berger, P., and Pullberg, S. (1965). Reification and the sociological critique of consciousness. *History and Theory* 4(2), 196–211.

Berman, M. (1982). *All That Is Solid Melts Into Air.* New York: Simon & Schuster.

Bradbury, M. (1976). The cities of modernism. In M. Bradbury and J. McFarlane (eds), *Modernism, 1890–1930.* Harmondsworth: Penguin.

Braidotti, R. (1994). *Nomad Subjects: Embodiment and Sexual Difference in Contemporary Feminist Theory.* New York: Columbia University Press.

Briggs, A. (1979). *The Age of Improvement, 1783–1867.* London: Longman.

Britton, S. (1991). Tourism, capital, and place: Towards a critical geography of tourism. *Environment and Planning D: Society and Space* 9, 451–78.

Butler, J. (1997). *The Psychic Life of Power: Theories in Subjection.* Stanford, CA: Stanford University Press.

Deleuze, G., and Guattari, F. (1987). *A Thousand Plateaus: Capitalism and Schizophrenia*, trans. B. Massumi. Minneapolis: University of Minnesota Press.

Edensor, T. (1998). *Tourists at the Taj.* London and New York: Routledge.

Foucault, M. (1990). *The History of Sexuality*, trans. R. Hurley. New York: Vintage.

Giddens, A. (1990). *The Consequences of Modernity.* Stanford, CA: Stanford University Press.

Giddens, A. (1991). *Modernity and Self-Identity.* Cambridge: Polity.

Heller, A. (1999). *A Theory of Modernity.* Oxford: Blackwell.

Herzfeld, M. (1991). *A Place in History: Social and Monumental Time in a Cretan Town.* Princeton, NJ: Princeton University Press.

Hetherington, K. (1997). *The Badlands of Modernity.* London and New York: Routledge.

Hodge, S. S., Persighetti, S., Smith, P., Turner, C., and Weaver, T. (2003). *An Exeter Mis-guide.* Exeter: Wrights & Sites.

Johnston, L. (2001). (Other) bodies and tourism studies. *Annals of Tourism Research* 23(1), 180–201.

Jokinen, E., and Veijola, S. (1997). The disoriented tourist: The figuration of the tourist in contemporary cultural critique. In C. Rojek and J. Urry (eds), *Touring Cultures: Transformations in Travel and Theory* (pp. 23–51). London and New York: Routledge.

Kaplan, C. (1996). *Questions of Travel: Postmodern Discourses of Displacement*. Durham: Duke University Press.
Lash, S. (1993). Reflexive modernization: The aesthetic dimension. *Theory, Culture, and Society* 10(1), 1–23.
Lash, S. (1999). *Another Modernity, A Different Rationality*. Oxford: Blackwell.
Lash, S., and Urry, J. (1994). *Economies of Signs and Space*. London: Sage.
Lefebvre, H. (1991). *The Production of Space*, trans. D. Nicholson-Smith. Oxford: Blackwell.
Marcuse, H. (1955). *Eros and Civilization*. London: Beacon Press.
MacCannell, D. (1989). *The Tourist: A New Theory of the Leisure Class*, 2nd edn. New York: Schocken.
Macdonald, S. (1997). A people's story: Heritage, identity, and authenticity. In C. Rojek and J. Urry (eds), *Touring Cultures: Transformations of Travel and Theory* (pp. 155–75). London and New York: Routledge.
Minca, C. (forthcoming). Re-inventing the square: Postcolonial visions in the Jamaa el Fna, Marrakech. In C. Minca and T. Oakes (eds), *Travels in Paradox: Remapping Tourism*. Lanham, MD: Rowman & Littlefield.
Minca, C., and Oakes, T. (eds) (forthcoming). *Travels in Paradox: Remapping Tourism*. Lanham, MD: Rowman & Littlefield.
Mitchell, T. (1988). *Colonizing Egypt*. Cambridge: Cambridge University Press.
Oakes, T. (2004). Tourism and the modern subject: Placing the encounter between tourist and other. In C. Cartier and A. Lew (eds), *Seductions of Place*. London and New York: Routledge (forthcoming).
Olsson, G. (2001). Washed in a washing machine. In C. Minca (ed.), *Postmodern Geography. Theory and Praxis* (pp. 255–81). Oxford: Blackwell.
Ritzer, G. (1996). *The McDonaldization of Society*, rev. edn. Thousand Oaks, CA: Pine Forge Press.
Rojek, C. (1993). *Ways of Escape: Modern Transformations in Leisure and Travel*. London: Macmillan.
Rojek, C., and Urry, J. (1997). Transformations in travel and theory. In C. Rojek and J. Urry (eds), *Touring Cultures: Transformations in Travel and Theory* (pp. 1–22). London and New York: Routledge.
Ryan, C. (ed.) (1997). *The Tourist Experience: A New Introduction*. London: Cassell.
Shields, R. (1991). *Places on the Margin: An Alternative Geography of Modernity*. London and New York: Routledge.
Simmel, G. (1950). The stranger. In K. Wolff (trans. and ed.), *The Sociology of Georg Simmel* (pp. 402–24). Glencoe, IL: Free Press.
Taylor, C. (2002). Modern social imaginaries. *Public Culture* 14(1), 91–124.
Tester, K. (ed.) (1994). *The Flâneur*. London and New York: Routledge.
Touraine, A. (1995). *Critique of Modernity*, trans. D. Macey. Oxford: Blackwell.
Urry, J. (1990). *The Tourist Gaze: Leisure and Travel in Contemporary Societies*. London: Sage.
Urry, J. (1995). *Consuming Places*. London and New York: Routledge.
Veijola, S., and Jokinen, E. (1994). The body in tourism. *Theory, Culture and Society* 11, 125–51.
Wang, N. (2000). *Tourism and Modernity: A Sociological Analysis*. Amsterdam: Pergamon.
Wilson, C. (1956). *The Outsider*. Boston: Houghton Mifflin.
Wilson, E. (1992). The invisible flâneur. *New Left Review* 191, 90–110.
Wolff, J. (1985). The invisible *flâneuse*: Women and the literature of modernity. *Theory, Culture, and Society* 2(3), 37–46.
Zukin, S. (1995). *The Cultures of Cities*. Oxford: Blackwell.

Chapter 23

Cultural Circuits of Tourism: Commodities, Place, and Re-consumption

Irena Ateljevic and Stephen Doorne

Introduction

The reconceptualization of geographic subdisciplines and the embrace of "de-differentiation of the economy and culture" (Crang and Malbon 1996) are central to the emergence of a "new" theorization of tourism. Within "the economic," contemporary cultural and social geography attempts to account for both the material conditions and the experiences of individuals, as well as the place of the individual within the structures of power and economy. Within "the cultural," contemporary economic geography embraces the economy as a cultural and social formation, opening up, as Thrift (2000) suggests, a Pandora's box of complexity. These processes have seen the integration of cultural politics in a more inclusive human geography, in which the challenge to transgress boundaries has produced a "new" discourse of tourism geography through which the interface between geography and tourism studies has begun to be re-examined (Squire 1994a, 1994b; Ioannides and Debbage 1998; Ringer 1998; Ateljevic 2000; Pritchard and Morgan 2000; Milne and Ateljevic 2001).

The transcendence of the boundaries between the economic and the cultural has seen the reconception of consumption as "circuits of culture" (Johnson 1986), that go beyond the linear, sequential act of monetary purchase "back into the social relations of production and forward into cycles of use and re-use" (Jackson and Thrift 1995: 205; see also Burgess 1990; Crang and Malbon 1996). As commodities move beyond their utility functions and assume certain cultural and symbolic meanings, production and consumption are seen as complements, feeding off each other in an endless cycle (Lury 1996). Further, the leisure and tourism context particularly reveals the mutual constitution of what are traditionally conceived as "independent objectivities" (Ateljevic 2000; see also du Gay 1996). The production of tourism takes place through its consumption, that is, "tourism" is *performed* rather than simply a series of products which are created and subsequently consumed (Kirshenblatt-Gimblett 1998; Edensor 1998; Aitchison 1999; Franklin and Crang 2001).

The study of the representation of culture through performance has an established lineage in tourism studies in terms of both critical examinations of staged authenticity and museumization (Turner and Ash 1975; Greenwood 1978; Smith 1978; Adams 1984; Britton and Clarke 1987; Crick 1989), and reflexive explorations of the social dynamics through which cultural production takes place (Boissevain 1996; Kirshenblatt-Gimblett 1998). In further readings of tourism as performance, Franklin and Crang (2001: 17–18) note the work of Edensor (1998), observing that: "it is not just those observed who are enacting culturally specific performances. The cultural competencies and required skills that make up tourist cultures themselves suggest a Goffmanesque where all the world is indeed a stage." Similarly, Perkins and Thorns (2001) reconceptualize the passive tourist gaze of sightseeing (Urry 1990) in the context of adventure tourism, observing the participation of tourists seeking active bodily involvement. In this context, the performance of tourism by tourists is itself the act of "production." Further more, as this chapter will illustrate, the process of production can be the performance of consumption practice beyond the scope of performing arts, but include a diversity of contexts, environments, and activities. In other words, producers themselves are consuming lifestyle, cultural context, or recreational activities in order to perform the act of production. Indeed, through the endless recycling of cultural circuits the act of production can be seen as an act of re-consumption and consumption as an act of re-production.

Rather than presenting tourism circuits as a theoretical point of arrival, we argue for the consideration of the concept as itself a gaze upon the traditional linear or dialectic renderings of tourism phenomena. In this chapter we offer three specific theoretical lenses in terms of touristic commodities, places, and acts of re-consumption. In doing so, we provide opportunities to examine circular cultural perspectives of tourism across a range of research contexts. Firstly, in the context of cultures of consumption, tourist commodities are revealed as objects around which subjective elements of personal and social identities are lived. Secondly, we discuss places where tourism happens in terms of the way in which meanings and identities of places are contested and produced through acts of consumption by people. Lastly, the lived experiences of tourism production are identified as opportunities to produce and re-consume cultural practices. Our discussion draws on a range of research projects incorporating diversity of market groups and cultural environments in New Zealand, Croatia, and China.

Touristic Commodities

In the contemporary global economy, the process of commodification of consumption has become characterized by intensity and sophistication to the extent that production is increasingly aestheticized, and meanings attached to visual representations and material objects (Britton 1991; Rojek 1995; Lury 1996; Ateljevic 2000). Consumption as a cultural form has emerged to acknowledge the importance of culture in ensuring consumption, through which leisure and tourism have become significant elements in contemporary capitalist societies (Featherstone 1987a, 1990; Rojek 1995; Sharpley 1996).

Britton (1991), with reference to Bourdieu (1984) and Urry (1990), placed tourism in the context of the contemporary cultural economy, within which groups and individuals increasingly engage in attempts to construct their identities through certain consumption preferences and lifestyle practices which signal taste and position in society. As the "culture of consumption" evolves in terms of Featherstone's (1987b) "you are what you buy" and you are "where you go away," an emerging contemporary literature offers depth and insight to issues surrounding material culture, consumption, and identity (e.g., Glennie and Thrift 1993; Crewe and Lowe 1995; Jackson and Holbrook 1995; Miller 1995b, 1998; Pearce 1997; Miller et al. 1998; Jackson 1999).

In the West, leisure and tourism consumption serves as an arena for social differentiation and the expression of identity (Featherstone 1990; Miller 1995a), in line with Bourdieu's (1984) notion of "cultural capital." Traffic in touristic goods creates aesthetic judgments of authenticity, yet also satisfies the urge to explore transnational cultural connections (Hannerz 1996). For example, building upon the work of Appadurai (1986, 1996), Thomas (1991) and Jackson (1999), we have traced the journey of touristic artifacts produced in rural China downstream to new locations in urban New Zealand where they become surrogates of human relations and signs of identity (Ateljevic and Doorne 2002a). In doing so, we explored the many ways in which travelers produced new meanings around these objects, reflecting their significance and role in their own personal development and growth. Thus, the act of consumption is motivated by the opportunity to produce and reproduce identities, as part of the prevailing cultural context.

The journey of the tie-dyed fabric we followed revealed dimensions of intercultural awareness and senses of connectedness that inform the creation of personal identities as a further reflection of Bourdieu's (1984) notion of "cultural capital" (see also Featherstone 1990; Jackson 1999). The women involved in its production had often little or no conception of the downstream interpretation of their cultural context, nor did they care what became of the goods they made. Their focus was more immediate and directed to their basic personal and collective needs. By contrast, the consumers of the fabric appropriated what they perceive of its cultural context to strategically facilitate their own social differentiation often based on a superficial understanding of the social relations of production.

The symbolic significance of these commodities in the identity formation of the consumer is often based on assumptions about the production process behind the "traditional hand-made craft" (Miller 1997, 1998). In this sense the values are attributed not to the objects in particular, but to their symbolic role within an identifiable genre of "ethnic" goods. In this context, specific objects can be readily assimilated into – or indeed discarded from – the life worlds of consumers depending on their capacity to enhance the individual's preferred identity image. Such representations are frequently constructed and read as expressions of life philosophies pertaining to the wearer/owner. The "traditional other" is embraced as a symbolic antithesis to the pressures of compartmentalized global consumer culture (Sharpley 1996). The example reflects the extent to which value coherence can be created through the act of juxtaposition and display of an otherwise random collection of objects when positioned within arenas of power-knowledge. It should be noted that the symbolic significance of objects is particular to time and place to the extent that specific objects may gain, change, or lose meaning depending on the dynamics of the cultural context in which they are positioned (Appadurai 1986).

Similarly, research on "wine tourists" in New Zealand has also focused on issues of understanding consumer identity, lifestyle, social class, and "cultural capital" (Abramovici and Ateljevic 2002). Wine tourism consumption was shown to be one of many aspects of cultural consumption and identity production within which people seek social belonging and class status. Social standing is frequently expressed as lifestyle reflected in fashionable clothes, housing, "healthy and real food," premium wine, coffee, "high" cultural practices, and "appropriate" leisure and travel pursuits, many of which have established associations with tourism directly. Travel in this context often emerges as a context through which the authentication of consumption practices, by association with particular places, confers status upon the individual (Kirshenblatt-Gimblett 1998).

Featherstone (1995) explains that it is only those individuals who participate in a particular activity, in other words who share particular consumption patterns, who appreciate the culturally appropriate behavior that goes with it. The sharing of the knowledge, values, and language that accompany lifestyle activities serves to form the common culture of a social group. Acquiring competence in assessing information, goods, and services is a lifelong investment in cultural and symbolic capital, and an investment in ongoing consumption as a medium of performance in "wine tourism."

The changing fashions in wine are informed by cultural references and events (such as the Wellington, New Zealand, International Art Festival), which are endlessly "redesigned," demanding continuous learning through material and cultural consumption. As such, the competition to acquire goods for this social group generates high admission barriers and effective techniques of exclusion. To define the criteria for membership of any set of objects is at the same time also to create a boundary, beyond which nothing belongs. In other words, the things that "we" have in common are our difference from "others." In the face of "their" difference, "our" similarity often comes into focus (Goodwin, Ackerman, and Kiron 1997). The whole romance behind the grape is clearly a circularity of the tangible and intangible, the wine and its associated meanings.

Tourism places

Within the preceding framework, in which consumption is identified as the practice of re-production, we can also recognize a corresponding multiplication of tourist *spaces* and *places*. Here, the discourses of television, brochures, and the web permeate and surround planes, buses, hotel rooms, restaurants, bars, attractions, beaches, campgrounds, lodges, forests, lakes, and, in fact, virtually every place. It is now well established in geography that space is not just an innocent backdrop or stage set in which events occur but rather a factor in itself (Knox 1994), "created out of social relations" (Massey 1993: 156), "increasingly being cast as actively produced, represented and contested" (Blomley 1996: 239).

A study of the contested spaces at New Zealand's Waitomo Glowworm Cave explored the notion of consumer sovereignty and place in the context of the rapid growth of Asian visitor markets (Doorne 2000). Following the adoption of market- and demand-driven management practices at the attraction, the collective ownership at a national natural heritage site was brought into question. Research revealed that north Asian visitors to the site registered higher tolerance of crowding compared to domestic visitors, resulting in the displacement of the crowd-intolerant domestic visitor population. The space and place implications of the consumer sovereignty concept assumed new significance not only in the context of its iconic symbolism for the domestic population, but also for indigenous landowners eager to reassert their historical claim to the site. Locked in a cycle of production and consumption, the domestic visitor market and traditional cultural claims were sacrificed in the interests of maintaining visitor numbers, revenues, and jobs in a stark reminder of the structural dynamics of the global tourism industry and its production of exclusionary territorial behaviors (Harvey 1993).

A study of backpacker travelers, also in New Zealand, revealed similar patterns of displacement within what has been widely perceived as a homogenous tourist consumer group (Ateljevic and Doorne 2001). The observed segmentation, particularly with respect to consumption patterns, was largely informed by the underlying cultural values that guide backpacker behavior. A key factor in the social differentiation among backpackers was each subgroup's perception of the "other." Traditional hippie drifters (see Cohen 1973), for example, frequently sought to distance themselves from the emerging more commercially oriented "mainstream" backpacker market by focusing on their respective ideology and exhibited behavior. These inclusive or exclusionary behavior patterns were inherently place-bound to the extent that destinations, regions, and activities were consumed (and created, or re-created) according to the behaviors produced in and around them. The study revealed the displacement of traditional drifters to places and spaces which were perceived to reflect their core values. Thus, on a regional level the backpacker landscape can be seen as a mosaic of value spaces reflecting particular codes of behavior and cultural practices, and modes of performance. While we focused our attention locally, the global nature of backpacking effectively interprets the whole world as "indeed a stage" (Franklin and Crang 2001: 17–18), with each destination a scene, an act within the completed production.

It is, of course, not only visitors who consume places. Perhaps most importantly, consumption by the "host" also demands reconsideration, for it is this act which is instrumental in the constitution of the host's lived identity, which is often taken as an initial reference for destination marketers. For example, the Wellington waterfront redevelopment project was conceived as "a place for people" – both locals and visitors. Yet, through its development, what was previously an unused and dormant space became the most contested landscape in the city (Doorne 1998). At the heart of the public controversy was the question of who the development was for. On one side were marketing and development initiatives transforming not only the image of the place but also the built environment, primarily for use by other people (tourists). On the other side were expressions of local identities and those appropriating the recreated image and place as their own. Underlying the situation was the notion of the waterfront as "public space," administered, owned, sold in places, and developed as a public–private partnership by the local authority (public sector) on behalf of the city and its people. Design values, however, conceived the place primarily as a site of conspicuous consumption, which included certain socioeconomic groups, but excluded others (such as skateboarders and the poor). The resolution of the conflict lay in the attempt to move beyond the serial production of "the tourist ghetto" to capture the essence of place from the perspective of the community. In doing so, commercial imperatives were satisfied through the reproduction of a living landscape necessarily differentiated from other places by its human geography and the consumption of its cultural spaces.

Tourism's contribution in the reconstruction of places via new spatialities of actors is being revealed as a network of circuits giving value to places in the evolving structures of the global tourism complex. In tourism a wide range of social groups and individuals (tourists, local residents, investors, travel writers, local entrepreneurs, marketing agencies, etc.) create spaces and places that convey a particular "identity" message. Meanings and values created within the circuits of cultural (tourism) production and consumption change over time, and reflect the material form of the environment because "real experiences can quickly become material out of which an individual can construct improved, imagined, scenarios" (Campbell 1995: 118). As Sack (1988) contends, threads of nature, meaning, and social relations of production and consumption are complexly interwoven in building place identities. A tourism landscape thus becomes "both a represented and presented space, both a signifier and signified, both a frame and what a frame contains, both a real place and its simulacrum, both a package and the commodity inside the package" (Mitchell 1994: 5). In this way, the production of places must also be considered as acts of re-consumption as the tourism complex voraciously appropriates surrounding economies, sociocultural landscapes, and built environments to reconstitute as "tourist destinations."

Acts of re-consumption

Here we turn our attention to the social relations that shape cultural economies of tourism (Lash and Urry 1994). Specifically, we firstly focus on the dynamics of "lifestyle entrepreneurship" in several different contexts, and secondly, historical analysis of the production of marketing discourses as a reflection of the sociocultural (con)text and underlying ideologies of leisure. Our studies of small tourism firms in New Zealand (Ateljevic and Doorne 2000) and Croatia (Ateljevic and Doorne 2003) illustrate the extent to which the cultural context is a significant element in the dynamics of entrepreneurship where producers consume places, experiences, and "activities" as lifestyle choices. Our earlier discussion of the segmentation of the backpacker traveler market highlighted both a rapid growth of small business activity in tourism and the corresponding emergence of "niche" markets. For example, the establishment of an underground "cave-tubing" business, also in Waitomo, New Zealand, was principally motivated by the desire for a prolonged lifestyle relationship with a particular landscape and recreational pursuit (see Ateljevic and Doorne 2000). The owner/manager's rejection of the traditional market-driven paradigm in favor of reciprocity and lifestyle management in effect created its own niche market of consumers actively seeking products which conveyed these values and eco-social orientation. The guides they employed were similarly consumers of re-creation, landscape, and caving culture through casual, often seasonal, contracts (see also du Gay 1996 regarding retailing).

It is no coincidence that many lifestyle entrepreneurs are former "travelers" who were actively engaged in the search for products articulating values of the broader sustainability paradigm. The arrival of foreign, and largely European, entrepreneurs in the Nelson and Golden Bay areas of New Zealand is an example.

They often came seeking environmental integrity and a sense of community. Their consumption of these has in turn reproduced the region in the image of their consumption values. Paradoxically, the search of lifestyle entrepreneurs who distance themselves from a "suffocating" business environment has provided a niche opportunity to simultaneously engage with markets on their own terms and to sustain their businesses in alternative socioeconomic ways. Thus, the process of production, while having a profound impact on future growth and development within the tourism industry, was largely a reflection of the entrepreneurs' consumption of particular places, landscapes, or recreational activities.

This concept can also be translated and transplanted across cultural contexts. The dynamics of entrepreneurship in the village of Murter on the Adriatic coast is set against a backdrop of economic transition and the post-war environment. The study of tourism entrepreneurship in Croatia focused on exploring the cultural context of decision-making by small business owners with respect to economy and lifestyle, the role of family, and the intergenerational nature of tourism businesses, gender issues, and relations of politics and the black market. The way in which many entrepreneurs of Murter constructed and articulated their preferred lifestyle and nostalgic associations of place reflected their desire to reproduce their own culture and to reaffirm their identity in the post-war context. The act of reproduction provided opportunities for individuals to engage in the collective consumption of "their" place, "their" cultural practices, and "their" social life in the face of political changes, social upheaval, and economic uncertainty. An emotional attachment, which underlay the personal and business commitment of many tourism entrepreneurs, was articulated as a nostalgic affection for the physical characteristics of the area together with its climate and pace of life. The "traditional" lifestyle of the region was commonly expressed as a relaxed, carefree approach to social relations and business activities, within which integrated economic and social rituals overtly revolved around drinking coffee and enjoying conversation in public areas and cafés. In this way, the consumption of lifestyle featured as a core element of the regional tourism product, simultaneously providing opportunities for consumers to in turn reproduce those elements of the culture.

While tourists readily engage the "visual" appeal of cafés and the relaxed Adriatic lifestyle, other elements of local culture provide the foundation for the social and economic stability of the community. Extended family structures were revealed as the primary units around which businesses were financed and employment roles based. One of the most persistent characteristics of the cultural environment was the stark gender division of labor roles and the perpetuation of exploitative relationships by a dominant macho male culture. These simultaneously provided references against which patriarchal and social relations were also reaffirmed within the community. Despite decades of change with respect to national and regional affiliations at the political level, the persistence of tourism and its representation provided a level of continuity for local and regional identity.

While the above discussion illustrates place construction and reproduction at the micro level, the process is predominantly subject to the complex structural machinery of dedicated agencies of government. The case of the national tourist administration of New Zealand, for example, reveals how over a hundred-year period tourist images have been central to shaping destinations through the interconnectedness of production and re-consumption. In other words, "producers" and "consumers" communicate and negotiate between each other in the economic, social, political, and cultural (con)texts they create, constitute, and re-consume, thereby constructing a particular realm of power-knowledge. In this way, hegemony is maintained by consent and coercion, rather than by domination (Ateljevic and Doorne 2002b).

The analysis of discourses and images in this study revealed tourism (re)imaging as a political process that reflects and reinforces the dominant ideologies of the time. By critically approaching tourism representations one can obtain insight into the ideological operations of the wider conditions of society within which tourism is constituted. More importantly, a historical perspective served to illustrate both a lineage of historical practices of tourism consumption and the continuity of cultural, social, and political significance. In colonial times, tourism served as a political agent to introduce, promote, and reinforce colonization. Socially, it served as an arena for social differentiation and the display of identity. Culturally, it expressed the dominant values and "life philosophy" of the classes from which tourists originated. Historical, longitudinal approaches illustrate that, in contemporary, postcolonial times, tourism continues "its purpose" to reinforce, reproduce, and maintain inequities in global structures of wealth and power that were established in the nineteenth century. What is significant is that class differentiation based on the political and economic capital of production has given way to consumption by emerging classes of the global cultural economy. Issues of social identity and the cultural context of particular forms of tourism consumption remain pertinent, mediated by the "cultural brokers" of tourism (Adams 1984), of which the New Zealand Tourism Board is but one example. The board's promotion strategy reveals the social relations underpinning the production of these texts, given that board marketing managers are themselves members of this service class, and thereby engaged in the act of producing and consuming the cultural (con)text in which they live.

Conclusions

This chapter has sought to appraise some of the new articulations that have emerged within the "cultural turn" in human geography, raising many issues for the geographical study of tourism. To accommodate emerging concerns, boundaries between economic and cultural questions have been blurred, disciplinary boundaries have been transgressed, theoretical and methodological strategies have been redefined – creating discourses of "new" geographies (Gregson 1992; Johnston 1993; Ioannides and Debbage 1998; Mansvelt and Perkins 1998). Reflecting upon these ideas of "new" geographies, this chapter has explicitly addressed the dualistic framing between production and consumption that has traditionally lain upon the dichotomy of economy and culture.

Establishing the cultural practice of tourism as an act of performance wherein individuals create their identities has served to be an insightful lens through which to view the dialectics of tourism production and consumption. This approach, generally concerned with broader analysis of culture, sees producers as "consumers" and consumers as "producers" who "feed off" each other in endless cycles of re-consumption. In this light, the framework of tourism circuits has been forged in order to finally resolve an endless dilemma of whether tourism is driven by either production or consumption processes. More importantly, the discussion reveals that geography lies at the heart of these processes, as tourism is inseparable from the spaces and places in which it is created, imagined, perceived, and experienced.

The conceptual challenge of removing the boundaries between production and consumption brings a powerful new vernacular that has the potential to open a wide range of new agendas. Tracing the processes of "consumption" in the context of social relations of tourism production to explore the personal, social, cultural, economic, and locality factors that influence re-consumption of tourism discourses can create potentially profitable literatures. In the process, the spatiality of a wide range of actors poses numerous questions. Multiple readings of local residents while working, living, playing, or, in other words, consuming and producing their localities through encounters with tourism should be explored and further revealed. The importance of identity "at work in tourism landscapes" raises issues related to employment and labor practices. How do managers, investors, and entrepreneurs negotiate the cultural (con)text in which they make economic decisions? How do employees invest their identities in their working lives and shape the spaces and places of tourism consumption? How do changing consumption tastes and lifestyle values influence the reconfiguration of corporate structures, and various forms of entrepreneurship? "Giving voice" to people while they collect, read, interpret, and communicate certain meanings of their tourist experience, in the context of their structural forces, can reveal how tourism is a socially negotiable concept.

In conclusion, by engaging with this approach this chapter has described circuits of tourism as a dynamic interconnected whole where players and stakeholders may (re)align themselves with any other player or stakeholder as need, desire, or opportunity allows. Furthermore, the idea offers boundless opportunity for the re-consumption of conceptual gazes and theoretical practices around the geographies of tourism.

REFERENCES

Abramovici, A., and Ateljevic, I. (2002). *What Lies Behind the Romance of the Grape? A Case Study of Wairarapa, New Zealand.* Paper presented at the Social Science in the 21st century, Sociological Association of Aotearoa (NZ), University of Canterbury, Christchurch.

Adams, K. M. (1984). Come to Tana Toraja, "Land of the Heavenly Kings": Travel agents as brokers in ethnicity. *Annals of Tourism Research* 11, 469–85.

Aitchison, C. (1999). New cultural geographies: The spatiality of leisure, gender and sexuality. *Leisure Studies* 18(1), 19–39.

Appadurai, A. (1986). *The Social Life of Things: Commodities in Cultural Perspective.* New York: Cambridge University Press.

Appadurai, A. (1996). *Modernity at Large: Cultural Dimensions of Globalisation.* Minneapolis: University of Minnesota Press.

Ateljevic, I. (2000). Circuits of tourism: Stepping beyond the "production/consumption" dichotomy. *Tourism Geographies* 2, 369–88.

Ateljevic, I., and Doorne, S. (2001). Nowhere left to run: A study of value boundaries and segmentation within the backpacker market of New Zealand. In J. A. Mazanec,

G. I. Crouch, J. R. Brent Ritchie, and A. G. Woodside (eds), *Consumer Psychology of Tourism, Hospitality and Leisure* (vol. 2, pp. 169–87). London: CAB International.

Ateljevic, I., and Doorne, S. (2002a). *Culture, Economy and Tourism Commodities: Social Relations of Production and Consumption.* Seminar presentation, the Auckland University of Technology, New Zealand.

Ateljevic, I., and Doorne, S. (2002b). Representing New Zealand: Tourism imagery and ideology. *Annals of Tourism Research* 29(3), 648–67.

Ateljevic, I., and Doorne, S. (2003). Unpacking the local: A cultural analysis of tourism entrepreneurship in Murter, Croatia. *Tourism Geographies* 5(2), 123–50.

Blomley, N. (1996). "I'd like to dress her all over": Masculinity, power and retail space. In M. N. Wrigley and M. Lowe (eds), *Retailing, Consumption and Capital: Towards the New Retail Geography* (pp. 238–56). Essex: Longman.

Boissevain, J. (1996). Ritual, tourism and cultural commoditization in Malta: Culture by the pound? In T. Selwyn (ed.), *The Tourist Image: Myths and Myth Making in Tourism.* Chichester: John Wiley.

Bourdieu, P. (1984). *Distinction.* London: Routledge.

Britton, S. (1991). Tourism, capital, and place: Towards a critical geography of tourism. *Environment and Planning D, Society and Space* 9, 451–78.

Britton, S., and Clarke, W. (1987). *Ambiguous Alternative: Tourism in Small Developing Countries.* Suva: University of South Pacific.

Burgess, J. (1990). The production and consumption of environmental meanings in the mass media: A research agenda for the 1990s. *Transactions of the Institute of British Geographers* 15(1), 139–61.

Campbell, C. (1995). The sociology of consumption. In D. Miller (ed.), *Acknowledging Consumption* (pp. 96–127). London: Routledge.

Cohen, E. (1973). Nomads from affluence: Notes on the phenomenon of drifter-tourism. *International Journal of Comparative Sociology* 14, 89–103.

Crang, P., and Malbon, B. (1996). Consuming geographies: A review essay. *Transactions of the Institute of British Geographers* 21(4), 704–11.

Crewe, L., and Lowe, M. (1995). Gap on the map? Towards a geography of consumption and identity. *Environment and Planning A* 27, 1877–98.

Crick, M. (1989). Representations of international tourism in the social sciences: Sun, sex, sights, savings, and servility. *Annual Review of Anthropology* 18, 307–44.

Doorne, S. (1998). Power, participation and perception: An insider's perspective on the politics of the Wellington Waterfront redevelopment. *Current Issues in Tourism* 1, 129–66.

Doorne, S. (2000). Caves, cultures and crowds: Carrying capacity meets consumer sovereignty. *Journal of Sustainable Tourism* 8, 116–30.

du Gay, P. (1996). *Consumption and Identity at Work.* London: Sage.

Edensor, T. (1998). *Tourists at the Taj: Performance and Meaning at a Symbolic Site.* London: Routledge.

Featherstone, M. (1987a). Lifestyle and consumer culture. *Theory, Culture and Society* 4, 55–70.

Featherstone, M. (1987b). Leisure, symbolic power and the life course. In J. Horne, D. Jary, and A. Tomlinson (eds), *Sport, Leisure and Social Relations.* London: Routledge & Kegan Paul.

Featherstone, M. (1990). Perspectives on consumer culture. *Sociology* 24(1), 5–22.

Featherstone, M. (1995). *Undoing Culture: Globalisation, Postmodernism and Identity.* London: Sage.

Franklin, A., and Crang, M. (2001). The trouble with tourism and travel theory? *Tourist Studies* 1(1), 5–22.

Glennie, P. D., and Thrift, N. J. (1993). Modern consumption: Theorising commodities and consumers. *Environment and Planning D, Society and Space* 11, 603–6.

Goodwin, N. R., Ackerman, F., and Kiron, D. (1997). *The Consumer Society.* Washington, DC: Island Press.

Greenwood, D. J. (1978). Culture by the pound: An anthropological perspective on tourism as cultural commoditization. In V. Smith (ed.), *Hosts and Guests: The Anthropology of Tourism* (pp. 129–38). Philadelphia: University of Pennsylvania Press.

Gregson, N. (1992). Beyond boundaries: The shifting sands of social geography. *Progress in Human Geography* 16(3), 387–92.

Hannerz, U. (1996). *Transnational Connections.* London: Routledge.

Harvey, D. (1993). From space to place and back again: Reflections on the condition of postmodernity. In B. C. J. Bird, T. Putnam, G. Robertson, and L. Tickner (eds), *Mapping the Futures: Local Cultures and Global Change* (pp. 3–29). London: Routledge.

Ioannides, D., and Debbage, K. G. (eds) (1998). *The Economic Geography of the Tourist Industry.* London: Routledge.

Jackson, P. (1999). Commodity cultures: The traffic in things. *Transactions of the Institute of British Geographers* 24, 95–108.

Jackson, P., and Holbrook, B. (1995). Multiple meanings: Shopping and the cultural politics of identity. *Environment and Planning A* 27, 1913–30.

Jackson, P., and Thrift, N. (1995). Geographies of consumption. In D. Miller (ed.), *Acknowledging Consumption* (pp. 204–38). London: Routledge.

Johnson, R. (1986). The story so far: And further transformations? In D. Punter (ed.), *Introduction to Contemporary Cultural Studies* (pp. 277–313). London: Longman.

Johnston, R. (1993). *The Challenge for Geography.* Oxford: Blackwell.

Kirshenblatt-Gimblett, B. (1998). *Destination Culture: Tourism, Museums, and Heritage.* Berkeley: University of California Press.

Knox, P. (1994). *Urbanisation: An Introduction to Urban Geography.* New Jersey: Prentice Hall.

Lash, S., and Urry, J. (eds) (1994). *Economies of Signs and Space.* London: Sage.

Lury, C. (1996). *Consumer Culture.* Cambridge: Polity.

Mansvelt, J., and Perkins, H. C. (1998). Putting recreation and leisure in their place: The geography of leisure. In H. C. Perkins and G. Cushman (eds), *Time Out? Leisure, Recreation and Tourism in New Zealand and Australia* (pp. 237–53). Auckland: Addison Wesley Longman.

Massey, D. (1993). Politics and space/time. In M. K. and S. Pile (eds), *In Place and the Politics of Identity* (pp. 141–61). London: Routledge.

Miller, D. (1995a). Consumption and commodities. *Annual Review of Anthropology* 24, 141–61.

Miller, D. (1995b). *Acknowledging Consumption.* London: Routledge.

Miller, D. (1997). *Capitalism: An Ethnographic Approach.* Oxford: Berg.

Miller, D. (1998). *Material Cultures: Why Some Things Matter.* London: University College.

Miller, D., Jackson, P., Thrift, N., Holbrook, B., and Rowlands., M. (1998). *Shopping, Place and Identity.* London: Leicester University Press.

Milne, S., and Ateljevic, I. (2001). Tourism, economic development and the global-local nexus: Theory embracing complexity. *Tourism Geographies* 3(4), 367–88.

Mitchell, W. J. T. (1994). *Landscape and Power.* Chicago: University of Chicago Press.

Pearce, S. (1997). *Experiencing Material Culture in the Western World.* London: Leicester University Press.

Perkins, H. C., and Thorns, D. C. (2001). Gazing or performing? Reflections on Urry's tourist gaze in the context of contemporary experience in the Antipodes. *International Sociology* 16(2), 185–204.

Pritchard, A., and Morgan, N. (2000). Privileging the male gaze: Gendered tourism landscapes. *Annals of Tourism Research* 27, 884–905.

Ringer, G. (1998). *Destinations: Cultural Landscapes of Tourism*. London: Routledge.
Rojek, C. (1995). *Decentring Leisure: Rethinking Leisure Theory*. London: Sage Publications.
Sack, R. D. (1988). The consumer's world: Place as context. *Annals of the Association of American Geographers* 78, 642–64.
Sharpley, R. (1996). Tourism and consumer culture in postmodern society. In M. Robinson, N. Evans, and P. Callaghan (eds), *Tourism and Culture Towards the 21st Century Cultural Change. Conference Proceedings*. Sunderland: Center for Travel and Tourism.
Smith, V. (1978). *Hosts and Guests: The Anthropology of Tourism*. Oxford: Blackwell.
Squire, S. J. (1994a). The cultural values of literary tourism. *Annals of Tourism Research* 21, 103–21.
Squire, S. J. (1994b). Accounting for cultural meanings: The interface between geography and tourism studies revisited. *Progress in Human Geography* 18(1), 1–16.
Thomas, N. (1991). *Entangled Objects*. Cambridge, MA: Harvard University Press.
Thrift, N. (2000). Pandora's box. In G. L. Clark, M. P. Feldman, and M. S. Gertler (eds), *The Oxford Handbook of Economic Geography* (pp. 689–704). Oxford: Oxford University Press.
Turner, L., and Ash, J. (1975). *The Golden Hordes: International Tourism and the Pleasure Periphery*. London: Constable.
Urry, J. (1990). *The Tourist Gaze: Leisure and Travel in Contemporary Societies*. London: Sage.

Chapter 24

Narratives of Being Elsewhere: Tourism and Travel Writing

Mike Robinson

Introduction

Writing about the experience of travel and visits to "other" places is as old as travel itself. Poets, novelists, evangelists, scientists, anthropologists, historians, journalists, comedians, cooks, and many others have all engaged in writing about their travels. From celebrated accounts of adventure and discovery, to schoolroom accounts of "what I did on my holidays," the desire to communicate our impressions, encounters, and emotions of travel is deep and persistent. This sharing of experiences in different places performs a number of functions. For the writer it legitimizes the episodes of travel as a lived/life event in a shared and social way. It indulges memory, allows interior reflection, and provides opportunities for cultural commentary, cross-cultural communication, or passionate polemic. It can generate and fuel personal status based on the acquisition of knowledge and insight (sometimes privileged knowledge), and it can, in those societies eager to "escape" through the journeys of others into worlds outside of themselves, make the travel writer popular or wealthy. For the reader, travel writings facilitate this escape and allow safe and easy passage to places they may never visit directly. At times they may actively spur readers to physically undertake journeys themselves (Robinson 1990; Hall and Kinnaird 1994). They enable engagement with distant, "other" peoples they are unlikely to meet, and foreign experiences they may otherwise never know about. In addition, and not to be overlooked, they also bring pleasure to the reader.

Travel writings also perform a valuable, if still under-explored, role for tourism researchers. This importance is accentuated when we consider that the vast majority of tourists do not write about their experiences. It is not because they don't have any, but they are seldom transcribed for a wider audience, except perhaps via postcard messages. Thus, the travel writer/travel writings, albeit unknowingly, feed a deeper generic understanding of the actualities and experiences of being "elsewhere." Dann (1996, 1999) has noted the relative neglect of travel writing within tourism studies. On the one hand this is surprising given the popularity of travel writing in contemporary society, its function as a promotional tool with the ability to influence holiday decision-making, and its "critical stance to the overall phenomenon it is treating" (Dann 1999: 160). On the other hand, the utilization of travel accounts as sources of knowledge and ways of seeing the world generates its own problematic set of ontological and epistemological issues and tensions which have arguably deterred tourism scholars from more sustained and rigorous investigations. These include finding ways through the tacit subjectivity of the texts, varying truths, and multiple authenticities of place, issues of authority and legitimacy, and overcoming the persistent reputation of travel writing as being "lightweight."

The interrelationships between the experience of travel and visited destinations, the varied narratives of that experience, and the textual and intertextual communicative processes between writer and reader and between readers and their own travel experiences, are complex and interactive. Tourists and travel writing are intimately connected by the ways each uses, consumes, and imagines the other. They collide in the formative spaces of home and away. It is indeed common to observe waiting passengers at airports or railway stations engrossed in the latest travel bestseller. Tourists-as-readers and readers-as-tourists are exposed to literature in a dynamic sense, as it carves out ways in which we see and structure the world. Travel writing can act as a precursory source of imagery of the tourist's destination, or as an endorsing, deeper reservoir of cultural location during and after a visit. It forms part of that larger collective of normative social practices that includes the consumption of literature, and which helps frame the tourist gaze. In relation to fictional texts, but also apposite in relation to travel writing, Robinson (2002: 67) reflects:

> Places, communities, history are imagined through the communicative power of literature. Furthermore, this power is cumulative, incessant, and difficult to counter-act. The creative writer has the beauty and poetic charm of language, plot and character to convey and represent places, as well as a long "shelf-life." The tourism promoter is armed with a few ephemeral brochures. It would appear to be a one-sided contest.

The focus of attention in this chapter is upon the complex relationships that exist between recorded narratives of travel and the practices and study of tourism. It explores the nature and dynamic of travel writing with reference to its internal textual qualities, and more so in terms of its wider impacts upon the phenomenon of tourism and our attempts to understand this. To begin with, the chapter is concerned to understand what travel writing is, where it fits in the literary sphere, and what roles it performs, particularly its resonance with the cultural contexts for travel and tourism. Three interrelated themes are then explored: first, the centrality of the romantic in travel writings and how this is transposed into our comprehension of tourism and tourist behavior; second, the idea of self within travel writing and the idea of struggle between writers and the spaces they inhabit; and third, the production of tourist space through travel narratives. These themes have been selected because they remain relatively under-researched in tourism studies, and also because they exemplify the relationships that exist between tourism and travel writing. At the outset, it is important to note the lack of academic attention given to the travel writing–tourism relationship, and it would not be feasible to expand much further beyond these points in the space available. In recognition of this the chapter suggests areas for future research.

Travel Writing as Literary Wandering

Attempting to place boundaries of genre on travel writing would seem to discount its very nature. Just as travelers continually cross geographical and cultural borders so their accompanying stories and accounts move disrespectfully within and between many different genres and subgenres, continuingly challenging the way we see the world. Beyond the first line of genre theory that distinguishes between poetry, prose, and drama, travel writing continually taxes those who seek to classify and typify it. Indeed, even these vast categories prove useless if one interprets Homer's *Odyssey* or Byron's *Childe Harold* as examples of travel writing. It is far beyond the scope of this chapter to fully examine travel writing as a genre, but it is nonetheless important to explore common elements that shed light upon its relationship with tourism. A starting point, following Fussell (1980), and picked up by Holland and Huggan (1998) and Dann (1999), is what travel writing is not. Travel books are not guide books. While we can identify a shift to more playful and elaborate textual infilling such as that found within the Rough Guides and the Lonely Planet series, guides more or less remain as repositories of "factual" (albeit value-laden) information that the tourist can reliably use to navigate him- or herself to, and around, spaces generally already designated as having touristic interest. Nor are travel books "travel-logs," or, as Dann (1999: 162) suggests, "travelogues," as epitomized in the Sunday newspaper supplements. Certainly journalistic reports of travel, or what Stowe (1994) terms "travel chronicles" ("letters from," newspaper travel columns, short "sketches," or collections of any of these), can feed into and from travel writing, but they are not one and the same.

But saying what travel writing actually *is* with any precision remains difficult. For Holland and Huggan (1998: 12) travel writing is best viewed as being "pseudoethnographic," reflecting some degree of objective reporting but invariably colored by personal experience. Following White's (1976) essay on "Fictions of factual representation," they use the term "factual fictions" to highlight the hybridity of the form. The spatial focus of travel is reflected, to a greater or lesser degree, in writing. Thus, Gregory (1999: 116) sees travel writing as a process of "scripting" through which "travel writing is intimately involved in the 'staging' of particular places; in the simultaneous production of 'sites' that are linked in a time-space itinerary and 'sights' that are organized into a hierarchy of cultural significance." Stowe (1994) highlights the ritualistic nature of travel, drawing upon Turner's (1982) work on ritual as cultural performance, and suggests that "an understanding of travel as a ritual activity suggests a related understanding of travel writings as quasi-religious texts, paralleling the scriptural, liturgical, and testimonial texts of Western religious traditions" (1994: 27). In a more secular way this spiritual undercurrent links also to Chard's (1999: 9) view of travel writings as involving "the construction of particular myths, visions and fantasies, and the voicing of particular desires, demands and aspirations." In essence these various conceptions are structured around what travel writing does – constructing/imagining spaces, dramatizing performances, feeding the reader with dreamscapes and psychic sustenance, and generating moments of liminality.

It is, of course, difficult to separate travel writing from the act of travel and engagement with destinations. If travel is at the core of modernity (Rothman

1998), then travel writing plays a major role in creatively documenting the processes of modernization and its associated problematics. Theorists of a globalizing world engaged with various "flows" (Hannerz 1992, 1996) across increasingly permeable boundaries refer to the new, virtual, electronic, and instantaneous modes of transfer, of images, ideas, and capital (Morely and Robins 1995). But in many ways these "flows" are soulless mechanisms of intercultural exchange while what remains central are physical flows of people. Not surprisingly, as people have become increasingly mobile (693 million recorded tourist trips in 2001: World Tourism Organization 2002) narratives of the practices and experience of travel have been constructed, building up a large, if diverse body of knowledge, what Davidson (2001) terms the "literature of movement." The idea of space is central to travel (de Certeau 1984; Urry 2000). As Duncan and Gregory (1999: 5) observe, travel writings are produced "by corporeal subjects moving through material landscapes." Thus an understanding of travel narratives requires some appreciation of the cultural context, motivation, and experience of movement across and within different spaces. In Fussell's (1980: 210) words: "They manipulate the whole alliance of between temporal and spatial that we use to orient ourselves in time by invoking the dimension of space. That is, travel books make more or less conscious an activity usually unconscious."

As expected, a historical view of travel writing closely mirrors the transformation of travel itself and its opening up of "new" spaces. Early travel writings, such as the accounts of Xenophon's incursion into Persia in the fourth century B.C., or the travels of Marco Polo in the thirteenth century, are very much documents of "essential" journeying, for military and mercantile purposes respectively. Antoninus's tours of Christian sites in the Middle East in the sixth century A.D., and Ibn Battuta's recorded trip to Mecca in the fourteenth century, provide examples of travel writings based upon religious pilgrimage, focused not only upon the journey in a spiritual sense but also on the sites, spectacle, and spaces of worship. Characteristically, though with exceptions, such narratives engage in ordered description and diachronic storylines and, though illuminating and entertaining on the margins, were nonetheless "serious" and meaningful *reports*. As Ohler (1989) identifies in his study of medieval travel, such accounts allow important historical insights into the experiences of travelers and early tourists.

But it was the great, secular, "world" explorations of the seventeenth, eighteenth, and nineteenth centuries (bound up with more extant developments in print technologies and the rise in literacy) that fired the development of travel writing and arguably delivered to the reader a format that is still readily recognizable. A detailed historical analysis of the evolution of travel writing as a generic process of communication remains a grand project beyond this review, and existing academic sources tend not to examine the devices of narrative and the communicative power of language, but examine specific themes, defined chronologies, and geographies relating to travel history (e.g., Porter 1991; Pratt 1992; Blanton 1998; Boehmer 1998; Mills and Foster 1998; Smith 1998; Chard 1999; Clark 1999; Cronin 2000; Gilroy 2000; Hadfield 2001; Hooper 2001; Korte 2001; Leask 2002). From a variety of different motivations, travel experiences, and encounters, narratives of travel are structured around a variety of literary styles and techniques that continue to vex those who would seek to identify it as a specific genre. It is useful to see travel writing as a metaphor of travel itself; as a discursive journey with points of departure and points of arrival, but with considerable digressions and deviations between object and self, the real and the imagined, the expected and the unknown, the comedic and tragic, the philosophic and the surreal, the romantic and the prosaic. Travel writers wander freely across a range of literary territories in the same way that travelers move through a variety of experiences, each needing a different voice and vocabulary.

Locating the Romantic and the Romanticized

The idea of the romantic is as central to travel writing as it is to travel. Here the romantic is taken to be the imaginative, fictitious, fabulous and the extravagant (Lamont 1987) ascribed to the vast majority of travel books and certainly well beyond the "romantic period" of 1775–1844, as identified by Gilroy (2000). Significantly, contemporary leisure travel is an important vehicle for people experiencing the distant, the exotic, the picturesque, the untouched, and the unknown, and all are elements that unfold to varying degrees in travel stories. Narratives are almost exclusively constructed around the themes of adventure and discovery. Moving between the here and the there, from the familiar to the unfamiliar, from the known to unknown, provides a rich source of matter and metaphor for the writer, who inhabits the experience of travel actively not passively, as Boorstin (1961) accuses "tourists" of doing. There is something innately fascinating about the experience of being elsewhere and the process of traveling, though it seems that in an academic framework of tourism/ist studies with its leanings (still) toward measurement and modeling, the centrality of the charm of travel and the emotion of the travel experience are frequently bypassed. Cousineau (1999: xxiii), in his well-observed deliberations on modern-day pilgrimage, speaks of "soulful travel," and "re-imagined" travel. Travel writing feeds heavily on travel as an event in itself. The act of journeying, by whatever means, is frequently very much in the foreground in travel books and not merely taken as a means of moving between destinations. The train journey, a car ride, or a walk are all imbued with significance beyond the boring functionality usually ascribed to them. In some cases the form of transport itself provides the romance through a combination of nostalgia and uniqueness; traveling on an old steam train or riding a Harley Davidson motor cycle.

Tradition in travel writing is one of romantic reimaginings of place. In part this relates to the linguistic turns and techniques used by writers to communicate their highly particular gazes. Sites and landscapes are constructed from, and interpreted by, highly Eurocentric ideas of the picturesque frame and via metaphorical devices that have long imparted this tradition. The travel writer (writing usually in retrospect) tells of places beyond the expectation of most of the reading public and thus descriptions are regularly crammed with intense superlatives of the aesthetic (wonder, awe, spectacular, stunning, dramatic, dazzling, etc.) and emotional value-laden descriptions relating to the status of the landscape (wild, pristine, remote, hidden, etc.). The reader may be charmed and inspired, but nonetheless at a distance from both the beauty of the landscape and the writer, apparently the sole witness. Narratives that mirror remote and distant travel (remote, that is, from the reader), seem especially to gravitate to romantic convention.

Somewhat removed from the notion of the romantic as the remote and beautiful is a stream of travel writing that focuses upon the nearby, the familiar, and, occasionally, the unsightly and the unpleasant. MacCannell (1976) touches upon this through his idea of "alienated leisure" and his examples of traveler's encounters in nineteenth-century Paris where (some) travelers engaged with sites of work and the distasteful, such as the sewers, the slaughterhouse, and the morgue. Such experiences of what maybe termed backyard travel are recounted by numerous writers including, in the UK, Defoe, Johnson, Gilpin, Butler, Orwell, Priestley, Morton, and more recently, Bainbridge, Danziger, and Murphy. At one level the travel writer focuses upon the ordinariness of the destination and travel. Examples include Murphy's (2000) *A Jaunt Around the Decaying Heart of England*, which takes in experiences of places such as Woking, Derby, Slough, and Luton; Sayle and Stratton's *Great Bus Journeys of the World* (1989); and Sinclair's (2002) traveling of the London orbital M25 motorway. In such examples we can detect a postmodern inversion of the picturesque and a shift from the exotic to the ordinary.

De Botton (2002) takes the idea of traveling and narrating the ordinary to new heights when he draws our attention to the work of Xavier de Maistre who, in 1790 and later in 1798, wrote accounts of day- and night-time journeys around the intimacies of his own bedroom. Without the burden of luggage de Maistre explores his sofa and his bed, not in the first instance as a resident of the familiar, but as a traveler. De Botton (2002: 246) notes, "De Maistre's work springs from a profound and suggestive insight: that the pleasure we derive from journeys is perhaps dependent more on the mindset with which we travel than on the destination we travel to." De Botton goes on to suggest that this "mindset" is effectively our receptiveness to the travel experience, where "We find a supermarket or hairdressers unusually fascinating. We dwell at length on the layout of a menu or the clothes of the presenters on the evening news. We are alive to the layers of history beneath the present and take notes and photographs." This idea of receptivity to travel is learned and travel writing feeds this learning process. But in presenting the ordinary, even in the harshest and most critical style, the travel writer is also romanticizing it. Accounts of the seemingly bland and mundane are subjected to exposure, revelation, and discovery as the practices of writing transfer people, places, and pasts into the realm of the romantic. The reader is taken to "the edge" of the writer's experience, following a series of reported encounters of equally "strange" landscapes and "colorful" characters.

Relatively little academic attention has focused upon issues surrounding tourists' search for the romantic, their changing conceptions of, and cross-cultural differences in, aesthetics, and where, how, and whether they find their imagined ideals. The (misplaced) distinction that somehow travel is a "serious" exploration of the world and that tourism is undertaken "simply for the 'fun' of it" (Leed 1995), conceals the reality that both traveler and tourist seek and have romantic experiences. Picking up on the predetermined mindsets that De Botton speaks of, to what extent do tourists follow and reproduce established narratives of romanticism (Adler 1989; Urry 1995)? To what extent does the tourism industry comply with such traditions? Where, in the increasingly diverse set of touristic forms, are tourists breaking away from, or reinventing, ideas of the romantic? Understanding the nature of the romantic tradition as constructed and compounded by travel writings of the past and present can assist in addressing questions that relate to the legacy they have left, and continue to leave, for tourism.

Self, Struggle, and Conflict

What is largely missing from travel guide books and is central to travel writing is the distinctive presence of the author's voice. Fussell (1980) speaks of the "internal freedom" of travel writing and of the reader's requirement of experiencing an interior journey as well as an exterior one. It is this interior exploration, juxtaposed against the experiences of the external world, that is at the core of a travel book. The act of travel is no value-neutral practice. It is imbued with purposes and actions that reveal, challenge, and subvert. The travel experience of the reader is then mediated through the writer, not only in terms of the latter's particular style, but more importantly through his or her ideologies, absorbed as they are into the text. It is the divulgence of "self" in the narrative that generates emplotments of the personal – desire, ambition, fulfillment, pilgrimage, love, loss, catharsis, etc. – and which helps to distinguish the field of travel writing.

From the recognition of the travel writer's self comes the reader's identification of experience, not in terms of geographical space but in a more empathetic, human way. The surveillance of places and peoples is interspersed, to varying degrees, with the feelings and emotions of the writer in a reflexive way. This reflexivity has evolved in travel writing as travelers/writers have jettisoned Enlightenment-informed formats of pseudo-scientific reporting and world-making didactics (Pratt 1992) in favor of self-exploration and struggle. The reader is momentarily part of the traveler/writer's internal conflicts and emotional upheavals. Take for example the following extract from Jan Morris's (1992: 15) depiction of Paris:

> I do not much like the songs of Edith Piaf, the boulevards of Baron Haussmann, the furniture of Louis XIV, the sound of Gertrude Stein, the vainglory of Napoleon or the conceit of Charles de Gaulle. I distrust, at one level, people who turn ideas into movements: at another, ideas themselves if too pressingly articulated. In a paranoia common but not often acknowledged among Britons of my World War II generation, deep in my semi-conscious I probably resent the fact that, while London was blitzed in victory, Paris remained inviolate in defeat.

Here Morris exemplifies that encounters with places can initiate a struggle with ourselves and the invisible cultural baggage we drag around when we travel. Paris for her is not a romantic idyll, but a plotting mass, absorbed with itself, a humorless city, grand but somehow sinister. Clearly there are numerous examples that would represent Paris in a completely different light. But this is the point; it is the recognition of the writer's challenge, conflict, and internal struggles, however petty, that illuminates the reader's experience. Furthermore, it is likely that to some degree the moral platforms and prejudices that travel writings carry are also carried by readers as they travel. The influence of the travel writer as ideologue as well as communicator of places and experiences, and how this manifests itself in tourism patterns, behavior, and tourist perceptions of destinations and peoples requires sustained examination.

Despite Fussell's (1980: 49) lament that "We are all tourists now," travel writers have frequently sought to maintain their distance from the tourist hordes and their status as lone explorers and exponents of the "real" adventure experience, and indeed as arbiters of taste. As Dann (1999: 160) suggests, the paradox remains "that the richer the portrayal of 'undiscovered' places of travel, the more likely it is that they will become transformed into 'discovered' tourist destinations." While some travelers/travel writers struggle with this, the profession can be seen as upholding its solitary, selfish role in apparent defiance of "mass" tourism. It is difficult not to see travel writers as champions and perpetuators of "anti-tourism" (Buzard 1993). There does exist a tacit elitism surrounding "travelers who write" (Hall and Kinnaird 1994), but arguably less so than amongst "writers who travel" (epitomized by Henry James, who famously labeled tourists as "vulgar, vulgar, vulgar"). The travel writer is culturally positioned as both critic and expert, and indeed is supported by a wider traveling/touring/reading public who turn to travel books for "inside" knowledge. The assumption seems to be that those engaging in "mass tourism" can somehow not fulfill these expert roles, maybe because of the transitory nature of their experiences and, more implicitly, because they have lost the idea of the critical "self" in the airport crowds. However, all tourists are critics and, increasingly, experts. They too undergo inner conflicts and struggles catalyzed by adventure and exploration, but these are rarely evidenced by texts or open to wider analysis. In the broader context of needing to undertake research focusing on tourist moments of experience, an agenda is required that explores the identification of "self" amongst tourists and how this self is articulated and changes.

The Production of Tourist Spaces?

Holland and Huggan (1998: 219) argue that travel writing (and by implication travel writers) is "complicit with the (mass) tourism it denounces: and while it may be given to see itself as an antidote to modern tourism, its usual effect may be to provide a further incentive for it." This view requires further examination for it hints at a direct relationship between travel writing and tourism. In a world pushing at the boundaries of experience and geographical/cultural space, travel writing can be seen in a promotional light encouraging an increasingly adventurous, Western, middle-class public to explore parts of the world previously inhabited by solitary writers. It would seem reasonable to argue, in line with Dann (1996), that travel books can play a role in holiday decision-making. They are amongst that pot pourri of textual influences that feed prospective tourists with information and opinion on destinations, although tracking, measuring, and disaggregating their specific affect is problematic (Robinson 2002). Notable recent examples of travel books influencing the development and extent of "tourist space" would include Peter Mayle's *A Year in Provence* (1989) and *Toujours Provence* (1991). These highly successful accounts of the author's relocation to Provence and the stories surrounding his integration into local culture have "led some to fear that his work has begun to change the imaginary and physical landscape, as more people seek the place and the experience that he describes" (Sharp 1999: 200). But, as Sharp goes on to argue, despite references to his work in British guide books and tourist maps, the area has not suffered unduly at the hands of mass tourism and changes that have taken place are part of a wider evolutionary process. Provence, for instance, has long been a favored destination for the British upper middle classes attracted to its associations with van Gogh and its proximity to established resorts on the Côte d'Azur. Moreover, changes in the social structure of Provence, as in many rural areas, have more to do with permanent settlement (second-home ownership, de-urbanization, etc.) than tourist influxes, though tourism may have contributed to the second-home phenomenon.

Further research is required to examine the relative role of travel books in the production of tourist space. Long-established fictive texts with a truly mass appeal, such as the novels of the Brontë sisters, have created tourist spaces and can influence tourism patterns (Robinson and Andersen 2002). Whereas, on the whole, travel writings do not act as an incentive for large-scale tourist influxes, their impacts are more selective in terms of readership and destination and more subtle as to any catalyzing effects. But this too is complicated when the intertextuality of travel writing is considered. Travel writing, with its accent on adventure and spectacle, can make an attractive genre for visual adaptation. It thus becomes difficult, for instance, to separate Mayle's *A Year in Provence* from the television drama series of the same name. Does the impact on the prospective traveler/tourist derive from encounter with the book, the television, or both? It is difficult to tell. In some cases the television series comes prior to the publication of the travel books, as with Michael Palin's (1992) *Around the World in Eighty Days*. Extracts read on the radio, serialized in the newspapers, and now on the internet, widen the audience for travel writing, but then again, only certain types of travel writing/travel writers are selected for dramatization.

While travel writings may have a marginal role in the production of tourist space they have had a significant part to play in the imagining and re-imaging of places and peoples. Said (1980, 1993), Anderson (1983), Pratt (1992), Darby (1998), Holland and Huggan (1998), Wheeler (1999), Gregory (1999), and Huggan (2001) have all focused on the power of literature in constructing, projecting, and maintaining Western white developed world hegemonies while subjugating the "rest" of the world. Travel writing, as a subset of a more extant politics of print and literature in general, has long assisted in scaping historical and contemporary attitudes to places, cultures, and societies that are persistent and more often than not, pernicious (see e.g., Parry (1993) on Kipling; Tambling (1995) on E. M. Forster; Teltscher (1995) on representations of India generally through travel writings). Space does not permit detailed coverage of the ways travel accounts have "othered" peoples, rewritten histories, and succeeded in generating and perpetuating myths from positions of colonial power. However, the legacy of travel accounts from previous centuries continues to play a role in shaping attitudes of contemporary tourists toward the world.

The disjuncture between "being" home and "being" away provides travel writing with its ultimate force and energy. It is the force we encounter when we experience the unfamiliar or, often, the familiar in other locations. The more elaborate the journey and the more exotic or remote the destination, the greater the sense of revelation and adventure for the reader. Often such journeys reproduce the paths of previous travelers to destinations during colonial times (Holland and Huggan 1998). But it is increasingly the case that, in examining travel writing in tourism studies, we also take into account those texts that document the travels of peoples from such destinations, which have often been obscured by the dominance of Westernized conceptions of the exotic and the romantic. Travel writings, such as those of V. S. Naipaul, Pico Iyer, Jamaica Kincaid, and Salman Rushdie, and Pettinger's (1998) edited collection of stories of Africans and people of African descent, provide a growing number of examples that tell of travels into the unknown, of adventure, the exotic, and of resistance in travel, but this time from the perspective of marginalized, subjugated communities traveling in "new" and "opposite" directions.

Concluding Remarks

The consumption of travel writing is widely seen as an antidote to a packaged or mass tourism that is frequently portrayed as trite, devoid of adventure, and unimaginative. At one level there would seem to be no link between the actions of the "armchair" readings of travel and the discourses and practices of contemporary tourism. Yet, each feeds the other and, as leisure activities, both have the capacity to shape geographies, histories, cultures and societies, and produce sets of real and imagined spaces in the world. Though tourists and the traveler continue to struggle with their identities, both share much in common. Both are shaped by notions of, and quests for, the romantic, and the romanticized, though each may experience this in different ways. Both are delightfully human in how they deal with the actual experience of getting to and being elsewhere. Each journey is constructed of a vast range of different experiences, intimate moments, emotional encounters, personal struggles, and diverse coping strategies. Travel writing opens up this personal and intimate world and in the absence of a body of "tourist writing" provides the tourism scholar with rich material that can inform much-needed research on the experiential dimensions of tourism.

The place of travel writing in tourism studies has been rather peripheral to date, partly due to the perceived tourist–traveler dichotomy. There is a need to look beyond this and to value all travel writings as providing ethnographies of tourism and tourist behavior – documenting change, detailing encounters, mapping out ways of living, recording traditions, providing cultural reflection – with their critical insights into tourism as a highly distinctive human practice. Future research needs to be bold to take on the intricacies and complexities of travel writing–tourism relationships. Closer examination of the relationships that exist between travel writing and the production/consumption of tourist space, and between narratives of travel and the motivations/experiences/performances of tourists should be central to an emergent research agenda in tourism studies. Such an agenda needs to be transdisciplinary, creatively drawing upon theory and method from literary and critical theory, cultural and media studies, social anthropology, history, and cultural geography, amongst others.

REFERENCES

Adler, J. (1989). Origins of sightseeing. *Annals of Tourism Research* 16(1), 7–29.
Anderson, B. (1983). *Imagined Communities*. London: Verso.
Blanton, C. (1998). *Travel Writing: The Self and the World*. Boston: Twayne.

Boehmer, E. (ed.) (1998). *Empire Writing: An Anthology of Colonial Literature, 1870–1918*. Oxford: Oxford University Press.
Boorstin, D. J. (1961). *The Image – or What Happened to the American Dream*. London: Penguin Books.
Buzard, J. (1993). *The Beaten Track: European Tourism, Literature and the Ways to "Culture", 1800–1918*. Oxford: Oxford University Press.
Chard, C. (1999). *Pleasure and Guilt on the Grand Tour: Travel Writing and Imaginative Geography, 1600–1830*. Manchester: Manchester University Press.
Clark, S. (ed.) (1999). *Travel Writing and Empire: Postcolonial Theory in Transit*. London: Zed Press.
Cousineau, P. (1999). *The Art of Pilgrimage*. Shaftesbury, Dorset: Element.
Cronin, M. (2000). *Across the Lines: Travel, Language, Translation*. Cork: Cork University Press.
Dann, G. S. (1996). *Tourism: A Socio-Linguistic Analysis*. Wallingford: CAB International.
Dann, G. S. (1999). Writing out the tourist in space and time. *Annals of Tourism Research* 26(1), 159–87.
Darby, P. (1998). *The Fiction of Imperialism: Reading Between International Relations and Post Colonialism*. London: Cassell.
Davidson, R. (ed.) (2001). *Journeys: An Anthology*. London: Picador.
de Botton, A. (2002). *The Art of Travel*. London: Hamish Hamilton.
de Certeau, M. (1984). *The Practice of Everyday Life*. Berkeley: University of California Press.
Duncan, J., and Gregory, D. (eds) (1999). *Writes of Passage: Travel Writing, Place and Ambiguity*. London: Routledge
Fussell, P. (1980). *Abroad: British Literary Travelling between the Wars*. New York: Oxford University Press.
Gilroy, A. (ed.) (2000). *Romantic Geographies: Discourses of Travel, 1775–1844*. Manchester: Manchester University Press.
Gregory, D. (1999). Scripting Egypt: Orientalism and the cultures of travel. In J. Duncan and D. Gregory (eds), *Writes of Passage: Travel Writing, Place and Ambiguity* (pp. 114–50). London: Routledge.
Hadfield, A. (ed.) (2001). *Amazons, Savages and Machiavels: Travel and Colonial Writing in English, 1530–1630*. Oxford: Oxford University Press.
Hall, D., and Kinnaird, V. (1994). A note on women travellers. In V. Kinnaird and D. Hall (eds), *Tourism: A Gender Analysis* (pp. 188–209). Chichester: John Wiley.
Hannerz, U. (1992). *Cultural Complexity*. New York: Columbia University Press.
Hannerz, U. (1996). *Transnational Connections*. London: Routledge.
Holland, P., and Huggan, G. (1998). *Tourists with Typewriters: Critical Reflections on Contemporary Travel Writing*. Ann Arbor: University of Michigan Press.
Hooper, G. (ed.) (2001). *The Tourist's Gaze: Travellers to Ireland 1800–2000*. Cork: Cork University Press.
Huggan, G. (2001). *The Post-Colonial Exotic: Marketing the Margins*. London: Routledge.
Korte, B. (2001). *English Travel Writing: From Pilgrimages to Postcolonial Explorations*, trans. C. Matthias. Basingstoke: Macmillan.
Lamont, C. (1987). The Romantic period 1780–1830. In P. Rogers (ed.), *The Oxford Illustrated History of English Literature*. Oxford: Oxford University Press.
Leask, N. (2002). *Curiosity and the Aesthetics of Travel Writing, 1770–1840: From an Antique Land*. Oxford: Oxford University Press.
Leed, E. (1995). *Shores of Discovery*. New York: Basic Books.
MacCannell, D. (1976). *The Tourist: A New Theory of the Leisure Class*. New York: Schocken Books.

Mayle, P. (1989). *A Year in Provence*. London: Pan Books.
Mayle, P. (1991). *Toujours Provence*. London: Pan Books.
Mills, S., and Foster, S. (eds) (1998). *British Women's Travel Writing: An Anthology*. Manchester: Manchester University Press.
Morely, D., and Robins, K. (1995). *Spaces of Identity: Global Media, Electronic Landscapes and Cultural Boundaries*. London: Routledge.
Morris, J. (1992). *Locations*. Oxford: Oxford University Press.
Murphy, B. (2000). *Home Truths: A Jaunt around the Decaying Heart of England*. Edinburgh: Mainstream Publishing.
Ohler, N. (1989). *The Medieval Traveller*. Woodbridge: Boydell.
Palin, M. (1992). *Around the World in Eighty Days* (reissue). London: BBC Consumer Publishing.
Parry, B. (1993) The content and discontents of Kipling's imperialism. In E. Carter, J. Donald, and J. Squires (eds), *Space and Place: Theories of Identity and Location* (pp. 221–40). London: Lawrence & Wishart.
Pettinger, A. (ed.) (1998). *Always Elsewhere: Travels of the Black Atlantic*. New York: Cassell.
Porter, D. (1991). *Haunted Journeys: Desire and Transgression in European Travel Writing*. Princeton: Princeton University Press.
Pratt, M. L. (1992). *Imperial Eyes: Travel Writing and Transculturation*. London: Routledge.
Robinson, J. (1990). *Wayward Women: A Guide to Women Travellers*. Oxford: Oxford University Press.
Robinson, M. (2002). Beyond and between the pages: Literature tourism relationships. In M. Robinson and H. C. Andersen (eds), *Literature and Tourism: Essays in the Reading and Writing of Tourism* (pp. 39–79). London: Continuum.
Robinson, M., and Andersen, H. C. (2002). Reading between the lines: Literature and the creation of touristic spaces. In M. Robinson and H. C. Andersen (eds), *Literature and Tourism: Essays in the Reading and Writing of Tourism* (pp. 1–38). London: Continuum.
Rothman, H. K. (1998) *Devil's Bargains: Tourism in the Twentieth-Century American West*. Kansas: University Press of Kansas.
Said, E. W. (1980). *Orientalism*. London: Routledge & Kegan Paul.
Said, E. W. (1993). *Culture and Imperialism*. New York: Random House.
Sayle, A., and Stratton, D. (1989). *Alexei Sayle's Great Bus Journeys of the World*. London: Methuen.
Sharp, J. P. (1999). Writing over the map of Provence: The touristic therapy of a "Year in Provence." In J. Duncan and D. Gregory (eds), *Writes of Passage: Travel Writing, Place and Ambiguity* (pp. 200–18). London: Routledge.
Sinclair, I. (2002). *London Orbital*. London: Granta Books.
Smith, V. (1998). *Literary Culture and the Pacific: Nineteenth-Century Textual Encounters*. Cambridge: Cambridge University Press.
Stowe, W. W. (1994). *Going Abroad: European Travel in Nineteenth-Century American Culture*. Princeton, NJ: Princeton University Press.
Tambling, J. (1995). *E. M. Forster: Contemporary Critical Essays*. Basingstoke: Macmillan.
Teltscher, K. (1995). *India Inscribed: European and British Writing on India 1600–1800*. New Delhi: Oxford University Press.
Turner, V. (1982). *From Ritual to Theatre: The Human Seriousness of Play*. New York: Performing Arts Journal Publications.
Urry, J. (1995). *Consuming Places*. London: Routledge.
Urry, J. (2000). *Sociology beyond Societies*. London: Routledge.

Wheeler, R. (1999). Limited visions of Africa: Geographies of savagery and civility in early eighteenth-century narratives. In J. Duncan and D. Gregory (eds), *Writes of Passage: Travel Writing, Place and Ambiguity* (pp. 14–48). London: Routledge.
White, H. (1976). The fictions of factual representation. In A. Fletcher (ed.), *The Literature of Fact* (pp. 21–44). New York: Columbia University Press.
World Tourism Organization (2002). <http://www.world-tourism.org/market_research/facts&figures.

Chapter 25

Gender and Sexuality in Tourism Research

Annette Pritchard

Introduction

It has long been contended that hetero-patriarchy infuses the sociocultural relationships that characterize tourism, yet women's and gay men's voices and lived experiences continue to remain on the margins of tourism studies. Perhaps the marginalization of women in tourism is unsurprising, given that the social science research collective remains dominated by a traditional research perspective grounded in male experiences, perceptions, and beliefs (DuBois 1983), which has long relegated women to the private domain. It *is* surprising, however, when one considers the impact feminism has had in other fields and disciplines – for example, social history has been reshaped by the fact that many of the pioneering researchers in recent years have been feminists interested in gender (Cannadine 2000). By contrast, the "malestream" philosophy of tourism research has marginalized other voices, which has compounded the field's dominance by a positivist, industry-oriented perspective. While the major strength of tourism studies has always been its interdisciplinary foundations, the field's epistemological and conceptual base remains poorly articulated. Much of its work is grounded in positivism, yet few studies acknowledge this, and fewer still explore the implications for tourism knowledge. This has a significant, although hidden, influence on tourism research on gender and sexuality. Positivism is rooted in the masculine, objective character of the hard sciences (Brunskell 1998), in the world of the public as opposed to the private, and requires researchers to succumb to the agenda of the scientific project of seeking "truth" by satisfying the demands of validity, sampling, and triangulation. In this philosophical tradition, gay and female voices have rarely been acknowledged and the result is a lack of critical conceptualization of the psychological, social, and cultural dimensions of both masculine and feminine identities in much tourism research. Although two seminal collections of work which foregrounded gender (Kinnaird and Hall 1994; Swain 1995) appeared almost a decade ago, an area of feminist tourism research still does not exist in the way that feminist leisure studies exists.

In leisure studies, the role of gender and, to a lesser extent, sexuality, as a shaper of leisure experiences is relatively established (Aitchison 2000). Indeed, researchers have explored how a range of social characteristics such as class (e.g., Deem 1986), race and ethnicity (e.g., Raval 1989), sexuality (e.g., Valentine 1993), and dis/ability (e.g., Henderson et al. 1995) combine to create points of empowerment or oppression in leisure worlds. In this chapter, I will focus on two of these characteristics – gender and sexuality – revealing the ways in which the practice, conceptualization, and academy of tourism continue to be structured by hetero-patriarchy. The chapter is framed by a theoretical analysis of tourism experiences that affirms or resists gendered and sexualized identities. Gendered societies contribute to gendered tourism practices and these in turn contribute to and reinforce the gendered nature of society. Thus, the chapter argues that tourism processes are gendered in their construction, presentation, and consumption in different and diverse ways, which are temporally and spatially specific. The chapter begins with a discussion of the multidimensionalities of gender, sexuality, identity, and power before briefly reviewing the extant literature on tourism, gender, and sexuality, although this neither tries to be, nor can it be, comprehensive. The chapter concludes by considering how a deeper insight into the manifestation of gender and sexuality in tourism worlds can contribute to the epistemological enrichment of tourism research.

Identity and Power

It is timely to reflect on identities, genders, and sexualities – to be reconstruing them as processes rather than artifacts. We are living through sharply transitional times, which are calling into question many conventions and orthodoxies that, until recently, felt relatively fixed. New perspectives are emerging across disciplines and research fields as Western consciousness seeks to evolve beyond the limitations of Newtonian and Cartesian thought – from relativity theory in physics, from the findings of depth psychologists, to new approaches in anthropological and ecological studies. As a result of these and other related developments, the postcolonial, post-industrial world is witnessing the increasing deconstruction of the largely masculine tradition of Western thought – developments which are combining to stimulate a new awareness of "reality" as a construction of human imagination. Place, space, time, and identity – none is now conceived as fixed but as mutable, represented, relative, and constructed. If relativity, fluidity, and imagination have replaced fixidity and objectivity, then reality becomes contested and, as a result – together with an increasing awareness that the intellectual tradition of the West is no longer the dominant wisdom tradition – there is greater interest in what was previously oppressed and unrecognized.

An element in these new approaches is an emphasis on the plural rather than the binary nature of gendered and sexual identities, and thus on multiple femininities and masculinities (Moore 1994). The fixity of gender, sexuality, and identity has been questioned as researchers have explored how the same individual may both experience and represent her or his femininity or masculinity differently in different contexts and in relation to different people (Pink 2001). This means we need to consider differences *among* as well as *between* female and male bodies and to confront the assumption that sex, gender, and sexuality are universal, essentialist, and definable experiences. The body is *the* site where our personal identities are constituted and social knowledges and meanings inscribed, and there are many ways in which bodies may be "sexualized." As Stephens (2002) notes, bodies may be biologically sexed as either male or female, they may be seen to exhibit certain gendered behavior (and thus be sexualized in terms of their masculinity or femininity), or they may be seen as sexualized because they engage in heterosexual or homosexual practices. In this sense, while sex and gender may seem inextricably linked, they are two separable and culturally constructed human status characteristics. As Swain (1995: 258) argues, gender is: "a system of culturally constructed identities, expressed in ideologies of masculinity and femininity, interacting with socially structured relationships in divisions of labor and leisure, sexuality and power between women and men."

It has been said that travel, travel writing, and the study of landscapes of colonialization and tourism have long been characterized in patriarchal, imperialist terms embedded in masculine conceptions of adventure, conquest, pleasure, and the exotic (e.g., Lewes 2000), while femininity has been defined in terms of the familiar and the domestic – the antithesis of independent experience. Thus, both the praxis and the scholarship of tourism have been heavily influenced by masculinist discourses which have determined what is considered "natural" and worthy of study. Over time, these constructed sets of expectations have become the norm because they are so prevalent and unquestioned. The time to confront the still influential all-subsuming male norm in tourism is long overdue and yet, as outlined above, a feminist critique of the gendered production and consumption of tourism products, experiences, and representations remains peripheral to tourism studies. The next section of this chapter reviews how tourism studies have failed to engage with gender and sexuality, resulting in a partial and incomplete analysis of the tourist experience.

Tourism Research, Gender, and Sexuality

To date, the objects of tourism gender research have almost exclusively been women (rather than women *and* men) and research has largely focused on employment patterns and sex tourism (Sinclair 1997; Pritchard and Morgan 2000a, 2000b). In addition, analysis of tourism marketing remains gender-blind (Westwood, Pritchard, and Morgan 2000) and there is little work that focuses on women's experiences as *consumers* rather than as *producers* of tourism (Apostologpoulos, Sonmez, and Dallen 2001). This is a serious omission as socioeconomic changes are increasingly creating enhanced opportunities for women to consume both leisure (e.g., Hashimoto 2000) and business (e.g., Harris 2002) tourism products. Moreover, much of the pioneering work in this area suggests that the tourism industry is failing to cater to differing needs amongst female consumers – for instance, as businesswomen (e.g., Lutz and Ryan 1993; Westwood, Pritchard, and Morgan 2000) or single travelers (e.g., Stone and Nichol 1999).

In so far as tourism studies have addressed women's experiences, an important research strand focuses on their employment in tourism. While by no means the first work, two collections of essays and papers in the mid-1990s (Kinnaird and Hall 1994; Swain 1995) made a considerable empirical and conceptual contribution to tourism gender studies. In the last decade this work has been supplemented by further studies of women and tourism employment (e.g., Sinclair 1997; Apostolog-poulos, Sonmez, and Dallen 2001). While much of this research has shown that tourism often benefits women in worldwide communities, improving their social, cultural, and economic positions (e.g., Creighton 1995; Scott 1995), employment for women in the tourism industry has not fundamentally challenged gender inequalities in society, while the industry is characterized by acute occupational segregation. Instead, it tends to confirm and reinforce gendered roles and relationships and, arguably, the tourism industry remains founded on an army of poorly paid women performing paid versions of what has traditionally been constructed as "women's work" (Enloe 1989). Such a situation is not peculiar to tourism employment and, indeed, it is well established that women tend to carry their traditionally constructed roles as carers into their formal, paid employment (McDowell 1997).

Women's involvement in the production of the tourism industry is not restricted to such employment, but also encompasses the sexual servicing of tourists. This is the second major strand of tourism gender research – examinations of host and guest relationships in destinations. The overwhelming focus of this work has been sex tourism and the gender relationships that characterize this activity (see Oppermann 1998; Kempadoo 1999; Clift and Carter 2000; Ryan and Hall 2001). Research has encompassed the romantic and sexual relations between tourists and hosts (e.g., Cohen 1986; Meisch 1995; Clift and Carter 2000; Herold, Garcia, and DeMoya 2001) and the impact of tourism on host cultures (e.g., Moore 1995). There is now substantial research that focuses on the range of paradigms that constitute sex tourism, as defined by Ryan and Hall (2001). This stretches from sexual encounters that are voluntary and non-commercial (romance and casual encounters), through to commodified and exploitative relationships (mail brides and prostitution) to interactions that are non-voluntary and assaults on individual integrity (sex slavery).

Sex is one of the oldest travel motivations, and the sex tourism industry is one outcome of a gendered tourism industry and a gendered international tourism system. The development of the industry is founded on three factors (Enloe 1989). The first is a poverty-stricken population, which encourages women to participate, either voluntarily or forcibly, in the sex industry. The second is Western male tourists who have been socialized into seeing women in developing countries as quintessential exotic temptresses. Finally, there are political and economic institutions and businesses that encourage men to travel to countries specifically to consume sexual services. The activities that constitute sex tourism are not, of course, exclusively male or exclusively heterosexual. As mentioned above, they also include relationships between female tourists and male hosts that create an opportunity for women to exploit men (Pruitt and Lafont 1995; Albuquerque 1998; Herold, Garcia, and DeMoya 2001). In effect, the economic emergence of women in the West has led to the development of so-called "romance tourism" – Western women engaging in romantic/sexual encounters with local men while touring in the Caribbean, Mediterranean, and elsewhere, for which they may offer some financial or other reward. Crucially, however, neither partner "considers their interaction to be prostitution, even while others may label it so" (Pruitt and Lafont 1995: 423), itself a significant commentary on gender and power relationships since the men offering sexual services are not described as prostitutes.

There is a small but growing body of research that explores the tourism experiences of the gay and lesbian communities (Hughes 2000; Pritchard, Morgan, and Sedgley 2000, 2002). Extant research in this area has examined a range of issues. These include: the relationship between holidays and homosexual identity (Hughes 1997, 1998, 2000); the sexual behavior of gay men in tourism spaces (Forrest and Clift 1998); the touristification of gay spaces (Pritchard et al. 1998); motivations of gay and lesbian tourists (Clift and Forrest 1999; Pritchard et al 2000). Significantly, with some exceptions (see Pritchard, Morgan, and Sedgley 2002), much of this work has focused on male rather than female experiences. As a result, once again, the tourism academy could be said to be marginalizing women, despite the fact that the homosexual community is clearly "a heterogeneous, culturally diverse group of men and women who, despite their common bonds, have diverse identities" (Greene 1997: xi). Notions of a homogeneous *gay* community inhabiting *gay* places potentially obscure lesbians' experiences while subsuming the female into the male gender-neutral "norm."

This conception of places as gay or heterosexual leads to a key contribution to tourism gender studies by, amongst others, cultural geographers. The so-called "cultural turn" in the social sciences has been reflected in tourism in the conceptualization of tourism places, spaces, and sites as political and contested. Today we see landscapes not as fixed, objective artifacts, but as symbolic, mutable, and culturally constructed mixtures of representation and form. They mean different things to different people at different times and represent, reinforce, idealize, and naturalize relations of gender and sexuality. Thus, feminist scholars have demonstrated that built environments – from the intimate place of the home to the public places and spaces of parks and shopping malls – are "remarkable in their desire to confine and control women" (Mitchell 2000: 126). In such everyday spaces, experiences, and interactions are gender segregations established, maintained, and reinforced (see McDowell 1997). Similarly, many cultural and feminist geographers have noted that landscapes are often portrayed and represented in feminine and sexualized terms. In fact, as Lewes (2000: 3) notes, "the idea that women and land are somehow analogous to each other is an ancient one." What she terms "somatopias" (from the Greek for body – *soma* – and for place – *topos*) are places which are simultaneously represented as female and designed for male bodily satisfaction; they act out the conflict between masculinized Culture and feminized Nature. In this way, representations of landscapes are grounded in wider gendered power relationships, so that both women and Nature are burdened with men's meaning and interpreted through masculinist discourse (Rose 1993). Yet despite this volume of geographical work on gendered space, only recently have tourism researchers begun to "acknowledge that the synergy between gender relations and spatial relations is a major contributor to leisure relations" (Aitchison 1999a: 19). This theme of tourism research, while recent, gathered pace during the 1990s and scholars explored how space, place, and landscape are sites where dominant discourses and wider hegemonic sociocultural relations are resisted, contested, or affirmed (Ringer 1998; Crouch 1999; Aitchison, MacLeod, and Shaw 2000). Much of this work explored how tourism landscapes and places have gendered and sexualized identities. For instance, Valentine (1993) and Pritchard et al. (1998) demonstrated that public leisure space is masculinized and heterosexually dominated. Similarly, Edensor and

Kothari (1994) and Aitchison (1999b) have critiqued the role of gendered representations of heritage in the creation of gendered spaces and places in cultural tourism.

Of course, representations of landscape do not exist in isolation, but are entwined in a circuit of culture, whereby texts utilize representations to construct meanings, which are then consumed, validated, and recycled. As a result, scholarship on the cultural construction of tourism landscapes also has much to say about the gendered and sexualized representation of tourism places and experiences (e.g., Cohen 1995; Pritchard and Morgan 2000a, 2000b). While research on tourism, gender, and space is emergent, there is a more developed literature on gender, tourism, and representation, although there remain many opportunities for further work. Research on gendered representations is established in media studies and sociology – from Goffman's (1979) work on magazine portrayals of women to Wright's (2001) examination of female representations in the western film genre. Such work has demonstrated that representations have been and continue to be stereotypical – typically attributing youth, beauty, and sexuality to women, and power and activity to men. Moreover, despite the social, cultural, and economic improvements in the position of many women worldwide and the wealth of academic work exploring sex, gender, and society, the essence or extent of these representations have hardly changed (Pritchard 2001).

Researchers have noted the same pattern in tourism gender representations. Kinnaird and Hall (1994) and Swain (1995), amongst others, have noted that in tourism brochures men are associated with action and power, while women are associated with passivity and availability. Such tourism marketing materials are carefully constructed texts, produced by governmental tourist organizations, tourism operators, and advertising agencies that draw on the wider cultural sphere (Morgan and Pritchard 1998). While their representations may convey many potential meanings, one meaning tends to be privileged over others and such is the power of this dominant ideology that it blinds consumers to other interpretations. The signs, symbols, myths, and fantasies privileged within tourism marketing are invariably male-orientated and heterosexual – what Valentine (1993) has termed "heteropatriarchy," or a process of sociosexual power relations which affirms and reproduces male dominance. Gendered and heavily sexualized representations of women have been seen to exoticize and eroticize destinations, to promote airlines, resorts, and hotels and, in some cases, are seen as the main reason for the visit. Tourism representations (like all representations) are mediated by cultural and ideological structures and the advertising agencies that create them have long been male-dominated, privileging particular masculine scripts (Pritchard and Morgan 2000a). It is unsurprising, then, that despite the diversity of the market, the representations seen in the travel media assume a particular kind of tourist – white, Western, male, and heterosexual (Richter 1995) – privileging the gaze of this "master subject" over others.

Gender, Sexuality, and the Epistemology of Tourism Research

The privileging of the male norm which has been identified in tourism representations is also evident in tourism scholarship. While one of the aims of this chapter was to critique the literature on tourism, gender, and sexuality, I also set out to argue that, through greater engagement with gender and sexuality and gender-aware approaches, we can arrive at a richer and more complex understanding of tourism epistemology and ontology. Since Descartes, philosophers have defined rational knowledge in masculine terms, assuming "a knower who believes he can separate himself from his body, emotions, values and past experiences so that he and his thought are autonomous, context-free and objective" (Rose 1993: 7). It is this "malestream" imperative to erase the researcher from the research process and to thus claim objectivity that must be challenged by feminist tourism studies, just as it has been by other fields and disciplines. Feminists' recognition of multiple realities, truths, and knowledge and acknowledgment of both participant and researcher voices has much to offer tourism studies, yet their influence remains peripheral. Researchers in the tourism academy need to confront the implications of their own identities for the research process. For many this remains an unrecognized challenge because as white, middle-class men they are the self, the same, the norm against which others are measured, they have "no class, no race, no gender... [they are] the generic person" (Kimmel 1996: 4). The tourism academy must thus incorporate *both* feminine and masculine voices if it is not to remain partial and unrepresentative, since, as the literature review above demonstrates, tourism studies have too often silenced feminine experiences by subsuming the plurality of female voices into some unstated male norm. Ironically, this has also simultaneously concealed heterosexual and masculine tourism experiences from full examination as researchers have shied away from foregrounding the self as the research subject in their obsession to research their other. Thus, in the coming years, not only do we need more conceptual and empirical studies of the multiplicity of female experiences as producers *and* consumers of tourism, but we also need to understand the diversity of male voices. In essence, research needs to embrace, articulate, and reflect the multiple identities and voices of all tourism producers and consumers, while not neglecting the political economy.

The currently dominant masculine and essentialist philosophy has also influenced the topics defined as legitimate areas of tourism study. Until the mid-1990s, sexuality and embodiment were regarded as inappropriate areas for geographical study, and today they remain very much on the margins of tourism scholarship, yet tourism researchers need to locate the body at the centre of their work. At the beginning of the twenty-first century, the body has emerged in consumer culture as *the* significant symbolization of self; it is a key metaphor for identity, and the media, advertising, fashion, and tourism industries (amongst others) all contribute to the discourses within which we manage and locate our own bodies (Evans and Lee 2002). It is through our bodies that we experience places and everyday interactions with people. The body symbolizes the self, it connects us with other people and places but also marks us as different and "out of place" (Cresswell 1996). The corporeal is therefore the ultimate basis for spatial exclusion and inclusion since whether we are white or black, young or old, female or male, able-bodied or disabled, determines others' responses to us and, on every scale from individual to nation, dictates what different bodies can or cannot do (Valentine 2001). In the same way as we need to conceptualize masculine and feminine identities in tourism, we need to examine the cultural meanings and practices which surround embodied spaces, bodies in spaces, represented bodies, and the tourist as a liminal, metamorphic body, transposed from "home" to "holiday." This call for the embodiment of tourism research, however, also asks for equal emphasis to be placed on male as well as female bodies. Ironically, much contemporary feminist research on the body has largely ignored the male body, thus paradoxically confirming "the dualism which links bodies and bodily matters to women and femininity" (Davis 1997: 19).

In calling for the embodiment of tourism research, it must be said that bodies are not merely empowered or oppressed through their gender and sexuality, although these two human characteristics have been the focus of this chapter. Colonialist and imperialist discourses, for example, drew heavily on both race and gender as a form of oppression and such overlays of power relations need to be acknowledged if we are to fully appreciate the broader discursive networks which structure gendered societies. Clearly there is also a pressing need for tourism research to examine the relationships between masculinist, heterosexual, and colonial discourses. While gender and sexuality have had to be separated out of the gamut of human status identifiers for ease of discussion here, the social processes constituting social relations are highly complex and differentiated. Gender and sexuality intersect with race, ethnicity, dis/ability, class, and nationality to form vectors of empowerment and oppression. In the same fashion, as students and writers of tourism research, each of us needs to remember that we all participate in a plurality of identities – ethnicities, genders, sexes, and races – and we need to turn our culturally diverse gazes to create alternative, inclusive, and insightful ways of knowing and understanding tourism.

REFERENCES

Aitchison, C. (1999a). New cultural geographies: The spatiality of leisure, gender and sexuality. *Leisure Studies* 18(1), 19–39.

Aitchison, C. (1999b). Heritage and nationalism: Gender and the performance of power. In D. Crouch (ed.), *Leisure/Tourism Geographies: Practices and Geographical Knowledge* (pp. 59–73). London: Routledge.

Aitchison, C. (2000). Poststructural feminist theories of representing Others: A response to the "crisis" in leisure studies' discourse. *Leisure Studies* 19(3), 127–44.

Aitchison C., MacLeod, N. E., and Shaw, J. (2000). *Leisure and Tourism Landscapes: Social and Cultural Geographies*. London: Routledge.

Albuquerque, K. de (1998). Sex, beach boys and female tourists in the Caribbean. *Sexuality and Culture* 2(2), 87–111.

Apostologpoulos, Y., Sonmez, S., and Dallen, J. T. (eds) (2001). *Women as Producers and Consumers of Tourism in Developing Regions*. Westport, CT: Praeger.

Brunskell, H. (1998). Feminist methodology. In C. Seale (ed.), *Researching Society and Culture* (pp. 37–47). London: Sage.

Cannadine, D. (2000). *Class in Britain*. London: Penguin Books.

Clift, S., and Carter, S. (eds) (2000). *Tourism and Sex: Culture, Commerce and Coercion*. London: Pinter.

Clift, S., and Forrest, S. (1999). Gay men and tourism: Destinations and holiday motivations. *Tourism Management* 20(3), 615–25.

Cohen C. (1995). Marketing paradise, making nation. *Annals of Tourism Research* 22(2), 404–21.

Cohen, E. (1986). Lovelorn farangs: The correspondence between foreign men and Thai girls. *Anthropological Quarterly* 59(3), 115–27.
Crang, M. (1998). *Cultural Geography*. London: Routledge.
Creighton, M. R. (1995). Japanese craft tourism liberating the crane wife. *Annals of Tourism Research* 22(2), 463–78.
Cresswell, T. (1996). *In Place/Out of Place: Geography, Ideology and Transgression*. Minneapolis: University of Minnesota Press.
Crouch, D. (ed.) (1999). *Leisure/Tourism Geographies: Practices in Geographical Knowledge*. London: Routledge.
Davis, K. (1997). Embodying theory: Beyond modernist and postmodernist readings of the body. In K. Davis (ed.), *Embodied Practices: Feminist Perspectives on the Body*. London: Sage.
Deem, R. (1986). *All Work and No Play? The Sociology of Women's Leisure*. Milton Keynes: Open University Press.
DuBois, B. (1983). Passionate scholarship: Notes on values, knowing and method in feminist social science. In G. Bowles and R. Duelli Klein (eds), *Theories of Women's Studies*. London: Routledge & Kegan Paul.
Edensor, T., and Kothari, U. (1994). The masculinisation of Stirling's heritage. In V. Kinnaird and D. Hall (eds), *Tourism: A Gender Analysis* (pp. 164–87). Chichester: John Wiley.
Enloe, C. (1989). *Bananas, Beaches and Bases: Making Feminist Sense of International Politics*. London: Pandora.
Evans, M., and Lee, E. (eds) (2002). *Real Bodies: A Sociological Introduction*. Basingstoke: Palgrave.
Forrest, S., and Clift, S. (1998). Gay tourist space and sexual behaviour. In C. Aitchison and F. Jordan (eds), *Gender, Space and Identity* (pp. 163–76). Brighton: Leisure Studies Association.
Goffman, E. (1979). *Gender Advertisements*. London: Macmillan.
Greene, B. (ed.) (1997). *Ethnic and Cultural Diversity among Lesbians and Gay Men: Psychological Perspectives on Lesbian and Gay Issues*, vol. 3. Thousand Oaks: Sage.
Harris, C. (2002). Women and power: A study of women business travellers in New Zealand. Unpublished Ph.D. thesis, Victoria University of Wellington.
Hashimoto, A. (2000). Young Japanese female tourists: An in-depth understanding of a market segment. *Current Issues in Tourism* 3(1), 35–50.
Henderson, K., Bedini, L., Hecht, L., and Schuler, R. (1995). Women with physical disabilities and the negotiation of leisure constraints. *Leisure Studies* 14(1), 17–31.
Herold, E., Garcia, R., and DeMoya, T. (2001). Female tourists and beach boys: Romance tourism or sex tourism? *Annals of Tourism Research* 28(4), 978–97.
Hughes, H. (1997). Holidays and homosexual identity. *Tourism Management* 18(4), 3–7.
Hughes, H. (1998). Sexuality, tourism and space: The case of gay visitors to Amsterdam. In D. Tyler, M. Robertson, and Y. Guerrier (eds), *Managing Tourism in Cities: Policy, Process and Practice* (pp. 163–78). Chichester: John Wiley.
Hughes, H. (2000). Holidays and homosexuals: A constrained choice? In M. Robinson, P. Long, N. Evans, R. Sharpley, and J. Swarbrooke (eds), *Reflections on International Tourism: Expressions of Culture, Identity and Meaning in Tourism* (pp. 221–30). Sunderland: Business Education Publishers.
Kempadoo, K. (ed.) (1999). *Sun, Sex and Gold: Tourism and Sex Work in the Caribbean*. Lanham, MD: Rowman & Littlefield.
Kimmel, M. (1996). *Manhood in America: A Cultural History*. New York: Free Press.
Kinnaird, V., and Hall, D. (eds) (1994) *Tourism: A Gender Analysis*. Chichester: John Wiley.

Kinnaird, V., and Hall, D. (1996). Understanding tourism processes: A gender-aware framework. *Tourism Management* 17(2), 95–102.

Kinnaird, V., and Hall, D. (2000). Theorizing gender and tourism research. *Tourism Recreation Research* 25(1), 71–84.

Lewes, D. (2000). *Nudes from Nowhere: Utopian Sexual Landscapes*. Lanham, MD: Rowman & Littlefield.

Lutz, J., and Ryan, C. (1993). Hotels and the businesswoman: An analysis of businesswomen's perceptions of hotel services. *Tourism Management* 14(5), 349–56.

McDowell, L. (1997) *Capital Culture: Gender at Work in the City.* Studies in Urban and Social Change. Oxford: Blackwell.

Meisch, L. A. (1995). Gringas and Otavalenos: Changing tourist relations. *Annals of Tourism Research* 22(2), 441–62.

Mitchell, D. (2000). *Cultural Geography: A Critical Introduction*. Oxford: Blackwell.

Moore, H. (1994). *A Passion for Difference: Essays in Anthropology and Gender.* Oxford: Polity.

Moore R. S. (1995). Gender and alcohol use in a Greek tourist town. *Annals of Tourism Research* 22(2), 300–15.

Morgan, N. J., and Pritchard, A. (1998). *Tourism Promotion and Power: Creating Images, Creating Identities*. Chichester: John Wiley.

Oppermann, M. (ed.) (1998). *Sex Tourism and Prostitution: Aspects of Leisure, Recreation and Work*. New York: Cognizant Communication Corporation.

Pink, S. (2001). *Doing Visual Ethnography.* London: Sage.

Pritchard A. (2001). Tourism and representation: A scale for measuring gendered portrayals. *Leisure Studies* 20(2), 79–94.

Pritchard, A., and Morgan, N. J. (2000a). Constructing tourism landscapes: Gender, sexuality and space. *Tourism Geographies* 2(2), 115–39.

Pritchard, A., and Morgan, N. J. (2000b). Privileging the male gaze: Gendered tourism landscapes. *Annals of Tourism Research* 27(3), 884–905.

Pritchard, A., Morgan, N. J., and Sedgley, D. (2000). Exploring issues of space and sexuality in Manchester's gay village. In M. Robinson et al. (eds), *Reflections on International Tourism: Expressions of Culture, Identity and Meaning in Tourism* (pp. 225–38). Sunderland: Business Education Publishers.

Pritchard, A., Morgan N. J., and Sedgley, D. (2002). In search of lesbian space: The experience of Manchester's gay village. *Leisure Studies* 21(2), 105–23.

Pritchard, A., Morgan, N. J., Sedgley, D., and Jenkins, A., (1998). Reaching out to the gay tourist: Opportunities and threats in an emerging market segment. *Tourism Management* 19(3), 273–82.

Pritchard, A., Morgan, N. J., Sedgley, D., Khan, E., and Jenkins, A. (2000). Sexuality and holiday choices: Conversations with gay and lesbian tourists. *Leisure Studies* 19(2), 267–82.

Pruitt, D., and Lafont, S. (1995). For love and money romance: Tourism in Jamaica. *Annals of Tourism Research* 22(2), 422–40.

Raval, S. (1989). Gender, leisure and sport: A case study of young people of South Asian descent – a response. *Leisure Studies* 8(3), 237–40.

Richter, L. K. (1995). Gender and race: Neglected variables in tourism research. In R. Butler and D. Pearce (eds), *Change in Tourism: People, Places, Processes* (pp. 71–91). London: Routledge.

Ringer, G. (ed.) (1998). *Destinations: Cultural Landscapes of Tourism*. London: Routledge.

Rose, G. (1993). *Feminism and Geography: The Limits of Geographical Knowledge.* Cambridge: Polity.

Ryan, C., and Hall, C. M. (2001). *Sex Tourism: Marginal People and Liminalities*. London: Routledge.

Scott, J. (1995). Sexual and national boundaries in tourism. *Annals of Tourism Research* 22(2), 385–403.

Sinclair, M. T. (ed.) (1997). *Gender, Work and Tourism*. London: Routledge.

Stephens, K. (2002). Sexualized bodies. In M. Evans and E. Lee (eds), *Real Bodies: A Sociological Introduction* (pp. 29–45). New York: Palgrave.

Stone, G. J., and Nichol, S. (1999). Older, single female holiday makers in the United Kingdom: Who needs them? *Journal of Vacation Marketing* 5(1), 7–17.

Swain, M. (1995). Gender in tourism. *Annals of Tourism Research* 22(2), 247–66.

Valentine, G. (1993). Hetero(sexing) space: Lesbian perceptions and experiences of everyday spaces. *Society and Space* 11(1), 395–413.

Valentine, G. (2001). *Social Geographies: Space and Society*. Harlow: Pearson.

Voskuil, C. M. (1998). Feminism, revolution and social change, or the art of squeezing square pegs into round holes. London: Paper presented at the British Sociological Association Sexual Divisions Study Group Conference.

Westwood, S., Pritchard, A., and Morgan, N. J. (2000). Gender-blind marketing: Businesswomen's perceptions of airline services. *Tourism Management* 21(4), 353–62.

Wright, W. (2001). *The Wild West: The Mythical Cowboy and Social Theory*. London: Sage.

Chapter 26

The Souvenir: Conceptualizing the Object(s) of Tourist Consumption

Jon Goss

Introduction

For most tourists, a trip is not complete without the purchase of souvenirs, whether for personal consumption or as gifts for friends and family back home, and in some cases shopping has become a major component of the tourist experience. This is not new, of course, as markets were established at ancient sites of pilgrimage to sell relics and other tokens of place, as well as provisions, to what might be called the first tourists (Leed 1991: 37), and shopping was already an essential part of the attraction of European and North American cities as tourism developed into a mass phenomenon in the nineteenth century (Harris 1991: 66). Tourism is, after all, simply the consumption of goods and services while in a leisure mode in another place. Similarly, the concept of "going shopping" explicitly contains a sense of displacement, and both medieval markets and modern department stores employed theatrical performance and exotic décor to sell new commodities imported from all corners of the world. Although some forms of consumption might be considered sedentary, the modern consumer is typically conceived to be at least virtually or metaphorically on a quest for value, and has thus been described as a "spiritual tourist" (Brown 1998). As Bauman (1998: 85) puts it, "the consumer is a person on the move and bound to remain so."

Nevertheless, contemporary globalization, which witnesses the progressive universalization of commodity consumption and discretionary travel, has produced a remarkable convergence of commodity consumption and tourism. The built environments of travel, for example, increasingly resemble shopping centers, and tourist sights might even be defined by the presence of gift shops. Destination shopping centers are often "themed" to evoke idealized tourist locations such as Polynesian tropical islands, European market towns, Mexican villages, or Bourbon Street, while some megamalls like Mall of America (USA), West Edmonton Mall (Canada), and Bluewater (UK), are tourist destinations in their own right. At the same time, individual commodity brands and retail concepts exploit images of elsewhere and past times to sell everyday household needs. Although, even in the advanced capitalist economies, consumers still avail themselves of some local products and quite often remain oblivious to the distant origins of many commodities, consumption increasingly trades upon images of spatio-temporal displacement from, and return to, idealized origins. A striking example is the dramatic role that images of imaginative and vehicular transport, and the aesthetics of motion and travel play in the environments of both consumption and tourism (Goss 1996, 1999).

The motivations for tourism and consumption, and the forms they take, are no doubt complex and diverse, and there is certainly no such thing as *the* tourist, let alone *the* consumer. Still, the discourses of tourism and consumption share a similar semiotic structure and social structuring in that they reproduce a generalized subjective sense of insufficiency in modern life, and play upon the differential distribution of both sensitivity to this condition and the means to address it. That is to say, discourses of tourism and consumption construct systems of objects and social relations that reproduce the master narrative of modernity that tells of progress at the price of the loss of authenticity under generalized conditions of increased mobility and the progressive commodification of "everything." This is not to say that all consumers and all tourists strive endlessly for authenticity as such, for again, there is a diversity of motivations for purchasing of commodities or visiting places. The term "authenticity" is also very slippery, applying both to the objects of experience and perceptions of objects and experiences (see Wang 1999), and what is hokey or tacky to one person may be of particular value to another. Nonetheless, the discourses of tourism and consumption, in general, work to "sell" the possibility of survival or restoration of authenticity and original value that is perceived to inhere in pristine nature, primitive culture, and pre-modern heritage – in other words, in contexts that are most accessible to those with enhanced personal means for mobility and commodity consumption.

Regardless of whether there is a radical difference in object relations between modern society and its Others, or whether things are hopelessly entangled in all social formations (Thomas 1991), tourism and consumption are invested in the possibility of authenticity, particularly in past times and distant places, traces of which are embodied in exotic and antique objects and which are brought into presence by personal acquisition and/or purchase. Thus, not only do tourists compulsively collect souvenirs from their travels, but commodities increasingly become "tourist objects," things that trade explicitly on their upon their spatio-temporal displacement from distant and past worlds (Lury 1997: 79).

Walter Benjamin (1985) argued that the souvenir is what modernity makes of the commodity, for it is emblematic of the modern subject's estrangement or alienation from the world, and desire for authentic presence. The souvenir is the commodity form that most effectively denies its commodity status: it is typically a purposive product that proclaims its "foundness" and, even if mass produced, it claims uniqueness through marketing narratives of its authentic production and the personal stories of its acquisition.

According to the *Oxford English Dictionary* (1971: 2924), the term "souvenir" refers to "a slight trace of something" that is no longer present. It is something both insubstantial, "a remembrance, a memory," and material, "a token of remembrance; something (usually a small article of some value bestowed as a gift) which reminds one of some person, place, or event." In making present something that is absent, the souvenir effects "the systematic transformation of the object into its own impossibility" (Stewart 1993: 135): by definition consumed under conditions of temporal-spatial estrangement, it embodies a material and spiritual trace its origins, and so works to signify simultaneously both absence and loss, and presence or restoration. In apparently issuing a "call to remembrance," the souvenir attests to our faith and desire for the persistence of meaning and preservation of life, what Giambattista Vico (1970: 78), calls the "credible impossibility...that bodies should be minds," that objects and images possess inherent meaning. The question, then, is how human experience constructs subjectivity of objects (Mitchell 1996: 72), how objects magically exceed their mere materialization to become metaphysical values, fetishes, and totems (Brown 2001: 5).

The Mysterious Object of Tourist Consumption

When Karl Marx (1977: 83. 165) sought to understand the mystery of the "very queer thing" called the commodity, or the double life of commodities as both "sensuous and supersensible things," he drew upon metaphors of "primitive" religiosity, conjuration, theatricality, and necromancy. He argued that, like the fetish, commodities come to life through anthropomorphic projection, casting a spell over modern consumers and thus appearing to possess value in themselves and in relation to each other, when in fact the "real" source of their value and sociality is the labor they embody. Marx here draws upon the original, anthropological sense of the fetish, in which an object appears to work magic, possession conferring power, when its real source is the social relations that confer legitimate possession. If modern capitalist society has eliminated traditional religion, it returns in repressed form in the fetishism of the commodity, and thus mythical thought and superstition underlie the veneer of universal rationality: as Raymond Williams puts it, for example, advertising is "a highly organized and professional system of magical inducements and satisfactions, functionally very similar to magical systems in simpler societies, but rather strangely coexistent with a highly developed scientific technology" (Williams 1980: 185; see also Horkheimer and Adorno 1972).

Similarly, developing the theatrical metaphor used by Marx, marketing and advertising are said to obliterate the "backstage" details of production and distribution of commodities so that they can perform in the context of highly staged displays, such as shop windows or advertisements on television and print media (Sack 1992: 118). Commodity production, in general, systematically obscures material connections to human labor and material origins, and subsequently invests them with fantastic and arbitrary meanings so that "it is an astute shopper indeed who has much idea about what most things are composed of and what kinds of people made them" (Leiss, Kline, and Jhally 1984: 274). This operation can be seen in many tourist sites, where souvenirs that evoke an association with a particular place, such as for example an aloha shirt in a gift shop or an orchid leis provided by greeters at Honolulu International Airport, prove, through the small print on the label or access to local knowledge, to originate in Pakistan or Thailand, respectively.

Such religious and dramaturgical analogies are similarly deployed in the critical analysis of tourism. The modern tourist, for example, is likened to the pilgrim, visiting secular sights as the religious once traveled to sacred sites to undergo experiences functionally equivalent to ancient rituals, thence returning to society personally transformed (Graburn 1983). Except of course the tourist's experience is of a degraded spirituality, the comfortable trip hardly comparable to the mortal and moral dangers of the pilgrim's progress, and thus "liminoid" rather than fully liminal (Turner and Turner 1978: 1–39; Leed 1991). Similarly, if tourism is conceived as a quest for authenticity in the world of the Other as compensation for its perceived lack in modern everyday life, the gullible tourist is presented only with "reconstructed ethnicity" and "staged authenticity" behind which lies a hierarchy of "backstage" regions, or reserves of more or less authentic culture to which they can have no access (MacCannell 1976, 1984; see also Graburn 1983).

Again, consumption and tourism cannot be reduced to a singular quest for authenticity (Urry 1990: 51), but their discourses do invite participants to search for "value," not just in the sense of an equitable exchange between money and utility – "value for money" – but in the sense of some kind of spiritual or emotional surplus that is precisely "beyond" the calculus of monetary exchange. The desire for a non-alienated commodity and for an intimate Other is manifest in oxymorons that abound in commodity and tourism marketing, such as "real nostalgia," "authentic reproductions," "live recordings," "original copies," "tropical paradise," "personal service," and "genuine hospitality." Now, it is all too easy to dismiss such constructions as a sign of a structurally necessary "bad faith" (Blythe 1990: 90) as often seems to be the case in Marxist analyses of consumption and tourism. In such analyses, the all too gullible consumer-tourist is assumed to be happily manipulated by the "consciousness industries" whose techniques of "mass deception" create "false needs," exploiting the ontological insecurity and sense of insufficiency that modern capitalism actually produces and offering to allay them through its own means of commodity and tourist consumption (Horkheimer and Adorno 1972; Marcuse 1972). Accordingly, consumer-tourists must willfully ignore the signs of contradiction in order to have it both ways: for example, to take the cheap mass-produced product as "Just for you," or "Aloha," as a personal gesture of hospitality. They must also deny the complicity of their own desires in the commodification of everything and the exoticization of the Other, which effectively undermine the very possibility of the authenticity of objects and ways of life that they purvey: for example, in the representation of "natural products" and "native people" innocent of the relations of exploitation involved in their production and performance.

The shopper and tourist always already suspects something of this critique, however, which then serves only to reinforce the simultaneous desire and self-contempt, the alternation between assertion and denial of identity that is characteristic of consumption and tourism (Frow 1991: 127). In condemning consumption and tourism, critical discourse only reproduces the structure of authenticity-in-authenticity on which tourist consumption depends (Frow 1991: 136). Moreover, the critique inevitably plays into the accompanying system of segmentation and social structuring, whereby consumer goods and tourist experiences are totemic marks of membership in particular "tribes" or "neo-tribes" (Sahlins 1976: 215–16; Maffesoli 1996), and/or mark "distinction" that depends upon possession of "cultural capital," and thus the differential distribution of the social knowledge of the means and relations of consumption and tourism (Bourdieu 1984). One might argue about the degree to which membership in collectivities of consumption and tourism "lifestyles" is by self-identification or determined by a hierarchy of cultural legitimacy, and one might acknowledge the "postmodern" consumer-tourist, conscious of the contradictions of consumption and tourism (Lash and Urry 1994: 58) and thus at home with the ironies of "genuine fakes" (Brown 1996). It is inevitably the master trope of authenticity, however, operating within narratives of loss and restoration, that organizes the "play" of multiple signs of identity and value.

The Aura of Objects

While Marx, the historical materialist, brilliantly diagnosed the dialectic materiality of the commodity, he placed faith in a "predeconstructive" ontology of presence, his project being to exorcize the contradictions of the commodity, to conjure away the "forgotten residue in things" (Bataille 1991: 35), or the ineffable "thingness" of the object world as the product of subjective imagination. Marx's argument paradoxically reproduces the "caricatural resurrection" performed by the commodity itself (Baudrillard 1998: 100), demystifying the object yet re-enchanting it with the spirits of "dead" labor and authentic use value, demonstrating the persistent and powerful desire for "the possibility of spectral survival" (Derrida 1994: 148).

For Benjamin the messianic materialist, however, the "specters of Marx" were not only ghosts of reified human labor, but manifestations of aura, the fleeting experience of temporal-spatial proximity with "the material origin – and finality – that human beings share with non-human nature, the physical aspect of creation" (Hanssen 1998: 212). Like personifications of allegory, commodities seem to speak of or upon some other plane, and thus like the objects we call art, antiques, primitive artifacts, nature, and souvenirs, they evince an uncanny ability to look at us, to return our look of desire (Benjamin in Wollen 1982: 237). The aura of an object is defined as "the unique appearance of a distance, however close it may be" (Benjamin 1969: 222–3), and is experienced as "temporal proximity, a fleeting moment in which the trace of an unconscious past is actualized" (Hansen 1987: 188).

While Benjamin (1969) describes the generalized decline of aura under conditions of modernity, with the intensification of commodity production with its capacity for serial reproduction of objects and images, he notes a certain "empathy of the soul with the commodity." This is particularly the case for the modern urban *flâneur,* the urban prototype of the global consumer-tourist, a "figure" who displays a relentless "allegorical intention": that is, under the sign of guilt and debt for the destruction of meaning under rapid social and technological changes of the nineteenth century, he or she pursues transitory images and accumulates obsolete objects of the commodity world in order to possess their residual aura, the traces of timeless and universal meanings (Buck-Morss 1989; Nägele 1991; Buci-Glucksmann 1994). In Western cultures, a generalized nostalgia pre-dates modernity, of course, and has theological expression in the concept of the Fall, with banishment from a state of prelapsarian innocence and the loss of the "Adamic language of Names." In the maelstrom of modern progress, however, it obtains secular expression in the felt loss of authentic relations with Nature, Objects, and the Other. Not that modernity has displaced the theology, exactly, for we can see that these come together nicely, for example, in the places and products that evoke "tropical paradise."

The discourses of consumption and tourism are informed by the "melancholic metaphysics" of allegory, a mode of figuration that "that signifies precisely the non-being of what it represents" (Benjamin in de Man 1983: 35). The etymological origins of allegory (from *allos* "other," and *agoreuin* "public space or marketplace") suggest speaking of the Other in the marketplace, of representing and recognizing the presence of something irreducible to material exchange, of the sacred within the profaned world of commerce (see Cohen 1989: 96). Allegory is peculiarly suited to the experience and contemplation of the commodity (Benjamin 1977), not only because of the peculiar "metaphysical subtleties" of the commodity system identified by Marx, but also because of the "dialectical trick" that they perform (Hanssen 1998: 100): that is, surrounded by overwhelming evidence of physical dissolution and temporal-spatial estrangement, and saturated in the pathos of death, decay, and departure, they nevertheless perform a "stunning reversal" (McCole 1993: 147) that celebrates the resurrection of life, restoration of value, return of the departed, and recovery of meaning. They deploy what Beatrice Hanssen (1998: 96) calls the "economy of salvation": representing socio-spatial process as progressive separation and temporal process as relentless "natural history," even as they confront the inevitability of distanciation and death, they nevertheless invite an imaginative "leap of faith" into intimacy and eternal life (Benjamin, in Buck-Morss 1989: 175). Allegory is often disdained for its contrived tendentiousness, and we might see in this phenomenon the operation of duplicity similar to that of the fetishism of the commodity, but it is ancient and universal, and intensified in periods of displacement and loss. Is it possible for consumer-tourists, relentlessly reminded of ongoing spiritual loss and material obsolescence, to take commodities simply as material objects present in themselves, or to see them merely as signs that represent something else, and not to be taken in by the object as if it actually presents or personifies that absent something?

The Lure of Tourist Consumption

Let us return to tourism's peculiar commodity, the souvenir, and to tourist objects, the more generalized commodity of contemporary consumption. How do the souvenir and the tourist object work? Is it simply that the thing jogs the memory and reminds us of the personal story of its acquisition or of the marketing hype that told of its originality and authenticity? Or does it also contain the essence of the temporally and spatially estranged Other, an object-soul that addresses us as such? I think that, somewhat paradoxically, it is both that tourist-consumers know, in one sense, that souvenirs are merely material, but that they nevertheless, not so much despite but precisely because of their semiotic selves, also inevitably take them to be possessed of an "impersonalised subjectivity" (Hansen 1987: 187). The metanarrative of modernity tells consumers and tourists that faith in the animation of objects and enchantment of the world is characteristic of a childlike and primitive "innocence," and thus that it is something once possessed and regretfully lost in their own personal and collective past. On the other hand, landscapes of consumption and tourism reproduce imagery of childhood, traditional societies, and exotic Others precisely in order to enhance the possibility of its imaginative restoration. By representing childish and primitive faith, for example, the discourses of consumption and tourism evoke a "subject supposed to believe" (Žižek 1997: 106), one through whom we can believe what we *in our very being* want to believe, and ultimately cannot help but believe, which is that meaning is immanent in the world.

To explain this, it is useful to consider the operation of the lure, which might provide a general model for the object of consumption and tourism, in that it is a complex and contradictory mechanism, simultaneously object and subject of desire. The lure is "originally" an apparatus constructed by falconers from the feathers of a dead bird to recall their hawks, but it also defines the birdlike call the falconer makes to attract the hawk, and thus refers to an "alluring cry." In the "belly" of the lure the hawk finds ground meat that it will take as its food, so that it will at once be tame to the hawker yet retain its wild capacity to kill. The hawk returns to hand, both because it has a memory of the last meal that was hidden within the lure and because it will be tricked by its powerful instinct to see in the flutter of the feathers the life of a bird that is the ultimate source of its own. Since we are not hawks, it is easy to see the deception of this decoy, but I believe that the aura of objects to us is like the fluttering of feathers to the hawk, a flash of life to which we owe a "primal response" due to the condition of our collective consciousness and capacity of language that are essential to our species being.

As Taussig (2001: 312) observes, a peculiarity of our susceptibility to the subjectivity of objects is that it is intensified by the experience of loss, and thus it is by the invocation of the dead that things become animated. Similarly, Žižek (1991: 22) has argued that the fundamental fantasy of contemporary mass culture is the return of the living dead, and whether as zombies in horror movies or "unalienated" nature or labor in objects of value, this represents the materialization of symbolic debt carried beyond physical death. Thus, in landscapes of consumption and at tourist sights/sites, which are saturated with images of loss, death, and departure, we are enjoined to mourn the transience of things, yet invited to celebrate restoration, resurrection, and return. Shopping centers come to resemble museums, stuffed with handicrafts and ethnographic objects; tourist sights become memorials to the death of nature, decline of culture, and loss of local ways of life, or even in the case of so-called "dark tourism" (Lennon and Foley 1999), literally shrines to martyred heroes and tragic victims of murder and mass killing. It is in the presence of overwhelming evidence of mortality and obsolescence that things seem particularly disposed take on a life of their own. In these contexts, commodities are souvenirs that not only evoke a personal memory of a particular person or place, but evoke a collective memory of the enchantment of the world, with its possibility of life beyond death, presence within absence, meaning in materiality, and subjectivity of objects.

Conclusion

As noted above, it has become something of a cliché to state that shopping and tourism are analogous to religion, and thus that shopping centers are "cathedrals of consumption" while tourist sites are the modern equivalent of the sacred sites of pilgrimage. Of course, the analogy is supposed to illustrate the corruption of spirituality by commerce, and the displacement of contemplation from its proper object – which is precisely not an object in the material sense, of course – on to the commodity. It is an ancient story, echoing biblical injunctions against idolatry and vain attempts to drive merchants and moneychangers from the temple.

What we seem to forget while adhering to our deist faith and materialist philosophies is that the church was the market, as divine presence was evoked to sanctify secular dealings, and secular dealings could in turn evoke divine presence. As Leed (1991: 37) points out, "pilgrimage devotion, the market, and the fair are all connected with voluntary, contractual activities (the religious promise, the striking of a bargain, the penny ride on the merry-go-round), and with a measure of joyful, 'ludic' communitas." At the sacred sites of pilgrimage, trade in currency, objects, and animals facilitated the ongoing rituals of exchange between profane and sacred objects, the material and spiritual realms, and life and death. As places of sacrifice, such sacred sites witnessed the ritual transaction between phenomenon and essence, material and spirit, and were thus the vital centers of public life, "the great sacred center of substitutions, of exchanges, the center of sacred consumption" (Williams 1991: 193). There is an inherent sacrificial structure to consumption and in many forms of tourism, and the tourist object or souvenir acts as the remainder from this transaction, acting as a reminder of the event of the sacrificial exchange, and embodying the possibility of its (re)enactment.

This is not to say that contemporary consumption and tourism are not qualitatively and quantitatively different from ancient religion and pilgrimage, but rather to point out that they exploit a similar sensitivity within us to what Schelling (1989: 34) calls "the incomprehensible basis of reality in things, the irreducible remainder, that which with the greatest exertion cannot be resolved in the understanding but remains eternally in the ground." Our relation to objects in general, and to the souvenir in particular, is defined by this longing for the possibility of exchange between the material and spiritual worlds. Its value as the object of consumption and tourism is precisely the possibility of commerce and transport between the realms of materiality and meaning, life and death, and substance and essence.

REFERENCES

Bataille, G. (1991). *The Accursed Shared: An Essay on the General Economy*, vol. 1: *Consumption*, trans. R. Hurley. New York: Zone Books.

Baudrillard, J. (1998). *The Consumer Society: Myths and Structures.* Thousand Oaks, CA: Sage.

Bauman, Z. (1998). *Globalization: The Human Consequences.* New York: Columbia University Press.

Benjamin, W. (1969). *Illuminations*, trans. H. Zohn. New York: Schocken Books.

Benjamin, W. (1973). *Charles Baudelaire: A Lyric Poet in the Era of High Capitalism*, trans. Harry Zohn. London: New Left Books.

Benjamin, W. (1977). *The Origin of German Tragic Drama*, trans. John Osborne. London: New Left Books.

Benjamin, W. (1985). Central Park. *New German Critique* 34, 32–58.

Blythe, M. (1990). The romance of Maoriland: Ethnography and tourism in New Zealand films. *East–West Film Journal* 4(2), 90–100.

Bourdieu, P. (1984). *Distinction*, trans. R. Nice. Cambridge, MA: Harvard University Press.

Brown, B. (1998). How to do things with things (a toy story). *Critical Enquiry* (Summer), 935–64.
Brown, B. (2001). Thing theory. *Critical Inquiry* 28, 1–16.
Brown, D. (1996). Genuine fakes. In T. Selwyn (ed.), *The Tourist Image: Myths and Myth Making in Tourism* (pp. 33–47). Chichester: John Wiley.
Buci-Glucksmann, C. (1994). *Baroque Reason: The Aesthetics of Modernity.* Thousand Oaks, CA: Sage.
Buck-Morss, S. (1989). *The Dialectics of Seeing: Walter Benjamin and the Arcades Project.* Cambridge, MA: MIT Press.
Cohen, M. (1989). Walter Benjamin's phantasmagoria. *New German Critique* 48, 87–107.
de Man, P. (1983). *Blindness and Insight: Essays in the Rhetoric of Contemporary Criticism.* Minneapolis: University of Minnesota Press.
Derrida, J. (1994). *Specters of Marx: The State of the Debt, the Work of Mourning and the New International*, trans. P. Kamuf. New York: Routledge.
Frow, J. (1991). Tourism and the semantics of nostalgia. *October* 57, 121–51.
Goss, J. (1996). Disquiet on the waterfront: Nostalgia and utopia in the festival marketplace. *Urban Geography* 17, 221–47.
Goss, J. (1999). Once-upon-a-time in the commodity world: An unofficial guide to Mall of America. *Annals of the Association of American Geographers* 89, 45–75.
Graburn, N. H. H. (1983). The anthropology of tourism. *Annals of Tourism Research* 10, 9–33.
Hansen, Miriam (1987). Benjamin, cinema and experience: The blue flower in the land of technology. *New German Critique* 40, 179–224.
Hanssen, B. (1998). *Walter Benjamin's Other History: Of Stones, Animals, Human Beings and Angels.* Berkeley: University of California Press.
Harris, N. (1991). Urban tourism and the commercial city. In W. R. Taylor (ed.), *Inventing Times Square: Commerce and Culture at the Crossroads of the World* (pp. 1–23). New York: Russell Sage Foundation.
Horkheimer, M., and Adorno, T. (1972). *Dialectic of Enlightenment*, trans. J. Cumming. New York: Seabury Press.
Lash, S., and Urry, J. (1994). *Economies of Signs and Space.* Thousand Oaks, CA: Sage.
Leed, E. J. (1991). *The Mind of the Traveler: From Gilgamesh to Global Tourism.* New York: Basic Books.
Leiss, W., Kline, S., and Jhally, S. (1984). *Social Communication as Advertising: Persons, Products and Images of Well-Being.* New York: Macmillan.
Lennon, J. J., and Foley, M. (1999). Interpretation of the unimaginable: The U.S. Holocaust Museum, Washington, DC, and "Dark Tourism." *Journal of Travel Research* 38, 46–50.
Lury, C. (1997). The objects of travel. In C. Rojek and J. Urry (eds), *Touring Cultures: Transformations of Travel and Theory* (pp. 75–95). New York: Routledge.
MacCannell, D. (1976). *The Tourist: A New Theory of the Leisure Class.* New York: Schocken.
MacCannell, D. (1984). Reconstructed ethnicity: Tourism and cultural identity in Third World communities. *Annals of Tourism Research* 11, 375–91.
McCole, J. (1993). *Walter Benjamin and the Antinomies of Tradition.* Ithaca, NY: Cornell University Press.
Maffesoli, M. (1996). *The Time of the Tribes: The Decline of Individualism in Mass Society*, trans. D. Smith. Thousand Oaks, CA: Sage.
Marcuse, H. (1972). *One-Dimensional Man.* London: Abacus.
Marx, K. (1977). *Capital: A Critique of Political Economy*, vol. 1, trans. B. Fowkes. New York: Vintage.
Mitchell, W. J. T. (1996). What do pictures really want? *October* 77, 71–82.

Nägele, R. (1991). *Theater, Theory, Speculation: Walter Benjamin and the Scenes of Modernity.* Baltimore: Johns Hopkins University Press.
Sack, R. (1992). *Place, Modernity and the Consumer's World: A Relational Framework for Geographical Analysis.* Baltimore: Johns Hopkins University Press.
Sahlins, M. (1976). *Culture and Practical Reason.* Chicago: Chicago University Press.
Schelling, F. W. J. (1989). *Philosophical Inquiries into the Nature of Human Freedom*, trans. James Guttman. New York: Open Court.
Stewart, S. (1993). *On Longing: Narratives of the Miniature, the Gigantic, the Souvenir, the Collection.* Durham, NC: Duke University Press.
Taussig, M. (2001). Dying is an art like everything else. *Critical Enquiry* 28(1), 305–16.
Thomas, N. (1991). *Entangled Objects: Exchange, Material Culture and Colonialism in the Pacific.* Cambridge, MA: Harvard University Press.
Turner, V., and Turner, E. (1978). *Image and Pilgrimage in Christian Culture: Anthropological Perspectives.* New York: Columbia University Press.
Urry, J. (1990). *The Tourist Gaze: Leisure and Travel in Contemporary Societies.* Thousand Oaks, CA: Sage Publications.
Vico, Giambattista (1970). *The New Science of Giambattista Vico*, trans. T. G. Bergin and M. H. Fisch. Ithaca, NY: Cornell University Press.
Wang, N. (1999). Rethinking authenticity in tourism experience. *Annals of Tourism Research* 26(2), 349–70.
Williams, J. G. (1991). *The Bible, Violence, and the Sacred: Liberation from the Myth of Sanctioned Violence.* New York: HarperCollins.
Williams, R. (1980). *Problems of Materialism and Culture.* NewYork: Columbia University Press.
Wollen, P. (1982). *Walter Benjamin: An Aesthetic of Redemption.* New York: Columbia University Press.
Žižek, S. (1991). *Looking Awry: An Introduction to Jacques Lacan through Popular Culture.* Cambridge, MA: MIT Press.
Žižek, S. (1997). *The Plague of Fantasies.* London: Verso.

Part VI Tourism, Place, Space, and Forms

Chapter 27

Tourism and Landscape

Theano S. Terkenli

The Place of Landscape in Tourism Geography: A Critical Assessment

On the basis of its imageability and tangible, experiential character, landscape constitutes a most significant geographical medium in the analysis of relationships that develop between tourist and visited location. Its easy and ready accessibility, as well as its representational and relational properties, render landscape both a veritable stage for play and recreation and a valuable means and tool of analyzing geographical change through tourism (Terkenli 2002). Its distinctive difference from other spatial units of analysis lies largely in the difference between seeing and gazing, where the latter activity, indispensable to the context of landscape, is emotionally laden, in contrast to the former, and thus central to the tourism nexus of activities. The complex nature of the relationship of tourism, or of the tourist, with the visited landscape, however, must be established at the outset. It is a complexity that is place-, time- and culture-contingent, representing specific social and cultural perceptions at particular historical periods. Thus, as a focus of research, the tourism landscape requires contextual interpretation and cannot be detached from questions of positionality and from its historical and sociocultural context – its relationship with *an observer.*

The tourism industry has been repeatedly denounced both as an exploiter or defiler of landscapes and as a quintessentially modern medium of globalizing standards of identity and development for contemporary landscapes (Jackson 1980: 3; Sack 1992; Urry 1995). On the other hand, the tourist, like a modern pilgrim, seeks regeneration in the realms of pleasure, dream, tradition, arts, and sports, which prompt and preserve the ongoing quest for novel tourism landscape destinations. The mechanisms of this essential connection between tourism and the landscape, however, remain largely unexplored. In the context of ambivalent and contested processes that constitute today's landscapes of tourism, this chapter aims to expose contemporary discourses that elucidate aspects of the relationship between tourism and landscape. This interdisciplinary field of study has so far hardly been embraced by geographers of tourism in a concerted, systematic way.

As the image or representation of a place, landscape represents the first and most enduring medium of contact between tourist and prospective or consumed place of travel; through acquired photographs it becomes a traveler's lasting memoir. Tourist landscapes, moreover, through promotion, sustenance, and transformation of their specific functions, are among the most significant cultural battling grounds on which much of today's sociocultural difference is increasingly created and development negotiated (Terkenli 2000: 180). Characteristics of modern European cultural landscapes were already established by the seventeenth century, imbuing the definition of the landscape with notions of vistas, prospects, or views of scenery. These notions have accompanied the development of landscapes up to the present times, for example in panoramic views, landscapes of characteristic forms, the ephemeral, the picturesque, and other landscape principles and models ubiquitous to the tourism industry, including photographic mementoes, postcards, advertisements, and tour-guide iconography. In all of these cases, the landscape has been *staged* by tourism planning and development initiatives for purposes of tourist consumption.

The visual aspect of the landscape has been widely emphasized and propagated (Daniels and Cosgrove 1988: 1–3). The evolution of particular trends in tourist demand inevitably led to, and reciprocally stemmed from, appropriate interventions in the visited landscape, through very specific principles and strategies of landscape design and planning that grew out of the art or science of the perspective. "Imagery is one of the most researched aspects of tourism marketing" (Pritchard and Morgan 2001: 167). Tourism marketing reproduces images and discourses about landscapes through representations of cultural signs, on the basis of which the tourist, through processes of experiential reinterpretation of the sign, may assess the sight and validate the meanings of the visited landscape within the predominant discourse. Iconographical methods of construction, signification, decodification, and deconstruction are central to the making of tourist landscapes (Norton 1996; Stefanou 2000). Supported and supplemented by other visual means of contemporary mass media (such as TV and video), they blur geographical differentiation and distinctions of *authentic*-staged and familiar-exotic in the landscape images conveyed.

Montaigne, the "father" of tourism according to J. B. Jackson, indicated the close connection of landscape to tourism and pointed out that the motive to travel, at least in his time, was essentially a geographical motive, closely linked to greater self-awareness: "this great world is a mirror where we must see ourselves in order to know ourselves" (Montaigne, in Jackson 1980: 5). This viewer–landscape relationship, as staged and played out in tourism landscapes, is increasingly explored in the context of tourism studies, for example in the analysis of aspects of tourism destinations as cultural landscapes (Norton 1996; Ringer et al., in Pritchard and Morgan 2001: 169), albeit so far inadequately. In this relationship, the positionality of the viewer or tourist, not easily delineated, is not inherently positive or negative. Decidedly, neither is it desirable to generalize the multiplicity of shifting positions of viewing or gazing, nor to dismiss or diminish the importance of historically predominant landscape interpretations. In other words, what is upheld here is not an essentialist notion of the tourist landscape, but rather a culturally ambivalent, socially constructed, and historically specific notion of the landscape that invites multiple and fluid interpretations, among which particular interpretations have historically prevailed.

Furthermore, the connection between landscape and tourism extends to the pleasure sought in the experience, a component of tourism that has become much more central and predominant in twentieth-century forms of tourism. Löfgren points out that since the eighteenth century the tourist industry has spearheaded new forms of tourist attraction, "it has developed the production sites of hedonism – a great weekend, an unforgettable event, a week of family fun, an exciting adventure" (1999: 6). Moreover, the enduring intensity of pleasure sought and found in the landscape since the Renaissance in the context of an emerging European bourgeoisie expresses something profound and constant about the human condition (Rose 1996: 345), something that links landscape and pleasure or attraction inextricably together, thus highlighting the significance of the human emotional component in the relationship of the visitor with the tourism landscape.

Key Issues and Research Advances in Tourism Landscapes

The cultural turn of the social sciences in the 1990s opened the ground for geographers to extend their more traditional areas of academic interest, such as the study of landscape, to issues of leisure and tourism spaces and places. Simultaneously the opening up to matters of space and geographical analysis of other tourism-related disciplines has encouraged the latter to turn their attention to the landscape in the context of leisure and tourism. In the larger context of tourism studies, this has not been so much a substantial turn to the tourism–landscape relationship, as the interest in this relationship has always existed, but rather its reorganization into a more concerted and conscious theoretical and empirical framework. Moreover, this newly emerging shift, which is only now becoming manifest, may no longer be situated in "a geography of tourism", but in a series of new "geographies of tourism."

This development of scientific interest in the relationship of tourism with the landscape comes at a time of convergence of three distinctive larger tendencies. The first is a widespread realization of the growing degree of modification that tourism development has been imparting to many landscapes around the world. High-impact alterations of land use, as well as intense seasonal and geographical tourist concentrations, in conjunction with the large-scale and/or environmentally degrading or incongruous construction of tourism infrastructure, result in landscape's carrying capacity being surpassed, leading to variable change in the preexisting landscape. "Sometimes the changes are so profound that it is possible to talk of tourism landscapes in which tourism dominates the uses of the land and the appearance of the area" (Wall, in Jafari 2000: 347). Secondly, international, and especially European, interest in the landscape, landscape policy, landscape values and assessment/analytical methodologies has skyrocketed in the very recent past, calling for organized action to evaluate, protect, and enhance the quality and multifunctionality of landscapes at the local, regional, national, and international levels (Klijn et al. 1999: 12; Terkenli 2001: 197; Tress and Tress 2001). Thirdly, the dominance of structuralist (and more recently postmodern and poststructuralist) perspectives on landscape in social and cultural geographies of tourism has been increasingly highlighting the complex interrelationships between the phenomenon of tourism and the construction, reconstruction, and consumption of landscape in and out of the context of everyday life.

The following overview of the scientific area(s) where landscape science(s) have developed a dialogue and interaction with the field of tourism will trace this relationship through an epistemological overview of the infusion of tourism-related issues into landscape geography and vice versa. Two larger periods in the recent history of geographical inquiry, corresponding to two distinct areas of geographical ontology and epistemology, may be identified here with regard to the description and interpretation of space/landscape in relation to leisure and tourism. The first overarching period – and epistemological approach – to landscape study gathers momentum through the quantitative revolution of the 1950s and 1960s. It finds application in a large body of work on tourism landscape analysis that is largely apolitical, informed more by economic concerns for landscape development. This body of work on the interrelationships of landscape and tourism constitutes the most extensive domain of landscape research in the field of tourism to date and continues to predominate in much of contemporary tourism research. The second period, and corresponding epistemological approaches, is formulated around more critical and radical perspectives revolving around the historical and material processes of space and landscape production, reproduction, and consumption. At the start of this chronological period, humanistic methodologies, also prevalent in geographical inquiry at the time, were not much explicitly employed in the study of the tourism–landscape relationship (Relph 1976; Meinig 1979; Jackson 1984), and thus it will receive no further discussion in the following overview. More recently, the dialectical relationships of society-individual and structure-culture, built into the landscape, as illustrated by structuralist interpretations of tourism landscapes in the 1970s and 1980s, have been in a process of renegotiation through postmodern and poststructuralist epistemological approaches.

In the course of the latter half of the twentieth century, geographical research thus shifted in scope and scale from the macro-analysis of symbolic landscapes of national scale to micro-analyses of townscape and resort landscapes (Hall and Page 1999: 12–13). Perspectives stressing the physical, material, and absolute nature of space more recently gave way to perspectives that emphasize its sociocultural, symbolic, and relative nature. One outcome of this shift is that many of these newly emerging geographical perspectives on the landscape have served to illuminate aspects of leisure and tourism research but have never been explicitly framed as leisure and tourism studies (Aitchison, MacLeod, and Shaw 2000: 7). The same trend is overwhelmingly apparent in the contributions to these more recent landscape tourism geographies of other tourism-related fields. The main difference between these social science discourses on tourism landscapes and those of other tourism-related disciplines is that the change that has occurred in the latter during the past few years has been of a far lesser degree than the change in the former. This change has also been more quantitative than qualitative, as was the case in the social sciences. In the remainder of this section, a series of themes that have attracted the interest of landscape geographies of tourism or tourism landscape analysis will be displayed and indicative examples of each of these themes will be provided. Without, obviously, intending to cover the entire field of tourism–landscape interrelationships, each of these themes represents a significant position in geographical discourses of leisure/tourism and culture, and as such will be discussed below. As will become obvious, an exhaustive presentation of even the most significant work in these fields would be impossible in the context of this brief overview.

Admittedly, the earliest geographical research on leisure and tourism landscapes, gaining momentum in the first half of the twentieth century, was purely concerned with the classification of scenic quality and land use (Aitchison, MacLeod, and Shaw 2000: 12). This preoccupation with landscape classification, assessment, and evaluation with the aid of land-use mapping and other quantitative methodologies adhering to positivist epistemologies, continues to inform a large portion of research in the area as conducted by various related academic disciplines. Such approaches to the landscape predominate in the environmental sciences, but are equally employed in the field of tourism geography by spatial analysts (Hall and Page 1999: 12–13; Garcia Perez 2002; Roovers, Hermy, and Gulinck 2002). Löfgren places the popularity of such landscape evaluation and measurement techniques in environmental studies and planning in a span of several decades, and especially the 1970s:

> Scores of studies appeared, with titles like "Eye Pupillary Measurement of Aesthetic Response to Forest Scenes" or "Modeling and Predicting Human Response to the Visual Recreation Environment". Hoping to create tools for natural resource management and planning, from wilderness aesthetics to scenic roads design, many of these studies put enormous amounts of energy and spectacular number crunching into what are good examples of social science trivia. They reflect a period in tourist and leisure management when hard facts, models, and clear taxonomies were in demand. (1999: 83)

Such work tended to appear in scientific journals such as *Landscape Architecture*, *Landscape Planning*, the *Journal of Environmental Sciences*, the *Journal of Environmental Management*, *Landscape Ecology*, the *Journal of Coastal Conservation*, and the *Journal of Coastal Research*.

Meanwhile, by the late 1930s and 1940s another quantitative approach to tourism landscape analysis had already gained ground, namely interest in the geography of seaside resorts, resort development, and coastal landscapes. This general interest aimed at tourism development and planning and focused on systematic geographical approaches to tourism landscape morphology through the employment of spatial analytical techniques. Resort morphology was recognized by tourism geographers and others as early as the 1930s, but not until the 1970s did detailed urban and economic analyses generate a considerable body of academic literature, today "a small but important research thread among planners and tourism geographers" (Meyer-Arendt, in Jafari 2000: 504–5). Concomitant to this development was the widespread employment of descriptive and predictive models in early recreation and tourism research within geography, a prevalent and ongoing trend in the geography of tourism to date (Pearce 1995). Aitchison, MacLeod, and Shaw point out that, "while leisure studies was embracing sociological concepts from Marxist, structuralist and humanist theory in the 1960s and 1970s, tourism studies and recreation research appeared to hold on to their more positivist paradigm" (2000: 12). They add that analyses of recreation and tourism continued to rely on quantitative methods to devise theories which mapped, modeled, coded, and classified recreation and tourism development, provision participation and impacts. Altogether, a number of models dealing with various aspects of the spatial structures of tourism emerged in the late 1960s, the 1970s, and the 1980s, most of which were developed independently of one another, with little or no recognition of, or attempt to build on, previous (Pearce 1995: 3, 14) or contemporary efforts. Consequently, this ongoing overall approach to spatial schemata of tourism has yet to produce either a strong conceptual or a theoretical base for tourism research. Rather, it remains highly unsystematic and fragmented.

Various types of models interpreting tourism development, tourism economics, and tourism psychology, as imprinted on the landscape, have thus been borrowed from or based on either geographical positivist and predictive models, such as those of Weber, Crystaller and Losch, Alonso, and including the gravity model and others, or sociological and anthropological conceptual tools and techniques. Themes under this umbrella of positivist modeling approaches to tourism and the landscape vary enormously: land-use change, planning, and management; landscape as a resource for urban, rural, regional, and national development; travel motives and tourist types; natural and cultural resource assessment for recreation and tourism; landscape impact analyses; tourism carrying capacity, etc. Journals exemplifying such work include *Tourism Management*, *Landscape and Urban Planning*, *Landscape Planning*, *Sustainable Tourism*, *Landscape Research*, *Tourism Geographies*, *Annals of Tourism Research*, and many others. Within this positivist paradigm, perhaps the most significant theme in tourism analysis emerging in tourism studies today becomes a series of perspectives revolving around sustainable development issues with applications in sustainable tourism development per se. Both interrelationships of tourism with broader sustainable development and sustainable tourism development itself appear to be closely connected to forms, functions, and symbolisms of landscapes of tourism, in an often normative approach.

A third strand of tourism landscape research that spans both chronological periods in the development of ontological and epistemological research perspectives to landscapes of tourism during the second half of the twentieth century is the historical perspective/overview of landscape change through tourism. Although the historical perspective has always been present in tourism studies as an introductory overview of current issues, complete historical geographical perspectives on tourism have emerged only very recently (Towner 1996). These have tended to examine the relationships between tourism and the landscape historiographically, stressing the impact of changing motives and socioeconomic constraints of travel on the landscape (Towner 1996). More recently, their tendency has been toward an analysis of the social history and cultural underpinnings of this relationship from a more critical point of view (Löfgren 1999). Though the spatial patterns that arise from locational attributes of supply and demand have predominated as an organizational concept in this type of tourism landscape approach, the particular role of place has also been explored (Towner 1996: 5–6). This third strand of tourism landscape research is also represented by anthropological and sociological journals such as *Journeys: The International Journal of Travel and Travel Writing*, but also the *Annals of Tourism Research*, *Ecumene*, and other journals with a more general interest in tourism geography.

Although a more critical shift to geographical research was already apparent in the 1960s, a Marxist and structuralist reorientation of landscape geography gained momentum only in the 1970s and 1980s. In this chronological context, cultural meanings were built into landscapes of the built environment and rural surroundings (Aitchison, MacLeod, and Shaw 2000: 15), illustrating dialectical relationships between structures and cultures, or society and the individual, with regard to landscapes of tourism. Although environmental issues have occasionally been raised, research on the relationship between tourism and the landscape appears rather scarce in the structuralist paradigm (Britton 1982, 1991; Shaw and Williams 1994; Porter and Sheppard 1998: 541), and, following contemporary trends in geography and the social sciences more generally, was soon superseded by postmodern, postcolonial, and poststructuralist approaches.

Postmodern/poststructuralist social and cultural geographies of landscapes of tourism demonstrate how the latter act as sites and sights of social and cultural inclusion/exclusion and are not fixed but are in a constant state of transition (Urry 1995). Such approaches to tourism landscapes acknowledge specific landscape contexts of transformation, rather than placing landscape in the context of an overall system of transformation. They include a wide variety of themes, such as landscape and place experiences and practices (Crang 1999), gender and identity formation (Kinnaird and Hall 1994), spectacle and performance (Hollinshead 1999), the gaze and surveillance (Urry 1990; Crang 1999; Hollinshead 1999), attraction and desire (Terkenli 2002), and the seduction of place (Cartier and Lew 2004). They call for the development of sociocultural *geographies* of leisure and tourism, rather than of a more systematic science of a geography of tourism. Two recently published books provide excellent illustrations of work within this paradigm. In *Leisure and Tourism Landscapes: Social and Cultural Geographies*, Aitchison, MacLeod, and Shaw (2000) identify a series of recent poststructuralist discourses on the spatiality of leisure and tourism landscapes, such as the role of gender in constructing and contesting leisure and tourism spaces, places, and landscapes; the place of ethnicity in the production and reproduction of urban landscapes; and interrelation between sexuality and spatiality in city landscapes. The other publication, *Leisure/Tourism Geographies: Practices and Geographical Knowledge*, is a collection of essays edited by David Crouch on the "fractured, multiple geographical knowledge . . . [that is] closer to our lived practice" (1999: 13). It considers leisure/tourism as an encounter that exists in place and landscape between people, people and space, people as socialized and embodied subjects, expectations, experience, and desire.

Contemporary Trends in Landscapes of Tourism and the Call for Theoretical Frameworks

The imprint and reflection on the landscape of contemporary forces of geographical transformation, including tourism and recreation, are invariably substantiated and articulated through changing landscape forms, practices, functions, and meanings indicative of a new cultural economy of space-time: a newly emerging cultural renegotiation and reinterpretation of landscape patterns and relationships (Terkenli 2002). In the case of landscapes of tourism, these trends are manifest in the dissolution of geographical particularity and identity, in the increasing breakdown of previously existing barriers and boundaries (geographical, categorical, or substantial) and in the simultaneous fusion of all parts of the world and of the human lifeworld in one. This transformation, whereby old socio-spatial schemata are dismantled and new forms and processes created, is characterized by a growing dissociation of these new schemata from geographical location and distinct place characteristics. Furthermore, processes of this new cultural economy of space take on increasingly global dimensions, through the dissemination and communication of all of the above changes through images – though their manifestations vary over space, time, and social context (Pritchard and Morgan 2001: 169; Terkenli 2002). Such developments, central and conducive to the transformation of landscape for purposes of tourism, clearly pose problems for hegemonic and totalizing discourses so far accommodated by tourism studies, and call for new theoretical frameworks in tourism landscape research. The first major problem of such an endeavor is that no theoretical framework has existed for landscapes of tourism thus far. The need for the development of such a body of interdisciplinary theory and epistemology for the study of landscapes of/and tourism remains indispensable, pressing, and of primary significance in this broader field.

In conclusion, much has been written and debated with regard to spatial forces and products of transformation through tourism as it relates to landscape. So far, however, this body of work lacks an adequate organizational framework of analysis, much more one that sufficiently addresses the spatial and social imprint of a rapidly changing world geography of tourism on the landscape. The challenge, then, for the study of interrelationships of tourism and landscape, as this emerges from such a brief overview of the contribution of landscape geographies to the study of tourism, is twofold. First, it lies in the rearticulation and reawareness of the place of landscape in the geography(ies) of tourism, at the same time as tourism and recreation need to gain a stronghold in various geographical as well as other social scientific discourses. This interdisciplinary dialogue and merging inevitably leads to the need to develop a theoretical framework for the study of landscapes and/of tourism out of disparate efforts and perspectives. While many such attempts from various sides have contributed to shedding light upon the interrelations between tourism and the landscape, these attempts have rarely been framed explicitly as tourism studies, much less as studies of landscapes of tourism. Second, this theory-building endeavor must be carried out while embracing the complexity of interrelationships between tourism and the landscape in the context of a newly emerging cultural economy of space informing *new geographies of tourism*. The latter indicate the need to study the ways in which space and landscape literally and metaphorically shape the experience of leisure and tourism, not only through the gaze, but also through multi-sensual sensitivity, materiality, embodiment, and expressive practice. Furthermore, they elicit future research into the ways in which contextualized, as well as overarching, leisure and tourism experiences inform and substantiate landscapes of tourism.

The development of new types of landscapes with the advent of new forms of tourism catering to new social needs, cultural preferences, and economic contingencies has certainly been an ongoing practice since the appearance of the phenomenon of tourism. The novelty of such landscapes in the present age, however, lies instead in their nature, scale, and geographical characteristics, cutting across many of the more traditional typologies of tourist environments (Shaw and Williams 1994: 172–3). The segregation, for instance, of leisure from home life that modernization instilled becomes more and more tentative and irrelevant in the postmodern Western world. Practices that we understand by leisure/tourism today merge with other areas of life (Harvey 1989; Crouch 1999: 2) in the society of spectacle where specific pleasures are not place-bound and objects of delight proliferate (Debord 1994). What ensues is a growing de-differentiation in space of leisure and tourism, shopping, work, culture, satisfaction of basic needs, comfort, play, familiarity, etc. Thus, in the context of this new cultural economy of space, a final major difficulty of our future task as outlined above becomes the increasing tendency for *all* landscapes to assume characteristics of landscapes of leisure and tourism, while the distinction between leisure and tourism is also becoming increasingly blurred.

REFERENCES

Aitchison, C., MacLeod, N. E., and Shaw, S. J. (2000). *Leisure and Tourism Landscapes: Social and Cultural Geographies*. London: Routledge.

Britton, S. G. (1982). The political economy of tourism in the third world. *Annals of Tourism Research* 9(3), 331–58.

Britton, S. G. (1991). Tourism, capital and place: Towards a critical geography of tourism. *Environment and Planning D: Society and Space* 9, 451–78.

Cartier, C., and Lew, A. A. (eds) (2004). *The Seduction of Place*. London: Routledge.

Crang, M. (1999). Knowing, tourism and practices of vision. In D. Crouch (ed.), *Leisure/Tourism Geographies: Practices and Geographical Knowledge* (pp. 238–56). London: Routledge.

Crouch, D. (ed.) (1999). *Leisure/Tourism Geographies: Practices and Geographical Knowledge*. London: Routledge.

Daniels, S., and Cosgrove, D. (1988). Introduction: Iconography and landscape. In D. Cosgrove and S. Daniels (eds), *The Iconography of Landscape: Essays on the Symbolic Representation, Design and Use of Past Environments* (pp. 1–10). Cambridge: Cambridge University Press.

Debord, G. (1994). *The Society of the Spectacle*. New York: Zone Books.

Garcia Perez, J. D. (2002). Ascertaining landscape perceptions and preferences with pair-wise photographs: Planning rural tourism in Extremadura, Spain. *Landscape Research* 27(3), 297–308.

Hall, C. M., and Page, S. J. (1999). *The Geography of Tourism and Recreation: Environment, Place and Space*. London: Routledge.

Harvey, D. (1989). *The Condition of Postmodernity*. Oxford: Blackwell.

Hollinshead, K. (1999). Surveillance of the worlds of tourism: Foucault and the eye-of-power. *Tourism Management* 20, 7–23.

Jackson, J. B. (1980). *The Necessity for Ruins and other Topics*. Amherst: University of Massachusetts Press.

Jackson, J. B. (1984). *Discovering the Vernacular Landscape*. New Haven: Yale University Press.

Jafari, J. (ed.) (2000). *Encyclopedia of Tourism*. London: Routledge.

Kinnaird, V., and Hall, D. (eds) (1994). *Tourism: A Gender Analysis*. Chichester: John Wiley.

Klijn, J. A., Bethe, F., Wijermans, M., and Ypma, K. W. (1999). Landscape assessment method at a European level: A case study of polder landscapes. *Report 173, Winand Staring Centre*. Wageningen: WSC.

Löfgren, O. (1999). *On Holiday: A History of Vacationing*. Berkeley: University of California Press.

Meinig, D. (1979). The beholding eye: Ten versions of the same scene. In D. Meinig (ed.), *The Interpretation of Ordinary Landscapes: Geographical Essays* (pp. 33–48). Oxford: Oxford University Press.

Norton, A. (1996). Experiencing nature: The reproduction of environmental discourse through safari tourism in East Africa. *Geoforum* 27(3), 355–73.

Pearce, D. (1995). *Tourism Today: A Geographical Analysis*, 2nd edn. London: Longman.

Porter, P. W., and Sheppard, E. S. (1998). *A World of Difference: Society, Nature, Development*. New York: Guilford Press.

Pritchard, A., and Morgan, N. J. (2001). Culture, identity and tourism representation: Marketing Cymru or Wales? *Tourism Management* 22, 167–79.

Relph, E. (1976). *Place and Placelessness*. London: Pion.

Roovers, P., Hermy, M., and Gulinck H. (2002). Visitor profile, perceptions and expectations in forests from a gradient of increasing urbanization in central Belgium. *Landscape and Urban Planning* 59(3), 129–45.

Rose, G. (1996). Geography and the science of observation: The landscape, the gaze and masculinity. In J. Agnew, D. N. Livingstone, and A. Rogers (eds), *Human Geography: An Essential Anthology* (pp. 341–50). Oxford: Blackwell.

Sack, R. D. (1992). *Place, Modernity and the Consumer's World*. Baltimore: Johns Hopkins University Press.

Shaw, G., and Williams, A. M. (1994). *Critical Issues in Tourism: A Geographical Perspective*. Oxford: Blackwell.

Stefanou, J. (2000). The contribution of the analysis of the image of a place to the formulation of tourism policy. In H. Briassoulis and J. van der Straaten (eds), *Tourism and the Environment: Regional, Economic, Cultural and Policy Issues*, 2nd edn. (pp. 229–37). Dordrecht: Kluwer Academic Publishers.

Terkenli, T. S. (2000). Landscapes of tourism: A cultural geographical perspective. In H. Briassoulis and J. van der Straaten (eds), *Tourism and the Environment: Regional, Economic, Cultural and Policy Issues*, 2nd edn (pp. 179–202). Dordrecht: Kluwer Academic Publishers.

Terkenli, T. S. (2001). Towards a theory of the landscape: The Aegean landscape as a cultural image. *Landscape and Urban Planning* 57(3–4), 197–208.

Terkenli, T. S. (2002). Landscapes of tourism: Towards a global cultural economy of space? *Tourism Geographies* 4(3), 227–54.

Towner, J. (1996). *An Historical Geography of Recreation and Tourism in the Western World 1540–1940*. New York: John Wiley.

Tress, B., and Tress, G. (2001). Capitalising on multiplicity: A transdisciplinary systems approach to landscape research. *Landscape and Urban Planning* 57 (3–4), 143–57.

Urry, J. (1990). *The Tourist Gaze: Leisure and Travel in Contemporary Societies*. London: Sage.

Urry, J. (1995). *Consuming Places*. London: Routledge.

Chapter 28

The Beach as a Liminal Space

Robert Preston-Whyte

Introduction

The beach is a place of strong magic. As a material space it is a boundary zone where the hint of celestial forces is whispered by the ebb and flow of tides, a space that is neither land nor sea, a zone of uncertainty that resonates with the sound of ever-changing seas, a setting that is, by turns, calm, tranquil, and soothing or agitated, unruly, and frightening. As a cultural space it is a borderland that allows both difference and hybridity while facilitating the tactile tug of land or sea to reveal for many, but not all, spaces of heightened sensibilities that are temporary, personal, and elusive – in short, liminal spaces.

Western scriptings of the beach through various forms of discourse or representation contribute to its popularity, and probably also toward a sense of disappointment when the text fails to meet expectations. In addition to these exchanges the beach does seem to contain liminal properties that sustain its allure for many visitors. These come in many forms. For some the simple act of stepping onto the sand may be accompanied by a feeling of upliftment, a frisson of awareness, and a holistic sensation in which action and consciousness are merged at the moment of crossing into what we can call a liminal space. According to Turner (1982: 56), Czikszentmihalyi (1974) calls this experience "flow" and describes it as "a unified flowing from one moment to the next, in which we feel in control of our actions, and in which there is little distinction between self and environment; between stimulus and response; or between past, present and future."

Liminality is an elusive concept. Some of the ways in which this notion has been incorporated into Western imagination are illustrated in the next section. Attention is then directed to the liminal properties of beaches. Drawn from a largely Western perspective, social, spiritual, surfing, and nudist beach spaces are offered as examples of spaces where liminality may be found and experienced in various ways. Visitors may seek, but not necessarily find, on these beaches a space where the stress of normal working lives is temporarily suspended, cultures merge, egalitarianism flourishes, and bonds of friendship are forged. The reliance on Western viewpoints and the paucity of empirical exploration in the literature is, however, a recognized weakness.

Czikszentmihalyi's notion of liminality as "flow" may be a useful starting point to support or deepen our understanding of how liminal beach spaces are perceived and experienced. The lack of distinction between self and environment in his description echoes the call for a more symmetrical view of human and nonhuman "actors" by actor-network theorists such as Callon (1986), Latour (1987), and Law (1994), while the combination of "past, present and future" is reflected in Harvey's claim that "space and time . . . are not realities but relations derived from processes and events" (Harvey 1997: 258). The implication of these issues is addressed in the concluding section, where actor-network theory is proposed as an approach that may be employed to explore the nature of liminal beach experiences empirically and across cultural divides.

Notions of Liminality

Van Gennep (1960) first used this concept in 1909 in his work *Les Rites de passage* to describe the intermediate stage in the transition from adolescence to adulthood. Liminal, from the Latin word *limen*, meaning boundary or threshold, seemed to be an appropriate word to describe the transitional stage in the initiation process. This is the boundary that lies between the separation of adolescents from their social environment and their incorporation into adult life. It is also a liminal space with "the ritual subject passing through a period and an area of ambiguity, a sort of social limbo which has few (though sometimes these are most crucial) of the attributes of either the proceeding or subsequent profane social statuses or cultural states" (Turner 1982: 24).

Since its introduction, the notion of liminality has been employed in many diverse cultural and social contexts. Temporal markers such as religious festivals, birthdays, and holidays are associated with prescribed rituals and symbols. While the arrival of each such event is customarily prescribed by calendar days, it is sensed as an enchanted period between the past and the present, between before and after. Each event is experienced differently in accordance with social and cultural demands or by the imagination of individuals. For example, while some may be conditioned to the choice of midnight as a boundary between days, for others dusk may be a more meaningful borderline time to relax and contemplate this transition.

The notion of liminality is employed here as a metaphor to facilitate "a way of proceeding from the known to the unknown" (Nisbet 1969: 4), from the accepted symbols of the profane to the blurred, ambiguous, and powerful symbols of the sacred. Liminal spaces are intangible, elusive, and obscure. They lie in a limbo-like space often beyond normal social and cultural constraints. In these spaces can be found brief moments of freedom and an escape from the daily grind of social responsibilities. As a place of desire they offer a "dreamtime" that resonates with spiritual rebirth, transformation, and recuperation. However, transitional states are also places of anxiety replete with darker images of threat and danger. Images of the no man's land of First World War trench warfare, the perception of crossroads as magical places, and pilgrim's reactions to sacred places are some examples of "in-between" spaces that evoke responses to an imagined geography (Trubshaw 2002).

In each case the liminal experience involves crossing some form of imagined threshold. While this transition from the known to the unknown may be accompanied by unease in some cases, it may also produce a feeling of heightened sensitivity or a deeper awareness of the special qualities of the place. Novelists such as William Golding (1954) and Alex Garland (1997) use the setting of the beach to great effect in capturing these feelings in their novels. For example, in Alex Garland's (1997) novel *The Beach*, the main character, Richard, endures the dangers of both land and sea to find a secret and secluded beach community living a supposedly utopian existence on a remote island off the coast of Thailand. Initially the ambience of the beach meets their expectations. In seemingly timeless space amongst the beach community, Richard reflects: "You fish, swim, eat, laze around, and everyone's so friendly. It's such simple stuff but . . . if I could stop the world and restart life, put the clock back, I think I'd restart it like this. For everyone" (Garland 1997: 133).

Beach Spaces

From a Western perspective, beach spaces incorporate the space of leisure activities in the material environment, provide measures of difference between them, and integrate the symbolic values socially and culturally attached to them. The social construction of these spaces (Giddens 1984; Harvey 1989; Soja 1989; Lefebvre 1991; Shields 1991; Gregory 1994; Massey 1994; Simonsen 1996; Young 1999) is the product of processes and practices that define their use on the basis of specific leisure activities. They include spaces for bathing, surfboarding, yachting, sunbathing, fishing, and promenading as well as spaces for those who seek enjoyment of beach environments in wild and lonely places. While social constructions of space are likely to differ between individuals, Golledge (1978, 1981) suggests that general agreement over their identification produces sufficient congruence to provide common ground for their effective definition and partition. People make decisions on their choice of beach space and periods of use by employing constructivist thought that draws on the desired activities to be experienced as well as romanticized *a priori* knowledge of the space.

The attraction of the beach with its many activity spaces turns it into a space of culture–nature interface between land and sea (Jeans 1990). It becomes a place where the cultural tastes and preferences of visitors leave their indelible imprint (Hugill 1975; Shields 1990; Tunstall and Penning-Rowsell 1998; Preston-Whyte 2001), and where changes in carrying capacities (Pearce and Kirk 1986), structure and morphology (Stansfield 1969; Pigram 1977; Pearce 1978; Franz 1985) and development history (Urry 1990; Haywood 1992; Ioannides 1992; Smith 1992; Agarwal 1997) impact on the socioeconomic, political, and natural environment.

The elusive quality of liminality does not seem to fit easily with either the social construction approach or the revelation of how development and use may change the beach. What is needed is an approach that expands our understanding of the nature of liminal spaces in places that range from wild, deserted, and remote beaches to those along settled coastlines. How and where is liminality experienced in association with beach activities such as fishing, surfing, and boardsailing? Do scuba divers become immersed in a placeless place between the familiar and the unfamiliar, the known and the unknown, beneath the waves? Do bathers and surfers experience a temporary suspension of time as they confront the raw energy unleashed by breaking waves? In what sense do piers built into and beyond the surf zone create a space suspended between land and sea, a connective tissue between two worlds? Can one assume that for some people liminal spaces may even be found in seaside resorts where paved promenades adjacent to the sand provide spaces of relaxation where, singly or in groups, they may move into a space of heightened sensitivity as they walk, run, cycle, or rollerblade? These questions need to be answered by employing appropriate epistemological, ontological, and methodological tools to discover why, where, and how people perceive and experience liminal beach spaces.

An approach that seeks to understand the notion of liminality must also accommodate factors that are thought to inhibit the experience. It is assumed, for example, that visitor recognition of the ugliness of overdeveloped, overcrowded, noisy, and polluted seaside resorts leads to disappointment and the frustration of their efforts to find the liminality they seek. In his novel, Alex Garland (1997) vividly captures this reaction through the eyes of Richard when he is sent to collect supplies for the secret beach community at Hat Rin, a nearby island resort:

> Before I'd been looking at Hat Rin with detached curiosity, and now I was looking at it with hatred . . . Most of all, I could pick up the scent of decay. It hung over Hat Rin like the sandflies that hung over the sunbathers, zoning in on the smell of sweat and sweet tanning lotion. The serious travelers had already moved on to the next island in the chain, the intermediate travelers were wondering where all the life had gone, and the tourist hordes were ready to descend on their freshly beaten track. (Garland 1997: 177)

It is also assumed that those who are engaged in their everyday duties such as lifeguards, rubbish collectors, and law enforcement officers, do not perceive the beach with the same enthusiasm as its visitors. The existence of these officials is also a sign that beaches can be a place of danger. Unpredictable currents are a threat to weak swimmers, and, where they occur, tsunamis and storm surges are a threat to all. Human waste and marine disturbances such as red tide threaten both visitors and sea creatures. The possibility of social and criminal violence threatens the viability of the beach as a space of relaxation. Despite this there is the ongoing transformation of many beaches to an environment in which Western cultural values signpost activities devoted to the consumption of pleasure and recreation. As Lencek and Bosker (1999: xix) note, "Nature's most potent antidepressant, the beach moves us with the power of a drug, the rhythm of its tides and shifting margins reorienting our sense of space and time, its aphrodisiacal cocktail of sun and water firing our slumbering hedonism."

These sensations of the seashore inspire social, spiritual, surfing, and nudist beach spaces, all of which have liminal potential. In each of these examples it is worth considering the extent to which natural and social elements of the beach environment are woven together in a framework of heterogeneous associations that may contribute toward the creation of a timeless space suspended between land and sea. In general attention is drawn only to the positive features of liminal beach spaces since it is these that attract those in search of such spaces. This does not mean, however, that tensions between individuals cannot develop within these spaces or that threats caused by social or natural elements cannot suddenly disrupt liminal states.

Social spaces

Beaches are generally perceived to present a smiling face to humanity. This makes them desirable places to socialize and relax (Shields 1990). So strongly do such spaces shape the lives of some that, "my great-uncle Arturo Manzoni was reputed to have said: 'there are three phases of life: birth, *beach* and death'" (Lencek and Bosker 1999: xix). However, whether or not the regeneration, relaxation, and recreation associated with beaches induce a sense of liminality in social settings is likely to depend on the nature of the conditions conducive to releasing the magic of the place.

There is no single imperative that sets out the conditions that shape the nature of liminal social spaces on beaches. Instead a variety of forms exist that may be as changeable as the beach itself. Alex Garland (1997) provides one setting in his novel that highlights a sense of belonging, and an unquestioned acceptance by a multicultural society, when Richard comments, "Assimilation: from day one we were working, everyone knew our names, we had beds allocated in the longhouse. I felt like I'd been living there all my life" (Garland 1997: 115). While this image of the beach may be portrayed as a "third space" (Bhabha 1994; Soja 1996) where hybridity is encouraged, such social conditions may be fragile and temporary. This too is vividly portrayed in Garland's novel when the social harmony of the beach community with its illusion of liminality is shattered by food poisoning and the death of two of its members through shark bites.

If hybridity is a feature of some beach spaces, difference may shape the social conditions in others as notions of group identity, formed on the basis of social and cultural attitudes, enhance the "We" of shared identity and exacerbate the perception and definition of "Others" as outsiders (Crang 1998). Preston-Whyte (2001) shows how such reasoning can lead to beach spaces that are socially and culturally identified, constructed, and contested. Garland (1997: 144) also portrays a fear of intrusion by uninvited visitors through his characters' belief that "The world is everything outside the beach." In this case the imaginary boundaries that people erect to reduce fear of the "Other" are symbolized by the cliffs and reef that protected the sanctuary of the secluded beach space.

Spiritual spaces

The beach provides a fascination for many religious sects that see the interface between land and sea as an auspicious environment in which seek intercession with their deity. The symbolism attached to dawn, and the cleansing act of immersion that takes place during religious ceremonies on beaches, are probably ages old. These actions seem to induce in believers a feeling of religious passion that imbues the beach with special meaning. It becomes a liminal space in which normal statuses are temporarily suspended: it becomes a sacred place.

The beach is recognized, symbolized, and used in different ways in different places as a meeting ground with the sacred. An internet search for "beach worship" reveals a startling number of religious groups that see the beach as a locale where its members can experience spiritual solace and support. However, the manner in which this activity takes place is likely to exhibit cultural variation.

Religious meetings of mainly black South Africans on the beaches of Durban, South Africa are regularly witnessed by the author and are offered as an example within a cultural context. On some weekends the sound of drums accompanied by singing heralds the start of a pre-dawn ceremony. The rising sun reveals a group of worshipers, most clad in white robes. Lighted candles may be arranged in a circle or semi-circle behind them. The officiant, identified by a blue sash or some other form of differentiating clothing, leads the prayers and singing. At some stage worshipers move to the sea and are ceremonially dowsed in the waves.

Throughout the ceremony the eye is drawn to the officiant, who orchestrates the vibrant singing, the spiritual engagement with the deity, and the pulsating throb of drums. The worshipers appear lost in a world of exaltation, a liminal space where faith and religious fervor create a sense of community, identity, and forged bonds. Bystanders gaze from a respectful distance, excluded from the experience and left to wonder and comment from their various cultural perspectives.

Although many religious groups are structured to accommodate communal worship, the beach is also a place to retreat from the turmoil of life in order to establish contact with one's inner self. In solitude the symbolic act of meditation is about entering a liminal space for the purpose of "setting aside time to attend to the hearth of your inner life" (Louden 2002: 1).

Surfing spaces

Surfing on waves that form and break along a shelving shore is a popular leisure activity on many beaches. For many surfers it becomes a compulsive pursuit that draws on a range of emotions. Augustin (1998: 589) notes "a changed relationship between body and nature that enhances spontaneity, imagination, and a need to be free," and draws attention to the attractive prospect of escaping institutional constraints for those who participate in *sport libre* (footloose sports) such as surfing. Entry into the sea to confront breaking waves induces a sense of well-being, a suspension of time, and a communion with self.

Surfers focus their attention on riding a board across the face of a building wave that is steep, smooth, high, and about to break. To the uninitiated this robust activity seems distant from the introspective spaces of religious groups and individuals. Yet the compulsive enthusiasm with which surfers daily confront waves suggest that surfing spaces provide a liminal experience that is equally intense. The short-lived adrenaline rush of a ride on or within a breaking wave is a place where time and space are concentrated. It is a moment of exhilaration in a liminal space before the collapse of a wave in a tumult of sound and fury. The desire to relive the experience is like an addictive drug.

The need to satisfy this addiction leads to a search for the best surfing spaces. Preston-Whyte (2002) shows that surfers gather in spaces where the wave shape is most suitable for surfing. This has two major outcomes. Firstly, surfers become socialized into a "subculture" that is companionable, competitive, and exclusive. Secondly, as the surfing population increases surfing space becomes a scarce resource. The issue of space and its control then becomes centered on notions of territoriality (Wesemann 1998) and identity. Territorial surfing groups possess a strong sense of identity honed through displays of skill and knowledge in coping with formidable waves, reinforced by their dedication and commitment to surfing and expressed through the use of "insider" vocabulary (Preston-Whyte 2002).

Under these conditions, access to prized and often scarce surfing space may require newcomers to participate in a rite of passage that is reminiscent of the transition discussed by van Gennep (1960). Before being accepted by exclusive groups newcomers must demonstrate their dedication and commitment to the sport, their surfing skill, knowledge about waves and currents, and respect for the rules and etiquette of the sport. The reward gained by the successful transition from newcomer to group member is the joy of riding the waves in the most liminal of surfing spaces.

Nudist spaces

The signs and symbols assigned to the wearing of clothes are associated with indicators of power, status, and gender in most Western societies. In these societies, public nudity commonly carries with it a level of social opprobrium, largely shaped by religious dogma, which tends to be articulated through expressions of disgust, disapproval, and suspicion. If the subject of nudist beaches is raised in social gatherings there are likely to be three responses. The first is a stern rebuke for even considering such aberrant sinful behavior. The second is a shifty-eyed denial of any interest in the practice of nudism. The third is enthusiastic acknowledgment of support for nudist beaches.

The third group of respondents appears to be growing in number. An exploration of the internet reveals a large number of nudist beaches on the continent of Europe, North America, and Australia. More relaxed attitudes on the part of local administrators and the police have accompanied the growing popularity of "clothing optional" public beaches. Many such beaches now have tacit recognition from local authorities and some have even progressed to the next stage of acquiring legal status. Morfa beach at Dyffryn Ardudwy near Barmouth in Wales is an example where 30 years of disrobing has finally received official recognition. Morfa beach is acclaimed to be the nation's first official nudist beach (BBC News 2002). What is the attraction of these beaches?

It would be naive to expect a simple answer to this question. There is little doubt, however, that "nudists" are attracted by the liminal nature of these beaches. The discourse of nature emphasizes tolerance, and a passive sensuality is tamed by individual self-regulation (Evans 2000). There is also a sense of liberation that comes with disrobing. "Nudity," according to Skye Delaney (2002), "is in fact a metaphor for peeling off false layers of the self. The many masks we wear in life, the many layers of falsehood that get us from one place to the next, can sometimes result in exhaustion." This suggests that nudist beaches are spaces of relaxation where the atmosphere of liminality allows the stressed and largely educated "free-thinkers" to relax and release the tensions of life. Evans (2000: 17) draws on Stam's (1988) critique of Mikhail Bakhtin's notion of Carnival in a searching analysis of motivation to suggest that

> Eros and nudity; the doffing of symbols of class and the mixing of distinct social groups; the ambiguity of a semiotics without clothes; communal rites of disrobing; and the background

discourses of utopian freedom; all these phenomena at Wreck Beach combine with its ideational and geographical marginality to produce a Carnival atmosphere in Bakhtin's sense.

The ease of access, liberation and sense of community that characterize the timeless atmosphere of nudist beaches is admirably captured by Evans (2000: 19):

> The cost of entry is small – a willingness to dispense with normative ideals of modesty and propriety. Once naked, people, no matter what their class, gender, or ethnic origins, are bona fide members of the community. In their nudity, they share a bond, a trans-personal sense of belonging. In their ritualized participation in the timeless space of sun-worship, they mutually step outside the tyranny of the clock and the tyranny of "normal" surveillance. They are, in a sense, united in a timeless space of ludic pleasure and sensual recuperation; they belong to a place out of time and out of normalcy.

The tolerance and lack of barriers of exclusion on nudist beaches also provide access to those who seem unable to tame their sexuality. A recurrent theme on these beaches worldwide appears to be the irritation of the masculine gaze by dressed men who persist in regarding women as objects of sexual consumption. This, and other forms of inappropriate behavior, can diminish the magic of the spaces that nudists seek. However, social opprobrium that could produce "a public politics of shame" (Evans 2000: 28), tends to be inhibited by the tolerant culture of nudist beaches.

A Way Forward?

The discussion on beaches as liminal spaces needs to be deepened. The dominance of a Western perspective that assumes liminality to be linked with heightened sensibilities associated with the temporary suspension of normal states, coupled with a paucity of empirical exploration of the nature of the symbolism of these threshold spaces, needs to be addressed by appropriate research strategies. Epistemologically and ontologically two main issues seem to be important in the choice of a suitable approach. First, the human actors, with their cultural discourse and symbols to conceptualize and tame the beach, and the non-human actors that constitute the material conditions of the beach itself with its attractions and dangers, must be dealt with on equal terms. Secondly, dualisms, such as nature/culture, that feature so strongly in socio-spatial analysis, need to be addressed (Demeritt 1996; Murdock 1997a; Watmore 1998, 2000).

Actor-network theory is one approach that may provide a way of extending our comprehension of liminality. Developed by Michel Callon, Bruno Latour, and John Law in their attempt to understand the construction of knowledge in science (e.g., Callon 1986; Latour 1987; Law 1994), actor-network theory has attracted considerable attention, not least because of the development of a philosophy focused on a unified theoretical perspective that promises a non-dualistic standpoint that combines the social and the material. Murdock (1997b) provides a good review.

Actor-network theorists maintain that the stability and durability of society is based on a network of interactions and associations that include non-human actors. Emphasis is placed on the symmetrical analysis of humans and non-humans, as they strive to build networks along the chain of associations that comprise them. Instead of agency being associated solely with human activity, in actor-network theory,

> agents (both human and non-human) emerge from a series of trials in which they are continually striving to become actors with powers; it is only at the end of the period of network stabilization that the actors/agents/actants can be distinguished from the lesser entities which by now are simple intermediaries, that is links in a network. (Murdock 1997a: 330)

The network ontology is concerned with the heterogeneity of networks in which subjects, objects, and the relations between them (social and material) are "seamlessly entwined within complex sets of association" (Murdock 1998: 359).

The use of actor-network theory as a philosophical discourse to deepen our understanding of liminal beach spaces will require epistemological and ontological shifts for many researchers. In particular it requires the incorporation of nonhuman actors in philosophical perspective. The study of social networks informed by social constructions would need to be replaced by networks that

> draw together materials, which have their own space-times, into new configurations which, to some extent, reflect the type of relations established in the network (that is networks and spaces are generated together). Thus each network traces its own particular space-time which reflects both the variety of the materials used in construction and the relations established between the combined elements. (Murdock 1998: 361)

The notion of liminal space as a transition between ways of being may also need revision or at least restructuring to reflect the manner in which the relations between actors, entities, and places are negotiated and represented in a process called *translation* (Callon 1986; Latour 1987). Networks may turn out to be stable or unstable depending upon the success of the translation process. A network becomes stabilized when the translation process allows successful integration of the component parts "thereby allowing the enrolling actor (the 'center') to 'speak' for all" (Murdock 1998: 362). It is through tracing networks along the path to the point of network stabilization (or destabilization) that actors/actants/agents may reveal the enigma of liminal spaces. A research agenda employing actor-network theory may be a useful approach to reveal cross-cultural views on the same beach as well as on different beaches across the world. We might then be in a better position to make sense of the cryptic comment made by Richard in Alex Garland's novel: "It doesn't matter why I found it so easy to assimilate myself into beach life. The question is why the beach life found it so easy to assimilate me" (Garland 1997: 116).

REFERENCES

Agarwal, S. (1997). The resort cycle and seaside tourism: An assessment of its applicability and validity. *Tourism Management* 18(2), 65–73.

Augustin, J.-P. (1998). Emergence of surfing resorts on the Aquitaine littoral. *The Geographical Review* 88(4), 587–95.

BBC News (2002). Wales has first nudist beach. <http://news.bbc.co.uk/hi/english/uk/wales/newsid_749000/749768.stm> (accessed February 14, 2002).

Bhabha, H. K. (1994). *The Location of Culture*. London: Routledge.

Callon, M. (1986). Some elements in a sociology of translation: Domestication of the scallops and fishermen of St Brieuc Bay. In J. Law (ed.), *Power, Action, Belief* (pp. 19–34). London: Routledge & Kegan Paul.

Crang, M. (1998). *Cultural Geography*. London: Routledge.

Czikszentmihalyi, M. (1974). *Flow: Studies of Enjoyment*. Chicago: University of Chicago, PHS Grant Report.

Delaney, S. (2002). Nude beaches: A link to spiritual transformation. <http://www.fiber-net.com/pub/he/NWM_Magazine_May_June_2000/NWM_Delaney_NudeBeaches_Page1.htm> (accessed February 14, 2002).

Demeritt, D. (1996). Social theory and the reconstruction of science and geography. *Transactions, Institute of British Geographers* NS 21, 484–503.

Evans, R. (2000). *Paradise on the Margins or Paradise Lost? Tolerance, Permissiveness and Conflict on Wreck Beach*. Arkleton Research Papers 5. Aberdeen: University of Aberdeen.

Franz, J. C. (1985). Pattaya–Penang–Bali: Asia's leading beach resorts. *Tourism Recreation Research* 10(1), 25–9.

Garland, A. (1997). *The Beach*. London: Penguin Books.

Giddens, A. (1984). *The Constitution of Society*. Cambridge: Polity.

Golding, W. (1954). *Lord of the Flies*. London: Faber & Faber.

Golledge, R. G. (1978). Representing, interpreting and using cognised environments. *Papers of the Regional Science Association* 41, 169–204.

Golledge, R. G. (1981). Misconceptions, misinterpretations and misrepresentations of behavioural approaches in human geography. *Environment and Planning A* 13(11), 1325–44.

Gregory, D. (1994). *Geographical Imaginations*. Oxford: Blackwell.

Harvey, D. (1989). *The Condition of Postmodernity*. Oxford: Blackwell.

Harvey, D. (1997). *Justice, Nature and the Geography of Difference*. Oxford: Blackwell.

Haywood, K. M. (1992). Revisiting the resort cycle. *Annals of Tourism Research* 19, 351–4.

Hugill, P. J. (1975). Social conduct on the golden mile. *Annals of the Association of American Geographers* 65(2), 214–28.

Ioannides, D. (1992). Tourism development agents: The Cypriot resort cycle. *Annals of Tourism Research* 19(4), 711–31.

Jeans, D. N. (1990). Beach resort morphology in England and Australia: A review and extension. In P. Fabbri (ed.), *Recreational Uses of Coastal Areas* (pp. 277–85). Dordrecht: Kluwer.

Latour, B. (1987). *Science in Action: How to Follow Scientists and Engineers through Society*. Milton Keynes: Open University Press.

Law, J. (1994). *Organizing Modernity*. Oxford: Blackwell.

Lefebvre, A. (1991). *The Production of Space*. Oxford: Blackwell.

Lencek, L., and Bosker, G. (1999). *The Beach: The History of Paradise on Earth*. London: Pimlico.

Louden, J. (2002). The call to retreat. <http://www.women-empowerment-women.org/spirituality04.html> (accessed February 14, 2002).

Massey, D. (1994). Double articulation: A place in the world. In A. Bammer (ed.), *Displacements: Cultural Identities in Question* (pp. 110–21). Bloomington: Indiana University Press.

Murdock, J. (1997a). Towards a geography of heterogeneous associations. *Progress in Human Geography* 21(3), 321–37.

Murdock, J. (1997b). Inhuman/nonhuman/human: Actor-network theory and prospects for a non-dualistic and symmetrical perspective on nature and society. *Environment and Planning D: Society and Space* 15, 731–56.

Murdock, J. (1998). The spaces of actor-network theory. *Geoforum* 29(4), 357–74.

Nisbet, R. A. (1969). *Social Change and History: Aspects of the Western Theory of Development.* London: Oxford University Press.
Pearce, D. G. (1978). Form and function in French resorts. *Annals of Tourism Research* 5(1), 142–56.
Pearce, D. G., and Kirk, R. M. (1986). Carrying capacities for coastal tourism. *Industry and Environment* 9(1), 3–6.
Pigram, J. J. J. (1977). Beach resort morphology. *Habitat International* 2(5–6), 525–41.
Preston-Whyte, R. A. (2001). Construction of seaside tourist spaces at Durban. *Annals of Tourism Research* 28(3), 581–96.
Preston-Whyte, R. A. (2002) Construction of surfing space at Durban, South Africa. *Tourism Geographies* 4(3), 307–28.
Shields, R. (1990). The "system of pleasure": Liminality and the carnivalesque at Brighton. *Theory, Culture and Society* 7, 39–72.
Shields, R. (1991). *Places on the Margin: Alternative Geographies of Modernity.* London: Routledge.
Simonsen, K. (1996). What kind of space in what kind of social theory? *Progress in Human Geography* 20, 494–512.
Smith, R. A. (1992). Beach resort evolution: Implications for planning. *Annals of Tourism Research* 19(2), 304–22.
Soja, E. (1989). *Postmodern Geographies: The Reassertion of Space in Critical Social Theory.* London: Verso.
Soja, E. (1996). *Thirdspace.* Oxford: Blackwell.
Stam, R. (1988). Mikhail Bakhtin and the left cultural critique. In E.A. Kaplin (ed.), *Postmodernism and its Discontents* (pp. 116–45). London: Verso.
Stansfield, C. A. (1969). Recreational land use patterns within an American seaside resort. *Tourist Review* 24(4), 128–36.
Trubshaw. B. (2002). Why Christopher Robin wouldn't walk in the cracks: An introduction to the liminality of place and space. <http://www.liminalspace.co.uk/edition%201.htm> (accessed February 14, 2002).
Tunstall, S. M., and Penning-Rowsell, E. G. (1998). The English beach: Experience and values. *The Geographical Review* 164(3), 319–32.
Turner, V. (1982). *From Ritual to Theatre: The Human Seriousness of Play.* New York: Performing Arts Journal Publications.
Urry, J. (1990). *The Tourist Gaze: Leisure and Travel in Contemporary Societies.* London: Sage.
van Gennep, A. (1960). *The Rites of Passage,* trans. M. B. Vizedom and G. L. Caffee. Chicago: University of Chicago Press.
Watmore, S. (1998). Wild(er)ness: Reconfiguring the geographies of wildlife. *Transactions, Institute of British Geographers* NS 23, 435–54.
Watmore, S. (2000). Elephants on the move: Spatial formations of wildlife exchange. *Environment and Planning D: Society and Space* 18, 185–203.
Wesemann, D. (1998). Unite, don't fight. *South African Bodyboarding Magazine* 7(8), 6.
Young, M. (1999). The social construction of tourist places. *Australian Geographer* 30(3), 373–89.

Chapter 29

Tourism, Shopping, and Retailing: An Axiomatic Relationship?

Tim Coles

Introduction: Toward Identification of the Latent Links

At face value the relationship between tourism and retailing is an obvious one. All tourism experiences inevitably begin with purchasing episodes. Flights are bought, accommodation is booked and paid for, currency is exchanged, and film, sun-tan lotion, guidebooks, and sundry other accouterments are acquired for the trip in prospect. The dynamics of the commodity-driven world don't stop with pre-travel planning and procurement. Once in the resort, tourists find a panoply of ways to part with their money: hospitality, services, and amenities are exchanged for the "tourist dollar," while trophies from the visit, souvenirs of those special memories, are outcomes of decisions to go shopping. Beyond such obvious, superficial connections several authors have pointed to the role of shopping in choreographing the tourism experience. Timothy and Butler (1995) note that shopping has become not only a major motivational component in the destination selection process, but also a key determinant in shaping activity patterns in tourism episodes. Increasingly tourists are making trips for the purpose of shopping, with sites, acts, and practices of consumption paramount in their travel planning. Shopping tourism – that is shopping as a distinctive form of tourism – is distinguished from shopping as a component of (another type of) tourism (activity).

Travel agents and tour operators have recognized this trend. Within the UK short breaks are marketed to the champagne region of France. Long-weekend coach tours are offered to the Rhine Valley in the run-up to Christmas to allow more imaginative shoppers the opportunity to give their loved ones gifts sourced from "authentic" German Christmas markets. Such practices have been recognized by retailers. Telfer (2001) notes how local wineries have joined forces to develop the Niagara Wine Route and thereby promote the Niagara region as a destination for wine tourism. Indeed, the Niagara Wine Route is hardly unique in this respect (Hall and Macionis 1998). Dedicated packages deliver acolytes to the high altars of consumption in North America, West Edmonton Mall (WEM) and the Mall of America. In addition to the vast expanses of retail space, hotels, hospitality, and recreational attractions are embedded in the mall environment to offer the tourist shopper a fully integrated leisure-shopping experience (Butler 1991; Goss 1993, 1999).

Trips motivated by purchase and consumption are not new. Fin-de-siècle department store owners encouraged shopping tourism by offering free delivery services and by participating in the earliest visitor guidebooks, which they gave away to their major patrons, many of whom visited the resorts for the season. By the fin-de-millennium, the principal transformations were more sophisticated linkages between retailers, tourists, and destinations as well as the more blurred distinctions between tourism, leisure, and shopping (see also Jackson 1991). As Jansen-Verbeke (1990: 4) notes, the role of shopping in leisure time has changed greatly as a "series of interconnected social, economic and cultural trends are creating new behavior patterns and new demands." Shopping is no longer merely an essential act of acquisition to maintain household units. Instead, as Shields (1992) argues, increasing emphasis in society on consumption and the acquisition of material goods has redefined the role of shopping. Beyond "shopping as quartermastering," shopping for discretionary, often non-essential goods has become an integral element in contemporary active recreation. Timothy and Butler (1995: 17) note that many people view shopping as a way of fulfilling part of their need for leisure, and ultimately tourism, as shopping offers enjoyment and even relaxation. Moreover, following Shields' reading more faithfully, the fusion of shopping as symbolic consumptive practice with tourism has resulted in entirely new product-driven modes of tourism directed at conspicuous displays of consumption. Global automotive brands such as Audi, Daimler-Chrysler (Mercedes Benz), Harley Davidson, and Morgan offer their customers the opportunity to visit their factories to view their products being made on the assembly line, and to preview their future purchases.

The relationship between tourism, retailing, and shopping should be of fundamental concern. On a more functional level, it helps to develop a much fuller understanding of people's motives for, and actual consumption of, time and space by fusing shopping with other leisure pursuits (cf. Wrigley and Lowe 2002). Distinctive spaces and place images are mediated to satisfy the new imperatives and modes of consumption (Butler 1991; Warnaby 1998). More importantly, the relationship engages with many contemporary critical debates in the social sciences. For instance, the interface between tourism and shopping endorses a prevailing paradigm of the world structured as a series of global networks of local places dominated by linkages and flows. Through tourists' shopping, goods, knowledge, and experiences flow from the extra-ordinary world of the tourist destination to the mundane, everyday world of home.

The more the relationship between tourism and shopping is teased apart, the more its apparently self-evident, obvious nature begins to be questioned, its full complexity revealed, and its prevailing orthodoxies challenged. The purpose of this chapter is to unravel some of the intricacies of this complex nexus and to explore some of the critical issues associated with the connectivities between tourism, shopping, and retailing. One of the principal themes here is the need for greater collaboration between interdisciplinary studies of retailing on the one hand and tourism on the other. Although both profess an interest in leisure, there has been little constructive dialogue between the two, a state of affairs hardly aided by the estrangement between the subdisciplines of retail and tourism geography. As will become clear, the tourism-shopping-retailing nexus is characterized by several contradictions. For instance, although it is both an axiomatic and hence pivotal association, in contrast to other themes in tourism research, it has not been the subject of widespread critical attention. Only one systematic treaty on the topic has been compiled (Timothy 2003). Equally, although it has not attracted the same volume of interest as other issues in tourism research, those aspects – such as souvenir purchasing – that have been prioritized, have been heavily reported. As such, the challenge is how to progress the agenda. Here it is argued that the adaptation of ideas from retail geography in tourism geography may offer one distinctive path forward.

The Supply Chain as an Organizing Principle

Ultimately, academic interest in the relationship between tourism, shopping, and retailing centers on one moment, the transaction. Interest in shopping tourism – or tourists shopping more widely – is predicated on the fact that tourists buy items, and to do so they require a retailer before the exchange of payment for commodity can take place. Like all other consumers, tourists are usually final participants in complex channels of distribution (cf. Gregson and Crewe 1997; but see also below), notwithstanding the fact that they are subject to special sets of circumstances and conditions. Conceptually, transactions may be read from either the retailer's or consumer's perspective; that is, from the demand or supply side. Primarily they have been viewed from the perspective of the tourist as consumer, while the necessity for, and role of, the retailer has been relatively overlooked. Semantics used in existing discourses accentuate "shopping," "purchasing," and "acquisition" as key descriptors of tourist exchanges: tourists shop, retailers offer; tourists purchase, retailers sell; tourists acquire, retailers proffer.

To date, work in this area has been highly fragmented and is in need of a robust framework through which to synthesize the multiple strands. The supply chain serves as a helpful structural framework for two principal reasons. First, rather than focusing exclusively on the tourist as shopper or the products tourists acquire, the supply chain as an organizing concept offers the opportunity to develop a much fuller understanding of the connections, meanings, and outcomes beyond the point of final transaction. The second reason is that it forms a central, albeit understated and assumed, idea within the new geography of retailing (Lowe and Wrigley 1996). Thus, it offers a medium by which the two sub-disciplines may be reconciled with one another to their mutual benefit.

At its simplest, the supply chain represents a basic linear model by which goods are distributed from the original producer to the final consumer. In the final stage of the supply chain the retail transaction takes place; the consumer buys the commodity from the retailer in exchange for money or other goods (barter). There are several variants of the supply chain depending on whether there are intermediaries such as wholesalers involved in conveying the goods from producer to retailer (or even consumer), or whether the producers, artisans, or craftsmen themselves are also the retailers to the final consumer. In more recent work, several authors have explored the concept of disposal; that is, consumers getting rid of goods after they have lost material value and, more usually, non-material relevance to their lives. Souvenirs of special trips, that may have taken pride of place on display in homes for visitors to gaze upon in awe, may lose their appeal or be replaced by the latest reminders and fashions. Gifts from generous relatives of their visits to far-flung and exotic places may lose their charm and are disposed of to precipitate a second cycle of consumption. The spaces and settings of disposal such as flea markets, car boot sales, secondhand book stores, and charity shops have themselves become leisure and consumption spaces in their own right, and a prime motive for journeys (Gregson and Crewe 1997; Gregson, Brooks, and Crewe 2000). Clearly, in connecting consumers with retailers and producers, the supply chain begins to draw our attention to the full dimensions and implications of marketing tourism merchandise, such as unfolding networks of entrepreneurial activity, the evolving social relations and organization of production, resource usage, community outcomes, and the impact on local culture.

Thomas Mann's 1912 novella *Death in Venice* hints at the full potential of the supply chain as a lens through which to project the critical issues, and to illuminate a path forward. Mann sketches an encounter between his anti-hero, Gustav von Aschenbach, and the gondoliers and artisans of Venice. Already world-weary, von Aschenbach "has some trouble getting to his destination, as the gondolier was in league with lace factories and glassworks and tried to land him at every place where he might view the wares and make a purchase; and whenever this bizarre journey through Venice might have cast his spell on him, he was effectively and irksomely disenchanted by the cutpurse mercantile spirit of the sunken queen of the Adriatic" (Mann 1998: 229).

What Mann's narrative reveals is that the supply chain is a flexible framework which makes it much easier to compare the dimensions and implications of marketing goods to tourists by different channels of distribution and forms of retail organization. Furthermore, it is a framework which allows the full economic, social, and cultural outcomes of the process to be interpreted simultaneously. The organization of distribution can be read alongside the social relations of distribution, the social politics of consumption, and the unfolding impress on community, culture, and environment. In von Aschenbach's case, his encounter is with the glass-blowers and lace-makers who are attempting to furnish him with mementoes of his stay. Contemporary discourses on souvenirs reflect the enduring role of small-scale artisanal producer-retailers in this respect (Hitchcock and Teague 2000). Tourists are not limited to these forms of distribution, as is demonstrated by work on their consumption of individual shops, shopping malls (Butler 1991), airport terminals (Freathy and O'Connor 1999; Hobson 2000), cooperatives (McGhee and Meares 1998), and street traders and itinerants (Timothy and Wall 1997). Furthermore, transactions between tourists and retailers do not always take place in formally regulated channels, but rather in informal situations (Timothy and Wall 1997) and sometimes through non-cash (i.e. barter) exchange (Zhao 1994).

Each of these forms of transaction and exchange setting exists in its own distinctive supply chain. As work by Foord, Bowlby, and Tillsley (1996) reminds us, supply chains and channels of distribution are not homogeneous and they vary in time and space, and in relation to the commodity conveyed. Retail organizations are not evenly distributed across space, and distinctive placial constellations of producers, intermediaries, and retailers are produced depending on local framing conditions of culture, society, economy, and regulation. These result, in turn, in singular sets of social relations of production and distribution. For instance, in relatively primitive systems of production and distribution, a surfeit of producers may put wholesalers and retailers at an advantage when dictating price, product form, and delivery date. Conversely, where commodities are scarce or brands are exclusive, distribution through retailers and wholesalers may be dictated more closely by producers. Thus, exchanges toward the end of the supply chain have consequences further "up" it. Power relations between actors vary in the supply chain, for instance between tourist and retailer, retailer and (wholesale) supplier, or between retailer and producer. Unfolding power relations of this variety, alone or in concert, have the ability to determine the nature of the transactions or the social relations of the interpersonal encounters; pricing and quality of goods; the "authenticity" of the products; and the impacts of the transaction on local communities, cultures, and environments. Von Aschenbach's unfortunate incident suggests that the power is ultimately in the hands of the craftsmen-retailers and their ability to draw the gondoliers (i.e. the transport infrastructure) into league. However, the general lessons of the combination of power and outcomes may be equally applied to Moreno and Littrell's (2001) work on retailers as key intermediaries in the delivery of contemporary Guatemalan textile goods to tourists. Similarly, cruise ships and coach drivers act as "gatekeepers" of visitor shopping experiences. Rather than influence the productive practices in the supply chain, these intermediaries choreograph the retail opportunities available to their passengers by dictating the settings of consumption and the time available to develop encounters (Dean 1991).

Finally, von Aschenbach's experience suggests a conspiracy of producers and tourists was unfolding, with important placial outcomes. Production, marketing, and distribution of artisanally produced goods had acknowledged, and been geared to (most certainly in terms of volume if not necessarily of quality, design, and style), the emergence of distinct demand from tourists. For many early tourists, shopping had become a central experience in the vacation. Infrastructure had developed to facilitate the effective, if not somewhat duplicitous delivery of the consumer to the products and their distributors, the craftsmen-retailers of Venice. For von Aschenbach, the imposition is unwelcome and to be resisted at all costs. In contrast, others before him clearly must have enjoyed the experience, and some must have submitted to it, unable to assert their will over the intermediaries; but either way it emboldened the producers and their agents, the gondoliers, to pursue their enterprise further. Whether this approach was wise or not is debatable, not least because the prevailing culture of commerce shapes von Aschenbach's very dim view of the destination. As Warnaby's (1998) work suggests, the importance of shopping in mediating a destination's place imagery is not a process unique to the early stages of mass tourism. Late twentieth-century towns and cities increasingly turned to culture, leisure, and shopping as a means of reinventing themselves in the eyes of investors and visitors.

In what remains of this chapter progress made toward understanding three main facets of the relationship between tourism, retailing, and shopping will be sketched out. These are: gearing production and products for the tourist market; the encounters, episodes, and performances of tourism shopping; and finally the settings and spaces for tourists' shopping.

Products, Producers, Production, and Distribution

When considering the purchases made by tourists there is a temptation to fall into the trap that they are predominantly, if not exclusively, souvenirs. According to Healy (1994: 138), it is important to distinguish between souvenirs and tourist merchandise, which he defines as "any tangible item purchased by tourists at a destination and intended to be transported subsequently off-site." Among tourist merchandise he includes five categories: natural products, handicrafts, other hand-made items (such as artisanally produced foodstuffs), local manufactures (such as alcoholic beverages, furniture, and other factory-made items), and non-local goods retailed at tourist sites such as film, postcards, guidebooks, T-shirts, and sporting equipment. Commodities in each of these categories have the potential to become souvenirs. According to Anderson and Littrell (1995: 328), "souvenirs help owners define and situate in time and place experiences they wish to remember. The souvenir is a tangible symbol and reminder of an experience that differs from daily routine and that otherwise would remain intangible, such as memories of people, places and events." What both these definitions gloss over is that tourists and residents often struggle over the same goods, services, and amenities in their consumption episodes. Although goods are often tailored and deliberately marketed for the tourist gaze (and purse strings!), this does not necessarily have to be the case. Straightforward lifestyle products such as CDs, clothes, food and drink, even cars and motorcycles, can function as tourism merchandise and souvenirs as well as (relatively) more routine, mundane signifiers of everyday life. They are transformed into tourism merchandise by the actions of tourists, how and where they are consumed, the settings and performances of purchase (see below), and hence how tourists imbue these items with meanings and experiences.

Retailing of tourism merchandise and souvenirs has widespread implications for producers, retailers, and consumers alike. One more obvious role of tourism merchandizing is, as Healy (1994) points out in the case of ecotourism, the generation of income for local producers and sales intermediaries from sales of goods and accompanying services. For local communities, production geared to tourism has the advantage of inducing new networks of entrepreneurship with several potentially positive economic and social outcomes. These can take several forms, including: linking merchandise to agricultural and forestry projects to provide a sustainable supply of inputs; the use of craft as "performance," an attraction in itself and also through financial accrual in a virtuous circle, as tourists gravitate to the locality; and the development of products in time that help educate visitors about local environments, resources, and cultures, that in turn help foster respect for local communities and their ways of life. Markwick (2001: 48) notes that tourism demand may help bolster traditional industries which would otherwise be facing stagnation or decline. Taking her cue from Cohen (1993), she describes how Maltese crafts that remain locally viable experience "complementary commercialization"; simply put, they undergo a further round of spontaneous commercial production. Conversely, "traditional" crafts threatened with decline, such as lace-making, experience a complex form of "substitutive commercialization" as they spontaneously reorientate themselves directly toward the demands and expectations of the unfolding contemporary tourist market.

These are by no means the only positive outcomes of gearing production toward tourists, but rather part of a wider taxonomy. McGhee and Meares (1998) explore the development of cooperatives in the rural communities of the Appalachians to market local crafts to visitors. They note that the internal form and organization of the cooperatives manifest themselves in the nature of the external contributions to the community. The precise form and appointment of the cooperative is not fixed permanently over time. As a result, the cooperative format through its flexibility, ability to react to changing commercial imperatives, and its inherent democracy forms a significant instrument through which retailing can contribute to local community development and empowerment in a more equitable, responsible, and – some would claim – "sustainable" manner.

Tourism merchandise production and distribution have also been demonstrated to deliver negative outcomes. Blundell (1993: 64) reports how the souvenir trade in Canada in the early 1990s was related to broader struggles by aboriginal peoples to sustain their cultures and transform their relations with the Canadian state. She describes how souvenirs that embody native Canadian iconography and themes were appropriated by non-native producers and commoditized in an almost endless array of ways. The result was a strained relationship between the native people and the state over calls for regulation of the production and distribution of these goods amid claims of postcolonial exploitation of minority peoples.

The dual concepts of authenticity and the stewardship of culture underpin Blundell's discussion. There is a mistrust among aboriginal people of non-natives' commitments toward preserving the authenticity of cultural (culture, or cultural goods) in the (mass) production of tourism merchandise. Moreno and Littrell (2001), in a study of Guatemalan textile retailers, suggest that this concern has some wider basis. As Cohen's (1988, 1993) research has emphasized, authenticity is negotiated, it is not static and may take emergent positions, and it may be influenced by tourists' interpretations of integrity and genuineness as well as their desires, expectations, and motivations (Markwick 2001: 34). Perceived authenticity is often a key consideration among tourists in their purchases (Asplet and Cooper 2000). Moreno and Littrell (2001: 682) note that Guatemalan textile retailers have acknowledged this to the point that they have procured, developed, produced, and sold products that exist on "traditionality continua" depending on their retail market contexts and the associated processes of negotiation over production and distribution in the supply chain. The concern for Moreno and Littrell is whether the insidious creep of mass tourism will lead to the transmutation of textiles into unrecognizable "new" forms of "tradition." This is in direct contrast to Cohen's (1992) position that cultural products such as mass-produced handicrafts that at first seem contrived and inauthentic might over time assume authenticity in their own right as a new manifestation of culture, which after all is continually unfolding and evolving (in Asplet and Cooper 2000).

Encounters, Experiences, Performance, and Demand

By considering the supply of products and their delivery to the tourist, it becomes clear that retailers and producers are active agents in the mediation of tourist shopping experiences and their outcomes. By focusing on the determinants for purchase such as motivations, tourism types, and background (di Matteo and di Matteo 1993; Littrell et al. 1994; Anderson and Littrell 1995; Kim and Littrell 1999; Onderwater, Richards, and Stam 2000), there has been a tendency to lose sight of the importance of human agency and experience as key features in the way that tourist shopping episodes are mediated.

Retail transactions in fact contain a highly experiential component, are heavily imbued with meaning for both retailer and tourist, are highly symbolic, and often integrate a significant performative element (Crang 1997). Nowhere is this more emphasized than in studies of souvenir purchasing (Hitchcock and Teague 2000). Tourism purchases, shopping acts, and the nature of souvenirs have meaning far beyond the acquisition of tangible reminders of extra-ordinary experiences. Tourists' acts of purchasing commodities to return to their everyday worlds exist within complex structures of social relations and cultural practices. These relationships transgress international boundaries from home into destination spaces to shape the acts, nature, and expectations of tourist purchase encounters. Park (2000) notes that, although there may be some similarities in the souvenir purchasing traits of Japanese and Korean tourists, the precise motives behind buying souvenirs differ subtly but significantly, based on the social, cultural, and historical contexts of gift-giving. Souvenir purchasing of both the Japanese (*omiyage*) and Koreans (*sunmul*) is geared toward providing friends and relatives at home with a gift when the tourist returns from travel (Park 2000: 83). The memento is part of a wider process to cement relationships within social groups. However, as Ko (1999: 72) reminds us, tourists from both cultures *must* buy travel gifts for their family members, relatives, friends, colleagues, or seniors. Japanese tourists are often given money as a travel budget (*senbetsu*) by these close acquaintances (Ko 1999), but with the obligation of purchasing souvenirs as an expression of social communication to indicate consideration for those people left behind at home (Park 2000). In contrast, Korean tourists view souvenirs as a medium for the mutual sharing of affection and a method for showing sincerity (Park 2000: 89). This extends to the gift itself. According to Park (2000), the Japanese concentrate on the concept of "giving/receiving" (i.e. not disappointing the recipient) to endorse social relations, while the Koreans focus on what to give because souvenirs play a role in self-expression and the attachment of the tourist to the recipient.

Wang and Ryan (1998) note that there are notable differences in what tourists seek in both material and non-material terms from a retail encounter at the point of delivery. Based on an exploratory study of 21 sales managers in Christchurch, New Zealand, there were notable differences in the meaning of purchasing experiences for Taiwanese, Japanese, and New Zealand tourists depending on how material considerations resolved with the non-material. As the authors warn, at the risk of stereotyping groups of tourists, the Taiwanese were most interested in discounts, the Japanese in additional services that could be obtained beyond price and product, while the New Zealanders were keen to nurture friendly relations with the salespeople. For Wang and Ryan (1998), tourists' shopping takes the form of a negotiation, a performance of an inter-cultural dialogue between retailer and tourist. The style of the negotiation and ultimately its resolution is in no small measure a function of background cultural influences. The accent in Taiwanese transactions on price is driven by the importance of keeping "face"; the unwillingness of the Japanese to bargain is interpreted as an outcome of the ideological side of a culture which emphasizes politeness, courteousness, and respect; and the more familiar, less confrontational approach of the New Zealanders is indicative of a greater willingness to be cooperative and flexible, and the absence of a local culture of discount-seeking. Mak, Tsang, and Cheung (1999) also focus on non-material values embedded in transactions. In comparing Taiwanese tourists' attitudes to shopping in Hong Kong and Singapore, they found that Hong Kong was valued for its wider choice of merchandise and shopping settings. There were, however, few differences in product and service quality. Most notably retailers in Singapore were perceived as more honest than their counterparts in Hong Kong.

As Mak et al. (1999) explicitly indicate, a more complete appreciation of the full dimensions of tourism shopping encounters has important policy implications. For instance, in their view, understanding the behavior and values of core market segments helps to maintain the competitiveness of destinations that have marketed themselves heavily on their shopping mix. Ko (1999) notes that intense competition between competing tourist shopping centers, the poor ethics and business practices of retailers, and the weak mediation by tour operators have discouraged many inbound Korean tourists from visiting Australia. Wang and Ryan (1998) suggest that detailed, firm-level retail operations geared to tourists need to be more culturally aware. Articulated in these terms such issues represent important lessons, but essentially local concerns. From a wider perspective, the value of such discourses is that they point to mechanisms by which spatial shifts in tourism production and consumption are negotiated in an increasingly interconnected world. Furthermore, they talk to wider debates on how the social politics of tourism, contestation of place, and power among stakeholders contribute to the unfolding nature of tourism spaces and flows.

Settings, Spaces, and Places

Considerable interest has been devoted to where tourist shopping takes place. The settings identified vary from the international, cross-border (Timothy and Butler 1995; Bygvrå 1998) to the regional, and from the urban (Getz 1993a) to the micro; that is, at the level of the individual retail organization – the airport (Freathy and O'Connor 1999; Hobson 2000), mall (Butler 1991), tourist shopping villages (Getz 1993b) – or individual enclaves, quarters or streets within cities (Getz 1993a; Paradis 2000). In addition to services and spaces which tourists share and contest with local users, dedicated, purpose-built settings, intended primarily for tourists' use, have been developed. Getz (1993b: 15) documents the emergence of tourist shopping villages in Canada which he defines as "small towns and villages that base their tourist appeal on retailing, often in a pleasant setting marked by historical or natural amenities." In contrast, Hobson (2000) outlines the recent development process by which airports have become major features of the UK retail market per se by virtue of their huge turnover and their distinctive forms, born of acute segmentation based on their through trade.

Far from a mere taxonomical identification of the types of spaces occupied by tourist shoppers, the value of such surveys is that they point to the conflation of retailing, shopping, and tourism as a key driver in contemporary urban affairs in two main respects. First, awareness of tourists as a key market segment is enticing retailers to produce new forms of shopping space addressed directly at them. For example, Nike Towns have become tourist attractions as much as retail outlets by drawing those as interested in having fun as in buying sports shoes. In perhaps the most extreme example of its type, the Blockbuster Video group persuaded the Florida legislature to allow it to build the 2,500 acre "Blockbuster Video Park," a "multi-jurisdictional tourism, sports and entertainment special district" of the state (Barber 2001: 132). Far from merely being recognized as another theme park or another "monster shop," these developments represent new types of urban space (Sorkin 1992). For instance, just as the shopping mall in the UK, by virtue of its role in decentralizing retailing and services, has been recognized as a new urban form (Wrigley and Lowe 2002), the same logic could be applied to the scale of appointment and business associated with airport retailing.

The second, more important, issue is the contestation which tourist shopping creates. More commonly this has been interpreted as the struggle between local shoppers and tourist shoppers for goods, services, and space (Snepenger et al. 1998; Paradis 2000). For instance, Coles and Shaw (2002) note that in the historic city of Bath the immense pressure on local services and space in high season produces distinctive behavioral strategies as local residents attempt to negotiate "their" town center. What begins to emerge from a more detailed inspection of this situation is that contestation born of connecting tourism to shopping is not limited to the consumers themselves, but also exists between the retailers, as well as between the retailers and the property agents. Not surprisingly, the emergence of large-scale retail businesses directed at tourists has diverted trade away from established retailers and their settings. However, more subtle dynamics are emerging at the micro level in individual property markets based on the value of leisure and questions over its ability to generate adequate rental values (Ravenscroft, Reeves, and Rowley 2000). Tourists, and the enhanced demand they are supposed to embody, have been used as a means to elevate property values and hence (re)structure the property market in UK cities. Winners emerge as those in prime sites with higher rents and more passing trade. Losers are those who exist in less popular locations, but whose rents still reflect the popularity of the destination, not the setting of the store. In cities such as Bath, the winners – often national and international chain stores – occupy the main retail strip and the adjacent thoroughfares. Those in more marginal locations, off the beaten track, commonly have their rents assessed based on gross visitor numbers with little recourse to detailed pedestrian counts. Such smaller, independent retailers complain that they contribute both to the shopping mix and diversity, and to the resultant vitality, atmosphere, and appeal of the destination. However, ironically, they are marginalized commercially because their viability is threatened in a negative feedback by elevated rents associated with destination "success."

Discussion: In New Directions

However obvious and self-evident the relationship between tourism and shopping would appear, it has not been at the forefront of tourism research. With the notable exception of some long-running individual research programs, the wider corpus on this theme is fragmented and only sporadic major treatises have pushed the scholarly agenda forward. One of the defining features of investigation thus far has been the fascination with exchange. Although it may seem contradictory, the research agenda must progress beyond the moment of transaction. To dwell exclusively on the final node in the supply chain is to fashion an artificial, ring-fenced understanding of the full extent and consequences of delivering goods to tourists. By adopting the supply chain as an organizing principle, it has become more apparent that production, distribution, and transaction are located in time and space and are embedded in and produce new sets of social relations and cultural politics in communities; and that retailing is imbued with complex sets of meanings for tourists, retailers, and other participants involved in the supply chain far divorced from the ultimate act of consumption.

One of the enduring problems is that interest in tourism, shopping, and retailing has not been matched by theoretical engagement. Although work on this nexus talks to and may contribute directly to many of the major critical debates in the contemporary social sciences, there has been an unwillingness among research workers to engage with theoretical discourses. According to Lowe and Wrigley (1996), much the same lack of theoretical engagement characterized not only geographical readings of retail change, but also wider interdisciplinary retail studies in the late 1980s and early 1990s. In an attempt to move the research agenda on, they advocated that geographical readings of retail should be more heavily informed by, and seek reflexively to shape, the latest developments in economic geography and cultural geography (which in turn were mutually reinforced by interdisciplinary developments). A conclusion is an inappropriate moment to introduce their arguments fully, but we can note that the new research agenda on retail geography has fostered a more nuanced understanding of the changing dynamics of retail location, the impress of corporate cultures and social relations on distribution, and the meaning and experience of consumption, to name but a few major contributions. Fundamentally these are issues with which tourism research workers will have to grapple if understanding of the tourism-shopping-retailing nexus is to progress. Tourism studies, by virtue of their nature and origins, have long borrowed heavily from contributing disciplines for inspiration, ideas, concepts, and theory. Now is the time to foster more seriously the links with retail studies.

REFERENCES

Anderson, L., and Littrell, M. A. (1995). Souvenir-purchase behaviour of women tourists. *Annals of Tourism Research* 22(2), 328–48.

Asplet, M., and Cooper, M. (2000). Cultural designs in New Zealand souvenir clothing: The question of authenticity. *Tourism Management* 21(3), 307–12.

Barber, B. J. (2001). *Jihad vs. McWorld: Terrorism's Challenge to Democracy.* New York: Ballantyne Books.

Blundell, V. (1993). Aboriginal empowerment and souvenir trade in Canada. *Annals of Tourism Research* 20(1), 64–87.

Butler, R. W. (1991). West Edmonton Mall as a tourist attraction. *Canadian Geographer* 35(3), 287–95.

Bygvrå, S. (1998). The road to the Single European Market as seen through the Danish retail trade: Cross-border shopping between Denmark and Germany. *International Review of Retail, Distribution and Consumer Research* 8(2), 147–64.

Cohen, E. (1988). Authenticity and commoditization in tourism. *Annals of Tourism Research* 15, 371–86.

Cohen, E. (1992). The study of touristic images of native people: Mitigating the stereotype of a stereotype. In D. G. Pearce and R. W. Butler (eds), *Tourism Research: Critiques and Challenges* (pp. 39–69). London: Routledge.

Cohen, E. (1993). Investigating tourist arts: Introduction. *Annals of Tourism Research* 20(1), 1–8.

Coles, T. E., and Shaw, G. (2002). Tourism, tourists and local residents: Management implications for the World Heritage City of Bath. In K. Wöber (ed.), *City Tourism* (pp. 230–40). Vienna and New York: Springer Verlag.

Crang, P. (1997). Performing the tourist product. In C. Rojek and J. Urry (eds), *Touring Cultures: Transformations of Travel and Theory*. London: Routledge.

Dean, C. (1991) Shopping trips by bus and coach. *International Journal of Retail and Distribution Management* 19(2), 34–7.

di Matteo, L., and di Matteo, R. (1993). The determinants of expenditures by Canadian visitors to the United States. *Journal of Travel Research* 31(4), 34–42.

Foord, J., Bowlby, S. R., and Tillsley, C. (1996). The changing place of retailer–supplier relations in British retailing. In N. Wrigley and M. Lowe (eds), *Retailing, Consumption, and Capital: Towards the New Retail Geography* (pp. 68–89). Harlow: Longman.

Freathy, P., and O'Connor, F. (1999). A typology of European airport retailing. *Service Industries Journal* 19(3), 119–34.

Getz, D. (1993a). Planning for tourism business districts. *Annals of Tourism Research* 20, 583–600.

Getz, D. (1993b). Tourist shopping villages: Development and planning strategies. *Tourism Management* 14(1), 15–26.

Goss, J. (1993). The magic of the mall: An analysis of form, function, and meaning in the contemporary retail built environment. *Annals of the Association of American Geographers* 83(1), 18–47.

Goss, J. (1999). Once-upon-a-time in the commodity world: An unofficial guide to the Mall of America. *Annals of the Association of American Geographers* 89(1), 45–75.

Gregson, N., and Crewe, L. (1997). The bargain, the knowledge and the spectacle: Making sense of consumption in the space of the car boot sale. *Environment and Planning D: Society and Space* 15, 87–112.

Gregson, N., Brooks, K., and Crewe, L. (2000). Narratives of consumption and the body in the space of the charity/shop. In P. Jackson, M. Lowe, D. Miller, and F. Mort (eds), *Commercial Cultures: Economies, Practices, Spaces* (pp. 101–21). Oxford: Berg.

Hall, C. M., and Macionis, N. (1998). Wine tourism in Australia and New Zealand. In R. W. Butler, C. M. Hall, and J. Jenkins (eds), *Tourism and Recreation in Rural Areas* (pp. 197–224). Chichester: John Wiley.

Healy, R. G. (1994). Tourist merchandise as a means of generating local benefits from ecotourism. *Journal of Sustainable Tourism* 2(3), 137–51.

Hitchcock, M., and Teague, K. (2000). *Souvenirs: The Material Culture of Tourism*. Aldershot: Ashgate.

Hobson, J. S. P. (2000). Tourist shopping in transit: The case of BAA. *Journal of Vacation Marketing* 6(2), 170–83.

Jackson, E. (1991). Shopping and leisure: Implications of West Edmonton Mall for leisure and leisure studies. *Canadian Geographer* 35(3), 280–7.

Jansen-Verbeke, M. (1990). Leisure + shopping = tourism product mix. In G. Ashworth and B. Goodall (eds), *Marketing Tourism Places* (pp. 128–35). London: Routledge.

Kim, S. Y., and Littrell, M. A. (1999). Predicting souvenir purchase intentions. *Journal of Travel Research* 38(2), 153–62.

Ko, T. G. (1999). The issues and implications of escorted shopping tours in a tourist destination region: The case study of Korean package tourists in Australia. *Journal of Travel and Tourism Marketing* 8(3), 71–80.

Littrell, M. A., Baizerman, S., Kean, R., Gahring, S., Niemeyer, S., Reilly, R., and Stout, J. (1994). Souvenirs and tourism styles. *Journal of Travel Research* 33(1), 3–11.

Lowe, M., and Wrigley, N. (1996). Towards the new retail geography. In N. Wrigley and M. Lowe (eds), *Retailing, Consumption, and Capital: Towards the New Retail Geography* (pp. 3–30). Harlow: Longman.

Mak, B. L. M., Tsang, N. K. F., and Cheung, I. C. Y. (1999). Taiwanese tourists' shopping preferences. *Journal of Vacation Marketing* 5(2), 190–8.

Mann, T. (1998). *Death in Venice*. London: Vintage. (1st pub. 1912, Hyperionverlag Hans von Weber.)

Markwick, M. C. (2001). Tourism and the development of handicraft production in the Maltese islands. *Tourism Geographies: An International Journal of Tourism Space, Place and the Environment* 3(1), 29–51.

McGhee, N. G., and Meares, A. C. (1998). A case study of three tourism-related craft marketing co-operatives in Appalachia: Contributions to community. *Journal of Sustainable Tourism* 6(1), 4–25.

Moreno, J., and Littrell, M. A. (2001). Negotiating tradition: Tourism retailers in Guatemala. *Annals of Tourism Research* 28(3), 658–85.

Onderwater, L., Richards, G., and Stam, S. (2000). Why tourists buy textile souvenirs: European evidence. *Tourism, Culture and Communication* 2, 39–48.

Paradis, T. W. (2000). Main Street transformed: Community sense of place for nonmetropolitan tourism business districts. *Urban Geography* 21(7), 609–39.

Park, M. K. (2000). Social and cultural factors influencing tourists' souvenir-purchasing behaviour: A comparative study on Japanese "omiyage" and Korean "sunmul". *Journal of Travel and Tourism Marketing* 9(1/2), 81–91.

Ravenscroft, N., Reeves, J., and Rowley, M. (2000). Leisure, property and the viability of town centres. *Environment and Planning A* 32(8), 1359–74 [TR].

Shields, R. (1992). *Lifestyle Shopping: The Subject of Consumption*. London: Routledge.

Snepenger, D. J., Reiman, S., Johnson, J., and Snepenger, M. (1998). Is downtown mainly for tourists? *Journal of Travel Research* 36(3), 5–12.

Sorkin, M. (1992). *Variations on a Theme Park*. New York: Noonday Press.

Telfer, D. J. (2001). Strategic alliances along the Niagara Wine Route. *Tourism Management* 22(1), 21–30.

Timothy, D. J. (2003). *Shopping, Tourism, Retailing and Leisure*. Clevedon: Channel View Books.

Timothy, D. J., and Butler, R. W. (1995). Cross-border shopping: A North American perspective. *Annals of Tourism Research* 22(1), 16–34.

Timothy, D. J., and Wall, G. (1997). Selling to tourists: Indonesian street vendors. *Annals of Tourism Research* 24(2), 322–40.

Wang, Z. H., and Ryan, C. (1998). New Zealand retailers' perceptions of some tourists' negotiation styles for souvenir purchases. *Tourism, Culture and Communication* 1, 139–52.

Warnaby, G. (1998). Marketing UK cities as shopping destinations: Problems and prospects. *Journal of Retailing and Consumer Services* 5(1), 55–8.

Wrigley, N., and Lowe, M. (eds) (1996). *Retailing, Consumption, and Capital: Towards the New Retail Geography.* Harlow: Longman.
Wrigley, N., and Lowe, M. (2002). *Reading Retail: A Geographical Perspective on Retailing and Consumption Spaces*. London: Arnold.
Zhao, X. (1994). Barter tourism along the China–Russia border. *Annals of Tourism Research* 21(2), 401–3.

Chapter 30

Tourism and the Countryside

Richard Sharpley

Introduction

Rural areas have long played host to tourists. Indeed, since the late 1700s, when there was a fundamental shift in the cultural appreciation of rural spaces, the countryside has rapidly evolved into a popular tourist destination throughout the developed world. Nevertheless, rural tourism has, for most of its history, remained a relatively small-scale, passive activity. In fact, it is only since the 1960s that it has emerged as a significant element of total tourism activity. For example, in England over three-quarters of the population now visit the countryside at some time during the year (Countryside Commission 1995a) while a quarter of all Europeans spend their main holidays in the countryside (Grolleau 1987; EuroBarometer 1998). The growth in rural tourism is also evident in other countries, manifested in the emergence of appropriate development policies (for example, Luloff et al. 1994; Long and Edgell 1997; Nylander 2001).

At the same time, the scope of rural tourism, in terms of its meaning and its demands upon rural resources, has also expanded significantly. That is, "until the last two decades or so, recreational and tourist activities in rural areas were mostly related closely to the rural character of the setting" (Butler, Hall, and Jenkins 1998: 8) and were, hence, passive, relaxing, and traditional. More recently, however, new demands and expectations have challenged the role of the countryside setting in defining the scope of rural tourism, requiring a new approach to the management and planning of rural tourism (Roberts and Hall 2001).

More importantly, both the socioeconomic structure of the countryside itself and its relationship with tourism have also undergone a fundamental transformation. The "traditional" countryside, characterized by a politically, economically, and socially dominant agricultural sector and associated settlement patterns, has been reshaped by the fragmentation of rural systems in general, and the declining role of the agrarian economy in particular (Marsden et al. 1993; Jenkins, Hall, and Troughton 1998). As a result, the countryside has become an arena in which a multitude of tensions and competing demands are played out, frequently reflecting wider social and economic differences and conflicts (Clark et al. 1994). Furthermore, the planning and management of rural areas, previously preoccupied with agricultural interests, has been obliged to embrace a diverse, yet interrelated array of political processes (Cloke 1992; Marsden and Murdoch 1998). At the same time, within this "new" countryside, tourism has assumed a more central role. Not only does it act as a focus for competing demands and processes, providing a potential vehicle for economic and social regeneration, particularly in peripheral rural regions, but it has also become an influential factor in the reshaping of the countryside (Gannon 1994; Cavaco 1995; Hoggart, Buller, and Black 1995; Fleischer and Pizam 1997; Jenkins, Hall, and Troughton 1998; Saeter 1998; Fleischer and Felenstein 2000).

To date, however, this broadening role of tourism within a changing countryside context has not been fully reflected in the study of rural tourism. In other words, although rural tourism has long been the focus of research, such research has been primarily tourism-centric. While generating substantial knowledge about, for example, the challenges of developing rural tourism businesses and, particularly, the management of the countryside as a resource for tourism, it has not, for the most part, been integrated into the wider, dynamic rural context (Hall and Page 1999: 178). This is not to say that the current body of knowledge does not contribute significantly to an understanding of the processes inherent in the demand and supply of rural tourism. Indeed, as the following review of key issues demonstrates, such knowledge is essential for the effective planning and management of tourism in the countryside; "rural tourism and recreation activities are distinctive, they require resources and management which are essentially different in content and scale from other forms of tourism activity" (Roberts and Hall 2001: 17).

However, as this chapter goes on to suggest, future research should reflect the fact that tourism is but one (albeit frequently dominant) of an enormous variety of interrelated activities and institutions that both exploit and contribute to the vitality and future development of the countryside. In other words, the principal issues relating to rural tourism management and development should not be addressed in isolation, but located within the frameworks of both overall tourism activity within a region or nation-state and also regional/national policy formulation for an integrated, multi-purpose countryside.

Defining the Rural

Although the term "rural tourism" itself is variously defined and interpreted (see below), it implicitly embraces tourism and leisure – or, collectively, recreational – activities that occur in countryside or rural spaces (Sharpley and Sharpley 1997). Therefore, the study of rural tourism has long been concerned with the concept of "the rural" in order to define not only the locational context within which rural tourism occurs but also, more importantly, the cultural context that determines tourists' activities, motivations, and expectations, as well as countryside management and planning philosophies (Harrison 1991).

Typically, definitions of the rural are based upon the rural–urban dichotomy, highlighting the perceived physical, social, economic, and cultural distinctiveness of the countryside as compared to urban areas. Most simplistically, the Organization for Economic Co-operation and Development (OECD) states that "rural areas comprise the people, land and other resources, in the open country and small settlements outside urban centers. Rural is a territorial or spatial concept. It is not restricted to any particular use of land, degree of economic health, or economic sector" (OECD 1993: 11). Inevitably, however, this definition overlooks not only the enormous physical, socioeconomic, and cultural diversity of the 90 percent of OECD territory that it embraces, but also the fact that "it may be a mistake to deny our common sense thoughts that rural areas can have distinctive characteristics or that these can have consequences for social and economic interactions in the countryside" (Bramwell 1994: 3).

Attempts have been made, therefore, to identify the particular qualities of areas that identify them as rural, the main approaches being summarized by Robinson (1990). In the specific context of rural tourism, Lane (1994) proposes three broad characteristics of rural areas that may also be related to their attraction to tourists. Firstly, and most commonly, (low) population density and (small) settlement size are considered a principal characteristic of rural areas, although the actual measurement criteria vary from one country to another. In the UK, for example, towns with less than 10,000 inhabitants are considered to be rural; in Australia, the figure is 1,000 and in Ireland, 100. Thus, it is the relative difference between urban and rural population densities that is crucial in terms of tourists' needs and expectations (Harrison 1991). Secondly, rural areas may be defined by traditional, agrarian land use and economies and, thirdly, traditional social structures, embracing "older ways of life and thinking ... combined with the scenic values and recreational opportunities of the countryside, attract tourists from urban areas" (Lane 1994: 11).

However, as Patmore (1983: 122) observes, there may be "no sharp discontinuity between urban and rural resources for recreation, but rather a complete continuum from local park to remote mountain peak." As a result, many researchers refer to an urban–rural continuum as a means of defining different degrees of rurality, from the economically integrated, "gentrified" areas on the urban fringe through to the remote, peripheral regions. According to Lane (1994), this continuum may, at a simplistic level, also reflect tourism demand, with countryside on the urban fringe enjoying a "strong day-visitor trade"; conversely, peripheral regions may attract lower levels of visitation although they may offer opportunities for more traditional or "pure" (Lane 1994) rural tourism activities. However, it may also be multidimensional when other factors, such as accessibility, are taken into account, meaning that one area may occupy different positions on several continua.

The urban–rural continuum concept also reflects the fact that there is no single "countryside" or "rural" space – indeed, it has been argued that the term "rural" can accommodate neither inter-rural differences nor similarities between urban and rural areas and should, therefore, be "done away with" (Hoggart 1990). Moreover, Shaw and Williams (1994: 223) suggest that "there is nothing inherent in any part of the countryside that makes it a recreational resource" and, therefore, as Hall and Page (1999: 182) argue, attempting to classify "tourism and recreational environments and their uses for specific reasons and purposes [is] rather meaningless if they are part of no more than a simple continuum of recreational and tourism resources." This, in turn, suggests that rural tourism, as a distinctive, identifiable form of tourism, is also a relatively meaningless term, a theme that will be returned to shortly.

Three other related issues further increase the complexity of defining the rural as the location and attraction of rural tourism. Firstly, the characteristics of rural areas as defined by Lane (1994) and others are themselves being challenged by transformations in the wider political economy which are impacting upon the socioeconomic structure and use of the countryside (Cloke 1992). For example, increasing mobility has reduced the autonomy and homogeneity of rural communities, counter-urbanization being a particular feature of many non-peripheral regions (Bolton and Chalkey 1990), rural economies have become de-localized, and new, non-rural use – including some tourism activity – is being made of rural spaces (Mormont 1990, cited in Roberts and Hall 2001: 14). Thus, while much of the research has been concerned with identifying the distinctive qualities of the rural as an attraction to primarily urban-based visitors, the political, economic, and social structures of rural areas are, in a sense, becoming increasingly urban in nature.

Secondly, the productive role of the countryside has diminished in tandem with a growth in "new markets for countryside commodities" (Cloke 1992: 293). In other words, the countryside is becoming less a place of (agricultural) production and more the object of consumption, whether by tourists, conservationists, or incoming residents (Kneafsey 2001). As a result, tensions exist not only between production and consumption in rural areas, such as between agriculture and conservation, development and landscape, or new middle-class opposition to the realities of farming (Cloke 1992), but also between different forms of production and consumption themselves (for example, between different recreational activities).

Thirdly, and consequently, the expected or perceived attraction of the countryside as, typically, the non-urban is, for the most part, an increasingly imagined or "virtual" reality (Sørensen and Nilsson 1999). That is, the countryside that tourists seek to consume is as much, if not more, an abstract, socially constructed concept as a place with tangible, unique qualities; it is seen as a "refuge from modernity" (Short 1991: 34), a rural utopia where visitors may escape from the present into an "authentic," nostalgic past. Thus, the rural, in the tourism context, is a constructed, negotiated experience, the symbolic significance of which may bear little resemblance to the reality of a dynamic countryside.

In order to address these definitional problems and, hence, the unclear relationship between the rural and tourism, Shaw and Williams (1994: 224) propose that, although "rural areas are highly esteemed as locales for leisure and tourism, their use is heavily contingent." In particular, the use of the countryside for tourism is contingent upon (a) a rural opportunity spectrum, whereby different rural areas are appropriate settings for different tourism activities; (b) accessibility, which is dependent upon not only spatial variation but also upon social factors and the political ownership of the countryside; and (c) space-time budget constraints, which determine both the nature and the location of tourism activities in the countryside. The advantage of this perspective is that it relates the demand for rural tourism not to the particular qualities (actual or imagined) of specific parts of the countryside – although the concept of rurality is fundamental to understanding the motivation for visiting rural spaces in general – but to the ability of tourists to exploit or consume the countryside for any variety of tourist activity. In other words, it emphasizes the role of the countryside as a tourism destination in general, rather than as the location for a specific type of tourist activity. This then, of course, raises the question: what is rural tourism?

Rural Tourism/Tourists or Tourism in the Countryside?

A key issue remaining unresolved in the literature is the nature or, indeed, existence, of rural tourism as a discrete sub-sector of tourism activity. In other words, despite the size of the rural tourism market and its relevance to rural economies – the latter starkly demonstrated by the impact of the outbreak of foot and mouth disease in the UK in 2001 (the policies designed to control the spread of the outbreak effectively "closed" the countryside to visitors, costing the British tourism industry some £5 billion (Sharpley and Craven 2001)) – there is little consensus within the literature as to what constitutes rural tourism and, consequently, who is a rural tourist.

A number of factors, some related to the problems associated with defining the rural, contribute to this lack of consensus. For example, in addition to variations between and transformations in rural areas, Lane (1994) observes that, amongst other things, not all tourism in the countryside is strictly rural in character (for example, inland resorts), while different forms of rural tourism predominate in different countries. Thus, farm tourism is virtually synonymous with rural tourism in Germany and Austria (Oppermann 1996) yet is rare in north America while, in Australia, rural tourism is, perhaps, most closely associated with "Outback," wilderness tourism (Sofield and Getz 1997). Lane goes on to suggest, therefore, that "pure" rural tourism should be rural in scale, character, control, and development (Lane 1994: 14) whereas, conversely, the European Community refers to rural tourism as all tourism activity in a rural area.

Two further points also deserve consideration. Firstly, a distinction is frequently drawn within the literature between tourism and recreation as "complementary and yet semantically different activities" (Hall and Page 1999: 181). Broadhurst (2001), for example, attempts to distinguish between leisure, recreation, and tourism, the defining elements being both the nature of the activity and the location (i.e. proximity to the home environment) where it occurs. While tourism is closely related to leisure and recreation, "our urge to explore our environment, and seek out new worlds, new settings and new people, is given almost totally free rein through tourism" (Broadhurst 2001: 9). Thus, in the countryside context, tourism is most frequently associated with more traditional rural pursuits undertaken during longer trips involving at least one night away, whereas more local, day trips are usually defined as leisure trips – certainly, in the UK, this dichotomy is exemplified in statistics which distinguish between "tourists" and "leisure day visitors" (Countryside Agency 2001). However, as Hall and Page (1999: 182) observe, "each use is a consumption of [rural] resources and space in relation to the user's discretionary time and income" and to distinguish between them, therefore, is somewhat illogical, in particular from a resource management perspective. Moreover, from a commercial perspective, to "most rural tourism entrepreneurs, the question 'What is rural tourism?' is largely of no great concern . . . a customer is a customer" (Sørensen and Nilsson 2001), although, of course, it is the customer who spends most (generally overnight stayers) who is of most relevance to rural tourism businesses.

Secondly, rural tourism is culturally defined. That is, rural tourism as an experience is as much defined by the expectations, perceptions, and cultural background of tourists as it is by the activities they participate in within a rural context. As Roberts and Hall (2001: 140) observe, "given the multidimensionality of people's social identities, rural tourism and recreation are likely to be consumed in different ways on different occasions" while, over time, the cultural role of the countryside as a tourism destination may also change (Shaw and Williams 1994). For example, from a postmodern perspective, the countryside has assumed greater importance as an object of consumption as it not only permits the "de-differentiation" (Lash 1990) of society and nature, but also provides the focus for environmental awareness, perhaps "the highest order discourse of postmodernisation" (Munt 1994).

Nevertheless, research into the demand for rural tourism (e.g., Curry 1994) has focused primarily on either identifying the characteristics of "rural tourists" (typically more affluent, better educated and, as Hummelbrunner and Miglbauer (1994) suggest, reflecting the behavior of the "new tourist") or their motivation for visiting the countryside. The latter, though limited, generally relates participation in rural tourism to the desire to experience the intrinsic qualities of the countryside (Grolleau 1987; Countryside Commission 1985). Indeed, only recently has research in Portugal identified different "ruralists," that is, different market segments which place varying degrees of importance on the "traditional" rural environment and/or the activities they are able to participate in (Kastenholz 2000).

Collectively, these points suggest that, just as there is no single "rural," there is no discrete rural tourism or tourist. Rather, there exists a "mass rural market distinguishable by activity" (Roberts and Hall 2001: 140), whether tourism, leisure, or recreational. This, in turn, suggests that future research should focus principally on exploring the needs, values, identities, and practices of the diverse range of visitors who consume the countryside for an equally diverse range of purposes, and on how the rural resource can be effectively managed to meet their needs.

Managing Tourism in the Countryside

Not surprisingly, much of the extant research into rural tourism is concerned with the planning and management of tourism in the countryside, a broad focus that embraces a variety of discrete yet interrelated issues. A complete review of these is beyond the scope of this chapter, although it is important to highlight the main areas of concern before considering the dominant research themes within the management context.

At a fundamental level, much of the literature addresses what may be described as the impacts or consequences of rural tourism, usually subdivided (as with tourism impact studies in general – for example, Mathieson and Wall 1982) into economic, environmental, and sociocultural impacts. Typically, economic impact studies focus upon the potential contribution of tourism to the growth and diversification of rural economies (Gannon 1994), the potential for pluriactivity or diversification on farms long being a common theme (Frater 1983; Pearce 1990: Dernoi 1991; Oppermann 1996; Weaver and Fennell 1997). Rural tourism has also emerged as a prominent issue within the wider study of the environmental impacts of tourism (Page and Getz 1997), the delicate balance between providing for the needs of tourists and protecting the environment often proving to be an elusive goal, particularly in popular destinations such as national parks (FNNPE 1993). More specifically, the interdependence of tourism and (traditionally) farmed landscapes as a principal attraction to visitors has assumed greater importance as farmers diversify into tourism. Similarly, the responses and transformations (both positive and negative) in rural society and culture resulting from the development of tourism have proved to be a fruitful area of research (e.g., Bouquet and Winter 1987; Perdue, Long, and Allen 1987; Getz 1994; Smith and Krannich 1998) and, collectively, these studies provide a substantial body of knowledge relevant to the more effective management of the countryside as a resource for tourism, albeit from an "impact" perspective.

In contrast, a number of issues are evident in the literature, exploring, again within a management context, the relationship between tourism, tourists, and rural spaces, the principal focus being the achievement of a balance between the needs of tourists, the tourism industry, and the rural resource base. As suggested shortly, this is the principal objective of sustainable rural tourism development, one of the current dominant themes within the rural tourism literature, but a variety of specific topics relevant to the management of tourism and the countryside deserve mention. These include:

- *Access and land use issues*. Rural tourism is dependent upon sufficient, suitable, and equitable access to the countryside to meet the growing and increasingly diverse demands of visitors (Millward 1993; Kaltenborn, Haaland, and Sandell 2001; McCool and Stankey 2001). However, such demands must be balanced with other legitimate uses and changing patterns of land ownership that call into question the viability of a "freedom to roam" (Shoard 1999), in particular the emerging issue of indigenous peoples' property ownership and rights (for example, McIntyre, Jenkins, and Booth 2001)
- *Visitor management techniques*. In recognition of the contribution of tourists to the appropriate use of rural resources, increasing attention has been paid to ways in which visitor behavior may be managed in general (Jim 1989) as well as specific approaches, including codes of conduct (Mason and Mowforth 1995), interpretation (Barrow 1994), zoning to match appropriate activities to specific types of countryside (Murphy 1985), and exclusion methods, such as the imposition of a speed limit on Lake Windermere in the English Lake District as an effective "ban" on motorized water sports.
- *Land management issues*. Inevitably, a significant body of literature is concerned with managing the countryside environment for tourism, either in general (Pigram 1983; Broadhurst 2001) or in the context of specific areas such as national parks (WTO/UNEP 1992; FNNEP 1993; Butler and Boyd 2000).
- *Transport issues*. In most industrialized countries, the motor car is the most popular means of both accessing and travelling around the countryside. Thus, reflecting wider concerns (Whitelegg 1993), sustainable transport policies have become a pressing issue within rural tourism planning.

Many, if not all, of these issues are represented within the prevailing research themes related to the management of rural tourism. Foremost amongst these is the concept of sustainable development, a perspective that has dominated tourism research in general and rural tourism research in particular since the early 1990s, and an approach adopted by many private and public sector rural tourism organizations (Countryside Commission 1995b). It also remains the subject of intense debate and is considered by some an oxymoronic and overly prescriptive perspective that actually restricts tourism-related development (Sharpley 2001).

Nevertheless, the notion of sustainable development has been catalytic in encouraging research into various aspects of rural tourism management, two principal areas being the integrated management of tourism destinations and the sustainability of rural tourism businesses. With respect to the former, attention is focused primarily on overall "environmental management systems" (Tribe et al. 2000) which seek to integrate appropriate management schemes that minimize on- and off-site environmental impacts, the multi-use of rural areas, the encouragement of community participation, and the education of visitors and employees in rural tourism enterprises.

In the case of the latter, it has long been recognized that tourism businesses in rural areas face a number of challenges (Wilson et al. 2001). For some years, private–public sector partnerships were a favored method of supporting and managing the development of local tourism businesses and addressing the problems faced by small, new businesses in a highly competitive market. More recently, however, attention has been increasingly focused on the contribution of clusters/networks as a means of generating regional competitiveness and positive economies for rural tourism businesses (Meyer-Cech 2001). A cluster is, simply, a collection of businesses or industries within a particular region that are interconnected by their products, their markets, and the other businesses or organizations, such as suppliers, with which they interact (Porter 1998). The benefits of clusters include increased competitiveness, economies of scale, opportunities for backward linkages, and a focus on cooperation and innovation, and they therefore represent a valuable model for the sustainable development of rural tourism businesses.

However, as suggested in the introduction to this chapter, most, if not all, of the research referred to here is highly tourism-centric. That is, the focus is primarily on rural tourism itself rather than on the broader social, political, and economic context within which it occurs. Therefore, as the final section argues, there is a need to widen the research base in order to relate it to the dynamic countryside environment within which tourism occurs.

Rural Tourism: A New Research Agenda?

From the preceding review, it is evident that a significant body of knowledge exists with respect to the impacts, planning, and management of tourism within the countryside. At the same time, however, it is evident that the research has been restricted by a variety of factors, such as definitional concerns, the artificially imposed parameters of "rurality" as a research framework, and an inward perspective on the processes and consequences of rural tourism development rather than on the wider rural context of which tourism is a part and also contributes to shaping.

Therefore, in order to explore more fully the relationship with, and role of, tourism in rural change and development, there is a need to adopt a fresh perspective that locates rural tourism research in a broader context. This new perspective should, firstly, view the countryside as a particular destination for tourism rather than "rural tourism" as a specific niche market and, secondly, relate tourism development to the broader political economy of rural areas where national rural tourism policies are the exception rather than the rule. In particular, the relationship between tourism, the rural economy, and national policies with respect to agriculture and rural development in general deserves attention, while the implications of the globalization of economies and culture should not be overlooked. In so doing, four research themes, usefully summarized by Roberts and Hall (2001: 220), then emerge:

1 *Change.* As rural areas themselves change in terms of social, economic, and political structures, research should be undertaken into emergent attitudes towards "rurality" and rural tourism from the point of view of both tourists and local, resident populations. At the same time, and perhaps more importantly, there is a need to research into how these changes may alter the relationship between rural and urban places (and indeed between different rural places) and the consequences for the development of rural tourism.
2 *Transparency.* Once there is a more transparent approach to recognizing the legitimacy of all forms of tourism and recreational activities in the countryside, research can then identify appropriate policies for providing and meeting the demands of all tourists to the benefit of rural economies and societies. In other words, there is a need for "transparency in recognizing the essential nature of new forms of tourism in rural areas" (Roberts and Hall 2001: 223), tourism which may be large-scale and hence demanding significant place commodification. An understanding of these forms of tourism in the rural context is, therefore, an essential foundation to appropriate management strategies.
3 *Integration.* At a general level, an understanding of how tourism is an integral element of rural economies and is hence deserving of inclusion in regional and national rural development policies should be a principal objective of future research. At the same time, there is also the need to focus research more specifically upon the link between rural tourism, rural development policy, and different household/business contexts, such as farms, village shops, and bed-and-breakfast accommodation providers.
4 *Unsustainability.* As noted above, adherence to the principles of sustainable tourism development may limit the potential for economic development; in short, sustainable tourism may result in unsustainable development. Future research should, therefore, be directed not only toward identifying means for optimizing tourism's developmental role in the countryside within environmental parameters, but also more generally toward the equitable recreational use of the countryside in terms of both production and consumption.

Collectively, these themes represent a new agenda for research that recognizes the realities of the demand, supply, and developmental role of tourism in a modern, dynamic countryside.

REFERENCES

Barrow, G. (1994). Interpretative planning: More to it than meets the eye. *Environmental Interpretation* 9(2), 5–7.

Bolton, N., and Chalkey, B. (1990). The rural population turnaround. *Journal of Rural Studies* 16(1), 29–43.

Bouquet, M., and Winter, M. (eds) (1987). *Who from their Labours Rest: Conflict and Practice in Rural Tourism*. Aldershot: Avebury.

Bramwell, B. (1994). Rural tourism and sustainable rural tourism. *Journal of Sustainable Tourism* 2(1/2), 1–6.

Broadhurst, R. (2001). *Managing Environments for Recreation and Leisure*. London: Routledge.

Butler, R., and Boyd, S. (2000). *Tourism and National Parks: Issues and Implications*. Chichester: John Wiley.

Butler, R., Hall, C. M., and Jenkins, J. (1998). Introduction. In R. Butler, C. M. Hall, and J. Jenkins (eds), *Tourism and Recreation in Rural Areas* (pp. 1–16). Chichester: John Wiley.

Cavaco, C. (1995). Rural tourism: The creation of new tourist spaces. In A. Montanari and A. Williams (eds), *European Tourism: Regions, Spaces and Restructuring* (pp. 129–49). Chichester: John Wiley.

Clark, G., Darrall, J., Grove-White, R., Macnaghten, P., and Urry, J. (1994). *Leisure Landscapes. Leisure, Culture and the English Countryside: Challenges and Conflicts*. London: Campaign for the Protection of Rural England.

Cloke, P. (1992). The countryside: Development, conservation and an increasingly marketable commodity. In P. Cloke (ed.), *Policy and Change in Thatcher's Britain* (pp. 269–95). Oxford: Pergamon Press.

Countryside Agency (2001). *The Economic Impact of Recreation and Tourism in the English Countryside*. Research Note CRN 15. Cheltenham: Countryside Agency.

Countryside Commission (1985). *National Countryside Recreation Survey 1984*. CCP 201. Cheltenham: Countryside Commission.

Countryside Commission (1995a). *National Countryside Recreation Survey 1990: Summary of Results*. Cheltenham: Countryside Commission.

Countryside Commission (1995b). *Sustainable Rural Tourism: Opportunities for Local Action*. CCP 483. Cheltenham: Countryside Commission.

Curry, N. (1994). *Countryside Recreation, Access and Land Use Planning*. London: E. & F. N. Spon.

Dernoi, L. (1991). About rural and farm tourism. *Tourism Recreation Research* 16(1), 3–6.

EuroBarometer (1998). *Facts and Figures on the Europeans' Holiday*. Brussels: EuroBarometer for DG XXIII, European Commission.

Fleischer, A., and Pizam, A. (1997) Rural tourism in Israel. *Tourism Management* 18(6), 367–72.

Fleischer, A., and Felenstein, D. (2000) Support for rural tourism; Does it make a difference? *Annals of Tourism Research* 27(4), 1007–24.

FNNPE (1993). *Loving them to Death? Sustainable Tourism in Europe's Nature and National Parks*. Grafenau: Federation of National and Nature Parks of Europe.

Frater, J. (1983). Farm tourism in England: Planning, funding, promotion and some lessons from Europe. *Tourism Management* 4(3), 167–79.

Gannon, A. (1994). Rural tourism as a factor in rural community economic development for economies in transition. *Journal of Sustainable Tourism* 2(1/2), 51–60.

Getz, D. (1994). Residents' attitudes towards tourism: A longitudinal study in Spey Valley, Scotland. *Tourism Management* 15(4), 247–58.

Grolleau, H. (1987). *Rural Tourism in the 12 Member States of the European Economic Community.* Brussels: EEC Tourism Unit, DG XXIII.

Hall, C. M., and Page, S. (1999). *The Geography of Tourism and Recreation: Environment, Place and Space*. London: Routledge.

Harrison, C. (1991). *Countryside Recreation in a Changing Society.* London: TMS Partnership.

Hoggart, K. (1990). Let's do away with rural. *Journal of Rural Studies* 16(3), 245–57.

Hoggart, K., Buller, H., and Black, R. (1995). *Rural Europe: Identity and Change*. London: Arnold.

Hummelbrunner, R., and Miglbauer, E. (1994). Tourism promotion and potential in peripheral areas. *Journal of Sustainable Tourism* 2(1/2), 41–50.

Jenkins, J., Hall, C. M., and Troughton, M. (1998). The restructuring of rural economies: Rural tourism and recreation as a government response. In R. Butler, C. M. Hall, and J. Jenkins (eds), *Tourism and Recreation in Rural Areas* (pp. 43–67). Chichester: John Wiley.

Jim, C. (1989). Visitor management in recreation areas. *Environmental Conservation* 16(1), 19–34.

Kaltenborn, B., Haaland, H., and Sandell, K. (2001) The public right of access: Some challenges to sustainable tourism development in Scandinavia. *Journal of Sustainable Tourism* 9(5), 417–33.

Kastenholz, E. (2000). The market for rural tourism in north and central Portugal: A benefit segmentation approach. In G. Richards and D. Hall (eds), *Tourism and Sustainable Community Development* (pp. 268–84). London: Routledge.

Kneafsey, M. (2001) Rural cultural economy: Tourism and social relations. *Annals of Tourism Research* 28(3), 762–83.

Lane, B. (1994). What is rural tourism? *Journal of Sustainable Tourism* 2(12), 7–21.

Lash, S. (1990) *Sociology of Postmodernism*. London: Routledge.

Long, P., and Edgell, D. (1997) Rural tourism in the United States: The Peak to Peak Scenic Byway and KOA. In S. Page and D. Getz (eds), *The Business of Rural Tourism* (pp. 61–76). London: International Thomson Business Press.

Luloff, A., Bridger, J., Graefe, A., Saylor, M., Martin, K., and Gitelson, R. (1994) Assessing rural tourism efforts in the United States. *Annals of Tourism Research* 21(1), 46–64.

Marsden, T., and Murdoch, J. (1998). The shifting nature of rural governance and community participation. *Journal of Rural Studies* 14(1), 1–4.

Marsden, T., Murdoch, J., Lowe, P., Munton, R., and Flynn, A. (1993). *Constructing the Countryside*. London: UCL Press.

Mason, P., and Mowforth, M. (1995). *Codes of Conduct in Tourism*. Occasional Papers in Geography 1. Plymouth: University of Plymouth,.

Mathieson, A., and Wall, G. (1982). *Tourism: Economic, Physical and Social Impacts*. Harlow: Longman.

McCool, S., and Stankey, G. (2001) Managing access to wildlands for recreation in the USA: Background and issues relevant to sustaining tourism. *Journal of Sustainable Tourism* 9(5), 389–99.

McIntyre, N., Jenkins, J., and Booth, K. (2001) Global influences on access: The changing face of access to public conservation lands in New Zealand. *Journal of Sustainable Tourism* 9(5), 434–50.

Meyer-Cech, K. (2001) Regional co-operation in rural theme trails. Lessons learned from the "Cheese Trail Bregenzerwald" and other Austrian examples. Proceedings of conference on

New Directions in Managing Rural Tourism and Leisure: Local Impacts, Global Trends. Ayr: SAC.

Millward, H. (1993). Public access in the west European countryside: A comparative survey. *Journal of Rural Studies* 9(1), 39–51.

Munt, I. (1994) The "other" postmodern tourism: Culture, travel and the new middle classes. *Theory, Culture and Society* 11(3), 101–23.

Murphy, P. (1985). *Tourism: A Community Approach*. London: Routledge.

Nylander, M. (2001) National policy for "rural tourism": The case of Finland. In L. Roberts and D. Hall (eds), *Rural Tourism and Recreation: Principles to Practice* (pp. 77–81).Wallingford: CAB International.

OECD (1993). *What Future for our Countryside? A Rural Development Policy.* Paris: OECD.

Oppermann, M. (1996). Rural tourism in southern Germany. *Annals of Tourism Research* 23(1), 86–102.

Page, S., and Getz, D. (1997). The business of rural tourism: International perspectives. In S. Page and D. Getz (eds), *The Business of Rural Tourism* (pp. 3–37). London: International Thomson Business Press.

Patmore, J. (1983). *Recreation and Resources: Leisure Patterns and Leisure Places.* Oxford: Blackwell.

Pearce, P. (1990) Farm tourism in New Zealand: A social situation analysis. *Annals of Tourism Research* 17, 337–52.

Perdue, R., Long, P., and Allen, L. (1987). Rural resident tourism perceptions and attitudes. *Annals of Tourism Research* 14, 420–9.

Pigram, J. (1983). *Outdoor Recreation and Resource Management.* Beckenham: Croom Helm.

Porter, M. (1998). *On Competition: A Harvard Business Review Book.* Boston: Harvard Business School Publishing.

Roberts, L., and Hall, D. (2001). *Rural Tourism and Recreation: Principles to Practice.* Wallingford: CAB International.

Robinson, G. (1990). *Conflict and Change in the Countryside.* London: Belhaven Press.

Saeter, J. (1998). The significance of tourism and economic development in rural areas: A Norwegian case study. In R. Butler, C. M. Hall, and J. Jenkins (eds), *Tourism and Recreation in Rural Areas* (pp. 235–45). Chichester: John Wiley.

Sharpley, R. (2001). Sustainable rural tourism development: Ideal or idyll? In L. Roberts and D. Hall (eds), *Rural Tourism and Recreation: Principles to Practice* (pp. 57–8).Wallingford: CAB International.

Sharpley, R., and Craven, B. (2001). The 2001 foot and mouth crisis. Rural economy and tourism policy implications: A comment. *Current Issues in Tourism* 4(6), 527–37.

Sharpley, R., and Sharpley, J. (1997). *Rural Tourism: An Introduction.* London: International Thomson Business Press.

Shaw, G., and Williams, A. (1994). *Critical Issues in Tourism: A Geographical Perspective.* Oxford: Blackwell.

Shoard, M. (1999). *A Right to Roam.* Oxford: Oxford University Press.

Short, J. (1991). *Imagined Country: Society, Culture and Environment.* London: Routledge.

Smith, M., and Krannich, R. (1998) Tourism dependence and resident attitudes. *Annals of Tourism Research* 25(4), 783–802.

Sofield, T., and Getz, D. (1997). Rural tourism in Australia: The Undara experience. In S. Page and D. Getz (eds), *The Business of Rural Tourism* (pp. 143–61). London: International Thomson Business Press.

Sørensen, A., and Nilsson, P. (1999). *Virtual Reality Versus Rural Reality in Rural Tourism: Contemplating the Attraction of the Rural.* Alta, Norway: 8th Nordic Symposium in Hospitality and Tourism Research.

Sørensen, A., and Nilsson, P. (2001). Are there any such things as rural tourists in Denmark? New Directions in Managing Rural Tourism and Leisure Conference, Scottish Agricultural College, Ayr.

Tribe, J., Font, X., Griffiths, N., Vickery, R., and Yale, K. (2000). *Environmental Management for Rural Tourism and Recreation*. London: Cassell.

Weaver, D., and Fennell, D. (1997) Rural tourism in Canada: The Saskatchewan vacation farm operator as entrepreneur. In S. Page and D. Getz (eds), *The Business of Rural Tourism* (pp. 77–92). London: International Thomson Business Press.

Whitelegg, J. (1993). *Transport for a Sustainable Future: The Case for Europe*. London: Bellhaven Press.

Wilson, S., Fesenmaier, D., Fesenmaier, J., and van Es, J. (2001). Factors for success in rural tourism development. *Journal of Travel Research* 40(2), 132–8.

WTO/UNEP (1992). *Development of National Parks and Protected Areas*. Madrid: World Tourism Organization/United Nations Environment Programme.

Chapter 31

Mobility, Tourism, and Second Homes

Dieter K. Müller

Mobility and the Geography of Second Home Tourism

Although an important tourism phenomenon, second home tourism has attracted only limited academic attention. Possibly this is due to second homes being considered to be at the edge of what is regarded as tourism. For example, Cohen (1974) identified second home owners as marginal tourists due to the lack of novelty in their travel behavior. However, Jaakson (1986) rejected this interpretation and, instead, argued that second home tourism constitutes a significant part of domestic tourism. Therefore, ignoring it would also mean neglecting important explanations for travel behavior and tourism infrastructure. More recently, second homes have also been considered an important international phenomenon and an important linking activity between tourism and migration, and tourism and daytripping (Müller 1999; Hall and Williams 2002).

The academic awareness of second homes reached a peak in the early 1970s when increased car ownership and interest in rural environments and outdoor activities, combined with the culmination of a long period of growth in disposable incomes in developed countries, led to a growth in second home tourism (Coppock 1977c). Berry (1970) predicted that *telemobility* – allowing people to move experiences to themselves instead of visiting these experiences – would lead to a second home owners' *invasion* of the countryside by the year 2000. In the case of this predicted invasion Rogers (1977: 100) argued that "there will have to be a revolution in our thinking on regional dynamics and on the role of second homes within the so-called *rural* and *urban* areas."

Today we know that this invasion did not occur, or at least not at the level that Berry had predicted. Instead, the oil crisis and the emergence of other destinations diverted tourist demand to other areas. In addition, academic interest – which peaked in Coppock's (1977b) seminal book *Second Homes: Curse or Blessing?* – became more localized in its concern and, hence, there was not the anticipated conceptual revolution regarding the role of second homes. However, by the 1990s second homes were once again on the academic agenda. This is probably due to two different phenomena. First, growing seasonal mobility among retired households put the issue of second homes on the agenda (King and Patterson 1998; King, Warnes, and Williams 2000). Second, the increasing internationalization of second home tourism generated new forms of conflict centered on foreign property ownership in some locations (Buller and Hoggart 1994b; Müller 1999). Such societal changes, as well as changing identities due to migration, increasing individual mobility and welfare, and new environmental interests, all suggest the need to revisit second home tourism.

On the Definition of Second Homes

In contrast to many other forms of tourism, second home tourism is covered relatively well in national statistics. In most Western countries second homes can be identified in census data. Nevertheless, there is a lack of comparable data, for example due to diverging definitions regarding the inclusion of caravans and boats as second homes, the difference between houses owned as second homes and for private rental for income, and the duration of occupancy (Coppock 1977c; King, Warnes, and Williams 2000). However, most researchers employ a pragmatic approach where data access determines the definition of second homes. Consequently, international comparisons are difficult to accomplish. Although urban second homes exist, they have generated little attention. Instead, the research focus has been on rural second homes, and this chapter, too, only discusses privately owned rural second homes.

Definitional approaches to second homes are also made more complicated because interest in second homes is not limited to tourism research but has also attracted attention from planning (Langdalen 1980; Gallent 1997; Gallent and Tewdwr-Jones 2000), rural geography (Pacione 1984; Buller and Hoggart 1994a) and population geography (Warnes 1994; King, Warnes, and Williams 2000). This is also mirrored in the terminology used to characterize second home tourism. For example, Casado-Diaz (1999) uses the term "residential tourism," Flognfeldt (2002) prefers "semi-migration," Finnveden (1960) "summer migration," and Pacione (1984) writes about "seasonal suburbanization."

Recently, the term – and also the concept of second homes – has been substantially brought into question (Kaltenborn 1997a, 1998; Müller 2002b) given that an increasing number of households have the ability to allocate their time independently from a workplace and, hence, adopt more mobile lifestyles and use several homes equally. Kaltenborn (1998) argues that second homes are seldom sold, but are sometimes passed on through generations. Hence, they may form true first homes due to emotional place attachment on the part of their owners. The extent of this phenomenon, however, is often concealed due to administrative practices which compel households to register one primary residence only (Müller 2002b).

The Historical Geography of Second Home Tourism

The roots of second homes can be traced back in ancient societies where the house in the countryside was an exclusive asset for the nobility (Coppock 1977c). During the eighteenth century second homes could be found in spa towns, and later on in places for sea bathing (Löfgren 1999), and were often used on a seasonal basis to escape city life (Bunce 1994). New means of transport were a substantial influence on the geography of second homes. In the Stockholm archipelago, for example, second homes were built along the steamboat lines (Ljungdahl 1938). During the first part of the twentieth century second home ownership spread to other groups outside of the upper classes, along with changing ideas regarding contact with nature and wilderness. In North America, second homes were constructed in wilderness areas as a cultural reminder of frontier development (Coppock 1977c; Wolfe 1977; Löfgren 1999). In the Nordic countries, second home construction was supported as a means of social tourism enabling an increasing number of households to take part in tourism, and entailed the construction of a large number of second homes in metropolitan hinterlands, particularly between 1950 and 1980 (Nordin 1993b).

Second Home Owners and their Motives

There are many reasons for purchasing a second home and these have to be understood in terms of the meaning of second home ownership for individual owners. Hence, most households purchase second homes to achieve some kind of lifestyle not available at the primary residence. These lifestyle decisions appear to be of increasing importance and imply, in some cases, greater mobility between different continents (Fountain and Hall 2002; Timothy 2002).

Jaakson (1986) provided a comprehensive overview of the meaning of second home tourism. Inversion from everyday life appears to be one major attraction of second homes. This inversion regards not only the focus on leisure, as opposed to work, but also a general relaxation and informality in the second home. Chaplin (1999) characterizes the behavior as an escape aiming to provide a balance in life. Moreover, second home ownership can be interpreted as a step "back to nature" (Jaakson 1986; Williams and Kaltenborn 1999), with some adaptation of the surroundings of the second home to the nature of their imagination, while others move toward an idealized simple rustic lifestyle (Jaakson 1986; Geipel 1989; Müller 1999).

Second home ownership also influences identity (Jaakson 1986). This is particularly true in cases where second homes represent emotional links to places of childhood or ancestry (Kaltenborn 1997a, 1997b; Löfgren 1999), which also influences the second home owners' possibilities of integration into the local community (Pacione 1979). Kaltenborn (1998) argues that second home ownership constitutes a turn to the local as a response to globalization. Similarly, Buller and Hoggart (1994a) argue that British second home owners are seeking a lost British countryside in rural France. However, in his study of German second home owners in Sweden, Müller (1999) draws a slightly different conclusion, suggesting that second home ownership mirrors a form of internationalization. Here European integration suggests that owning a property abroad forms a self-evident right within the new Europe, and becomes an expression of a changing geographical identity. Inevitably, the strength of such feelings differs amongst the member states of the European Union.

Jaakson (1986) also mentions certainty, aiming at keeping the family together, as a further reason for second home ownership. Further, Jaakson (1986) and Kaltenborn

(1997a, 1997b) note the importance of continuity represented by second homes. Many second home owners have inherited their properties and thus it represents a place of family heritage. In fact, some second home owners state that they invest in a second home in order to pass it on to the next generation (Jansson and Müller 2002). Another reason for purchasing a second home is related to creative work. Maintaining and changing the interior and exterior of the second home can itself be an important motive for second home ownership (Jaakson 1986; Müller 1999). Chaplin (1999) sees such creative work as a means whereby owners express their identities.

Depending on the national context, second home ownership can also be an expression of elitism (Wolfe 1977; Jaakson 1986; Halseth and Rosenberg 1995; Halseth 1998). Halseth (1998) argues that second home landscapes are turning more and more into elite playgrounds. In contrast, second homes are part of everyday life in many Scandinavian countries. Even there, however, second home ownership in certain amenity-rich locations can be perceived as attaching status to owners.

Recent developments in Europe and North America indicate that second home ownership can also, usefully, be approached from a life-cycle perspective, particularly in the context of retirement second home ownership which attracts retirees to amenity-rich and often sunny places (Buller and Hoggart 1994a; Warnes 1994; Williams, King, and Warnes 1997; King, Warnes, and Williams 2000). In general it can be noted that most owners of second home are over 40 (Jansson and Müller 2002). After becoming established in the housing and labor markets, often with teenage children, households identify second homes as objects for investment and creative focus. It is also obvious that a proportion of second home owners actually purchase a property for later retirement (Hoggart and Buller 1994; Müller 1999). Hence, second home ownership sometimes represents a pre-stage to permanent migration. However, in many cases permanent migration is not registered, because households choose to retain a link to their formerly permanent home (Müller 1999). Therefore, it is almost impossible to pinpoint accurately the households that retire to their second homes. Without doubt, second homes for retirement are not only of interest from a national perspective. Instead, second home ownership often implies international mobility from the north to the sunbelts of North America and Europe.

Second home patterns

Research into geographical patterns dominated the early research agenda on second homes, and entailed a large number of studies providing comprehensive overviews of second home ownership in various regions (Tombaugh 1970; Clout 1971, 1972, 1977; Bielckus 1977; Henshall 1977; Thissen 1978; Pacione 1979; Barke 1991). The majority of these studies followed the tradition of regional geography, placing the focus on the second home region, mapping volumes and distributions. Some studies addressed second home patterns from a more theoretical point of view. For example, Aldskogius (1968, 1969) developed quantitative models of the diffusion of second homes in Sweden. Similarly, Burby, Donnelly, and Weiss (1972) simulated second home patterns for a hypothetical island.

More recently, second home patterns were addressed with regard to mobility and origin–destination relationships (Hoggart and Buller 1994, 1995; Müller 1999). In terms of spatial distance the majority of second home owners live relatively close to their property. Even in an international context, long-distance second home ownership is still the exception. These studies follow the tradition started by Wolfe (1951), scrutinizing second homes in Ontario. Similarly, Lundgren (1974) addressed second home development from an urban point of view. He showed, for Montreal, how urban growth caused a relocation of second home areas to the outer limits of the metropolitan hinterlands.

The role of real-estate agents in the distribution of second home ownership, at least in international second homes, should not be underrated. Second home owners are channeled to certain destinations by the promotional activities of real-estate agents, although this is mainly true for the more inexperienced segment of the demand market (Hoggart and Buller 1994). The agents not only act as gatekeepers to the second home area, but also play an important role in offering post-purchase services and social activities (Müller 1999). For instance, the agents organize meetings with other second home owners, help to fill in taxation forms, and give advice regarding administrative matters even years after the purchase.

The constraints of working lives also favor the location of second home ownership within the weekend traveling zone around the owner's primary residence and thus most second homes can be labeled weekend homes. These weekend homes can be visited frequently and also for short periods. In contrast, second homes outside the weekend zone, vacation homes, are only visited occasionally but often for longer periods (Müller 2002b). These patterns mirror geographical assumptions regarding spatial interactions and gravity models (Bell 1977). Müller (1999) established empirically that second home demand decreases in a logistic curve with increasing distance from the primary residence, implying that second home ownership loses attractiveness as soon as the weekend leisure zone is passed. That means that second home ownership outside the weekend zone is relatively independent of the location of the primary residence; the second home is visited once or twice annually. Instead, second home locations are dependent on the geography of amenity-rich landscapes, which tends to concentrate the geographical distribution, at least of purpose-built second homes, to coastal and mountain areas (Tombaugh 1970). Nevertheless, second homes, often converted former permanent rural housing, can be found in virtually all locations, simply because they also represent links to places of childhood and family origin.

Impacts and Planning Implications

The spatial distribution of second home ownership also influences the geography of change induced by second homes. For example, impacts on society and the environment can differ between areas characterized by converted second homes as opposed to purpose-built second homes. A common problem is the seasonality in resident populations induced by second home tourism, an issue that may be neglected within some planning systems (Ragatz 1970; Casado-Diaz 1999), although it may be highly contentious in others, such as that of the UK. This issue is discussed in more detail below.

The impacts of second home tourism are, however, primarily dependent on the extent to which second home ownership displaces permanent residents, or complements them by utilizing otherwise empty houses. In this context, Müller (1999) argues that second home tourism is mainly a consequence of rural change. Accordingly, second home tourism is considered a symptom of the declining traditional countryside. In contrast, Gallent and Tewdwr-Jones (2000) interpret second home tourism as a cause for rural decline. Certainly, evidence for both arguments can be found. Differing local and national contexts entail, however, difficulties in drawing general conclusions regarding the impact of second home tourism. Instead, second homes have to be seen in the context of different planning regimes and place traditions.

Economic impacts

Achieving a positive economic impact from second home development is a central concern of rural planners and politicians when making decisions about land use and tourism development (Green et al. 1996). For example, Shucksmith (1983) lists impacts related to second home acquisition, improvements, and the consumption of other goods and services as forms of economic impact. Generally, second home development is considered an option to sustain rural environments which have experienced economic and population decline, due to the additional contributions second homes make to the regional economy (Clout 1972; Deller, Marcouiller, and Green 1997). However, the economic effects of second homes are not always positive. Increases in property values are often considered a threat to sustainable rural development (Boschken 1975; Shucksmith 1983). In a study in Vermont, USA, it is argued that second home development increases the tax burden for the local population (Fritz 1982), although Gartner (1987) states the opposite, arguing that costs are shared between more households. For the United States, it is estimated that second homes generate revenues that just cover the increased expenses of public services (Deller, Marcouiller, and Green 1997). Nevertheless, infrastructure investments and other adverse economic impacts of second home development are usually not assessed comprehensively, and hence systematic accounts of the economic effects of second homes are not self-evident.

In this context it can be observed that the distance between second home and primary residence substantially influences the expenses of second home owners' households (Bohlin 1982a; Nordin 1993a; Müller 2002c). The longer the distance between second home and primary residence, the smaller the quantity of goods that can be taken from home (Bohlin 1982b). Müller (1999) established that, during their period of residence, six German second home owners in Sweden spend as much as a permanent household. Moreover, second home owners tend to favor small rural shops and therefore substantially contribute to the maintenance of retail services in the countryside (Nordin 1993a; Müller 1999).

Social impacts

During the 1960s and 1970s, the social impact of second home ownership initiated concern among rural populations and planners (Coppock 1977a, 1977d; Rogers 1977; Jordan 1980). In the 1990s these concerns were still alive despite the fact that the fears of "an invasion" of the countryside, expressed in the 1970s, had not been realized (Gallent and Tewdwr-Jones 2000). These concerns usually focus on the exclusion of the local population as a result of the increase in property prices produced by second home demand, particularly when it is perceived that local young families are unable to purchase a property (Coppock 1977d; Gallent and Tewdwr-Jones 2000). Where such processes occur, formerly permanently used villages are transformed into seasonal resorts, implying, for example, increased crime rates and reduced local services (e.g., Jordan 1980). In addition, Jordan (1980) argued that the second home owners may disrupt long-established sociocultural norms and practices. In the Welsh case, significant sociocultural impacts are perceived due to the fact that the second home owners were primarily English, and were not only seen as external agents depriving the local population of houses, but were also English-speakers in areas where Welsh was commonly the language of everyday life (Coppock 1977d; Rogers 1977; Shucksmith 1983; Gallent and Tewdwr-Jones 2000). In addition, second home owners may benefit from government grants aimed at modernizing rural housing which are implicitly for local residents (Gallent 1997).

A reason for resentment toward second home development seems to be the differing social and economic backgrounds of second home owners and locals (Halseth and Rosenberg 1995). Second home development can be perceived as a form of rural gentrification that implies an encounter between traditional rural lifestyles and urban imaginations of the rural (Müller 1999). Halseth (1998) argues that this may entail a transformation of the countryside into an elite landscape. However, Flognfeldt (2002) draws a different picture for a second home area in Norway. There, second home owners are partly perceived as "local patriots" and, hence, are more and more seen as a resource that can be utilized to attract additional businesses.

The social integration of second home owners into the local community is, however, not automatic but is dependent on the ambitions and strategies of the second home owners, as well as the attitudes of the locals (Albarre 1977; Buller and Hoggart 1994b). Limited social distance may enhance the opportunity for second home owners to become fully integrated in the local community (Pacione 1979). International second home ownership causes problems regarding language and traditions (Buller and Hoggart 1994b; Müller 1999). Moreover, contact with the local population is limited. Hence, contact with other second home owners, often of the same nationality, may substitute for the desired countryside life among the locals (Müller 1999), and may even be the goal of some second home owners – such as the British in the Costa del Sol (King, Warnes, and Williams 2000).

Environmental impacts

Second home ownership does not always imply new environmental impacts. In cases of formerly permanent rural homes, usually no new infrastructure is needed, although this is not so in the case of purpose-built second homes. Unplanned developments around lakes and rivers, which are particularly attractive to second home development, are a particular concern because of pollution risks (Ragatz 1977; Gartner 1987). Indeed, concerns over environmental impacts led Langdalen (1980) and Clout (1971) to argue for planning restrictions in order to limit the impact of second home development on the landscape.

Second home owners tend to appreciate the same aspects of a locality, such as landscape and calmness, as the local population. However, there may be substantial differences in their view of future development in the second home community. Second home owners are usually more conservative and less positive about change

(Boschken 1975; Aronsson 1993; Girard and Gartner 1993; Green et al. 1996). Instead, they focus more on the physical aspects of their second home environment and thus favor land use control and preservation (Burby, Donnelly, and Weiss 1972).

Moreover, sometimes second home owners have romanticized images of rural areas born of earlier tourism experiences. However, the rural reality differs from these images. German second home owners in Sweden, for example, react to this by constructing a landscape around them that represents their image of the Swedish countryside, which is strongly influenced by the work of a Swedish children's author (Müller 1999). This search for an ideal and authentic countryside also entails the fact that they are usually interested in restricting further tourism development (Aronsson 1993). Obviously, there is no space for other tourists within the rural idyll.

Conclusions

Research has mainly addressed the impacts of second home tourism. In particular, the impact of second homes on the rural property market and the consequences for the rural society have attracted academic interest (Coppock 1977b; Gallent and Tewdwr-Jones 2000). To some extent these studies of impacts have been abstracted from analyses of underlying social, political, and economic processes and, therefore, tend to be relatively rudimentary and simplistic. Hence there is a need for further impact studies, set in the context of analyzing broader processes of production, consumption, and regulation. For example, there is a need to study the economic dimension of second home development in the context of the property market. Moreover, it is important that the local population is understood not only as a victim of societal change, but also as an agent of it. In other words, its members are reflexive actors, who contribute not only to the process of second home development and integration, but also to the significant place differences which exist with respect to these processes. In addition, it is desirable to assess many of the social and political issues related to participation in second home tourism.

The emergence of new mobile lifestyles, and of new patterns of international mobility, requires new perspectives that focus on the role of second homes beyond the rural arena (Williams and Hall 2002). Recent second home development cannot be understood or managed effectively without examining the reasons and changes that caused the newly awakened interest in owning such a property. Consequently, the resulting patterns of second home location also require a fresh assessment.

There is also an urgent need to ask new questions regarding planning and second homes. The predominating perception of second home owners as outsiders within rural societies increasingly fails to acknowledge the emergence of new mobile lifestyles among both the second home owners and the rural population. This new geography of human mobility entails profound questions regarding concepts such as place attachment, identity, and home. Consequently, it has to be asked how planning can adapt to this and how second home owners can be represented in the planning process. This is vital considering the presence and the absence of the second home owners in the host communities and home communities.

In conclusion, it can be stated that second home tourism is truly an expression of globalization and today's highly mobile societies, and at the same time it is an expression of maintaining family roots and traditions. Hence, second home tourism is not only about tourism, but goes beyond it. It represents the changing conditions of production and consumption, and thus it challenges a core concept of the social sciences, i.e. the distinction between migration and tourism.

REFERENCES

Albarre, G. (1977). Second homes and conservation in southern Belgium. In J. T. Coppock (ed.), *Second Homes: Curse or Blessing?* (pp. 139–46). Oxford: Pergamon.

Aldskogius, H. (1968). Studier i Siljansområdets fritidshusbebyggelse. *Geografiska Regionstudier* 4. Uppsala: Department of Social and Economic Geography.

Aldskogius, H. (1969). Modelling the evolution of settlement patterns: Two studies of vacation house settlements. *Geografiska Regionstudier* 6. Uppsala: Department of Social and Economic Geography.

Aronsson, L. (1993). *Mötet: En studie i Smögen av Turisters, Fritidsboendes och Bofastas Användning av Tid och Rum* [Encounter: A Study of the Use of Time and Space among Tourists, Cottagers, and Permanent Residents in Smögen]. Research Report 1993:1, Unit for Regional Science, University College Karlstad.

Barke, M. (1991). The growth and changing pattern of second homes in Spain in the 1970s. *Scottish Geographical Magazine* 107, 12–21.

Bell, M. (1977). The spatial distribution of second homes: A modified gravity model. *Journal of Leisure Research* 9, 225–32.

Berry, B. J. L. (1970). The geography of the United States in the year 2000. *Transactions of the Institute of British Geographers* 51, 21–53.

Bielckus, C. L. (1977). Second homes in Scandinavia. In J. T. Coppock (ed.), *Second Homes: Curse or Blessing?* (pp. 35–46). Oxford: Pergamon.

Bohlin, M. (1982a). The spatial and economic impact of recreational expenditures and sales in the Pigeon Lake area of Alberta. *Forskningsrapporter från Kulturgeografiska institutionen vid Uppsala universitet* 77. Uppsala: Department of Social and Economic Geography.

Bohlin, M. (1982b). Fritidsboende i den regionala ekonomin: Vart fritidshusägarnas pengar tar vägen. *Geografiska Regionstudier* 14. Uppsala: Department of Social and Economic Geography.

Boschken, H. L. (1975). The second home subdivision: Market suitability for recreational and pastoral use. *Journal of Leisure Research* 7, 63–75.

Buller, H., and Hoggart, K. (1994a). *International Counterurbanization: British Migrants in Rural France*. Aldershot: Ashgate.

Buller, H., and Hoggart, K. (1994b). The social integration of British home owners into French rural communities. *Journal of Rural Studies* 2, 197–210.

Bunce, M. (1994). *The Countryside Ideal: Anglo-American Images of Landscape*. London: Routledge.

Burby, R. J. III, Donnelly, T. G., and Weiss, S. F. (1972). Vacation home location: A model for simulating the residential development of rural recreation areas. *Regional Studies* 6, 421–39.

Casado-Diaz, M. A. (1999). Socio-demographic impacts of residential tourism: A case study of Torrevieja, Spain. *International Journal of Tourism Research* 1, 223–7.

Chaplin, D. (1999). Consuming work/productive leisure: The consumption patterns of second home environments. *Leisure Studies* 18, 41–55.

Clout, H. D. (1971). Second homes in the Auvergne. *Geographical Review* 61, 530–53.

Clout, H. D. (1972). Second homes in the United States. *Tijdschrift voor Economische en Sociale Geografie* 63, 393–401.

Clout, H. D. (1977). Résidences secondaires in France. In J. T. Coppock (ed.), *Second Homes: Curse or Blessing?* (pp. 47–62). Oxford: Pergamon.

Cohen, E. (1974). Who is a tourist? A conceptual clarification. *Sociological Review* 22 527–55.

Coppock, J. T. (1977a). Issues and conflicts. In J. T. Coppock (ed.), *Second Homes: Curse or Blessing?* (pp. 195–216). Oxford: Pergamon.

Coppock, J. T. (ed.) (1977b). *Second Homes: Curse or Blessing?* Oxford: Pergamon.

Coppock, J. T. (1977c). Second homes in perspective. In J. T. Coppock (ed.), *Second Homes: Curse or Blessing?* (pp. 1–16). Oxford: Pergamon.

Coppock, J. T. (1977d). Social implications of second homes in mid and north Wales. In J. T. Coppock (ed.), *Second Homes: Curse or Blessing?* (pp. 147–54). Oxford: Pergamon.

Deller, S. C., Marcouiller, D. W., and Green, G. P. (1997). Recreational housing and local government finance. *Annals of Tourism Research* 24, 687–705.

Finnveden, B. (1960). Den dubbla bosättningen och sommarmigrationen: Exempel från Hallandskustens fritidsbebyggelse. *Svensk Geografisk Årsbok* 36, 58–84.

Flognfeldt, T., Jr. (2002). Second home ownership: A sustainable semi-migration? In C. M. Hall and A. M. Williams (eds), *Tourism and Migration: New Relationships between Production and Consumption* (pp. 187–281). Dordrecht: Kluwer.

Fountain, J., and Hall, C. M. (2002). The impact of lifestyle migration on rural communities: A case study of Akaroa, New Zealand. In C. M. Hall and A. M. Williams (eds), *Tourism and Migration: New Relationships between Production and Consumption* (pp. 153–68). Dordrecht: Kluwer.

Fritz, R. G. (1982). Tourism, vacation home development and residential tax burden: A case study of the local finances of 240 Vermont towns. *American Journal of Economics and Sociology* 41, 375–85.

Gallent, N. (1997). Improvement grants, second homes and planning control in England and Wales: A policy review. *Planning Practice & Research* 12, 401–11.

Gallent, N., and Tewdwr-Jones, M. (2000). *Rural Second Homes in Europe: Examining Housing Supply and Planning Control.* Aldershot: Ashgate.

Gartner, W. C. (1987). Environmental impacts of recreational home developments. *Annals of Tourism Research* 14, 38–57.

Geipel, R. (1989). Territorialität auf dem Mikromaastab. *Münchener Geographische Hefte* 62, 111–29.

Girard, T. C., and Gartner, W. C. (1993). Second home second view: Host community perceptions. *Annals of Tourism Research* 20, 685–700.

Green, G. P., Marcoullier, D., Deller, S., Erkkila, D., and Sumathi, N. R. (1996). Local dependency, land use attitudes, and economic development: Comparisons between seasonal and permanent residents. *Rural Sociology* 61, 427–45.

Hall, C. M., and Williams, A. M. (eds) (2002). *Tourism and Migration: New Relationships between Production and Consumption.* Dordrecht: Kluwer.

Halseth G. (1998). *Cottage Country in Transition: A Social Geography of Change and Contention in the Rural-Recreational Countryside.* Montreal: McGill-Queen's University Press.

Halseth, G., and Rosenberg, M. W. (1995). Cottagers in an urban field. *Professional Geographer* 47, 148–59.

Henshall, J. D. (1977). Second homes in the Caribbean. In J. T. Coppock (ed.), *Second Homes: Curse or Blessing?* (pp. 75–84). Oxford: Pergamon.

Hoggart, K., and Buller, H. (1994). Property agents as gatekeepers in British house purchases in rural France. *Geoforum* 25, 173–87.

Hoggart, K., and Buller, H. (1995). Geographical differences in British property acquisitions in rural France. *Geographical Journal* 161, 69–78.

Jaakson, R. (1986). Second-home domestic tourism. *Annals of Tourism Research* 13, 367–91.
Jansson, B., and Müller, D. K. (2002). *Fritidsboende i Kvarken*. Umeå: Department of Social and Economic Geography.
Jordan, J. W. (1980). The summer people and the natives: Some effects of tourism in a Vermont vacation village. *Annals of Tourism Research* 7, 34–55.
Kaltenborn, B. P. (1997a). Nature of place attachment: A study among recreation home-owners in Southern Norway. *Leisure Sciences* 19, 175–89.
Kaltenborn, B. P. (1997b). Recreation homes in natural settings: Factors affecting place attachment. *Norsk Geografisk Tidsskrift* 51, 187–98.
Kaltenborn, B. P. (1998). The alternate home: Motives of recreation home use. *Norsk Geografisk Tidsskrift* 52, 121–34.
King, R., and Patterson, G. (1998). Diverse paths: The elderly British in Tuscany. *International Journal of Population Geography* 4(2), 157–82.
King, R., Warnes, A. M., and Williams, A. M. (2000). *Sunset Lives: British Retirement to the Mediterranean*. London: Berg.
Langdalen, E. (1980). Second homes in Norway: A controversial planning problem. *Norsk Geografisk Tidsskrift* 34, 139–44.
Ljungdahl, S. G. (1938). Sommar-Stockholm. *Ymer* 58, 218–42.
Löfgren, O. (1999). *On Holiday: A History of Vacationing*. Berkeley: University of California Press.
Lundgren, J. O. J. (1974). On access to recreational lands in dynamic metropolitan hinterlands. *Tourist Review* 29, 124–31.
Müller, D. K. (1999). *German Second Home Owners in the Swedish Countryside: On the Internationalization of the Leisure Space*. Umeå: Department of Social and Economic Geography.
Müller, D. K. (2002a). German second home development in Sweden. In C. M. Hall and A. M. Williams (eds), *Tourism and Migration: New Relationships between Production and Consumption* (pp. 169–86). Dordrecht: Kluwer.
Müller, D. K. (2002b). German second home owners in Sweden: Some remarks on the tourism–migration nexus. *Revue Européenne des Migrations Internationales* 18, 67–86.
Müller, D. K. (2002c). Second home ownership and sustainable development in northern Sweden. *Tourism and Hospitality Research* 3, 343–56.
Nordin, U. (1993a). Fritidshusbebyggelse för skärgårdsbor? Studier av fritidsboendets betydelse för sysselsättningen i Blidö församling, Norrtälje kommun 1945–1987. *Meddelanden från Kulturgeografiskalnstitutionen vid Stockholms Universitet* B86. Stockholm: Department of Social and Economic Geography.
Nordin, U. (1993b). Second homes. In H. Aldskogius (ed.), *Cultural Life, Recreation and Tourism* (pp. 72–9). Stockholm: National Atlas of Sweden.
Pacione, M. (1979). Second homes on Arran. *Norsk Geografisk Tidsskrift* 33, 33–8.
Pacione, M. (1984). *Rural Geography*. London: Harper & Row.
Ragatz, R. L. (1970). Vacation homes in the northeastern United States: Seasonality in population distribution. *Annals of the Association of American Geographers* 60, 447–55.
Ragatz, R. L. (1977). Vacation homes in rural areas: Towards a model for predicting their distribution and occupancy patterns. In J. T. Coppock (ed.), *Second Homes: Curse or Blessing?* (pp. 181–94). Oxford: Pergamon.
Rogers, A. W. (1977). Second homes in England and Wales: A spatial view. In J. T. Coppock (ed.), *Second Homes: Curse or Blessing?* (pp. 85–102). Oxford: Pergamon.
Shucksmith, D. M. (1983). Second homes: A framework for policy. *Town Planning Review* 54, 174–93.
Thissen, F. (1978). Second homes in the Netherlands. *Tijdschrift voor Economische en Sociale Geografie* 69, 322–32.

Timothy, D. J. (2002). Tourism and the growth of urban ethnic islands. In C. M. Hall and A. M. Williams (eds), *Tourism and Migration: New Relationships between Production and Consumption* (pp. 135–52). Dordrecht: Kluwer.

Tombaugh, L. W. (1970). Factors influencing vacation home location. *Journal of Leisure Research* 2, 54–63.

Warnes, T. (1994). Permanent and seasonal international retirement migration: The prospects for Europe. *Nederlandse Geografische Studies* 173, 69–79.

Williams, A. M., and Hall, C. M. (2002). Tourism, migration, circulation and mobility: The contingencies of time and place. In C. M. Hall and A. M. Williams (eds), *Tourism and Migration: New Relationships between Production and Consumption* (pp. 1–52). Dordrecht: Kluwer.

Williams, A. M., King, R., and Warnes, A. (1997). A place in the sun: International retirement migration from the UK to Southern Europe. *European Urban and Regional Studies* 4, 115–34.

Williams, D. R., and Kaltenborn, B. P. (1999). Leisure places and modernity: The use and meaning of recreational cottages in Norway and the USA. In D. Crouch (ed.), *Leisure/Tourism Geographies* (pp. 214–30). London: Routledge.

Wolfe, R. (1951). Summer cottages in Ontario. *Economic Geography* 27, 10–32.

Wolfe, R. I. (1977). Summer cottages in Ontario: Purpose-built for an inessential purpose. In J. T. Coppock (ed.), *Second Homes: Curse or Blessing?* (pp. 17–34). Oxford: Pergamon.

Chapter 32

Gaming and Tourism: Issues for the New Millennium

Patricia A. Stokowski

In current trends in tourism, gambling is big news. A sentiment of unbridled optimism and competitive business fervor has accompanied the rapid expansion of gambling (the activity) and gaming (the term used by entrepreneurs to describe their business) across the United States and internationally over the past two decades. Acclaimed as a new means of economic stimulation, job creation, and enhancement of tax revenues, gaming development has become, by some measures, a success story in the midst of worldwide economic uncertainty. The new permissiveness for gambling activity and gaming development is evident in North and South America, Britain, Australia, Africa, the newly independent states of eastern and central Europe, and in some areas of Asia (Thompson 1998; Cosgrove and Klassen 2001). In fact, many state and national governments now find gambling revenues integral to supporting public functions.

Favoring these new development strategies are transformations in public values, as moral concerns that once limited the spread of gambling have moderated in the twenty-first century. For example, in the United States, in contrast to public opinions expressed in earlier decades, a 1999 poll showed that about two-thirds of Americans (63 percent) approved of gambling, about 57 percent of adults had purchased a lottery ticket in the prior year, and about 31 percent had gambled in a casino (Gallup Poll 1999). Attitudes toward gaming as a growth strategy, however, were mixed. That same survey reported that 47 percent of respondents thought gambling should stay at current levels and only 22 percent thought gambling should be expanded. Concerns over increased negative community impacts, evidence of the spread of pathological and problem gambling behavior, and unaccounted costs of gaming development have become central in public debate and controversy (Nichols, Giacopassi, and Stitt 2002).

This chapter provides an assessment of the contemporary relationships between gaming and tourism. Key issues and themes are identified, and evolving debates are evaluated. Many of the examples below derive from US gaming locales because these types of "open market" developments seem especially problematic in their social and economic consequences. But the considerable social transformations introduced by the spread of gambling all over the world in recent decades, even in the more controlled gaming environments of other countries, also have implications for the future of tourism.

The topic of gambling is particularly interesting for tourism geographers and other social scientists, whose interests range widely across environmental and social issues. Geographers interested in the physical and environmental aspects of tourism have studied gaming development-related land use changes, the manipulation of community spaces to accommodate gambling venues, the extent and persistence of gaming impacts, and the design and interpretation of built landscapes and tourist attractions associated with gaming. Geographers interested in the social and cultural aspects of tourism have analyzed the transportation and communication networks of gamblers, laborers, and businesses, the mobility of people and capital, the social and cultural impacts of new gaming developments, and gaming tourist behaviors and practices. Though interest in these topics is increasing, many issues remain relatively under-studied, and future research into the policy implications of relationships between gaming and tourism is warranted.

The Recent Proliferation of Gaming in the US

A brief discussion of trends associated with gambling activity and gaming development in the US can demonstrate the expansion of the industry as well as provide a context for the recent flourishing of academic interest in this topic. In 1960, all legal betting in the US was conducted at horse and dog tracks in about 20 states, or at casinos in just one state (Nevada had legalized casinos in 1931). Atlantic City, New Jersey, legalized casino gambling in 1976, and state-sanctioned lotteries – common in colonial and early decades of American history, but later made illegal – took their contemporary form when New Hampshire adopted a lottery in 1964 (Clotfelter and Cook 1989; Mason and Nelson 2001). Over the past 15 years, though, there has been unparalleled growth and expansion of gaming across the country. Now, all but two states (Hawaii and Utah) allow some form of gambling, and Americans can legally gamble at horse and dog tracks, take chances in state-sanctioned lotteries in 37 states, bet at privately owned and managed land-based casinos and at river-boat and dockside casinos in 11 states, gamble at casinos on Native American reservations in 31 states, drop coins in thousands of "convenience gambling" machines scattered throughout select communities across the country, or go online to participate in internet-based gambling from the convenience of their home.

The corporate-driven, free-market model of gaming development exhibited in the US shares with its international counterparts an interest in maximizing economic returns. Though the primary beneficiary of gaming in some countries is government rather than corporations, the economic impacts associated with the spread of gaming are often dramatic. For example, Americans are reported to wager over $600 billion a year (up from $117 billion in 1984; see Mason 2000). The American Gaming Association reports that gross gambling revenues (wagers minus winnings returned to bettors) for all types of gambling increased from about $27 billion in 1991 to over $63 billion in 2001; nearly $26 billion of the 2001 industry total was from commercial casinos (American Gaming Association 2003). A 1996 Arthur Anderson study of the economic effects of casino gambling, cited in the final report of the National Gaming Impact Study Commission (1999: 7–6), noted that, "in 1995 the casino industry recorded $22–25 billion in total revenues, paid a total of $2.9 billion in direct taxes (including federal and state, property, construction sales and use, and gambling taxes), directly employed almost 300,000 people and paid $7.3 billion in wages." These data show that gambling is a formidable tourism activity: "In dollar terms, legalized gambling is bigger than movies, bigger than spectator sports, bigger than theme parks, bigger than all the books, magazines and newspapers published in the United States put together" (Mason and Nelson 2001: 2).

Similar growth patterns are associated with commercial gaming development in Canada. Mandal and Vander Doelen (1999) reported that over 50 casinos operated across the country in 1998, and that Canadians wagered over $27 billion in 1999. Canadian support of casino development rests on the expectation of new revenues for government and industry, and the anticipation of new jobs and economic stimulation. An additional rationale is that of controlling cross-border tourist markets. Provincial governments attempt to keep in their country monies that Canadian gamblers would otherwise spend in US casinos across the border.

The Canadian model of legalized casinos differs in an important way from the American approach: the provinces themselves own and operate their casinos (similar to some European approaches), or they have created public–private partnerships for casino development and management. These alternative models represent different philosophies in regulating casino gaming. The American approach has been for federal and state governments to exert strong regulatory authority while letting private corporate competition and the market determine the scope of gaming development. Most other countries have limited the number of casinos and access to those facilities, and have retained monopoly government ownership so as to direct gaming revenues toward social goals (Thompson 1998).

Key Issues and Debates

In the US, the extraordinarily rapid expansion of commercial gambling opportunities over the last two decades led to the creation of the federally designated National Gaming Impact Study Commission in 1997. Charged with coordinating a comprehensive analysis of the social and economic consequences of gaming in the US, this body eventually recommended a pause in the expansion of gambling across the country. Their review of prior studies, interviews with experts, and limited primary data collection led Commissioners to believe that "The available information on economic and social impact is spotty at best and usually inadequate for an informed discussion let alone decision" (NGISC 1999: 1–6). As the most visible review of gambling in recent decades, the Commission's final report raised critical questions about the role and dispersion of gaming across American society, but it carried no legal mandate for action.

The NGISC report raised many questions about gambling behavior and gaming development. The international expansion of gambling places these questions in even broader contexts of tourism analysis. Do people who gamble have similar social and economic characteristics? Is gaming entertainment, or is it deviant behavior? Is gaming exploitative – does it disproportionately affect those who can ill afford the costs? To what extent does gaming development stimulate economic development, including tourism? How do the effects of gambling differ across regulatory settings? Do the social goods supported by taxes on gambling behavior (scholarships and education, revenues for historic preservation, open space purchases, and social welfare programs) exceed the costs? Who should benefit from gaming development? What effects does gaming development have on communities and adjacent regions? How does the introduction of gaming affect public institutions, other sectors of the economy, or political power and influence? Does the increase in gambling activity create societies that value risk?

The questions outlined above can be summarized in three general categories, each representative of a different level of social analysis: (1) individual tourist behavior; (2) the social, cultural, and environmental impacts of gaming; and (3) the structure of the gaming industry. Each of these is reviewed below, with the discussion framed around recent research advances and evolving public and academic debates.

Gambling behavior

Gambling has become such a routine form of leisure activity that even the opening of a new casino captures only modest national attention. The New Year's Eve 2003 opening of the Seneca Nation's Seneca Niagara Casino in Niagara Falls, New York, is a case in point. Only a few hours after it opened, 4,600 eager gamblers were reported to be inside the casino (Burlington Free Press 2002: 2A). The motives of these visitors – and others like them visiting casinos around the world each day – have emerged as topics of interest to social scientists. To what extent is gambling simply a "playful activity"? Who gambles, and what are their demographic characteristics? To what extent do people substitute gambling for other recreation activities?

Data about the socioeconomic characteristics of gamblers are available in academic studies about tourist behavior and in industry-generated surveys of casino, lottery and race-track patrons. Results vary, though, by gaming locale. For example, Park et al. (2002) found that respondents to a survey of gamblers in Black Hawk, Colorado, were predominantly female (60 percent), had a mean age of 57 (67 percent were over 50), and largely lived in Colorado (85.5 percent). Almost half (47 percent) had only a high school degree or less, and about 53 percent had an income of less than $40,000 a year. But, a 1999 US nationwide Gallup Poll found that men tended to gamble more than women, and the poll results "counter a stereotype of gamblers as lower class and lower income." While these studies suggest that there is no single type of gambler, comparative domestic and international analyses would be desirable to learn if there are consistent patterns in types of gamblers visiting types of gaming sites or destinations.

Researchers have also studied the leisure and pleasure motives of gamblers. In a study of the personal characteristics and activity involvement levels of patrons to a sample of Colorado casinos, Jang et al. (2000: 235) found that three factors (self-identification as a gambler, centrality of the activity to one's lifestyle, and the pleasure/importance of gambling) explained much of the variance in a visitor's "enduring involvement" with gambling, though there were differences between males and females. Applying an approach based on ethnographic participant observation, Cotte (1997) examined the motivations of gamblers visiting a large casino in the northeastern US. She derived a taxonomy of gambling motives organized around the ultimate purpose of the activity, its focus, and the nature of the consumption experience. These two studies provide exemplars for motivation research, but also indicate a need for broader research covering a wider range of respondents and types of locales.

Beyond understanding the basic characteristics and motivations of gamblers, a topic of increasing academic and public interest is that of problem and pathological gambling. Volberg (2001) explained that people defined as at-risk gamblers and problem gamblers experienced personal difficulties resulting from their gambling behaviors; that is, they have "patterns of gambling behavior that compromise, disrupt, or damage personal, family, or vocational" aspects of their lives (2001: 4). Pathological gambling, on the other hand, refers to addictive behavior in which people lose control over their gambling participation. Volberg's research suggests that about 2.5 million American adults are pathological gamblers (about 1 percent of the US population), and another 3 million are likely problem gamblers. The availability of a casino being located within 50 miles of home "is associated with about double the prevalence of problem and pathological gambling" (2001: 50). A study of German gamblers (Fabian 1995) also suggested that slot-machine gambling may lead to instances of pathological gambling.

Taken together, these studies suggest interesting hypotheses about gambling and tourist behavior. Research that extends across cases, and that compares the structural characteristics of gaming locales (and betting games), the personal motivations and socioeconomic characteristics of gamblers, and the travel and participation patterns of gamblers drawn to different kinds of gaming experiences or attractions, are also desirable. Such research would also provide a broader basis on which to judge the future expansion of markets, as baby boomers enter retirement, as populations and markets become more culturally diverse, and as market saturation occurs with industry expansion.

The social and cultural impacts of gaming

In the late 1980s, as gaming was introduced in rural communities, on reservations, and on riverboats across the US, and in major metropolitan areas around the world, academic attention turned to analyzing the impacts of this new approach to economic development. Much of that research has focused on casino gaming, and two types of studies have prevailed: survey research on community perceptions of, and support for, new casino developments; and mixed-methods analyses of the impacts of casino gaming in host communities (see the 1996 special issue of the *Journal of Travel Research* for examples). In general, research findings from this body of work have shown that benefits tend to be economic, while costs are both social and economic. Additionally, people with business interests in the gaming industry tend to be more favorable to its expansion and less worried about its impacts. But, many impacts issues remain unaddressed even today, and theoretical and practical understanding has been slowed by a lack of comparative longitudinal studies.

Several traditional tourism topics have received little attention in the current literature about gambling behavior and the business of gaming, including host–guest encounters in tourism destinations offering gaming opportunities, the marketing of place, and the reinterpretation of local history under gaming development. Another overlooked topic is that of the effects of gaming development on a community's natural and cultural environments. These issues are at the heart of a community's sense of place, and how such issues are managed during development processes is a reflection of residents' social cohesion, their abilities to identify meaningful aspects of local life, and their skills in managing a planning process. Stokowski's (1996) analysis of the introduction of casino gaming in Colorado mining towns, along with other studies of gaming development in historic communities (Chadbourne, Walker, and Wolfe 1997), indicate that strong political will is needed to protect significant local places, to apply consistent design and architectural guidelines, and to plan effectively in the face of external corporate pressure.

Clearly, development impacts will vary by the scope and scale of the gaming enterprise. Nevertheless, a pattern observed in many new casino gaming locales is that Butler's destination life cycle model has a very pronounced, steep upwards slope very early on in the process. Many communities (especially in rural areas) are unprepared for the pace of change and the single-minded focus of highly sophisticated gaming entrepreneurs seeking early entry into new markets, or the number of gamblers who ensue. Planning thus becomes a key ingredient in a community's pursuit and adoption of gaming. Traditional approaches to planning assume that benevolent public leaders will guide and manage a rational, data-based, participatory planning process. The fallacy of this model is illustrated by the evidence of growth machine politics (Stokowski 1996) that have accompanied many gaming developments. As Chadbourne, Walker, and Wolfe (1997: 51) observed, though, "casinos are not interested in an elongated public review process. Time is money."

The issues associated with community impacts of gaming offer a wide range of research questions and hypotheses for interested researchers. These topics are complex, as Raento (2001) observed in analyzing the intersections of local history, geography, and multi-scale development of gaming and heritage industries. In her study of gaming development in western US mountain towns, she noted (2001: 99) that, "The Rocky Mountain case exemplifies how local geographies interact over time with regional, national, and global processes and constantly shape the most intimate environments of routine and leisure. These local geographies are spaces where meaning and experience are created and contested." Further research on these topics would advance understanding of the geography of tourism and gaming, and would offer practical application in the areas of community planning processes, the protection of special local places, and ways of creating communities that are good places to live, not merely good places to work.

The structure of the gaming industry

The notion of gambling as "play" – as unstructured and free leisure activity – may be almost irrelevant in today's highly commercialized, electronic casino and lottery businesses. Casinos, for example, are creative arrangements of entertainment features (free drinks, low-cost meals, flashing lights, live shows, costumed "hosts," and so on) that are cleverly designed to entice people to part with their dollars. These controlled settings carefully regulate sensory elements (sight, sound, and smells) to offer consumers an aura of fun and socially acceptable risk. While betting payoffs are structured to allow visitors the illusion of gambling success, it is a truism that the house always wins in the end.

Gaming represents "profit-making ventures on a vast commercial scale... Gambling is being commercialized and institutionalized more rapidly than at any previous era in... history" (Abt 1996: 179–80). This is only possible with the approval of the state, which seeks from the process of legalization substantial direct and indirect tax revenues. In locales around the world, though, states are involved in gaming development in different ways. As Thompson (1998) pointed out, European casinos are typically government-owned monopolies, are highly restricted in access and hours, are limited in number (usually one per town), are taxed at a high rate, and are relatively small (compared with US casinos owned and operated by corporations). While laws regulating casinos are highly restrictive in Europe, though, non-casino gambling activities such as lotteries and electronic gambling machines proliferate. Other countries favor a mix of North American and European gaming models (for example, Australia, which has developed the corporate, mass-market approach of the US within the European model of one casino per city).

There are advantages and disadvantages to each of these models of gaming development. For example, under the corporate model adopted in the US, gaming has become not only a *desirable* source of revenue but a *necessary* source of revenue for some state and national governments. In Colorado, for example, casinos revenues are taxed on a multi-tier tax system, and the State Historical Society receives 28 percent of the gaming taxes. These monies are used for preservation and restoration projects in the gaming towns and other communities across Colorado. The annual income to the State Historical Society's Preservation Fund has grown from $2.5 million in 1992 (gaming began October 1, 1991) to $23.6 million in 2001 (Gaming in Colorado 2002), which makes Colorado one of the richest states in the US in terms of funding for historic preservation. The sacrifice of the towns, though, has not gone unnoticed. Colorado's three gaming towns have been placed on the National Trust for Historic Preservation's (1998) list of most endangered historic places, and that organization's website noted, "the price of prosperity is the loss of irreplaceable remnants of Colorado's colorful mining history."

The role of the state in promoting (or at least allowing) gaming is not without its problems. Abt (1996: 197) noted, "The problems of creating real economic opportunities for people through a combination of their own hard work and government investment in new capital-producing infrastructures have been ignored in the growing reliance on 'luck', 'chance' and unearned 'windfall' profits." There are reasons for state involvement in legal gaming, though. One of these is that "legal gaming brings consumers and purveyors of gaming services under the protection of contract" (Eadington 1996: 7), and so regulation reduces opportunities for illegal gambling, organized crime, and political corruption. Yet, the long-term consequences of state reliance on gaming revenues are unclear. Because gambling losses are borne by individuals, the state becomes a tacit partner in seeking individual loss – a questionable role for government.

Gaming corporations (which are increasingly large, multinational firms with powerful lobbyists) focus on profits as their measure of success. Lucrative markets tend to be those in large urban areas, in existing tourist destinations, or in border areas where competitors are already operating. In these social, political, and cultural environments, entrepreneurs seek to tailor and market gaming opportunities that suit long-term business goals. Thus, some riverboats are reconceived as "dockside casinos" (i.e., they do not "cruise" but simply "float" at a dock), and new games, betting limits, and entertainment features are proposed to encourage broader participation. (An example is the careful transformation of Las Vegas during the 1990s from "adult entertainment" to "family destination" and back to "adult entertainment" center, all in response to competition from emerging gaming locales around the country; see Hannigan 1998.) Global corporate linkages and local marketing strategies are the two faces of gaming industry viability. Moreover, the proliferation of new games and technologies, expanded forms of gambling, and development of new gaming locales raise issues about competition and the "substitution effects" (Siegel and Anders 2001), as gamblers choose among all the options. Few researchers have studied the politics of gaming, the institutional linkages that support the industry, or the business practices that preserve its competitive markets. These topics are important areas of research that would improve knowledge of the influence exerted by the gaming industry on all types of tourism the world over.

Conclusions

With the public acceptance of legal gambling around the world, policy-makers, academics, and citizens have become attentive to the impacts of the new developments (Abt, Smith and Christiansen 1985; Goodman 1995; Eadington and Cornelius 1997). There is now a wealth of popular writing about the rise of powerful new gaming enterprises (O'Brien 1998; Benedict 2000; Bridges 2001; Eisler 2001), and academic researchers are providing scholarly analysis in studies about lotteries (Clotfelter and Cook 1989); analyses of the impacts of casino gaming (Dombrink and Thompson 1990; Long, Clark and Liston 1994; Stokowski 1996; Jensen and Blevins 1998; Meyer-Arendt and Hartmann 1998; Hsu 1999); reviews and analyses of gaming tourism on Native reservations (d'Hauteserre 1998, 2001; Lew and Van Otten 1998); and analyses of gambling behaviors, especially problem and pathological gambling (Pavalko 1999; Barker and Britz 2000; Volberg 2001).

Researchers studying gambling behavior and gaming development face particular challenges. Gambling participation data are sometimes available, but are compromised by the year-to-year expansion and decline of markets, difficulties in measuring impacts indicators, and the self-interests of industry and organizations that survey gamblers. Studies of the social and community impacts of gaming and gambling suffer from difficulties associated with quantifying individual, community, and organizational consequences of gaming, and few studies consider the environmental impacts of gaming developments. One of the newest and most rapidly growing areas of gaming development – that of casino development on Native American reservations, particularly in Canada and the US – is of substantial interest, but has received relatively little scholarly attention. This is, in part, because data about tribal gaming are often proprietary and unavailable to researchers, but there are also cultural barriers to research. Yet, the largest gambling facility in the US, and one of the largest in the world, is Foxwoods Resort Casino, opened by the Mashantucket Pequot tribe in Connecticut in 1992. The Foxwoods website (Foxwoods Casino 2003) indicates that this casino has about 6,500 slots and over 350 table games, yet detailed research about the social and economic effects it has on the surrounding region and communities is limited (though see early studies by Carmichael, Peppard, and Boudreau 1996 and d'Hauteserre 1998).

How should we advance efforts to develop the geography of gaming and tourism? This chapter has proposed a range of questions that would serve as the basis for an expanded social science of gaming development and gambling behavior. The relatively recent and extraordinary transformation of gambling from a highly restricted and isolated activity to one considered to be recreational and available to many citizens within driving distance of their homes is an illustration of the merging of powerful industry forces, federal and state governments in fiscal need, and citizens willing to relax moral standards. The speed at which gambling has become an acceptable form of leisure and tourism pursuit around the world suggests that this industry will – intentionally or inadvertently – radically change the way people view the pursuits of free time, leisure, and tourism in the future.

Even recent periods of economic downturn have not slowed gaming industry expansion or the interest of individuals in spending their discretionary income on gambling. In the coming decade, there will be increasing efforts to expand computer-based internet gambling (both on land and offshore), and use of electronic gaming devices. A new culture of gambling has taken root world-wide, and geographers interested in tourism, gambling, and the gaming industry now have many opportunities for research. The notion of "landscape" may offer a starting point for these future investigations. Landscapes can be conceived in a variety of ways – as space, as nature, as places of communal meaning, as the basis for identity formation, as public settings, as political maneuvering, as cultural representation, as reproduction of social systems, as aesthetics, as spectacle, as marketed image, and so on. Researchers from all social sciences might find in the concept of landscapes a starting point for applying a wide range of theories that can elaborate the characteristics of gambling behavior and gaming as these relate to the tourism. The need is evident: *gambling* has become a predominant metaphor for social life after the millennium.

REFERENCES

Abt, V. (1996). The role of the state in the expansion and growth of commercial gambling in the United States. In J. McMillen (ed.), *Gambling Cultures: Studies in History and Interpretation* (pp. 179–98). London: Routledge.

Abt, V., Smith, J. F., and Christiansen, E. M. (1985). *The Business of Risk: Commercial Gambling in Mainstream America*. Lawrence: University Press of Kansas.

American Gaming Association. (2003). AGA fact sheet gaming revenue: 10 year trends. <http://www.americangaming.org/casinoentertainment/aga_facts/facts.cfm/ID/8>(accessed March 20, 2003).

Barker, T., and Britz, M. (2000). *Jokers Wild: Legalized Gambling in the Twenty-First Century*. Westport, CT: Praeger.

Benedict, J. (2000). *Without Reservation: The Making of America's Most Powerful Indian Tribe and Foxwoods, the World's Largest Casino*. New York: HarperCollins.

Bridges, T. (2001). *Bad Bet on the Bayou: The Rise of Gambling in Louisiana and the Fall of Governor Edwin Edwards*. New York: Farrar, Straus & Giroux.

Burlington Free Press (2002). Seneca casino opens in Niagara Falls, NY. *Burlington Free Press* (p. 2A). Burlington, VT.

Carmichael, B., Peppard, D., and Boudreau, F. (1996). Megaresort on my doorstep: Local resident attitudes toward Foxwoods Casino and casino gambling on nearby Indian reservation land. *Journal of Travel Research* 34(3), 9–16.

Chadbourne, C., Walker P., and Wolfe M. (1997). *Gambling, Economic Development, and Historic Preservation.* Chicago: American Planning Association.

Clotfelter, C. T., and Cook, P. J. (1989). *Selling Hope: State Lotteries in America.* Cambridge, MA: Harvard University Press.

Cosgrove, J., and Klassen, T. R. (2001). Gambling against the state: The state and legitimation of gambling. *Current Sociology* 49(5), 1–15.

Cotte, J. (1997). Chances, trances, and lots of slots: Gambling motives and consumption experiences. *Journal of Leisure Research* 29(4), 380–406.

d'Hauteserre, A.-M. (1998). Foxwoods Casino Resort: An unusual experiment in economic development. *Economic Geography* (special issue), 112–21.

d'Hauteserre, A.-M. (2001). Representations of rurality: Is Foxwoods Casino Resort threatening the quality of life in southeastern Connecticut? *Tourism Geographies* 3(4), 405–29.

Dombrink, J., and Thompson, W. N. (1990). *The Last Resort: Success and Failure in Campaigns for Casinos.* Reno: University of Nevada Press.

Eadington, W. R. (1996). The legalization of casinos: Policy objectives, regulatory alternatives, and cost/benefit considerations. *Journal of Travel Research* 34(3), 3–8

Eadington, W. R., and Cornelius, J. A. (eds) (1997). *Gambling: Public Policies and the Social Sciences.* Reno: University of Nevada Press.

Eisler, K. I. (2001). *Revenge of the Pequots: How a Small Native American Tribe Created the World's Most Profitable Casino.* New York: Simon & Schuster.

Fabian, T. (1995). Pathological gambling: A comparison of gambling at German-style slot machines and classical gambling. *Journal of Gambling Studies* 11(3), 249–63.

Foxwoods Casino (2003). Gaming at Foxwoods. <http://www.foxwoods.com> (accessed June 15, 2003).

Gallup Poll (1999). *Gambling in America – 1999: A Comparison of Adults and Teenagers.* <http://www.gallup.com/poll/specialReports/socialAudits/Gamblingrelease.asp>.

Gaming in Colorado (2002). *Fact Book and 2001 Abstract.* Denver: Colorado Division of Gaming.

Goodman, R. (1995). *The Luck Business: The Devastating Consequences and Broken Promises of America's Gambling Explosion.* New York: The Free Press.

Hannigan, J. (1998). *Fantasy City: Pleasure and Profit in the Postmodern Metropolis.* London: Routledge.

Hsu, C. H. C. (ed.) (1999). *Legalized Casino Gaming in the United States: The Economic and Social Impact.* New York: Haworth Hospitality Press.

Jang, H.-C., Lee, B., Park, M., and Stokowski, P. A. (2000). Measuring underlying meanings of gambling from the perspective of enduring involvement. *Journal of Travel Research* 38, 230–8.

Jensen, K., and Blevins, A. (1998). *The Last Gamble: Betting on the Future in Four Rocky Mountain Mining Towns.* Tucson: University of Arizona Press.

Lew, A. A., and Van Otten, G. A. (eds) (1998). *Tourism and Gaming on American Indian Lands.* New York: Cognizant Communication Corporation.

Long, P., Clark, J., and Liston, D. (1994). *Win, Lose or Draw? Gambling with America's Small Towns.* Washington, DC: Aspen Institute.

Mandal, V. P., and Vander Doelen, C. (1999). *Chasing Lightning: Gambling in Canada.* Toronto: United Church Publishing House.

Mason, J. L., and Nelson, M. (2001). *Governing Gambling*. New York: Century Foundation Press.

Mason, W. D. (2000). *Indian Gaming: Tribal Sovereignty and American Politics*. Norman: University of Oklahoma Press.

Meyer-Arendt, K., and R. Hartmann (eds) (1998). *Casino Gambling in America: Origins, Trends, and Impacts*. New York: Cognizant Communication Corporation.

National Trust for Historic Preservation (1998). National Trust for Historic Preservation's 11 most endangered historic places. <http://www.nationaltrust.org/11Most/1998>(accessed March 20, 2003).

NGISC (National Gambling Impact Study Commission) (1999). National Gambling Impact Study Commission Final Report. <http://govinfo.library.unt.edu/ngisc/reports/fullrpt.html> (accessed March 20, 2003).

Nichols, M., Giacopassi, D., and Stitt, B. G. (2002). Casino gambling as a catalyst of economic development: Perceptions of residents in new casino jurisdictions. *Tourism Economics* 8(1), 59–75.

O'Brien, T. L. (1998). *Bad Bet: The Inside Story of the Glamour, Glitz, and Danger of America's Gambling Industry*. New York: Random House.

Park, M., Yang, X., Lee, B., Jang, H.-C., and Stokowski, P. A. (2002). Segmenting casino gamblers by involvement profiles: A Colorado example. *Tourism Management* 23, 55–65.

Pavalko, R. M. (1999). *Risky Business: America's Fascination with Gambling*. Belmont, CA: Wadsworth/Thompson Learning.

Raento, P. (2001). Gambling in the Rocky Mountains. *Fennia* 179(1), 97–127.

Siegel, D., and Anders., G. (2001). The impact of Indian casinos on state lotteries: A case study of Arizona. *Public Finance Review* 29(2), 139–147.

Stokowski, P. A. (1996). *Riches and Regrets: Betting on Gambling in Two Colorado Mountain Towns*. Niwot, CO: University Press of Colorado.

Thompson, W. N. (1998). Casinos de juegos del mundo: A survey of world gambling. In J. H. Frey (ed.), *Gambling: Socioeconomic Impacts and Public Policy* (pp. 11–21). Annals of the American Academy of Political and Social Science 556. Thousand Oaks, CA: Sage Periodicals Press.

Volberg, R. A. (2001). *When the Chips are Down: Problem Gambling in America*. New York: Century Foundation Press.

Chapter 33

Geographic Perspectives on Event Tourism

Donald Getz

Introduction

In 2002 Japan and Korea jointly hosted the World Cup of soccer/football. A mega-event such as this or the Olympics illustrates a number of questions and issues about event tourism that lend themselves to geographic analysis. A resident of the host community might want to know why the event is being held and who arranged for it to be brought there. There will certainly be local interest in knowing how many tourists are likely to travel to the event, and what exactly will attract them. It might even become controversial when people start asking about costs and potentially negative impacts. Who stands to gain or lose from the event can be a divisive issue.

While most events are not big enough to warrant such probing by the average person, many events are significant enough for their host community to cause debate, protest, and even serious political turmoil. So why bother with them? Almost every city and destination in the world has a portfolio of events, many of which appeal to tourists. Event tourism has become highly competitive in part because of their widespread appeal and the ability of every place to hold events. They are highly valued by tourism and government agencies for strategic reasons. Corporations are attracted to sponsor events for marketing reasons, so growth of the events sector is assured.

Event studies

Most of the literature on events and event tourism concerns their management, marketing, and economic impacts. Many colleges and universities have introduced event management programs and degrees, helping to fuel demand for applied research and "how to" materials. But little has been written about the field of event studies, and how the traditional academic disciplines, including geography, can make a contribution. "Event studies" is an interdisciplinary field of research and teaching focused on the nature and importance of events in society and the economy. While "event management" concentrates on planned, professionally produced events, "event studies" can also consider unplanned and news events (such as spontaneous political protests) or very personal celebrations.

As an academic field, event studies is in its infancy – very few researchers would think of themselves as being part of it. Yet much of what has been written about event management, marketing, and impacts makes a direct contribution to greater understanding of the *phenomenon* of events. Event studies borrows from other fields and academic disciplines, including anthropology, history, sociology, psychology, leisure studies, sport and business management, art administration, geography, planning, design, and economics. Figure 33.1 describes event studies as an interdisciplinary field, meaning that its underpinning theories and methods are generally borrowed from well-established disciplines. Over time, event studies should acquire some unique theories and methods.

Event geography

To determine the nature of "event geography" it is useful to examine the main traditions of "human geography" research. This discipline has concentrated on human–resource interactions, especially spatial and temporal patterns of human activity and including impacts on the environment. Human-to-human interactions are a related theme, encompassing social or economic reasons for meeting other people and how these are shaped by space and places (Shaw and Williams 2002). With these comments in mind, event geography would consist of the major themes and topics illustrated in table 33.1, namely: the temporal dimension that events bring to tourism; distribution patterns and resource dependencies; the impacts of events and sustainable development, and contributions to policy, planning, and management.

The conceptual linking of event geography and event studies is shown in figure 33.1. Event studies concerns the understanding of the phenomenon of events in society and the economy, and is the starting point for learning about event management. Event geography is one of the contributing disciplines, with event tourism being a specific application of event management.

Events and event tourism

An event is a time-limited occurrence. When it is over it can never be perfectly replicated, so each event is by definition unique. We are talking mostly about

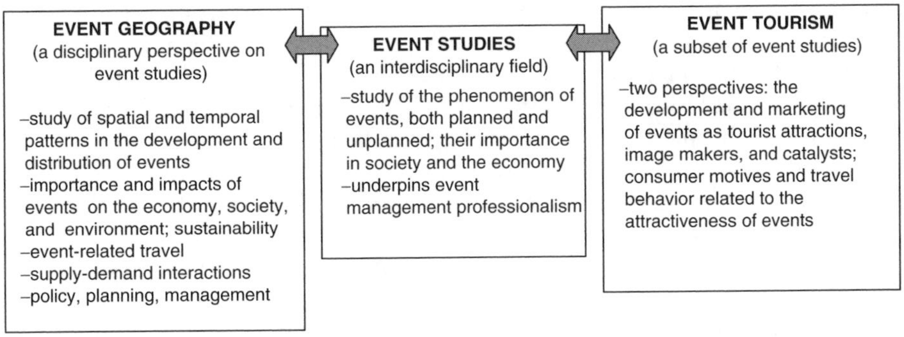

Figure 33.1 Event studies, event geography, and event tourism: conceptual interrelationships

planned events, and they can be one-time or periodic in nature. A general classification of planned events (Getz 1997) includes the following: festivals and other cultural celebrations; sports; meetings and conventions; exhibitions and sales; political and state occasions; entertainment, arts, and cultural performances. Personal and corporate events can also be included. Many events are rather independent of place, in that they could potentially be held anywhere, or in many competing venues. However, events can make their place or venue memorable, and places increasingly market themselves through events.

Several perspectives can be taken on event tourism. The first is derived from consumer behavior and is defined by the phenomenon of travel related to events: who is motivated to travel to an event, and why? what are their travel characteristics and effects? A second perspective is that of tourism organizations and other agencies who produce and/or market events as attractions and image-makers for communities and destinations, making it part of place marketing (see, e.g., Hiller 2000a). These agents see event tourism mostly in economic terms. A humanistic or cultural-geography perspective on event tourism would also be concerned with identities and meanings shaped by events, or attached to events, in specific places.

Themes and Topics in Event Geography

Table 33.1 summarizes the main themes and points of discussion that follow. Event geography is fairly broad, but our focus on tourism narrows it down somewhat. The sequence of themes is based on the belief that events are first and foremost temporal phenomena – that is what separates them from other tourist attractions. Although events are usually short-lived (from one-day festivals to six-month world's fairs) their planning can take years, and their impacts can be permanent. In this context, Hiller (2000b) examined the mega-event and its urban impacts in the pre-event, event, and post-event periods.

Temporal dimensions of event tourism

Of all the elements of tourism, events offer a special advantage: timing. Although some are tied to the calendar (e.g., holiday celebrations), others can be moved temporally or purposefully created in order to take advantage of opportunities and to develop demand in the low seasons. It is the very nature of events that each one is truly unique, being a once-only combination of setting (the environment and venue), management (including the program), and people (those producing it and those attending). No matter how many times they are offered, as with annual festivals or sports, every one is somewhat different. Because of this, events are ever-increasing in popularity as people search for novelty and authenticity. However, as more events are created for economic or corporate reasons, there is a tendency for them to become imitative in terms of program and marketing. These two forces of inherent uniqueness and standardization are in constant tension.

An excellent geographic study of the timing of events was conducted by Janiskee (1996a). His database of American festivals showed the peak and low festival seasons and how they varied in different parts of the country, and he more specifically studied the American Oktoberfest, which is a season-specific type of festival (Janiskee 1996b). Anthropologists and sociologists (e.g., Manning 1983) have long

Table 33.1 Major event geography themes

A. Temporal Dimensions
- the inherent uniqueness of events as timed attractions
- seasonal distribution linked to resources and climate
- value of events in broadening the tourist season
- concentration in time and resultant competition (i.e., the peak season for events)
- the event life cycle (is decline predictable?)
- media events and virtual reality events related to the absence of a sense of place
- time-switching (travel patterns affected by events)

B. Locating Events (Distribution Patterns)
- the resource base for events
- resource dependency and population ecology as factors explaining life cycles and failures
- supply–demand interactions (attractiveness, drawing power; market area linked to the distance-decay function; displacement of other tourists)
- event places (settings for events – their cultural significance, planning, and management)
- events and urban renewal
- crowd behavior and attendance estimation/forecasting
- motivation to travel to events
- spatial planning of events

C. Events, the Environment, and Sustainability
- sustainability principles applied to events
- economic impacts (nature and distribution of economic costs and benefits)
- ecological effects of events; green practices; contribution to conservation
- social and cultural impacts (interaction of hosts and guests; resident perceptions and attitudes)
- crowding and capacity issues

D. Policy, Planning, and Management
- development of community and destination event portfolios in place marketing
- management of impacts; research and evaluation
- diffusion and standardization; authenticity
- policy (who controls events?)
- values (who supports events? who cares if they disappear? whose values are reflected?)
- political: events as propaganda or diversion
- globalization (bidding on events globally)

been interested in the nature of celebration and how it both stems from and helps define culture. This viewpoint includes a focus the annual calendar of celebrations related to factors such as the harvest and changing seasons.

Most contemporary festivals are held in summer or fair-weather months (e.g., Ryan et al. 1998, regarding New Zealand events), although it should be stressed that other types of events, like business meetings and conventions, peak in the spring and fall and some sport events are most frequent in winter. Cultural factors and traditions help keep certain seasons dominant for specific types of events, but many are now being created specifically to overcome the traditional seasonality pattern of tourism. One of the rare studies of event tourism seasonality was undertaken by Yoon et al. (2000), who examined the event market in Michigan.

There is no doubt that people alter their travel plans because of events. For example, they are going to a certain destination for business or pleasure anyway, but decide to time their visit with an event because it provides additional value to the trip. This "time-switching" is an important limitation in estimating the economic impact of events, because the spending of time-switchers cannot be attributed as a benefit of the event itself (Dwyer et al. 2000a, 2000b). Switching is more likely to occur in major cities and resorts that have considerable drawing power all year round, as opposed to small towns and rural areas where an event might be the only reason for people to make the trip. Accordingly, economic and image-related impacts of events can be expected to be greater in smaller population centers.

Other temporal dimensions have to be considered for events. Every consumer "product," including events, has a life-cycle. A life-cycle is not fully predictable, nor is the model deterministic. Stages in the life-cycle are not always clear, but events do have a birth, they grow and mature, and many die or require rejuvenation. This temporal aspect of events, and factors shaping the life-cycle, has been studied by several researchers (Getz and Frisby 1988; Frisby and Getz 1989; Getz 1993a, 1993b, 2000a; Walle 1994).

Television and certain types of events are good friends, generating a class of events that can be called "media events." TV produces many events, especially sports, for later broadcast, and it does not really matter if they attract very many live spectators. Destinations can benefit by managing the event to ensure positive images are conveyed to the broadcast audience. However, the very limited research on media impacts suggests that enhanced image is very difficult to obtain, let alone prove (Mossberg 2000). The biggest of events, such as the Olympics or the soccer World Cup, always attract global media attention so they might be in a different league when it comes to media-generated benefits. This is an issue in need of much more research.

Will media or virtual-reality events ever replace "real" events? For some functions, such as buying from an online trade show, they work well. But what is missing is the sense of place, the dynamics of crowds, and the emotions associated with being physically a part of something special. Growth in virtual and media events is expected, including expositions, entertainment, and sport, but they will probably not diminish the appeal of attending live events.

Locating events (distributional patterns)

The spatial distribution of events is clearly a topic for geographers, such as the mapping of American festivals by Janiskee (1994). Event distribution patterns are at least partially dependent on the natural resource base, such as those themed or derived from agricultural products or other primary economic activities like mining. But the pattern of events in the landscape has been changing dramatically in response to powerful forces. Specifically, the resource base of events has shifted away from natural resources. All events require a venue (often specific facilities, but sometimes a street or open space), people to organize and manage them, customers to pay, and often sponsors to subsidize them. As communities and destinations become more competitive for tourism and investment, more economic resources are committed to events. So the nature and distribution of events is increasingly shaped by politics (i.e., is tourism perceived to be an important industry?) and consumer economics (what target audiences can be reached?).

It has been observed by several authors that growth in event numbers, and their concentration in certain areas or times of the year, could result in event failure (Jones 1993; Janiskee 1996a; Richards 1996). Population ecology offers a theoretical basis for examining the distribution and failure of events. The theory is that only so many events can exist in a given area owing to competition for scarce resources (including money, venues, volunteers) and for customers. To endure, an event has to find its best "niche" wherein resource acquisition can be assured. Well-established events not only have found the survival formula, but their success almost guarantees that corporate sponsorship and government grants will remain available.

Supply–demand interactions

Supply–demand interactions are fertile ground for event geographers. Analysis and forecasting of demand for a particular event or a region's events will in part depend on population distribution, competition, and intervening opportunities. Along these lines, Bohlin (2000) used a traditional tool of geographers, the distance-decay function, to examine festival-related travel in Sweden. He found that attendance decreased with distance, although recurring and well-established events have greater drawing power. The difficulties of forecasting event attendance have been well noted in the literature (Mules and McDonald 1994; Teigland 1996; Pyo and Cook 1988; Spilling 1998). Demand mapping (e.g., Verhoven, Wall, and Cottrell 1998) has also been used as an event marketing tool.

Arising from numerous event visitor studies it can be concluded that most events rely on local and regional (day-trip) visitors, not long-distance tourists. Even world's fairs and the Olympics must sell most of their tickets to residents. The concept of "tourist attractiveness" must therefore be assessed for each event. How powerful an attraction is the event for various target segments? Who will travel and stay overnight, versus those who will only stay a few hours then return home? Event-related travel motivation in general has been reviewed by Getz and Cheyne (2002), and motivations to attend specific types of events have frequently been examined (e.g., Uysal et al. 1993; Nogawa, Yamaguchi and Hagi 1996; Crompton and McKay 1997; Formica and Uysal 1998; Green and Chalip 1998; Pitts 1999; Travel Industry Association of America 1999).

Another theoretical and methodological concern when conducting impact evaluations is the matter of displacement. Regular tourists can be displaced when events take up available accommodation, and it is therefore often counterproductive to hold major events in the peak tourist season. For example, Hultkrantz (1998) was able to demonstrate that the World Championship of Athletics held in Goteborg, Sweden in 1995, had the effect of displacing as many expected tourists as were attracted by the event, resulting in no gain in tourist volumes. Of course, it is possible that event tourists generate greater economic impact owning to their spending patterns.

Major events also motivate people to travel to one place as opposed to another, so that during the World's Fair (Expo) in Vancouver, Canada (1986) normal travel patterns were disrupted – Vancouver and British Columbia gained, but the rest of Canada lost traffic (Lee 1987).

At the site level, attention is frequently given to the spatial component in estimating event attendance, such as through aerial mapping of crowds (Raybould et al.

2000) or spatial stratification in sampling (Denton and Furse 1993). A real need is for comparative studies of crowd behavior at events, including analysis of their movements, interactions, reactions to management systems, and preferences.

Event places

The study of event places has barely been addressed in the literature. Traditionally, many events have been associated with specific places that take on, at least temporarily, special cultural significance. Falassi (1987) called this process "valorization," involving rites and symbols to ensure that people entering the place recognize that its function has temporarily been altered.

Historically town squares and parks, even streets, have fulfilled this important civic function, but in recent decades the trend is to purpose-build festival and event places, including multi-purpose sport and arts complexes, festival squares and parks, and waterfront facilities for community event programming. The result of these capital and social investments are special places that can be identified by their monuments, special-purpose buildings, attractive landscape and vistas, and frequent ceremonial use. They definitely attract visitors, who view them as must-see urban icons. Several authors have reported on the roles of events in urban renewal projects (Hughes 1993; Mules 1993), and it can be concluded that event programming and creation of event places has become a necessary element in urban development.

What is the nature of an event place? Getz (2001) examined festival places, comparing a number in Europe and North America. A conceptual model was developed, but its testing and elaboration will require collaboration from the fields of environmental psychology, urban design, arts, event management, and sociology. The model focuses on the interdependence of elements of setting (location and design), management systems (including the program), and people. An important issue for researchers is to examine the interactions of event places with tourists and residents.

Spatial planning of events

Getz (1991) illustrated several models of potential event tourism patterns in a region. One option is clustering events in service centers, as opposed to dispersing them over a large rural area. These are related to the concept of "attractiveness" discussed above, and also have implications for the distribution of benefits and costs. Analysis of the zones of influence of events has been undertaken by Teigland (1996) specific to the Lillehammer (Norway) Winter Olympics, and this method has implications for event planning, especially regarding mega-events with multiple venues. The elements of these zones of influence are the gateways, venue locations, tourist flows, transport management, and displacement of other activities.

Event impacts, the environment, and sustainability issues

The economic impacts of events have been given prominence in the literature and in public policy, and there are comprehensive models and ample advice available on how to validly conduct economic impact assessments (e.g., Crompton and McKay 1994; Getz 1994; Crompton 1999; Dwyer et al. 2000a, 2000b). The spatial distribution of costs and benefits is of particular interest in event geography, and so too are issues of social equity. Two very specific geographic questions are those of defining the region for which economic benefits are to be estimated, and measuring the spatial distribution of spending by visitors.

The "greening" of events will remain a major issue, with the Olympics leading the way by implementing its own environmental program. A good example of how an event can become more environmentally friendly is that of the Cherry Creek Arts Festival in Denver, Colorado (profiled in Getz 1997). Events can also be positive tools in conservation, such as festivals and shows held to raise awareness or funds.

Events will increasingly be evaluated by reference to principles of sustainable development. Currently many events are not sustainable when it comes to some or all of the following criteria:

- minimization of waste, energy consumption, and pollution
- keeping private travel to a minimum
- protecting resources for the future
- fostering a positive environmental attitude
- reusing facilities; not building needless infrastructure
- avoiding damage to wildlife habitat and ecological systems

Additional research on impacts and evaluation of management practices will be required to foster improved event sustainability.

The social and cultural impacts of events

The entire realm of host–guest interactions is fertile ground for event geographers. Events can be used to erect boundaries (Buck 1977) or to foster direct contact between hosts and guests. Travelers who are looking for authentic cultural experiences can find them at cultural festivals and events. Economic benefits can be maximized when money flows directly from tourists into a community-controlled event and locally owned businesses.

Events generally produce positive impacts for some, and negative effects for others, often with spatial implications. Impacts of noise, congestion, crime or other disruption to community life occur in spatial and temporal patterns. The first landmark study of event impacts (of Adelaide's Grand Prix, by Burns, Hatch and Mules 1986) examined how residents were affected in their homes and while conducting their normal business, such as by increased commuting times. Accident rates were also analyzed, revealing a so-called "hoon effect" attributed to the atmosphere of the races and the nature of those attracted to them. Researchers studying the Gold Coast (Australia) Indy races determined that where one lived in relation to the races, and respondent's occupations, helped explain positive and negative attitudes towards the event (Fredline and Faulkner 1998, 2002). Delamere (2001) has developed a scale to measure attitudes toward the social impacts of community festivals.

Crowding and capacity issues

The capacity of sites or communities to host events is an important topic in need of further research. While crowds often add to the appeal of events, how much is too much? One study (Wickham and Kerstetter 2000) examined the relationship between place attachment and perceptions of crowding in an event setting. Abbott and

Geddie (2001) argued that effective crowd management techniques can reduce management's legal liability.

Policy, Planning, and Management

Why should a government or tourism agency invest in events? There are clear benefits to be realized for place marketing in general and economic development in particular; therefore on purely economic grounds a case can be made for sustaining an attractive event portfolio. Each portfolio will contain events classified by type, season, place, and target markets. However, few tourism agencies have a mandate to invest in events or other tangible infrastructure, and instead they focus on marketing (Getz, Anderson, and Sheehan 1998).

Unfortunately, the widespread preoccupation with economic objectives in event tourism detracts from comprehensive impact evaluation and impedes the pursuit of multiple goals, including the social and environmental. Communities and destinations require a management system for events, encompassing spatial and temporal dimensions in the data. A major policy question is that of identifying who shares responsibility for event tourism development and its management and marketing.

Little has been said about globalization and its impacts on the event sector. Is authenticity being compromised by the diffusion of standardized events? Does aggressive bidding on events lead to a hierarchy of cities or destinations ranked according to their event attractiveness? Do media events threaten the appeal of travel? These are all policy issues needing attention.

Finally, events have always had a political dimension (see Hall 1992), going back at least as far as the Roman games, and can be used quite effectively to legitimize causes, political parties, or corporate activities. A number of authors have questioned the motivations of government involvement in producing mega-events, and the resultant effects on society.

Ultimately, the question of worth arises: how can the investment in festival places or one-time events be justified? It is an inherently political question involving a discourse among citizens, organizations, and government about the worth of events in society and to the economy, their real and imagined impacts, and the distribution of costs and benefits. Regarding one-time events it is desirable to get a full, post-event evaluation – but this is seldom undertaken. Researchers might also ask: when an event disappears, does anyone miss it? Who supports an event, and why, is another political question.

Conclusions

Event geography is an important element in the field of event studies, with particular relevance to the study of event tourism. Geographical analysis is necessary to contribute both theory and practical marketing implications to the event tourism field. The major themes discussed in this chapter all suggest multiple research questions and methods, including those pertaining to the timing of tourism, its distribution, supply–demand interactions and spatial planning, impact evaluation, and policy development.

The main themes of event-related research have been identified and general research needs discussed by several authors (Formica 1998; Getz 2000b; Harris et al. 2000). Specific to event geography, the more obvious themes of temporal and spatial distribution have been examined, but other geographic themes have been largely ignored. Geographers can make a greater contribution to event studies through theory-building, and to event management through applied research.

In terms of theory-building, a crucial question is the extent to which certain types of events are resource-dependent or rooted in specific environments. The matter of authenticity should be explored more from a geographic point of view, such as addressing the issue of how, for example, a food festival can both emerge from and reinforce a distinct sense of place. While economic and environmental impacts of events and event tourism have been explored by many, there is still a need for attention to the process by which events help shape and define urban environments, particularly in the context of urban renewal, mega-events, and event venues. More attention should also be paid to explaining, rather than mapping, spatial and temporal variations in events. What are the relative contributions of resources, culture, policy, and economics in accounting for patterns?

Applied geographic research will specifically help advance event management. Geographers have the tools to do market area analysis and evaluate event attractiveness (or drawing power). Hierarchies of event places could be determined through analysis of existing events and event venues, leading to implications for place marketing. Better measurement of the spatial distribution of event tourist activities and spending will aid in forecasting event impacts, as will studies of time-switching and displacement. Finally, analysis of event patterns in time and space is essential to gaining a better understanding of event trends and potential competition.

Event geography is an emerging field of inquiry with great potential to contribute to theory, policy, and management. While the number of practitioners and related research to date has been very limited, this chapter has demonstrated that the contributions have been very important. Future research directions have been suggested, and it is to be hoped that continued theoretical and practical work will achieve greater recognition for this specialization.

REFERENCES

Abbott, J., and Geddie, M. (2001). Event and venue management: Minimizing liability through effective crowd management techniques. *Event Management* 6(4), 259–90.

Bohlin, M. (2000). Traveling to events. In L. Mossberg (ed.), *Evaluation of Events: Scandinavian Experiences* (pp. 13–29). New York: Cognizant Communication Corporation.

Buck, R. (1977). Making good business better: A second look at staged tourist attractions. *Journal of Travel Research* 15(3), 30–1.

Burns, J., Hatch, J., and Mules, T. (eds) (1986). *The Adelaide Grand Prix: The Impact of a Special Event*. Adelaide: Centre for South Australian Economic Studies.

Crompton, J. (1999). *Measuring the Economic Impact of Visitors to Sports Tournaments and Special Events*. Ashburn, VA: National Recreation and Park Association.

Crompton, J., and McKay, S. (1994). Measuring the economic impact of festivals and events: Some myths, misapplications and ethical dilemmas. *Festival Management and Event Tourism* 2(1), 33–43.

Crompton, J., and McKay, S. (1997). Motives of visitors attending festival events. *Annals of Tourism Research* 24(2), 425–39.

Delamere, T. (2001). Development of a scale to measure resident attitudes toward the social impacts of community festivals, part 2: Verification of the scale. *Event Management* 7(1), 25–38.

Denton, S., and Furse, B. (1993). Visitation to the 1991 Barossa Valley Vintage Festival: Estimating overall visitor numbers to a festival encompassing several venues and events. *Festival Management and Event Tourism* 1(2), 51–6.

Dwyer, L., Mellor, R., Mistilis, N., and Mules, T. (2000a). A framework for assessing "tangible" and "intangible" impacts of events and conventions. *Event Management* 6(3), 175–89.

Dwyer, L., Mellor, R., Mistilis, N., and Mules, T. (2000b). Forecasting the economic impacts of events and conventions. *Event Management* 6(3), 191–204.

Falassi, A. (ed.) (1987). *Time out of Time: Essays on the Festival.* Albuquerque: University of New Mexico Press.

Formica, S. (1998). The development of festivals and special events studies. *Festival Management and Event Tourism* 5(3), 131–7.

Formica, S., and Uysal, M. (1998). Market segmentation of an international cultural-historic event in Italy. *Journal of Travel Research* 36(4), 16–24.

Fredline, E., and Faulkner, B. (1998). Resident reactions to a major tourist event: The Gold Coast Indy Car Race. *Festival Management and Event Tourism* 5(4), 185–205.

Fredline, E., and Faulkner, B. (2002). Variations in residents' reactions to major motorsport events: Why residents perceive the impacts of events differently. *Event Management* 7(2), 103–14.

Frisby, W., and Getz, D. (1989). Festival management: A case study perspective. *Journal of Travel Research* 28(1), 7–11.

Getz, D. (1991). *Festivals, Special Events, and Tourism.* New York: Van Nostrand Reinhold.

Getz, D. (1993a). Case study: Marketing the Calgary Exhibition and Stampede. *Festival Management and Event Tourism* 1(4), 147–56.

Getz, D. (1993b). Corporate culture in not for profit festival organizations. *Festival Management and Event Tourism* 1(1), 11–17.

Getz, D. (1994). Event tourism: Evaluating the impacts. In B. Ritchie and C. Goeldner (eds), *Travel, Tourism and Hospitality Research: A Handbook for Managers and Researchers*, 2nd edn (pp. 437–50). New York: John Wiley.

Getz, D. (1997). *Event Management and Event Tourism.* New York: Cognizant Communication Corporation.

Getz, D. (2000a). Festivals and special events: Life cycle and saturation issues. In W. Gartner and D. Lime (eds), *Trends in Outdoor Recreation, Leisure and Tourism* (pp. 175–85). Wallingford, UK: CAB International.

Getz, D. (2000b). Developing a research agenda for the event management field. In J. Allen et al. (eds), *Events Beyond 2000: Setting the Agenda, Proceedings of Conference on Event Evaluation, Research and Education* (pp. 10–21). Sydney: Australian Centre for Event Management, University of Technology.

Getz, D. (2001). Festival places: A comparison of Europe and North America. *Tourism* 49(1), 3–18.

Getz, D., Anderson, D., and Sheehan, L. (1998). Roles, issues and strategies for convention and visitors bureaux in destination planning and product development: A survey of Canadian bureaux. *Tourism Management* 19(4), 331–40.

Getz, D., and Cheyne, J. (2002). Special event motives and behaviour. In C. Ryan (ed.), *The Tourist Experience: A New Introduction*, 2nd edn. London: Continuum Books.

Getz, D., and Frisby, W. (1988). Evaluating management effectiveness in community-run festivals. *Journal of Travel Research* 27(1), 22–7.

Green, B., and Chalip, L. (1998). Sport tourism as the celebration of subculture. *Annals of Tourism Research* 25(2), 275–91.

Hall, M. (1992). *Hallmark Tourist Events: Impacts, Management and Planning*. London: Belhaven.

Harris, R., Jago, L., Allen, J., and Huyskens, M. (2000). A rearview mirror and a crystal ball: Past, present and future perspectives on event research in Australia. In J. Allen et al. (eds), *Events Beyond 2000: Setting the Agenda, Proceedings of Conference on Event Evaluation, Research and Education* (pp. 21–9). Sydney: Australian Centre for Event Management, University of Technology.

Hiller, H. (2000a). Mega-events, urban boosterism and growth strategies: An analysis of the objectives and legitimations of the Cape Town 2004 Olympic bid. *International Journal of Urban and Regional Research* 24(2), 439–58.

Hiller, H. (2000b). Toward an urban sociology of mega-events. *Research in Urban Sociology* 5, 181–205.

Hughes, H. (1993). Olympic tourism and urban regeneration. *Festival Management and Event Tourism* 1(4), 157–62.

Hultkrantz, L. (1998). Mega-event displacement of visitors: The World Championship in Athletics, Goteborg 1995. *Festival Management and Event Tourism* 5(1/2), 1–8.

Janiskee, R. (1994). Some macroscale growth trends in America's community festival industry. *Festival Management and Event Tourism* 2(1), 10–14.

Janiskee, R. (1996a). The temporal distribution of America's community festivals. *Festival Management and Event Tourism* 3(3), 129–37.

Janiskee, R. (1996b). Oktoberfest American style. *Festival Management and Event Tourism* 3(4), 197–9.

Jones, H. (1993). Pop goes the festival. *Marketing Week* 16(23), 24–7.

Lee, J. (1987). The impact of Expo '86 on British Columbia markets. In P. Williams, J. Hall, and M. Hunter (eds), *Tourism: Where is the Client?* Conference Papers of the Travel and Tourism Research Association, Canada Chapter.

Manning, F. (ed.) (1983). *The Celebration of Society: Perspectives on Contemporary Cultural Performance*. Bowling Green, OH: Bowling Green University Popular Press.

Mossberg, L. (2000). Effects of events on destination image. In L. Mossberg (ed.), *Evaluation of Events: Scandinavian Experiences* (pp. 30–46). New York: Cognizant Communication Corporation.

Mules, T. (1993). A special event as part of an urban renewal strategy. *Festival Management and Event Tourism* 1(2), 65–7.

Mules, T., and McDonald, S. (1994). The economic impact of special events: The use of forecast. *Festival Management and Event Tourism* 2(1), 45–53.

Nogawa, H., Yamaguchi, Y., and Hagi, Y. (1996). An empirical research study on Japanese sport tourism in sport-for-all events: Case studies of a single-night event and a multiple-night event. *Journal of Travel Research* 35, 46–54.

Pitts, B. (1999). Sports tourism and niche markets: Identification and analysis of the growing lesbian and gay sports tourism industry. *Journal of Vacation Marketing* 5(1), 31–50.

Pyo, S., and Cook, R. (1988). Summer Olympic tourist market: Learning from the past. *Tourism Management* 9(2), 137–44.

Raybould, M., Mules, T., Fredline, E., and Tomljenovic, R. (2000). Counting the herd. Using aerial photography to estimate attendance at open events. *Event Management* 6(1), 25–32.

Richards, G. (1996). European cultural tourism: Trends and future prospects. In G. Richards (ed.), *Cultural Tourism in Europe* (pp. 311–33). Wallingford, UK: CAB International.

Ryan, C., Smee, A., Murphy, S., and Getz, D. (1998). New Zealand events: A temporal and regional analysis. *Festival Management and Event Tourism* 5(1/2), 71–83.

Shaw, G., and Williams, A. M. (2002). *Critical Issues in Tourism: A Geographical Perspective*, 2nd edn. Oxford: Blackwell.

Spilling, O. (1998). Beyond Intermezzo? On the long-term industrial impacts of mega events: The case of Lillehammer 1994. *Festival Management and Event Tourism* 5(3), 101–22.

Teigland, J. (1996). *Impacts on Tourism from Mega-Events: The Case of Winter Olympic Games*. Sogndal: Western Norway Research Institute.

Travel Industry Association of America (1999). *Profile of Travelers Who Attend Sports Events*. Washington, DC: TIAA.

Uysal, M., Gahan, L., and Martin, B. (1993). An examination of event motivations: A case study. *Festival Management and Event Tourism* 1(1), 5–10.

Verhoven, P., Wall, D., and Cottrell, S. (1998). Application of desktop mapping as a marketing tool for special events planning and evaluation: A case study of the Newport News Celebration in Light. *Festival Management and Event Tourism* 5(3), 123–30.

Walle, A. (1994). The festival life cycle and tourism strategies: The case of the Cowboy Poetry Gathering. *Festival Management and Event Tourism* (2), 85–94.

Wickham, T., and Kerstetter, D. (2000). The relationship between place attachment and crowding in an event setting. *Event Management* 6(3), 167–74.

Yoon, S., Spencer, D., Holocek, D., and Kim, D. (2000). A profile of Michigan's festival and special event tourism market. *Event Management* 6(1), 33–44.

Part VII Tourism, the Environment, and Society

Chapter 34

Tourism and the Natural Environment

Klaus Meyer-Arendt

Although the historic roots of tourism may be traced to human attraction to cultural phenomena (e.g., the Seven Wonders of the World and the Grand Tour), the natural environment has been an "object of desire" for Western tourists since at least the onset of the Industrial Revolution. The natural environment today comprises a significant proportion of the tourist experience. The demand for nature experiences, be they at the seaside, in the mountains, or in a rainforest, has brought tourists and tourism developers to the most far-flung corners of the earth. While this phenomenon has made the world seem a smaller planet, and brought more of its inhabitants into a tourism-based economy, it has also been accompanied by a variety of impacts, both positive and negative.

This chapter examines (1) the variety of origins of tourist attraction to the physical environment and the present-day manifestation of those origins, and (2) human–environment relationships as presented in conceptual models and summarized in recent literature. Although tourism typologies and conceptual models are, by definition, simplified and necessarily arbitrary constructs of a large and complex phenomenon – and real-world tourism quite often cuts across "types" and is not easily modeled – such frameworks still provide a means of understanding and assessing tourism impacts upon the natural environment.

Origins of Nature-Based Tourism

Nature-based tourism has multiple origins. Probably the most significant have been Romanticism, the springs tradition, the seaside tradition, nature in religion, the exploration theme, the parks and recreation movement, hunting and fishing, curiosity about animals, and the search for the perfect climate. All of these have contributed to the development and expansion of tourism in natural environmental settings.

Romanticism: the search for the sublime and picturesque in nature

Large-scale nature-based tourism began in the West as a response to the Industrial Revolution in the late eighteenth and nineteenth centuries (Johnson 1990). The natural environment that Europeans and Americans had previously taken for granted shrank under the demand for natural resources to fuel new industries and expanding urban areas. In Germany, a Romanticist school of artists began to paint natural landscapes seemingly untouched by human hand. Philosophically, the Romantic movement was a subjective response to the objectivity and classification of nature that began with the Enlightenment (Hall 1998). As Russell (1946: 653) noted, "the romantic movement is characterized, as a whole, by the substitution of the aesthetic for utilitarian standards." Landscapes that were previously feared, including mountains and wilderness, now became objects of awe and admiration (Nicolson 1962; Tuan 1979; Honour 1981).

This new orientation toward nature made its way across the Atlantic, where artists of the so-called Hudson River School romanticized New York's Hudson River Valley, and especially its Catskill Mountains area. Literature also romanticized the natural environment, and early tourists were drawn to venues described in art and literature in both Europe and the United States (Nash 1967; Butler 1985; Durie 1994). Somewhat ironically, industrial-era railways and steamships provided an easy means of travel by urban dwellers to these as yet unspoiled landscapes (Butler 1985). The Hudson River Valley became America's first true tourism corridor, and the Catskills – where the Mountain House Hotel opened in 1824 – the first natural environment destination for urban tourists (Sears 1989).

In the US, both artists and tourists were inspired by the sublime and picturesque in nature. Picturesque was defined as a "pleasing quality of nature's roughness, irregularity, and intricacy" (Nash 1967). Sublime referred to "picturesque" but on a grander scale, and it became associated with the hand of God in creating the "wild" in nature (Nash 1967; Demars 1990). The Catskills and Niagara Falls were among the first nature-based areas venerated by artists and tourists, but as the American frontier pushed westward, the search for the sublime followed.

Artists soon discovered Yosemite, Yellowstone, Mount Hood, and the Grand Canyon, and tourists were not far behind (Sears 1989; Demars 1991). To the romantics the New World was perceived as a new Eden in which man could draw close to wild nature. In the writings of the Romantics, and more particularly the American transcendentalists such as Emerson and Thoreau, nature came to be endowed with a spiritual property, wholeness and wellness (Hall 1998). For tourists, railroad companies provided both marketing and infrastructure by extending railroad spurs, building hotels, and organizing package tours (Pyne 1998). As rampant tourism development threatened to destroy the attractiveness of the various natural wonders, visionaries such as George Perkins Marsh pressed hard to create a national park system to protect the natural beauty from commercialization (Nash 1967; Hall 1998).

The search for the sublime and picturesque in the early American landscape was, in part, stimulated by the need to compete with the cultural and historical monuments of Europe that had inspired the Grand Tour, and, by extension, modern tourism (Sears 1989). The Grand Canyon National Park, Yosemite National Park, and Yellowstone National Park represented the coliseums and cathedrals of the New World and gave rise to a new form of nature-based tourism that not only continues to this day but has also been exported across the globe through the development of national parks and nature reserves.

At a less imposing scale, tourism also romanticized the pastoral and rural, which provided a more accessible natural landscape for urban dwellers. Hiking and bicycling were early forms of enjoying the pastoral countryside which continue to this day. With the popularization of the automobile came the "Sunday drive," a term synonymous with a leisurely day trip through a natural or rural environment. The establishment of parkways and scenic highways in the 1920s and 1930s was a result of this countryside "motoring" tradition (Hugill 1985).

The springs tradition

A second origin of nature-based tourism is the "taking of the waters" at natural springs. Probably originating in the early centers of civilization in the Middle East, bathing in natural springs became associated with gods and spirits in ancient Greece (Valenza 2000). The Romans, who believed in the therapeutic as well as the spiritual value of springs, established springs resorts throughout the Italian peninsula and Europe, including Britain. Many of the best-known springs resorts, including Bath, Vichy, Baden-Baden, and Espa, claim descent from the Roman era.

Hydrotherapy, or thermalism, enjoyed a revival in the late Middle Ages, as abandoned Roman springs sites as well as new ones were (re)discovered in England and continental Europe (Lowenthal 1962; Lavery 1971). The tradition diffused to the English colonies in the seventeenth century, and later spread westward and southward across the US (Lawrence 1983). There were many types of springs, including hot springs and sulfur springs, but all attracted tourists for both therapy and recreation. And although a natural resource was the attraction, the sites of the springs soon became highly modified by entrepreneurs who sought to create the service infrastructure that they felt the thermalists required, including cottage accommodations, fitness and therapeutic centers, and music and dance venues (Valenza 2000). As the spa resort infrastructure came to dominate the resorts, the role of nature became reduced to only the waters that initially attracted the thermalists, as at Bath, England or the German bath (*Bad*) resorts.

Although the springs tradition has waned in North America since the 1930s, it remains popular in much of Europe (especially in Germany and central Europe) and Japan, and is still locally important in the US and other parts of the world. Much of the natural springs environment, however, has been converted by the construction of swimming pools and jacuzzi spas into which the spring waters are piped. The popularity of the home "hot tub" may also be an outgrowth of the historic springs experience.

The seaside tradition

Touristic attraction to seashores is also rooted in classical Roman Europe, although the modern tradition is more directly traced to the springs tradition. Thallasotherapy, a salt-water form of hydrotherapy, was practiced by the early Romans, and some coastal urbanization in modern-day Italy is traced to that period. Modern sea bathing, however, is traced to Scarborough, England circa 1700, where a natural springs emptied onto a beach near the base of a cliff (Stansfield 1970). Some springs aficionados decided to brave the open sea, and this activity was quickly reinforced by doctors who began to endorse salt-water bathing (as well as drinking and breathing) as a cure for a variety of ailments. Coastal tourism was quickly popularized. As with the springs, the natural resource that attracted the tourists soon became modified by extensive development, and the natural environment began to play almost a subservient role to the resort environment.

At the same time that pristine coastal environments were being discovered by tourists and developers, a pioneering set of artists and elite tourists ventured out to find as yet undiscovered beaches to enjoy before mass tourism set in. This search for the ideal coastal landscape, in which to bathe, breathe the salt air, and enjoy the sunset continues today as the tourism industry scouts out ever more remote and exotic sites to develop. The film *The Beach* (released in 2000), for example, dramatized the quest of the backpacking adventure tourist to find the last, perfect, and unspoiled beach.

Even in general terms, the human attraction to water accounts for a huge proportion of world tourism, both international and domestic. People like to spend extended periods of leisure time along a littoral, be it the sea, a lake, or a river. Much of the urbanization associated with shoreline areas is of a recreational or touristic variety. The coasts of Spain, Italy, the Balearic Islands, and Florida represent one extreme of water-oriented commercial tourism, whereas cottages around arboreal lakes and northern seas in Canada and Norway reflect the opposite extreme of a wilderness coast experience (Mullins 1991; Halseth 1998; O'Reilly 2000).

Nature as a religious experience

Wilderness has played a key role in religion for thousands of years, and for the Romanticists the wilderness experience was often a religious experience (Nash 1967; Graber 1976; Hall and Page 2002). In the US, as a result of several religious "Great Awakenings" in the eighteenth and nineteenth centuries, the natural environment took on a spiritual role not unlike that imparted to Nature during the contemporaneous search for the sublime and picturesque. Among Methodists in particular, the "camp-meeting" became an important event both for proselytizing isolated rural dwellers and for reaffirming one's faith in God. In rural areas, where churches were few and far between, camp meetings were held in groves of trees (Sullivan 1990). Trees served as the natural equivalents of church spires, and "forest groves" and similar toponyms came to dot the American landscape as once isolated clumps of trees became developed as recreational camps or even towns. Coastal areas also became revered by people seeking a religious experience, and religious resorts appeared on all US coasts during the nineteenth century (Demars 1988). And while beaches and tree groves remained the natural attraction, the growing built environments surrounding them often came to obscure the natural environment.

Religious pilgrimage and ritual is structurally similar to tourism, and some consider tourism a form of secular pilgrimage (Graburn 1977). In some religions, the natural environment plays a "sacred" or health role (Bhardwaj 1998). The Ganges River for Hinduism, Buddhist shrines and lamaseries, and isolated Christian monasteries are examples of religious destinations in natural settings that attract spiritual and secular pilgrims in search of special places and experiences.

Latter-day exploration

Another origin of nature-based tourism lies in the tradition of exploration, *terra incognita*, and adventure travel. Historically, explorers pushed into *terra incognita* – the unknown regions on early European maps of the world. This also took them to the extremes of nature, including its highest peaks, longest rivers, widest deserts, and most remote rainforests. Such explorations were followed vicariously by armchair explorers in nineteenth- and early twentieth-century England, continental Europe, and the United States. Scientific societies such as the Royal Society, the Royal Geographical Society, the Explorers' Club, and the National Geographic Society promoted and capitalized upon this popular interest. By the 1950s, classical exploration – consisting of discovery and ideographic descriptions – was largely restricted to only a few remaining "white spaces" on the world map, including parts of New Guinea, the Amazon Basin, a few remaining unconquered mountain peaks, the polar areas, and the ocean depths. Like religious pilgrims, explorers shared much in common with tourists, and beginning in the 1950s armchair explorers started to take to the road, retracing the steps of classical adventurers and recreating their experiences in increasingly more exotic settings, often organized by a tour operator. The appeal of tourist-as-explorer is greater among some cultures (e.g., Germany and England) than others, and thus a greater proportion of residents from such places venture out to explore their personal *terra incognita*.

Although exploration tourism is sometimes focused on culture (e.g., pre-contact Amazonian tribes, isolated hill people in southeast Asia, or archaeological traces of earlier peoples), the natural environment plays a key, if not dominant, role even in this form of exploration tourism. The types of tourists who participate in such trips may range from the truly adventurous to those who need their modern comforts. But the environments that lure them are strikingly similar. Arctic and Antarctic tourism are examples of exploration tourism, as are Amazon cruises. It can be argued that even some climbers of Everest or Kilimanjaro are not true mountain climbers but rather relatively wealthy tourists in search of exotic and extreme experiences. Since true exploration of the classical variety has practically vanished, or is at least restricted to extremely costly ventures in submarine environments or to outer space, softer forms of exploration tourism have become more popular.

The parks and recreation movement

Another origin of tourism in the natural environment evolved from the parks and recreation movement of the nineteenth and early twentieth centuries. Rooted in Industrial Age urbanism, this movement called for the creation of urban parks to provide opportunities for enjoying greenery as well as providing physical exercise to the working classes of the inner cities (Patmore 1983). The movement led to the creation of neighborhood parks and opportunities for sports. Wealthier urban residents would to send their children to "summer camps" where the wilderness experience and opportunities for physical exercise were even greater. In the early twentieth century, the establishment of the Boy Scouts and the Girl Scouts were further extensions of this movement.

Modern outdoor recreation (or activity-based tourism) is a direct outgrowth of the parks and recreation movement. While the term "recreation" refers to leisure-time activities in or close to one's home base, recreationists are increasingly going to more distant venues. Whitewater rafting in Costa Rica, sailing in the Caribbean, skiing in the Alps, trekking through northern Thailand, mountain-biking in Utah, windsurfing in the Columbia River Gorge, and scuba-diving in Honduras are all examples of activity-based tourism dependent upon the natural environment. Even playing golf at California's Pebble Beach country club or at St. Andrews in Scotland could fall into this category. In a similar vein, many resorts have added activities (e.g., windsurfing or horse-riding) to expand their offerings and attract more activity-oriented tourists. The increasing popularity of nature-based adventure tourism has been related to the social spatialization at tourist destinations, market differentiation, and a yearning to transcend the metaphorical "tourist gaze," among other factors (Cloke and Perkins 1998).

Because of the demand and competition for activity-based leisure opportunities, the world's natural resources continue to be explored for their potential for such development. Scuba-diving in sinkholes and underground rivers on the Yucatán Peninsula, hang-gliding at Angel Falls in Venezuela, and bungee-jumping over the Zambezi River in southern Africa, are among the vanguard of activity-based outdoor recreation and adventure attractions.

Hunting and fishing

Hunting, fishing, and gathering were the primary food-acquiring activities of pre-agricultural humans. To some extent, these three activities remained important cultural traditions long after plant and animal domestication was introduced. Hunting and fishing, especially, are considered more than just sport activities, but are also cultural legacies of the "good old days." As natural habitats for hunting and fishing have slowly disappeared under the expansion of agriculture, urbanization, industrialization, and related pollution in the nineteenth and twentieth centuries, grass-roots movements were initiated to establish game reserves, nature preserves, and clean rivers. Fish camps, hunting clubs, private and public game reserves and hunting lands, safaris, and fishing rodeos are all traced to the mostly male compulsion for hunting and fishing. In Mongolia, Genghis Khan has been proclaimed the first "ecotourist," perhaps because he established the first national park – for hunting (Wheeller 1994). Since the nineteenth century, the hunting of big game has led to the development of a major segment of the tourist industry, especially in Africa, South Asia, and North America. The negative side of the hunting and fishing has been that several animal species have been hunted to extinction and many more are threatened and endangered.

Today, tourism associated with hunting and fishing continues to be big business. Wildlife populations are better managed than in decades past, and licenses to shoot big game cost in the thousands of dollars, thereby reducing pressure on their survival. Recreational fishing supports a large charter-boat industry worldwide (Gill 1989), and fishing "rodeos" attract anglers internationally. The US not only has a large fishing-based domestic tourism industry, but is also a source for international tourists seeking fishing opportunities in Canada and Central America. Lake Yojoa in Honduras, for example, attracts Americans in search of the world's largest largemouth bass.

Curiosity about exotic fauna in nature

Ever since the days of the Greeks and Romans, humans have been curious about exotic animals. Lions, elephants, zebras, chimpanzees, and giraffes excited the imaginations of people who were more accustomed to cattle, sheep, goats, deer, rabbits, bears, and wolves. Exotic animals were put on display, both for show and also for sporting events. In the nineteenth century, the concept of zoos was introduced to the Western world. Soon tourists wanted to see exotic wildlife in its natural habitat, and wildlife preserves and national parks were established in places such as east and south Africa, both to save dwindling animal populations and to allow them to be viewed by tourists. Exotic wildlife preserves were also established in places such as Texas and Florida, where drive-through photo safari vacations provided all the sights of Africa or Asia. However, those who could afford it preferred to see the genuine habitat, and modern safari tourism (with a camera replacing the gun) to Africa and south and southeast Asia continues to be popular. Concern over the future survival of endangered wildlife lures many tourists to these remaining habitats. Large primates, including mountain gorillas and orangutans, are luring tourists to Africa and Indonesia, and exotic birds and monkeys are attractions in many other rainforests. The giant tortoises of the Galapagos, the komodo dragons of Indonesia, penguins in the Antarctic, polar bears in Manitoba, and the sea turtles in the Caribbean are additional examples of animals that have spawned a tourist industry centered upon "ecotourism" (Weaver 2002).

Climate and health

The last major category of nature-based tourism is that of climate. Since the Romans fled to soothing springs and seaside villas, Western tourists have adopted the habit of seasonally taking advantage of more salubrious climates. In addition to seasonal touristic transhumance, many people – both young and retired – often permanently migrate to such favored destinations.

Hot summers led to an escape to cool mountain air or soothing sea breezes. As Spain colonized her New World territories, the muggy lowland tropics were often bypassed in favor of cooler mountainous environs. Similarly, England's golden age of imperialism led to the development of "hill stations" in tropical and subtropical colonies throughout Asia and parts of Africa (Spencer and Thomas 1948). In the mid-latitudes mountains (e.g., the Alps, the Appalachians, and the Sierra Nevada) became popular recreation destinations in the nineteenth century for cooling off and enjoying the scenery.

Colder climates, however, have probably resulted in the largest temporary migration of all time. Winter "snowbirds" (elderly retirees) and summer school vacationers flee the colder northern latitudes at all times of the year in search of warmth along the Mediterranean, in the Caribbean, and in other tropical, subtropical, and desert environments. By the early nineteenth century, winter tourists were traveling to the French Riviera and the Bahamas to soak up the warmth. The singer-songwriter Jimmy Buffett popularized coconut-rimmed tropical beaches in his 1970s music, and North American and European expatriates have been scouting out venues in the greater Caribbean ever since to recreate their own "Margaritavilles." In general, locations with plenty of sunshine and few clouds or natural hazards are favored by tourism developers. In countries such as Mexico, Costa Rica, and the Dominican Republic, drier areas have been more favored because of the greater reliability of sunshine. When the Banco de Mexico's computer searched for the ideal east coast Mexican seaside resort location in the late 1960s, the undeveloped site of Cancún beat out the Veracruz coast hands down (Collins 1979). Over time, many of the temporary tourist colonies that have been created by summer and winter sunshine-seekers have been turned into sites of permanent residence, especially for the English in Spain and Americans in Mexico.

Conceptualizing the Tourist–Natural Environment Relationship

The natural environment attracts tourists for reasons that generally fall into the various categories described above, and the relationship between the tourist and the environment depends both upon the type of tourism as well as the type of tourist. A whitewater rafter, a rainforest ecotourist, a soft-adventure explorer, or a latter-day Romantic would require, and most enjoy, a natural environment relatively free of human modification (or at least modified *only* to enhance nature's attributes). A seaside tourist or a religious pilgrim/tourist, on the other hand, may not object to man-made (or even commercial) attractions augmenting the primary natural attraction. Although tourism is perceived by many to have only negative impacts upon the physical environment, the relationship between the two is multifaceted. Several scholars have tried to model the tourist–natural environment relationship, but none of these models has successfully addressed all aspects of that complex relationship.

Over half a century ago, Roy Wolfe proposed a direct inverse relationship between recreational urbanization and environmental quality (Wolfe 1952). As lakeside cottage resorts became more urbanized and commercialized through expanding summer tourism, they increasingly became "divorced from their geographic environment" (Wolfe 1952: 57). According to Wolfe, the initial attractions of a site – serene wilderness and pristine shores – become obscured by "honky-tonk" cultural overlays. Subsequent studies, including the classic *Man's Role in Changing the Face of the Earth* (Thomas 1956), have correlated increases in recreational usage with environmental degradation. In that landmark volume, Davis (1956) summarized human impacts upon shorelines – from shell middens to the construction of seawalls – and noted that the most recent era of environmental impacts was attributed primarily to coastal recreation and tourism.

However, the popular perception that the tourist–natural environment relationship is necessarily one of inverse linearity began to be questioned in the 1970s and 1980s. Cohen (1978) identified four major factors that contributed to decline in environmental quality under pressure from tourism:

1 the intensity of tourism
2 the resilience of the ecosystem
3 the time perspective of the developer, and
4 the transformational character of recreational development (i.e., during the course of resort evolution, the type of tourist attracted to that particular resort changes, as may well the recreational resource).

Landscape architects and planners have argued that, with effective design and management, a coexistence or "symbiosis" between tourism and the environment is possible (Budowski 1976; Pigram 1980; Mathieson and Wall 1982; Romeril 1985; Gunn 1988). Such a "symbiosis" is necessary to "sustain" the environment in the face of tourism, and "sustainability" of the environment is now often interchangeably used with "sustainable tourism." In fact, the term "ecotourism," first used in the mid-1980s (Romeril 1985), is now meant to suggest that a symbiotic relationship between tourists and the natural environment is not only possible but perhaps also the ideal.

As idealized as the term "ecotourism" is, it quickly became misapplied and misused. Sixty small boats filled with "ecotourists" snapping photographs of flamingos in a Yucatán lagoon is not a symbiotic relationship between humans and nature. Several investigators have questioned the validity of the term as well as the validity of the concept (well summarized in Wheeller 1994). Some have questioned the sustainability aspect of the relationship (Butler 1991), and others have argued that the natural environment cannot be regarded as an environment devoid of humans (Wheeller 1994). Perhaps in recognition of a "social" component of the natural environment, several newly established parks and preserves in Central America have established resource-use agreements with local populations (see e.g. Place 1991). The debate over whether ecotourism really exists, and whether it can really be sustainable, rages on in various outlets such as the *Journal of Sustainable Tourism*. Numerous case studies of ecotourism and "ecotourism development" are also sprinkled throughout the tourism literature and occasionally aggregated in conferences proceedings (e.g., Kusler 1991). Absent from the various discussions are scientific rigor and conceptual models.

Models of tourism development that incorporate environmental components remain few. Wolfe (1982), re-evaluating previous research on recreational travel (Wolfe 1966), proposed a conceptual model of resort evolution that included both economic and environmental components. In his "normative typology of tourist destinations" (also known as the "Ellis Curve"), the x axis measures relative environmental impacts and the y axis represents the level of economic impact (see figure 13.3, this volume). When describing the course of evolution of a resort, the early stages of tourism development are characterized by positive economic and environmental impacts. This is attributed by the initial attention paid by developers to aesthetics of landscape in order to attract the tourist as well as by the initially low number of visitors. In time, however, environmental degradation sets in, and even the economic benefits, while still positive, decrease as more profits are pocketed by outside investors and developers.

One of the most cited theoretical models of resort evolution is one proposed by Butler in 1980 (cf. this volume, chapter 13). The "resort-cycle" model has been applied, often in modified form, in the study of various social, economic, and planning aspects of tourism (Agarwal 1994). It has perhaps become the most commonly referenced model for framing tourism research in spite of its generalized nature and multiple shortcomings (Haywood 1986). However, few researchers have used the Butler model to examine environmental impacts of tourism. This author correlated environmental changes at Grand Isle, Louisiana to resort cyclicity (Meyer-Arendt 1985), and in subsequent analyses provided models of tourism–environment relationships patterned after Butler's model (Meyer-Arendt 1990, 1993). Although these models were designed to understand environmental modifications in urbanizing seaside settings, similar models for broader analyses of the tourism–natural environment relationship can be and need to be developed.

The lack of clearly defined modeling of the tourist–environment relationship is also evident in textbooks that have explored the relationship between tourists and the natural environment. Such books have typically recognized the complexity of this interrelationship, but only one of those reviewed here contained conceptual models of the relationship. Three books emphasized the importance of sustainability in tourism–environment relationships and the importance of environmental planning and management (Hunter and Green 1995; Mieczkowski 1995; Holden 2000). Hunter and Green (1995) concentrated on tourism impacts upon the environment, whereas environmental impacts upon tourism as well as both positive and negative tourism impacts upon the environment were discussed at length by Mieczkowski (1995) and Holden (2000). Conceptual models exploring both the complex reciprocal relationships between tourists and the environment, as well as the concept of carrying capacity, were presented in only one textbook (Mieczkowski 1995). The use of environmental impact analyses (EAs, EISs) to assess tourist development in natural areas was presented in detail in another text (Hunter and Green 1995).

In summary, understanding the tourist–natural environment relationship within a scientific framework is not easy, and even conceptual models have not adequately addressed all aspects of this relationship. The Ellis Curve, while pedagogically popular, has produced few follow-up case studies. Butler's resort-cycle model, perhaps the leading organizational framework in site-specific tourism analysis, has largely been ignored when evaluating environmental relationships. Even recent textbooks on the tourism–environment relationship have shied away from conceptual models and relied instead upon case studies or abstract planning matrices. Perhaps there are no universal guidelines or models, and tourism impacts upon the natural environment can be assessed only on a case-by-case basis. This would, by definition, make planning and management in natural areas more difficult and dependent upon case studies of successful tourism management practices in similar environmental settings. Rigorous methodological examinations still need to be made.

Conclusion

Human attraction to the natural environment in the form of tourism is best described as a complex relationship that is not easily understood or conceptually modeled, let alone scientifically analyzed. The reasons humans are attracted to the physical environment have their origins in various traditions, including Romanticism, the tradition of "taking the waters," a love for the sea, religion or spiritualism, exploration of the unknown, hunting and fishing, love of exercise and outdoor recreation, attraction to exotic wildlife, and a quest for a salubrious climate. Because of the wide range of motivations to similar nature destinations, it is difficult to summarize the tourist–natural environment relationship by means of matrices or conceptual models. The few real models that exist in tourism geography have not yet been applied widely to tourism's impacts upon the physical environment, even though "ecotourism" and "sustainable tourism" have become ubiquitous buzzwords in the tourism industry.

As Wong Poh Poh points out in this volume (chapter 36), little headway has been made in the past 20 years of research into the environmental impacts of tourism.

Scholars from various academic disciplines have employed a variety of research methodologies in a variety of tourism-impacted environmental settings, and thus the number of case studies has increased over time. In spite of a lack of research paradigms or conceptual models of the tourist–environment relationship, knowledge gleaned from increasing numbers of case studies around the world is increasingly providing a basis for sound environmental management and planning in natural environments affected by tourism.

REFERENCES

Agarwal, S. (1994). The resort cycle revisited: Implications for resorts. In C. P. Cooper and A. Lockwood (eds), *Progress in Tourism, Recreation and Hospitality Management* (vol. 5, pp. 194–208). Chichester: John Wiley.

Bhardwaj, S. M. (1998). Non-hajj pilgrimage in Islam: A neglected dimension of religious circulation. *Journal of Cultural Geography* 17(2), 69–87.

Budowski, R. (1976). Tourism and environmental conservation: Conflict, coexistence, or symbiosis. *Environmental Conservation* 3, 27–31.

Butler, R. W. (1980). The concept of a tourist area cycle of evolution: Implications for management of resources. *Canadian Geographer* 24, 5–12.

Butler, R. W. (1985). Evolution of tourism in the Scottish highlands. *Annals of Tourism Research* 12, 371–91.

Butler, R. W. (1991). Tourism, environment, and sustainable development. *Environmental Conservation* 18(3), 201–9.

Cloke, P., and Perkins, H. C. (1998). Cracking the canyon with the Awesome Foursome: Representations of adventure tourism in New Zealand. *Environment and Planning D: Society and Space* 16(2), 185–218.

Cohen, E. (1978). Impact of tourism on the physical environment. *Annals of Tourism Research* 5, 215–37.

Collins, C. O. (1979). Site and situation strategy in tourism planning: A Mexican case study. *Annals of Tourism Research* 6, 351–66.

Davis, J. H. (1956). Influence of man upon coast lines. In W. L. Thomas, Jr. (ed.), *Man's Role in Changing the Face of the Earth* (pp. 504–21). Chicago: University of Chicago Press.

Demars, S. E. (1988). Worship by-the-sea: Camp-meetings and seaside resorts in 19th century America. *American Geographical Society's Focus* 38(4), 15–20.

Demars, S. E. (1990). Romanticism and American national parks. *Journal of Cultural Geography* 11(1), 16–24.

Demars, S. E. (1991). *The Tourist in Yosemite, 1855–1985.* Salt Lake City: University of Utah Press.

Durie, A. J. (1994). The development of Scotland as a tourist destination. In A. V. Seaton (ed.), *Tourism: The State of the Art* (pp. 494–9). Chichester: John Wiley.

Gill, D. A. (1989). *The Social Structure and Economics of the Charter and Party Boat Fishing Industry in Mississippi.* Mississippi State: Mississippi Agriculture and Forestry Experiment Station.

Graber, L. H. (1976). *Wilderness as Sacred Space.* Washington, DC: Association of American Geographers.

Graburn, N. (1977). Tourism: The sacred journey. In V. Smith (ed.), *Hosts and Guests: The Anthropology of Tourism* (pp. 17–32). Philadelphia: University of Pennsylvania Press.

Gunn, C. A. (1988). *Tourism Planning.* New York: Taylor & Francis.

Hall, C. Michael (1998). Historical antecedents of sustainable development and ecotourism: New labels on old bottles? In C. M. Hall and A. A. Lew (eds), *Sustainable Tourism: A Geographical Perspective* (pp. 13–24). London: Addison Wesley Longman.
Hall, C. M., and Page, S. J. (2002). *The Geography of Tourism and Recreation: Environment, Place, and Space.* Montreal: McGill-Queen's University Press.
Halseth, G. (1998). *Cottage Country in Transition*, 2nd edn. London Routledge.
Haywood, K. M. (1986). Can the tourist-area life cycle be made operational? *Tourism Management* 7(3), 154–67.
Holden, A. (2000). *Environment and Tourism.* London: Routledge.
Honour, H. (1981). *Romanticism.* Harmondsworth: Penguin.
Hugill, P. (1985). The rediscovery of America: Elite automobile touring. *Annals of Tourism Research* 12, 435–47.
Hunter, C., and Green, H. (1995). *Tourism and the Environment.* London: Routledge.
Johnson, K. (1990). Origins of tourism in the Catskill Mountains. *Journal of Cultural Geography* 11(1), 5–16.
Kusler, J. A. (1991). *Ecotourism and Resource Conservation.* Papers compiled by J. A. Kusler from two international symposia on ecotourism sponsored in part by the Association of Wetland Managers. Madison: Omni Press.
Lavery, P. (1971). Resorts and recreation. In P. Lavery (ed.), *Recreational Geography.* New York: John Wiley.
Lawrence, H. W. (1983). Southern spas: Source of the American resort tradition. *Landscape* 27(2), 1–12.
Löfgren, O. (1999). *On Holiday: A History of Vacationing.* Berkeley: University of California Press.
Lowenthal, D. (1962). Tourists and thermalists. *Geographical Review* 52, 124–7.
Mathieson, A., and Wall, G. (1982). *Tourism: Economic, Physical and Social Impacts.* New York: Longman.
Meyer-Arendt, K. J. (1985). The Grand Isle, Louisiana resort cycle. *Annals of Tourism Research* 12, 449–65.
Meyer-Arendt, K. J. (1990). Modelling environmental impacts of tourism development along the Gulf Coast. *The Compass* 67, 272–83.
Meyer-Arendt, K. J. (1993). Geomorphic impacts of resort evolution along the Gulf of Mexico coast: Applicability of resort cycle models. In P. P. Wong (ed.), *Tourism vs. Environment: The Case for Coastal Areas* (pp. 125–38). Dordrecht: Kluwer Academic Publishers.
Mieczkowski, Z. (1995). *Environmental Issues of Tourism and Recreation.* Lanham, MD: University Press of America.
Mullins, P. (1991). Tourism urbanization. *International Journal of Urban and Regional Research* 15(3), 326–42.
Nash, R. (1967). *Wilderness and the American Mind.* New Haven: Yale University Press.
Nicolson, M. H. (1962). *Mountain Gloom and Mountain Glory.* New York: Norton.
O'Reilly, K. (2000). *The British on the Costa del Sol.* London: Routledge.
Patmore, J. A. (1983). *Recreation and Resources: Leisure Patterns and Leisure Places.* Oxford: Basil Blackwell.
Pigram, J. J. (1980). Environmental implications of tourism development. *Annals of Tourism Research* 7, 554–83.
Place, S. E. (1991). Nature tourism and rural development in Tortuguero. *Annals of Tourism of Research* 18, 186–201.
Pyne, S. J. (1998). *How the Canyon Became Grand.* New York: Penguin.
Romeril, M. (1985). Tourism and the environment: Towards a symbiotic relationship. *International Journal of Environmental Studies* 25, 215–18.
Russell, B. (1946). *A History of Western Philosophy.* London: Counterpoint Unwin.

Sears, J. F. (1989). *Sacred Places: American Tourist Attractions in the Nineteenth Century.* New York: Oxford University Press.

Spencer, J. E., and Thomas, W. L. (1948). The hill stations and summer resorts of the Orient. *Geographical Review* 38, 637–51.

Stansfield, C. A., Jr. (1970). The development of modern seaside resorts. *Parks and Recreation* 5(10), 14–17, 43–6.

Sullivan, C. L. (1990). *Gathering at the River: South Mississippi's Methodist Camp Meetings.* Perkinston, MS: Mississippi Gulf Coast Community College Press.

Thomas, W. L. (ed.) (1956). *Man's Role in Changing the Face of the Earth.* Chicago: University of Chicago Press.

Tuan, Yi-fu (1979). *Landscapes of Fear.* New York: Pantheon.

Valenza, J. M. (2000). *Taking the Waters in Texas.* Austin: University of Texas Press.

Weaver, D. B. (2002). Asian ecotourism: Patterns and themes. *Tourism Geographies* 4, 153–72.

Wheeller, B. (1994). Egotourism, sustainable tourism and the environment: A symbiotic, symbolic or shambolic relationship. In A. V. Seaton (ed.), *Tourism: The State of the Art* (pp. 647–54). Chichester: John Wiley.

Wolfe, R. I. (1952). Wasaga Beach. The divorce from the geographic environment. *Canadian Geographer* 2, 57–66.

Wolfe, R. I. (1966). Recreational travel: The new migration. *Canadian Geographer* 10, 1–14.

Wolfe, R. I. (1982). Recreational travel: The new migration, revisited. *Ontario Geography* 19, 103–24.

Chapter 35

Tourism and Touristic Representations of Nature

Jarkko Saarinen

Introduction

Dean MacCannell (1976), in his highly influential book *The Tourist: A New Theory of the Leisure Class*, approaches tourism within a framework of modernity and its evolution in Western societies. For him, the progress of modernity depends on its very sense of instability and non-authenticity. The alienation process taking place in industrialized and increasingly post-industrialized societies is a consequence of modernity, and to cope with alienation in everyday life, people seek for authenticity and mythical structures as tourists on their holidays. More specifically, MacCannell states that tourists are both searching for and also creating and recreating those structures which modernity has demolished and caused to vanish elsewhere.

One "place" where modern people think they can still find "authenticity" and "real" experiences is nature, in that the natural environment may reflect a past connection between people and the land, a link which arguably has disappeared from contemporary urban and suburban life (Tuan 1974; Relph 1976; Oelschlaeger 1991). This lost connection with the past not only has a time dimension, but it has also a geographical dimension: in many people's minds the past, authenticity, and real experiences can still be found on the peripheries of the modern world, where nature, wildernesses, and indigenous or other cultural groups untouched by modernity are situated (see Saarinen 2001; Shaw 2001).

Authenticity is a problematic and hotly debated concept in tourism research (see Cohen 1988; Selwyn 1996). It is approached here as a constructed idea. According to Ning Wang (1999: 351), certain "objects, such as nature, are in a strict sense irrelevant to authenticity in MacCannell's sense." However, nature is not seen here as an object in the context of socially, economically, and politically determined activity, as modern tourism is (see Mels 1999; Markwell 2001; Meethan 2001). On the contrary, nature and the attractiveness, images, and representations of natural environments that motivate people to visit and consume nature are approached as social constructions, the authenticity of which can also be emphasized "through cultural representations of reality" (MacCannell 1976: 92).

Thus authenticity refers here to the socially constructed idea of tradition – genuine, real, natural, unique – which has its historically and ideologically conditioned determinants and spatial contexts. This does not necessarily lead, however, to a total relativism in which any idea or representation of nature is as good as the next, for space as a social construct is a moral category and the production of spatial representations and possible "staged authenticity" (e.g. the situation in which a certain representation is not related to the space to which it actually aims to refer) can be evaluated (see Sack 1992; Proctor 1998; Little 1999; Pritchard and Morgan 2000; Ateljevic and Doorne 2002). On the other hand, contrary to MacCannell's approach (1976), authenticity is not understood here as a foundation for explaining contemporary tourism (see Meethan 2001), but as a partial, although important, argument for understanding and explaining the role and idea of nature and its representations in tourism and the production of tourism spaces.

The spatial dimension of the socially constructed past, authenticity and stability, along with the assumption of modern alienation made by MacCannell (1976), forms a basis upon which the tourism industry can use nature and produce representations of nature with references to authenticity and real experiences for visitors to consume. Indeed, nature has become a major tourist attraction and nature-based tourism is one of the central components of tourist activities today. In fact, many authors state that this is one of the fastest-growing segments of the whole tourism industry (Ceballos-Lascuráin 1996; Mowforth and Munt 1998; Fennell 1999). Nature-based or nature tourism relies on the attractiveness of "undeveloped" natural areas and the associated activities that can be pursued there. It is sometimes linked to the idea of alternative and sustainable tourism (see Whelan 1991; Burton 1998), but this is grounded in a contradiction. Nature forms a resource for nature-based tourism, as a city does for urban tourism, and from that perspective sustainability is not a condition. In order to maintain the resource as "nature," however, there must be some limits to the development that takes place, although such limits are not necessarily integrated into the idea of sustainability. Rather, the limits of development can be greatly modified in tourism while maintaining images of a certain kind. For this development purpose, the tourism industry actively produces representations in which a destination is depicted through images such as those of natural landscapes, wilderness, and wild animals.

The rapid development of nature-based tourism has gained concrete expression in certain places within each country. In Finland, for example, the total number of visits to national parks almost tripled during the 1990s (Saarinen and Vaara 2002). Indeed, nature is "today universally regarded as a source of pleasure" (Wang 2000: 80), but natural attractions and wilderness environments have not always been the focus of positive attention for visitors, nor have they always been a source of pleasant experiences. According to Short (1991: 6) "fear of the wilderness was one of the strongest elements in European attitudes to wilderness up to the Nineteenth Century", and this attitude was taken across the seas (see Nash 1982; Hall 1998). Thus, the history of nature as a significant tourist attraction is quite short, in fact. In the days of the Grand Tour, for example, early visitors made no real reference to the beauty or sublime character of the Alps (Macnaghten and Urry 2001: 6), and the famous late eighteenth-century Swedish natural scientist and traveler Carl von Linné (1969[1889]: 68) described Lapland, which is nowadays marketed in terms of positive images of wild land and as a source of vitality, as a hell on earth for which "the right name should be Styx." Today, these same "landscapes of evil" are visited internationally by millions of tourists every year, simply to experience the natural beauty of the wild landscapes and mountain scenery (see Hall and Page 1999; Saarinen 2001).

Natural environments or other attractions are not static or uncontested categories within tourism; rather, they are constantly changing products of certain combinations of social, political, and economic relationships that are specific in space and time. From that perspective, the attractions of nature are not "out there" waiting to be discovered, seen, and admired: they are our and others' constructions (see Allen, Massey, and Cochrane 1998). What we see and especially value in natural landscapes are cultural projections created by tourism and modernization in general. MacCannell (1992) sees the Yosemite National Park, for example, as a human product, a piece of nature which is marked off, interpreted, and museumized for the purposes of visitors and society (see also Mels 1999). In our age of modernity, nature has become a product, a general trademark with certain qualities attached to particular places, which can be wild, untouched, untamed, scenic, beautiful, rough, and the like.

The focus of this chapter is closely linked to the idea of nature as a social construction and a changing product in the commoditization and representation processes of tourism. The purpose is to introduce some of the earlier changes in Western societies that have served to accentuate the role of nature and its representations in present-day tourism and to analyze on a conceptual level how nature is produced and represented in tourism. First, the transformation of production in Western countries will be discussed, giving special attention to current changes characterized by the ideas of the new tourism and the experience economy, which have created new needs for tourists to consume nature. Second, some current approaches of human geography will be integrated into the discussion of representations in tourism. In this sense geography as a discipline can be regarded as "the art of recognizing, describing and interpreting the personalities of regions" and other spaces (Gilbert 1960: 158). One of the major aspects creating personalities or identities for (tourism) regions is the process of representation, which has been studied increasingly by tourism geographers.

The Changing Structures of Tourism: New Tourism, the Experience Economy, and the Consumption of Nature

Structural changes have been visible in the development of tourism since the early 1990s, with the growth of nature-based tourism and the decrease in the relative importance of mass tourism being especially highlighted in the literature (see Fennell 1999; Hall and Page 1999). The demand for nature-based tourism grew rapidly in the late 1980s, leading to the creation of new products and types of tourism.

Supposedly "new," "alternative" forms of tourism, such as ecotourism, are not only outcomes of the perceived problems of (mass) tourism but also results of changes that have taken place in Western societies, where the economy has developed toward post-Fordist production and disorganized capitalism (see Harvey 1989; Williams and Shaw 1998). Within this context it is argued that the tourist industry and its destinations are changing and are creating products that conform better to the new structures of motivation, tourist segments, and trends in general consumption (see Poon 1993; Ryan, Hughes, and Chirgwin 2000), with consumers becoming increasingly differentiated, and markets expanding and changing more fluidly than ever before (see Shaw, Agarwal, and Bull 2000).

As a term, "new tourism" does not represent a specific form of tourism, but rather a new style of production, with increasing flexibility, individuality, and hybridity (Poon 1993); features which are also present in the representations and new uses of the natural environment. One of the new uses of nature is linked to the present growth of the experience economy, with its increased tendency for individualization in production and consumption (see Beck and Beck-Gernsheim 2001; Thrift 2001). For Pine and Gilmore (1999), the experience economy represents a logical development in production and the progression of economic value. Agricultural commodities are extracted, fungible market-based products, while the goods in the next phase are manufactured, tangible, and user-oriented products. This is followed by the production of services, characterized by their delivered nature and intangible activities for a particular client. They argue that the production of experiences therefore represents the higher mode of production, in the form of nature tourism, staged experiences, and memorable events that engage individuals in a personal way as guests.

The experience economy ties space, time, and human experiences together in systems in which individuals seek to perform a wide variety of new activities. The products of the experience economy are good examples of this development and connection between spatiality, time, and experiences, which often involves spectacles, exercise, and speed (see Ryan, Hughes, and Chirgwin 2000; Thrift 2001). Natural areas in the Nordic countries, for example, have traditionally offered activities such as backpacking, hiking, hunting, and fishing in summer and cross-country skiing in winter (see Kauppi 1996; Fredman et al. 2001), but the use of such areas for tourism has experienced both quantitative and qualitative changes during the last decade. The volume of activity has grown, and snowmobile trekking has become one of the central new nature-based activities in northern Finland, for example, and clearly the most visible. This modernization of tourism and recreation in nature is a global process with changing elements in different places. For example, in "Northwoods" region, Wisconsin (USA), traditional activities such as fishing and hunting have almost been replaced by snowmobiling, mountain biking, and cross-country skiing, which all represent modern new activities for North American tourists (see Williams and Kaltenborn 1999).

New activities such as snowmobile trekking, dog sledge safaris, mountain biking, and canoeing/kayaking are pursued through enterprises that are related specifically to the experience economy. In fact, 20 years ago these new activities would not been seriously listed with the traditional ones in Nordic countries. Many of them rely on changes in production and consumption, international influences, and new images of nature. Dog sledge safaris, for example, are mainly grounded in representations of the Arctic and cold, snowy areas promoted by French tourist operators, who most probably evaluate northern nature, its uses and its attractions, in the light of their historical relations with Canada. The local equivalent of the husky dog in Lapland is the reindeer, the role of which is growing in the nature tourism market but is still marginal compared with that of the sledge dog.

The Production of Touristic Nature and its Representations

Representing nature in tourism

Modern tourism is an industry grounded in ideas. In order to develop, it must produce, construct, and use socio-spatial representations of nature and culture for marketing purposes. The question of representations, their production and the changes that take place in them, can be seen as crucial for tourism (Squire 1994; Crang 1997; Cloke and Perkins 1998; Edensor 1998; Del Casino and Hanna 2000; Pritchard and Morgan 2000). People attach meanings and representations to faraway places, and these have a very significant influence on their choice of destination and their motives and behavior as tourists.

Representations can be understood as forms of presenting an object not by copying it but by re-presenting it in a new form and/or a new textual environment (Hall 1997). Touristic representations are based on discourses producing meanings for places, cultures, attractions, and activities in connection with tourism. As stated by Stuart Hall (1992: 291), discourse is "a particular way of representing" a particular topic. Thus, the concepts of discourse and representation are closely connected. Discourses are socially and historically produced coherent meaning systems and practices which both manifest power structures and are power structures at the same time. Discourses are constructed in social practices, such as place promotion and local politics, and at the same time they construct and transform social reality and the physical environment by virtue of the practices and policies attached to them. Discourse as a term refers to both the process and its outcome, but discourses or representations are in no sense static outcomes. They evolve with time and can change our ideas and practices.

Power issues are always involved in discourses and representations (see Cheong and Miller 2000; Lefebvre 1991; Hall 1992). In fact, one of the major practices manifesting power in tourism is the production of representations for the purposes of place promotion, which is in effect a "means of designing a place to satisfy the needs of its target markets" (Kotler, Haider, and Rein 1993). Place promotion spatializes meanings, representations, and history for tourists to consume. Its aim is to make the natural and cultural features of the destination known and popular by packaging real or imagined representations into a marketable product. However, while this process makes the natural and cultural features of the destination known, it also stereotypes and modifies the signs and symbols involved (see Meethan 2001).

Representations are specific descriptions that manifest a power to represent "Something by Someone to Somebody". This three-S nature of representations in the production of tourist destinations is illustrated in figure 35.1 by reference to two brochures produced by the Finnish Tourist Board (MEK) in the late 1970s. The one on the right-hand side (winter 1977–8) is aimed at depicting and marketing Saariselkä in northeastern Lapland, by means of a map and three pictures: a snowy fell landscape, a fell in its autumn colors and a lake view. For the next winter season 1978–9 (on the left), identical pictures were used to advertise the Aavasaksa region!

Thus both destinations are represented in a stereotypical way, with similar references to natural beauty, wilderness, and possibilities for nature activities. Geographically, Aavasaksa is situated in southwest Lapland, close to the Swedish border,

Figure 35.1 An example of the production of touristic representations of nature. Two virtually identical tourist brochures for the winter season, advertising different destinations in Finnish Lapland, Saariselkä and Aavasaksa, produced by the Finnish Tourist Board (MEK) in the late 1970s (see Saarinen 2001)

while Saariselkä lies in northeast Lapland, near the border with Russia. The pictures used in the brochures are not in fact from either of these places, however. The fell landscapes are from two other well-known destinations in Lapland, and the lake view could be from anywhere in Finland, but they are certainly not from Saariselkä or Aavasaksa, because neither has any lakes. As if there were not enough misrepresentations, only one of the scenes depicts the tourist season that the brochure is supposed to be advertising, i.e. winter.

The "Someone" in the above example was MEK, a central government organization based in Helsinki. MEK was simply engaged in marketing the two destinations ("Something") to Finnish and foreign tourists (the other "Someone"). As a result, both were constructed on the basis of southern and foreign stereotypes of the landscape and nature of Lapland in general, the representation of which would be more or less the same regardless of where the actual destinations might be located. In this case the logic of the production of representations lies in the generally stereotyped perception of Lapland as a natural landscape of fells, mountains, and lakes, and thus different destinations can be represented through images of basically the same kind. The landscapes represented are also entirely free of human influence. Even today, after several phases of rapid development, with the creation of beds for about 10,000 visitors, restaurants, discos, a spa, a brewery, and shops, the representations of Saariselkä still make use of similar wilderness images. These images are also supported by physical modifications of environment, for example the "planting" of old dead trees inside the area of tourism infrastructure, such as along the roads and parking lots, to represent wild, untouched nature (Saarinen 2001). These grey trees do indeed characterize the wilderness of Lapland and produce positive images for Finnish tourists, but for those from central Europe, the Germans, for example, they refer more obviously to the negatively perceived forest deaths caused by air pollution in their own environment. Thus representations are social constructs, the interpretations and uses of which for the purposes of place promotion should always be based on an analysis of the cultural context.

The homogenization of nature

On a physical level, Williams and Shaw (1997) identify a similar process of change in the United Kingdom to that discussed above. They argue that seaside resorts have suffered from a loss of distinctiveness, so that they have begun to resemble each other. Indeed (mass) tourist destinations are often seen as products that have developed or are developing toward spatial homogenization – a general tendency described in geography by Edward Relph (1976). This implies that destinations are being converted into places with similar physical and symbolic features, attractions, and images. In addition, their tourist infrastructures, facilities, and "sense of place" may also increasingly come to imitate and refer to the places from which most of the tourists – the consumers – and the capital for development and construction originate (see Meethan 2001; Saarinen 2001). However, there are still other kinds of perspectives and positions, such as local or non-touristic ones, from which destination, its identity, and uses can be perceived and evaluated differently. Thus, the hegemonic representations of tourist destinations can be contested through different kinds of sociocultural processes from which destination and its nature(s) are constituted (see Macnaghten and Urry 1998).

The homogenization process demonstrates in a way the idea of time-space compression propounded by Harvey (1989), in which space and spatial experience shrink as a result of increasing movement of capital and information. Time and space are not the only elements compressed by this circulation and (over)accumulation of capital, for tourist "destinations come in and out of fashion and tourism moves on elsewhere" (Mowforth and Munt 1998: 30). During this "circulation," which could also be described by means of the Butlerian life-cycle metaphor (see Butler 1980), tourist destinations are modified and developed toward homogenization and mass-scale industry in order to effectively serve the accumulation of capital and provide a larger spatial structure for tourism. This process may lead to the physical loss of the original character of the place, including the attractiveness of its natural environment, even though this environment may still play an important role in the associated representations. At the same time, the representations of nature may become abstract and placeless, losing all connection with the physical place that they are marketing. Relph (1976) calls this "an erosion of place," a change in the original natural and cultural landscape and a loss of its unique and authentic sense of place, which relates to the idea of staged ("objective") authenticity put forward by MacCannell (1976).

From one perspective (Morgan 1994), spatial homogenization is a "natural" process in the development of tourism and in the current trend toward globalization, but not necessarily a desirable one. Destinations are spaces designed and built up on the premises of attracting non-local people and capital. Getz (1999: 24), for example, defines a tourist space as "an area dominated by tourist activities or one that is organized for meeting the needs of visitors." The needs and values of the customers are therefore the leading guidelines in a market-driven economic activity such as tourism and in the representations produced by it. From the local perspective, one possible result of this process can be the marginalization of local communities and lifestyles, in which traditional livelihoods and other such uses of natural environment are evaluated in public discussions and images as pre-modern, economically inferior, and non-profitable comparing to tourism development. Finally, such rhetoric may be concretized in land-use planning, regional politics, and economic investments favoring non-locally oriented tourism development.

Conclusions: The Politics of Nature Representations

The present significant role of tourism and its constantly evolving new forms are connected with developments in Western societies, post-Fordist production, and the rise of the experience economy and a new middle class with a capacity and need to consume wide varieties of products and ideas (see Urry 1990; Pine and Gilmore 1999; Meethan 2001). The economic significance of tourism and the fact that nature-based tourism is developing rapidly mean that new destinations and attractions for activities in nature are constantly evolving. Partly due to this process, tourism directed at protected areas is one of the most rapidly growing sectors of the industry at the present time (Mowforth and Munt 1998; Hall and Page 1999). Different places and regions are being planned and transformed in order to attract more nature tourists. Even whole countries and national economies can be highly dependent on the needs of modern tourism, the tourist trade, and the representations used for its promotion.

Nature has become a tourist product, a quality of a certain destination that can be commoditized and represented in various ways, and the growing flow of tourists to natural areas, along with the increasing circulation of touristic representations of nature, has played an important role in how we perceive nature and different destinations and regions and in what we think nature is for. In that sense, tourism for its part also defines and maps what is allowed and suitable, preferable or unwanted, in a certain spatial context. As stated by Macnaghten and Urry (1998: 1), there is "a diversity of contested natures" constructed in specific social practices and positions, some of which even conflict with each other, being produced by and through different stakeholders, local and non-local groups and actors, for example. The production of space and representations for the purposes of tourism also involves a discursive spatial struggle inside the destinations and host communities, over land use, resources, and economics. This may include a process whereby local values and attitudes toward nature are depicted as the "other" by constructing them as different, distinctive, and even "lower" relative to non-local tourist value systems and representations of nature.

The homogenization process transforms the representation of local geographies to conform better to the images that exist outside the region and to fulfill the historically and touristically constructed expectations of potential visitors. Thus, evolving tourism often produces its own spaces, landscapes representing the values and needs of the tourism industry rather than those of other local interests or identities (see Hall 1994). As pointed out by Lefebvre (1991: 58), peripheral tourist destinations characterized by natural, amenity-rich landscapes are constructed and represented as "leisure-oriented spaces" to meet the needs of Western urbanized and industrialized societies.

Many peripheral natural areas and places are nowadays tied to the "centres," to global economies and to larger cultural/political networks, through the development of tourism. The development of tourism and touristic transformations of nature and its different elements at peripheral destinations, often represent manifestations of larger processes. In general, the growth of tourism may create welfare and new opportunities for obtaining work, and nature-based tourism can play a significant role in regional development, but it may also create problems. For example, the touristic idea and its representations of wilderness areas as places of aesthetic and scenic value may first contest ideologically and then displace in practical terms the local uses of nature as a resource for traditional livelihoods.

Modern tourism has become a major element in constructing and constituting the way in which we see our environment, other places, cultures, and nature, and the way in which "others" see and represent us and our daily environment. The tourism industry operates as a link and medium between local and larger spatial scales, and this can lead to the creation, re-creation, and experiencing of non-authenticity, homogeneity, and unsustainable practices, and finally to a loss of attractiveness and a decline in tourism. Thus, the politics associated with representations of nature and critical evaluation of the basis of such representations and related discourses may be regarded as both crucial topics for academics to study and also crucial issues for the industry if it is to achieve long-term sustainability. The questions which should be addressed in the future are therefore related to the ideological background of the representations of nature and their different uses in tourism. The essential questions in the context of the critical theory are whose nature and construction of nature are represented when one sets out to develop tourism in amenity-rich natural landscapes, and what potential contradictions in ideas, uses, and practices may exist between touristic and other interests and values in such destinations.

REFERENCES

Allen, J., Massey, D., and Cochrane, A. (1998). *Rethinking the Region*. London: Routledge.

Ateljevic, I., and Doorne, S. (2002). Representing New Zealand: Tourism image and ideology. *Annals of Tourism Research* 29(3), 648–67.

Beck, U., and Beck-Gernsheim, E. (2001). *Individualization*. London: Sage.
Burton, R. (1998). Maintaining the quality of ecotourism: Ecotour operators' responses to tourism growth. *Journal of Sustainable Tourism* 6(2), 117–42.
Butler, R. (1980). The concepts of a tourist area cycle of evolution: Implications for management of resources. *Canadian Geographer* 24(1), 5–12.
Ceballos-Lascuráin, H. (1996). *Tourism, Ecotourism, and Protected Areas*. Gland: IUCN.
Cheong, S.-M., and Miller, M. (2000). Power and tourism: A Foucauldian observation. *Annals of Tourism Research* 27(2), 371–90.
Cloke, P., and Perkins, H. (1998). Cracking the canyon with the Awesome Foursome: Representation of adventure tourism in New Zealand. *Environment and Planning D: Society and Space* 16(2), 185–218.
Cohen, E. (1988). Authenticity and commodisation in tourism. *Annals of Tourism Research* 15(3), 371–86.
Crang, M. (1997). Picturing practice: Research through the tourist gaze. *Progress in Human Geography* 21(3), 359–73.
Del Casino, V. J. Jr., and Hanna, S. P. (2000). Representation and identity in tourism map spaces. *Progress in Human Geography* 24(1), 23–46.
Edensor, T. (1998). *Tourists at the Taj: Performance and Meaning at a Symbolic Site*. London: Routledge.
Fennell, D. (1999). *Ecotourism: An Introduction*. London: Routledge.
Fredman, P., Emmelin, L., Heberlein, T., and Vuorio, T. (2001). Tourism in the Swedish mountain region. In S. Benght (ed.), *Going North: Peripheral Tourism in Canada and Sweden* (pp. 123–46). Stersund: ETOUR.
Getz, D. (1999). Resort-centred tours and development of the rural hinterland: The case of Cairns and the Atherton Tablelands. *The Journal of Tourism Studies* 10(2), 23–34.
Gilbert, E. W. (1960). The idea of the region. *Geography* 45, 157–75.
Hall, C. M. (1994). *Tourism and Politics: Policy, Power and Place*. Chichester: John Wiley.
Hall, C. M. (1998). Historical antecedents of sustainable development and ecotourism: New labels on old bottles? In C. M. Hall and A. A. Lew (eds), *Sustainable Tourism: A Geographical Perspective* (pp. 3–24). New York: Longman.
Hall, C. M., and Page, S. J. (1999). *The Geography of Tourism: Environment, Place and Space*. London: Routledge.
Hall, S. (1992). The west and the rest. In S. Hall and B. Gieber (eds), *Formations of Modernity*. London: Polity/Open University.
Hall, S. (1997). The work of representation. In S. Hall (ed.), *Representation: Cultural Representations and Signifying Practices* (pp. 13–64). London: Open University/Sage.
Harvey, D. (1989). *The Condition of Postmodernity*. Oxford: Blackwell.
Kauppi, Matti. (1996). Finnish nature as an international tourism product (in Finnish). *Suomen Matkailun Kehitys Oy:n julkaisuja* A70.
Kotler, Philip, Haider, D., and Rein, I. (1993). *Marketing Places*. New York: Macmillan.
Lefebvre, Henri. (1991). *The Production of Space*. Oxford: Blackwell.
Little, Jo. (1999). Otherness, representation and the cultural construction of rurality. *Progress in Human Geography* 23(3), 437–42.
MacCannell, D. (1976). *The Tourist: A New Theory of the Leisure Class*. New York: Schocken Books.
MacCannell, D. (1992). *Empty Meeting Ground: The Tourist Papers*. London: Routledge.
Macnaghten, P., and Urry, J. (1998). *Contested Natures*. London: Sage.
Macnaghten, P., and Urry, J. (2001). Bodies of nature: Introduction. In P. Macnaghten and J. Urry (eds), *Bodies in Nature* (pp. 34–57). London: Sage.
Markwell, K. (2001). An intimate rendezvous with nature? *Tourist Studies* 1(1), 39–57.
Meethan, K. (2001). *Tourism in Global Society*. New York: Palgrave.

Mels, T. (1999). *Wild Landscapes: The Cultural Nature of Swedish National Parks*. Lund: Lund University Press.
Morgan, M. (1994). Homogenous products: The future of established resorts. In W. F. Theobald. (ed.), *Global Tourism: The Next Decade* (pp. 378–95). Oxford: Butterworth-Heinemann.
Mowforth, M., and Munt, I. (1998). *Tourism and Sustainability: A New Tourism in the Third World*. London: Routledge.
Nash, R. (1982). *Wilderness and the American Mind*, 3rd edn. London: Yale University Press.
Oelschlaeger, M. (1991). *The Idea of Wilderness*. London: Yale University Press.
Pine, J., and Gilmore, James (1999). *The Experience Economy. Work is Theatre and Every Business a Stage: Goods and Services are No Longer Enough*. Boston: Harvard Business School Press.
Poon, A. (1993). *Tourism, Technology and Competitive Strategies*. Wallingford: CAB International.
Pritchard, A., and Morgan, N. (2000). Constructing tourism landscapes: Gender, sexuality and space. *Tourism Geographies* 2(2), 115–39.
Proctor, Jim (1998). Ethics on geography: Giving moral form to the geographical imagination. *Area* 30(1), 8–18.
Relph, Edward (1976). *Place and Placelessness*. London: Pion.
Ryan, C., Hughes, K., and Chirgwin, S. (2000). The gaze, spectacle and ecotourism. *Annals of Tourism Research* 27(1), 148–63.
Saarinen, J. (2001). The transformation of a tourist destination: Theory and case studies on the production of local geographies in tourism in Finnish Lapland. *Nordia Geographical Publications* 30(1), 1–105.
Saarinen, J., and Vaara, M. (2002). *A Cottage Beside the National Park* (in Finnish, summary in English). Research Paper 845. Finnish Forest Research Institute.
Sack, R. (1992). *Place, Modernity and Consumer's World*. Baltimore: Johns Hopkins University Press.
Selwyn, T. (1996). Introduction. In T. Selwyn (ed.), *The Tourist Image: Myths and Myth Making in Tourism* (pp. 1–32). Chichester: John Wiley.
Shaw, G., Agarwal, S., and Bull, P. (2000). Tourism consumption and tourist behaviour: A British perspective. *Tourism Geographies* 2(3), 264–89.
Shaw, J. (2001). Winning territory: Changing place and change pace. In J. May and N. Thrift (eds), *Timespace: Geographies of Temporality* (pp. 120–32). London: Routledge.
Short, R. (1991). *Imagined Country: Environment, Culture and Society*. London: Routledge.
Squire, S. (1994). Accounting for cultural meanings: The interface between geography and tourism studies re-examined. *Progress in Human Geography* 18(1), 1–16.
Thrift, N. (2001). Still life in nearly present time: The object of nature. In P. Macnaghten and J. Urry (eds), *Bodies in Nature* (pp. 34–57). London: Sage.
Tuan, Yi-Fu (1974). *Topophilia: A Study of Environmental Perception, Attitudes, and Values*. Englewood Cliffs: Prentice-Hall.
Urry, J. (1990). *The Tourist Gaze: Leisure and Travel in Contemporary Societies*. London: Sage.
von Linné, Carl. (1969[1889]). *A Journey to Lapland 1732* (in Finnish). Hämeenlinna: Karisto.
Wang, N. (1999). Rethinking authenticity in tourism experience. *Annals of Tourism Research* 26(2), 49–70.
Wang, N. (2000). *Tourism and Modernity*. Amsterdam: Pergamon.
Whelan, T. (ed.) (1991). *Nature Tourism: Managing for the Environment*. Washington, DC: Island Press.

Williams, A. M., and Shaw, G. (1997). Riding the big dipper: The rise and decline of the British seaside resort in the twentieth century. In G. Shaw and A. Williams (eds), *The Rise and Fall of British Coastal Resorts: Cultural and Economic Perspectives* (pp. 1–18). London: Mansell.

Williams, A. M., and Shaw, G. (1998). Tourism and the environment: Sustainability and economic restructuring. In C. M. Hall and A. A. Lew (eds), *Sustainable Tourism: A Geographical Perspective* (pp. 49–59). New York: Longman.

Williams, D., and Kalterborn, B. (1999). Leisure place and modernity: The use and meaning of recreational cottages in Norway and the USA. In D. Crouch (ed.), *Leisure Tourism Geographies: Practices and Geographical knowledge* (pp. 214–30). London: Routledge.

Chapter 36

Environmental Impacts of Tourism

P. P. Wong

In their book, still considered a classic, Mathieson and Wall (1982) classified the impacts of tourism as economic, physical, and social. They further examined the physical impacts in terms of environmental components or ecosystems and made a distinction between the natural and the built environment. This chapter will keep to this broad distinction of the environment and discuss the impacts on the natural environment. This is underpinned by the fact that the natural environment forms a significant basis of tourism. The increasing demand for ecotourism and nature-based tourism in recent years (Page and Dowling 2001; Weaver 2001; Newsome, Moore, and Dowling 2002) has also created more concern for tourism impacts on the natural environment.

It is only in the last three decades that the seriousness of the environmental impact of tourism on a global scale has become more evident. Globally, air travel and the use of vehicles for travel contribute to the increasing sources of greenhouse gas emissions, biodiversity loss resulting from habitat loss, consumption of resources, and degradation of various types of environments, such as coastal areas, mountains and wilderness areas, rural areas, and small islands. All these are translated into environmental changes affecting air, land, and water (Wong 2002).

The environmental impacts of tourism have distinct geographical patterns with specific areas identified in terms of the type, extent, and intensity of the impacts (Mieczkowski 1995). On a global scale, the major areas are in western Europe – the Mediterranean, the Alps, and the coasts of the North Sea and Baltic Sea. The Mediterranean Basin is the most touristically overdeveloped region in the world, accounting for 30 percent of international arrivals (EEA 2001). The spatial pattern or intensity of environmental impacts can be complicated by its temporal intensity (seasonality). Normally, seasonal impacts provide a chance for nature to recover from damage suffered during the tourist season (Mieczkowski 1995). But impacts can also proceed in different dimensions. They can be cumulative in terms of space and time, leading to a threshold and a critical level of negative impact. For example, tourism-related air and road travel adds to the cumulative impact of global climate change, which in turn affects tourism negatively, especially in alpine areas (Elsasser and Burki 2002) and on many small islands (Nurse et al. 2001). On the other hand, economic recession can sometimes slow down environmental impacts. For example, the environmental impacts of Japanese leisure and tourism would have been more severe if not for the collapse of the country's "bubble economy" in the 1990s, leading to a slowdown in the development of resorts, golf links, skiing grounds, and hotels (Gielsen, Kurihara, and Moriguchi 2001).

Serious research on the environmental impacts dates from the 1970s. It took a more systematic approach from the 1980s, and by the 1990s also included the notion of sustainable development (Briassoulis and van der Straaten 1999). While research has been carried out from various perspectives, research from a geographical perspective has not progressed since the publication of Mathieson and Wall's book (Butler 2000). More basic contributions have come from non-geographical sources. This chapter starts by classifying the environmental impacts and examines various aspects of research on the environmental impacts of tourism – the constraints, methodologies, contributions from various disciplines, and selective examples of issues. It concludes with the nature of future research and how it relates to measures to reduce negative environmental impacts.

Classifications

As the impacts of tourism on the environment are varied and complex, there is a need to classify them for various reasons, such as research design and analysis, project appraisal, policy development, and programme applications (Hunter and Green 1995). A reductionist approach is evident in recent research on the environmental impacts of tourism and this can take various forms. The environmental impacts of tourism can be considered in terms of:

1. broad or general categories that relate closely to the categorization of tourist assets or attractions found in physical, biological, socioeconomic, natural, built, and cultural environments;
2. the nature of the impacts over time or space, including: short-term or long-term impacts (ESCAP 1992); positive or negative impacts; local, regional, and even global impacts; and direct, indirect, or induced impacts. To some extent these reflect the characteristics of the tourism industry; and
3. environmental components, some examples of which include approaches by Mathieson and Wall (1982) and Mieczkowski (1995) that focus on ecosystems to understand negative environmental impacts; Ceballos-Lascuráin's (1996) classification of direct tourism impacts on geological exposures, minerals and fossils, soils, water resources, vegetation, animal life, sanitation, landscape aesthetics, and the cultural environment; and GFANC's (1997) identification of seven ecosystems impacted by coastal tourism activities alone.

A summary of the adverse impacts on the natural environment is given in table 36.1. More details can be obtained from recent summaries on activities impacting on the coastal ecosystems (GFANC 1997), impacts associated with mountain resorts

Table 36.1 Summary of adverse impacts on the natural environment

A. Pressure on natural resources
1 Energy depletion
2 Water supply
3 Land use
4 Soil erosion
B. Harm to wildlife/habitat and biodiversity loss
1 Trampling and clearance of vegetation
2 Loss of forest cover
3 Disturbance to wildlife
4 Damage to coral reefs
5 Damage to species
C. Pollution
1 Air pollution
2 Untreated wastewater
3 Solid waste and litter
4 Noise pollution

Sources: Genot 1997; Wong 2002.

(Buckley, Pickering, and Warnken 2000), effects of downhill skiing upon the environment (Holden 2000), and impacts on Pacific islands (Hall 1996). Holden (2000) also considers the environmental impacts of viewing wildlife in its habitat.

Research Constraints

Studies of the environmental impacts of tourism face several methodological and conceptual constraints, from the nature of the tourism phenomenon to the variety of disciplinary perspectives that are involved. In their earlier overview, Mathieson and Wall (1982) noted the uneven coverage of research on tourism's environmental impacts, which was particularly sparse in the areas of soils, and air and water quality. The research undertaken has usually referred to one particular environmental component and was mostly conducted in Britain and North America. Another important feature was the "post factum" (after the fact) analysis, which made it difficult to establish a baseline against which future changes could be determined (Mathieson and Wall 1982; Mieczkowski 1995).

This situation has not improved greatly over the past 20 years. Hunter and Green (1995) found that research on the environmental impacts of tourism was usually limited to a defined, and often relatively small, geographical area and from the viewpoint of a single discipline, taking for example an ecological, geographical, sociological, or economic perspective. Overall, research has been relatively poorly developed and not truly multidisciplinary, lacking coherence and being relatively fragmented and unstructured. It should be emphasized that it is difficult to distinguish the impacts of tourism from other anthropogenic factors and it is not easy to attribute specific impacts solely to tourists and to tourist activities, differentiate deliberate or incidental impacts, and assign cause and effect (Butler 2000).

This situation is due to the complex nature of the environmental impacts (Mieczkowski 1995; Holden 2000). Most impacts are non-linear in character, while others build up slowly and cumulatively, resulting in long-term dramatic changes that are not evident until it is too late. Others cause a disproportionately high rate of change initially and then level off. There are also complications from spatial and temporal discontinuities of impacts, as noted earlier (that is, where and when the impacts occur). Although most tourist phenomena are highly localized, their effects can be felt far away, as in the case of air, water, and noise pollution related to tourism activities in pristine nature reserves.

In one of the early attempts to provide an overview of the environmental impacts of tourism, Cohen (1978) suggested that the impacts are dependent on: (1) the intensity of tourist site use and development; (2) the resilience of the ecosystem; (3) the time-perspective of the tourist developer; and (4) the transformational character of tourist development. Based on research in Australia, Sun and Walsh (1998) provided additional details on these factors. The nature and degree of environmental impacts appeared to depend on the interaction among: (a) usage rates (including both intensity and frequency); (b) the type of recreational activity; and (c) site-specific vegetation, climate, and edaphic factors. Most of the studies reviewed by Sun and Walsh (1998) showed that the degree of impact increased with the level of recreational use, although not always. Vegetation and soils had different impact thresholds for recreational use. A full understanding of how different factors influenced the resulting environmental impacts remained unclear from their research, except that, overall, impacts do increase with use. Some overseas studies have shown that this relationship becomes less strong once the impacts reach the threshold of particular environments. However, in order to understand the differences in tolerance levels of the ecosystems and their environmental components, there is a need for adequate base-reference data – which are seldom available.

Research Methodologies

Despite the various constraints on research into the environmental impacts of tourism, sufficient common scientific methodologies have been widely enough applied to review here (Sun and Walsh 1988):

1 *Experimental studies*. These studies generate more reliable information on the process of impact on the natural environments as they are statistically measurable and quantifiable (for example, the quantification of vegetation and soil response to trampling). However, experiments are more costly and time-consuming than other research methods, and sometimes they are physically or politically impossible. For instance, it is difficult to set up an experimental protocol elaborate enough to monitor the impacts of coastal tourism in complex marine ecosystems (Bellan and Bellan-Santini 2001). Thus, the experimental approach is only suitable for specific environmental components and specific tourist activities.
2 *Field survey studies*. These have the advantage of producing quick results within a relatively short period of time at relatively low costs. Field surveys often measure surrogate variables based on general appearance and other features.

They lack the direct quantification that is characteristic in experimental studies. Examples include increases in the number and size of flood events as an indicator of excess land development, or insect infestations due to vegetation changes resulting from tourism development. Field surveys can be very useful, but do not provide enough accurate information on the intensity of visitor use and the impacts of environmental management policies. They cannot fully quantify the relationship between environmental changes and intensity of use. That being said, field survey studies will likely improve with better technology and through continuous and long-term monitoring.

3 *Questionnaires.* Survey questionnaires range from a limited number of closed-ended questions to detailed interviews and focus groups. They are conducted on both users and managers and measure perceptions of impacts. They can be useful in clarifying issues caused by recreation and tourism and to help us understand user experiences and perceptions of environmental impacts (Hillery et al. 2001). As a methodology, questionnaires are used mostly by social scientists and have the potential to quantify responses to specific environment issues and investigate the level where environmental impacts become critical in changing tourist behavior.

Studies on the environmental impacts of tourism will benefit from a combination of traditional research techniques, the incorporation of techniques from multiple disciplines, and the development of new procedures. For example, in their study on the impacts of ecotourism in eight protected areas, Farrell and Marion (2001) examined a range of available rapid assessment methods in developing standardized procedures to record trail and recreation site impacts.

Research Contributions

Interest in the environmental impacts of tourism grew with the increasing awareness of environmental issues in the 1970s (Hudman 1991; Tangi 1977; Baud-Bovy and Lawson 1977), combined with growing unease over tourism as a form of economic development, and a desire to bring conservation and tourism issues together (Farrell and McLellan 1987). Geographers provided some useful reviews of research on the impacts of tourism on the environment during this earlier period (Pearce 1985; Farrell and McLellan 1987; Farrell and Runyan 1991). More recent summaries have focused on the impacts of specific forms of tourism, such as coastal tourism (GFANC 1997; Orams 1999), alpine tourism (Godde, Price, and Zimmerman 2000), and ecotourism (Buckley 2001). Sun and Walsh (1998) reviewed tourism's biophysical impacts (vegetation and soils). And studies of cave tourism have found that the respiration of visitors to limestone caves has negatively affected the growth of speleothems (stalagmites, stalactites, etc.) (Baker and Genty 1998).

Research on the environmental impacts of tourism has been geographically uneven, with the greatest number, scope and depth of studies having been undertaken in the US. Europe is behind the US, and in the UK almost all work relating environment to recreation and tourism is done within the context of recreation (Butler 2000).To a large extent, research on the environmental impacts of tourism is still "relatively immature and a true multidisciplinary approach to investigation has yet to be developed" (Holden 2000: 69). Considering the constraints discussed earlier, a true multidisciplinary approach may not be possible. Research on the environmental impacts will continue to benefit from specialized studies by ecologists and other natural scientists, as well as broader studies by geographers, sociologists, planners, and economists. Pearce (1985), in one of the early reviews on environmental research, noted that there is also a wide range of organizations involved in such research, ranging from the international organization down to park boards and local authorities.

Ecology and related natural sciences have been the traditional base for the study of the environmental response to pressures from outdoor recreation (and tourism). Many of these studies have come from temperate countries, particularly the US, and few reflect the special circumstances of the tropics and less developed countries. Edington and Edington (1986) was one of the early texts to provide a fuller understanding of the ecological factors that influence the scale of environmental damage caused by recreational and tourism development. Liddle (1997), in an important text on recreation ecology, classified the impacts of tourism on four ecological groups: plants, soils, wildlife, and aquatic. Some impacts show a curvilinear use-impact relationship, in which the initial impact is associated with a steep fall in number of species, which is followed by a more shallow decline, the impact apparently reduced by the introduction of other species. In the species-rich environment of the tropics, the possibility of such relationships should be investigated for trampling in tropical forests, off-road vehicle impacts on vegetation, and underwater walks (with breathing helmets) on coral reefs (Hammitt and Cole 1998).

Studies on the environmental impacts of tourism have also come from geography and other social sciences. Mathieson and Wall (1982) remains a useful summary; according to Brown (1998), their treatment of the impacts on different ecosystems and different components of the natural environment is still valid. Contributions on this subject in recent years have varied. For example, Holden (2000) provided a useful classification based on resource usage, tourists' behaviour, and environmental pollution; Newsome, Moore, and Dowling (2002) gave an overview of impacts on nature areas; Bauer (2001) examined the impact of tourism in Antarctica; and more studies on tourist perceptions of environmental impacts are likely (cf. Hillery et al. 2001).

There is also an increasing concern related to the impacts of ecotourism, a form of tourism that was supposed to minimize environmental degradation. Buckley (2001) found that ecotourism-related travel, accommodation, and activities affected a variety of ecosystem components. Birds have been the most extensively studied species in relations to tourism and recreation impacts. Conversely, almost no work has been done on reptiles, except for sea turtles and Galapagos iguanas (Burger 2002). There is still much that needs to be learned about the nature, magnitude, and permanence of tourism-induced environmental changes.

Further research relating to the environmental impacts of tourism needs to be conducted on the identification and isolation of impacts; impact variation over time and space; long-term monitoring of environmental changes; the provision of reliable and empirical data; better research paradigms and models; and the examination of variability among explanatory factors (cf. Briassoulis and van der Straaten 1999). Bellan and Bellan-Santini (2001), in their bibliographic research on the impacts of coastal tourism in Europe, found a large area of "grey" literature (consulting reports and other applied research publications), which were not quoted, analyzed, or used by scholars and academics. Gielsen, Kurihara, and Moriguchi (2001) also found such literature in their survey of the environmental impacts of coastal tourism, which was made more difficult by fact that many of these reports were in Japanese. They also warned that, although knowledge about coastal tourism impacts has increased, and better management has resulted from the observed effects of tourism, some of the research results have been of dubious practical value.

Considering the major forms of tourism found worldwide, our knowledge is most developed in respect of environmental impacts in coastal and alpine regions. Research issues related to these two areas, with particular focus on coral reefs and biophysical impacts, is examined below.

Coral reefs

Scuba diving has an impact on coral reefs. With increasing demand for recreational diving, there is obviously a concern about the negative impacts on the reefs (Van Treeck and Schumacher 1998). The main issues are: What are the results from studies conducted on the impacts of recreational diving? Can they provide some idea of what is considered an acceptable limit to the number of divers in a particular diving site?

The Great Barrier Reef World Heritage Area has been the site of extensive research on the impact of recreation on coral. In areas where monitoring has been carried out, there is enough knowledge about the effect of diving on coral ecology to predict future changes to the flora and fauna, and to implement and monitor policies to reduce unacceptable impacts. Where monitoring is not possible much less information has been available and the cumulative impacts of recreation and tourism have not been satisfactorily addressed (Hillman 1996). The results from one study on the experimental opening of two new scuba diving sites in the Great Barrier Reef Marin Park showed that the impacts were related to more to variability in diver behavior, while repeated use did not necessarily lead to cumulative deterioration (Rouphael and Inglis 2002).

Studies on the impacts of recreational diving in other parts of the world have found mixed results. On Bonaire (an island in the Netherlands Antilles), even relatively low levels of diving have had an impact on the dominance patterns in which, rather than damaging the overall coral cover, branching corals were found to have increased at the expense of large, massive colonies (Hawkins et al. 1999). On Grand Cayman Island, the diver numbers and distance from buoys were related to the hard coral cover and the cover of the major reef-building coral (Tratalos and Austin 2001). In the northern Red Sea, the suitable diving level is difficult to determine, but high levels of use were shown to be detrimental to corals, even stony coral colonies (Zakai and Chadwick-Furman 2002).

These studies have shown that the nature of the impact of diving on corals is site-specific. The results are useful in identifying and mitigating damaging behavior by divers; they can help to estimate a diver-carrying capacity; and they can provide a better understanding of impacts and their management. Coral reefs exist in a delicate balance with the diving industry, and a host of other ecological factors must be considered. There are, for example, still difficulties in developing proper bio-indicators to monitor human impacts on coral, despite many years of research (Hughes 2002).

Biophysical impacts

A fair amount of knowledge of the biophysical impacts of tourism has come from recreation ecologists working on tourism impacts on soils, plants, wildlife, and aquatic systems in a wide variety of habitats. For example, Liddle (1997) provided a useful classification of disturbances to animals: disturbance type 1, where the animal is aware of the physical presence of the recreationist; disturbance type 2, where its habitat is affected; and disturbance type 3, where direct and damaging contact is made with the animal.

Research on the biophysical impacts needs to address several issues (Sun and Walsh 1998): What are the long-term effects of tourism on wildlife and plants? What regional effects can result from cumulative local impacts? To what extent would physical and biological effects eventually change species abundance and diversity, with consequent effects on the wilderness value of nature areas? To date, studies have mainly focused on the short-term effects of recreational use. The need for more long-term studies is illustrated in the following two examples. A New Zealand study indicated that, while wildlife species may appear to be tolerant of tourists, significant impacts still occur. Higham (1998), however, noted that the research results were both site- and species-specific, and that the long-term monitoring of such impacts was crucial to better understanding. Another study found that nearly all animals avoided a 5 km zone around a winter resort in the Rondane National Park in Norway (Nellemann et al. 2000). In addition, the maternal reindeer avoided a 10 km zone around the same resort. The avoidance by animals of such resorts, and related anthropogenic disturbances, could be further complicated by long-term impacts (e.g. carrying capacity) and could be more serious than the implied impact of direct physiological stress.

Such long-term changes are especially an issue in relatively untouched nature areas, such as national parks, conservation reserves, and other fragile environments (Buckley 2000, 2001). In the light of growing demand for ecotourism, increased consideration has to be given to appropriate impact studies and the use of the results to minimize the biophysical damage. Evaluations should also include the benefits to the local human population, as well as reducing environmental impacts (Anon. 2001).

Among the world's more fragile environments, Antarctica remains the only region well protected from tourism impacts. Although commercial tourism to Antarctica began in late 1950s, the continent is well protected by an international environmental protocol and industry-generated visitor and tour operator guidelines (Splettstoesser and Folks 1994). Based on an analysis of both academic and popular literature on Antarctica tourism, and from his own observations, Bauer (2001: 139) concluded "that given the demonstrated goodwill of Antarctic tourists and the keen financial interest in the maintenance of the near-pristine Antarctic environment by Antarctic tour operators, as well as the watchful eye of the Antarctic Treaty Parties, tourism in Antarctica is at present a sustainable activity." One important lesson is that high tour costs and strict enforcement are ingredients that can minimize the negative environmental impacts of tourism.

Conclusion

Two major conclusions can be drawn about research on the impacts of tourism on the natural environment. The first is that more studies of a holistic nature or perspective are required. For example, in the coastal environment, Bellan and Bellan-Santini (2001) proposed studies on the direct and indirect impacts of tourism for each of the large biotopes or ecosystems, taking into account quantitative and qualitative changes to their physical, chemical, and biological components. They envisaged an alliance of natural scientists with social scientists to conduct the research and also to involve others who apply the information. In a small way, the industrial ecology approach provides a holistic view, which was used by Buckley (2001) in providing a more complete view of the major environmental impacts of ecotourism: (1) travel to and from destination or site; (2) accommodation on site or on tour; and (3) specific recreational activities that may involve local travel.

The second major conclusion is related to environmental management. In general, the results from tourism impact studies could be used in environmental management. However, the environmental impacts of tourism should not be assessed in a vacuum, but rather weighed against other economic activities and trade-offs. The environment cannot be isolated from the political economy of place (Brown 1998). The direction of future impact studies will also be influenced by how such studies help to clear up the environmental mess caused by tourism. As more is known about the impacts of travel, tourism, and recreation on plants, animal life, soils, water, and air, that information can be used to mitigate negative impacts.

To date, the Environmental Impact Assessment (EIA) approach has been the most widely used measure for preventing the negative impacts of tourism (Ravenscroft 1992). Although the technical information for such assessments is often available, the quality of baseline monitoring data can be a problem. For example, in Australia, the baseline data are frequently collected for terrestrial flora, though less so for marine flora, while the least attention is given to the physical environment (Warnken and Buckley 1998). In contrast, monitoring is emphasized in the Great Barrier Reef Park and this has translated into better environmental management (Warnken and Buckley 1998, 2000). For developing countries, EIA is still not widely used, and when it is applied it is often not effectively enforced (Wong 1998).

Much less effective are ecolabels and related measures (Font and Buckley 2001). As currently practiced in the developed countries, ecolabels can be a valuable environmental management tool if critical conditions are enforced (Buckley 2002). For developing countries, these labels have been limited to marketing tourism services to high-spending, environmentally conscious Western tourists, and are frequently considered a threat to local tourism enterprises (Sasidharan, Sirakaya, and Kerstetter 2002). For example, the Blue Flag awards, a scheme for European beaches that fulfill a number of exacting criteria (FEEE 1996), are not suitable in southeast Asia, as the environmental conditions are different and the scheme gives the wrong impression that non-Blue Flag coastal resorts are already associated with a polluted environment (Wong 2001).

The environmental impacts of mass tourism are generally known to be overwhelmingly negative, based on many case studies. In some instances, the causal links to tourism are still debated. There is a place for better understanding benefits and good practices. Forms of self-regulation have been attempted by the tourism industry itself, and environmental and sustainable development good practices have been spread by the WTTC (World Travel and Tourism Council) and the WTO (World Tourism Organization). Bellan and Bellan-Santini (2001) have indicated that perhaps it is also crucial to carry out research into forms and tourist activities which prove to be indirectly beneficial and for more documentation of good practices – thus pointing to another potential direction of environmental impact studies.

REFERENCES

Anon (2001). Ecotourism: Facts and figures. *UNEP Industry and Environment*, 24, 3–4, 5–9.

Baker, A., and Genty, A. (1998). Environmental pressures on conserving cave speleothems: Effects of changing surface land use and increased cave tourism. *Journal of Environmental Management* 53, 165–75.

Baud-Bovy, M., and Lawson, F. (1977). *Tourism and Recreation Development*. London: The Architectural Press.

Bauer, T. G. (2001). *Tourism in the Antarctic: Opportunities, Constraints, and Future Prospects*. New York: Haworth Press.

Bellan, G. L., and Bellan-Santini, D. R. (2001). A review of littoral tourism, sport and leisure activities: Consequences on marine flora and fauna. *Aquatic Conservation: Marine and Freshwater Ecosystems* 11, 325–33.

Briassoulis, H., and van der Straaten, J. (1999). Tourism and the environment: An overview. In H. Briassoulis and J. van der Straaten (eds), *Tourism and the Environment*, 2nd edn (pp. 1–20). Dordrecht: Kluwer Academic Publishers.

Brown, F. (1998). *Tourism Reassessed: Blight or Blessing?* Oxford: Butterworth-Heinemann.

Buckley, R. (2000). Tourism in the most fragile environments. *Tourism Recreation Research* 25, 31–40.

Buckley, R. (2001). Environmental impacts. In D. B. Weaver (ed.), *The Encyclopedia of Ecotourism* (pp. 379–94). Wallingford: CAB International.

Buckley, R. (2002). Tourism ecolabels. *Annals of Tourism Research* 29, 183–208.

Buckley, R. C., Pickering, C. M., and Warnken, J. (2000). Environmental management for alpine tourism and resorts in Australia. In P. Godde, M. F. Price, and F. M. Zimmerman (eds), *Tourism and Development in Mountain Regions* (pp. 27–45). Wallingford: CAB International.

Burger, J. (2002). Tourism and ecosystems. In I. Douglas (ed.), *Causes and Consequences of Global Environmental Change* (*Encyclopedia of Global Environmental Change*, vol. 3, pp. 597–609). Chichester: John Wiley.

Butler, R. W. (2000). Tourism and the environment: A geographical perspective. *Tourism Geographies* 2, 337–58.

Ceballos-Lascuráin, H. (1996). *Tourism, Ecotourism, and Protected Areas*. IUCN. Gland: World Conservation Union.

Cohen, E. (1978). Impact of tourism on the physical environment. *Annals of Tourism Research* 5, 215–37.

Edington, J. M., and Edington, M. A. (1986). *Ecology, Recreation and Tourism*. Cambridge: Cambridge University Press.

EEA (European Environment Agency) (2001). *Environmental Signals 2001*. Copenhagen: EEA.

Elsasser, H., and Burki, R. (2002). Climate change as a threat to tourism in the Alps. *Climate Change* 20, 253–7.

ESCAP (1992). *A Preliminary Study on Environmental Management of Tourism Development in the ESCAP Region*. New York: UN.

Farrell, B. H., and McLellan, R. W. (1987). Tourism and physical environment research. *Annals of Tourism Research* 14, 1–16.

Farrell, B. H., and Runyan, D. (1991). Ecology and tourism. *Annals of Tourism Research* 18, 26–40.

Farrell, T. A., and Marion, J. L. (2001). Identifying and assessing ecotourism visitor impacts in eight protected areas in Costa Rica and Belize. *Environmental Conservation* 28, 215–25.

FEEE (Foundation for Environmental Education in Europe) (1996). *Awards for Improving the Coastal Environment: The Example of the Blue Flag*. Paris: UNEP/WTO/FEEE.

Font, X., and Buckley, R. C. (eds) (2001). *Tourism Ecolabelling: Certification and Promotion of Sustainable Management*. Wallingford: CAB International.

Genot, H. (1997). Tourism. In D. Brune et al. (eds), *The Global Environment: Science, Technology and Management* (vol. 1, pp. 64–75). Weinheim: VCH Verlagsgesellschaft.

GFANC (German Federal Agency for Nature Conservation) (ed.) (1997). *Biodiversity and Tourism*. Berlin: Springer.

Gielsen, D. J., Kurihara, R., and Moriguchi, Y. (2001). The environmental impacts of Japanese leisure and tourism: A preliminary analysis. Draft 19 December 2001. <http://www.resourcemodels.org/page8.html> (accessed March 11, 2003).

Godde, P., Price, M. F., and Zimmerman, F. M. (eds) (2000). *Tourism and Development in Mountain Regions*. Wallingford: CAB International.

Hall, C. M. (1996). Environmental impact of tourism in the Pacific. In C. M. Hall and S. J. Page (eds), *Tourism in the Pacific: Issues and Cases* (pp. 65–80). London: International Thomson Business Press.

Hammitt, W. E., and Cole, D. N. (1998). *Wildland Recreation*, 2nd edn. New York: John Wiley.

Hawkins, J. P., et al. (1999). Effects of recreational scuba diving on Caribbean coral and fish communities. *Conservation Biology* 13, 888–97.

Higham, J. E. S. (1998). Tourists and albatrosses: The dynamics of tourism at the Northern Royal Albatross Colony, Taiaroa Head, New Zealand. *Tourism Management* 19, 521–31.

Hillery, M., et al. (2001). Tourist perception of environmental impact. *Annals of Tourism Research* 28, 853–67.

Hillman, S. (1996). The state of the Great Barrier Reef World Heritage Area report. *Reef Research* 6(2) <http://www.gbrmpa.gov.au/corp_site/info_services/publications/reef_research/issue2_96/2wot.html> (accessed March 11, 2003).

Holden, A. (2000). *Environment and Tourism*. London: Routledge.

Hudman, L. E. (1991). Tourism's role and response to environmental issues and potential future effects. *Revue de Tourisme* 4, 17–21.

Hughes, G. (2002). Environmental indicators. *Annals of Tourism Research* 29, 457–77.

Hunter, C., and Green, H. (1995). *Tourism and the Environment*. London: Routledge.

Liddle, M. (1997). *Recreation Ecology*. London: Chapman & Hall.

Mathieson, A., and Wall, G. (1982). *Tourism: Economic, Social and Physical Impacts*. London: Longman.

Mieczkowski, Z. (1995). *Environmental Issues of Tourism and Recreation*. Lanham, MD: University Press of America.

Nellemann, C., et al. (2000). Cumulative impacts of tourist resorts on wild reindeer (*Rangifer tarandus tarandus*) during winter. *Arctic* 53, 9–17.

Newsome, D., Moore, S. A., and Dowling, R. K. (2002). *Nature Area Tourism: Ecology, Impacts and Management*. Clevedon: Channel View Publications.

Nurse, L. A., et al. (2001). Small island states. In J. J. McCarthy et al. (eds), *Climate Change 2001: Impacts, Adaptation, and Vulnerability* (pp. 843–75). Cambridge: Cambridge University Press.

Orams, M. (1999). *Marine Tourism: Development, Impacts and Management*. New York: Routledge.

Page, S. J., and Dowling, R. K. (2001). *Ecotourism*. New York: Prentice Hall.

Pearce, D. G. (1985). Tourism and environmental research: A review. *International Journal of Environmental Studies* 25, 247–55.

Pearce, D. G. (1989). *Tourist Development*. Harlow, Essex: Longman.

Ravenscroft, N. (1992). Environmental impact of recreation and tourism development: A review. *European Environment* 2(2), 8–13.

Rouphael, A. B., and Inglis, G. J. (2002). Increased spatial and temporal variability in coral damage caused by recreational scuba diving. *Ecological Applications* 12, 427–40.

Sasidharan, V., Sirakaya, E., and Kerstetter, D. (2002). Developing countries and tourism ecolabels. *Tourism Management* 23, 161–74.

Splettstoesser, J., and Folks, M. C. (1994). Environmental guidelines for tourism in Antarctica. *Annals of Tourism Research* 21, 231–44.

Sun, D., and Walsh, D. (1998). Review of studies on environmental impacts of recreation and tourism in Australia. *Journal of Environmental Management* 53, 323–38.

Tangi, M. (1977). Tourism and the environment. *Ambio* 6(6), 336–41.

Tratalos, J. A., and Austin, T. J. (2001). Impacts of recreational SCUBA diving on coral communities of the Caribbean island of Grand Cayman. *Biological Conservation* 102, 67–75.

Van Treeck, P., and Schumacher, H. (1998). Mass diving tourism: A new dimension calls for new management approaches. *Marine Pollution Bulletin* 37, 499–504.

Warnken, J., and Buckley, R. (1998). Scientific quality of tourism environmental impact assessment. *Journal of Applied Ecology* 35, 1–8.

Warnken, J., and Buckley, R. (2000). Monitoring diffuse impacts: Australian tourism developments. *Environmental Management* 25, 453–61.

Weaver, D. B. (2001). *The Encyclopedia of Ecotourism*. Wallingford: CAB International.

Wong, P. P. (1998). Coastal tourism development in Southeast Asia: Relevance and lessons for coastal zone management. *Ocean and Coastal Management* 38, 89–109.

Wong, P. P. (2001). Southeast Asian tourism: Traditional and new perspectives on the natural environment. In P. Teo, T. C. Chang, and K. C. Ho (eds), *Interconnected Worlds: Tourism in Southeast Asia* (pp. 215–30). Amsterdam: Pergamon.

Wong, P. P. (2002). Tourism as a global driving force for environmental change. In I. Douglas (ed.), *Causes and Consequences of Global Environmental Change* (*Encyclopedia of Global Environmental Change*, vol. 3, pp. 609–23). Chichester: John Wiley.

Zakai, D., and Chadwick-Furman, N. E. (2002). Impacts of intensive recreational diving on reef corals at Eilat, northern Read Sea. *Biological Conservation* 105, 179–87.

Chapter 37

Tourism and Resource Management

David Mercer

Introduction

Bowler (1992: 504) has reminded us that "Fear of environmental degradation began in the mid-nineteenth century but did not become a major concern for most people until the later decades of the twentieth." Subsequently, there has been an explosion of interest around the world in issues surrounding sustainable development, ecological restoration, and resource "management." An exponential growth in specialist legislation and environmental reporting requirements, high-level conferences, think-tanks and degree programs, as well as a steady outpouring of new books and journals and the spawning of government and non-government agencies, all bear witness to what appears to be a reformed intellectual and policy environment. This revolution in thinking in some circles has also impacted to some extent upon the business world, with the "triple bottom line" now frequently being invoked as a key corporate objective. This involves corporations paying attention not just to profit levels but also to their social and environmental impacts and responsibilities. There is also growing interest in affluent countries in ethical investment, industrial ecology, and the production and marketing of a wide variety of "green" products and services, ranging from organic food products to "clean and green" energy and ecotourism experiences (Frankel 1998).

Notwithstanding these developments, each year also sees the publication of often conflicting surveys about the state of the environment. More often than not the reports are deeply pessimistic, cataloguing ever-worsening data on biodiversity decline, coral bleaching, land degradation, global warming, water scarcity, and so on (Wackernagel et al. 2002). But set against these trends there are commentators like Lomborg (2001) who, controversially, argue that all the indicators point to continuing environmental improvement. Such writers invariably highlight local success stories – cases where water or air quality has been improved dramatically, where fish stocks are now rebuilding, or where flora and fauna species have been pulled back from the brink of extinction (Suzuki and Dressel 2002). In most such situations improvements have come about because of a localized commitment to "strong" rather than "weak" sustainability and the presence of an appropriately robust regulatory framework curbing the worst excesses of private enterprise (Thompson 2002). Less commonly, as will be discussed below, markets have been created for ecosystem services and tourism benefits have flowed from this.

So where, exactly, does tourism sit in this rather confused picture? The simple answer, of course, is that it depends upon precisely what kind of "tourism" one is talking about, its context, and where it is situated along the spectrum between "hard" and "soft" tourism (Krippendorf 1982), or – to use Eagles' (1980) useful continuum – on the ten-point scale between *negativism* and *moralism*. It also depends upon the extent to which one is taking into account the long-term cumulative impacts of innumerable, individual project-related and consumer decisions impacting upon both local and global environments. For example, given the growing popularity of air travel there has been a parallel call from eco-groups for tourists to holiday closer to home, for a hefty levy on jet fuel, and for aviation to be included in the Kyoto Protocol as partial redress for the 600 million tonnes of carbon dioxide that are pumped out by commercial passenger aircraft each year (Rao 2002).

"Managing" the Environment

Implicit in much of the discourse and associated policy development surrounding natural resource management in affluent Western societies, as well as, increasingly, in indigenous and traditional cultures (Milton 1998), is the idea that natural systems somehow can be "managed" or "designed" for human ends, just as one might plan – or "engineer" – an entirely new city or mend or maintain a machine. Traditionally, such hubris has manifested itself in large-scale engineering projects such as those undertaken, for example, by the Tennessee Valley Authority in the United States or the coastal defense works of the Dutch government (Louisse and Kuik 1991; Miller and Reidinger 1998). The contemporary genetic modification of crops is also representative of this "technical-fix" mind-set which has recently come under fierce attack for the poor understanding it demonstrates of the workings of complex ecosystems and the pivotal role played by so-called "hub" species (Buchanan 2002).

"Management" can also be interpreted as referring to policies driving resource allocation, the regulation of environmental quality and/or the mitigation of environmentally damaging processes. Olson (1995: 560), for instance, defines resource management simply as "the attempt to maximize present net benefits derived from the utilization of resources," but then proceeds to explain that invariably there are diverse views on *intertemporal assignment*, or the "best" time to exploit resources. He argues that with reference to any kind of resource – whether depletable, renewable, or environmental – there are no recognized standards for "appropriate" discount rates (i.e. the rate at which a resource can or should be exploited) but that it is often the case that private actors favor both the widespread privatization of resources and higher discount rates, or more rapid exploitation. In addition to there being no recognized standards for discount rates, since 1933 the "functional" or "appraisal" approach to the study of resources has become progressively mainstream. In that year Zimmerman's classic *World Resources and Industries* was first published, laying the groundwork for an intellectual shift away from viewing resources as relatively easily quantifiable "stocks" and toward seeing them much more as being constantly evaluated and re-evaluated through human eyes for anthropocentric ends (Sewell and Burton 1971).

Three Economic Models

In the economics literature three broad models of resource representation and appraisal can be identified, differentiated in terms of their ideological underpinnings. The first, which will receive attention in this chapter, takes an ethical stand in favor of ecocentrism and argues – often passionately – against viewing environmental goods and services as existing exclusively for human use. This standpoint holds that many environmental values (scenic amenity, wilderness, etc.) cannot be expressed simply in dollar terms. It is often better described as "ecosystem management" rather than resource management in that it "integrates scientific knowledge of ecological relationships within a complex sociopolitical and values framework toward the general goal of protecting native ecosystem integrity over the long term" (Grumbine 1994: 27). At marked variance with this position is the neoclassical viewpoint which maintains that "rational" individuals assign values to individual resources and that the unfolding preferences and scarcity are reflected in "true" market values. This position also insists that resources are interchangeable, i.e. as scarcity occurs, one resource can easily be *substituted* for another (Krieger 1971). For example, if tourists perceive that the outdoor "natural" environment is not providing a satisfactory experience then they pay for an alternative, or substituted, experience in a controlled indoor setting. The world's largest indoor beach – the Ocean Dome at Miyazaki in Japan (2,800 square meters of sand, and a constant 30°C) is perhaps an extreme example of this kind of thinking. The final model, often referred to as the "London school," takes a position midway between the above and argues that there are certain crucial "unsubstitutable" resources, such as water and the atmosphere, that must not have their value assigned by individuals, but by the whole of humanity for the benefit of future generations.

Regardless of the ideological underpinnings, the resource management decision framework consists of two basic components, the *management* and *ecological subsystems*. Bonnicksen (1991) has summarized the interactions between these two in the form of a conceptual diagram, reproduced here as figure 37.1. *People* operate within this framework both as resource *users* and as *managers*, while in the real world the *boundaries* of the resource systems being "managed" are defined in numerous different ways and at varying scales. Commonly, too, resource systems are divided among one or more variants of public and private property regimes, a situation that can militate against optimum management outcomes.

As an exploitative economic activity, tourism in most of its forms makes demands on the complete range of both renewable and non-renewable resources. As well, popular tourist destinations like Florida or Australia's Gold Coast are often also centers of high population growth rates, so the resource demands can be exponential. In late 2002, for example, the Gold Coast was in the midst of the worst drought on record and the main reservoir supplying the region was at 34 percent capacity.

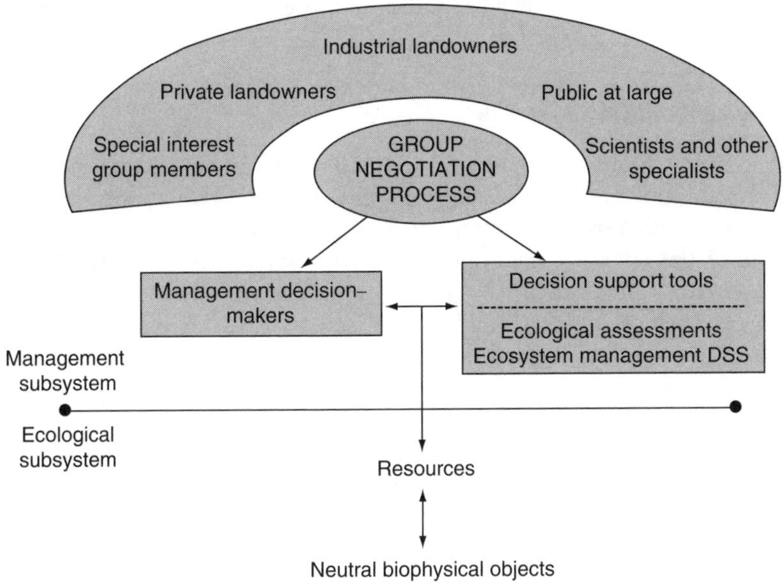

Figure 37.1 The ecosystem management decision environment
Source: After Bonnicksen 1991.

At that time, with limited prospects of rain, the outlook for both residents and potential tourists was decidedly bleak (see <www.goldcoast.qld.gov.au>).

In many places, too, the annual tourist incursion far exceeds the normal resident population and tourism has become such a damaging activity that "eco-taxes" have been levied on visitors to help fund desperately needed infrastructure and environmental remediation. A sharp decline in government investment in management of the Great Barrier Reef Marine Park in Australia has led to the imposition of a "reef tax" on visitors (Lawrence, Kenchington, and Woodley 2002); and, amid much controversy, a similar solution has recently been implemented in Spain's Balearic Islands, where the resident population is 800,000 by contrast with annual tourism visitation of 10.2 million (Croft 2002). One can perhaps anticipate a similar policy response in the future in order to protect the threatened coral reef biodiversity of Malaysia's Perhentian and Sipadan island cays, two of the world's most highly prized diving destinations. In this situation – as with Australia's Great Barrier Reef – there are strong pressures from governments as well as from local and international private enterprise interests to encourage tourism. The reefs are also subject to many other negative impacts, often making it difficult to isolate the precise role that tourism is playing.

There are other, related resource issues, too. Mangroves, for example, are highly productive wetland ecosystems in tropical and subtropical areas, but they are under serious threat in popular tourist countries like Thailand. Escalating visitor demands for coastal resort accommodation, as well as for sea food derived from aquaculture projects, have triggered an unprecedented level of mangrove destruction in that country with the total area being reduced by more than 50 percent between 1960 and 1990 (Middleton 2000).

Biodiversity Decline

Because so many different "resources" are involved in any particular tourism development, for the purposes of this chapter some dramatic reductionism and concentration on a few case studies is essential. From here on this discussion focuses only on aspects of the complex relationship between wildlife tourism and biodiversity preservation (Ross and Wall 2001). Arguably, biodiversity decline is *the* most serious global environmental problem and is representative of an emerging set of new problems in tourism management that is the subject of ongoing, and at times acrimonious, debate. These issues in turn are a subset of one of the central questions in environmental policy: how we can best design resource management regimes for protection of the commons (Ostrom et al. 2002). The tourism/biodiversity nexus has been explored in the 1997 Berlin Declaration on Biological Diversity and Tourism (United Nations Environment Program 2001). *Inter alia*, the declaration notes that tourism:

- is largely based on a healthy environment and beautiful landscapes;
- has the potential for degrading the natural environment, social structures, and cultural heritage; and
- can create revenues for the maintenance of natural areas.

Whether delineated at the gene, species, or ecosystem level, biodiversity is a fundamental resource. It provides natural ecosystems with an essential buffer against natural disasters and is vital to such commercial sectors as agriculture (Tilman, Wedin, and Knops 1996). In addition, the aesthetic features of natural ecosystems are frequently highly valued by urban dwellers and have always played a central role in the cultural identity of indigenous people. In the United States, for example, the rapid colonization of Indian lands in 13 contemporary states resulted in the slaughter of all but several hundred buffalo out of an estimated Great Plains population of some 60 million. As Native Americans gradually assert their treaty rights to the independent management of their traditional lands, this beast that is so pivotal to their identity is successfully returning and their numbers are now in excess of 200,000 (Lott and Greene 2002). Indeed, in many countries, the public discourse surrounding biodiversity is taking place against a background of mounting calls for greater recognition of animal rights (Fjellstrom 2002). In June 2002, for example, in a landmark vote, the German Constitution was amended (Paragraph 20a) to grant animals, like humans, the right to be respected by the state and to have their dignity respected. As we shall see, such moves are not necessarily a barrier to tourism development. In Iceland, for example, whale watching is now far more profitable for that economy than was whaling prior to an internationally enforced ban in 1989, and many former whaling ports around the world have now been reinvented as successful whale-watching centers (Hagalin 2002).

The challenge for humans is to halt or slow the dramatic biodiversity decline process by protecting habitats and endangered species, stopping illegal poaching, and/or instituting captive breeding programs. As in eastern Poland and Yellowstone National Park, the process may involve the highly controversial reintroduction and protection of what are considered by some to be "dangerous" predatory animals into areas that have been set aside primarily for human enjoyment. But this in turn can have dramatic consequences for other species and surrounding landowners. In 1995, after an absence of 60 years, 31 gray wolves were released into Yellowstone. Within six years their numbers had grown to 168 and, as well as wreaking havoc on the park's coyote population, they had also expanded their range beyond the reserve's boundaries to adjoining pastoral properties (Tollefson 2001; Kleese 2002). At the other extreme, tourism management often involves removing certain "inappropriate" species from protected environments or killing native animals to "protect" tourists. At the time of writing, the controversial removal of brumbies (wild horses) is taking place in the alpine areas of Kosciusko National Park in Australia (Dennis 2002). As well, around 35 tourists have been killed by black bears in the United States in the last 100 years, and the fatal mauling by wild dingoes of a 9-year-old boy camping on Australia's World Heritage-listed Fraser Island in 2001 resulted in a "revenge" cull that could have been avoided had the recommendations of a 1998 draft dingo management strategy been implemented (*The Australian* 2001). Interestingly, the cull of the country's purest strain of dingo was strongly opposed by the island's traditional Aboriginal owners. Similar revenge responses are commonplace following shark and crocodile confrontations with tourists in Australia and elsewhere. So intense has been the long-term "war" on some shark species – like the critically endangered grey nurse shark – that the Australian Commonwealth government has belatedly embarked on an urgent recovery plan (Pollard, Lincoln Smith, and Smith 1996).

Following Rittel and Webber (1973) and Macnaghten and Urry (1998) in *Contested Natures*, such cases are all illustrative of so-called "wicked problems," that is, problems that are unstructured, highly complex, and pose considerable ethical and strategic dilemmas for both managers and policy-makers. For example, whaling is still permitted on "cultural" and "subsistence" grounds by the Alaskan Inuit. Yet the obvious question to ask of the Fraser Island "solution" is: in cases where tourists are intruding into the territory of a potentially dangerous animal, and one that has enormous cultural significance to Aboriginal Australians, why is it that the interests of the tourism sector are privileged? A similar question could be posed in relation to the long-standing practice in Australia of "protecting" surfers and swimmers from sharks through shark-netting, a blanket technique that, out of all proportion to the potential risks, indiscriminately kills a wide range of marine creatures.

Biodiversity Protection and Tourism: The Australian Example

With 11,046 species currently estimated to be threatened with extinction worldwide, we have now entered the sixth great extinction period (i.e. a period of very rapid mass extinction; see Leakey and Lewin 1996). The main difference, though, between this and previous phases is that humans are largely to blame. All species are affected, but for illustrative purposes around 1 percent of mammals and birds are now made extinct every 100 years, a figure that is anywhere between 1,000 and 10,000 times the "natural" rate (IUCN 2000). Because Australia has been isolated for much of its geological history, it has evolved a highly distinctive biota. Indeed, it has been identified as one of the twelve most "megadiverse" countries in the world and the only one of these that is an advanced industrial society (Amos, Kirkpatrick, and Giese 1993).

However, the record of biodiversity destruction, especially since the time of European settlement, is one of the worst in the world. Over the last century Australia accounted for 50 percent of all the mammals that became extinct worldwide, 25 percent of the country's mammal species are now either threatened or extinct, and the expectation is that 50 percent of the country's birds will have disappeared by the end of the twenty-first century (Recher 1999). While this record – and the concomitant devastation of native fauna – is appalling, there is mounting interest, both in Australia and elsewhere, in fauna and flora protection for its own sake as well as for potential pharmaceutical products and as a drawcard for eco-tourists (so-called wildlife tourism, or WT) (United Nations Environment Program 2001). Indeed, the Commonwealth government registered its commitment by ratifying the International Convention on Biological Diversity (the Biodiversity Convention) in June 1993. We now turn to a discussion of the potential benefits of WT, first in Australia, then in other countries.

At the "negativistic" extreme, WT involves wildlife hunting and other actions that are destructive of fauna (Eagles 1980). By contrast, the "moralistic" dimension is characterized by deep respect for animals and the protection of habitat. This discussion is largely concerned with the latter category. McNeely (1997) has argued that tourism and biodiversity represent a "natural partnership"; and, drawing on published data, Braithwaite and Reynolds (2002) have estimated that anywhere between 10 and 50 percent of all tourism experiences/expenditures contain some component of wildlife tourism. In 1996 this would have contributed between $US600 billion and $US3 trillion worldwide. Moreover, for some countries and regions wildlife tourism is the main source of foreign exchange earnings. Costa Rica and Ecuador have long regarded biodiversity as perhaps their most significant natural resource, and the Cape Floral Kingdom in South Africa represents a regional example (Stoll-Kleemann and O'Riordan 2002).

As noted, Australia is well endowed with unique flora and fauna and this is commonly a prime reason for visiting the country (Braithwaite and Reynolds 2002). Over 80 percent of the country's mammals, reptiles, and frogs, and 45 percent of its land birds, are found nowhere else. Hundloe and Hamilton (1997) report that 75 percent of inbound tourists stated that they hoped to see a koala (*Phascolartos cenereus*) during their stay and that this species alone contributes in excess of $A300 million to the Australian economy each year. Indeed their study found that, for 11 percent of Australian inbound visitors, the unique wildlife was the primary drawcard, leading them to calculate that wildlife is worth up to $A1.8 billion to the Australian economy per annum. Increasingly in Australia, large private investments are being made in wildlife tourism, especially in relation to species that are attractive to overseas visitors.

For example, in the late 1960s, John Wamsley, the founder of what later became Earth Sanctuaries (ESL), purchased a degraded property in the Adelaide Hills. The property was fenced, all feral animals were removed from the site, and native flora and fauna were reintroduced. The Warrawong Sanctuary was first opened to the public on January 1, 1985 and then became a public company in September 1993. Subsequently, ESL purchased an additional nine properties in diverse biogeographical regions (totaling 90,000 hectares), mainly in South Australia. In each case the expensive recovery and transformation process was the same as that carried out at Warrawong, with the main emphasis being on the removal of threats to birds, small native mammals, and reptiles. The company's assets are valued according to a formula that assigns a monetary value to the number of species in different categories of rarity, and the main income is derived from tourist revenue (Productivity Commission 2001).

Developing Countries

There are also many examples from developing countries of tourism coming to the rescue of areas of habitat that otherwise might have succumbed to the ravages of illegal logging, poaching, or agricultural expansion. The *Paseo pantera* (path of the panther) project is an ambitious land purchase project that aims to develop a chain of protected reserves – and associated ecotourism enterprises – across Central America (<www.garrobo.org/mosquitia/paseo>).

In Kenya, too, only 400 km^2 now remain of a biologically rich coastal forest that once covered a vast area of East Africa between Mozambique and Somalia. Since 1993, encouraged by conservationists from Europe and North America, former farmers in the vicinity of the Arabuko-Sokoke forest have turned successfully to ecotourism based around butterfly breeding and the trading of pupae on the international market (Salmon 2002). Similarly, in northern Pakistan tourism has come to the aid of the endangered snow leopard. Prior to 1998 poor local farmers regularly killed the leopards when they attacked their livestock. A foreign-based snow-leopard trekking company now pays money into a central fund that is used to compensate farmers for livestock losses. The company and overseas tourists benefit because snow leopards are a great tourist drawcard and the local farmers also benefit (Richards 2002).

Conclusion

As has been shown with the above examples, tourism ventures – whether run by private enterprise and the state or partnerships of NGOs and the state and the private sector – and biodiversity conservation need not necessarily be in conflict. The hope is that a growing proportion of the $463 billion currently spent by tourists worldwide will be targeted at saving habitat for wildlife (Chalmers 2002). Unfortunately, it is usually much easier to find instances where private developments have had negative environmental and social impacts (Buckley 1999). Nor is it the case that private sanctuaries are universally applauded. The North American-owned, 400,000 hectare, Pumalin Park in Chile, for example, has been denounced as a new form of colonialism. And in the case of the Moreton Bay Marine Park in Australia and similar areas around the world there are ongoing issues in terms of indigenous dispossession in the name of "environmental protection" (Johnston 1999). At the start of the twenty-first century there is no shortage of "wicked problems" involving resource management issues and tourism.

This chapter has sought to provide a brief overview of some of the ethical dilemmas, proposed solutions, and research challenges that lie ahead. In particular, using the yardstick of "ecosystem health" (Capra 2002) we can anticipate considerable research activity in the near future focused on the detailed monitoring and analysis of the successes and failures of various ecotourism models – in both the private and public sectors – in terms of biodiversity preservation and rehabilitation. There is also a need for closer research attention to the ethical and power-sharing issues involved, for example, when Western "experts" seek to impose non-indigenous management "solutions" in areas of longstanding significance to indigenous people.

Issues relating to "scale" and "boundaries" will also be central to the tourism research agenda in the coming years. For example, the 35,000 km^2 Great Limpopo Transfrontier Park has recently been proclaimed. Straddling, as it does, Mozambique, South Africa, and Zimbabwe, there are immense challenges ahead in terms of international cooperation over management for which policy-oriented researchers will need to develop a whole new set of interdisciplinary skills.

REFERENCES

Amos, N., Kirkpatrick, J. B., and Giese, M. (1993). *Conservation of Biodiversity, Ecological Integrity and Ecologically Sustainable Development.* Melbourne: Australian Conservation Foundation and World Wide Fund for Nature.

Bonnicksen, T. M. (1991). Managing biosocial systems: A framework to organize society–environment relationships. *Journal of Forestry* 89(10), 10–15.

Bowler, P. J. (1992). *The Fontana History of the Environmental Sciences.* London: Fontana.

Braithwaite, R. W., and Reynolds, P. C. (2002). Wildlife and tourism. In D. Lunney and C. Dickman (eds), *A Zoological Revolution: Using Native Fauna to Assist in its Own Survival* (pp. 108–15). Sydney: Royal Zoological Society of New South Wales and Australian Museum.

Buchanan, M. (2002). *Small World: Uncovering Nature's Hidden Networks.* London: Weidenfeld & Nicolson.

Buckley, R. (1999). Sustainable tourism and critical environments. In T. V. Singh and S. Singh (eds), *Tourism Development in Critical Environments* (pp. 21–34). New York: Cognizant Communication Corporation.

Capra, F. (2002). *The Hidden Connections: A Science for Sustainable Living.* London: HarperCollins.

Chalmers, P. (2002). World's ecotourism promoters promise dollars, sense. *Reuters News Service* (Malaysia), October 25.

Croft, A. (2002). Spanish islands buffeted by storm over "eco-tax." *Reuters News Service* (Spain), June 21.

Dennis, A. (2002). Challenge to tame snowy brumbies. *Sydney Morning Herald*, June 25.

Eagles, P. (1980). An approach to describing recreation in the natural environment. *Recreation Research Review* 8(1), 28–36.

Fjellstrom, R. (2002). Specifying speciesism. *Environmental Values* 11, 63–74.

Frankel, C. (1998). *In Earth's Company: Business, Environment, and the Challenge of Sustainability (Conscientious Commerce).* Gabriola Is., BC: New Society Publishers.

Grumbine, R. E. (1994). What is ecosystem management? *Conservation Biology* 8(1), 27–34.

Hagalin, S. (2002). In Iceland whales may be worth more alive than dead. *Reuters News Service* (Iceland), June 28.

Hundloe, T., and Hamilton, C. (1997), with contributions from L. Wilks. *Koalas and Tourism: An Economic Evaluation.* Discussion Paper 13. Canberra: The Australian Institute.

IUCN (International Union for the Conservation of Nature) (2000). Red list of threatened species. <http://www.redlist.org/> (accessed June 15, 2003).

Johnston, A. (1999). Threats and opportunities presented by international policy debates on tourism developments. *Cultural Survival Quarterly* 23(2), 57–9.

Kleese, D. (2002). Contested natures: Wolves in late modernity. *Society and Natural Resources* 15, 313–26.

Krieger, M. H. (1971). *What's Wrong With Plastic Trees? Rationales for the Preservation of Natural Environments.* Working Paper 152. Berkeley: Institute of Urban and Regional Development, University of California.

Krippendorf, J. (1982). Towards new tourism policies: The importance of environmental and sociocultural factors. *Tourism Management* 3, 135–48.

Lawrence, D., Kenchington, R., and Woodley, S. (2002). *The Great Barrier Reef: Finding the Right Balance.* Melbourne: Melbourne University Press.

Leakey, R., and Lewin, R. (1996). *The Sixth Extinction.* New York: Anchor.

Lomborg, B. (2001). *The Skeptical Environmentalist: Measuring the Real State of the World.* Cambridge: Cambridge University Press.

Lott, D. F., and Greene, H. W. (2002). *American Bison: A Natural History.* Berkeley: University of California Press.

Louisse, C. J., and Kuik, T. J. (1991). Coastal defence alternatives in the Netherlands. In B. L. Edge (ed.), *Proceedings of the Twenty-Second Coastal Engineering Conference* (pp. 1862–75). Reston, VA: American Society of Civil Engineers.

Macnaghten, P., and Urry, J. (1998). *Contested Natures.* London: Sage.

McNeely, J. (1997). Tourism and biodiversity: a natural partnership. Paper presented at UNEP Symposium on Tourism and Biodiversity, Utrecht, Netherlands, April 17.

Middleton, N. (2000). Mangroves: Forests of the sea. *GeoDate* 13(1), 1–4.

Miller, B. A., and Reidinger, R. B. (1998). *Comprehensive River Basin Development: The Tennessee Valley Authority.* Washington, DC: World Bank.

Milton, K. (1998). Nature and the environment in indigenous and traditional cultures. In D. E. Cooper and J. A. Palmer (eds), *Spirit of the Environment: Religion, Value and Environmental Concern* (pp. 86–99). London: Routledge.

Olson, K. H. (1995). Resource management. In R. Paehlke (ed.), *Conservation and Environmentalism: An Encyclopedia* (pp. 560–1). New York: Garland.

Ostrom, E., Dietz, T., Dolsak, N., Stern, P. C., Stonich, S., and Weber, E. E. (eds) (2002). *The Drama of the Commons.* Washington, DC: National Academy Press.

Pollard, D. A., Lincoln Smith, M. P., and Smith, A. K. (1996). The biology and conservation status of the grey nurse shark (*Carcharias taurus*) in New South Wales, Australia. *Aquatic Conservation: Marine and Freshwater Ecosystems* 6, 1–20.

Productivity Commission (2001). *Constraints on Private Conservation of Biodiversity.* Canberra: Productivity Commission.

Rao, S. (2002). Cheap air travel adding to global warming woes. *Reuters News Service* (London), June 27.

Recher, H. (1999). The state of Australia's avifauna: A personal opinion and prediction for the new millennium. *Australian Zoologist* 31(1), 11–27.

Richards, C. (2002). Invest in partnership. *New Internationalist* 352, 25.

Rittel, H., and Webber, M. M. (1973). Dilemmas in a general theory of planning. *Policy Sciences* 4, 155–69.

Ross, S., and Wall, G. (2001). Wallace's Line: Implications for conservation and ecotourism in Indonesia. In D. Harrison (ed.), *Tourism and the Less Developed World: Issues and Case Studies* (pp. 223–34). Wallingford: CAB International.

Salmon, K. (2002). Profit from principle. *New Internationalist* 352, 24–5.

Sewell, W. R. D., and Burton, I. (eds) (1971). *Perceptions and Attitudes in Resources Management*. Ottawa: Department of Energy, Mines, and Resources.

Stoll-Kleemann, S., and O'Riordan, T. (2002). From participation to partnership in biodiversity protection: Experience from Germany and South Africa. *Society and Natural Resources* 15, 161–77.

Suzuki, D., and Dressel, H. (2002). *Good News for a Change: Hope for a Troubled Planet*. Toronto: Stoddart.

The Australian (2001). Dithering on dingoes brings tragedy. May 2.

Thompson, D. (2002). *Tools for Environmental Management. A Practical Introduction and Guide*. Gabriola Is., BC: New Society Publishers.

Tilman, D., Wedin, D., and Knops, J. (1996). Productivity and sustainability influenced by biodiversity in grassland ecosystems. *Nature* 379(6567), 718–20.

Tollefson, J. (2001). Wily coyote outgunned by bigger canine cousin. *Reuters News Service* (USA), July 3.

United Nations Environment Program (2001). *Report of the Workshop on Biological Diversity and Tourism*, Santo Domingo, June 4–7. Santo Domingo: United Nations Environment Program.

Wackernagel, M., Schulz, N. B., Deumling, D., Linares, A. C., Jenkins, M., Kapos, V., Monfreda, C., Loh, J., Myers, N. and Norgaard, R. (2002). Tracking the ecological overshoot of the human economy. *Proceedings, National Academy of Sciences* 99(14), 9266–71.

Zimmerman, E. (1933). *World Resources and Industries*. New York: Harper & Row.

Chapter 38

National Parks: Wilderness and Culture

Stephen Boyd

Introduction

National parks have become tourist icons with many countries promoting some of their parks as "must-see attractions." In some cases the attraction to visit individual parks is as much a product of marketing as it is of accessibility. In other cases, the uniqueness of place is often the sole reason why tourists visit them. While most countries' national parks represent remnants of a particular region's past, it is important at the outset of this chapter to note that national parks are established against a cultural landscape that has been shaped and modified over time. Culture plays as important a role as nature does in explaining the origins of most national park systems, and it is therefore important to view national parks as elements of the cultural landscape of regions.

This chapter is in two parts. First, a historical perspective is provided on key elements that characterized early parks systems (e.g., US, Canada, New Zealand) such as worthless lands, preservation thinking, frontier development and peripheral lands, and leading personalities. This discussion highlights that early parks established within New World countries set precedents, which others would follow. Second, emerging and future challenges for national parks are addressed as spaces for tourism, to include conflicting park mandates, the challenge of creating sustainable spaces, controlling visitation and park management as a few. In many cases, parks are not just places for recreation and tourism, but where this focus is most prominent, the argument to be put forth later in the chapter is that planning and managing national parks must include both their natural and cultural components, as the attraction of visiting national parks is both their outstanding natural elements and the uniqueness of the culture or cultural remnants that they contain.

Early National Parks, History and Commonalities

A number of common elements may be identified in the evolution of the early parks, which would set precedents that later parks would follow (Boyd and Butler 2000).

These include the fact that parks could only be established on worthless lands, often as a remnant of frontier regions, and that preservation of wilderness spaces was a driving factor in safeguarding areas from commercial development and change. These elements are taken up and addressed in this section of the chapter, where the argument is made that, in the early establishment of parks and park systems, wilderness and nature took precedence over culture.

Worthless lands

Much has been written regarding the establishment of national parks and the "worthless lands" concept, as many of the early national parks were created out of wastelands (Hall 1992). It is no coincidence that the locations of the first national parks were in regions of the New World countries that were peripheral to economic development and population growth. The landscapes of Yellowstone, declared the world's first national park in 1872, and Yosemite, declared a state park in 1864, had within them certain aspects of outstanding natural quality, but also elements that were of limited economic use such as geysers, sulfur pools, and towering granite cliffs, hence the thinking that they were "worthless" (Boyd and Butler 2000). Tongariro, New Zealand's first national park, was established in 1887, consisting of three central volcanoes within the North Island. Chief Te Heu Heu Tukino of the Ngati Tuwharetoa was concerned that the mountains would be subdivided and lost to his tribe and so he decided to protect them by gifting them to the Crown. Although the nucleus of the land was deeded in 1887, it took until 1894 before the park was legally designated. The delay between deeding of the land and the establishment of the park was rooted in the government's concern that only worthless land would be set aside in the establishment of the park, and that there had to be absolute certainty that land being added to the park had no economic value (Simmons and Booth 2000).

The idea of national parks emerged at a time when Western nations were modernizing, industrializing, and urbanizing, where the focus was on evolving capitalist economies, and maximizing the use of spaces, and it was therefore critical to ensure that no areas that had economic potential be removed from development interests. In contrast to this, however, was the strength of the preservation movement in pushing for areas to be assigned formal protection status, and as such the desire to preserve areas from development would emerge from the middle of the nineteenth century as a strong factor in early park establishment.

Preservation

The first national parks in the New World countries were influenced by the Romantic and aesthetic perception that started to emerge of nature in the early to mid-nineteenth century, where emphasis was placed on the beauty within nature but also the need to protect these landscapes for future generations (Nelson 1976). In the 1830s Catlin had argued the case for the protection of much of the Great Plains of America's Midwest as they quickly came under the eye of the speculator and developer as the railroads pushed northward and westward. By the middle of the nineteenth century there had emerged in North America concerns over the impact of settlement and its expansion on the natural landscape and its inhabitants. For example, in 1864 George Perkins Marsh drew attention to the loss of natural environment in many settled parts of eastern North America and called for a reconsideration of the approach taken toward environmental management; rethinking that would later see the emergence of the conservation movement and the rise of utilitarian thinking, where the wise use of resources was espoused to serve the greatest good (Marsh 1965).

Arguably, the preservation ethic that emerged was a by-product of a desire to make use of these "wastelands." Tourism quickly emerged as an integral aspect of the early national parks in the New World countries. The establishment of parks was quickly followed by railroad developments that linked settled areas to parks and which were primarily responsible for the development of accommodation and other visitor-related infrastructure within parks. In the case of New Zealand, for example, Roche (1987) noted early enthusiasm for Tongariro to be perceived as having value as a resort for those requiring change from city life, and made accessible through a rail link to settled regions within North Island.

Despite the focus on using the parks for tourism, from the outset of the early parks being developed there was strong sentiment that the uniqueness of flora and fauna also be preserved. Commentary associated with the early parks is replete with statements about the need to create "indigenous parks," "preserve wildlife in its habitat," and be "left as near as possible in its natural state" (Hall 2002). Despite having the support of preservation organizations like the Sierra Club and proponents of preservation like John Muir, national parks suffered an identity crisis: were they to be bastions of untrammeled nature, or were they to be used for tourism? Early park legislation would imply they tried to be both as dual mandates were often read in the wording of the legislation that saw the passing of National Park Acts in many of the New World countries. Phrases like "conserving the scenery and the natural and historic objects and the wildlife therein" and "so as to leave them unimpaired" would be followed by "provide for the enjoyment, benefit and education," signaling that from the start parks were aiming to be all things to all people (Nelson 1976; Boyd and Butler 2000). The inability to set forth clear mandates as to the purpose of national parks has been a root cause of the problematic relationship that tourism has had with parks. It could be argued, though, that the small numbers of visitors to parks at the time meant that the relationship was not problematic. Nelson (1976) noted that it surely became so with the increased mobility provided by the motor car and the development of national highway systems. The early parks and the nature of the legislation passed helped to set a precedent as to what a national park should be and what activities are deemed acceptable within parks.

Frontier remnant

Hall (2002) argued that the first national parks established in New World countries represented remnants of the frontier that was quickly disappearing. His argument is that "wilderness" was what lay beyond the frontier of civilization in North America, and that the establishment of national parks was in a way an attempt to "capture" wilderness characteristics given that, by 1890, the American frontier had closed. Frederick Jackson Turner had argued that the customs, traditions, and values of the American people had been founded and shaped on the frontier, and that the perceived loss of wilderness and a "frontier" synonymous with "abundance," "opportunity," and "difference" offered in the New World meant the link to the past had been severed. Hall (2002) notes that the loss of the frontier had two effects: first it saw the rise of what has been termed "the progressive conservation movement" where a more scientific approach to conservation was adopted, and, second, it reinforced nature and wilderness as being important to people's lives, and meant that wilderness started to take on cultural and spiritual values for the American people, who thought it should therefore be preserved. The implication of these two contrasting effects would see preservationists pitted against conservationists. The thinking behind the progressive conservation movement was epitomized by the policies adopted in forestry by Gifford Pinchot, under the Theodore Roosevelt administration, for sustainable yield management, and a philosophy of the wisest use of resources for the greatest good, with economic motives prevailing over aesthetic ones (Pinchot 1947). This was challenged by preservationists like John Muir, who wanted government to protect forested regions from being developed for timber production (Nash 1967).

Not surprisingly, the approach to how wilderness areas should be managed varied between preservationist and conservationist, with the former favoring no change and the absence of exploitative human activity within wilderness areas, and the latter recognizing the merits of selective usage of forests, allowing wilderness areas to change over time, but be managed in a manner that ensured their overall conservation. While the preservation movement (Muir) was critical of such an approach, the progressive conservation movement was nevertheless very instrumental in advancing the idea of a national park system.

The second effect of the closing of the frontier, namely a change in the perception of wilderness, saw peripheral areas as romantic places, while to many they took on a spiritual dimension. To others, wilderness areas were places where one reaffirmed and tested one's "manliness" (Nash 1967) and the cultural values of the frontier as a difficult physical environment were refashioned in the 1880s and 1890s in the emergence of clubs for hunting, mountaineering, and walking (Hall 2002). By the start of a new century, wilderness places and their landscapes had emerged as part of America's consciousness, were the subject of books, had taken on the mantle of being national symbols (Grand Canyon, Yellowstone), and at last were recognized as "cherished parts of former environments" (Hall 2002) worthy of being maintained and protected. While national parks may represent remnants of a past frontier within individual countries, it would be the use of these areas, and not their outright protection, that would later fuel the growth and proliferation of national parks and subsequent systems.

Value of Wilderness Areas

Many authors have emphasized that the perception of national parks over time changed from areas of wilderness with limited benefit to places of recreation and tourism, and with scientific and aesthetic values (see the summary offered by Hall and Page 2002). One factor responsible for seeing change in the use of wilderness areas, and in many cases national parks, was linked to the ambiguity attached to national park mandates. In many of the early national park systems, wilderness areas would be established as fundamental spaces within individual national parks. This was common in the early national parks in the New World countries (see Butler and Boyd 2000).

Designation of wilderness areas as preserves took place under the Wilderness Act in the United States in 1964, which helped establish areas that were free of human occupancy. While legal recognition of the wilderness concept occurred in New Zealand as early as 1952 as part of the National Parks Act, with the first wilderness areas being established under the Act as early as 1955, wilderness was quickly viewed from an anthropocentric perspective, as opposed to one where the ecological integrity of areas took priority over use (Hall and Higham 2000). Wilderness in New Zealand quickly came to be recognized as a cultural and recreational concept rather than one designated for preservation of nature, often viewed as part of a recreational spectrum. As recently as the 1980s wilderness policy identified wilderness areas as places for recreational use as opposed to areas offering qualities that helped shape recreational experience. Presently, there exists no official policy that emphasizes the importance of ensuring the ecological integrity of places over their recreational use and potential.

Other New World country park systems took a different approach to wilderness areas and the role that ecological integrity played. In Canada, the development of zoning as an integral part of national park management saw the inclusion of a wilderness category, and the establishment of a systems plan for national park creation identified a distinct number of natural terrestrial regions that comprised the Canadian land base within which the preference was to have at least one national park in each terrestrial region where priority would be given to ensuring the ecological integrity of each region over its recreational and tourism use. Furthermore, amendments to the National Parks Act in the 1980s in Canada from the original Act of 1930 would see ecological integrity, and hence the survival of wilderness qualities of areas, be assigned as having priority over use (Boyd 2000).

Discussion

The above common elements, namely the idea that national parks be established in peripheral areas, have a high element of wilderness present, and be places where use, albeit recreation and tourism, over protection was quickly established from the outset, and where they would develop into a system of parks and be managed by the highest authority within respective countries, shaped how national parks have been defined and come to be viewed and accepted with the "New World" conservationist and national park tradition.

This viewpoint, however, fails to accommodate those parks systems that have developed under different conditions and where the timeline in establishing parks is relatively recent. National parks in parts of Europe (e.g., England and Wales) have a relatively short history and have been established within "working" landscapes as opposed to "protected" landscapes, where protection has to be balanced against other uses such as development, urban growth, and private lands (Parker and Ravenscroft 2000). This then raises a challenge as to what model new park systems should emulate. In particular, many parks are being established in less developed countries, and the challenges of developing a system of parks may be compromised by the absence of areas able to satisfy New World country thinking regarding parks (see Cresswell and Maclaren (2000) for discussion on the establishment of national parks and their tourism potential within Cambodia and Vietnam).

New World thinking about national parks established the primacy of wilderness and nature over culture. At the outset of this chapter it was noted that national parks are in essence cultural constructs, and that nature and the wilderness present is often that modified and/or shaped by current society and the generations that have been custodians of those spaces. The focus in this chapter is not with the place that national parks play in wider cultures, but rather in how national parks have played a role in helping to conserve distinctive local cultures, as well as safeguarding commemorative integrity present within parks. The irony of this is, however, that the history of early park establishment and the common elements of parks is one that has excluded culture, indigenous, and local people as part of that mix. Writings about the early parks focused on the natural qualities of places and the need to preserve the ecological mix, and lip service was paid to the fact that national parks were created from the cultural landscape present in regions. Catlin, in his infamous quote about preserving the North American Indians in their natural surroundings in a nation's park, indirectly established the importance that culture could play in national park creation, but because of the emphasis on worthless lands, wilderness, and preservation a cultural component received little attention (Boyd and Butler 2000).

The early parks in New World countries were established for a clientele that was not local, but rather distant and elite. In fact, the setting aside of land for the safari national parks of eastern Africa required the removal of traditional peoples from their lands, where locals would not benefit from being in close proximity to the parks (Goodwin 2000). With regard to national parks in eastern Africa, the idea of partnerships between the managers of parks and local peoples is a relatively recent development. Where international tourism is concerned, Goodwin (2000) has noted that culture offers some potential as the foreign visitor is interested in experiencing local culture as well as viewing wildlife. It is this mix of wildlife viewing and local culture which is encouraging local communities across eastern Africa to develop wildlife sanctuaries, where the benefits of offering tourism services and a product are reinvested into local communities with limited loss through leakage. In many cases, the culture present within national parks is often presented to visitors as a key component of the experience. This will be addressed later in this chapter, but too often this cultural product is in the form of viewing the lifestyle of traditional peoples, an experience that may in turn be questioned in terms of authenticity.

Where culture and the cultural landscape have been appreciated it is in the development of sites that have been given world heritage status, but the majority of national parks that have received this status have done so because of their natural, as opposed to cultural, properties. As at the end of 2002 there were 730 world heritage sites: 563 were cultural, 144 were natural, and 23 were mixed (<www.unesco.org>, accessed January 4, 2003). Experiencing the cultural property within national parks of world heritage status is unfortunately reduced to those inscribed as mixed sites, Tongariro, New Zealand, being one.

Emerging and Future Challenges for National Parks

Space does not permit a detailed discussion of all the challenges that face national parks today from tourism. Instead the following sections outline key areas that will continue to shape how national parks adapt to tourism.

Park mandates

Despite the fact that institutional arrangements are in place within some systems to protect national parks and ensure their ecological integrity for present and future generations in the form of Park Acts, policy, and planning and management frameworks, national parks have increasingly become places for recreation and tourism. This can be illustrated using Canada's national park system. Here park policy may be traced back to the 1930 Parks Act, which stressed that the parks be left in an unimpaired state. Although the term ecological integrity was not specifically used, the wording of the Act implied that the natural qualities of parks be safeguarded. Between the 1930 Parks Act and the release of the 1994 park policy (Parks Canada 1994), the focus shifted from tourism (1964 policy) to protection of park ecosystems (1994 policy) (see Boyd 2000; Boyd, forthcoming). The 2001 Canada National Parks Act (<www.parkscanada.gc.ca/apps/cp-nr/index.asp>, accessed February 2, 2003) reaffirmed that the priority of park mandates was to maintain as well as restore ecological integrity through the protection of natural resources and natural processes.

Park policy is actualized through individual park management plans. For example, Sheila Copps, then Deputy Prime Minister and Minister of Canadian Heritage, in the foreword to the Banff National Park Management Plan (Parks Canada 1997) states clearly that, first and foremost, Banff is a place for nature in which ecological integrity is the cornerstone of the park as well as the key to its future, but that it is also a place for people, a place for heritage tourism, a place for community, and a place for environmental stewardship. The plan is strategic, offering a clear core vision shaped around a range of themes such as an integrated approach to decision-making, and with the view that a parks tourism strategy shaped around heritage will serve as a model of integrated management. This last point illustrates that parks cannot remain as ecological reserves: economic reality necessitates that they encourage and develop forms of tourism that will have a minimized impact on the parks' ecological structure. While the mandate may have shifted in favor of ecological integrity, the emphasis of a tourism strategy shaped around heritage may suggest that, while legislation places emphasis on ecological integrity, in practice parks will encourage tourism in order to ensure the system is adequately financed.

The picture becomes increasingly more complex when national park systems such as that in the UK are considered, where the vast majority of parks have been created relatively recently compared to the history of the park development elsewhere, as individual national parks are superimposed on "working landscapes" compared to the early parks in the New World countries where parks were created as part of "protected landscapes" (Butler and Boyd 2000). In the case of parks in "working" environments, the challenge to promote ecological integrity over certain types of park use will be all the greater.

Parks and wilderness spaces

Wilderness spaces, within national parks, today take on a different role than in the past. Backcountry regions are becoming favored as the playground of the nature-based tourist, and with improvements in transportation and technology, wilderness regions in parks are more easily accessed. One consequence of this is that parks are in danger from new forms of tourism that use the wilderness purely as the backdrop to non-mechanized and mechanized activities. Conventional management strategy in national parks has been to zone parks according to different levels of use and type of activity. In the past, the majority of visitors confined themselves to the frontcountry areas of parks. Today, and most likely in the future, the increased pressure placed on national parks to self-fund and the growth of heritage and nature-based tourism will see further use made of the backcountry and wilderness spaces. Parks have had a long and uneasy relationship with tourism, and because tourism was present in the early parks it has been expected that tourism should remain a key feature of any national park landscape.

Parks and sustainability

It is important to remember that parks are more than tourism spaces, and that they have a nature preservation function, and are places for wildlife, aboriginal people, interpretation and education, communities (in some park systems), and research, and need to be planned and managed to ensure they carry out their mandates. As such, a major contemporary issue that national parks face today is the challenge to be sustainable landscapes (Boyd 2000). A reasonable argument to be made is that parks can only be true examples of sustainable landscapes if all activities, including tourism, are placed on a sustainable path. This challenge is often hampered by the reality in most park systems that the competent authority assigned to managing parks has to attempt to balance use with protection by employing trade-offs between uses and park users based on the priority assigned to park mandates if sustainability is to ever move beyond a visionary dream.

Linked to achieving sustainability, parks today are faced with issues such as resource conflicts in the form of activities incompatible with park goals, illegal use of park resources, and external threats from surrounding areas (Dearden 2000). Although citing Banff National Park in Canada as an example of all three conflicts, Dearden stresses that there is no generic solution to these problems and that because problems arise locally, a localized approach to resolution is best. Other major issues facing national parks today are how to manage tourists and mitigate tourism impacts. With reference to the latter, the last two decades have witnessed a range of planning frameworks designed for national parks that focus on opportunity, activity management, impact management, and what are acceptable limits of change that park landscape can cope with (Vaske, Donnelly, and Whittaker 2000). In most cases there are common elements: opportunity, indicators, standards and collaboration. Actions are often linked to standards to identify approaches that can be taken to mitigate visitor impacts, including capital development, education (enforcing regulations) and restricting the level of use by imposing limits. Vaske, Donnelly, and Whittaker (2000) point to new thinking which suggests that a normative approach be used to establish management standards, and to limit levels of impact to those considered acceptable, based on the frequency of encounters.

Culture and commemorative integrity

Much of this chapter has focused on the wilderness or natural attributes of national parks. The following two examples illustrate that more attention is starting to be paid to the cultural attributes within parks. The first example looks at the role of aboriginal peoples in park management, whereas the second looks at shifts in park policy where equal attention is given to protecting cultural and commemorative resources as well as natural ones.

Uluru (Ayers Rock) is internationally recognized as one of Australia's leading tourist attractions. Tourists are overwhelmingly motivated by the desire to see the spectacular inselberg, but they unfortunately rank learning about Aboriginal culture in the area low (Hall 2000). Aboriginal communities take a different view and have decided to become involved in tourism, defining their relationship with tourism as having control and exercising choice (Mercer 1994). They have representation on the management board that administers the park, and have control over how tourism is presented ensuring that the cultural and religious significance that Aboriginal people attach to the park is accorded the highest degree of protection and respect. Much of this involvement has recently become symbolized by the interpretive and educational services they offer visitors at the Uluru-Kata Tjuta Cultural Center located in the park (Mercer 1994). There may be issues over the authenticity of this experience, but at least local traditional cultures are beginning to have some representation and say over how culture is presented within parks.

As for policy developments that pay attention to culture, the current Canadian national parks policy in setting out guiding principles assigned ecological and commemorative integrity as having equal priority, saying that "protecting ecological integrity and ensuring commemorative integrity take precedence in acquiring, managing and administering heritage places and programs . . . the integrity of natural and cultural heritage is maintained by striving to ensure that management decisions affecting these special places are made on sound cultural resource management and ecosystems-based management practices" (Parks Canada 1994: 16). One section of the policy is given over to cultural resource management, noting that the objective is to manage cultural resources in accordance with the principles of value, public benefit, understanding, respect, and integrity. The policy details what is involved in the practice of cultural resource management (inventory, evaluation, consideration of historic value in actions affecting conservation and presentation, and monitoring and review) and the activities of cultural resource management (planning, research, conservation, presentation) (Parks Canada 1994). In short, it has taken policy with respect to the Canadian national park system to a position where cultural resources in parks are seen as being important as natural resources in parks.

Conclusions

National parks are places containing naturalness (wilderness) and culture. Unfortunately, attention has often been paid more to their naturalness tendencies as opposed to the cultural resources they provide. With the likelihood that tourism will continue to grow in national parks in the future, park agencies would do well to promote both nature and culture to a market that will probably demand it.

National parks have emerged as important for tourism. Yet, there has been limited attention by academic scholars toward writing about tourism and national parks. While tourism and national parks have been the focus of academic journal articles over the years, there has been a relative paucity of single texts on the subject. The edited work of Butler and Boyd (2000) was the first academic book to be produced that specifically discussed the issues and implications that arise from the relationship between tourism and national parks. One area where that relationship is critical is how parks are managed to accommodate, and maybe in some cases accept, tourism. Some of the discussion in the previous section alludes to this challenge. Butler (2000: 301) noted that "tourism in national parks will not only remain a significant problem to management, but most likely will become *the* major issue in national parks in many countries in the decades ahead," basing this on the argument that tourism in national parks will remain dynamic, developing new forms of tourism and adding new parks to existing systems. Taken on its own, the relationship between tourism and national parks is one which deserves greater attention by scholars in the future as opposed to being addressed within thematic texts that present studies on national parks but where the focus is directed at specific types of tourism such as ecotourism and heritage.

REFERENCES

Boyd, S. W. (2000). Tourism, national parks and sustainability. In R. W. Butler and S. W. Boyd (eds), *Tourism and National Parks: Issues and Implications* (pp. 161–86). Chichester: John Wiley.

Boyd, S. W. (forthcoming). The TACE model and its application to national parks: A Canadian example. In R. Butler (ed.), *The Tourism Area Life Cycle: Applications and Modifications*. Clevedon: Channel View Publications.

Boyd, S. W., and Butler, R. W. (2000). Tourism and national parks: The origin of the concept. In R. W. Butler and S. W. Boyd (eds), *Tourism and National Parks: Issues and Implications* (pp. 13–27). Chichester: John Wiley.

Butler, R. W. (2000). Tourism and national parks in the twenty-first century. In R. W. Butler and S. W. Boyd (eds), *Tourism and National Parks: Issues and Implications* (pp. 323–35). Chichester: John Wiley.

Butler, R. W., and Boyd, S. W. (2000). Tourism and parks: A long but uneasy relationship. In R. W. Butler and S. W. Boyd (eds), *Tourism and National Parks: Issues and Implications* (pp. 3–11). Chichester: John Wiley.

Cresswell, C., and Maclaren, F. (2000). Tourism and national parks in emerging tourism countries. In R. W. Butler and S. W. Boyd (eds), *Tourism and National Parks: Issues and Implications* (pp. 283–99). Chichester: John Wiley.

Dearden, P. (2000). Tourism, national parks and resource conflicts. In R. W. Butler and S. W. Boyd (eds), *Tourism and National Parks: Issues and Implications* (pp. 187–202). Chichester: John Wiley.

Goodwin, H. (2000). Tourism, national parks and partnerships. In R. W. Butler and S. W. Boyd (eds), *Tourism and National Parks: Issues and Implications* (pp. 245–62). Chichester: John Wiley.

Hall, C. M. (1992). *Wasteland to World Heritage: Preserving Australia's Wilderness*. Carlton: Melbourne University Press.

Hall, C. M. (2000). Tourism, national parks and Aboriginal peoples. In R. W. Butler and S. W. Boyd (eds), *Tourism and National Parks: Issues and Implications* (pp. 29–38). Chichester: John Wiley.

Hall, C. M. (2002). The changing cultural geography of the frontier: National parks and wilderness as frontier remnant. In S. Krakover and Y. Gradus (eds), *Tourism in Frontier Areas* (pp. 283–98). Lanham: Lexington Books.

Hall, C. M., and Higham, J. E. S. (2000). Wilderness management in the forests of New Zealand: Historical development and contemporary issues in environmental management. In X. Font and J. Tribe (eds), *Forest Tourism and Recreation: Case Studies in Environmental Management* (pp. 143–60). Wallingford: CAB International.

Hall, C. M., and Page, S. (2002). *The Geography of Tourism and Recreation*, 2nd edn. London: Routledge.

Marsh, G. P. (1965[1864]) *Man and Nature; or, Physical Geography as Modified by Human Action*, ed. D. Lowenthal. Cambridge, MA: Harvard University Press.

Mercer, D. (1994). Native peoples and tourism: Conflict and compromise. In W. F. Theobald (ed.), *Global Tourism: The Next Decade* (pp. 124–45). New York: Butterworth-Heinemann.

Nash, R. (1967). *Wilderness and the American Mind*. New Haven: Yale University Press.

Nelson, J. G. (1976). *Man's Impact on the Western Canadian Landscape*. Ottawa: McClelland and Stewart/Carleton University.

Parker, G., and Ravenscroft, N. (2000). Tourism, national parks and private lands. In R. W. Butler and S. W. Boyd (eds), *Tourism and National Parks: Issues and Implications* (pp. 95–106). Chichester: John Wiley.

Parks Canada (1994). *Guiding Principles and Operational Policies*. Ottawa: Canadian Heritage.

Parks Canada (1997). *Banff National Park Management Plan*. Ottawa: Government of Canada.

Parks Canada (2001). The Government of Canada announces action plan to protect Canada's natural heritage. <www.parkscanada.gc.ca/apps/cp-nr/index> (accessed February 2, 2003).

Pinchot, G. (1947). *Breaking New Ground*. New York: Harcourt Press.

Roche, M. M. (1987). A time and a place for national parks. *New Zealand Geographer* 43(2), 104–7.

Simmons, D. G., and Booth, K. L. (2000). Tourism and the establishment of national parks in New Zealand. In R. W. Butler and S. W. Boyd (eds), *Tourism and National Parks: Issues and Implications* (pp. 39–49). Chichester: John Wiley.

UNESCO (2002). World Heritage sites. <www.unesco.org/> (accessed January 4, 2003).

Vaske, J., Donnelly, M., and Whittaker, D. (2000). Tourism, national parks and impact management. In R. W. Butler and S. W. Boyd (eds), *Tourism and National Parks: Issues and Implications* (pp. 203–22). Chichester: John Wiley.

Chapter 39

Ecotourism: Theory and Practice

Erlet Cater

Introduction

In a world where one in five of the population (1.2 billion people) live in extreme poverty on less than a dollar a day, around 10 million children under the age of 5 died of mostly preventable diseases in 1999, and more than 113 million children do not attend school (DFID 2001), it is somewhat bemusing that a tourism niche market should seemingly command sufficient universal interest to lead to the UN designation of 2002 as the International Year of Ecotourism (IYE). This designation also flies in the face of the fact that, despite extravagant claims to the contrary concerning its global significance (see, for example, the various estimates cited by TIES 2000), the World Tourism Organization estimates that ecotourism constitutes only 2–4 percent of global tourism (WTO 2002).

Ecotourism in Theory

The endorsement of ecotourism by the UN via the designation of IYE bears testament to the internationalization of the concept. We witness its universality as various interests across the world embrace this apparently sustainable strategy of natural resource utilization. Why does a relatively small, specialist, market hold such magnetic attraction for academics and practitioners from the developing and developed countries alike? What are the characteristics of this undeniably charismatic, but sometimes dangerously deceptive, construct?

The appeal of ecotourism

The allure of ecotourism to stakeholders can be attributed to the fact that it is presented as a theoretically non-destructive operationalization of the "use it or lose it" philosophy: simultaneously making conservation pay and paying for conservation. It represents a symbiotic, win-win scenario with environmental protection resulting both *from* and *in* improved local livelihoods; continued, and possibly enhanced, profits for the tourism industry; sustained visitor attraction and satisfaction; and revenue as well as popular support for conservation. Consequently, ecotourism strategies have not only been endorsed by tourism destinations and businesses, but also advocated by international environmental agencies and promoted by international lending and bilateral development agencies. Support from the latter group is remarkable considering that, in the past, tourism development was seen as inappropriate for overseas development assistance (IRG 1992).

The characteristics of ecotourism

As with sustainable development, nailing ecotourism to a precise definition proves a slippery task, leading one commentator to the tongue-in-cheek observation that "Defining ecotourism is as elusive as the animals on some ecotours" (Ecoclub 2001). This has led to such a proliferation of definitions, since the term was first given popular airing in the early 1980s by Ceballos-Lascuarian, that Fennell (2001) could conduct a content analysis of 85 of them just over a decade later. Rather than expand on these multifarious definitions and their evolution (see, e.g., Fennell 1999; Page and Dowling 2002), it is illuminating to examine the principal features of ecotourism outlined in the Quebec Declaration on Ecotourism (UNEP/WTO 2002). Emanating from the World Ecotourism Summit, the focal event of IYE, and with a caveat that the 1,200 participants were aware of the limitations of this consultative process to incorporate the input of the large variety of ecotourism stakeholders, the declaration recognizes:

> that ecotourism embraces the principles of sustainable tourism, concerning the economic, social and environmental impacts of tourism. It also embraces the following specific principles that distinguish it from the wider concept of sustainable tourism:
>
> - Contributes actively to the conservation of natural and cultural heritage,
> - Includes local and indigenous communities in its planning, development and operation, and contributing to their well-being,
> - Interprets the natural and cultural heritage of the destination to visitors,
> - Lends itself better to independent travelers, as well as to organised tours for small size groups. (UNEP/WTO 2002)

Deconstructing these principles throws light on the complexities and interdependencies implied in both the theory and practice of ecotourism

Ecotourism as a subset of sustainable tourism

By declaring that ecotourism embraces the principles of sustainable tourism, the Quebec declaration implicitly acknowledges that ecotourism is not the only manifestation of the latter. Many writers have positioned ecotourism as a subset of sustainable tourism, situating it in relation to this and other tourism types, for example alternative, nature, adventure, cultural tourism (Fennell 1999) and even mass tourism (Weaver 2001).

It is now commonly agreed that sustainable tourism should be regarded as a generic term that covers all forms of tourism that not only incorporate the essential dimensions of sustainability but also contribute to sustainable development in general (Hunter 1995). The aim of sustainable tourism development is "to meet the needs of present tourists and host regions while protecting and enhancing environmental, social and economic values for the future" (Page and Dowling 2002: 16). There has been much debate regarding sustainability in the context of tourism. Tourism researchers have identified additional elements to the classic "trinity" of sustainable development consisting of economic, social, and environmental criteria. For example, Bramwell et al. (1996) add cultural, political, managerial, and governmental dimensions.

Insofar as ecotourism embraces the essential elements of sustainability, it is one variant of sustainable tourism, but under that umbrella term are many types of tourism, whether based on natural or human resources, that contribute to sustainable development (Page and Dowling 2002), and even mass tourism, providing it adheres to the essential criteria outlined above. While ecotourism should, by definition, be sustainable tourism, not all sustainable tourism is ecotourism. What are its specific attributes?

Distinguishing Principles of Ecotourism

Active engagement

The Quebec Declaration's first principle, refining ecotourism from the wider concept of sustainable tourism, is that it should contribute *actively* (author's italics) to the conservation of cultural and natural heritage. Orams (2001) classifies ecotourism types along a continuum from "better" operations that actively contribute to the improvement of the natural environment, through "neutral" operations that passively seek to minimize their impacts on the natural environment to "worse" operations that are more exploitative and irresponsible, thus detracting from the quality of the natural environment. Hence, the requirement to contribute actively to nature conservation positions true ecotourism at the "better" end of the spectrum, emphasizing that ecotourism requires not only behavioral/lifestyle changes amongst the participants but also involves actions that contribute to environmental well-being (Weaver 1998). A similar case can be made for cultural heritage. While writers such as Fennell (1999) are uneasy with the inclusion of culture as a fundamental principle of ecotourism, regarding it as a secondary motivation to the overall ecotourism experience, others point to the inextricability of the natural and cultural in many locations (Hall 1994), where so-called natural landscapes are frequently the product of long histories of indigenous land management. Fennell's purist stance is theoretically defensible, positioned as it is at the ecocentric end of the spectrum, but in practice it would confine ecotourism to the ever-shrinking wilderness areas of the world, or to protected areas. Some writers subscribe to this restrictive view, for example Honey (1999) defines ecotourism as "travel to fragile, pristine, and usually protected areas," while Bottrill and Pearce's (1995) British Columbian study implicitly confines ecotourism to legally protected areas. However, while such areas constitute popular, if not exclusive, venues for ecotourism in most parts of the world, the insights provided into ecotourism participation would be partial. For example, less than 1 percent of the world's marine area is within established protected areas (Cater and Cater 2001) yet whale-watching experiences in diverse marine locations across the globe (admittedly not all sustainable) attracted 9 million participants in 1999 (Hoyt 2001).

Inclusivity

The Declaration's second principle, the inclusion of local and indigenous communities in ecotourism planning, development, and operations while contributing to their well-being, echoes the most vaunted principle of ecotourism in recent years: community involvement. This has important implications not only for development, hence donor agencies' interest in ecotourism as a pro-poor strategy (Ashley, Goodwin, and Roe 2001), but also for conservation, cultural sustainability, distributive justice, and efficient use of human resources. Early approaches toward community involvement in ecotourism were largely tokenist, involving manipulative, passive, consultative, or for-material-reward participation, none of which brings enduring effects on people's lives (Pretty 1995). The Quebec Declaration, however, stresses the need for more active participation in decision-making from the outset, so that "participative planning mechanisms are needed that allow local and indigenous communities, in a transparent way, to define and regulate the use of their areas at a local level, *including the right to opt out of tourism development*" (UNEP/WTO 2002; italics in original).

Educative

The third specific ecotourism principle outlined at Quebec emphasizes the need to interpret the natural and cultural heritage of a destination for visitors. Indeed, Page and Dowling (2002) suggest that the educative element of ecotourism is a key to distinguishing it from other forms of nature-based tourism, arguing that ecotourism education can influence tourist, community, and industry behavior and assist in the longer-term sustainability of tourist activity in natural areas. They argue that interpretation helps to advance the cause of conservation as tourists see the big picture regarding the environment.

Small-scale

The declaration's final specific principle is that ecotourism lends itself better to independent travelers, as well as to organized tours for small-sized groups. Despite the wording of this codicil, which would allow for larger groups, the obvious preference is for small-scale visitation. Scale is one of the most contested characteristics of ecotourism. Pointers toward its conceptualization as primarily a small-scale activity include: first, the fact that early ecotourism was represented by a few hardy individuals traveling alone or in small tour groups (Page and Dowling 2002); second, smallness of scale is implicit if ecotourism is viewed as a subset of alternative tourism (i.e. to mass tourism) that is characterized by small-scale operations reliant on local inputs (Weaver 1998); third, the International Ecotourism Society emphasizes the functional aspects, with the market segment concentrated on leading and accommodating small groups in natural areas in an educational manner using interpretive materials and local specialist guides (Epler-Wood 2002).

Confining ecotourism to small-scale participation not only brings the danger of preaching to the converted but also the irrationality of denying the designation of ecotourism to large-scale nature-based tourism if it adheres to all the requirements of sustainable tourism. As Williams and Shaw (1998: 56) state, "While sustainability is often popularly associated with 'smallness'... the link between scale and sustainability has not been empirically (or theoretically) tested." Weaver (2001) also argues that it neither makes economic sense nor acknowledges the potent lobbying force constituted by increased participation. He observes a two-way relationship. On the one hand, ecotourism can strengthen the mass tourism product by offering opportunities for "green" diversification as well as helping to impart an ethos of sustainability and environmental awareness to mainstream tourism. On the other, mass tourism supplies a large market of soft ecotourists that helps position ecotourism as a significant stakeholder capable of lobbying on an equal footing with stakeholders in other sectors such as agriculture and logging. Furthermore, mass tourism can introduce sophisticated environmental management strategies to ecotourism that are beyond the capability of most traditional small-scale operations. Weaver does, however, recognize that power differentials between the two sectors mean that the influence of mass tourism over ecotourism is likely to be much greater than vice versa. Consequently, mass tourism may effectively appropriate ecotourism for its own purposes.

The debate about scale illustrates the heterogeneity of ecotourism. There is increasing recognition of a spectrum of participation and involvement from hardcore specialist groups, frequently undertaking scientific observation, to more casual natural-resource-based activities, such as whale-watching, providing they are sustainably managed. Weaver (2001) identifies the latter as a "soft" ecotourism market which may largely consist of "mass tourists engaged in such activities as part of a broader, multi-purpose vacation that often places emphasis in the 3S realm." Such a pragmatic view is adopted by Queensland, Australia where three broad styles of ecotourism are distinguished – self-reliant, small group, and popular ecotourism – with the latter involving the transport of larger numbers of visitors to, through, or across the country's best-known and most popular natural attractions (Page and Dowling 2002).

Ecotourism in Practice

There has been considerable disappointment concerning the failure of ecotourism to deliver its promises. For example, an early analysis of 23 Integrated Conservation-Development Projects (ICDPs), most with ecotourism components, found that few benefits went to local people or served to enhance protection of adjacent wildlands (Wells and Brandon 1992).

As with all ideals faced with harsh market realities, it is hardly surprising that there is considerable divergence between theory and practice. This is not the fault of ecotourism *per se* but can be attributed to two major factors. The first is the failure to recognize the wider context of ecotourism; the second is that its "sexiness" as a concept has meant that, either through a failure to understand or blatant opportunism, ecotourism has frequently been misinterpreted, misappropriated, and misdirected.

The wider context

The wider context in which ecotourism is set as a process and as a principle is vitally important, because it plays a vital role in prospects for sustainable outcomes. The aim must be "to understand, in a theoretically informed way *how* the processes of interaction between tourism and sets of place characteristics operate, and develop over time, in different contexts" (Gordon and Goodall 2000: 292). It is essential to recognize that these place characteristics both shape and are shaped by economic, sociocultural, political, ecological, institutional, and technical forces that are exogenous and endogenous as well as dynamic. These forces may have enabling or constraining effects (Hall and Page 1999) and are highly contingent on scale and circumstance (Lew and Hall 1998). However, there are certain general, recurrent, themes which give rise for concern. One of the most significant is the failure to recognize the broader economic milieu of ecotourism.

Co-dependencies and confrontations

There is an inherent danger of regarding ecotourism as an isolated alternative, dissociated from other economic activities. Instead, it should be viewed as a complementary or supplementary economic activity, not a substitute. There are various scale levels to consider. First, it is imperative that ecotourism is viewed in the context of nature-based tourism. While ecologically based, it is by no means certain that nature-based tourism is ecologically sound, socioculturally responsible, or even, if any of these qualities are compromised, ultimately economically viable.

Second, ecotourism needs to be considered with respect to other tourism market segments that are dependent upon, and consequently impact on, the natural environment. Any one location is likely to host a variety of frequently incompatible recreational pursuits with the requirements of one activity prejudicing the needs of another, for example the possible confrontation between ecotourism and resort-based tourism. Specialist, largely international, visitation also needs to be examined in parallel with domestic or regional tourism. The characteristics of domestic tourism in general are poorly understood. This is surprising given that in most countries domestic travel, recreation, and leisure involve significantly greater numbers of people and economic activity than international tourism. Similarly, while research is dominated by international tourist flows originating in the West, regional participation is increasingly significant, with a concomitant relative diminution of the traditional "Western" inbound ecotourist markets (Weaver 2002). Ghimire (2001) documents how, in 1998, 55 percent of tourists in the ASEAN (Asian and South-East Asian) countries came from the Asian and Pacific developing countries; 73 percent of visitors to the SADC (South African Development Community) region originated from Africa; and 70 percent of visitors to the Mercosur (Mercado Comun del Cono Sur) countries were from Latin America. Whether domestic or regional, these tourists are likely to construct different "imaginative geographies" of the natural and cultural resources of the destination compared with Western ecotourists. In China, domestic tourists favor artificial site enhancement compared with preservation in a pristine state, and have a higher tolerance of crowding and litter (Lindberg et al. 1997). Weaver (2002) cites the work of Hashimoto, who describes the different aesthetics, attractions, and crowding thresholds in the Japanese context. While, as Weaver suggests, the extent to which Asian markets will be influenced by Western models of ecotourism participation is unknown, he argues for peculiarly "Asian" models of ecotourism that, for cultural reasons, deviate from the conventional Eurocentric constructs. Visitor ethnicity is important not only because of potentially conflicting needs but also because we have a poor grasp of the relative contribution of international, intra-regional, or domestic visitors toward sustainable livelihoods in destination areas. Place (1998), for example, argues that in Costa Rica domestic tourists are more likely to stay in modest accommodation and patronize locally owned establishments, thus supporting village-based development. It is vital, therefore, that ecotourism is viewed not only in the context of nature-based tourism, but also in that of tourism in general. Milne (1998) warns against creating a dichotomy between "alternative" and "mass" tourism because all types of tourism development are interlinked.

Third, with regard to the overall picture of sustainability, it is vital to consider the interactions between ecotourism and all other forms of economic activity. It is crucial to move beyond a tourism-centric view, as "we cannot hope to achieve sustainability in one sector alone, when each is linked to and dependent upon the others" (Butler 1998: 28). Sectoral conflicts may compromise the success, if not the very existence, of ecotourism.

Finally, it is essential to consider the global context. Despite ecotourism's emphasis on local involvement, it is not exempt from the center–periphery relations inherent in international tourism. Ecotourists originate largely from the more developed countries and consequently their tour, travel, and accommodation needs are largely coordinated by firms based in those countries. This dominance has led to accusations of ecotourism as "eco-imperialism" or "eco-colonialism" (Hall 1994; Mowforth and Munt 1998). A 1997 study on an ecotourism project in Taman Negara, Malaysia, concluded that only a tiny proportion of tourist expenditure reaches ecotourism destinations in the South. Two-thirds of the expenditures of European and North American ecotourists went to foreign airlines and travel agencies, with a large proportion of the remainder being spent, before and after the visit to the ecotourism destination, in the large cities and well-established tourist centers (TWN et al. 2001).

Economic viability

Concern has also been voiced over the economic viability of ecotourism, an essential but frequently skated over aspect of its long-term sustainability. Hillel (2002) describes how "In Brazil 80% of small and medium enterprises . . . close doors within their first two years. Why should ecotourism be different? Entrepreneurship at SME level is risky." There is also the question of finance and support for ecotourism marketing, particularly given the relatively small size of the market and the burgeoning number of ecotourism enterprises. Mader (2002) notes that "Too many noble eco-friendly projects have failed because there has been no investment in marketing . . . How many ecotourism projects funded by the international development banks or agencies still exist?" Ironically, because ecotourism strategies are being endorsed, and even financed, by multilateral agencies the threat of oversupply is omnipresent. Garcia (2002) describes how European regional development funding through the LEADER initiative contributed toward rural tourism becoming virtually a "mass product" with supply outgrowing demand by 1998. Consequent price-cutting, with dramatic discounts, in many European destinations, constituted a difficult environment for such fragile enterprises. Such outcomes legitimize concerns voiced that:

> If the IYE is to suggest that all UN member countries should encourage ecotourism projects in rural and natural areas, the danger of an oversupply of ecotourism facilities is very real... who will take the responsibility, when ecotourism initiatives make investments based on miscalculated demand and later face decline, local businesses go bankrupt and entire communities are pushed into crisis? (TWN et al. 2000)

There are many examples where ecotourism has to be buoyed up by financial support, either through public sector subsidies or through individual altruism. Wilkie and Carpenter (1999) are skeptical of the prospects for a viable tourist industry in more isolated, less well endowed protected areas in the Congo Basin when even the most well-established and accessible sites, with abundant and charismatic wildlife, have marginal revenue-generating capacity. Consequently, ecotourism there constitutes a net financial cost to protected area management. In Jamaica, Gaymans (1996) describes how the government is creating and maintaining costly trails, allowing visitors free access, assuming that tourist expenditures will boost local and national economies. He argues that this strategy "reinforces the absurd notion that nature itself has no economic value." The potential pitfalls of individual altruism are pointedly illustrated by a small-scale ecotourism operator summing up his situation as being "five years and two family savings accounts" later (Shores 2002).

Structural inequalities

As with any other economic activity, ecotourism is both shaped by and shapes the markedly inequitable structures, both internationally and intranationally, in which it is cast as a process. There is no empirical substantiation of the claim that ecotourism generally contributes to a more equitable distribution of tourism income and a reduction in poverty. Indeed, ecotourism may exacerbate, or even create, divisions. Entus (2002) describes how:

> many projects which have set out to be community-based... have, at some point or another in their evolutionary cycles, engendered or exacerbated pre-existing internal divisions of power, and led to the formation of new business elites who represent but a small fraction of the "local community."

Amongst the many concerns voiced by critics of the IYE was that it did not "confront the structural inequalities that characterize ecotourism's origins and practice" (Vivanco 2002).

The contextual examination above has focused primarily on political-economic structures. Many other considerations are equally significant in shaping the fortunes of ecotourism, but, overall, it can be seen that it is an easy scapegoat for more fundamental causal relationships. It is also true that much of the criticism leveled at ecotourism derives from its frequent bastardization, intentional or otherwise.

The Misinterpretation and Misappropriation of Ecotourism

Purists would argue that some of the wider conceptions of ecotourism outlined earlier open the door to misinterpretation. The most common misinterpretation is a tendency to equate it with the much wider concept of nature tourism. While the latter may be ecologically based, it is not necessarily sustainable. There are countless examples of eco-opportunism where the prefix "eco" has been unjustifiably attached, such as eco(ad)ventures, ecocruise, and ecosafari (Wight 1994).

There is also increasing concern, particularly from indigenous rights groups and NGOs based in the South, that ecotourism misappropriates nature and culture, not only imposing an essentially Western-centric ethos on societies which have different values, but also effectively commodifying the environment and traditional practices.

Ethnocentrism

The accusation is that ecotourism, as constructed by the West, attempts "to force people everywhere into the same cultural, economic, and political mould" which "is bound to generate insecurity, resentment, conflict, and even ecological degradation" (Vivanco 2002: 26). Mowforth and Munt (1998) cite Colchester's observation that "the generally holistic (or cosmovision) view of nature held by indigenous peoples is radically different from the cultural notion of wilderness held by western conservationists." Even the much-lauded concept of conservation-for-development draws fire from indigenous people as "that is not necessarily consistent with our traditional view of guardianship and protection. We wouldn't even use the word conservation" (Taylor, cited in Vivanco 2002: 26).

One of the most important issues in the arena of cross-cultural difference is the consumptive orientation of indigenous people versus the non-consumptive orientation of ecotourists:

> Given their traditional lifestyles and values, indigenous peoples are very protective of their right to harvest the resources in their territories... indigenous people have traditionally tended to harvest their resources in a sustainable fashion... In contrast, most ecotourists explicitly seek out non-consumptive activities while traveling... Given these contrasting perspectives, conflict is likely to occur should a group of ecotourists stumble across the harvesting of wildlife while they are visiting an indigenous territory. (Hinch 2001: 352)

Anti-developmentalist stance

As noted earlier, traditional cultures frequently constitute an important component of the composite ecotourism attraction for the Western visitor. However, in the same way that anti-developmentalists romanticize the lifestyles of indigenous peoples (Corbridge 1995), so, too, may Western-constructed ecotourism assume an artificial, "zooified" lifestyle in local populations. Again, Hinch (2001: 353) argues:

> The romantic image that non-indigenous people have of natives living by traditional means is no longer accurate and in many cases never was... The contrast between tourist expectations of indigenous people living traditional lifestyles and the preferences of many indigenous people for modern lifestyles presents challenges for ecotourism within indigenous territories.

Furthermore, anti-developmentalists tend to ignore local people's aspirations for higher living standards founded on a clear understanding of the costs and benefits of development (Corbridge 1995). This may mean that a wholesale, unconditional, acceptance of ecotourism as a sole development strategy by local people is both unlikely and unrealistic. Consequently, Brandon and Margoluis (1996) argue that it may be a false assumption that poor households may switch from illegal, unsustainable, and difficult activities such as fuelwood collection or goldmining to legal activities that generate equal revenues, such as ecotourism, and will be content to substitute similar money incomes from different activities. Their income needs are not fixed and they aspire beyond just holding their own economically. Brandon and Margoluis also highlight the frequently seasonal nature of ecotourism and question "at what point will it act as an economic incentive – for the part of the year when the person receives the income or for the whole year? Or will the person work in ecotourism and undertake illegal and/or unsustainable activities during other times of the year?"

Commodification

Another aspect of misappropriation is that ecotourism appropriates and commodifies both nature and culture. This is problematic for three major reasons. First, indigenous peoples voice their concern that outside interests have no right to expropriate local resources in this way; for example, the Cordillera People's Alliance (1999: 3) (Philippines) argues that "the Department of Tourism does not own 'nature'. Neither does it own the 'culture' it so aggressively sells in national and international markets. The Cordillera region and its people's culture are not commodities; they are not for sale."

Second, as Hinch (2001: 347) points out, "Indigenous people have a much deeper connection with the land than non-indigenous peoples. Because they do not see the land as a possession, they are very wary of treating it as a commodity, even in the purportedly benign context of ecotourism." Complex nature–culture relationships mean that cultural erosion may result in the disintegration of social mechanisms governing resource use and allocation. Absence of cultural identity may lead to an individualistic approach to property rights that eventually leads to resource commercialization (Daoas 1999).

Third, ecotourism inevitably attaches a financial value to nature. Should it present an unattractive investment prospect because of market conditions, or fail because of unfair competitive advantage, there is the danger that ecotourism entrepreneurs will look to other more financially advantageous, but less environmentally and culturally considerate, investments. These may ultimately out-compete ecotourism.

Biopiracy

Not only may ecotourism result in misappropriation, but it is itself frequently misappropriated. This was seen in the eco-opportunism of unsustainable operators operating under the guise of ecotourism. Another insidious form of eco-opportunism is the increasing phenomenon of "biopirates" masquerading as ecotourists. TWN (2002) present case studies from South America, Africa, and southeast Asia, demonstrating how biopirates can easily sidestep existing regulations and laws in southern countries by traveling there as "tourists" to illegally collect genetic resources, plants, and wildlife as well as associated indigenous knowledge with commercial value for the biotechnology industry.

Misdirection of ecotourism

Much concern has been voiced, in particular by southern NGOs, that ecotourism opens the door to exploitation of nature and culture, not only by the tourism industry:

> for the Mekong region at least, ecotourism is not an approach that implies persistence and the capability to continue as a small-scale and community-based activity in a longer term. It is rather used by official agencies and private industry as a springboard to develop mainstream mass tourism in less developed territories, without addressing the self-destructive processes inherent in tourism evolution. (TWN 2001)

but also by other sectors:

> because tourism provides the physical infrastructure for freer movement of people and goods within countries and across borders, ecotourism has opened opportunities for investors to gain access to remote, rural forest, coastal and marine areas. The more transportation systems that are established, the more encroachments, illegal logging, mining and plundering of biological resources occur. (TWN 2001)

It is evident from the above discussion that, while IYE sought to legitimize ecotourism, there are powerful interests that subvert and corrupt this theoretically sustainable construct.

Conclusion

It is misleading to take issue with the broader philosophy behind ecotourism. Problems arise when there is a failure to recognize it as a process set in an interdependent world characterized by difference and diversity. When the concept is translated into a universal template, largely Western-conceived, it becomes clear that it is not a case of "one size fits all." Contexts vary enormously across space and time.

Ecotourism also suffers from being manipulated, and thus tainted, in many instances by unscrupulous eco-opportunists, furnishing ample ammunition for its wholesale condemnation. While sustainable operations may be identified, and "rewarded" via certification programs (Honey and Rome 2001), penalizing those who corrupt the ideals of ecotourism will be not be easy. Market forces, coupled with powerful vested interests, represent formidable obstacles, as with sustainable development in general.

Too much is expected of ecotourism. To ensure more sustainable outcomes requires far more than tinkering at the margins. In the same way that Hall (2000) describes how both tourism and the environment constitute "a meta-problem, characterized by highly interconnected planning and policy 'messes'," it is essential that ecotourism is positioned within a larger discourse. This should encompass issues such as environmental and habitat protection, sustainable development, traditional knowledge, intellectual property regimes, biological diversity, access and benefit sharing, biopiracy, and cultural property (Bobiwash, cited in Environment News Service 2002). Situated in this way, ecotourism can make a positive contribution towards sustainable development. It may be but a small pebble cast into the murky waters of unsustainable human activity, but its ripple effects have the potential to facilitate an understanding and appreciation of the complex interlinkages and interdependencies at work. This should define the agenda for future research on ecotourism.

REFERENCES

Ashley, C., Goodwin, H., and Roe, D. (2001). *Pro-Poor Tourism Strategies: Expanding Opportunities for the Poor.* Pro-Poor Tourism Briefing 1. London: ODI.

Bottrill, C. G., and Pearce, D. G. (1995). Ecotourism: Towards a key elements approach to the concept. *Journal of Sustainable Tourism* 3(1), 45–54.

Bramwell, B., Henry, I., Jackson, G., Prat, A. G., Richards, G., and van der Straaten, J. (1996). *Sustainable Tourism Management: Principles and Practice.* Tilburg: Tilburg University Press.

Brandon, K., and Margoluis, L. (1996). Structuring ecotourism success: Framework for analysis. In *The Ecotourism Equation: Measuring the Impacts.* New Haven, CT: International Society of Tropical Foresters, Yale University.

Butler, R. (1998). Sustainable tourism. Looking backwards in order to progress? In C. M. Hall and A. A. Lew (eds), *Sustainable Tourism: A Geographical Perspective* (pp. 25–34). Harlow: Longman.

Cater, C., and Cater, E. (2001) Marine environments. In D. Weaver (ed.), *The Encyclopedia of Ecotourism* (pp. 265–82). Wallingford: CAB International.

Corbridge, S. (1995). Editor's introduction. In S. Corbridge (ed.), *Development Studies: A Reader* (pp. 1–16). London: Edward Arnold.

Cordillera People's Alliance (1999). Tourism in the Cordillera, HAPIT 6(2), <http://www. inkarri.net/ ingles/indioeng/fil31.htm>.

Daoas, D. (1999). Efforts at protecting traditional knowledge: The experience of the Philippines. In *Roundtable on Intellectual Property and Traditional Knowledge.* WIPO/ IPTK/ RT/99/6A. Geneva: World Intellectual Property Organization.

DFID (2001). *Poverty: Bridging the Gap.* London: DFID.

Ecoclub (2001) *Ecotourism News* 22 <http:/ /ecoclub.com/news/22.html>.

Entus, S. (2002). Re participative (business) community development. Discussion list <trinet@hawaii.edu> (accessed June 19, 2002).

Environment News Service (2002). UN urged to rethink Ecotourism Year <http://ens.lycos. com/ens/nov2000/2000L-11-28-11.html> (accessed June 12, 2002).

Epler-Wood, M. (2002). *Ecotourism: Principles, Practices and Policies for Sustainability.* Paris and Burlington, VT: UNEP/International Ecotourism Society.

Fennell, D. (1999). *Ecotourism: An Introduction.* London and New York: Routledge.

Fennell, D. (2001). A content analysis of ecotourism definitions. *Current Issues in Tourism* 4(5), 403–21.

Garcia, A. (2002). Public funding for ecotourism. Discussion list <ecotourism_financing@ yahoogroups.com> (accessed August 8, 2002).

Gaymans, H. (1996). Five parameters of ecotourism. In *The Ecotourism Equation: Measuring the Impacts.* Bulletin 99. New Haven: Yale School of Forestry and Environmental Science.

Ghimire, K. B. (2001). *The Native Tourist.* London: Earthscan.

Gordon, I., and Goodall, B. (2000). Localities and tourism. *Tourism Geographies* 2(3), 290–311.

Hall, C. M. (1994). Ecotourism in Australia, New Zealand and the South Pacific: Appropriate tourism or a new form of ecological imperialism? In E. Cater and G. Lowman (eds), *Ecotourism: A Sustainable Option?* (pp. 137–57). London and Chichester: Royal Geographical Society/John Wiley.

Hall, C. M. (2000). Rethinking collaboration and partnership: A public policy perspective. In B. Bramwell and B. Lane (eds), *Tourism Collaboration and Partnerships Politics, Practice and Sustainability* (pp. 143–58). Clevedon: Channel View.

Hall, C. M., and Page, S. J. (1999). *The Geography of Tourism and Recreation*. London: Routledge.

Hillel, O. (2002) Re [iye2002] ecotourism and guides. Discussion list <iye2002@yahoogroups.com> (accessed July 8, 2002).

Hinch, T. (2001). Indigenous territories. In D. Weaver (ed.), *The Encyclopedia of Ecotourism* (pp. 345–57). Wallingford: CAB International.

Honey, M. (1999). *Ecotourism and Sustainable Development*. Washington, DC: Island Press.

Honey, M., and Rome, A. (2001). *Protecting Paradise: Certification Programs for Sustainable Tourism and Ecotourism*. Washington, DC: Institute for Policy Studies.

Hoyt, E. (2001). *Whalewatching*. London: IFAW.

Hunter, C. J. (1995). On the need to re-conceptualise sustainable tourism development. *Journal of Sustainable Tourism* 3(3), 155–65.

IRG (1992). *Ecotourism: A Viable Alternative for Sustainable Management of Natural Resources in Africa*. Washington, DC: Agency for International Development Bureau for Africa.

Lew, A. A., and Hall, C. M. (1998). The geography of sustainable tourism: Lessons and prospects. In C. M. Hall and A. A. Lew (eds), *Sustainable Tourism: A Geographical Perspective* (pp. 199–203). Harlow: Longman.

Lindberg, K., Goulding, C., Zhongliang, H., Jianming, M., Ping, W., and Guohui, K. (1997). Ecotourism in China: Selected issues and challenges. In M. Oppermann (ed.), *Pacific Rim Tourism* (pp. 128–43). Wallingford: CAB International.

Mader, R. (2002) Marketing and development. Discussion list <iye2002@yahoogroups.com> (accessed January 30, 2002).

Milne, S. S. (1998). Tourism and development: The global–local nexus. In C. M. Hall and A. A. Lew (eds), *Sustainable Tourism: A Geographical Perspective* (pp. 35–48). Harlow: Longman.

Mowforth, M., and Munt, I. (1998). *Tourism and Sustainability*. London: Routledge.

Orams, M. B. (2001). Types of ecotourism. In D. Weaver (ed.), *The Encyclopedia of Ecotourism* (pp. 23–36). Wallingford: CAB International.

Page, S. J., and Dowling, R. (2002). *Ecotourism*. Harlow: Pearson.

Place, S. (1998). Ecotourism: Viable route to rural development. In C. M. Hall and A. A. Lew (eds), *Sustainable Tourism: A Geographical Perspective* (pp. 107–18). Harlow: Longman

Pretty, J. (1995). The many interpretations of participation. *In Focus* 16, 4–5.

Shores, J. (2002). *Ecotourism_financing*, introd. John Shores. Discussion list <ecotourism_financing@yahoogroups.com> (accessed August 1, 2002).

TIES (2000). *Ecotourism Statistical Factsheet*. Vermont: The International Ecotourism Society.

TWN (2001). Cancel the year of ecotourism. An open letter to UN Secretary Kofi Annan. *Earth Island Journal* 16, 3. <http://www.earthisland.org/eijournal/new_articles.cfm?articleID = 237&journalID = 48>.

TWN (2002) *Clearinghouse for Reviewing Ecotourism* 6. <http://www.twnside.org.sg/title/eco6.htm>.

TWN et al. (2001). *Call for a Fundamental Reassessment of the International Year of Ecotourism*. Letter to Oliver Hillel, October 20, 2000, reproduced in forwarded email from D. Buhalis, January 18, 2001. Discussion list <trinet-l@hawaii.edu>.

UNEP/WTO (2002). Quebec declaration on ecotourism. <www.ecotourism2002.org>.

Vivanco, L. (2002). Seeing the dangers lurking behind the International Year of Ecotourism. *The Ecologist* 32(2), 26.

Weaver, D. (1998). *Ecotourism in the Less Developed World*. Wallingford: CAB International.

Weaver, D. (2001). Ecotourism in the context of other tourism types. In D. Weaver (ed.), *The Encyclopedia of Ecotourism* (pp. 73–83). Wallingford: CAB International.

Weaver, D. (2002). Asian ecotourism: Patterns and themes. *Tourism Geographies* 4(2), 153–72.

Wells, M., and Brandon, K. (1992). *People and Parks: Linking Protected Area Management with Local Communities*. Washington, DC: World Bank, WWF, and USAID.

Wight, P. (1994). Environmentally responsible marketing of tourism. In E. Caterand G. Lowman (eds), *Ecotourism: A Sustainable Option?* (pp. 39–55). London and Chichester: Royal Geographical Society/John Wiley.

Wilkie, D. S., and Carpenter, J. F. (1999). Bushmeat hunting in the Congo Basin: An assessment of impacts and options for mitigation. *Biodiversity and Conservation* 8(7), 927–55.

Williams, A. M., and Shaw, G. (1998). Tourism and the environment: Sustainability and economic restructuring. In C. M. Hall and A. A. Lew (eds), *Sustainable Tourism: A Geographical Perspective* (pp. 49–59). Harlow: Longman.

WTO (2002) International Year of Ecotourism Launched in New York. <http://www.world-tourism.org/newsroom/Releases/more_releases/january2002/launch>.

Chapter 40

Tourism, Sustainability, and Social Theory

George Hughes

What a transformation is contained within the passage of half a century. In the late 1940s, in the aftermath of the Second World War, tourism was nurtured to help restore social normality across western Europe. Against the background of the traumatic depths of the recent conflict, the assertion that tourism could make a valuable contribution to peacemaking was highly credible. To this was quickly added the merit of tourism's economic potential as Western countries, in efforts to regenerate their war-torn economies, responded to the vigorous post-war growth in tourist numbers. During the 1960s this rhetoric had, in turn, been commended to "developing countries" as part of more comprehensive strategies to "modernize" the "underdeveloped" parts of the world. However, this enthusiasm was soon tempered by the growing concern of the political left. Here "underdevelopment" was recast in more critical terms as "dependency" and tourism conceived as an expression of neocolonial relations of power (Britton 1982). More liberally inclined economic analysts also began to question the "benefits" of tourism, which were argued to be greatly overstated (Bryden 1973), and social analysts reflected on the social and cultural threats posed to traditional ways of life (Greenwood 1989). This growing ambiguity about the value of tourism was contemporaneously captured in the title of Young's (1973) book *Tourism: Blessing or Blight?*

This ambivalence continued and reached new heights as the environmental debate became progressively incorporated into the critique of tourism. At the beginning of the 1980s Cohen was calling for the defense of the environment "from" tourism (Cohen 1978) yet, by the close of the decade, theorists were pointing to the advantages of integrating tourism and environmental strategies (Farrell and Runyan 1991). Following the publication of the Brundtland Report (WCED 1987), and the subsequent influence upon the global political agenda exercised by the Rio Convention of 1992, it became inevitable that the principles of sustainable development would be incorporated by the industry. As signatories to the Rio Convention, governments began to explore ways of reshaping their national tourism policies to accord with the environmental objectives of Agenda 21 while the World Tourism Organization formally adopted the principles of sustainable development. Cynically this might all be interpreted as a public relations exercise in which the tourism industry applied a "green wash" merely to keep it abreast of ideological change. However, the support given to the principles of sustainable tourism by the World Wide Fund for Nature, the Audubon Society of America, the Nature Conservancy, and sundry green pressure groups lends credibility to claims that at least parts of the tourism industry may be endeavoring to become more environmentally friendly.

Many environmentally orientated types of new tourism have since proliferated, including nature tourism, green tourism, ecotourism, responsible tourism, and sustainable tourism. Analysts have coined such diverse terms in an attempt to capture a supposed shift that is taking place from mass package tourism to more individualistic and differentiated types of holiday making (Poon 1993). Theorists have been struggling to make sense of these diverse categories and the ambiguous relationships they have with the environment. In a capitalist world this expanding market sector could hold the key to environmental sustainability. New tourism has been seized upon supposedly because some of these tourists exhibit consumption tastes that have been influenced by debates about global environmental responsibility. They are also prepared to pay for the kinds of environmental experience that are consistent with prevailing interpretations of sustainable development. Sustainable tourism is thus being advanced by both the industry and conservation organizations as tourism's response to sustainable development.

New Tourism

Krippendorf (1987) and Poon (1993) account for the growth in new kinds of tourism as part of wider shifts in the socioeconomic character of Western societies. For the last quarter of the twentieth century the industrialized heartlands of western Europe and North America had been experiencing significant change, summarily described by the term de-industrialization. This change has proved to be not only economic but also social and cultural. The demise of semi-skilled and unskilled occupational categories under the twin pressures of automation and global relocation of production, and the contemporaneous expansion in service employment, coincided with, and contributed to, transformations in institutional structures including those of class, family, gender, and nation. Western economies have been in transition from industrial (or Fordist) to post-industrial (or post-Fordist) modes of production with associated, but theoretically contested, claims that their sociocultural structures have also been in transition from modern to postmodern (Featherstone 1991; Lash and Urry 1994). Hence the growth in new forms of tourism may be explained by the changing composition of consumers, who are increasingly drawn from the expanding new middle classes employed within the post-industrial service economy.

Poon (1993) caricatures new kinds of tourists as those who focus upon travel that involves enjoyment of the natural environment while respecting the integrity of local communities. Fewer in number than the mass holiday market, new tourists are highly sought after because they are alleged to be more discerning. They look for authenticity, novelty, spontaneity, and adventure and are keen to learn about the natural environment and new cultures. While they demand a high-quality product new tourists are also willing to pay for it as long as it represents good value for money. Poon differentiates these new kinds of tourist from the old-style mass holiday tourists using a range of dualistic criteria (table 40.1).

Using the analogy of the product life-cycle Poon predicts the gradual running down of standardized mass holiday tourism in favor of these more individualized new holiday practices. She insists that this is inevitable because of changes in the marketplace brought about by the advent of new kinds of consumers, technologies, production practices, management techniques, and social and cultural conditions. If Poon is correct this may present a very productive and convenient solution to the growing environmental problems being laid at the door of tourism.

However, the definition of the new tourist is a fuzzy one and not altogether environmentally coherent. While interest in the physical and cultural environment is a defining feature of new tourism it does not follow that all new tourists are environmentally conservationist in either intention or practice. This dilemma has been approached relatively unproblematically in much of the research into new tourism where, historically, the concentration has been upon defining ecotourism and its more recent variant sustainable tourism. Ecotourism, as defined by Scace et al., "is an enlightening nature travel experience that contributes to conservation of the ecosystem while respecting the integrity of host communities" (Scace et al., 1992 cited in Wight 1994: 39). On the other hand, sustainable tourism is the "tourist use of natural environments where long-term economic benefits, continuous environmental protection and local community development are inherent" (Eagles 1995: 25).

The similarities between these two definitions, for allegedly different expressions of new tourism, illustrates the ambiguous character of the terms being employed and the considerable overlap that exists between supposedly different activities. However, tourism theorists continue to insist that there are legitimate bases for differentiating between types of new tourism. Thus Eagles (1995), for example, proposes differentiating the category of sustainable tourism into the four niche markets of ecotourism, wilderness tourism, adventure travel, and car camping. Although all four are admitted to have "similarities," Eagles claims the market segments are rooted in different philosophical bases. Ecotourism involves travel for the discovery of and learning about wild natural environments. Wilderness travel involves

Table 40.1 Characteristics of old and new tourists

Old Tourist	New Tourist
Search for the sun	Experiencing something different
Follow the masses	Want to be in charge
Here today, gone tomorrow	See and enjoy but do not destroy
Just to show that you have been	Just for the fun of it
Having	Being
Superiority	Understanding
Like attractions	Like sports
Take precautions	Adventurous
Eat in hotel dining room	Try out local fare
Homogeneous	Hybrid

Source: Adapted from Poon 1993.

personal recreation through primitive travel in natural environments that are devoid of human disturbance. Adventure travel is personal accomplishment through the thrills of dominating dangerous environments. Car camping is safe family travel at the interface between the wild and the civilized.

Lew (1998) adds a further cultural twist to this ambiguity when he claims that the term nature is more readily used to describe ecotourism in the Asia-Pacific region while North Americans prefer to use the term adventure. Thus what might be a soft adventure tour to a North American could be a simple nature tour to a resident of an Asia-Pacific country (Lew 1998: 98). The point is that there is considerable slipperiness involved in differentiating between new tourism's market segments and, despite the objections of theorists (Wall 1997), market researchers continue to roll these together into terms like ecotourism and sustainable tourism. Such studies are open to charges of misrepresenting the character and size of the ecotourism market and Filion et al. (1992, cited in Eagles 1995) have been criticized for inflating the estimated world-wide demand for ecotourism because they included adventure tourists, wilderness tourists, and campers in their analysis. This raises question marks over the environmental integrity of the eco- or sustainable components of new tourism. Ecotourists, and sustainable tourists, are alleged to be not merely interested in the natural environment, as adventure tourists would be, but concerned for its conservation and protection, which adventure tourists don't necessarily claim.

Environmentally Responsible Consumption?

A structuralist reading of the growth of new tourism would locate it firmly within the developing needs of global capitalism. Theorists, such as Harvey (1989), explain the general character of post-industrial change as an effect of the over-accumulation of capital. He argues that profitability crises are an expected and routine aspect of market capitalism because it is in the nature of capitalism, through competition and a tendency toward market saturation, to threaten profit margins and market demand. Hence, in the interests of maintaining profitability, new markets have to be continuously created to maintain and accelerate the pace of consumption. Products, fashions, ideas, and technology become increasingly ephemeral and consumption increasingly instantaneous. Things are disposed of long before their natural life is complete. Adapting Harvey's general analysis would thus suggest that the growth of new tourism is a reflection of the changing needs of the market. New, more differentiated and profitable, types of holiday product have had to be introduced to counter the immense competitive pressures upon the standardized and price-sensitive package holiday. The consumer, following the dictates of fashion, has simply responded to these new market opportunities.

This depiction renders the individual as an essential cog in the wheel of consumer capitalism. Schooled from early childhood in the consumption practices necessary to maintain consumer capitalism, the consumer is duped into the illusion that life satisfaction can be attained through the consumption of marketed goods and services. But it is not conducive to profit maximization if consumer satisfaction is allowed to endure. The expansion of production requires that consumer desire be stretched far beyond the natural limits set by biological needs. Thus the compulsion to consume no longer has anything to do with the traditional notion that it satisfies needs. The post-industrial consumption culture has reversed this relationship. In post-industrial consumer culture the promise of satisfaction now precedes the stimulation of need (Baudrillard 1988). Consumption is therefore not so much a successful attainment of satisfaction as a restless and disaffected activity which consumers have been deluded into believing they undertake entirely voluntarily (Bauman 1998: 26). Such hysterical consumption would be unlikely to conserve and protect the environment, at best rendering it as a passing fashion in the rapid circulation of consumption signs. In its most extreme form such a dystopic view would leave little room for authentic human–environment relationships.

However, Urry (1990, 2000) and Lash and Urry (1994) use the theoretical insights of Bourdieu (1984) to offer a more subtle class-based interpretation of this structural paradigm. This recognizes that the process of consumption can be used to critique the problems of environmental degradation as well as contribute to them. Bourdieu (1984) suggests that class structure is maintained in a very dynamic way. Each class, to maintain its relative social position with respect to others, engages in struggles that seek to increase the volume and value of its capital stock. This struggle extends far beyond the immediate acquisition of economic capital, and it is Bourdieu's particular theoretical contribution to recognize the significance of cultural capital in this process. Cultural capital is essentially a dispute over taste. It is mobilized through cultural institutions that are used to endorse some tastes at the expense of others. It is thus a hegemonic process in which cultural institutions become arbiters of taste. Whoever controls the institutional structure exercises considerable power in determining the constituents of "good" taste. For example, class dominance may be promoted through a facility to appreciate the fine arts but this facility is influenced by differential access to the resources of education. In this kind of way a class may seek to maintain and promote its socioeconomic dominance using seemly non-political assertions about taste.

Urry argues that de-industrialization, during the last quarter of the twentieth century, has brought about a class transformation with the rise of what he terms a new "service class." Members are drawn from the ranks of those employed in the expanding service industries and share a range of characteristics:

> The service class consists of that set of places within the social division of labour whose occupants do not own capital or land to any substantial degree, are located within a set of interlocking social institutions which collectively "service" capital; enjoy superior work and market situations generally resulting from the existence of well-defined careers, either within or between organisations; and have their entry regulated by the differential possession of educational credentials. (Urry 2000: 80)

Paradoxically, in the accelerating consumerism of postmodern society, one aspect of taste, promoted by the new service class in its struggle for cultural dominance, is selective consumption restraint. This expresses itself in a range of practices such as green consumerism, vegetarianism, natural childbirth, the rejection of synthetic fibres, and a host of recreational activities motivated by concerns about health. Service class consumers have bought into the ideology of consumer capitalism but they also believe that they have certain consumer rights, i.e. those of the citizen as consumer (Lash and Urry 1994: 297). Such rights include a belief in the entitlement to certain qualities of the environment, including rights to clean air and water, as well as less tangible aesthetic demands for attractive scenery. Fractions of the new service class have thus become engaged in ideological struggles to resist a range of environmentally damaging developments and to press diverse environmental issues. In application to tourism Urry (1995a, 1995b, 1997) has been able to interpret the decline of the traditional British seaside resort, and the rising preference for the rural environment, as a cultural effect of such shifts in class structure. "To be a tourist, to look on landscapes with interest and curiosity... has become a right of citizenship from which few in the 'West' are formally excluded" (Urry 1995a: 176). Hence the cultural tastes of new middle-class tourists may be used to account for the attraction of the environment within many of the new types of tourism.

However, this does not necessarily guarantee that the particular forms that this tourism takes will be necessarily any better for the environment than their mass tourist predecessors. Some analysts conceive the attraction to pristine environments as but the latest variant in "ego-tripping" (Munt 1994). Where Lash and Urry (1994) interpret the contradictory emergence of green consumption practices in terms of consumer citizenship, Mowforth and Munt (1998) explain the appeal of nature to a sub-group of new tourists, whom they call ego-tourists, as a competition for personal uniqueness. Rather than a deep-seated concern for the environment, ego-tourists search out styles of travel to reflect the "alternativeness" of their lifestyle. Environmental rhetoric is used by ego-tourists to claim the moral high ground and to obfuscate their part in the exploitation of the destinations they visit. Here environmental interest is being used as a structurally differentiating device to assert the cultural superiority of a class fraction from those conceived to be amongst the lower orders. This is an appealing way of interpreting the hedonistic characteristics of adventure travel, but its excessive structuralism interprets individual agency in a very limited way. Individuality is asserted, contradictorily, primarily for the purpose of reaffirming the superiority of a class position and status (Mowforth and Munt 1998: 135).

Yet, as Krippendorf argues, an individual's central motivation for leisure travel is, more simply, a personal desire to recuperate in a world that is different from the everyday:

> The much maligned tourist is a person looking, quite legitimately, for his/her happiness, badly needing the subjective freedom supplied by travelling... The tourist is his own advocate and not an international ambassador; he is not there to aid development or protect the environment. It goes without saying, then, that he behaves in an egoistic way. Nobody has ever explained to him the consequences of his actions and drawn his attention to the responsibility that is his. (Krippendorf 1997: 46)

For Krippendorf the tourist is a carefree, but ignorant, agent whose actions unintentionally contribute to the realization of mass effects. His environmental failings come from his having "been left out of all discussion on the subject, even though he is one of the main protagonists" (Krippendorf 1997: 46). However, this too has its conceptual weakness as ignorance becomes progressively more difficult to sustain as an explanation for environmental damage. The modern individual has access to unprecedented resources of knowledge about the world, with the result that ignorance is increasingly becoming a matter for individual culpability. Indeed it is this very enriched knowledge base that supports the individualistic and differentiated character of new tourism as post-industrial consumers use the process of consumption to map out personal identities.

The Reflexive Tourist?

Recent theory emerging from debates about globalization and risk society may, however, offer some prospects for conceiving a more ethically grounded thesis for sustainable tourism. In the work of Anthony Giddens (1991, 1994, 1998, 2000) and Ulrich Beck (1992, 1997, 1998, 1999, 2000) compatible explanations for the general growth in environmentalism have been offered which might be adapted to account for the rise in environmentally orientated types of new tourism. Both these theorists offer complex arguments that can only be understood as part of their broader project to theorize the structuring of Western society. Neither addresses tourism directly, although Beck discusses the more general concept of leisure in the context of his analysis of work and civil labor (Rojek 2001). However, the principles involved in the work of these two theorists warrant the constructive critical attention of tourism scholars.

Giddens argues that the modern individual possesses capabilities of self-reflexive management that distinguish him or her from individuals in pre-modern or traditional societies. Reflexivity has become the mechanism through which an individual is subjected to socially structuring influences but whose reflexive practices, in turn, reproduce social structure. This is a recursive relationship that Giddens terms structuration. To facilitate this process the individual draws on a substantial, and expanding, knowledgeability about the world that derives from modern society's preoccupation with surveillance, including the collection, storage, and manipulation of data. From a profusion of expert systems such as DIY guides, consultancy, advice programs, scientific and technological reports, and the like, the reflexive individual can exert significant control over what amounts to his or her personal lifestyle. Beck and Beck-Gernsheim (2002) see this enhanced control as both emancipating and anxiety-creating because individuals, faced with an extended array of lifestyle possibilities, no longer simply choose but are forced to choose by the nature of modern society. This is stress-inducing because there is always the possibility of making unrewarding and potentially lifestyle-damaging choices over things like marriage, career, family, and friends. So while lifestyle management has become a principal mechanism in the reproduction of modern social structures, and critical for the maintenance of the "everyday," it is also tinged with anxiety and risk. In Beck's words, "people are condemned to individualization" (Beck 1997: 96).

Beck (1997) also believes that risk, and particularly environmental risk, has become institutionalized as a result of industrialized production. This is a particularly modern phenomenon since Beck insists that traditional society had no equivalent notion of risk. Pre-industrial society experienced its hazards in a fatalistic way. They came from the gods, demons, or nature. However, the gradual extension of social control has turned externally generated hazards into internally calculable risks and hence the consequences of risk have become a political issue. This argument is central to both Beck's and Giddens' notion of life politics and is bound up with the exercise of rational control. Insurance, for example, plays a key role in the rational management of risk where private insurance buffers individuals against a range of risks to person and property and the "providential welfare state" (Giddens 1991) functions on behalf of the collective. But Beck argues that globalization has changed the nature of risk to the extent that we can no longer fully understand, or calculate, the scale of the risks society faces. The consequence is that while nations devise more and more environmental laws and regulations aimed at controlling risks, "no individual or institution seems to be held specifically accountable for anything" (Beck 1998: 18). Beck describes this state of affairs as one of "organized irresponsibility" in which the power and credibility of regulatory institutions have been eroded.

Giddens arrives at a similar conclusion from his analysis of the relations between individuals and modern institutions. He (1991) argues that in modern society the more functional aspects of social interaction take place between individuals, defined as clients or customers, and abstract systems whose operatives remain largely anonymous. Giddens asserts that this kind of interaction differs from the character of relations between acquaintances and requires individuals to place trust in the proper functioning of abstract systems. However, recent years have seen a growth of public distrust in the probity of many abstract systems and, in particular, those responsible for regulating environmental impacts. There has been increasing public disquiet over an array of environmental issues. Examples include the nuclear accident at Chernobyl, the genetic modification of life, food safety, global warming, biodiversity loss, soil degradation, and atmospheric pollution. There have also been questions raised about the extent to which these are the consequences of unacceptably exploitative economic systems.

Thus, in being reflexive, the individual has become a prisoner of lifestyle choice, forced to confront a world of enhanced environmental risk that is managed by institutions that no longer command public confidence. There is enhanced public awareness that risks are systemically produced but a collective refusal to recognize these as failings of the social system. Rather, when something goes wrong, it is individuals that are blamed rather than the system. Prompted by anxiety about the risks posed by tampering with nature, and a diminished trust in the institutions charged with environmental regulation, individuals have been pressed into engaging with a wide range of environmental issues, which has resulted in self-conscious adjustments to their lifestyles. This helps to explain the way in which environmentalism, or what Dunlap and Van Liere (1978) earlier considered to be a New Environmental Paradigm (NEP), has become incorporated into everyday life. Against a background of risks, dangers, and hazards a new level of environmental awareness has entered the everyday. The supposed environmental inflection of new tourism might therefore be conceptualized, on one level, as a simple extension of this lifestyle management to the practice of tourism.

However, Beck and Giddens foresee the spread of reflexive self-monitoring into all areas of life. They reject the conclusion that this would produce narcissistic individuals besotted only with personal self-actualization. Rather, both Giddens and Beck point to deeper existential concerns about the global commons motivated by, but extending beyond, self-centered concern with personal risk. Giddens points to the current reassertion of the kind of moral questions that had supposedly been emptied of relevance under the onslaught of postmodernity.

> The tremendous extension of human control over nature...comes up against its limits... These consist not so much in the environmental degradation and disruption that is thus brought about, as in the stimulus to reintroduce parameters of debate external to modernity's abstract systems. In other words repressed existential issues as such, press themselves back on to the agenda...moral/existential problems are actively recovered and brought forward into public debate. The specific moral arena of such debates concerns, not just what should be done for human beings to survive in nature, but how existence itself should be grasped and "lived": this is Heidegger's "question of Being." (Giddens 1991: 224)

This concern with the grand questions of life is also a feature of Beck's theorizing. In *The Brave New World of Work* Beck (2000) posits a new relationship between work, leisure, and society in which the overall goal is to sustain the commons and meet the obligations of society. Activities that do not contribute to wider social goals do not contribute to social capital. It is not clear precisely how tourism would figure in this relationship, but it is evident that Beck would entertain ethical objections to the pursuit of any leisure activity that was undertaken entirely for its own sake and without reference to the global commons. "Apathy, indifference, sloth, and subordination are not on the menu" (Rojek 2001). Tourism, while contributing to self-actualization, would always face the necessity to protect and enrich the commons. One might thus expect this to be a world in which more environmentally responsible forms of tourism would flourish.

Conclusion

Since the publication of the Brundtland Report (WCED 1987), and the Rio Convention of 1992, a considerable literature has developed that addresses the application of sustainability principles to tourism. While strong on the advocacy, definition, and examples of sustainable development, a defect of this literature is its perplexing weakness when it comes to offering a plausible account of why, in the context of consumer capitalism, a tourist might voluntarily choose to adopt consumption restraint. This is a far from trivial matter since tourism is not only constructed in terms of commodity capitalism but frequently also characterized by an intensity of consumption that borders on the hyper-real. A scan of travel agents' windows, travel supplements, and adverts will quickly confirm the credibility gap that exists between the rhetoric of sustainable tourism and the empirical reality of current high-street retailing. Given the centrality of consumption in post-industrial capitalist societies it is hardly surprising that environmental claims for diverse forms of new tourism have attracted vigorous critical attention (Munt 1994; Mowforth and Munt 1998).

Yet, in the aftermath of Brundtland and Rio, there has been a tentative awakening of environmental sensitivity amongst consumers. In application to tourism Mowforth and Munt (1998) and Urry (1995a) both advance interpretations that privilege the role of aesthetics over moral or ecological responsibility in accounting for the growth of environmentally orientated new forms of tourism. Indeed Mowforth and Munt promote aesthetic taste in direct opposition to the thesis of environmentally responsible tourism. These are conceptually powerful interpretations that illustrate the potential for misconceiving the motivations ascribed to environmental interest. They also illustrate the importance of conceptualizing tourism in terms of the larger socioeconomic structure of which it is part. For example, under Fordism it was the consumer's experience of social alienation and the possibility of an authentic "center-out-there" (Cohen 1979) that dominated the conceptual agenda of tourism during the 1960s and 1970s. Tourism became part of an emancipatory package that labor movements wrested from employers and governments. Similarly the arrival of new tourism reflects the widespread de-industrialization of tourist-generating areas and a growth in demand for more post-industrial forms of tourism, i.e. those that offer a greater sense of individuality. In both cases, because particular geographies of tourism emerged that have responded to the consumption tastes of visitors, there seem to be compelling reasons for turning the spotlight onto the tourist whose consumption tastes will influence the production of sustainable tourism development. This is particularly pertinent given emerging critiques of environmental impact management, where concepts such as carrying capacity, threshold, and indicators seem to be empirically problematic (Butler 2000; Hughes 2002).

At the risk of further contributing to the proliferation of hybridity I have introduced the concept of a "reflexive tourist" by adapting the work of Beck and Giddens. However, this is intended not so much to designate a particular package of tourist consumption practices as to suggest a mode in which tourism is consumed. Reflexivity is an empirical phenomenon, identified by Beck and Giddens as a response to the internally referential character of modernity. Environmentally responsible practices have become institutionalized in the public and private sectors and promoted lifestyle adaptations amongst individuals cognizant of the existential risks inherent in what Giddens terms the "juggernaut" of high capitalism. The work of Beck and Giddens opens the possibility that tourists, by virtue of their growing recognition of environmental risks, might regulate their lifestyles in support of the global commons. Such environmentally self-reflexive tourism would be an ideological gift under neoliberal capitalism since it would both maintain the virtuousness of consumption and realign it in conformity with the principles of sustainability. But such a rationalistic and instrumental approach, while capturing many aspects of our social relations, hardly represents their full significance. The motivation for holiday-taking, as Krippendorf and others have pointed out, is precisely to escape the rationalism and instrumentalism of the everyday. Hence, while offering a very tantalizing prospect for the sustainable management of tourism, it remains an open question as to how far tourism will be shaped by environmental reflexivity and how far by self-indulgence.

REFERENCES

Baudrillard, J. (1988). *Selected Writings*, ed. M. Poster. Stanford: Stanford University Press.

Bauman, Z. (1998). *Work, Consumerism and the New Poor*. Buckingham: Open University Press.

Beck, U. (1992). *Risk Society: Towards a New Modernity*. London: Sage.

Beck, U. (1997). *The Reinvention of Politics: Rethinking Modernity in the Global Social Order*. Cambridge: Polity.

Beck, U. (1998). Politics of risk society. In J. Franklin (ed.), *The Politics of Risk Society* (pp. 9–22). Cambridge: Polity.

Beck, U. (1999). *World Risk Society*. Cambridge: Polity.

Beck, U. (2000). *The Brave New World of Work*. Cambridge: Polity.
Beck, U., and Beck-Gernsheim, E. (2002). *Individualization: Institutionalized Individualism and its Social and Political Consequences*. London: Sage.
Bourdieu, P. (1984). *Distinction*. London: Routledge & Kegan Paul.
Britton, S. G. (1982). The political economy of tourism in the Third World. *Annals of Tourism Research* 9(3), 331–58.
Bryden, J. M. (1973). *Tourism and Development: A Case Study of the Commonwealth Caribbean*. Cambridge: Cambridge University Press.
Butler, R. W. (2000). Tourism and the environment: A geographical perspective. *Tourism Geographies* 2(3), 337–58.
Cohen, E. (1978). Impact of tourism on the physical environment. *Annals of Tourism Research* 5(2), 215–37.
Cohen, E. (1979). A phenomenology of tourist experiences. *Sociology* 13(2), 179–201.
Dunlap, R. E., and Van Liere, K. (1978). The new environmental paradigm: A proposed measuring instrument and preliminary results. *Journal of Environmental Education* 9(1), 10–19.
Eagles, P. F. J. (1995). Understanding the market for sustainable tourism. In S. F. McCool and A. E. Watson (eds), *Linking Tourism, the Environment and Sustainability. Proceedings of a Special Session of the Annual Meeting of the National Recreation and Park Association* (pp. 25–33). Minneapolis: National Recreation and Park Association.
Farrell, B. H., and Runyan, D. (1991). Ecology and tourism. *Annals of Tourism Research* 18(1), 26–40.
Featherstone, M. (1991). *Consumer Culture and Postmodernism*. London: Sage.
Giddens, A. (1991). *Modernity and Self-Identity*. Cambridge: Polity.
Giddens, A. (1994). Living in a post-traditional society. In U. Beck, A. Giddens, and S. Lash (eds), *Reflexive Modernization: Politics, Tradition and Aesthetics in the Modern Social Order* (pp. 56–109). Cambridge: Polity.
Giddens, A. (1998). *The Third Way*. Cambridge: Polity.
Giddens, A. (2000). *The Third Way and its Critics*. Cambridge: Polity.
Greenwood, D. J. (1989). Culture by the pound: An anthropological perspective on tourism as cultural commoditization. In V. L. Smith (ed.), *Hosts and Guests: The Anthropology of Tourism*, 2nd edn (pp. 171–85). Philadelphia: University of Pennsylvania Press.
Harvey, D. (1989). *The Condition of Postmodernity*. Oxford: Blackwell.
Hughes, G. (2002). Environmental indicators. *Annals of Tourism Research* 29(2) 457–77.
Krippendorf, J. (1997). Behaviour and experiences while travelling. In L. France (ed.), *The Earthscan Reader in Sustainable Tourism* (pp. 45–6). London: Earthscan.
Lash, S., and Urry, J. (1994). *Economies of Signs and Space*. London: Sage.
Lew, A. A. (1998). The Asia-Pacific ecotourism industry: Putting sustainable tourism into practice. In C. M. Hall and A. A. Lew (eds), *Sustainable Tourism: A Geographical Perspective* (pp. 92–106). Harlow: Longman.
Mowforth, M., and Munt, I. (1998). *Tourism and Sustainability: New Tourism in the Third World*. London: Routledge.
Munt, I. (1994). Eco-tourism or ego-tourism? *Race and Class* 36(1), 49–60.
Poon, A. (1993). *Tourism, Technology and Competitive Strategies*. Wallingford: CAB International.
Rojek, C. (2001). Leisure and life politics. *Leisure Sciences* 23, 115–25.
Urry, J. (1990). *The Tourist Gaze*. London: Sage.
Urry, J. (1995a). The tourist gaze and the environment. In J. Urry, *Consuming Places* (pp. 173–92). London: Routledge.
Urry, J. (1995b). A middle-class countryside? In T. Butler and M. Savage (eds), *Social Change and the Middle Classes* (pp. 205–19). London: UCL Press.

Urry, J. (1997). Cultural change and the seaside resort. In G. Shaw and A. M. Williams (eds), *The Rise and Fall of British Coastal Resorts: Cultural and Economic Perspectives* (pp. 102–13). London: Pinter.

Urry, J. (2000). *The Tourist Gaze*, 2nd edn. London: Sage.

Wall, G. (1997). Sustainable tourism – unsustainable development. In S. Wahab and J. J. Pigram (eds), *Tourism, Development and Growth: The Challenge of Sustainability* (pp. 33–49). London: Routledge.

WCED (World Commission on Environment and Development) (1987). *Our Common Future*. Oxford: Oxford University Press.

Wight, P. (1994). Environmentally responsible marketing of tourism. In E. Cater and G. Loman (eds), *Ecotourism: A Sustainable Option* (pp. 39–55). London: John Wiley.

Young, G. (1973). *Tourism: Blessing or Blight?* Harmondsworth: Penguin.

Chapter 41

Tourism and the Elusive Paradigm of Sustainable Development

David B. Weaver

Introduction

Interest in and alleged adherence to the goal of sustainable tourism development is ubiquitous. Concurrently and paradoxically, it can be argued that examples of tourism sites and destinations that meet a demonstrable standard of sustainable development are relatively rare, and perhaps non-existent. What factors account for this apparent discrepancy between intent and implementation, which constitutes a major issue within the tourism industry and the field of tourism studies? This chapter begins by outlining the contemporary origins and evolution of "sustainable tourism" as a concept. The four tourism platforms of Jafari (1989, 2001) are used to organize this discussion. Subsequent sections focus on the problems and contradictions that have impeded the implementation of "sustainable tourism."

Evolution of "sustainable tourism"

Jafari (1989, 2001) argues that the post-Second World War evolution of the tourism sector has been influenced by a succession of tourism philosophies or "platforms," each of which is influenced in turn by broader ideologies. Each has had its own crucial influence on the evolution of sustainable tourism, and perception of what constitutes "development" and how it can best be achieved. Initially, tourism in the 1950s and 1960s was dominated by an *advocacy platform* that regarded tourism as a crucial vehicle of economic development. This platform emerged from the then prevalent tenets of modernization theory (see Rostow 1960), which asserts that economic development diffuses from nodes of focused activity (usually an urban area) to more "traditional" peripheral areas, gradually leading to the evolutionary modernization of the entire country. Tourism was cited as one example of a propulsive activity that could stimulate this "trickle-down" effect if established in areas possessing appropriate natural and cultural resources (Sharpley 2000). Government could initiate this process through the creation of strategically located growth poles (as in Cancún, Mexico), but the primary impetus for development, especially once a critical mass of population in the growth pole triggered self-propelled growth, would come from the private sector. Beyond this association with modernization theory, the advocacy platform has come to be associated with virtually any support for mass tourism that derives from laissez-faire market forces.

The large-scale, laissez-faire tourism development that emerged with support from the advocacy platform, however, resulted in perceived negative economic, environmental, and sociocultural impacts, especially within the emerging "pleasure periphery" destinations of the Caribbean, South Pacific, and Africa (Turner and Ash 1975; de Kadt 1979; Lea 1988). In reaction to these impacts and inspired by the broader anti-modernization and core/periphery rhetoric of Dependency theorists such as Frank (1967) and Beckford (1972), the antithetical *cautionary platform* emerged in the 1970s as the dominant paradigm within tourism studies, if not as widely in the destinations themselves. Dependency-inspired academics such as Harrigan (1974) and Finney and Watson (1975) provided the most overtly political expressions of this platform by equating tourism in the Third World with plantation agriculture as a vehicle that systemically perpetuated the exploitation (or "under-development") of peripheral destinations by the North American and European core, thereby fostering interdependent but unequal patterns of economic, social, and cultural development.

More moderate is Butler's (1980) destination life-cycle model, which Weaver and Lawton (1999) regard as the culmination of the cautionary platform because of its core assertion that continued laissez-faire tourism development eventually results in the breaching of any destination's economic, environmental, and sociocultural carrying capacities, and eventual "decline" if no remediation is undertaken (see chapter 16). Although the terminology of "sustainability" was not yet employed in their rhetoric, the Butler model and the cautionary platform in general clearly regarded conventional mass tourism as unsustainable, given also that the concept of "development" was perceived as involving issues of equity and autonomy, and not simply the increase in per capita GNP. Supporters of the cautionary platform vary in the extent to which capitalism is regarded as playing a legitimate role in the development process, with some Dependency theorists arguing for a complete withdrawal from the global capitalist system.

While all highly critical of conventional mass tourism, exponents of the cautionary platform did not articulate models of tourism development that would avoid the fundamental problems it had identified. The appearance of these purportedly more appropriate options in the early 1980s signifies, according to Jafari, the emergence of the *adaptancy platform*. Because the cautionary platform emphasized the contradictions of mass tourism, it is not surprising that the adaptancy platform focused on the virtues of small-scale "alternative tourism" (Dernoi 1981; Singh, Theuns, and Go 1989) or allied concepts such as *sanfter Tourismus* (CIPRA 1985). Supporters presented mass tourism and alternative tourism as diametrically opposed "ideal types," wherein the former is described as contrived, obtrusive, externally controlled, and growth-oriented while the latter is authentic, unobtrusive, "community"-controlled and equilibrium-oriented (Weaver 1991; Clarke 1997). This indicates a perception of "development" that augments Dependency impulses with neo-Malthusian "limits to growth" influences (e.g., Erlich and Erlich 1970; Meadows et al. 1972) and the "small is beautiful" ideas of Schumacher (1974).

Early manifestations of alternative tourism were sociocultural (as for example in the "meet the people" programs in India and the "cultural villages" of Senegal) and political (including work on cooperatives in Cuba and Israel, and "awareness" trips to Nicaragua), with church groups such as the Ecumenical Coalition on Third World Tourism (ECTWT) playing a prominent role in the diffusion of this sector. Nature-based manifestations of alternative tourism, with an emphasis on environmental sustainability, appeared in the late 1980s under the rubric of "ecotourism" (Ziffer 1989; Boo 1990) (see chapter 46), which reflected the added influence of the contemporary environmentalist movement.

The knowledge-based platform and sustainable tourism

The perceived contradictions within the advocacy platform (i.e., that laissez-faire tourism growth eventually degrades the resources that attract tourists in the first place) gave rise to the cautionary platform, and the adaptancy platform in turn built on the latter by proposing purportedly more appropriate tourism alternatives. Subsequently, contradictions within the adaptancy platform combined with overall limitations in the existing structure of tourism platforms to promote the rise in the early 1990s of the so-called *knowledge-based platform.* These contradictions included the potentially harmful intrusions of alternative tourists into the private "backstage" of the local community, and the damage that these visitors can cause to sensitive natural and cultural environments that have not been site-hardened to accommodate even small levels of visitation. Alternative tourists can inadvertently serve as "explorers" who expose such destinations to more intensive forms of tourism development, and can generate or exacerbate intra-community rivalries as locals compete to provide goods and services. Furthermore, the small numbers of visitors that are inherent to alternative tourism may generate insufficient revenue to foster the level of economic development desired by the local population (Weaver 2001) or, in the case of ecotourism, to trigger an incentive effect in protecting natural environments from more destructive forms of resource exploitation. Community involvement, a cornerstone of alternative tourism, is potentially impeded by problems of definition (who belongs to the "local community"?), internal politics, cost and benefit distribution and public apathy. Moreover, the small businesses and operations that form the core of alternative tourism are notorious for their high failure rate (McKercher 1998). Hence, engagement with alternative tourism is more likely to result in no tourism at all due to difficulties in attaining *financial* sustainability.

The above all provide reasonable counter-arguments to the assertion of adaptancy platform supporters that small-scale tourism is an intrinsically superior vehicle for fostering economic and sociocultural development, even allowing for a model of development that emphasizes autonomy, equity, and equilibrium. Moreover, the concomitant to each contradiction is that large-scale tourism can potentially mitigate the impact. That is, mass tourism is usually confined to site-hardened areas, and it generates enough revenue to induce the incentive effect. Economies of scale also allow substantial resources to be allocated for cost-effective sustainability-related practices such as sewage treatment systems, recycling, and rigorous auditing procedures (Weaver and Lawton 2002). Another basic contradiction is that alternative tourism by definition only accounts for a small portion of the world's tourism activity, which leaves open the status of mass tourism. The options of converting the latter to alternative tourism or phasing it out are both unrealistic. Mass tourism is here to stay, alternative tourism is no more than a partial and location-specific remedy (Jafari 2001), and the real issue is the imperative of ensuring that the dominant large-scale mode of tourism operates in an environmentally and socioculturally sustainable way.

This is not to argue the case for mass tourism as per the advocacy platform, which is committed and constrained ideologically to laissez-faire market forces and a pro-growth ethic that induce a cycle of destination expansion and degradation. Rather, the argument is that the cautionary and adaptancy platforms are also limited and prone to contradiction, but by their adherence to dependency and limits-to-growth ideologies. What is required, according to Jafari (2001), and what fundamentally characterizes his knowledge-based platform, is a new perspective in which science rather than the dogma of the left or right dictates the mode of tourism development and management that is most appropriate to any given destination. According to this perspective, mass tourism and alternative tourism can be both suitable and unsuitable, depending on circumstances. These circumstances include the legitimacy of different developmental goals, wherein a heavily built-up area such as Majorca or Miami might focus more on economic development, while a small rural community of indigenous people might choose to place a higher priority on cultural preservation and self-sufficiency. The knowledge-based platform, moreover, accommodates the idea that alternative and mass tourism represent gradually converging poles of a continuum within a single tourism system, wherein most tourism activity increasingly combines characteristics of both models (Clarke 1997; Jafari 2001).

The construct of "sustainable tourism," which embodies this perspective and is central to the knowledge-based platform, is an adaptation of the concept of "sustainable development," which is commonly interpreted as development that meets the needs of the present without compromising the ability of future generations to meet their own needs (WCED 1987). Sustainable development emerged from earlier science-based models of sustained yield resource management, progressive conservation and integrated resource management (Hall 1998), and was popularized through the World Conservation Strategy (WCS) of 1980, the Brundtland Report (WCED 1987), and the Rio Earth Summit of 1992 and its Agenda 21 manifesto. The Brundtland Report in its sweeping discussion of global environmental issues made no mention of tourism despite the growth and ubiquity of this sector in the mid-1980s. However, the affiliated concept of sustainable tourism appeared soon thereafter in the tourism literature and has since developed into a central paradigm for tourism academics, organizations, and practitioners (Inskeep 1991; Nelson, Butler, and Wall 1993; Middleton 1998; Mowforth and Munt 1998; Swarbrooke 1999).

Of note is the widespread engagement with sustainability within the conventional mass tourism industry, which involves the proliferation of codes of conduct (UNEP 1995) and ecolabels such as "Green Globe 21" and "Blue Flag" (Font and Buckley 2001), as well as the implementation of "green" practices such as recycling and energy use reduction (Webster 2000). Affiliated organizational initiatives include the adaptation of Agenda 21 to the travel and tourism industry, the creation of a sustainable tourism unit within the World Tourism Organization, and the creation of the global Alliance for Sustainable Tourism (WTTC 2002a). The European Union has been especially proactive in the field of sustainable tourism through programs such as Natura 2000 and LEADER (Blangy and Vautier 2001).

Factors Impeding the Attainment of Sustainable Tourism

Despite the apparently high level of engagement with sustainability principles and practices within the tourism sector, it is doubtful whether any destinations, much less tourism as a whole, can claim to have achieved a meaningful level of sustainability as of the early 2000s. The following subsections outline various factors that cumulatively help to account for this discrepancy between engagement and accomplishment. In the process, emerging contradictions within the paradigm of sustainable tourism and the knowledge-based platform are revealed.

Malleability of sustainable tourism

Smith (2001) describes "sustainable tourism" and "sustainable tourism development" as cultural constructs. As such, they are ambiguous and malleable terms that inspire multiple interpretations. This is also the case, and for similar reasons, with the parent construct of "sustainable development." The near-consensus of support for the latter is therefore deceptive, as it simply masks support for different selective interpretations of the seemingly oxymoronic construct and its vague emphasis on "wise use" and "balance" (Hall 1998). Apparent support for continued "development" is semantically appealing to advocacy platform supporters, while cautionary and adaptancy supporters find favor with the adjective "sustainable" and its implications of environmental stewardship and equilibrium dynamics. Notwithstanding the alleged neutrality of the knowledge-based platform, the same ideological residue is evident in the engagement with "sustainable tourism." Wearing and Neal (1999), like Jafari (2001), describe the latter as a bridge that spans the gap between the advocacy and cautionary/adaptancy platforms. However, it usually continues to be interpreted and implemented from either an advocacy or cautionary/adaptancy perspective. Science, far from being ideologically neutral, is selectively employed to generate "knowledge" that supports the agenda of one platform or another, and gives them credibility. Mowforth and Munt (1998), among others, further allege that many corporations employ the rhetoric of "veneer" or "pragmatic" environmentalism to "greenwash" business-as-usual products and practices that do not stand up to scrutiny.

As suggested earlier, the diversity of destinations does still provide a compelling reason for a flexible approach toward "sustainable tourism." Hunter (1997), for example, regards malleability as an asset, extolling sustainable tourism as an "adaptive paradigm" whose objectives and strategies (and the underlying ideologies of stakeholders) are likely to vary according to the type of destination being considered. Nevertheless, in addressing this contradiction of previous platforms (i.e., that a particular ideology and model of development embraces all destinations), a new contradiction emerges wherein "sustainable tourism" can mean just about anything to anyone, and in the process becomes essentially and effectively meaningless, and even diabolical.

Tourism and complexity

Even were it possible to arrive at a consensus on the developmental goals of sustainable tourism, formidable problems arise from the complexities of tourism itself, which, ironically, were cited by Jafari (2001) as a factor that spawned the need for the knowledge-based platform. Fuzzy boundaries are one aspect of this complexity, wherein the accommodation and travel agency sectors are almost wholly embedded within tourism, but restaurants and transportation are not. To what extent, therefore, is the tourism industry culpable and responsible for environmental performance in the latter sectors? Equally confounding is the quantification of tourism's indirect and induced impacts, including backward linkages in food processing and agriculture as well as other affiliated activities that do not involve face-to-face contact with tourists.

The magnitude of these affiliated effects is reflected in the difference between the tourism *industry* (activities involving face-to-face contact with tourists), which accounted for 3.6 percent of global GDP in 2002, and the tourism *economy* (i.e., direct and indirect activity together), which accounted for 10 percent (WTTC 2002b). The Gold Coast of Australia illustrates this broader influence, as only a small proportion of its labor force, and a smaller portion of its land base, is directly involved in tourism. However, most of the population and most of the area's urban growth is indirectly dependent on that sector through various backward and forward linkages. The engagement with sustainable tourism must therefore take into account physical and social effects (i.e., suburban sprawl in the Gold Coast, drilling for oil in the outback) that have no immediate or obvious linkage with tourism.

Fuzzy boundaries are one aspect of tourism's increasingly recognized status as a complex system that cannot be readily isolated or subjected to analysis in classic positivist terms (Faulkner and Russell 1997, 2000; McKercher 1999). This is germane to sustainability, since the monitoring of relevant indicators is often predicated on the "simple system" assumption of linear extrapolation, wherein a given increase in input (i.e., "cause") is associated with a predictable increase in output (i.e., "effect") (see (a) in figure 41.1). Hence, a certain amount of sewage discharged into the sea by a hotel should produce a predictable increase in the coliform count. Assuming that a threshold of environmentally "safe" coliform levels can be

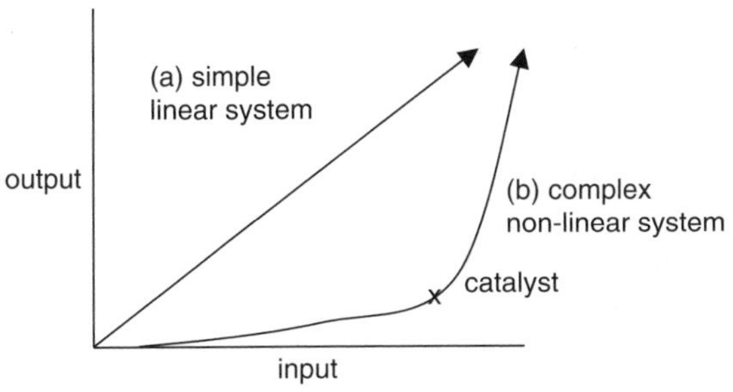

Figure 41.1 Linear and non-linear cause–effect relationships

identified, it is a simple matter to determine sustainable levels of discharge that do not breach these thresholds.

In complex non-linear systems, a period of predictable input–output relationships such as that just described may suddenly give way, through a positive feedback loop or an "avalanche effect" catalyst, to exponential increases in output, indicating a disparity between cause and effect (Bradbury 1998) (see (b) in figure 41.1). This is evident when normal levels of hotel sewage discharge suddenly give rise to a red tide, or repeated stress on infrastructure by cruise ship passengers induces a spontaneous riot by local residents. In other cases, the catalyst is an unpredictable, catastrophic event. This could potentially apply to the Gold Coast, where current rates of development appear to be sustainable, but only because the resilience of the local environment has not been tested in recent decades (that is, since most of the dunes and mangroves were modified or removed by a 100-year cyclone). The litmus test of sustainability is whether the Gold Coast and its environment can survive such an event. However, this cannot be determined in advance of the event, and hence it is not possible at present to assess whether the current intensive tourism landscape of the Gold Coast is really sustainable.

Complex systems are also characterized by spatial and temporal discontinuities between cause and effect. This is relevant because of the tendency for sustainable development and sustainable tourism initiatives to be pursued within specified parameters of space (e.g., a particular municipality or country) and time (e.g., a five-year strategic plan) due to the nature of the political process. In the spatial scenario, the cause of an unsustainable outcome within a particular destination is found beyond that destination (see figure 41.2), as when the beaches in one jurisdiction are fouled by effluent originating in another destination. Ironically, these causes may have been actions that were taken to achieve sustainable tourism. For example, the introduction of strict zoning controls in the alpine resort of Aspen, Colorado, diverted tourism-related development to nearby communities ill prepared to accommodate intensification (Gill and Williams 1994). In the temporal scenario (see figure 41.2), actions such as the construction of a pier or the decision to commodify a local cultural ceremony may yield unsustainable outcomes (e.g., erosion and loss of cultural authenticity, respectively) long after the action was taken. In both the spatial and temporal scenario, the discontinuity may make it difficult to identify the actual cause and origin of the unsustainable outcome.

A third form of discontinuity is sectoral, wherein actions in agriculture or mining have a direct or indirect impact on tourism. For example, deforestation and agricultural colonization threaten the viability of ecolodges in southern Peru (Yu, Hendrickson, and Castillo 1997), while the scuba diving industry in Indonesia is undermined by the use of poison and dynamite by reef fishers (Elliott et al. 2001). Both situations reflect the critical interrelationships between tourism and other complex systems over which the former exerts little influence. Yet, the tourism literature and tourism planners tend toward parochialism, as if the sustainability of the sector could be achieved without taking into consideration these external systems (Weaver 2001). The difficulty in engaging sustainability is compounded if these sectoral discontinuities in cause and effect are combined with the spatial and temporal discontinuities, as when clear-cutting undertaken years ago in an upstream jurisdiction has a negative effect in the present time on tourism in a downstream jurisdiction.

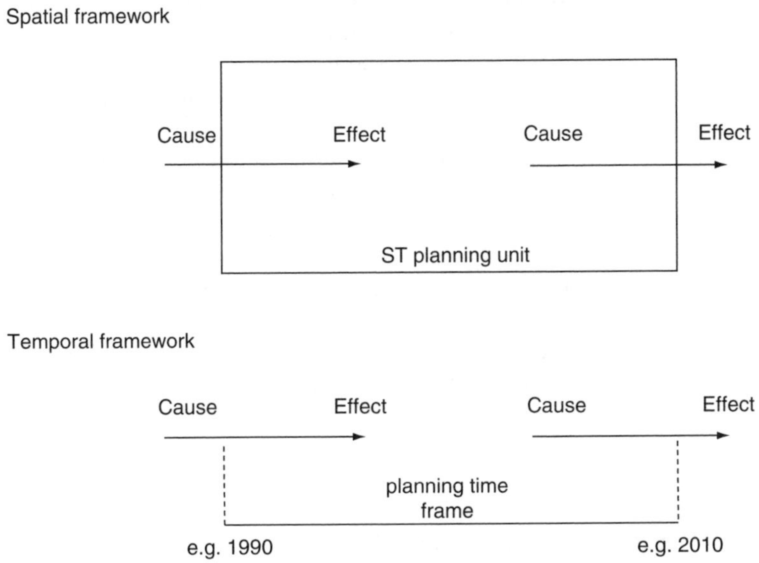

Figure 41.2 Spatial and temporal discontinuities between cause and effect
Source: From D. B. Weaver © 2000: Sustainable tourism: Is it sustainable? In B. Faulkner, G. Moscardo, and E. Laws (eds), *Tourism in the 21st Century: Lessons from Experience*. London: The Continuum International Publishing Group (p. 306). Reproduced with the permission of the publisher.

Sustainable tourism indicators

Hamilton and Attwater (1997) define indicators as variables that provide information about something so that appropriate management decisions can be made. Indicator selection, weighting, measurement, and monitoring are therefore essential to the pursuit of sustainability (however defined). Comprehensive efforts to identify tourism-related indicators have been made by the World Tourism Organization (1996) and the Groupe Développement, a Paris-based sustainable development institution. The compilation of such inventories, however, is quite different from their meaningful application, given the above critique. For example, the effective selection, measurement, and monitoring of sustainable tourism indicators is impeded by the subjectivity of the construct of sustainable tourism, the complexities of the tourism system, the uniqueness of each destination, and budgetary as well as political realities. Only a limited number of indicators can therefore be selected for effective long-term engagement. The initial efforts of the World Tourism Organization (1996), for example, yielded 11 specific measures associated with an equal number of core indicators.

Once these are selected (and assuming that they reflect the optimum combination of variables), significant benchmark and threshold values must be identified. These values, again, are determined by ideology and concomitant development objectives, and hence are highly flexible. Once these values are determined, effective measurement and monitoring procedures must be implemented. Each indicator, ideally, should be continuously assessed through time and space, but since this is not feasible for all indicators, appropriate sampling protocols need to be established. Periodically, all the indicators must be evaluated and some assessment of "sustainability" made. This raises several problems, including the weight that should be assigned to each variable and the contribution that can be attributed to tourism. Overall assessments may also be confounded by trade-offs among variables. The alienation of local communities, for example, may offset the positive environmental indicator of establishing high-order protected areas, as documented in Kenya (Akama 1996). Geographic scale is another important consideration, since it is possible to gerrymander an area so that its tourism can be pronounced internally "sustainable." In addition, the fact that the complexity of the process increases with the size of the area being considered encourages micro-level engagement (e.g., at the level of individual businesses) that is unsystematic and fragmented.

Conclusion

This analysis considers contradictions and problems that seriously impede the attainment of sustainable tourism and challenge the premises of the knowledge-based platform with which it is associated. A major concern is the oxymoronic nature of the term "sustainable tourism" and its amenability to appropriation by supporters of various ideologies, thus allowing it to be used to represent and support just about any model of development. The complexity of tourism systems, and practical problems in identifying, weighting, measuring, and monitoring sustainability indicators, are associated challenges that impede the implementation of sustainable tourism.

It may thus be asked whether the effort to pursue sustainable tourism is worthwhile or merely an unfruitful distraction. One argument in favor is that its abandonment virtually guarantees unsustainable outcomes, as per the Butler tourism life-cycle sequence (Weaver and Lawton 1999). However ambiguous and elusive, the construct of sustainable tourism provides an ideal and goal to work toward, and one moreover that is widely embraced in principle. Clarke (1997), in this vein, argues that sustainable tourism is more important as a directive than a concrete objective. Related to this is the need to fully appreciate the inherent nature of indicators – that is, they are *indications* of the status of some phenomenon, and not necessarily the basis for definitive assessments of that status. They at least usually reveal the *direction* in which the phenomenon is heading, which may be a less contentious issue than identifying specific benchmarks or thresholds (Maclaren 1996). When assessing the progress of the tourism sector with respect to these directions, it must also be stressed that engagement with sustainability is a recent phenomenon. The knowledge and progress generated since the late 1980s have been exponential (albeit generated from a very small base) as well as more scientifically informed, and as a result the appropriate paths toward sustainability are more discernible. Rapidly advancing information technologies and the creation of relevant networks and institutional frameworks suggest that this exponential growth in knowledge and capacity will continue. The amalgamation of tourism research with investigations in other systems such as agriculture and forestry is essential, since a cross-systems or integrated approach is vital to engaging successfully with sustainability. Ultimately, it will never be possible to assess any destination or product as being environmentally and socioculturally sustainable beyond any doubt. Perhaps the best that can be expected therefore is honest engagement with the objective, marked by continued dialogue, demonstrated intent to improve on the status quo, and a willingness to address problems promptly and effectively as they are identified.

REFERENCES

Akama, J. (1996). Western environmental values and nature-based tourism in Kenya. *Tourism Management* 17, 567–74.

Beckford, G. (1972). *Persistent Poverty: Underdevelopment in Plantation Economies in the Third World*. New York: Oxford University Press.

Blangy, S., and Vautier, S. (2001). Europe. In D. Weaver (ed.), *The Encyclopedia of Ecotourism* (pp. 155–71). Wallingford: CAB International.

Boo, E. (1990). *Ecotourism: The Potentials and Pitfalls*, vol. 1. Washington, DC: World Wildlife Fund.

Bradbury, R. (1998). Sustainable development as a subversive issue. *Nature and Resources* 34(4), 7–11.

Butler, R. W. (1980). The concept of a tourist area cycle of evolution: Implications for management of resources. *Canadian Geographer* 24, 5–12.

CIPRA (1985). *Sanfter Tourismus: Schlagwort oder Chance für den Alpenraum?* Vaduz, Liechtenstein: Commission Internationale pour la Protection des Régions Alpines.

Clarke, J. (1997). A framework of approaches to sustainable tourism. *Journal of Sustainable Tourism* 5, 224–33.

de Kadt, E. (1979). *Tourism: Passport to Development?* Oxford: Oxford University Press.

Dernoi, L. (1981). Alternative tourism: Towards a new style in North–South relations. *International Journal of Tourism Management* 2, 253–64.

Elliott, G., Mitchell, B., Wiltshire, B., Manan, I., and Wismer, S. (2001). Community participation in marine protected area management: Wakatobi National Park, Sulawesi, Indonesia. *Coastal Management* 29, 295–316.

Erlich, P., and Erlich, A. (1970). *Population, Resources, Environment*. San Francisco: W. H. Freeman.

Faulkner, B., and Russell, R. (1997). Chaos and complexity in tourism: In search of a new paradigm. *Pacific Tourism Review* 1, 93–102.

Faulkner, B., and Russell, R. (2000). Turbulence, chaos and complexity in tourism systems: A research direction for the new millennium. In B. Faulkner, G. Moscardo, and E. Laws (eds), *Tourism in the 21st Century: Lessons from Experience* (pp. 328–49). London: Continuum.

Finney, B., and Watson, K. (eds) (1975). *A New Kind of Sugar: Tourism in the Pacific*. Honolulu: East-West Center.

Font, X., and Buckley, R. (eds) (2001). *Tourism Ecolabelling: Certification and Promotion of Sustainable Management*. Wallingford: CAB International.

Frank, A. (1967). *Capitalism and Underdevelopment in Latin America*. New York: Monthly Review Press.

Gill, A., and Williams, P. (1994). Managing growth in mountain tourism communities. *Tourism Management* 15, 212–20.

Hall, C. (1998). Historical antecedents of sustainable development and ecotourism: New labels on old bottles? In C. Hall and A. Lew (eds), *Sustainable Tourism: A Geographical Perspective* (pp. 13–24). Harlow: Longman.

Hamilton, C., and Attwater, R. (1997). Measuring the environment: The availability and use of environmental statistics in Australia. *Australian Journal of Environmental Management* 4(2), 72–87.

Harrigan, N. (1974). The legacy of Caribbean history and tourism. *Annals of Tourism Research* 2, 13–25.

Hunter, C. (1997). Sustainable tourism as an adaptive paradigm. *Annals of Tourism Research* 24, 850–67.

Inskeep, E. (1991). *Tourism Planning: An Integrated and Sustainable Development Approach*. New York: Van Nostrand Reinhold.

Jafari, J. (1989). An English language literature review. In J. Bystrzanowski (ed.), *Tourism as a Factor of Change: A Sociocultural Study* (pp. 17–60). Vienna: Centre for Research and Documentation in Social Sciences.

Jafari, J. (2001). The scientification of tourism. In V. L. Smith and M. Brent (eds), *Hosts and Guests Revisited: Tourism Issues of the 21st Century* (pp. 28–41). New York: Cognizant Communication Corporation.

Lea, J. (1988). *Tourism and Development in the Third World*. New York: Routledge.

Maclaren, V. (1996). Urban sustainability reporting. *Journal of the American Planning Association* 62, 184–206.

McKercher, B. (1998). *The Business of Nature-Based Tourism*. Elsternwick, Victoria: Hospitality Press.

McKercher, B. (1999). A chaos approach to tourism. *Tourism Management* 20, 425–34.

Meadows, D. H., Meadows, D. L., Randers, J., and Behrens, W. (1972). *The Limits to Growth*. New York: Signet.

Middleton, V. (1998). *Sustainable Tourism: A Marketing Perspective*. Oxford: Butterworth-Heinemann.

Mowforth, M., and Munt, I. (1998). *Tourism and Sustainability: New Tourism in the Third World*. London: Routledge.

Nelson, J. G., Butler, R. W., and Wall, G. (1993). *Tourism and Sustainable Development: Monitoring, Planning, Managing*. Waterloo, Canada: University of Waterloo.

Rostow, W. (1960). *The Stages of Economic Growth*. Cambridge: Cambridge University Press.

Schumacher, E. (1974). *Small Is Beautiful*. London: Abacus.

Sharpley, R. (2000). Tourism and sustainable development: Exploring the theoretical divide. *Journal of Sustainable Tourism* 8, 1–19.

Singh, T. V., Theuns, H., and Go, F. (eds) (1989). *Towards Appropriate Tourism: The Case of Developing Countries*. Frankfurt: Peter Lang.

Smith, V. L. (2001). Sustainability. In V. L. Smith and M. Brent (eds), *Hosts and Guests Revisited: Tourism Issues of the 21st Century* (pp. 187–200). New York: Cognizant Communication Corporation.

Swarbrooke, J. (1999). *Sustainable Tourism Management*. Wallingford: CAB International.

Turner, L., and Ash, J. (1975). *The Golden Hordes: International Tourism and the Pleasure Periphery*. London: Constable.

UNEP (1995). *Environmental Codes of Conduct for Tourism*. Paris: United Nations Environment Programme.

WCED (World Commission on Environment and Development) (1987). *Our Common Future*. Oxford: Oxford University Press.

Wearing, S., and Neal, J. (1999). *Ecotourism Impacts, Potentials and Possibilities*. Melbourne: Butterworth-Heinemann.

Weaver, D. B. (1991). Alternatives to mass tourism in Dominica. *Annals of Tourism Research* 18, 414–32.

Weaver, D. B. (2000). Sustainable tourism: Is it sustainable? In B. Faulkner, G. Moscardo, and E. Laws (eds), *Tourism in the 21st Century: Lessons from Experience*. London: Continuum.
Weaver, D. B. (2001). *Ecotourism*. Brisbane: John Wiley.
Weaver, D. B., and Lawton, L. J. (1999). *Sustainable Tourism: A Critical Analysis*. Research Report No. 1. Gold Coast, Australia: CRC for Sustainable Tourism.
Weaver, D. B., and Lawton, L. J. (2002). *Tourism Management*, 2nd edn. Brisbane, Australia: John Wiley.
Webster, K. (2000). *Environmental Management in the Hospitality Industry: A Guide for Students and Managers*. London: Cassell.
WTO (1996). *What Tourism Managers Need to Know: A Practical Guide to the Development and Use of Indicators of Sustainable Development*. Madrid: World Tourism Organization.
WTTC (2002a). AGENDA 21 for the travel and tourism industry towards environmentally sustainable development. <http://www.wttc.org/stratdev/agenda21.asp> (accessed May 1, 2002).
WTTC (2002b). The impact of travel and tourism on jobs and the economy – 2002. <http://www.wttc.org/ecres/TSA%202002/TSA%20%202002%20Executive%20Summary.pdf> (accessed May 6, 2002).
Yu, D., Hendrickson, T., and Castillo, A. (1997). Ecotourism and conservation in Amazonian Peru: Short-term and long-term challenges. *Environmental Conservation* 24, 130–8.
Ziffer, K. (1989). *Ecotourism: The Uneasy Alliance*. Washington, DC: Conservation International.

Part VIII Policies, Planning, and Governance

Chapter 42

Tourism and Public Policy

C. Michael Hall and John Jenkins

This chapter seeks to present an overview of studies in tourism politics and public policy. It begins by defining "politics" and "public policy," moves on to examine studies of tourism policy, and then discusses ways forward. The massive growth of tourism, the involvement of governments, and the perceived negative impacts of tourism in developing countries helped bring about an increase of activity in tourism policy analysis especially in the late 1980s and early 1990s, with the work of Matthews (1975, 1978, 1983; Matthews and Richter 1991) and Richter (1980, 1983, 1984, 1989; Richter and Waugh 1986) providing a seminal contribution to scholarship. It is only since the 1970s that tourism public policy has become a high priority of governments in developed and less developed countries. Among other things, interrelated processes in the globalization of economies, internationalization of financial markets, massive growth of multinational corporations, economic restructuring, environmental damage, and, most recently, terrorism have collectively sparked public sector decision and action (or in some cases debate followed by non-decision and inaction) with respect to tourism. Many institutions of the state in developing and developed countries are now enveloped in important tourism matters. Some such institutions have been born out of specific tourism concerns, for example with respect to national and regional tourism promotion (Pearce 1992). Nevertheless, many agencies of the state have an interest in tourism although they are not tourism-specific institutions. For example, customs and immigration departments which police the entry of international visitor arrivals, or national parks agencies which have a major conservation mandate even though they also manage a significant attraction to tourists in many parts of the world (Hall 2000). In other words, there is need for a broadly based approach to understanding the regulatory framework for tourism.

Politics and public policy are extremely significant aspects of tourism matters, whether they be local, regional, national, or global in scale (or are constituted as multi-level governance), because of their role in regulating the tourism industry and tourist activity. Multi-level analysis of tourism policy has tended to be traditionally focused on tourism decision-making in federal systems (Richter 1989; Craik 1991a,

1991b; Jenkins 1997). Nevertheless, tourism policy is increasingly becoming related to broader government strategies with respect to trade and promotion at both national and regional levels, while the significant role of sub-national tourism authorities as actors in international relations is only just beginning to be recognized (Hall 2000). This situation also highlights the interplay between tourism policy development and multi-level governance and processes of economic globalization. Authors such as Jessop (1999) and Higgott (1999) point to this strategic interpretation of globalization, which refers to individual and institutional policy actors' attempts to promote the global coordination of activities on a continuing basis within different orders or functional systems. Examples of such processes may include:

- the formation of regional economic and trading blocs – particularly in the triadic regions of North America (North American Free Trade Area (NAFTA)), Europe (European Union (EU)) and East Asia-Pacific (Asia-Pacific Economic Cooperation) – and the development of formal links between those blocs (e.g. the Asia–Europe Meetings);
- the growth of "local internationalization," "virtual regions," through the development of economic ties between contiguous, for example "border regions," or non-contiguous local and regional state authorities, for example growth regions and triangles, in different national economies which often bypass the level of the nation-state but which still retain support at the national level; and
- the widening and deepening of international and supranational regimes which cover economic and economically relevant issues and which may also provide for regional institutionalized governance.

All of these shifts in economic globalization have substantial implications for tourism policy. For example, Hall (2001a) highlighted the increasing role of tourism in new supranational structures in relation to the specific goals of such organizations to not only encourage greater tourist flows but also mobility of labor for the tourism industry. Similarly, within the European Union there are substantial tourism policy stresses and strains which play out in the interplay between local, regional, national, and supranational levels of governance and which have substantial implications for economic development and political citizenships, including the level of participation in the development of policy (Williams and Shaw 1998). Nevertheless, despite the practical significance of tourism politics and policy for the character and nature of tourism, the field is relatively poorly developed in relation to other areas of tourism research in terms of theoretical developments, empirical understandings, and the extent of published works.

Politics, Public Policy, and Political Systems

Society's understandings of the *polis* (political association) and *polity* (constitution) have certainly changed since Aristotle's time (see, e.g., Dahl 1965). Politics and policy are not easily separated in English, while in major European languages, there is no distinction (see Colebatch 2002). As Colebatch (2002: 68) observed, there "is always an element of politics in the policy process, but the distinction between politics and policy is drawn on in shaping the action." We very often see references to politics as a form of struggle and policy as an outcome (e.g., books and papers titled "the politics of 'something' policy"), but they are difficult to separate in practice. Indeed, Considine (1994: 4) takes a view that "policy is the continuing work done by groups of policy actors who use available public institutions to articulate and express the things they value."

Public policy is more than what governments do. Policy-making is a political activity, influenced by (and constitutive of) the economic and social characteristics of society, as well as by the formal structures of government and other features of the political system. The nature of the policy-making process in any nation-state varies over space and time, and varies among policy sectors or policy communities. Attempts to analyze policy are made complex not only by decisions, actions, and events, but by the knowledge that there is no coherent or universally accepted theory of public policy processes, and no single means of explaining events. "Analysis has come to centre on a search for patterns and relationships that explain as well as describe the actions of governments. Central to this concern has been the view that political authorities are not simply receptors of political demands and the state not simply a mechanism for sorting out and pronouncing on them" (Atkinson and Chandler 1983: 3). As Minogue put it, "any satisfactory explanatory theory of public policy must also explain the inter-relations between the state, politics, economy and society" (Minogue, n.d.: 5, in Ham and Hill 1984: 17). Policy is therefore a consequence of the political environment, values and ideologies, the distribution of power, institutional frameworks, and of decision-making processes (Simeon 1976).

Given the interaction of numerous forces in the policy-making process (e.g., individuals, agencies, laws, perceptions, ideas, choices, processes, and the distribution of power), it is not surprising to find that there is little agreement in public policy studies as to what public policy is, how to identify it, and how to clarify it. Nevertheless, a common element in definitions is that "public policies stem from governments or public authorities... A policy is deemed a public policy not by virtue of its impact on the public, but by virtue of its source" (Pal 1992: 3).

Thomas Dye defined public policy as "whatever governments choose to do or not to do" (Dye 1992: 2). Following on from this Hall and Jenkins described tourism public policy as whatever governments choose to do or not to do with respect to tourism (e.g., Jenkins 1993, 2001; Hall 1994, 2000; Hall and Jenkins 1995). However, there is increasing skepticism about the effectiveness of government, particularly central government, and the intended consequences and impacts of much government policy with respect to tourism (Jenkins 1997, 2001; Jenkins, Hall, and Troughton 1998). For example, as Richter (1989: 21) observed, "critics of current tourism policies are becoming aware and are more than a little cynical about the excesses and 'mistakes' occasioned by national tourism development schemes." Nevertheless, even given demands for "smaller government" in much of the Western world, market failure still provides a number of rationales for state intervention in tourism, including:

- improving economic competitiveness;
- amending property rights;
- enabling state decision-makers to take account of externalities;

- providing widely available public benefits;
- reducing risk and uncertainty;
- supporting projects with high capital costs and involving new technologies; and
- educating and providing information.

Nevertheless, what is regarded as appropriate in terms of state intervention in tourism is not a constant but is affected by changing political ideologies. The tendency to privatize and commercialize functions that were once performed by government which has been almost universal in Western nations since the late 1970s has substantially affected the nature of many national governments' involvement in the tourism industry (Pearce 1992; Hall and Jenkins 1995; Elliott 1997; Hall 2000). According to Davis et al. (1993: 24) three principal economic reasons for this trend can be identified: "governments are interested in reducing the dependency of public enterprises on public budgets, in reducing public debt by selling state assets, and in raising technical efficiencies by commercialization." However, the economic reasons are themselves shrouded in political rationales that relate to broader philosophical perspectives which have most often been associated with a "New Right," corporatist or neo-conservative economic agenda which in various countries was labeled as "Reaganism" (USA), "Thatcherism" (UK), or "Rogernomics" (New Zealand).

In such a political climate the role of government in tourism has undergone a dramatic shift from a traditional public administration model which sought to implement government policy for a perceived public good, to a corporatist model which emphasizes efficiency, investment returns, the role of the market, and relations with stakeholders, usually defined as industry (Hall 1999). Corporatism, here, is used in the sense of a dominant ideology in Western society which claims rationality as its central quality and which emphasizes a notion of individualism in terms of self-interest rather than the legitimacy of the individual citizen acting in the democratic interest of the public good (see Saul 1995). However, in many policy areas, including tourism, the changed role of the state and the individual's relation to the state provides a major policy quandary. On the one hand there is the demand for less government interference in the market and allowing industries to develop and trade without government subsidy or assistance, while, on the other, industry interest groups seek to have government policy developed in their favor, including the maintenance of government funding for promotion and development. This policy issue has generally been resolved through the restructuring of national and regional tourist organizations to (a) reduce their planning, policy and development roles and increase their marketing and promotion functions and (b) engage in a greater range of partnerships, networks, and collaborative relationships with stakeholders. Such a situation has been described by Milward (1996) as the hollowing out of the state in which the role of the state has been transformed from one of hierarchical control to one in which governing is dispersed among a number of separate, non-government entities. This has therefore led to increased emphasis on governance through network structures as a "*new* process of governing; or a changed condition of ordered rule; or the *new* method by which society is governed" (Rhodes 1997: 43).

The implications of the restructuring of government involvement in tourism have been well documented (e.g. Craik 1991b; Hall and Jenkins 1995; Bonham and Mak 1996). For example, in the United States the state of Colorado's tourism offices were abolished by voters, while Oregon and Virginia privatized their state offices in the desire to gain greater levels of private sector funding (Bonham and Mak 1996). Similarly, in Australia and Canada, state tourism offices have been corporatized, with greater emphasis being given to the establishment of partnerships with industry in joint marketing and promotional campaigns (Hall and Jenkins 1995). Such a situation clearly indicates that, far from being abstract, government tourism policy, may have very practical affects on tourism.

The definition of public policy used by Hall and Jenkins (1995) covers government action, inaction, decisions, and non-decisions as it implies a *deliberate* choice between alternatives. Seen in this way, public policy is a process (see Ham and Hill 1984; Hogwood and Gunn 1984; Dye 1992; Davis et al. 1993). Policies are formulated and implemented in dynamic environments where there is a complex pattern of decisions, actions, interaction, reaction, and feedback. An extremely influential perspective is that of Dye (1978), who noted that the focus of political science was

> shifting to *public policy* – to the *description and explanation of the causes and consequences of government activity*. This involves a description of the content of public policy; an assessment of the impact of environmental forces on the content of public policy; an analysis of the effect of various institutional arrangements and political processes on public policy; an inquiry into the consequences of various public policies for the political system; and an evaluation of the impact of public policies on society, in terms of both expected and unexpected consequences. (1978: 5)

"Policy, then, involves *conscious* choice that leads to deliberate action – the passage of a law, the spending of money, an official speech or gesture, or some other observable act – or inaction" (Brooks 1993: 12). For a policy to be regarded as public policy, at the very least it must have been processed, even if only authorized or ratified, by public agencies (Hall and Jenkins 1995). This is an important caveat because it means that the "policy may not have been significantly developed within the framework of government" (Hogwood and Gunn 1984: 23). Pressure groups (e.g., tourism industry associations, conservation groups, community groups) (Tyler and Dinan 2001), significant individuals (e.g., local government councillors, business leaders), members of the bureaucracy (e.g., employees within tourism organizations or development agencies) and others (e.g., academics and consultants), all influence and perceive public policies in significant and often markedly different ways (Craik 1991a; Hall and Jenkins 1995; Hall 2000). Furthermore, policy outputs, i.e. a policy statement or plan, need to be distinguished from policy outcomes, the actual effects of policies, as policy outcomes may be unintended even if policy itself is rational choice in action. Nevertheless, as Cunningham (1963: 229) suggested, "policy is like the elephant – you recognize it when you see it but cannot easily define it." Cunningham's statement is significant in that it implicitly contributes to the numerous approaches which tourism policy studies can take.

Studying Tourism Public Policy: A Context

Public policy is a separate academic discipline in its own right. It is an important area of academic scholarship that generates much debate, research, and literature. Interest in public policy research has grown considerably since the 1960s. That growth began in the United States and Britain as social scientists were attracted to the applied, socially relevant, multi-disciplinary, integrative, and problem-directed nature of policy analysis (Hogwood and Gunn 1984). Pleas for more policy relevance (Easton 1969), the speedy growth of public policy activity, and government intervention after the Second World War, and the failure of many policy initiatives, also contributed to the growth in public policy research and mirrored the call for greater relevance in other social science disciplines, such as geography (Harvey 1974). Arguably, however, such policy foci have had only limited impact on the study of tourism (see Williams and Shaw 1988; Hall 1994, 2000; Hall and Jenkins 1995). Similarly, the subject of tourism has had little direct impact on public policy with extremely few articles on tourism actually appearing in policy studies journals, although cognate fields such as the environment, national parks, and coastal zone studies have received significant attention in the policy literature.

A conceptual understanding of the policy-making process is fundamental to the analysis of public policy in the tourism policy arena, because policies imply theories (Brooks 1993). Public policy theory serves as the basis for explaining decision-making and policy-making processes, and for identifying the causal links between events. "A theory serves to direct one's attention to particular features of the world, thus performing the essential task of distinguishing the significant from the irrelevant" (Brooks 1993: 28). Yet, the importance, use and relevance of particular public policy theories often rest on the research philosophy and world views of the analyst or those who designed the study. Put simply, *people* decide on definitions and theories that are relevant to the scope and features of the policy process under investigation. *People* tend to view policies and policy-making through their own world-views, and these will, more or less, dictate a study's outcomes (see, e.g., Allison 1971; Brooks 1993; Majone 1980, 1989; Mitchell 1989).

"Problem solving for the policy analyst is as much a matter of creating a problem (1) worth solving from a social perspective and (2) capable of being solved with the resources at hand, as it is of converging to a solution when given a problem" (Wildavsky 1979: 388). Policy analysis "is synonymous with creativity" (Wildavsky 1979: 3) and is akin to an "art" or "craft" (Holt and Turner 1974; Wildavsky 1979; Majone 1980, 1989). Both Majone and Wildavsky see policy analysis as an activity for which there can be no fixed program. Theory is the tool of the artisan. Description, analysis, and explanation, and the use of appropriate theory to help explain events, are necessarily influenced by the researcher's ability and desire to manipulate data, and by his or her intellectual bias. Different theoretical perspectives – for example pluralist, elitist, Marxist, corporatist (Ham and Hill 1984), or pluralist, public choice, and Marxist (Brooks 1993) – while not mutually exclusive, conceptualize the policy process in distinct ways. For example, the analysis of tourism could be undertaken within a neo-Marxist framework, emphasizing power relations among classes in society and the relationships between economic and political power. Such a perspective was quite significant in the 1970s and 1980s (Papson 1981; Thurot and Thurot 1984), particularly with respect to analyses of tourism in underdeveloped countries (Britton 1982a, 1982b; Francisco 1983) as well as influencing the development of post-structural approaches to the study of tourism (Aitchison, McLeod, and Shaw 2000). "In the neo-Marxist view of the state, public policies are portrayed on a large canvas, and the key to understanding the actions of the state is to recognize that the capitalist class enjoys certain structural advantages. These advantages derive from the fact that in a capitalist system investment decisions (what is to be produced and how resources are to be allocated) are decisions made in large measure by business" (Atkinson and Chandler 1983: 4). Such neo-Marxist perspectives have also been extremely important in developing an appreciation of the political economy of tourism and the role of the state (Hall 1998c; Dieke 2000; Bianchi 2002; see also chapter 5, this volume). In contrast a public choice approach derived from neoclassical economics which stresses the role of rational utility-maximizing decision-making and presents the state as a rational provider of public goods provides a substantially different conception of the tourism policy process and the role of government within it (Michael 2001). Moreover, theories can be distinguished from one another by their *level of analysis*, in terms of their *world view*, and by the *methods* they typically employ in studying public policy (Brooks 1993). Each perspective therefore differs in its assumptions about political conflict, the appropriate level of analysis, and the research method.

The above situation has contributed to the lack of a dominant or coherent approach in tourism policy studies as with public policy studies in general. Nevertheless, policy research, and, indeed, research throughout the sciences, can be built on two main types of theory: that which adopts prescriptive models and that which adopts descriptive models (Mitchell 1989; Brooks 1993). "Prescriptive or normative models seek to demonstrate how policy-making should occur relative to pre-established standards," whereas "descriptive models document the way in which the policy process actually occurs" (Mitchell 1989: 264). Prescriptive (normative) models serve as a guide to an ideal situation. However, a descriptive approach is preferred when exploring a new territory in a particular policy arena. Descriptive (positive) theories/models hopefully give rise to explanations about what happened during the decision-making and policy-making processes. They help analysts to understand the effects that choice, power, perception, values, and process have on policy-making. In other words, although prescriptive models are deductive, one cannot deduce in the absence of prior knowledge. Examples of prescriptive policy studies in tourism include the work of Edgell (1990) as well as the policy publications of organizations such as the World Tourism Organization or the World Travel and Tourism Council, and many government bodies (Hall 2000). However, although here has been a substantial growth in descriptive policy studies in tourism in recent years (e.g., Richter 1989; Pearce 1992, 2001; Jenkins 1997; Hall 1998a, 1998b, 2001b; Hall and Oehlers 2000; Chambers and Airey 2001; d'Hauteserre 2001; Henderson 2001; Tyler and Dinan 2001; Wearing and Huyskens 2001; Whitford, Bell, and Watkins 2001), only a small number of policy studies have explicitly sought to link accounts of tourism policy-making to theories of public policy (e.g., Doorne 1998; Dredge 2001; Jenkins 2001; Hall 2002).

Unfortunately, the study of tourism, politics, and public policy lacks a coherent thread and a broader comparative perspective (Hall and Jenkins 1995). This is perhaps not surprising. Globally, academic research in tourism did not become widespread until the 1990s, and there is still little in-depth analysis of tourism policies in many countries. There are few tourism researchers with backgrounds in political science, public policy, and politics, and hence a lack of critical engagement with public policy theory. In addition, there is a relative absence of formal international research groups, such as academic associations, which explicitly examine tourism policy, in the way such groups exist for tourism geography, anthropology, marketing, or history. Nonetheless, Hall and Jenkins (1995) provided a conceptual framework for the study of tourism public policy, which has been adapted to studies of tourism policy and planning in locations such as the Wellington waterfront in New Zealand (Doorne 1998), and Northern Territory (Pforr 2001) and Lake Macquarie in Australia (Dredge 2001). Hall and Jenkins (1995) note several aspects as essential to critical analysis of tourism public policy:

- analyze public policy at a number of levels (macro, middle, and micro) over time and space;
- incorporate the historical imprint of earlier decisions, actions, procedures, and programs, as a short-term account of the public policy process might provide misleading findings;
- utilize the case-study approach;
- link description, theory, and explanation;
- give explicit recognition to ideology, power, and values as well as institutional arrangements;
- acknowledge that the values of the researcher surround all that is done in the course of a study. Subsequent to available information, the values of any researcher may constrain information sources, methodology, analysis, and findings. The researcher may also influence who has access to the research, and the sources he or she cites may be politically motivated. Some, perhaps much, information will remain uncaptured, will not be detected, or will not be accessible.

As one or more of the above approaches is omitted, the explanatory powers of any study will likely be weakened. Moreover, critical to the analysis of tourism public policy is the explicit study of the linkage between power, ideology, values, and institutions. However, substantial differences exist over how notions of power can be applied to our understanding of how decisions are made. Aitchison, McLeod, and Shaw (2000) seek to utilize a post-structural perspective on power in their understanding of tourism landscapes, and cite the work of Elstain (1981), who described structuralist or socio-structuralist theories, such as neo-Marxist understandings of the state discussed above, as "narratives of closure" in reference to their supposedly totalizing explanations of social phenomena as products of material relations. Nevertheless, despite the popularity with post-structuralists of applying Foucauldian notions of power with respect to ideas of the gaze (Urry 1990) and social and cultural surveillance (Fyfe 1998), substantial reservations have been expressed about the usefulness of such an approach. Hartsock (1990: 169) notes that "Foucault has made it very difficult to locate domination... he has on the one hand claimed that individuals are constituted by power relations, but he has argued against their constitution by relations such as the domination of one group by another." In reflecting on these comments Aitchison, McLeod, and Shaw (2000: 4) noted that "with no systematic power there can be no overall system of domination and oppression, only specific contexts of subordination, resistance and transformation." Indeed, one of the most surprising aspects of the so-called "cultural turn" in social and cultural geography, and the cultural dimensions of tourism studies, given the supposed interest in power as expressed through postcolonial, minority, and gendered issues, is the lack of recognition of the substantial literature which exists in policy studies with respect to power and decision-making.

Power may be conceptualized as "all forms of successful control by A over B – that is, of A securing B's compliance" (Lukes 1974: 17). The use of the concept of power is inextricably linked to a given set of value assumptions which predetermine the range of its empirical application. Lukes constructed a typology of power and related concepts in an effort to clarify their meaning and relationship (table 42.1).

In drawing on the public policy literature when seeking to analyze community-based tourism, Hall (2003) utilized the work of Lukes (1974) who identified three different approaches, or dimensions, in the analysis of power, each focusing on different aspects of the decision-making process:

- a one-dimensional view emphasizing observable, overt behavior, conflict, and decision-making;
- a two-dimensional view which recognizes decisions and non-decisions and observable (overt or covert) conflict, and which represents a qualified critique of the behavioral stance of the one-dimensional view; and

Table 42.1 Typology of power and related concepts

Concept	Meaning
Authority	B complies because he recognizes that A's command is reasonable in terms of his own values, either because its content is legitimate and reasonable or because it has been arrived at through a legitimate and reasonable procedure
Coercion	Exists where A secures B's compliance by the threat of deprivation where there is a conflict over values or course of action between A and B
Force	A achieves his objectives in the face of B's non-compliance
Influence	Exists where A, without resorting to either a tacit or overt threat of severe deprivation, causes B to change his course of action
Manipulation	Is an "aspect" or sub-concept of force (and distinct from coercion, power, influence, and authority) since here compliance is forthcoming in the absence of recognition on the compiler's part either of the source or the exact nature of demand upon him
Power	All forms of successful control by A over B – that is, of A securing B's compliance

Source: Bachrach and Baratz 1970; Lukes 1974, in Hall 2003.

- a three-dimensional view which focuses on decision-making and control over the political agenda (not necessarily through decisions), and which recognizes observable (overt or covert) and latent conflict.

Each of the three dimensions arises out of, and operates within, a particular political perspective as the concept of power is "ineradicably value-dependent" (Lukes 1974: 26). For example, a pluralist conception of the tourism policy-making process, such as that which underlies the notion of community-based tourism planning (e.g., Murphy 1985), will focus on different aspects of the decision-making process, than structuralist conceptions of politics which highlight social relations within the consumption of tourist services (e.g., Urry 1990; Britton 1991). These distinctions are significant for our understanding of tourism. As Britton recognized,

> we need a theorization that explicitly recognizes, and unveils, tourism as a predominantly capitalistically organized activity driven by the inherent and defining social dynamics of that system, with its attendant production, social, and ideological relations. An analysis of how the tourism production system markets and packages people is a lesson in the political economy of the social construction of "reality" and social construction of place, whether from the point of view of visitors and host communities, tourism capital (and the "culture industry"), or the state – with its diverse involvement in the system. (1991: 475; see also chapter 5, this volume)

However, given the need to understand the dominant groups and ideologies operating within the political and administrative system which surrounds tourism, it seems reasonable to assume that the use of a wide conception of power, capable of identifying decisions, non-decisions, and community political structure, will provide the most benefit in the analysis of the political dimensions of tourism (Hall and Jenkins 1995).

Where Are We Now?

According to Kosters (1984: 612), "if a multi-disciplinary tourism science develops without the necessary ingredient of political analysis, it will remain imperfect and incomplete." Tourism public policies are enmeshed in a dynamic, ongoing process, and it has become increasingly evident that governments struggle to comprehend the tourism industry, its impacts and future, and how they should intervene (Williams and Shaw 1988; Pearce 1992; Elliott 1997). Indeed, the impact on tourism of global events such as the terrorist attacks in the United States on September 11, 2001, the American-led invasion of Iraq in 2003, the Bali bombings in 2002, and other aspects of political instability have only served to heighten the need for a better understanding of the policy dimensions of tourism (Sönmez 1998; Anson 1999; Ioannides and Apostolopoulos 1999; Sönmez, Apostolopoulos, and Tarlow 1999; Hall 2001, 2002). For example, national security concerns in the post-September 11 environment have not only influenced travel behavior but have also affected the direct personal security measures employed to protect the traveling public (see chapter 12, this volume). By extension, and as Hall (2002) argued, not only are the media therefore significant in terms of the images that surround travel and specific destinations and which influence travel decision-making (Carter 1998), but they also have a substantial impact on the policy measures which governments take with respect to tourist safety and security:

> The stringency of application of security measures has previously ebbed and flowed in light of responses to terrorist attacks and hijackings and perceptions of risk and security and subsequent commercial and consumer pressures for convenient and cheaper travel. Even given the undoubted enormity of the events of September 11 it is highly likely that they will ebb and flow again. (Hall 2002: 462, 465)

In developed countries, the state, and government itself, has many responsibilities including defense, security, economic development, education, health, and law and order. These particular responsibilities that rest mainly with government have been the subject of much public policy inquiry. However, tourism has only relatively recently emerged as an obvious commitment and important consideration in the public sector. As a result, analysis of tourism policies is often constrained by:

- the lack of consensus concerning definitions of such fundamental concepts as "tourism," "tourist," and the "tourist industry";
- the lack of recognition given to tourism policy-making processes and the consequent lack of comparative data and case studies;
- the lack of well-defined analytical and theoretical frameworks; and
- the limited amount of quantitative and qualitative data.

The present state of tourism policy studies can now partly be said to refute Richter's contention that

> Research has bypassed the political reasons that tourism is pursued and developed in ways often seen as dysfunctional in economic and social terms. Seldom are policies scrutinized in terms of what Harold Lasswell says are the core issues of politics – who gets what, when, and how. Seldom is tourism considered in terms of the political needs of those who wield power or of the government as a whole . . . No social science discipline has evidenced less interest in tourism than political science. (1989: 18–19)

Over the years, the evidence in a broad spectrum of journals (see, e.g., *Annals of Tourism Research*, *Culture and Policy*, *Current Issues in Tourism*, *Environment and Planning D*, *Geojournal*, *Leisure Studies*, *Tourism Geographies*, *Tourism Management*), texts (e.g., Edgell 1990; Craik 1991a; Johnson and Thomas 1992; Hall 1994; Hall and Jenkins 1995; Elliott 1997), conference proceedings, and postgraduate theses testifies to the growing interest in grappling with diverse tourism public policy issues. Nevertheless, in relative terms the study of tourism policy and decision-making remains a minor area of tourism research as compared to the study of tourism marketing, economics, or geography. Yet the study of tourism policy offers the opportunity to examine many topics which should be of interest not only to the tourist industry, government agencies, and students of tourism, but to researchers working within and on the boundaries of many other disciplines (e.g., economics, geography, history, sociology). These topics include:

- the political nature of the tourism policy-making process;
- public participation in the tourism planning and policy process;
- the sources of power in tourism policy- and decision-making;
- the exercise of choice by public servants in complex policy environments;
- the means by which government and state institutions at all levels intervene in tourism;
- the means by which the tourism industry and tourist behavior are regulated; and
- perceptions as to the effectiveness of tourism policies.

Indeed, it is remarkable that, given the significance attached to cooperation and coordination in tourism development and planning (Bramwell and Lane 2000), the potential contribution of public policy to understanding these issues has only received limited recognition (Hall 1999; Jenkins 2001). Instead, much tourism planning and development literature tends to ignore or gloss over many of the political dimensions to tourism decision-making which are arguably central to understanding not only the processes of tourism development but also how they may be made more sustainable. Furthermore, given the growing awareness of the economic contribution of tourism to much of the developed world in the aftermath of September 11 it is also evident that a more sophisticated understanding of tourism policy at the international and supranational levels is required. Decisions with respect to national tourism policies, broadly interpreted, and with respect to visa requirements and security, clearly have repercussions at the local and individual levels not only within the country in which they may be made but also in locales in other countries. Perhaps more than ever tourism policy needs to be understood as occurring not only at different scales but also between institutions in different parts of the world.

Governments and their critics have become more aware of and interested in the study of the process, outcomes, and impacts of tourism public policies. Hence, the evaluation of government decisions, actions, and programs, and therefore of tourism public policies, is receiving growing recognition. "Understanding public policy is both an art and a craft" (Dye 1992: 17), and so is making tourism policy. Complex programs require extensive investigations to examine process, outcomes, and adjustments. Performance in policy analysis "depends crucially on an intimate knowledge of materials and tools, and on a highly personal relationship between the agent and his task" (Majone 1989: 45). Given the dynamic and sometimes turbulent environments in which most tourist organizations operate, the discretion of bureaucrats in policy implementation, the numerous interests that want a say in government policy, and the difficulties in balancing interests and values, it is argued that studies of tourism public policies might provide useful insights into who gets what, when, and why in the tourism policy process, and might also make a contribution to better-informed government decision-making and policy-making.

REFERENCES

Aitchison, C., McLeod, N. E., and Shaw, S. J. (2000). *Leisure and Tourism Landscapes: Social and Cultural Geographies*. London: Routledge.

Allison, G. (1971). *The Essence of Decision*. Boston: Little, Brown.

Anson, C. (1999). Planning for peace: The role of tourism in the aftermath of violence. *Journal of Travel Research* 38(1), 57–61.

Atkinson, M. M., and Chandler, M. A. (1983). Strategies for policy analysis. In M. M. Atkinson and M. A. Chandler (eds), *The Politics of Canadian Public Policy* (pp. 3–20). Toronto: University of Toronto Press.

Bachrach, P., and Baratz, M. S. (1970) *Power and Poverty: Theory and Practice*. New York: Oxford University Press.

Bianchi, R. V. (2002). Towards a new political economy of global tourism. In R. Sharpley and D. J. Telfer (eds), *Tourism and Development: Concepts and Issues* (pp. 265–99). Clevedon: Channel View Publications.

Bonham, C., and Mak, J. (1996). Private versus public financing of state destination promotion. *Journal of Travel Research* 35(2), 2–10.

Bramwell, B., and Lane, B. (eds) (2000). *Tourism Collaboration and Partnerships: Politics, Practice and Sustainability*. Clevedon: Channel View Publications.

Britton, S. G. (1982a). International tourism and multinational corporations in the Pacific: The case of Fiji. In M. J. Taylor and N. Thrift (eds), *The Geography of Multinationals* (pp. 252–74). Sydney: Croom Helm.

Britton, S. G. (1982b). The political economy of tourism in the Third World. *Annals of Tourism Research* 9(3), 331–58.

Britton, S. G. (1991) Tourism capital and place: Towards a critical geography of tourism. *Environment and Planning D: Society and Space* 9(4), 451–78.

Brooks, S. (1993). *Public Policy in Canada*. Toronto: McClelland & Stewart.

Carter, S. (1998). Tourists' and travelers' social construction of Africa and Asia as risky locations. *Tourism Management* 19, 349–58.

Chambers, D., and Airey, D. (2001). Tourism policy in Jamaica: A tale of two governments. *Current Issues in Tourism* 4(2/4), 94–120.

Colebatch, H. (2002). *Policy*. Buckingham: Open University Press.

Considine, M. (1994). *Public Policy: A Critical Approach*. South Melbourne: Macmillan Education Australia.

Craik, J. (1991a). *Resorting to Tourism: Cultural Policies for Tourist Development in Australia*. North Sydney: Allen & Unwin.

Craik, J. (1991b). *Government Promotion of Tourism: The Role of the Queensland Tourist and Travel Corporation*. Brisbane: Centre for Australian Public Sector Management, Griffith University.

Cunningham, G. (1963). Policy and practice. *Public Administration* 41, 63.

Dahl, R. A. (1965). *Who Governs? Democracy and Power in an American City*. New Haven: Yale University Press.

Davis, G., Wanna, J., Warhurst, J., and Weller, P. (1993). *Public Policy in Australia*, 2nd edn. St Leonards: Allen & Unwin.

d'Hauteserre, A.-M. (2001). The role of the French state: Shifting from supporting large tourism projects like Disneyland Paris to a diffusely forceful presence. *Current Issues in Tourism* 4(2/4), 121–50.

Dieke, P. U. C. (ed.) (2000). *The Political Economy of Tourism Development in Africa*. New York: Cognizant Communication Corporation.

Doorne, S. (1998). Power, participation and perception: An insider's perspective on the politics of the Wellington waterfront redevelopment. *Current Issues in Tourism* 1(2), 129–66.

Dredge, D. (2001). Local government tourism planning and policy-making in New South Wales: Institutional development and historical legacies. *Current Issues in Tourism* 4(2/4), 355–80.

Dye, T. (1978). *Understanding Public Policy*, 3rd edn. Englewood Cliffs: Prentice Hall.

Dye, T. (1992). *Understanding Public Policy*, 7th edn. Englewood Cliffs: Prentice Hall.
Easton, D. (1969) *A Framework for Political Analysis*. New Jersey: Prentice Hall.
Edgell, D. (1990) *International Tourism Policy*. New York: Van Nostrand Reinhold.
Elliott, J. (1997) *Tourism: Politics and Public Sector Management*. London: Routledge.
Elstain, J. B. (1981). *Public Man, Private Woman*. Princeton: Princeton University Press.
Francisco, R. A. (1983). The political impact of tourism dependence in Latin America. *Annals of Tourism Research* 10, 363–76.
Fyfe, N. R. (1998). *Images of the Street: Planning, Identity and Control in Public Space*. London: Routledge.
Hall, C. M. (1994). *Tourism and Politics: Policy, Power and Place*. London: Belhaven Press.
Hall, C. M. (1998a). The legal and political dimensions of sex tourism: The case of Australia's child sex tourism legislation. In M. Oppermann (ed.), *Sex Tourism and Prostitution: Aspects of Leisure, Recreation, and Work* (pp. 87–96). New York: Cognizant Communication Corporation.
Hall, C. M. (1998b). The politics of decision making and top-down planning: Darling Harbour, Sydney. In D. Tyler, M. Robertson, and Y. Guerrier (eds), *Tourism Management in Cities: Policy, Process and Practice* (pp. 9–24). Chichester: John Wiley.
Hall, C. M. (1998c). The institutional setting: Tourism and the state. In D. Ioannides and K. Debbage (eds), *The Economic Geography of the Tourist Industry: A Supply-Side Analysis* (pp. 199–219). London: Routledge.
Hall, C. M. (1999). Rethinking collaboration and partnership: A public policy perspective. *Journal of Sustainable Tourism* 7(3/4), 274–89.
Hall, C. M. (2000). *Tourism Planning*. Harlow: Prentice Hall.
Hall, C. M. (2001a). Territorial economic integration and globalisation. In C. Cooper and S. Wahab (eds), *Tourism in the Age of Globalisation* (pp. 22–44). London: Routledge.
Hall, C. M. (2001b). Tourism and political relationships in South-East Asia. In P. Teo (ed.), *Interconnected Worlds: Tourism in South-East Asia* (pp. 13–26). Oxford: Elsevier.
Hall, C. M. (2002). Travel safety, terrorism and the media: The significance of the issue-attention cycle. *Current Issues in Tourism* 5(5), 458–66.
Hall, C. M. (2003). Politics and place: An analysis of power in tourism communities. In S. Singh, D. Timothy, and R. Dowling (eds), *Tourism in Destination Communities* (pp. 99–114). Wallingford: CAB International.
Hall, C. M., and Jenkins, J. M. (1995). *Tourism and Public Policy*. London: Routledge.
Hall, C. M., and Oehlers, A. (2000). Tourism and politics in south and southeast Asia: Political instability and policy. In C. M. Hall and S. J. Page (eds), *Tourism in South and South-East Asia: Critical Perspectives* (pp. 77–94). Oxford: Butterworth-Heinemann.
Ham, C., and Hill, M. (1984). *The Policy Process in the Modern Capitalist State*. New York: Harvester Wheatsheaf.
Hartsock, N. C. M. (1990). Foucault on power: A theory for women. In L. Nicholson (ed.), *Feminism/Postmodernism* (pp. 157–75). London: Routledge.
Harvey, D. (1974). What kind of geography for what kind of public policy? *Transactions of the Institute of British Geographers* 63, 18–24.
Henderson, J. (2001). Regionalisation and tourism: The Indonesia–Malaysia–Singapore growth triangle. *Current Issues in Tourism* 4(2/4), 78–93.
Higgott, R. (1999). The political economy of globalisation in East Asia: The salience of "region building." In K. Olds, P. Dicken, P. F. Kelly, L. Kong, and H. W. Yeung (eds), *Globalisation and the Asia-Pacific: Contested Territories* (pp. 91–106). London: Routledge.
Hogwood, B., and Gunn, L. (1984). *Policy Analysis for the Real World*. Oxford: Oxford University Press.
Holt, R. T., and Turner, J. E. (1974). The scholar as artisan. *Policy Sciences* 5, 257–70.

Ioannides, D., and Apostolopoulos, Y. (1999). Political instability, war and tourism in Cyprus: Effects, management and prospects for recovery. *Journal of Travel Research* 38(1), 51–6.

Jenkins, J. M. (1993). Tourism policy in rural New South Wales: Policy and research priorities. *Geojournal* 29(3), 281–90.

Jenkins, J. (1997). The role of the Commonwealth Government in rural tourism and regional development in Australia. In C. M. Hall, J. M. Jenkins, and G. Kearsley (eds), *Tourism Planning and Policy in Australia and New Zealand: Cases, Issues and Practice* (pp. 181–91). Sydney: Irwin.

Jenkins, J. (2001). Statutory authorities in whose interests? The case of Tourism New South Wales, the bed tax, and the Games. *Pacific Tourism Review* 4(4), 201–18.

Jenkins, J., Hall, C. M., and Troughton, M. (1998). The restructuring of rural economies: Rural tourism and recreation as a government response. In R. Butler, C. M. Hall, and J. Jenkins (eds), *Tourism and Recreation in Rural Areas* (pp. 43–68). Chichester: John Wiley.

Jenkins, W. I. (1978). *Policy Analysis: A Political and Organisational Perspective*. London: Robertson.

Jessop, B. (1999). Reflections on globalisation and its (il)logic(s). In K. Olds, P. Dicken, P. F. Kelly, L. Kong, and L. and H. W. Yeung (eds), *Globalisation and the Asia-Pacific: Contested Territories* (pp. 19–38). London: Routledge.

Johnson, P., and Thomas, B. (eds) (1992). *Perspectives on Tourism Policy*. London: Mansell.

Kosters, M. (1984). The deficiencies of tourism science without political science: Comment on Richter. *Annals of Tourism Research* 11, 610–12.

Lukes, S. (1974). *Power: A Radical View*. London: Macmillan.

Majone, G. (1980). The uses of policy analysis. *Policy Studies Review Annual* 4, 161–80.

Majone, G. (1989). *Evidence, Argument and Persuasion in the Policy Process*. New Haven and London: Yale University Press.

Matthews, H. G. (1975). International tourism and political science research. *Annals of Tourism Research* 2(4), 195–203.

Matthews, H. G. (1978). *International Tourism: A Social and Political Analysis*. Cambridge: Schenkman.

Matthews, H. G. (1983). Editor's page: On tourism and political science. *Annals of Tourism Research* 10(4), 303–6.

Matthews, H. G., and Richter, L. K. (1991). Political science and tourism. *Annals of Tourism Research* 18(1), 120–35.

Michael, E. (2001). Public choice and tourism analysis. *Current Issues in Tourism* 4(2/4), 308–30.

Milward, H. B. (1996), Symposium on the hollow state: Capacity, control and performance in interorganizational settings. *Journal of Public Administration Research and Theory* 6(2), 193–5.

Mitchell, B. (1989). *Geography and Resource Analysis*. Harlow: Longman Scientific and Technical.

Murphy, P. (1985) *Tourism: A Community Approach*. New York and London: Methuen.

Pal, L. A. (1992). *Public Policy Analysis: An Introduction*. Nelson, Canada: Scarborough.

Papson, S. (1981). Spuriousness and tourism: Politics of two Canadian provincial governments. *Annals of Tourism Research* 8(2), 220–35.

Pearce, D. G. (1992). *Tourist Organisations*. Harlow: Longman Scientific and Technical.

Pearce, D. G. (2001). Tourism, trams and local government policy-making in Christchurch, New Zealand. *Current Issues in Tourism* 4(2/4), 331–54.

Pforr, C. (2001). Tourism policy in Australia's Northern Territory: A policy process analysis of its tourism development masterplan. *Current Issues in Tourism* 4(2/4), 275–307.

Rhodes, R. A. W. (1997). From marketisation to diplomacy: It's the mix that matters. *Australian Journal of Public Administration* 56(2) 40–53.
Richter, L. K. (1980). The political uses of tourism: A Philippine case study. *Journal of Developing Areas* 14, 237–57.
Richter, L. K. (1983). Tourism politics and political science: A case of not so benign neglect. *Annals of Tourism Research* 10, 313–35.
Richter, L. K. (1984). A search for missing answers to questions never asked: Reply to Kosters. *Annals of Tourism Research* 11, 613–15.
Richter, L. K. (1989). *The Politics of Tourism in Asia*. Honolulu: University of Hawaii Press.
Richter, L. K., and Waugh, W. L., Jr. (1986). Terrorism and tourism as logical companions. *Tourism Management* December, 230–8.
Saul, J. R. (1995). *The Unconscious Civilization*. Concord: Anansi.
Simeon, R. (1976). Studying public policy. *Canadian Journal of Political Science* 9(4), 558–80.
Sönmez, S. (1998). Tourism, terrorism, and political instability. *Annals of Tourism Research* 25(2), 416–56.
Sönmez, S., Apostolopoulos, Y., and Tarlow, P. (1999). Tourism in crisis: Managing the effects of terrorism. *Journal of Travel Research* 38(1), 13–18.
Thurot, J. M., and Thurot, G. (1984). The ideology of class and tourism confronting the discourses of advertising. *Annals of Tourism Research* 10, 173–89.
Tyler, D., and Dinan, C. (2001). The role of interested groups in England's emerging tourism policy network. *Current Issues in Tourism* 4(2/4), 210–52.
Urry, J. (1990). *The Tourist Gaze*. London: Sage.
Wearing, S., and Huyskens, M. (2001). Moving on from joint management policy regimes in Australian national parks. *Current Issues in Tourism* 4(2/4), 182–209.
Whitford, M., Bell, B., and Watkins, M. (2001). Indigenous tourism policy in Australia: 25 years of rhetoric and economic rationalism. *Current Issues in Tourism* 4(2/4), 151–81.
Wildavsky, A. (1979). *Speaking Truth to Power*. New York: John Wiley.
Williams, A. M., and Shaw, G. (1988). Tourism policies in a changing economic environment. In A. M. Williams and G. Shaw (eds), *Tourism and Economic Development: Western European Experiences* (pp. 230–9). London: Belhaven Press.
Williams, A. M., and Shaw, G. (eds) (1998). *Tourism and Economic Development: Western European Experiences*, 3rd edn. London: Belhaven Press.

Chapter 43

Partnerships, Participation, and Social Science Research in Tourism Planning

Bill Bramwell

Introduction

The growth in partnership activity in many Western nations since the late 1970s has reflected a tendency for the state to shed or reduce many of its functions. This trend emerged in the context of substantial government fiscal problems, criticisms of state activity from the neoliberal agenda of the "New Right" that have been highly politically effective, and sometimes also pressure from civil society for more direct involvement in public policies. A case can be made that all of these trends have been influenced by an undermining or "hollowing out" of nation-states related to the diverse processes of globalization (Bramwell and Lane 2000; Hall 2000a; Lovelock 2001). In developing countries the calls for decentralization and for a reduced role for the state have often resulted from concern about an excessive concentration of decision-making and authority within central government and about the poor performance of public bureaucracies (Turner and Hulme 1997). Partnerships have also been encouraged by the increased influence of sustainable development agendas, such as Agenda 21, that advocate subsidiarity and the expansion of participation in policy-making by local community groups that are directly affected by the policies (Lafferty 2000). It is in these broad contexts that partnerships involving various actors have become fairly common for tourism planning in developed countries and are also emerging in some developing nations. Partnerships are increasingly advocated as a part of "good governance," together with wider community participation and the empowerment of groups and individuals by engaging them more fully in tourism decision-making (Murphy 1985; Hall 2000b).

The term partnership is used here to describe a relatively formal process of regular, face-to-face meetings between parties, with these meetings being based on at least some agreed rules and on intentions to address shared issues. These collaborative arrangements can bring together stakeholders in the public and private sectors, as well as environmental and community groups, in order to discuss and make policy decisions about how tourism should be managed and developed (Selin and Beason 1991; Jamal and Getz 1995; Carr, Selin, and Schuett 1998). There is growing recognition of the potential benefits of collaborative tourism planning that includes various industry segments, public sector agencies, and (rather less often) other groups in civil society (Hall 2000b; World Tourism Organization 2000). The presumed potential benefits of partnership meetings include that they have the potential to promote discussion, negotiation, and the building of mutually acceptable proposals about tourism issues (Gray 1989; Healey 1997; Hall 2000b). By such means they can help to promote stakeholder democracy, and encourage capacity-building and skill acquisition among the participants. They have potential to increase the involvement of socially and economically marginalized peoples in the decision-making that affects their own lives. It has also been suggested that such collaborative arrangements may help to pool the knowledge and other resources of stakeholders, and may encourage better coordination between policies (Selin and Beason 1991).

There is perhaps less appreciation of the substantial problems associated with shared decision-making. For example, there are notable barriers to involving all relevant parties in partnerships and to ensuring that their views are listened to and considered equally. Powerful groups in joint working have many advantages that can mean that their perspectives and priorities will prevail. In addition, partnerships may "be set up simply as 'window dressing' to avoid tackling real problems head on with all interests" (Bramwell and Lane 2000: 9), or they may be used to create a semblance or illusion of broad participation in order to diffuse tensions with other parties or to legitimize projects in bureaucratic and donor circles (Few 2001). A further potential difficulty is that recent forms of partnership are normally based on approaches to "rational" management that have been developed in Western developed nations, and in some countries or areas and for some parties these partnerships may be considered irrelevant, politically unwanted, or a hindrance to effective governance. These multi-party arrangements, with their associations with "rational" management, can also operate as symbols of dominance that serve to undervalue other useful ways of influencing tourism policies. The road of apparent good intentions with regard to partnerships is rough indeed.

This chapter focuses on tourism planning partnerships that are concerned with the development process and that work across sectors by including stakeholders representing tourism, environmental, and community interests as well as various state agencies, sometimes explicitly seeking to promote more sustainable forms of development. It examines some of the obstacles to these partnerships encouraging greater inclusiveness and participation. It is also suggested that the difficulties of collaborative working mean that there may be circumstances when the goals of sustainable development are not best achieved using this approach. Consideration is given to three strategies that might be adopted in response to the problems that limit stakeholder participation in multi-party working. First, effort can be directed at making collaborative relations more inclusive, thereby widening involvement in this participatory democratic form, usually as a supplement to a representative democratic system based on elections (Prior, Stewart, and Walsh 1995; Painter 1999). Second, steps can be taken to assist the parties that are not engaged in partnerships to build their own institutional capacities and self-confidence. And, finally, actors not engaged in joint working can be consulted so that their views may be conveyed to the partnership members, who might then adjust their policies. A specific focus here is on the potential to use various approaches to social science research in order to better understand the views of these parties.

Potential Difficulties Associated with Partnerships

Tourism partnerships are much less likely to emerge and thrive in developing nations where there is no tradition of wide stakeholder participation in decision-making. For example, in some countries there is only a limited experience of democracy. Sometimes this is reflected in political decision-making resting with a narrow economic or social elite, or in clientelistic relations between individuals and politicians that include mutual obligations to grant favors and support (Tosun 2000; Mitchell 2002). Ladkin and Bertramini (2002: 86) interviewed public sector tourism officials in Cusco, a major tourist destination in Peru, and they conclude that the political culture there "engenders the need amongst public and private sector leaders to gain power and public recognition which makes coordination and collaboration between stakeholders difficult. Individual power struggles take precedence over collective opportunities." In some developing countries, poor social groups may be discouraged from becoming involved in tourism planning by a cultural acceptance that planning decisions are made by a narrow group of people, or by their long history of being excluded from such decisions. For example, in an assessment of tourism planning in Yogyakarta province in Indonesia, Timothy (1998, 1999) found a strong tradition of reverence toward people in positions of power and with high social standing, as well as an acceptance that political and social control rests in the hands of central government or a few social or political leaders. There was little pressure in this society to extend decision-making because the center was regarded as being responsible for making policy choices. Poor groups in developing countries may also be uninterested in participatory planning as they are preoccupied with economic survival. In this context, Timothy (1999: 385–6) describes how some Indonesian government planners contended that "because of their low socioeconomic status, residents are not interested in becoming involved in tourism planning; they are merely concerned with making ends meet."

Power relations are a pervasive feature of society, and consequently the concerns of less influential groups can easily be marginalized as a result of partnership arrangements (Reed 1997; Holland 2000). Dominant parties may have a disproportionate influence on which stakeholders are invited to the collaborative meetings, as well as on the agendas and deliberations in the meetings, and on the outcomes. Unless partnerships take into account the relative bargaining power of the various parties there is a real danger that they simply provide opportunities for the more powerful. For example, Hall (2000a) concludes that business interests have tended to dominate participation in collaborative tourism forums in Australia, with only limited inputs from environmental organizations and the community at large. Local communities are also divided by power relations, such as by the influence of local hegemonic elites, by the demands of different sectors of the community, and by the social distance and communication gaps between local government decision-makers and the people they represent (Mowforth and Munt 1998). Jamal and Getz (2000) identify various inequitable outcomes resulting from the round-table meetings set up to agree a growth management strategy for the tourism center of Canmore in

Canada. These meetings did not involve the less visible segments of the community or the advocates of a "no growth" strategy, and the actors who did participate in them were not listened to equally, with this being affected by the perceived legitimacy of their views and by the aggressive tactics of some participants. Such power relations mean that assumptions that stakeholders will be empowered through partnerships are often misplaced unless there are also changes within the wider economic and political context (Brown 2002). Most actors affected by a partnership organization are engaged in complex webs of social networks, possibly including participation in other collaborative arrangements, and these networks affect the actors' relations with partnership members, including the likelihood that they will be invited to partnership meetings, their perceived legitimacy and their power, and their potential alliances with partnership members (Araujo and Bramwell 2002).

The interactions between participants in multi-party meetings may be hindered by their cultural differences, based on their varying frames of reference, systems of meaning, and modes of discourse. The cultural values or sense-making frameworks of less powerful indigenous groups may mean that they are at a considerable disadvantage in partnership discussions, as the contemporary project of "modernity" means that influential groups often give priority to scientific knowledge, to instrumental and systematic discourses, and to "rational" management approaches. Consequently, in partnership negotiations the forms of knowledge, and the rationality and values of indigenous groups, may be regarded as the "other," and as inherently inferior to those of dominant groups (Healey 1997).

Another obstacle to equitable participation in planning partnerships is that these partnerships may be managed deliberately in order to achieve preconceived planning goals. For example, in a study of a government-funded, community-based program of natural resource management in Botswana, Twyman (2000) argues that the district-level government officers strategically asserted their power in their consultations with the community for the purpose of securing their own prior policy objectives. This can be described as a "containment" strategy. Few (2001) argues further that community-based conservation projects in protected parks often involve such "containment" strategies because the primary purpose of the designation of these parks is biodiversity protection rather than resource-consumptive activities such as tourism, and because the priority for conservation may be contested by the stakeholders using park resources.

While a few groups may have a hegemonic influence on partnership members, it must be remembered that collaborative relations create new spaces or sites for struggle and for the reformulation of dominant paradigms (Wearing and Huyskens 2001). It is also important to recognize that people are not passive recipients and that some individuals with less power do have the skills to manipulate and rearticulate the discourses with which they are presented (Twyman 2000). Thus, in a study of planning in two of Belize's protected coastal areas that face pressures from diving and sport fishing tourism, Few (2001: 119) concludes that, while the public sector adopted various "containment" strategies, "The very fact that planners entered negotiations with stakeholders, sought their support and sought to demonstrate their involvement in planning, opened up the opportunities for conflict, dissent and disruption." For example, projects involving multi-party working allow participants to "withhold their participation in the project as a form of control, either overtly through boycotting meetings, or implicitly through 'apathy' and 'lack of enthusiasm' for the project process" (Twyman 2000: 331). It should also be recognized that partnerships that engage several stakeholder groups potentially are more democratic and equitable than earlier approaches where tourism and environmental planning were mostly driven by a few state agencies. But, while partnerships can help to widen participation, their unequal power relations need to be taken into account explicitly.

When Not To Set Up Partnerships

The many endorsements of partnership approaches to tourism management can suggest that they must be the most appropriate organizational form in all circumstances. In particular, it might be concluded that this type of governance, based on increased organization and cooperation, is invariably the best when seeking to promote sustainable development objectives. Such conclusions have begun to be challenged. Thus, Lovelock (2002: 8) has recently called for a closer "examination of the potential advantages of underorganisation and conflict in the implementation of sustainable tourism." For example, conflict can be constructive if it raises public awareness of environmental problems, or if it alerts people to the priorities of community groups that have previously gained little attention. Non-cooperation may be particularly effective for stakeholders that lack power in the sense of formal authority, political access, or financial resources, but that have "discursive legitimacy" due to their ability to manipulate public understanding and concern (Lovelock 2002). In such circumstances, these relatively "powerless" actors may succeed in achieving their goals by using various forms of non-cooperation and conflict. For example, environmental organizations with a marginal influence on policy-makers may engage in protest activities in order to raise their profile, gain public support, and recruit members. And the parties that lack formal authority may be expressing views and policy options that could help to advance the aims of sustainability.

Contemporary partnership models are usually based on developed world or "Western" views on organizational forms that are conducive to "rational" management, and thus they may also be considered important for "modernization" (Wearing and Huyskens 2001). The increasingly prevalent rhetoric of partnership approaches to development may result in "traditional" forms of governance being discarded as backward on the grounds that they hold back a historical trajectory that is supposed to be necessary, based on the experience of the economically developed countries in the "West" (Mitchell 2002). But these partnerships may be imposed in places where the traditional approaches to collective decision-making have been relatively successful in encouraging resource conservation and in restricting unsustainable practices. These places may include those where there are long-established communal management systems for "common pool" or communally shared resources, such as applies to the resources of some reefs and upland pasture land (Berkes 1989; Bromley 1992; Healy 1994). In such circumstances the "Western" or contemporary models of partnership may be both unwanted by local communities and also inappropriate in relation to encouraging greater sustainability.

More Inclusive Relations within Partnerships

One response to some of the difficulties associated with partnerships is to work to make their operation more inclusive and participatory. This may involve working to ensure they are less planner-centered and more people-centered instead (Twyman 2000). With planner-centered approaches, the outcomes sought tend to focus on administrative and financial efficiency and on facilitating local people's acceptance of planners' views, while people-centered perspectives often seek to enhance local management capacity, increase confidence in indigenous potential, raise collective consciousness, and also meet local needs and priorities.

A more people-centered focus may be promoted by encouraging participation in partnership meetings from representatives of a broader range of relevant actors. A study of participants in a tourism and outdoor recreation alliance in the United States found that they frequently mentioned the diversity of participants as a factor in the alliance's effectiveness (Selin and Myers 1998). There is potential to use the explicit steps involved in stakeholder analysis to assist in identifying the many potential participants, as well as their main interests and their relative influence on the issues (Gregory and Keeney 1994; Araujo and Bramwell 2000). A study of a partnership set up to manage the impact of pilgrims and tourists on the surroundings of a Hindu temple complex at Changu Narayan in Nepal illustrates the importance of such organizations evaluating and adjusting to the political context and the actors with political influence. The partnership involved numerous "community" representatives and had several practical successes, but it subsequently faced a serious political challenge due to its failure to adjust to the Nepal government decentralizing key powers to a local organization not involved in the partnership (Sofield 2001). A continuing process of stakeholder evaluation or mapping might have recognized the need to involve this agency and thus might also have avoided the political difficulty. Warner (1997: 418) also argues that stakeholder analysis can be used to identify those actors that need their capacities raising, on the basis that "a 'consensus' model of participation should direct early effort towards those stakeholders who are most polarised from a capacity to negotiate collaboratively."

A more people-centered focus may also be encouraged by working to make the routines and styles of dialogue in partnership meetings more inclusive and equitable. This can involve encouraging more respectful listening, more open discussion, and a fuller exploration of what each participant really cares about and why (Healey 1997). It may then be possible to draw more successfully from local people's practical consciousness and local knowledge. Local knowledge has its own reasoning processes, and it may weave together technical reasoning, moral attitudes, and emotive feelings. Some people are familiar with the language of consequences, grounded in economic reasoning or scientific evidence. Others are more accustomed to the language of belief or the political assertion of rights. Others again may be more comfortable with the expression of fears and dangers. If the hegemony of the powerful is to be reduced, all these forms of reasoning need to be learned about and shown respect in the collaborative process. The difficult translation between these different "world views" is fundamental to the building of confidence and trust across the often deep fractures between the participants in joint working (Bramwell and

Sharman 1999). But, while steps can be taken to improve matters, in practice there are often profound tensions behind these differences in communication, and they are unlikely to be completely overcome.

There are many other, perhaps intractable, difficulties involved in widening participation in shared decision-making. One problem is that it is difficult to decide on an appropriate balance between representatives of the various interests, such as between those most concerned with economic issues and those defending the environment (Yuksel, Bramwell, and Yuksel 1999). The number of participants in multi-party meetings should also not be increased to a point where dialogue and negotiation are hindered (Williams, Penrose, and Hawkes 1998). One approach to widening participation in partnerships can be to provide training programs to build the capacities of marginalized groups. However, while training may provide representatives with the knowledge necessary to participate in meetings, it may also inculcate a series of obligations that "persuade" participants to adhere to a particular set of rules and encourage specific modes of thinking, argumentation, and language, these tending to reinforce the particular "modes of rationality" that are congruent with the sponsors of the partnership (Clegg 1989). Training and capacity-building are clearly key aspects of empowerment, yet question marks remain over the extent to which they will function to create genuine community empowerment rather than merely serving to "manage the community" (Atkinson 1999).

Capacity-Building among Parties Outside Partnerships

A different response to the difficulties of collaborative working is for partnerships to provide assistance to the parties that are not engaged in their meetings so that they can build their own capacities and self-confidence. Particular attention might be directed to those groups that are socially and economically marginalized, and this help may be provided whether or not they might subsequently join in multi-party initiatives. Such assistance may enable these groups to build their own social and intellectual capital and institutional resources, and encourage them to find their own responses to particular issues. This may involve outsiders adopting the role of advisors or enablers so as to promote the "self-mobilization" of these groups, encouraging them to retain control (Shepherd 1998; Wearing and Huyskens 2001). Shepherd argues that far more attention should be paid in developing countries to strengthening local people's organizations in order to encourage them to become much more fully engaged in their own right in rural development. He also suggests that this approach should recognize that the "community" is not just the local economic and political elites, but also the poor, women, and marginal groups, and moreover that conflict is normally a consistent feature of the life of communities. His contention is that, in rural areas in less developed nations, "Viable, sustainable organisations which can be run by the rural poor and exert an influence in the wider development arena are the mechanisms for participation" (1998: 182).

Mowforth and Munt (1998: 240) further extend this argument by contending that, in the context of tourism decision-making in developing countries, "the only forms of local participation that are likely to break the existing patterns of power and unequal development are those which originate from within the local communities themselves." In the context of eastern Europe, Pickvance (1997) argues that the tendency toward decentralization of the political arena to more local geographical scales does not lead automatically to democratization without the simultaneous development of the ability of citizens to exercise democratic rights in practice. He takes as a key index, of this ability to apply democratic rights, the activities of non-governmental organizations and social movements in civil society: "The questions I ask are whether such groups find it easy to form and develop and whether they are successful in achieving their aims, or whether they encounter resistance and repression" (Pickvance 1997: 137).

Consultation with Parties Outside Partnerships: Drawing on Social Science Research

While partnerships usually involve a relatively small number of individuals in regular, face-to-face meetings, they can be combined with other types of participation involving many more people outside of these. For example, the organization leading a multi-party partnership that used tourism to encourage sustainable development in a poor region of Brazil had consulted with many stakeholders not directly engaged in the partnership by hosting a three-day workshop at the start of the project and one-day workshops in different local areas (Araujo and Bramwell 2000, 2002). However, the resulting increase in stakeholder democracy was limited because a high proportion of workshop participants were public sector staff, and because there was only one such consultation exercise in each local area. Further, there was little local control over the process of community engagement, which appears to have had a greater focus on community inputs in order to further the project's objectives rather than on adjusting those goals.

In fact, numerous consultation techniques can be used in combination with a partnership involving a few stakeholder representatives in order to better understand the views of other non-participating stakeholders. For example, various social science research approaches and techniques can be utilized to examine the concerns and policy preferences of various actors, and the resulting findings about these concerns and preferences can help partnerships in their decision-making about tourism. This research can employ traditional surveys from a quantitative perspective, or else qualitative approaches that seek to be more processual, contextual, comparative, and emic (Cohen 1979). Emic approaches stress empathy with the actors being studied and their perspectives in order to gain a more complete understanding of their emotions, views, and interpretations. Such qualitative research may encourage greater reflexivity and self-critique, thereby providing new insights to inform the work of partnerships. The potential for such benefits encouraged Wearing and Huyskens (2001: 196–7) to advocate wider use in tourism management of "hybridised management supported by social science research."

Support for more widespread applications of ethnographic research techniques in tourism planning comes from Sandiford and Ap (1998), who highlight relevant advances in the use of these techniques in fields such as anthropology. The application of emic approaches in tourism research can entail exploring people's "world views" and seeking to understand their perspectives in their own terms. The intention behind these approaches is to give "voice" to the research subjects, and some researchers using these techniques have a particular interest in the less powerful and the marginalized (Alasuutari 1995). Pearce, Moscardo, and Ross (1996: 4) argue that in-depth studies of residents' attitudes to tourism should use emic approaches in order to "draw upon the actors' interpretations and local inside knowledge of the meaning of the behaviour under study." The potential insights from adopting an actor-oriented approach are illustrated by Verbole's (2000) examination of social changes related to the development of rural tourism in Slovenia, where she reveals the deeply ingrained influence of family clans, networks, and cliques in gaining and controlling access to relevant decision-making processes.

Obtaining more profound understanding of the "world views" of different actors through ethnographic research is not a simple task, as researchers need to challenge their own beliefs and perceptions, which are often very different to those of their subjects. Researchers need to approach the task reflexively, identifying their own "position," challenging their own interpretations, embracing ambiguity, and being candid about uncertainty (Dann and Phillips 2001; Jamal and Hollinshead 2001). One approach to understanding varied stakeholder perspectives is to use interactive or participatory action research. Here the subjects being studied are encouraged to take part in shaping the research, such as by defining their own criteria and identifying their own ways of representing and interpreting the issues being examined. Action research is particularly reliant on establishing mutual trust between the researcher and the people being studied. Such participatory research is proposed by Wearing and Huyskens (2001) and Wearing and McDonald (2002) in order to help make tourism management more democratic, notably when the intention is to help oppressed groups or communities to find solutions for themselves and to control their own destinies more effectively.

A range of social science approaches is incorporated in the action research process used by Brown (2002) and colleagues in order to assist in management decision-making in relation to Buccoo Reef Marine Park in Tobago in the eastern Caribbean. While this park is a protected area, its reef is the most visited tourist attraction in Tobago. The action research was based on "an approach to decision-making that aimed to be inclusive and consensus-based," with this approach being used in work with stakeholders affected by the Park's management (Brown et al. 2000; Brown, Tompkins, and Adger 2001; Brown 2002: 13). Several specific tasks were involved in this approach. First, the affected stakeholder groups were identified, together with their interests, influence, and impacts, and then they were involved in "envisioning" exercises to develop future development options. Estimates were made of the environmental, economic, and social impacts of the development options based on a range of surveys as well as stakeholder perceptions of likely changes. Small group sessions were later used to review the issues and to identify stakeholder priorities for development, with the resulting priorities providing the basis for subsequent consensus-building in a plenary workshop that brought together all the stakeholders. Finally, the more participatory management was institutionalized through the formation of a partnership organization, the Buccoo Reef Stakeholder Group. Based on the program at Buccoo Reef, Brown (2002: 13) argues that "two aspects – respecting stakeholder knowledge and sharing information – are critical contributions to a process of empowerment." It is stressed that the researchers "must be willing to share the information they collect and transform possibly complex economic, social or ecological data into accessible information for lay-people" (Brown, Tompkins, and Adger 2001: 5).

Despite the significant achievements of Brown's (2002: 14) action research, she concludes that the stakeholders were "enabled to make decisions, but were not empowered to implement them themselves nor to sufficiently influence others to implement them, and thus further institutional development and innovation were necessary." This illustrates why it is misleading to assume that sophisticated consultation techniques will serve to empower indigenous groups or local communities, as such fundamental change is only likely to occur when there are also substantial changes in broader economic, social, and political structures. Another necessary qualifying note is that consultative participation involves people being asked to express their opinions, and a few stakeholders, usually professionals, listen to the views expressed. While these professionals may modify their decisions in the light of the resulting opinions, they are under no obligation to take these views on board. The professionals can retain their power to define the problems, as well as to conduct the information-gathering process, control the analysis, and make decisions about how to respond (Pretty 1995; Araujo and Bramwell 2002). Mowforth and Munt (1998: 246) identify further reasons for caution in relation to applying the consultation techniques of rural appraisal to tourism projects in developing countries. They stress that, although

> the techniques of local appraisal are well-intentioned by those who lead and conduct them, the critical questions concerning the balance of power are who leads them and to what ends. In the end they are led, or at least significantly advised, by First World professionals, and the idea that a group of outsiders visiting for a short period of time can appreciate, let alone solve, the problems experienced by local communities is rather pretentious and patronising, and suggestive of neo-colonialist attitudes.

Conclusion

The chapter has suggested several ways in which tourism planning partnerships may encourage greater inclusiveness and participation. Use may be made of hybrid participation practices, such as by combining varying collaborative and consultative approaches either at the same time or consecutively at different stages. Another approach can be to assist the parties that are not directly engaged in a partnership to build their own institutional capacities and self-confidence, which may or may not be intended to promote their future involvement in the partnership. Such assistance might be directed in particular to those groups that are socially and economically marginalized. Prominence was given in the discussion to the use of social science research approaches to better understand the views of stakeholders who are not directly involved in a partnership, with consideration given to one application in Buccoo Reef Marine Park. From a normative perspective, there is notable potential for more widespread applications of ethnographic research techniques in order to gain insights into people's "world views," so that this can assist partnerships in making better decisions. The discussion suggests that there is a need for more research to identify the specific approaches to partnerships and consultation that have been employed in varying contexts in relation to tourism planning.

It has also been argued that, while tourism planning partnerships might promote inclusiveness and can widen their consultation activities, there are also substantial dangers and constraints in relation to what is achieved in practice. Looked at critically, partnerships and other approaches to widening participation in tourism policy-making could be seen largely as providing improved means for economic and political elites to incorporate dissenting groups and to manage potential conflicts more effectively broadly within their own agendas. Public–private sector partnerships might also be depicted as intended primarily to challenge and transform the bureaucratic nature of public agencies. And there are more general fears about the wider dispersal of power and influence in more complex, flexible, and discontinuous policy-making arrangements as part of a general "hollowing out" of the traditional nation-state. For example, Painter (1999: 131) argues that the "danger is that with conventional liberal democracy tied so tightly to the institutions and discourses of the nineteenth-century nation-state, these new centers and arenas of politics and governance will become undemocratic sites of exclusion". Looked at more positively, however, one might conclude that these forms of governance can establish more democratic and more open decision-making procedures and can set important precedents. Indeed, once more open procedures are used that involve more participants it may prove difficult to avoid such procedures and to exclude a wider range of groups in the future without arousing suspicion and prompting opposition (at least from more articulate and well-organized groups) (Bassett, Griffiths, and Smith 2002; Hastings 1999). Of course, these differing interpretations may be more or less appropriate in different instances and situations. One avenue for future study in the tourism field will be to evaluate how specific approaches to partnerships and consultation in particular circumstances affect the power relations between actors, issues of democracy and accountability, and the final distribution of the benefits and costs of tourism development.

REFERENCES

Alasuutari, P. (1995). *Researching Culture: Qualitative Method and Cultural Studies*. London: Sage.

Araujo, L. M. de., and Bramwell, B. (2000). Stakeholder assessment and collaborative tourism planning: The case of Brazil's Costa Dourada Project. In B. Bramwell and B. Lane (eds), *Tourism Collaboration and Partnerships: Politics, Practice and Sustainability* (pp. 272–94). Clevedon: Channel View.

Araujo, L. M. de., and Bramwell, B. (2002). Partnership and regional tourism in Brazil. *Annals of Tourism Research* 29(4), 1138–64.

Atkinson, R. (1999). Discourses of partnership and empowerment in contemporary British urban regeneration. *Urban Studies* 36(1), 59–72.

Bassett, K., Griffiths, R., and Smith, I. (2002). Testing governance: Partnerships, planning and conflict in waterfront regeneration. *Urban Studies* 39(10), 1757–75.

Berkes, F. (ed.) (1989). *Common Property Resources: Ecology and Community-Based Sustainable Development*. London: Belhaven.

Bramwell, B., and Lane, B. (2000) Collaboration and partnerships in tourism planning. In B. Bramwell and B. Lane (eds), *Tourism Collaboration and Partnerships: Politics, Practice and Sustainability* (pp. 1–19). Clevedon: Channel View.

Bramwell, B., and Sharman, A. (1999). Collaboration in local tourism policy-making. *Annals of Tourism Research* 26(2), 392–415.

Bromley, D. (ed.) (1992). *Making the Commons Work: Theory, Practice and Policy.* San Francisco: Institute for Contemporary Studies.

Brown, K. (2002). Innovations for conservation and development. *The Geographical Journal* 168(1), 6–17.

Brown, K., Adger, W., Tompkins, E., Bacon, P., Shim, D., and Young, K. (2000). *Trade-off Analysis for Marine Protected Area Management.* Centre for Social and Economic Research on the Global Environment Working Paper GEC 02. Norwich: University of East Anglia.

Brown, K., Tompkins, E., and Adger, W. (2001). *Trade-off Analysis for Participatory Coastal Zone Decision-Making.* Norwich: Overseas Development Group, University of East Anglia.

Carr, D., Selin, S., and Schuett, M. (1998). Managing public forests: Understanding the role of collaborative planning. *Environmental Management* 22(5), 767–76.

Clegg, S. (1989). *Frameworks of Power.* London: Sage.

Cohen, E. (1979). Rethinking the sociology of tourism. *Annals of Tourism Research* 6(1), 18–35.

Dann, G., and Phillips, J. (2001). Qualitative tourism research in the late twentieth century and beyond. In B. Faulkner, G. Moscardo, and E. Laws (eds), *Tourism in the 21st Century: Lessons from Experience* (pp. 247–65). London: Continuum.

Few, R. (2001). Containment and counter-containment: Planner/community relations in conservation planning. *The Geographical Journal* 167(2), 111–24.

Gray, B. (1989). *Collaborating: Finding Common Ground for Multi-Party Problems.* San Francisco: Jossey-Bass.

Gregory, R., and Keeney, R. (1994). Creating policy alternatives using stakeholder values. *Management Science* 40(8), 1035–48.

Hall, C. M. (2000a). Rethinking collaboration and partnership: A public policy perspective. In B. Bramwell and B. Lane (eds), *Tourism Collaboration and Partnerships: Politics, Practice and Sustainability* (pp. 143–58). Clevedon: Channel View.

Hall, C. M. (2000b). *Tourism Planning: Policies, Processes and Relationships.* Harlow: Prentice Hall.

Hastings, A. (1999). Analysing power relations in partnerships: Is there a role for discourse analysis? *Urban Studies* 36(1), 91–106.

Healey, P. (1997). *Collaborative Planning: Shaping Places in Fragmented Societies.* London: Macmillan.

Healy, R. (1994). The "common pool" problem in tourism landscapes. *Annals of Tourism Research* 21(3), 596–611.

Holland, J. (2000). Consensus and conflict: The socioeconomic challenge facing sustainable tourism development in Southern Albania. *Journal of Sustainable Tourism* 8(6), 510–24.

Jamal, T., and Getz, D. (1995). Collaboration theory and community tourism planning. *Annals of Tourism Research* 22(1), 186–204.

Jamal, T., and Getz, D. (2000). Community roundtables for tourism-related conflicts: The dialectics of consensus and process structures. In B. Bramwell and B. Lane (eds), *Tourism Collaboration and Partnerships: Politics, Practice and Sustainability* (pp. 159–82). Clevedon: Channel View.

Jamal, T., and Hollinshead, K. (2001). Tourism and the forbidden zone: The undeserved power of qualitative inquiry. *Tourism Management* 22(1), 63–82.

Ladkin, A., and Bertramini, A. (2002). Collaborative tourism planning: A case study of Cusco, Peru. *Current Issues in Tourism* 5(2), 71–93.

Lafferty, W. (2000). *Sustainable Communities in Europe.* London: Earthscan.

Lovelock, B. (2001). Interorganisational relations in the protected area–tourism policy domain: The influence of macro-economic policy. *Current Issues in Tourism* 4(2/4), 253–74.

Lovelock, B. (2002). Why it's good to be bad: The role of conflict in contributing towards sustainable tourism in protected areas. *Journal of Sustainable Tourism* 10(1), 5–30.

Mitchell, J. (2002). *Ambivalent Europeans: Ritual, Memory and the Public Sphere in Malta*. London: Routledge.

Mowforth, M., and Munt, I. (1998). *Tourism and Sustainability: New Tourism in the Third World*. London: Routledge.

Murphy, P. (1985). *Tourism: A Community Approach*. London: Routledge.

Painter, J. (1999). New geographies of democracy in contemporary Europe. In R. Hudson and A. Williams (eds), *Divided Europe: Society and Territory* (pp. 107–31). London: Sage.

Pearce, P., Moscardo, G., and Ross, G. (1996). *Tourism Community Relationships*. Oxford: Pergamon.

Pickvance, C. (1997). Decentralization and democracy in eastern Europe: A sceptical approach. *Environment and Planning: Government and Policy* 15(2), 129–42.

Pretty, J. (1995). The many interpretations of participation. *In Focus* 16 (Summer), 4–5.

Prior, D., Stewart, J., and Walsh, K. (1995). *Citizenship: Rights, Community and Participation*. London: Pitman.

Reed, M. (1997). Power relations and community-based tourism planning. *Annals of Tourism Research* 24(3), 566–91.

Sandiford, P., and Ap, J. (1998). The role of ethnographic techniques in tourism planning. *Journal of Travel Research* 37(1), 3–11.

Selin, S., and Beason, K. (1991). Interorganizational relations in tourism. *Annals of Tourism Research* 18(4), 639–52.

Selin, S., and Myers, N. (1998). Tourism marketing alliances: Member satisfaction and effectiveness attributes of a regional initiative. *Journal of Travel and Tourism Marketing* 7(1), 79–94.

Shepherd, A. (1998). *Sustainable Rural Development*. London: Macmillan.

Sofield, T. (2001). Sustainability and pilgrimage tourism in the Kathmandu Valley of Nepal. In V. Smith and M. Brent (eds), *Hosts and Guests Revisited: Tourism Issues of the 21st Century* (pp. 257–71). New York: Cognizant Communication Corporation.

Timothy, D. (1998). Co-operative tourism planning in a developing destination. *Journal of Sustainable Tourism* 6(1), 52–68.

Timothy, D. (1999). Participatory planning: A view of tourism in Indonesia. *Annals of Tourism Research* 26(2), 371–91.

Tosun, C. (2000). Limits to community participation in the tourism development process in developing countries. *Tourism Management* 21(6), 613–33.

Turner, M., and Hulme, D. (1997). *Governance, Administration and Development: Making the State Work*. Basingstoke: Macmillan.

Twyman, C. (2000). Participatory conservation? Community-based natural resource management in Botswana. *The Geographical Journal* 166(4), 323–35.

Verbole, A. (2000). Actors, discourses and interfaces of rural tourism development at the local community level in Slovenia: Social and political dimensions of the rural tourism development process. *Journal of Sustainable Tourism* 8(6), 479–90.

Warner, M. (1997). "Consensus" participation: An example for protected areas planning. *Public Administration and Development* 17(4), 413–32.

Wearing, S., and Huyskens, M. (2001). Moving on from joint management policy regimes in Australian national parks. *Current Issues in Tourism* 4(2–4), 182–209.

Wearing, S., and McDonald, M. (2002). The development of community-based tourism: Rethinking the relationship between tour operators and development agents as intermediaries in rural and isolated area communities. *Journal of Sustainable Tourism* 10(3), 191–206.

Williams, P., Penrose, R., and Hawkes, S. (1998). Shared decision-making in tourism land use planning. *Annals of Tourism Research* 25(4), 860–89.

World Tourism Organization (2000). *Public–Private Sector Cooperation: Enhancing Tourism Competitiveness*. Madrid: World Tourism Organization.

Yuksel, F., Bramwell, B., and Yuksel, A. (1999). Stakeholder interviews and tourism planning at Pamukkale, Turkey. *Tourism Management* 20(3), 351–60.

Chapter 44

Local and Regional Tourism Policy and Power

Andrew Church

In a locality many forces will determine how tourism evolves but, increasingly, regional and local policies have been seeking to influence different aspects of tourism development. In some countries organized local government support for tourism dates back to the nineteenth century (Jeffries 2001) but in other localities, especially in less developed countries, local and regional tourism policy is a relatively recent phenomenon (Sharpley 2002). A full understanding of the processes and geographies of tourism requires an examination of the role of regional and local policy organizations. Williams (1998: 147) claims this is "a truly extensive topic" due to the variety of tourism policies. But, by taking a broad overview of theoretical and empirical research, the next four sections of the chapter identify some important common features and changes in the roles, aims, structures, and impacts of regional and local tourism policies. Recent research (Elliott 1997; Morgan and Pritchard 1999; Hall 2000; Sharpley and Telfer 2002) has also sought to understand the processes that shape policies and these are considered in a further section on power relations and the broader political and economic drivers of policy changes.

Conceptual Categories, Policy Roles, and Geographical Scales

"Regional government" usually refers to the first tier down from the national level of government and this is the definition used in this chapter, while "local government" refers to the remaining scales of government below the regional. The involvement of local organizations and governments in tourism policy is usually justified on the grounds that such bodies are well placed to understand how tourism interacts with local needs and environments, and how it can be managed (Elliott 1997; Hall 2000). The justifications for strategic regional policies are more complex but often include the need to balance national and local interests, to integrate national, urban, and rural development and to guide the spatial location of tourism (Jenkins 2001). Local and regional government is defined by the formal institutions of the state (Hambleton, Savitch, and Stewart 2002) and in most countries includes democratically elected organizations, such as provinces, councils, or communes, along with the laws, policies, officers, and structures that enable these organizations to operate. In states where national government is totalitarian or military, local and regional government may be controlled by unelected centrally appointed officials. The term governance has become increasingly used to encapsulate the growing cooperation between a range of public, private, and voluntary organizations. Often governance involves official government organizations but this is not always the case and governance structures can be constructed by social partnerships and networks involving private, voluntary, and community sector bodies. Indeed, critiques of urban and regional governance in neoliberal capitalist states have identified how governance partnerships dominated by private sector interests favoring policies for economic competitiveness have resulted in turbulent and often destructive changes in the role of local governments concerned with social priorities (Brenner and Theodore 2002). Over the last 20 years many local and regional tourism policies could be categorized as governance because governments have developed policies through alliances and partnerships with other bodies (see Bramwell, chapter 43 this volume). This chapter will consider both government and governance, but will concentrate on the role played by local and regional government. It will also follow Pearce's (1992) approach and refer to the bodies responsible for tourism policy as regional tourism organizations (RTOs) and local tourism organizations (LTOs) to acknowledge that local and regional governments frequently do not act alone. Relations between RTOs and LTOs are often complex. In Australia, Jenkins (2000) claims that the RTOs at the state and territory level are statutory bodies, but the LTOs, which are very varied, are not always members of their respective RTOs and often don't support their RTO.

The variety of local and regional tourism policies is highlighted by the recent attempts to produce conceptual categorizations of the roles, planning approaches, and geographical scales of tourism policy. Hall (2000) identified eight functional roles played by tourism policy: coordination, planning, legislation, entrepreneurial support, stimulation, promotion, social tourism, and public interest protection. Of these different roles, promotion is often ubiquitous to all tourism organizations at national, regional, and local levels. Zhang, Chong, and Ap (1999) utilized an adaptation of these roles to examine tourism policy in China after 1978. They argue that ideally these differing roles will be mutually reinforcing but they are often conflictual, especially at the local and regional scale. In China between 1978 and 1985 the decentralization of certain responsibilities for tourism to regional and urban organizations produced marked conflict between the stimulation and regulation roles (Zhang, Chong, and Ap 1999). In a broader discussion of southeast Asian countries, Smith (2000) merges these different functional roles into conceptual categories for tourism planning, arguing that there are four basic strategic approaches: ad hoc, limited growth, integrated, and comprehensive. Local and regional organizations may of course be involved in initiatives using different planning approaches concurrently and will develop their own mix of approaches. Smith's (2000) own example of Nusa Dua (Bali) reveals that the first integrated tourism development in southeast Asia has been accompanied, just outside the resort boundary, by ad hoc tourism development opposed by local communities. Indeed, in many locations in developing countries, local communities who wish to resist major tourism projects have found themselves unable to prevent the combined onslaught of planned and unplanned tourism development (Mowforth and Munt 1998). All these categorizations are idealized, but despite their limitations they are useful for organizing knowledge of local and regional tourism policy. In many localities and regions, however, tourism policies can not be neatly placed into categories. Pearce (2001) and Jenkins (2000) both provide recent empirical examples of the ad hoc nature of policy, and while it is important to identify where policies fit categories, it is also important to examine policies which seem to highlight tensions and contradictions between conceptual categories.

Some useful generalizations are drawn from this overall picture of complexity by Williams (1998), who summarizes the connections between tourism planning and policy at different geographical scales of government. The role of a planning hierarchy is to allow higher tiers to provide a framework for lower ones. In many countries the key concerns carried through from national to regional level tourism planning are generating regional economic growth and identifying key tourism locations through spatial planning, marketing, and infrastructure provision. Local plans, in turn, carry through the concern for economic impacts and spatial planning by focusing on the key locations for tourism identified at higher scales. LTOs, however, will place a much greater emphasis on the physical layout, design, and management of developments (Williams 1998). Alongside these concerns that connect tiers of planning it is also possible to identify some distinctive features of LTOs and RTOs (Williams 1998). Both tiers will be more involved with visitor management than the national scale. Regional plans are sometimes distinctive in their concern with environmental impacts, although in many countries this is also a key local issue. Regional tourism plans often focus on the type and location of tourism attraction whereas local plans are more concerned with the local organization of tourism resources and the control of development (Williams 1998). In discussing the distinctive roles of different tiers of government it is important to recognize that strategies are not neatly passed between tiers. Regional and local governance, generally, over the last 20 years has experienced some complex rescaling of both functions and power as a consequence of neoliberalism and the increasingly globalized economy. Goodwin and Painter (1996) identified how local governance was becoming increasingly multiscalar as local partnerships involved bodies from different tiers of governance. Smith (2002: 87) claims that "Certainly, specific functions and activities previously organized at the national scale are being dispersed to other scales up and down the scale hierarchy. At the same time, however, national states are reframing themselves as purer, territorially rooted economic actors in and out of the market." The result of this process, according to Smith (2002), is that over the last 20 years city governments have had to adopt new neoliberal policies to replace the liberal policies of earlier periods. The increasing complexity of tourism policy identified by Williams (1998) stems to a considerable degree from this rescaling of governance under neoliberalism. The functional boundaries between different tiers of tourism governance will have become more porous, resulting in some of the ad hoc polices identified by Jenkins (2000) and Pearce (2001).

The specific tourism plans considered by Williams (1998) will not encapsulate all the local and regional government activities that affect tourism. For example, local government tourism officers in many countries are closely involved in promotional activities but are not part of the land use planning process which will influence the local buildings and facilities they have to promote (Jeffries 2001). Often the mainstream roles of local government, such as planning and infrastructure provision, are as important as any tourism policy in shaping the nature of tourism development (Elliott 1997). Of Australia's Gold Coast, a major destination with 4 million visitors per year, Elliott (1997: 167) notes that in the late 1990s, although the local city council had responsibility for the local public management of tourism, "it is surprising, if not alarming, that the City of the Gold Coast has no committee, department, director or senior manager responsible exclusively for tourism management." In the Gold Coast tourism was managed through two strategic council directorates, one for planning, development, and transport and one for city projects. Local and regional tourism policy research has concentrated on tourism strategies, departments, and officers and in future more attention needs to be given to the influence of other governance processes, such as waste management and transport. Recently, however, urban analysts have begun to reveal how tourism policy is influenced by the wider context of city management and politics (Judd and Fainstein 1999).

The Broad Aims of Regional and Local Tourism Policy

The various roles of policy are used by RTOs and LTOs to achieve certain broad aims. To some degree, changes in the aims of tourism policy locally will reflect changes occurring at the national level. This is not because local and regional policy is simply driven by the national level. Rather, as noted earlier, policy at all levels reflects wider economic, social, and environmental changes, especially globalization and the rise of neoliberal governance. Hall (2000: 156), in relation to the aims of tourism policy, argues "that at the broad level government involvement has been shifting from a developmental to a promotional role," a change he claims has increased the importance of local government. Timothy (2001: 149) presents a slightly different view, arguing that there has been a shift in the aims of tourism planning from the "narrow concerns with physical planning and blind promotion aimed at the masses towards a more balanced approach that supports the development and promotion of more sustainable forms of tourism." Both authors, however, identify the growth of more measured tourism policy aims and a desire to address sustainability issues. This shift has been accompanied by a growing emphasis on a holistic approach to tourism policy that aims to encourage community participation to increase local ownership and to limit negative environmental impacts (Timothy 2002). Alongside these wider changes in policy aims it is possible, over the last 20 years, to identify for RTOs and LTOs three distinctive broad aims: economic diversification in non-tourism locations, resort renewal strategies, and addressing social divides. These are not present in all localities but are arenas where RTOs and LTOs have taken a distinctive lead.

Tourism policy, at all geographical scales of the state, usually aims to diversify the economy. National-level tourism policies often target either areas where tourism already exists or those where the physical and social features appear to have considerable tourism potential (Baum 1994). Jenkins (1997), however, highlights how the geographical focus of national tourism policies can be highly politicized and the allocation of regional funds often reflects party political priorities and favoritism. RTOs and LTOs, however, have often taken the lead in developing initiatives to attract visitors to areas where, traditionally, tourism had a minor economic role and its future potential appeared limited. This typically involved local governments in declining urban areas aiming to use tourism to support economic diversification (Page 1995). This has contributed to the widespread growth of heritage and cultural tourism, drawing on the symbols and environments of an industrial past (see chapter 17, this volume). Cities with strong locational advantages for tourism have also developed significant tourism policies but, in less advantageous locations, local authorities were often instrumental in implementing initiatives where few measures had existed before (Hope and Klemm 2001). In the European Union, however, the growth of local tourism initiatives in less advantageous areas was additionally stimulated by a combination of local authorities wishing to support tourism and the availability of European Commission funds to assist locations experiencing problematic industrial restructuring. The European Regional Development Fund and the Commission's Community Initiatives have provided local authorities with sources of funding to support tourism initiatives in problem regions (Williams 1996).

Similarly, in rural areas with seemingly limited tourism potential, the growth of tourism policies with economic diversification aims has been led by local and regional bodies. This has occurred in very different geographical circumstances. Lewis (1998) claims that, in the USA, a surge of tourism initiatives in rural areas was driven by local community leaders. In the Maramures region of Romania, there are significant constraints on tourism development, but local communes, associations, and church bodies have led the development of a range of tourism initiatives (Turnock 2002). In the European Union the availability of funds from the European Commission again plays an important role in relation to the actions of LTOs and RTOs. Ribeiro and Marques (2002: 212) argue that in the European Union the agricultural crisis in many disadvantaged rural areas has resulted in a "tourism canonization" in which tourism policy, like a saint, is unquestioningly revered. LTOs and RTOs in many areas, often lacking tourism infrastructure and competitive attractions, are still grasping at tourism as the route to diversification, often encouraged by national governments and the European Union (Ribeiro and Marques 2002).

Economic diversification has also been a key aim of policy in some declining coastal resorts and spa towns, especially in some European countries (Shaw and Williams 1997; Williams and Balaz 2000). In the UK, the national-level body – the English Tourism Council – has encouraged local government in resorts to develop distinctive approaches by urging them to target marketing more precisely (English Tourism Council 2001). Local government in Bulgaria, however, is viewed as an obstacle to new strategies for the redevelopment of Black Sea resorts due to a "parasitic attitude" toward the taxes generated by resort complexes (Bachvarov 1999: 200). Nevertheless, a second distinctive aim of local and regional tourism policy is that, in the vast majority of declining resorts and spas, RTOs and LTOs have been the main bodies responsible for developing renewal strategies. Central government, if it plays a role, typically limits itself to providing supporting funds. In eastern Europe, tourism organizations in resorts and spa towns have had to struggle against neglect by national governments concerned either with more pressing priorities or the implementation on non-interventionist neoliberal economic strategies (Williams and Balaz 2000).

A third distinctive broad aim of local and regional tourism policies has been to use tourism policy to address social divides. This is not widespread but has developed in communities with a history of nationalistic or ethnic conflict and difference. LTOs in many countries have a long history of managing conflicts relating to tourism, but addressing social divides involves rather different approaches. Under apartheid, South African tourism was manipulated to maintain divides, but subsequently local tourism and leisure initiatives based on shared spaces have been part of the attempt at urban "peace building" in Johannesburg (Bollens 1999). Often, however, seemingly socially progressive tourism policies conceal blatant neoliberal economic priorities. Hiller (2000) argues that Cape Town's Olympic bid, which was driven by the market priorities of a business elite, sought legitimation in claims that it would unite different nationalities and ethnic groups. In Northern Ireland the representations of heritage and history developed by LTOs and RTOs have been highly contested but often can present a shared heritage that lessens the distinctions between Unionist and nationalist communities (Boyd 2000). Local tourism policies can be divisive and even used to deny human rights (Mowforth and Munt 1998), but carefully managed cultural and heritage tourism can have a unifying effect. It is important not to be too optimistic, but initiatives that aim to reach out across social divides are often led by LTOs and RTOs sensitive to ethnic, nationalistic, and community difference.

Changing Structures, Innovation, and the Impacts of Tourism Policy

The expansion of local and regional tourism policy has been accompanied by three broad innovations in policy structures and implementation: the development of partnerships, transnational cooperation, and community involvement. These innovations are not particular to tourism policy and increasingly have been features of regional and urban governance. LTOs and RTOs have historically been involved in local alliances and international cooperation; recently, however, partnerships have become more regularized and innovative but also problematic (see chapters 43 and 46, this volume, on partnerships and transnational cooperation). Transnational cooperation can involve the transfer of policy practice and benchmarking at a number of scales of governance. Increasingly, however, concerns are being raised that such policy transfer leads to policy conformity and stimulates competition rather than the intended cooperation (Church and Reid 1996). Hambleton, Savitch, and Stewart (2002: 7) claim that "too often governments have simply borrowed ideas from other countries without considering issues of transferability and application." The other major form of local and regional tourism policy innovation is measures to ensure community participation, which have also been strongly promoted by international development agencies encouraging international policy transfer (Sharpley and Telfer 2002). Timothy (2002) argues that participatory tourism planning is more developed in advanced industrialized nations and identifies the barriers in developing countries as being power structures that exclude (especially women and certain ethnic groups), a lack of information and community awareness, peripherality, insufficient public funds, and poorly developed partnerships. Even in industrialized countries, however, holistic community-based tourism strategies have encountered numerous obstacles (Grant 1998).

These broad innovations are also linked to general shifts in local and regional governance which can have an important influence on tourism policy. In some major cities, Hambleton argues, a "new city management" has emerged involving changes to leadership and the rise of influential mayors (Hambleton, Savitch, and Stewart 2002). These urban governance innovations may affect tourism policy but not in a uniform manner. In US cities, Judd (2000) notes that mayors have often led the political process, supporting the construction of new tourism attractions such as stadia and exhibition centers. The mayor of London has produced a tourism strategy which, rather than emphasizing new facilities, concentrates on marketing (Greater London Authority 2002).

Despite policy innovations, a number of studies have revealed that the social and economic impacts of local and regional tourism policies have not lived up to expectations. Judd and Fainstein (1999) suggest that urban tourism strategies often fail to achieve planned economic goals and some cities are left with significant costs of maintaining new facilities. In a rural context, Ribeiro and Marques (2002) review a wide range of evidence and argue that rural tourism can make effective contributions to rural development, but income and employment effects are often below expectations. They claim, however, that local and regional tourism policy has had important beneficial impacts on rural policy processes, leading to "a rethink of attitudes and motivations, a catalysis of ideas, initiatives and energies" (Ribeiro and Marques 2002: 218). Other studies in rural and urban areas, however, reveal the problematic political impacts of new forms of local and regional tourism policy. New tourism partnerships in southwest England have led to policy conformity that limits local innovation (Meethan 1998). Similarly, in the former German Democratic Republic, new local tourism strategies are increasingly presenting a standardized, homogenous representation of history and heritage (Coles 2003). The growth of collaborative tourism partnerships has also been accompanied by problematic competition between local governments. In the Yunan Great Rivers National Park in China, despite the presence of a national park coordinating authority, local provinces are still involved in haphazard competition to attract tourists (Cater 2000).

Recent initiatives in less developed countries to involve local communities in tourism development have also had mixed impacts. Attempts to connect major resorts in Indonesia to local food chains to increase local economic impacts have had some positive outcomes (Telfer and Wall 2000). Bianchi (2002) suggests, however, that, in many countries, national and local government pay only lip service to the "new language" of fair trade and community development. Many studies in less developed countries have highlighted the relative lack of influence of local government on powerful interest groups (Mowforth and Munt 1998). Hall (1994) claims that the environmental degradation of tourism areas in southeast Asia and Pacific Rim countries stems not from a lack of awareness amongst governments but a local failure to enforce legislation. In Thailand, even where resort plans were developed in areas like Pattaya, local government appeared powerless or unwilling to implement them in the face of powerful interest groups and the rapid tourism development which was prevalent in the country (Elliott 1997). For theorists developing a broader critique of neoliberal governance, these contradictions and failings of community participation in the face of the economic priorities of tourism development come as little surprise. For Peck and Tickell (2002: 43) the growth of the "neoliberal policy repertoire" involved "the selective appropriation of 'community' and nonmarket metrics, the establishment of social-capital discourses and techniques, the incorporation (an underwriting) of local-governance and partnership-based models of policy development."

Power, Theory, and the "Drivers" of Local and Regional Tourism Policy

Theoretical frameworks concerned with organizations and power have been developed to explain the changing nature of local tourism policy and the role played by interest groups. Organizational theory was used by Pearce (1992) to examine, particularly in European countries, how RTOs and LTOs evolved and their degree of stability. Jenkins (2000) suggests that Pearce's approach, while useful, has some limitations since in Australia it does not encapsulate the range and complexity of interest groups involved in local and regional tourism governance. The need to understand the power of interest groups in local tourism policy has drawn researchers to theoretical perspectives developed to examine governance in major cities. The urban growth machine (Molotch 1976) and the urban regime (Stone 1989) were theoretical frameworks developed to understand the power and role of business interests in urban policy, and the emergence of coalitions involving business and other interests. Schollman, Perkins, and Moore (2001) claim that the power of business interests in the place promotion of Christchurch, New Zealand has some of the features of the urban growth machine model. In a study of the London borough of Islington, Long (2000) argues that regime theory provides a useful framework for understanding how a tourism partnership was developed. Theoretical analysis has enabled research on tourism policy to go beyond the mainly descriptive approaches and normative arguments that dominated early studies (Hall and Page 2000a). But caution is needed when applying theories developed to understand the broad process of urban politics to the specific field of urban tourism policy, which can be a very limited element of growth strategies in some cities. Some of the original proponents of growth machine and regime theories have found that there are often close relations between local business and city leaders, but this does not mean business interests have a significant impact on the development of growth policies and the nature of growth (Logan, Whaley, and Crowder 1997). Furthermore, these theories lack insight when managed or slow-growth policies are developed (Clark 2002). As local tourism policy becomes more concerned with sustainability and managed growth, theoretical frameworks concerned with urban growth become of less value or need considerable adaptation to focus on growth management (Gill 2000; see also chapter 45, this volume).

In order to go beyond the focus on interest groups, broader social and political theories concerned with social relations have also been used in studies of local and regional tourism. Drawing on Foucauldian concepts, Morgan and Pritchard (1999) argue that power is not simply concentrated in interest groups but permeates all aspects of society, and for all social groups power is both constraining and productive. An empirical study of southwestern coastal resorts in England is used to claim that the variations in resort performance, place promotion, and symbolic representation can be understood as the outcome of social processes rooted in the struggles for power between different interest groups, classes, genders, sexes, and races.

Michael (2001) analyzes tourism policy from the very different theoretical perspective of public choice theory, and views government power as being based on its role in the market system. The origins and value of these contrasting theoretical perspectives have been subject to dispute in geography and social science. In the study of local tourism policy, it is unclear whether such theoretical perspectives can be so readily applied to less developed countries. A political economy of tourism in less developed countries is gradually emerging (Bianchi 2002), but local and regional governance is noticeably absent from many studies which focus on national government and international agencies (Timothy 2002). The analysis of local and regional tourism policies in less developed countries faces some distinctive challenges, not least of which will be examining the impacts on policy of corruption and graft, a topic barely mentioned in recent texts on tourism and development, even though crime is addressed (e.g., Hall and Page 2000b; Sharpley and Telfer 2002). Local tourism policy in industrialized countries has also been significantly affected by corruption and this requires further research (see Bachvarov 1997; Perry 1997; Williams and Balaz 2000 for some examples). This is a highly contentious topic and often local voices best encapsulate the complex role of corruption in local and regional tourism policy and planning. A good example is provided by Pholpoke's (1998) study of Doi Suthep mountain near Chaing Mai in Thailand, where plans to develop a cable car route to this important pilgrimage site and visitor attraction were fiercely opposed by some local community and religious groups:

> opportunities for graft and insider investments mean that the government's role in promoting tourism frequently conflicts with its social responsibility functions. Professional consultants therefore help to legitimate its planning and approval processes. Local government tourism marketers may defer to the "specialist" who proposes and executes plans for "national development" projects. Thus, the tourism marketers, whether state officials or private professionals, want to be perceived as possessing an established body of systematic knowledge, a commitment to client-centred service, and the right to control their own work. In predominantly tourist-centred regions, local government officials perceive themselves as tourism professionals first, and only secondarily as state officials with public service obligations. On the theory that tourism development is always in the public interest, the government official as marketer can ultimately be made only accountable to the policy makers and investors as opposed to the local community. The overlapping interests of consultants, planners, promoters and investors prevent any possibility of presenting an "independent" view in "master plans" presented to the government. (Pholpoke 1998: 271)

This encapsulates how the power structures shaping tourism development in north Thailand are based on the complex relationships between corruption, local and national government, business interests, and international consultants' tourism knowledge. In any locality, however, the power structures that shape local tourism development will also driven by broader economic and political processes. These include key processes that are the focus of other chapters of this book, especially globalization, state restructuring, and changes to civil society. The increasingly globalized economy and political restructuring mean that local and regional tourism policy is subject to the same contradictions that confront cities and regions in general (Brenner and Theodore 2002). In particular LTOs and RTOs face the typical neoliberal contradiction of being both more competitive and more collaborative.

Local organizations will compete more vigorously for increasingly fluid inward investment, but globalization also heightens mutual vulnerability, encouraging co-operation (Hambleton 2002). Globalization has been accompanied by often dramatic transformations in international and national governance. RTOs and LTOs will be significantly shaped by central–local state relations and the governance structures laid down by national and international bodies (Hall and Jenkins 1995). Regional tourism policies are often well developed in federal countries with strong provincial/regional government, such as the USA, Canada, and Germany (Elliott 1997). By contrast, in post-communist states tourism governance has undergone dramatic changes as a result of deregulation and the removal of state-socialist tourism organizations. In the Czech Republic and Slovakia this has left an "organizational vacuum" in tourism development at the regional and local levels, leading to problems for promotion and coordination (Williams and Balaz 2000: 57). In many countries LTOs and RTOs have also had to respond to changes in civil society. A more active citizenship has often sought to influence the social and environmental aspects of local and regional tourism policy. Urry (1990) argues that the conservation and cultural concerns of the expanding "new service class" lay behind the expansion of urban heritage tourism in the UK. The broad processes of globalization and neoliberal state restructuring that significantly construct tourism policy are, in turn, affected by the activities of RTOs and LTOs that encourage some of the international flows of people (especially the rich and powerful), culture, and information that are a key part of the problematic globalization process.

Conclusions: Local and Regional Tourism Policy and Future Research Agendas

Jenkins (2000, 2001) recently argued that tourism policy research was still a fragmented research field requiring considerably more theoretical and empirical work, possibly drawing on theories of political organization, human behavior, and organizational systems. These conclusions undoubtedly apply to local and regional tourism policies. In developing countries the research agenda is relatively simple since there is a need for more academic studies of local and regional tourism policies because past research has concentrated on national and international organizations (Bianchi 2002). However, researchers must be realistic concerning the role of local and regional government. In many less developed countries tourism policy is still dominated by national governments, although there are exceptions such as India and South Africa, where tourism policy is relatively devolved to regional organizations. Also in more developed countries, Gordon and Goodall (2000) argue that, in many localities outside big cities, public stakeholders lack the organizational and institutional structures to develop influential tourism policies. Overall, however, the research summarized in this chapter suggests that a key research priority for tourism geography is to reveal the power structures shaping policy and how the ongoing rescaling of governance and the development of multiscalar policies impacts on power relations. A further priority is to identify the influence of the mainstream non-tourism activities of local and regional government on tourism development. Local case studies have shown how ad hoc, incremental, and expedient tourism policy can be (Pearce 2001; Leberman and Mason 2002). More comparative studies of localities would also be valuable for understanding how the different sources of power interact with local geographies to produce the current mixes of tourism policies (Church et al. 2000). This raises questions over how power should be conceptualized in studies of tourism. The study of power in tourism policy has tended to follow the approach of Hall (2000: 10), and focus on the "play of interest and values in the influence and determination of tourism planning and policy processes." Recent research has shown that power over tourism development is not just wielded by interest groups but is rooted in social relations and can be used to set social norms and wield influence over other social groups (Morgan and Pritchard 1999). Smith (2002: 88) summarizes the nature of social power as being "who is empowered and who contained, who wins and who loses." Tourism research has increasingly identified who is empowered by local and regional tourism policy, but the way in which tourism policy can contain certain social groups remains less well understood.

REFERENCES

Bachvarov, M. (1997). End of the model? Tourism in post-communist Bulgaria. *Tourism Management* 18(1), 43–50.

Bachvarov, M. (1999). Troubled sustainability: Bulgarian seaside resorts. *Tourism Geographies* 1(2), 192–203.

Baum, T. (1994). The development and implementation of national tourism policies. *Tourism Management* 15(3), 185–92.

Bianchi, R. (2002). Towards a new political economy of global tourism. In R. Sharpley and D. J. Telfer (eds), *Tourism and Development: Concepts and Issues* (pp. 265–99). Clevedon: Channel View Publications.

Bollens, S. A. (1999). *Urban Peace-Building in Divided Societies: Belfast and Johannesburg*. Oxford: Westview Press.

Boyd, S. W. (2000). "Heritage" tourism in Northern Ireland: Opportunity under peace. *Current Issues in Tourism* 3(2), 150–74.

Brenner, N., and Theodore, N. (2002) Cities and the geographies of "actually existing neoliberalism." In N. Brenner and N. Theodore (eds), *Spaces of Neoliberalism: Urban Restructuring in North America and Western Europe* (pp. 2–32). Oxford: Blackwell.

Cater, E. A. (2000). Tourism in the Yunnan Great Rivers National Parks System Project: Prospects for sustainability. *Tourism Geographies* 2(4), 472–89.

Church, A., Ball, R., Bull, C., and Tyler, D. (2000). Public policy engagement with British tourism: The national, local and the European Union. *Tourism Geographies* 2(3), 312–36.

Church, A., and Reid, P. (1996). Urban power, international networks, and competition: The example of cross-border co-operation. *Urban Studies* 33(8), 1297–1318.

Clark, T. N. (2002). Globalisation and transformations in political cultures. In R. Hambleton, H. V. Savitch, and M. Stewart (eds), *Globalism and Local Democracy: Challenge and Change in Europe and North America* (pp. 67–94). New York: Palgrave Macmillan.

Coles, T. E. (2003). The emergent tourism industry in eastern Germany a decade after unification. *Tourism Management* 24(2), 217–26.

Elliott, J. (1997). *Tourism Politics and Public Sector Management*. London: Routledge.

English Tourism Council (2001). *Sea Changes: Creating World Class Resorts in England*. London: English Tourism Council.

Gill, A. (2000). From growth machine to growth management: The dynamics of resort development in Whistler, British Columbia. *Environment and Planning A* 32(8), 1083–1103.

Goodwin, M., and Painter, J. (1996). Local governance, the crisis of Fordism and the changing geographies of regulation. *Transactions of the Institute of British Geographers* 21(4), 635–49.

Gordon, I., and Goodall, B. (2000). Localities and tourism. *Tourism Geographies* 2(3), 290–312.

Grant, M. (1998). *Sustainable Tourism in Bristol: Local Opportunities.* Mimeo available from Environmental Stewardship, 33 Cornwall Rd., Bristol BS7 8LJ, UK.

Greater London Authority (2002). *Visiting London: A Tourism Strategy for London.* London: Greater London Authority.

Hall, C. M. (1994). *Tourism in the Pacific Rim: Development, Impacts and Markets.* Melbourne: Longman Cheshire.

Hall, C. M. (2000). *Tourism Planning: Policies, Processes and Relationships.* Harlow: Pearson Education.

Hall, C. M., and Jenkins, J. (1995). *Tourism and Public Policy.* London: Routledge.

Hall, C. M., and Page, S. (2000a). *The Geography of Tourism and Recreation: Environment, Place and Space.* London: Routledge.

Hall, C. M., and Page, S. (2000b). *Tourism in South and South East Asia.* Oxford: Butterworth-Heinemann.

Hambleton, R. (2002). The new city management. In R. Hambleton, H. V. Savitch, and M. Stewart (eds), *Globalism and Local Democracy: Challenge and Change in Europe and North America* (pp. 147–68). New York: Palgrave Macmillan.

Hambleton, R., Savitch, H. V., and Stewart, M. (2002). Globalism and local democracy. In R. Hambleton, H. V. Savitch, and M. Stewart (eds), *Globalism and Local Democracy: Challenge and Change in Europe and North America* (pp. 1–18). New York: Palgrave Macmillan.

Hiller, H. (2000). Mega-events, urban boosterism and growth strategies: An analysis of the objectives and legitimations of the Cape Town 2004 Olympic bid. *International Journal of Urban and Regional Research* 24(2), 439–58.

Hope, C. A., and Klemm, M. S. (2001). Tourism in difficult areas revisited: The case of Bradford. *Tourism Management,* 22(6) 629–35.

Jeffries, D. (2001). *Governments and Tourism.* Oxford: Butterworth-Heinemann.

Jenkins, J. (1997). The role of the Commonwealth Government in rural tourism and regional development in Australia. In C. M. Hall, J. Jenkins, and G. Kearsley (eds), *Tourism Planning and Policy in Australia and New Zealand: Cases, Issues and Practice.* (pp. 181–91). Sydney: Irwin.

Jenkins, J. (2000). The dynamics of regional tourism organisations in New South Wales, Australia: History, structures and operations. *Current Issues in Tourism* 3(3), 175–203.

Jenkins, J. (2001). Editorial: Special issue on tourism policy. *Current Issues in Tourism* 4(2), 69–77.

Judd, D. (2000). Strong leadership. *Urban Studies* 37(5/6), 951–61.

Judd, D., and Fainstein S. (1999). *The Tourist City.* New Haven: Yale University Press.

Leberman, S. I., and Mason, P. (2002). Planning for recreation and tourism at the local level: Applied research in the Manawatu region of New Zealand. *Tourism Geographies* 4(1), 3–21.

Lewis, J. B. (1998). The development of rural tourism, *Parks and Recreation* 2(2), 99–107.

Logan, J. R., Whaley, R. B., and Crowder, K. (1997). The character and consequences of the growth regimes: An assessment of 20 years of research. *Urban Affairs Review* 32(May), 603–30.

Long, P. (2000). Tourism development regimes in the inner city fringe: The case of Discover Islington, London. In B. Bramwell and B. Lane (eds), *Tourism Collaboration and Partnerships: Politics, Practice and Sustainability* (pp. 183–99). Clevedon: Channel View Publications.

Meethan, K. (1998). New tourism for old? Policy developments in Cornwall and Devon. *Tourism Management* 19(6), 583–93.

Michael, E. (2001). Public choice and tourism analysis. *Current Issues in Tourism* 4(2), 308–30.

Molotch, H. (1976). The city as growth machine. *American Journal of Sociology* 82(3), 483–99.

Morgan, N. J., and Pritchard, A. (1999). *Power and Politics at the Seaside*. Exeter: University of Exeter Press.

Mowforth, M., and Munt, I. (1998). *Tourism and Sustainability: New Tourism in the Third World*. London: Routledge.

Page, S. (1995). *Urban Tourism*. London: Routledge.

Pearce, D. G. (1992). *Tourist Organisations*. Harlow: Longman.

Pearce, D. G. (2001). Tourism, trams and local government policy-making in Christchurch, New Zealand. *Current Issues in Tourism*, 4(2) 331–54.

Peck, N., and Tickell, A. (2002). Neoliberalizing space. In N. Brenner and N. Theodore (eds), *Spaces of Neoliberalism: Urban Restructuring on North America and Western Europe* (pp. 33–57). Oxford: Blackwell.

Perry, P. J. (1997). *Political Corruption and Political Geography*. Aldershot: Ashgate.

Pholpoke, C. (1998). The Chiang Mai cable-car project: Local controversy over cultural and eco-tourism. In P. Hirsch and C. Warren (eds), *The Politics of Environment in Southeast Asia: Resources and Resistance* (pp. 262–80). London: Routledge.

Ribeiro, M., and Marques, C. (2002). Rural tourism and the development of less favoured areas: Between rhetoric and practice. *International Journal of Tourism Research* 4(3), 211–20.

Schollmann, A., Perkins, H. C., and Moore, K. (2001). Rhetoric, claims making and conflict in touristic place promotion: The case of central Christchurch, New Zealand. *Tourism Geographies* 3(3), 300–25.

Selwyn, T. (2000). De-Mediterraneanisation of the Mediterranean. *Current Issues in Tourism* 3, 226–45.

Sharpley, R. (2002). Tourism: A vehicle for development? In R. Sharpley and D. Telfer (eds), *Tourism and Development: Concepts and Issues* (pp. 11–34). Clevedon: Channel View Publications.

Sharpley, R., and Telfer, D. J. (eds) (2002). *Tourism and Development: Concepts and Issues*. Clevedon: Channel View Publications.

Shaw, G., and Williams, A. M. (eds) (1997). *The Rise and Fall of British Coastal Resorts*. London: Pinter.

Smith, N. (2002). New globalism, new urbanism: Gentrification as global urban strategy. In N. Brenner and N. Theodore (eds), *Spaces of Neoliberalism: Urban Restructuring in North America and Western Europe* (pp. 80–103). Oxford: Blackwell.

Smith, R. A. (2000). Tourism planning in tourism in south and southeast Asia. In C. M. Hall and S. Page (eds), *Tourism in South and Southeast Asia* (pp. 104–16). Oxford: Butterworth-Heinemann.

Stone, C. (1989). *Regime Politics: Governing Atlanta 1946–1988*. Lawrence: University Press of Kansas.

Telfer, D. J., and Wall, G. (2000). Strengthening backward economic linkages: Local food purchasing by three Indonesian hotels. *Tourism Geographies* 2(4), 421–47.

Timothy, D. J. (2001). *Tourism and Political Boundaries*. London: Routledge.

Timothy, D. J. (2002). Tourism and community development issues. In R. Sharpley and D. J. Telfer (eds), *Tourism and Development: Concepts and Issues* (pp. 149–64). Clevedon: Channel View Publications.

Turnock, D. (2002). Prospects for sustainable rural cultural tourism in Maramure, Romania. *Tourism Geographies* 4(1), 62–94.

Urry, J. (1990). *The Tourist Gaze: Leisure and Travel in Contemporary Societies*. London: Sage.

Warren, C. (1998). Tannah Lot: The cultural and environmental politics of resort development in Bali. In P. Hirsch and C. Warren (eds), *The Politics of Environment in Southeast Asia: Resources and Resistance* (pp. 229–61). London: Routledge.

Williams, A., and Balaz, V. (2000). *Tourism in Transition: Economic Change in Central Europe*. London: I. B. Tauris.

Williams, R. H. (1996) *European Union Spatial Policy and Planning*. London: Paul Chapman.

Williams, S. (1998). *Tourism Geography*. London: Routledge.

Zhang, H. Q., Chong, K., and Ap, J. (1999). An analysis of tourism policy development in modern China. *Tourism Management* 20, 471–85.

Chapter 45

Tourism Communities and Growth Management

Alison Gill

The success of a tourism destination is often measured in terms of growth in the visitor numbers and their expenditures. From a business perspective growth is a fundamental objective of a tourism-based economy. However, over the past couple of decades attitudes towards tourism growth have been affected by two major, and not unrelated, forces: increasing public awareness of the potentially negative impacts of tourism development, and the introduction of the concept of sustainable development. As tourist numbers have increased worldwide, the negative impacts of tourism development have been increasingly evident in destination communities. These impacts have been primarily related to the degree or amount of development, the rate or speed of growth, and the level of community control over development. Unsightly commercial strip development along roads and beach frontage, oversized and competitive signage, and a lack of design uniformity are common visual indicators of the absence of planning and growth control in tourism destinations. However, the problems associated with uncontrolled growth go far beyond the immediate visual effects on the landscape and may include deteriorating environmental quality, an inability to provide adequate infrastructure to keep up with spatial expansion, and concerns by residents about a declining quality of life. Ultimately, if unchecked, these negative impacts will result in declining tourist visits and a downmarketing of tourist products.

In concert with this broader public awareness that tourism is not an environmentally or socially benign activity, the concept of sustainability has entered academic and popular discourses, leading to a growing concern for environmental issues. The ideas of sustainability have also entered the policy arena and, while yet in their infancy in terms of being fully operationalized, have resulted in changing approaches and concerns at all levels of government. The management of tourism, while still heavily weighted to a "demand-driven" perspective, is, in some places, shifting to a "supply-driven" approach whereby the ability of the resource to sustain tourism is the basis for growth decisions. The degree to which this is regulated by government or self-regulated within the industry varies considerably between places and nation-states.

The purpose of this chapter is to examine approaches that communities use to control tourism-related growth. A discussion of the relationship between communities and tourism growth serves as a frame for a more critical examination of the concept of growth management. This includes a consideration of how growth management evolved over time and how it has been applied in a tourism context, and an assessment of management tools that have been employed. Issues and challenges are then considered, including defining and sustaining environmental quality, scale factors in enacting growth management, and the challenges of participatory planning and community capacity-building. The chapter concludes by highlighting research needs associated with tourism growth management.

Communities and Tourism Growth

Tourism has been viewed as an attractive economic opportunity for many communities. In some instances global economic restructuring has resulted in the decline of traditional resource-based activities. In rural communities, tourism has been seen as one of the few alternatives when extractive industries such as fishing, forestry, agriculture, and mining cease to be economically viable. Elsewhere, especially in the developing world, ecotourism has often been promoted as the key to development in areas that have long been on the periphery of the global economy. In some cases communities actively pursue tourism opportunities, while in other instances tourism is thrust upon them. Regardless of the circumstances, experience has shown that unless tourism is effectively planned and managed there will be negative consequences (Gunn 1994).

The problems associated with tourism growth have been recognized within the academic realm for over 20 years and Butler's (1980) seminal concept of the resort cycle has remained a core idea of how, over time, tourism development can lead to stagnation and decline. Others have identified the critical stage at which growth stagnates as the limits of an area's carrying capacity (Coccossis and Parpairis 1992; Williams and Gill 1998). Growth, in particular a rapid rate of growth together with uncontrolled development, has been demonstrated in numerous studies as a reason for negative host community attitudes towards tourism (e.g., Canaan and Hennessy 1989; Long, Perdue, and Allen 1990; Prentice 1993; McCool and Martin 1994). In tourism communities, as elsewhere, local opposition to growth is grounded in a perceived decline in the quality of life caused by such factors as environmental degradation, traffic congestion, and increased cost of living (Schneider and Teske 1993). Opposition to growth may vary depending on such variables as length of residence or the degrees of dependency individuals have on the tourism industry (Johnson, Snepenger, and Akis 1994). However, the relationship between dependency and attitudes is not clear-cut. As Williams, Shaw, and Greenwood (1989) demonstrate in their study in Cornwall, entrepreneurs do not necessarily make decisions based solely on maximization of economic benefits, but balance such decisions with other quality-of-life issues related to their role as residents.

As noted above, a significant change that is affecting tourism growth in communities is the rise in environmental awareness amongst the general public. However, while public opinion polls invariably reflect positive responses to questions concerning good environmental practices, the implementation of such practices is often constrained when faced with "real-world" trade-off situations, such as jobs versus environmental protection. Local decisions concerning growth and competitiveness must be set within this broader and more complex global frame.

A further significant change during the past decade has occurred in response to globalization. With the declining influence of nation-states and the increased importance of trading alliances, communities have experienced new forms of governance that involve increasing devolution of the responsibilities of senior government to the local level. This has resulted in increased powers for local decision-makers and greater involvement of the public in decision-making (Walzer 1995). In this more competitive environment, local governments have been encouraged to develop stronger initiatives for private–public sector partnerships in their pursuit of growth (Moore and Pierre 1988). Private–public partnerships are increasingly being promoted as the model upon which tourism development should depend. As Jamal and Getz (1995: 187) observed, "Achieving coordination among government agencies, between the public and private sector, and among private enterprises is a challenging task . . . and requires the development of new mechanisms and processes for incorporating the diverse elements of the tourism system."

An important influence on growth policies is being felt as the result of increased lobbying by environmental non-governmental organizations (ENGOs) who frequently oppose growth and development – including tourism development. The enhanced role of NGOs reflects changes in the "new economy" whereby decisions are increasingly influenced by NGOs, private industry, and the public at large. Environmental organizations exert pressure not only directly on local governments but also on the corporate sector. The corporate sector is responding by engaging in a variety of self-regulation practices, although often NGOs seek independent certification of sustainable practice (e.g., Green Globe) (Font 2002). Levels of private–public sector partnership have increased and, as discussed more fully below, collaborative approaches between communities have been advocated.

The Development of Growth Management Ideas

Tourism businesses and activities occupy space within communities alongside other land uses, and as such are controlled by the same legislation and regulations that govern all community land use. In most developed countries, communities have land-use plans that identify designated uses for commercial, industrial, residential, and open space purposes (Gunn 1994), although tourism is often not a core element of such plans (Page and Thorn 1998). Market forces determine the rate of growth and, as most communities have welcomed growth and possess available land, towns and cities have expanded outwards. The idea of growth management as a conscious governmental program to control growth was developed in the United States in the 1970s as the result of rapid population growth during the 1950s and 1960s that led to suburbanization of towns and cities. While growth management legislation in the US is enacted at the state level in states that have experienced rapid growth (e.g. Oregon, California, Florida, Hawaii, Vermont) municipalities are responsible for the development of their own plans. From a growth management perspective this entails a public participatory approach, although the degree to which this is enacted is variable.

Initially, the objectives of growth management were embedded in environmental concerns (Zovanyi 1998), but this central concern was subsumed under other concerns such as the provision of affordable housing and community infrastructure and services. Growth management has been described as a "guidance system" to implement a desirable community vision (Chapin and Kaiser 1979) by attempting to capture the benefits of growth while mitigating the consequences. Growth management does not represent a no-growth approach. As Gill (2000) observed in the mountain resort community of Whistler (British Columbia, Canada), an approach which is grounded in environmental concerns and yet does not necessarily constrain development is appealing to both the environmental sentiments of the public who support the "management" element and the developers who are comfortable with the "growth" label.

In a tourism context, growth management considerations at the community level must not only respond to local concerns but necessarily balance the needs of residents with those of tourists. Tourism resources are frequently common pool resources (Healey 1994), such as public lands or water bodies that are used for recreational purposes or scenic enjoyment and valued by residents and tourists alike. Bosselman, Peterson, and McCarthy (1999) suggest that equity, sustainability, efficiency, and resiliency are principles that should guide growth decisions in relations to such resources. Elaborating on these ideas, they suggest that successful tourism management systems should include the following six components: "(i) they should define resource boundaries clearly; (ii) identify the players affected by the system; (iii) let the players make the rules; (iv) localize the rules as much as possible; (v) give the players a sense of permanence; and, (vi) monitor and mediate violations of the rules efficiently but effectively" (Bosselman et al. 1999: 21–2).

Growth Management Strategies

Underlying growth management decisions, the tasks of coordination and consensus-building lie at the heart of the process (Innes 1992). Growth management goes beyond more traditional planning processes by articulating a community-defined iterative process for formulating policy decisions and guiding capital budgets and improvement programs (Gill and Williams 1994). Growth management is a more radical departure from traditional planning approaches in the United States than it is for example in the United Kingdom. In the United States zoning, rather than the site-specific development control applied in the United Kingdom, is the primary tool of land-use regulation. Growth management employs both traditional methods of physical planning and land-use control, such as zoning and subdivision control, as well as newer processes of participatory land-use planning. These tools are used to influence and control the rate, amount, type, location, and quality of proposed new developments. Bosselman, Peterson, and McCarthy (1999) identify three categories of growth management strategy – those that manage quality, quantity, and location (table 45.1). Quality is most frequently addressed through design guidelines and controls, while quantity is often an issue of carrying capacity. While some planning techniques focus on only one of the strategies, others, such as community visioning, serve more comprehensive and multiple objectives. In a tourism context, many of these strategies are elements of community tourism planning processes (Murphy

Table 45.1 Examples of tourism growth management tools

Tools	Examples
Quality	
Special districts	Santa Fe, NM; New Orleans, LA
Zoning	Park City, Utah; Lake Tahoe, NEV
Environmentally sensitive area maps	Aspen, CO
Performance standards, e.g.	
Development density Building height/setback Floor area ratio Architectural and design Landscaping Sign controls Viewscape controls Noise regulation	Whistler, BC; Vail, CO; Stowe, VT; Bonaire, Netherlands Antilles; Jackson WY; Park City, Utah; Seaside, FL; Bermuda
Restrictive covenants	Whistler, BC
Trade-off strategies	
Density bonuses	Coral Gables, FL; Teton County, WY
Quantity	
Preservation strategies, e.g.	
Permit limits	Great Barrier Reef, Australia
Usage settings (e.g. low, moderate, high)	Cancún–Tulum Corridor, Mexico
Development rights transfer	Peninsula Township, MI
Zoning and mapping	Stowe, VT
Growth limitation strategies, e.g.	
Entrance/usage fees	Westminster Abbey, London
Parking limits, restricted access	Hanauma Bay, Hawaii; Yosemite National Park
Building caps and quota systems (residential, commercial)	Sanibel Island, FL; Bermuda; Bonaire, Netherlands Antilles
Incremental growth strategies	
Rate of growth restrictions	Whistler, BC; Aspen, CO; Ambergrise Caye, Belize
Location	
Tourist dispersion strategies	Languedoc-Roussillon, France
Tourist concentration strategies	Canterbury, UK; Bruges, Belgium, Nusa Dua, Bali
Comprehensive tools	
Comprehensive growth management plans	Seattle, WA
Comprehensive community plans	Banff, Alberta
Visioning	Jackson, WY

Source: Gill and Williams 1994; Wark 1995; Bosselman, Peterson, and McCarthy 1999.

1985). Indeed, community tourism planning processes embody many of the principles of tourism growth management, especially with respect to the role of community stakeholder involvement in determining the nature of future development.

Likewise, planning for sustainable tourism (Nelson, Butler, and Wall 1994; Bramwell et al. 1996), which embodies notions of carrying capacity, also has much in common with the principles of growth management.

Design control

Although quality is an attribute that is desirable in any urban setting, it is even more critical in a tourism context. The overall quality of the visitor experience, and the quality of life for residents, are dependent on good management. Without management controls, aesthetic quality is easily eroded by inappropriate designs, blocked or degraded viewscapes, and polluted environments. The basic tools for addressing such issues pre-date growth management approaches and include zoning and performance standards. While zoning has been widely used to ensure the spatial segregation of incompatible uses, design standards, which are often supplementary to zoning regulations, have been less widely applied. Zoning traditionally restricted its design criteria to height, density, and setback (yard) requirements. However, especially in heritage areas and comprehensively designed or redeveloped tourist environments, design criteria have also included architectural and design standards specifying building materials, style, and color (Lew 1988). In tourist settings standards relating to signage, viewscape control, and landscaping, and even noise regulations are of particular importance. Not infrequently, trade-off strategies are used to tailor specific community needs (for example the need for more urban park space or facilities) with the desire of the developers to make a profit. Thus, a developer may get a higher density bonus (i.e., be allowed to build more densely in one area) in return for park creation or the protection of viewsheds in another area.

Bosselman, Peterson, and McCarthy (1999) caution that communities must make sure that their regulations are not so stringent that they deter desired development. This is a complex challenge that evolves over time and is related to the competitive position of the destination at various stages of development (Cooper 1997; Gill 2000). For example, Gill (2000) found that during the early stages of Whistler's resort development, economic imperatives drove decisions and growth responded to market forces. Rapid growth was seen by the municipality, as a desirable objective until a "critical mass" was achieved, at which point the resort was competitive within the market. At this stage, the power of the local growth machine was contested by local residents as they became organized as community lobbyists raising concerns about the rate of growth and the effects of tourism on quality-of-life issues. Over time the priorities of growth management in Whistler have changed from a primary concern with matching growth in community infrastructure to the overall growth of the resort, to an increasing concern with the impacts of growth on environmental sustainability. Indeed, growth management is by definition a dynamic and iterative process responding to changing circumstances and attitudes.

Carrying capacity

Growth management shares a number of characteristics with other mechanisms that have been utilized to control the numbers of visitors in parks or outdoor recreation contexts (Wight 1998). The most widely known concept is that of carrying capacity which suggests growth within acceptable limits (Martin and Uysal 1990; Williams and Gill 1998). However, the application of carrying capacity is controversial

(Wight 1998; McCool and Lime 2001; Shaw and Williams 2002) as it is difficult to link simply raising or lowering a specific carrying capacity standard to resultant changes (McCool 1994). As Wight (1998) notes, this comes in part from the confusion between "impact" and "damage." Carrying capacity is very complex and involves understanding not only the physical and ecological limits but also the social and psychological responses of tourists and residents. Such factors as the type of tourist activities, seasonal distribution, and above all management decisions are all variables that must be considered. Although there are environmental limits that can be more objectively determined – for example, water supply or sewage treatment capacity – social and psychological carrying factors, such as crowding, are also important in determining visitor satisfaction levels. This type of approach requires involvement and participation of the community in establishing values and priorities.

One approach to carrying capacity that has been adopted more often in tourist destinations than in other types of community is the establishment of a development cap in the form of a "bed unit" or "pillow limit." This has been applied in some mountain tourist destinations where there are limitations on the amount of available land suitable for development as well as fragile ecosystems, such as alpine meadows and valley wetlands. Further, tourists visiting mountain destinations are generally seeking more natural settings and a non-urban experience, best catered to in smaller resorts with limited bed space (Dorward 1990). Thus, establishing a maximum limit for development is seen as desirable. However, under a growth management regime, this limit is not set in stone and can be adjusted in response to a community's desires. As Bradshaw (1989: viii) observed, it is a "a statement of local preferences... with proper mitigation practically any level of growth can be tolerated if it is preferred." For example, in the case of Whistler, the bed unit level was adjusted upwards from an initial limit of 40,000 in 1989 to a level of 52,500 in 2000 (Gill 2000). However, even this limit does not represent the actual agreed-upon limit as there is a clause that allows employee housing units to exceed the development cap. Further, in 1999, following a public referendum on the issue, extra bed units that exceeded the limit were approved in a trade-off whereby a developer gave the community a parcel of parkland that completed a wetlands ecosystem plan in return for the right to build a hotel elsewhere in the resort. Although the scientific basis for establishing Whistler's development cap is questionable, it has had the effect of establishing in people's minds the idea that to exceed the cap is in some way undesirable. If future growth is deemed to be desirable (perhaps in association with the community's selection as the 2010 Winter Olympics site), then opposition to such growth will be inevitable from those who "believe" in the validity of the bed unit limit. Another destination that set limits and then expanded them is the Galapagos Islands, where the permit system used to control visitor numbers has gradually allowed more over time (Wight 1998). Bermuda has successfully implemented a limit of 550,000 on the number of tourists it believes is optimum for the island (Conlin 1996). In part thanks to its island setting, it has been able to successfully employ regulatory mechanisms that limit the number of hotel rooms, time-share units, cruise vessels, and charter flights. As in the case of Whistler, these measures have been embedded within a broader growth management approach that also addresses the quality of the visitor and resident experience.

Despite a significant body of research that suggests the limitations of using a carrying capacity approach, many tourist destinations still seek a fixed number (Wight 1998). Elsewhere it is the rate of growth within a tourist destination that is the major concern for residents and thus some growth management approaches have adopted a targeted growth rate approach. For example, Aspen, Colorado, initially established an annual growth limit of 3.47 percent, although a subsequent plan reduced this to 2 percent (Gill and Williams 1994). However, despite the desirability of establishing limits (Bramwell et al. 1996), few development proposals include such limits, in large part because of the difficulty of developing appropriate measures (Butler 1996, 1999).

Community visioning

Although there are many tourist destinations employing some form of growth management strategy to address development concerns, fewer practice more comprehensive approaches. The need to develop a long-term vision or strategy for growth is increasingly acknowledged and tourism communities are increasingly identifying goals and objectives around a "vision statement." These strategic visioning exercises are often set within the broader objective of "sustainable development" and they may or may not be referred to as "growth management" (which can sometimes have a negative connotation to pro-development interests). However, regardless of what the processes are called, the results are very similar. Given the many and various stakeholder groups involved in community visioning exercises, it can take a considerable amount of time to reach consensus. For example, Jackson, Wyoming's vision took two years to formulate (Jamal and Getz 1997). In Jackson's vision statement support for a growth management approach was articulated to achieve the enhancement of natural resources; maintenance and enhancement of the community's small-town, Western heritage; preservation of historical heritage; and diversification of the economy (Jamal and Getz 1997). The utility of community-based vision statements as a management tool varies depending on such variables as the specificity of community values, the process and type of public involvement in the visioning process, and the degree to which the vision guides strategic planning and development initiatives.

There are numerous problems associated with stakeholder involvement in participatory processes (Simmons 1994; Gill 1996; Reed 1997). The degree to which participants actually influence outcomes is very much dependent on power relations (Jamal and Getz 1995; Reed 1997). Public participation covers a spectrum of involvement, from processes in which the public are little more than informed of issues (for example in a public meeting), to a much less common situation of actual shared decision-making where stakeholder representatives have legislated power to make decisions (Williams, Penrose, and Hawkes 1998). Further, especially in a tourism context where there is often a wide diversity of interests, representativeness can be a problem. For example, the views of seasonal employees are often not well represented in tourist destination planning processes (although often this is because they choose not to be involved). Understanding their needs for affordable housing and community services is, however, an important element in overall planning. Uneven power relations also occur in the not uncommon circumstance where the interests of large tourism enterprises override those of smaller tourism operators, or where other resource users (e.g., the forest industry) have greater political influence (Reed and Gill 1997). A further problem is volunteer burnout. Participatory processes rely on volunteerism, and in any community this falls in large part to a committed group of individuals. In long-drawn-out processes, such as the example given above of Jackson, the commitment of time and energy leads to attrition amongst participants.

Growth monitoring

Monitoring is also a fundamental element of growth management. Without an adequate database it is impossible to ascertain if strategies need amending. As in many urban settings, the data in tourist destinations are invariably inadequate and incomplete. Some advances have been made recently with the development of tools such as environmental management systems and environmental auditing (Hawkes and Williams 1993). In addition to environmental monitoring, tracking economic and social indicators relating to both residents and visitors is desirable. Given the technical and administrative realities of implementing a comprehensive monitoring system relatively few places have implemented them (Butler 2000). Whistler has attempted to develop a comprehensive resort and community monitoring program that collects a wide range of economic, social, and environmental data (Gill 1997; Williams and Gill 1998). However, its utility is limited by a lack of analysis to determine the relationships between the data. The information does, however, provide a useful basis for trend analysis, which, in keeping with growth management principles, is shared annually with residents in a community meeting. While attempts are made to engage the community in the process, those attending meetings tend to be a core of residents committed to participating in community affairs as well as representatives of various interest groups.

Issues and Challenges of Growth Management

The central challenge for growth management in a tourism destination is how to maintain the critical balances among sustaining environmental quality, stimulating a healthy tourism industry, and maintaining community viability and support. Sustaining environmental quality in the face of growing demand is a key ingredient in the long-term viability of a destination. While this has been seen as the domain of the public sector, especially in the provision of protected areas, new approaches are emerging within the industry. The rapid growth of ecotourism, in which operators and tourists engage in forms of tourism that exhibit greater responsibility to both the environment and society, reflects the response of the market to heightened environmental awareness amongst the public as a whole. These market forces are also influencing other tourism operations. To remain competitive and to maintain growth, there is evidence that sectors of the tourism industry are recognizing the need to position themselves as innovators with respect to corporate ethical behavior. A number of hotel chains have already subscribed to environmental management systems, as have some resort developers. In the US for example, the "Sustainable Slopes" environmental charter for ski areas is subscribed to, in varying degrees, by over 70 percent of the mountain sports operators (<http://www.nsaa.org/nsaa2002/_environmental_charter.asp>, accessed September 10, 2002). Business models of sustainable practice are also beginning to be adopted by tourism communities. The resort municipality of Whistler, British Columbia, has, for example, adopted "The Natural Step" approach to guide its future development (Natrass and Altomare 2002). This approach, developed as a corporate tool for sustainability, offers a process of development that "uses a science-based systems framework to help organizations, individuals and communities take steps towards sustainability" (<www.naturalstep.ca>, accessed September 10, 2002).

Another overlooked issue is the relationship between growth and land values, and the resultant implications of this. Assuming that a destination maintains its competitive position, land prices will invariably rise as supply fails to meet growing demand. Under such circumstances, the provision of affordable housing for the workforce becomes an even more difficult issue to resolve. Rising land prices are a reality of any tourist community experiencing growth and create problems that are not readily resolved. Communities that have established caps on growth are even more seriously affected. The consequences of not having adequate affordable housing present problems for any resort as affordability is the key driver of displacement (Culbertson and Kolberg 1991). Some communities, such as Aspen, Colorado, are now largely composed of second home residents, which in turns leads to a deterioration of a sense of "community." The presence of bedroom communities to house workers surrounding the main tourist destination is another common feature of resort communities as real estate within a successful destination becomes overpriced for minimum wage workers. In time, growing demand in the nearby bedroom communities will increase their prices, triggering a further outmigration. In some places, to protect residential neighborhoods there are restrictions on property owners with respect to their rights to rent out their properties as tourist accommodation. A common problem in resorts where there are no restrictions is that rental accommodation occupied by employees is often only seasonally available. While the issue of affordable housing is an important outcome of tourism growth, only a few academic studies have explored this topic (Culbertson and Kolberg 1991; Heid 1995; Lewis 1991).

From a geographic perspective, the fact that tourist communities are not closed systems but integrally connected to the surrounding region raises the issue of the appropriate scale at which growth management should be enacted. In the US the degree to which growth management is practiced at the local level varies widely from one community to the next. In cases where municipalities have enacted strong growth management controls, displacement effects are seen in the surrounding region. This calls for growth management to be embedded in larger regional or state systems, which the states of Hawaii and Vermont have attempted. In most cases, however, community-driven growth management policies apply only within municipal boundaries, even though the destination is dependent on both public and private externalities, including transportation systems and natural areas, as well as external political decisions and the vagaries of tourist decision-making (Gill and Williams 1994). Ackerman (1999) suggests that the major reason there is a lack of growth management at a regional, state, or national scale is because in many instances geographically larger planning areas cut across local jurisdictions and it is at this local level that land-use decisions are frequently made. Elsewhere, for example in the United Kingdom, regional planning has gained importance in recent years and offers opportunities for managing growth in a more comprehensive manner (Counsell and Haughton 2002).

In the absence of legislation at the regional level, voluntary collaboration becomes an imperative, although in many instances it is competition rather than collaboration that characterizes relationships between communities (Gill 1997). A collaborative approach, best when involving public–private sector partnerships, is essential in the tourism sector because of the dependence of the industry on common pool resources. For example, scenery is a significant element of many tourist attractions and in some cases is the primary attraction. Yet rarely does the industry control the "use" of a scenic viewshed. In many cases legislation is required to protect that viewshed from deterioration caused by such activities as logging or development.

While, in the United States, growth management legislation has introduced a comprehensive framework within which communities can strive for balanced development, its implementation is hampered by several factors. Conceptually, community values and participatory approaches drive the process. In reality the degree of participatory input is limited by problems associated with such processes as representativeness, the capacity of planning professionals to integrate public input, and the resources of the community to acquire good data on which sound decisions can be based. For smaller communities, in particular, capacity issues relating to expertise and resources are a serious barrier to the implementation of growth management practices. Further, studies suggest that in many places growth control initiatives do not necessarily result in good planing (Ackerman 1999).

Conclusions

In most tourist destinations growth is often encouraged and uncontrolled in the early stages of development when associated problems are not evident. This results in the need for post hoc action when problems of declining environmental quality, overcrowding, traffic congestion, or the lack of affordable housing emerge. At this stage growth is more difficult to manage, but management is essential if the destination is to become sustainable. Tourism communities face unique challenges. How does one, for example, achieve a vision such as the one developed by the residents of Squamish, British Columbia? In common with many other smaller communities they wish to "build and strengthen a diverse four-season tourism sector while maintaining our small town atmosphere and preserving our heritage" (Gill and Reed 1997). Growth implies change which residents often resist; however, lack of growth can also lead to undesirable impacts associated with a stagnant or declining economy.

Growth management approaches have been adopted as the guiding principles for many communities, particularly in the United States, with the primary concern being control of land use. For tourism communities where meeting the complex needs of diverse resident stakeholders (e.g., second home owners, seasonal workers, and resident entrepreneurs) and tourists is a challenging task, growth management practices are best embedded within a broader approach to sustainability. While researchers have usefully critiqued and expanded upon Butler's (1980) resort-cycle model, new models of growth within a framework of sustainability are called for. The edited works by Wahab and Pigram (1997) and Bramwell et al. (1996) offer some thoughts on this relationship. Butler (1999, 1996) elaborates on the constraints of effectively integrating tourism into concepts of sustainable development. These include its relationship to carrying capacity; control of tourist development and operation; mass tourism; and problems of measurement and monitoring. A constraint on the implementation of methods such as monitoring is the lack of community capacity for planning and implementation. Indeed, in the examples given of growth management planning, the communities are often elite destinations that have the ability to hire planners and managers. In some cases, such as in developing countries, comprehensive tourism planning is often carried out by outside consultants, supported by aid agencies such as the World Bank. The degree to which there is an implementation gap between plans and action is worthy of investigation. Further, as Butler (1999: 17) observes, "Tourism researchers with few exceptions have tended to ignore the issues of control of tourism and, by implication, the politics of tourism."

Given that decisions about growth are ultimately political (Hall 1994), the roles and responsibilities of various community growth management approaches need to be considered from a "new economy" perspective. This would situate growth decisions in the changed global economy and consider the significance of emerging public–private partnerships (Augustyn and Knowles 2000), and the role of industry and NGOs. This presents significant challenges with respect to the existing institutional arrangements in many places. It calls for a closer integration of tourism planning (at various levels) with municipal, and regional, land-use and resource planning. Such integration as Godfrey (1998) observes in his study of local government attitudes towards sustainable tourism in the UK can be problematic. In particular, the need for integrated planning that meaningfully engages a wide range of stakeholder representatives in the planning process is desirable. This is happening in some places, for example in British Columbia, where a regional strategic land and resource management planning process (LRMP) has brought together representatives from all levels of government, industry (including tourism operators), residents, environmental groups, and outdoor recreation groups (Williams, Penrose, and Hawkes 1998). While local governments will continue to be responsible for land-use decisions related to growth, the manner in which they engage others in decision-making will (at least in the developed world) change with pressure for greater involvement and greater decision-making power shared with stakeholders,

The examples given in this chapter are drawn primarily from the United States, where there is a history of growth management legislation in many jurisdictions. There are lessons to be learned from this experience and future research could usefully engage in comparative studies in tourism growth management under various institutional arrangements, including those across international boundaries and cultures.

REFERENCES

Ackerman, W. V. (1999). Growth control versus the growth machine in Redlands, California: Conflict in urban land use. *Urban Geography* 20(2), 146–67.

Augustyn, M., and Knowles, T. (2000). Performance of tourism partnerships: A focus on York. *Tourism Management* 21(4), 341–51.

Bosselman, F. P., Peterson, C. A., and McCarthy C. (1999). *Managing Tourism Growth: Issues and Applications*. Washington, DC: Island Press.

Bradshaw, T. K. (1989). Foreword. In I. Schiffman (ed.), *Alternative Techniques for Managing Growth*. Berkeley, CA: Institute of Governmental Studies, University of California.

Bramwell, B., Henry, I., Jackson, G., and van der Straaten, J. (1996). A framework for understanding sustainable tourism management. In B. Bramwell, I. Henry, G. Jackson, A. G. Prat, G. Richards, and J. van der Straaten (eds), *Sustainable Tourism Management: Principles and Practice* (pp. 23–72). Tilburg, Netherlands: Tilburg University Press.

Butler, R. W. (1980). The concept of a tourist area cycle of evolution: Implications for management of resources. *The Canadian Geographer* 24(1), 5–12.

Butler, R. W. (1996). The concept of carrying capacity for tourist destinations: Dead or merely buried? *Progress in Tourism and Hospitality Research* 2(3/4), 283–93.

Butler, R. W. (1999). Sustainable tourism: A state-of-the art review. *Tourism Geographies* 1(1), 7–25.

Butler, R. W. (2000). Tourism and the environment: A geographical perspective. *Tourism Geographies* 2, 337–58.

Canaan, P., and Hennessy, M. (1989). The growth machine, tourism and the selling of culture. *Sociological Perspectives* 32, 227–43.

Chapin, F. S. Jr., and Kaiser, E. J. (1979). *Urban Land Use Planning*. Urbana: University of Illinois Press.

Coccossis, H., and Parpairis, A. (1992). Tourism and the environment: Some observations on the concept of carrying capacity. In H. Briassoulis and J. van der Straaten (eds), *Tourism and the Environment* (pp. 23–33). Dordrecht: Kluwer.

Conlin, M. V. (1996). Revitalizing Bermuda: Tourism policy in a mature island destination. In L. C. Harrison and W. Husbands (eds), *Practicing Responsible Tourism: International Case Studies in Tourism Planning Policy and Development* (pp. 80–102).Toronto: John Wiley.

Cooper, C. (1997). The contribution of life cycle analysis and strategic planning to sustainable tourism. In S. Wahab and J. J. Pigram (eds), *Tourism Development and Growth: The Challenge of Sustainability* (pp. 78–94). New York: Routledge.

Counsell, D., and Haughton, G. (2002). Complementary or conflict? Reconciling regional and local planning systems. *Town and Country Planning* 71(6), 164–8.

Culbertson, K., and Kolberg, J. (1991). Worker housing in resorts: Aspen's experience. *Urban Land* 50(4), 513–27.

Dorward, S. (1990). *Design for Mountain Communities: A Landscape Architectural Guide*. New York: Van Nostrand Reinhold.

Font, X. (2002). Environmental certification in tourism and hospitality: Progress, process and prospects. *Tourism Management* 23, 197–205.

Gill, A. M. (1996). Rooms with a view: Informal settings for public dialogue. *Society and Natural Resources* 9, 633–43.

Gill, A. M. (1997). Competition and the resort community. In P. E. Murphy (ed.), *Quality Management in Urban Tourism*. Chichester: John Wiley.

Gill, A. M. (2000). From growth machine to growth management: The dynamics of resort development. *Environment and Planning A* 32, 1083–1103.

Gill, A. M., and Reed, M. G. (1997). The reimaging of a Canadian resource town. Post-productivism in a North American context. *Applied Geographic Studies* 1(2), 129–47.

Gill, A. M., and Williams, P. W. (1994). Managing growth in mountain tourism communities. *Tourism Management* 15(3), 212–20.

Godfrey, K. B. (1998). Attitudes towards "sustainable tourism" in the UK: A view from local government. *Tourism Management* 19(30), 213–24.

Gunn, C. (1994). *Tourism Planning: Basics, Concepts, Cases*, 3rd edn. Washington, DC: Taylor & Francis.

Hall, C. M. (1994). *Tourism and Politics: Politics, Power and Place*. Chichester: John Wiley.

Hawkes, S., and Williams, P. (1993). *The Greening of Tourism*. Burnaby, BC: Simon Fraser University, Centre for Tourism Policy and Research.

Healey, R. G. (1994). The "common pool" problem in tourism landscapes. *Annals of Tourism Research* 21, 596–611.

Heid, J. (1995). A strategic approach to affordable housing in resort communities. *Urban Land* August, 34–81.

Innes, J. E. (1992). Group processes and social construction of growth management. *Journal of the American Planning Association* 58, 440–53.

Jamal, T., and Getz, D. (1995). Collaboration theory and community tourism planning. *Annals of Tourism Research* 22(1), 186–204.

Jamal. T., and Getz, D. (1997) "Visioning" for sustainable tourism development: Community-based collaborations. In P. E. Murphy (ed.), *Quality Management in Urban Tourism*. Chichester: John Wiley.

Johnson, J. D., Snepenger, D. J., and Akis, S. (1994). Residents' perception of tourism development. *Annals of Tourism Research* 21(3), 629–42.

Lew, A. A. (1988). Tourism and place studies: An example of Oregon's older retail districts. *Journal of Geography* 87(4), 122–6.

Lewis, S. (1991). Building affordable housing in unaffordable places. *Planning* 57, 24–7.

Long, P. T., Perdue, R. R., and Allen, L. (1990). Rural residents' tourism perceptions and attitudes by community level of tourism. *Journal of Travel Research* 28(3), 3–9.

Martin, B. S., and Uysal, M. (1990). An examination of the relationship between carrying capacity and the tourism lifecycle: Management and policy implications. *Journal of Environmental Management* 31, 327–33.

McCool, S. F. (1994). Planning for sustainable nature-dependent tourism development: The limits of acceptable change system. *Tourism Recreation Research* 19(2), 51–5.

McCool, S. F., and Lime, D. W. (2001). Tourism carrying capacity: Tempting fantasy or useful reality? *Journal of Sustainable Tourism* 9(5), 372–88.

McCool, S. F., and Martin, S. (1994). Community attachment and attitudes towards tourism. *Journal of Travel Research* 32(2), 29–34.

Moore, C., and Pierre, J. (1988). Partnerships or privatisation? The political economy of economic restructuring. *Policy and Politics* 16(3), 169–78.

Murphy, P. (1985). *Tourism: A Community Approach*. London: Routledge.

Nattras, B., and Altomare, M. (2002). *Dancing with the Tiger: Learning Sustainability Step by Natural Step*. Gabriola Island, BC: Newsociety Publishers.

Nelson, J. G., Butler, R., and Wall, G. (eds) (1994). *Tourism and Sustainable Development: Monitoring, Planning, Managing*. Department of Geography Publication Series 37. Waterloo, Canada: University of Waterloo

Page, S., and Thorn, K. (1998). Sustainable tourism development and planning in New Zealand: Local government responses. In C. M. Hall and A. A. Lew (eds), *Sustainable Tourism: A Geographical Perspective* (pp. 173–84). New York: Addison Wesley Longman.

Prentice, R. (1993). Community-driven tourism planning and resident preferences. *Tourism Management* 14, 218–27.

Reed, M. (1997). Power relations and community-based tourism planning. *Annals of Tourism Research* 23(3), 566–91.

Reed, M. G., and Gill, A. M. (1997). Tourism, recreational and amenity values in land allocation: An analysis of institutional arrangements in the postproductivist era. *Environment and Planning A* 29, 2019–40.

Schneider, M., and Teske, P. (1993). The antigrowth entrepreneur: Challenging the "equilibrium" of the growth machine. *Journal of Politics* 55, 214–30.
Shaw, G., and Williams, A. M. (2002). *Critical Issues in Tourism: A Geographical Perspective*, 2nd edn. Oxford: Blackwell.
Simmons, D. (1994). Community participation in tourism planning. *Tourism Management* 15, 98–108.
Wahab, S., and Pigram, J. J. (eds) (1997). *Tourism Development and Growth: The Challenge of Sustainability*. New York: Routledge.
Walzer, N. (ed.) (1995). *Local Economic Development: Incentives and International Trends*. Boulder, CO: Westview Press.
Wark, R. J. (1995). Tourism growth management: An examination of opportunities for Salt Spring Island, B.C. Unpublished Master's thesis on natural resources management, Simon Fraser University, Burnaby, BC.
Williams, A. M., Shaw, G., and Greenwood, J. (1989). From tourist to tourism entrepreneur, from consumption to production: Evidence from Cornwall. *Environment and Planning A* 21, 1639–53.
Williams, P., and Gill, A. M. (1998). Tourism carrying capacity management issues. In W. Theobald (ed.), *Global Tourism: The Next Decade*, 2nd edn (pp. 231–46). Oxford: Butterworth-Heinemann.
Williams, P., Penrose, R., and Hawkes, S. (1998). Shared decision making in tourism land use planning. *Annals of Tourism Research* 225(40), 860–99.
Wight, P. (1998). Tools for sustainability analysis in planning and managing tourism and recreation in the destination. In C. M. Hall and A. A. Lew (eds), *Sustainable Tourism: A Geographical Perspective* (pp. 75–91). New York: Addison Wesley Longman.
Zovanyi, G. (1998). *Growth Management for a Sustainable Future: Ecological Sustainability as the New Growth Management Focus for the 21st Century*. Westport: Praeger.

Chapter 46

Political Boundaries and Regional Cooperation in Tourism

Dallen J. Timothy and Victor B. Teye

Introduction

International borders and their adjacent territories have long functioned as tourist attractions and important destinations, while also mediating tourism flows as physical and psychological barriers (Timothy 1995, 2001; Williams, Baláž, and Bodnárová 2001). According to the political geography literature, international boundaries have several functions: to mark the physical limits of sovereignty; to mediate the flows of certain goods and services; to filter undesirable elements out and keep desired elements in; to provide a line of military defense; and to monitor flows of people.

Owing to these functions, borders traditionally have been perceived by travelers as somewhat burdensome; immigration formalities are commonly seen as intimidating and inconvenient, and crossing some boundaries, even friendly ones, can be daunting and time-consuming. In national administrative terms, borders have long dictated the extent of sovereign control, and historically few cross-boundary partnerships have developed except in instances of limited trade in goods, because problems were generally more localized in nature. However, during the past century, political isolationism, which was the norm in many parts of the world for centuries, has diminished. In its place, there has been rapid globalization and integration. Manifestations of this exist in many parts of the world as sections of countries, entire countries, large multination regions, and continents begin to cooperate and collaborate in social, economic, political, and ecological ways to achieve goals which are to the mutual benefit of all parties (Balassa 1961; Williams 1994; Jessop 1995; Bhalla and Bhalla 1997; Bach 1999).

Cross-border and multinational alliances have gone from near non-existence 70 years ago to become the norm in the twenty-first century, with important implications for tourism. This chapter highlights the main issues surrounding cross-border and international collaboration in tourism, with a special focus on the scale of cooperation, critical areas of cooperation, and the reasons why true cross-national collaboration is difficult to achieve. While we recognize that there are subtle differences between the meanings of cooperation and collaboration, the two terms are used interchangeably in this chapter, as are the terms border, boundary, and frontier.

Forms and Scales of Cross-Border Cooperation

In recent years, countries have begun examining the notion of cross-border regional (supranational) cooperation, especially in areas of economic development, trade, human mobility, and political stability. As a result, since the middle of the twentieth century, several supranational alliances have been created which aim to decrease the barrier effects of political boundaries primarily in trade terms. Many of these alliances have also begun to branch into other areas of human welfare and economic development, including cross-border migration, education, environmental conservation, and tourism. Four scales of supranational alliances are identified in figure 46.1 and discussed below.

Global alliances

Many alliances have been formed since the mid-1900s, which involve membership at a global level. Perhaps the best-known example is the United Nations (UN), which aims to promote human welfare in economic, social, military, and political terms. While tourism was not originally one of the primary concerns of the UN, it is now an important part of the UN mandate to improve social and individual welfare. Many of the UN's efforts regarding tourism are conducted under the auspices of the United Nations Educational, Scientific and Cultural Organization (UNESCO), the United Nations Development Programme (UNDP), and the United Nations Environment Programme (UNEP).

UNESCO's mandate is extensive in many aspects of science, education, and culture. However, in 1972 the organization enacted the World Heritage Convention, which has been instrumental in the conservation of many cultural and natural sites throughout the world. The Convention established the World Heritage List and the World Heritage Commission, whose goal is to protect and provide global status to

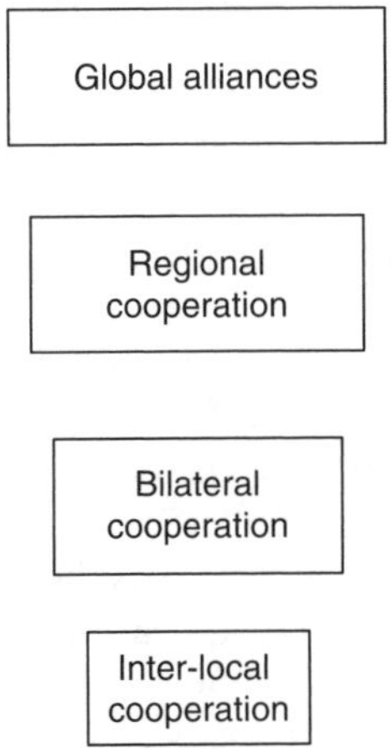

Figure 46.1 Levels of cross-border cooperation

cultural and natural properties of outstanding universal value. One of the Commission's most critical responsibilities is to provide technical support under the World Heritage Fund in less affluent states. By the end of 2001, 167 nations had joined the Convention and 721 sites had been listed – 554 cultural sites, 144 natural sites, and 23 mixed properties (Timothy and Boyd 2003). While UNESCO itself is somewhat indifferent to tourism, its efforts work hand in hand with tourism, as most of the properties on the list are significant visitor attractions.

The World Tourism Organization (WTO) is the largest and most geographically widespread international coalition of states that deals directly with tourism. Its responsibilities include overseeing changes in tourism worldwide by collecting data from all countries, providing educational resources and training programs, and assisting less developed countries in planning their tourism industries in a sustainable manner. Another critical organization is the International Air Transport Association (IATA), which helps regulate international air travel, negotiate flight routing, and deal with some aspects of flight safety standards.

Several other international trade coalitions also have specific interests in tourism. These include the International Maritime Organization (IMO), the International Civil Aviation Organization (ICAO), the Customs Cooperation Council (CCC), the International Monetary Fund (IMF), the Organization for Economic Cooperation and Development (OECD), and the General Agreement on Tariffs and Trade (GATT – now the World Trade Organization) (Hall 1994, 2000). Despite this wide range of interest, there is relatively little regulation of tourism on a truly global scale, the exceptions being the WTO and international regulations pertaining to air transportation (Hall 1994).

Regional/pan-continental cooperation

On this scale, alliances tend to be more geographically condensed and cohesive. The most common example is regional trading blocs, also known as free trade areas, economic communities, and regional alliances. Balassa (1961) and Williams (1994) noted seven stages, or types, of economic integration, namely free trade areas, customs unions, common markets, economic unions, monetary unions, economic and monetary unions, and full economic unions. The move toward regionalism can be described as cooperation and integration between adjoining nations, which share a sense of individual inadequacy in areas of socioeconomic welfare (Renninger 1979; Teye 2000). In other words, by uniting to some degree with cross-border neighbors, national development objectives, particularly among smaller and less developed nations, can best be met through a collective regional effort (Hussain 1999: 27). The underlying premise of economic communities is that nations can enlarge their trading regions for imports and exports. With the elimination of protective tariffs and other trade barriers, products that have customarily been produced for domestic use and limited export can more easily circulate within the region.

While the European Union is usually cited as the most successful and integrated of these communities, several others have appeared during the past 30 years and have achieved some level of success. While none of these has tourism as its primary focus, tourism has come to the forefront of socioeconomic negotiations in many of these alliances. This is particularly so in NAFTA (North America Free Trade Area), the European Union, ASEAN (Association of South East Asian Nations), and SADC

(Southern African Development Community), where the industry has received significant deliberate consideration at the supranational level.

On a smaller scale, several growth triangles have been formed in Asia. This concept refers to three or more countries or parts of countries working together in a complementary fashion to improve their economies. The idea of growth triangles originated in 1990 when Singapore partnered with Indonesia's Riau province and Malaysia's Johor state in a sub-ASEAN economic alliance, which became known as the SIJORI Growth Triangle. The goal of the alliance was to strengthen the economic and social linkages between the three partners and to promote the entire area as an open investment region for multinational corporations (Timothy 2000b). Other goals included decreasing the barrier effects of state borders by increasing flows of capital, labor, and goods across their common boundaries (Parsonage 1992; Hall 2001).

Considerable efforts have focused on tourism in recent years as tourism has grown to a significant level in Johor, Riau, and Singapore. Joint marketing efforts, resort development, ecotours, golf courses, and agritourism are among the common tourism elements being undertaken under the auspices of the growth triangle. The SIJORI Triangle was the first of its kind and has served as a model for more recent growth triangles throughout Asia, although these have been mixed in their degree of success. The main problem in SIJORI and other triangles has been a chronic unbalance in benefits among member countries; usually one or two signatories reap most of the benefits at the expense of the other party nations (Timothy 2000b).

Bilateral cooperation

This refers to collaborative efforts between two sovereign nations. Examples of this exist throughout the world, where neighboring countries cooperate in a variety of areas of tourism. Often there is a strong economic dependence by one country on its neighbor. Liechtenstein, for example, is heavily dependent on Switzerland for much of its economic welfare, and in the international arena Switzerland represents its smaller neighbor in many diplomatic circles and in the area of tourism promotion.

Since 1994, Israel and Jordan have devoted considerable efforts to develop tourism jointly along their common boundary in the Jordan River Valley. Such efforts include developing common cultural and natural areas and infrastructure (Gradus 1994; Kliot 1996). Likewise, dozens of international parks have been developed since the 1930s throughout the world in an effort to conserve natural and cultural resources that spill over national boundaries. It takes considerable effort and serious negotiations on the part of both nations to create bi-national parks (Timothy 1999, 2000a).

Inter-local cooperation

Local-level, cross-border networks are the fourth and final level of international cooperation. Despite political tradition dictating that cross-boundary partnerships are under the domain of central governments, not local administrators (Dupuy 1982; Gaines 1995), this form of collaboration is becoming more common today, and it is critical in areas where tourism activities take place at or near international boundaries. Often such collaborative efforts occur informally, without authorization from national governments, and are often the most successful because at this level there are generally fewer bureaucratic obstacles to hinder cross-border relations. Hansen (1983) and Bufon (1994) stressed the importance of local international partnerships, which they suggested might be the forerunners to more official bilateral and multilateral agreements.

This level of cooperation can have positive social, economic, and political impacts. Leimgruber (1989: 57) recognized that "cooperation on a local scale on matters such as tourist promotion . . . effectively contributes to reduce the separative role of the boundary [because] the common problems in a peripheral region prevail over nationalist considerations." One of the best illustrations of this phenomenon is the establishment of Euroregions, which were formed in Europe in the late 1980s as a way of solving traditional economic problems in border areas and reducing regional disparities in preparation for EU integration (Bertram 1998; Timothy 2002). These cross-boundary areas are volunteer associations of border region governments, which gear their transboundary activities toward specific economic, sociopolitical, and technical issues (Scott 1998: 608). Likewise, the European Commission's Interreg and Regis programs have actively sought to boost the economic development of Europe's borderlands and peripheral regions, based on the notion of local international cooperation. A considerable amount of Interreg's efforts have included tourism initiatives in peripheral areas of Europe (Anderson and O'Dowd 1999; Timothy 2001, 2002; Williams, Baláž, and Bodnárová 2001).

Cross-border networks are common in situations where cities and villages are divided. Officially border communities should resolve "city-level problems through foreign policy channels" (Herzog 1991: 261), but these official channels are often skirted, where possible, to solve problems and promote tourism at the grassroots level.

The Importance of Cross-Border Cooperation

In part, supranational cooperation has grown rapidly in recent years because of its potential to enhance sustainable development strategies, boost individual national economies, and assist in peacemaking between neighbors. Tourism has come to play an important role in these partnership efforts.

Sustainable development

Because environmental and economic problems are increasingly international in scope, cross-border and multinational cooperation has the potential to enhance sustainability in the context of tourism, for it can decidedly form more equitable relationships, enhance ecological and cultural harmony, improve efficiency, create holistic management approaches, and improve sociocultural and ecological integrity (Timothy 1999). However, it must be realized that cooperation is not the only answer and it must be approached with caution, for it can create additional challenges where building effective stakeholder partnerships is concerned.

Peace

Cross-frontier collaboration in vital areas of tourism may be a useful tool in enhancing the peace-building benefits that tourism possibly possesses (Fineberg 1993; Gradus 1994; Kliot 1996; Saba 1999). Even in situations where hostility is strong between neighbors, cooperation in matters of tourism might help build friendship and understanding. Sönmez and Apostolopoulos (2000) recognized this on the divided island of Cyprus and suggested several ways in which north–south relations might be mended through tourism cooperation: (1) set policies to facilitate free tourist migration between sides; (2) remove restrictions on contact between Turkish and Greek Cypriots; (3) build free trade agreements; (4) enact cooperative marketing/promotion efforts; and (5) encourage contact between peoples.

Traditionally, international boundaries and their protectionist roles have created competitive relationships between adjacent nations where neighbors offer similar goods and services, thereby creating competitive, sometimes unhealthy, market environments. While goodwill and sustainable tourism development can be critical outcomes of cross-border cooperation, they do not automatically follow. Nonetheless, early signs from the EU, ASEAN, and North America show that supranational cooperation can begin to break down competition and advance symbiotic, complementary relationships, so that entire cross-border regions benefit from the growth of tourism and neighbors do not have to work in competition for a limited demand (Apostolopoulos and Sönmez 2000; Timothy 2002).

Critical Areas of Cross-Border Cooperation and Related Constraints

As the discussion above demonstrates, tourism in one form or another can be considered at all levels of cooperation. However, even when the goals for collaboration are essentially the same for all participating nations, they must be operationalized within the social systems and political frameworks that exist with different values, prejudices, and perceptions (Graizbord 1986). Strong dissimilarities in economics, culture, politics, and social structure frequently obstruct partnership efforts (Saint-Germain 1995; Scott 1998), so when cooperation takes place between entities where similar cultures, values, and political views exist, it has a much better chance of success (Bufon 1994; Blatter 1997; Bertram 1998). The most common elements of tourism considered in international alliances include trade in goods and services, promotion and marketing, flow of people, environmental conservation, and transportation and infrastructure (Teye 1991; Timothy 2001). Each of these is examined briefly below.

Trade in goods and services

Supplies including building materials, foodstuffs, and fuel are necessary for tourism to function. While the ideal tourism system would utilize local products and services as much as possible, completely locally derived product use is not always achievable. In this case, governments might consider easing import and export restrictions on industry-related goods, which cannot be produced domestically. Such efforts are nearly always met with considerable resistance as governments balk at the notion of reducing the protectionist measures for domestic industries.

To maximize the benefits of tourism, providers of services, such as tour companies and resort developers, should be able to function in member countries in cooperation with local service providers with minimal interference and business restrictions. Similarly, other services, such as rental agencies and hotels, should be permitted and even encouraged to function across borders with few hindrances. Such allowance would likely improve foreign investments at a regional level and enhance economic balance as complementarity is created in cross-border areas.

Promotion and marketing

Promotion and marketing have traditionally been the most successful and most common forms of cross-border cooperation in tourism, and there are many examples throughout the world where this is done on regional (e.g., South African Regional Tourism Council and Visit ASEAN Years), bi-national (e.g., Ireland–Northern Ireland), and inter-local (e.g., special events and sporting competitions) levels. Such efforts are said to improve representation in foreign markets (Teye 2000) and expand the resource and attraction base in such a way that "the sum is greater than the parts" (Richard 1993: 603). Some of the most important areas of marketing cooperation include joint advertising campaigns, shared promotional budgets, equal exposure in the promotional literature, and joint marketing research. With joint advertising campaigns and promotional budgets, funds in each nation can be saved and utilized in other important pursuits, such as personnel training, infrastructure development, and conservation (Aulakh, Kotabe, and Sahay 1996; Timothy 2001).

Despite its apparent success, this area of cooperation is not without problems. It is difficult to manage, can create harmful competition, is value-laden and time-consuming, and can end up favoring elites on both sides of the border through political opportunism (Church and Reid 1996, 1999; Blatter 1997; Timothy 1999), thereby marginalizing further the positions of less affluent community members and communities.

Movement of people

In the realm of tourism, cross-border collaboration affects both tourists and industry workers. Human resource cooperation might encourage more equitable and efficient management, and improve ecological and cultural integrity as ideas are shared and knowledge gained via personal exchanges and common training exercises (Timothy 1999). It is also sometimes a way of gaining cheap labor (Williams and Hall 2002), which may perpetuate stereotypical images of certain people and reinforce the divide between the rich and the poor.

Liberalizing policies regarding passports, visas, currency controls, health requirements, immigration procedures, and customs controls would likely increase travel between countries to the benefit of entire regions, as an element of the barrier effect is diminished (Teye 2000; Timothy 2001). However, such efforts are rarely achieved on a large scale because participating nations realize that this requires surrendering some degree of sovereignty for the cause of collaboration (Blake 1994; Scott 1998). Likewise, this extreme may cause borders to become too open to undesirable forces (e.g., drugs and terrorism), so a careful and delicate balance ought to be the goal. Arrangements can also be made so that visitors are allowed to drive their own vehicles across borders, and special provisions could permit citizens of one country to purchase vacation homes and property in another country. Some alliances allow people with certain skills, language abilities, and cultural experience to work in the tourism industries of other nations. This could help fill gaps in the workforce of one or more countries and may also be used to encourage better international understanding through staff exchanges and co-sponsored joint training programs. Such endeavors might create new jobs, higher standards of living, and increased regional incomes. Nonetheless, they could also result in displaced or underemployed workers in the destination country, dependency on foreign sources of income, and high levels of remittance leakages by professionals as money earned is sent to the home country rather than being spent in the place of employment.

Conservation issues

Nature and culture provide the foundations and the attraction base of tourism. Since ecosystems and cultural amenities commonly transcend international boundaries, many observers argue that they need to be managed and conserved holistically as a single entity (Gradus 1994; Johnstone 1995). Cooperation can be helpful in the conservation and use of resources. Conservation efforts might include the protection of shared heritage sites, parklands and preserves, ecosystems, and urban areas. Culture and nature interpretation is also an important area of collaboration, together with conservation planning, for the negative effects of tourism on the environment can be mitigated more broadly at the regional level. Additionally, cooperation may help prevent one country's over-utilization of resources at the expense of others as conservation policies are planned in concert on both sides of a border (Timothy 1999).

While this goal is a noble one and is beginning to see some degree of success in various parts of the world, as in the case of international parks described earlier, it is very difficult to attain. Balanced cross-national partnerships in ecological terms are difficult to achieve when significant socioeconomic differences exist on two sides of a border (Herzog 1991; Williams, Baláž, and Bodnárová 2001). Concerns that appear to be so urgent and which receive so much political and media attention in most affluent countries (e.g., environmental conservation and infrastructure development) are of secondary importance in less affluent nations, because their primary goal is to provide food, jobs, and education for their citizens. Imbalances result when one partner nation has knowledge and financial resources for tourism development but the others do not, as in the case of SIJORI above and along the US–Mexico border (Parent 1990). Likewise, uneven levels of development usually mean that there will also be varying standards of environmental protection, largely a result of political relationships more than economic ones.

Infrastructure and transportation

Accessibility to places and shared resources can be improved when governments collaborate on infrastructure efforts (Ingram, Milich, and Varady 1994). Very often, adjacent countries have overlapping, or parallel, infrastructures and transportation systems, which is an inefficient use of resources – something that could potentially be helped by cross-frontier collaboration as budgets are reduced and directed to other needs. Some of the most crucial areas of collaboration include telecommunications, railways and highways, airports, and jointly operated bus and taxi services – all affected in terms of cost and efficiency. Examples of long-term successes can be found in western Europe and more nascent efforts in the Middle East and eastern Europe.

Sometimes these efforts are hampered by contrasting planning regulations, labor laws, environmental standards, social and bureaucratic attitudes, and land management differences (Herzog 1991; Ingram, Milich, and Varady 1994; Wu 1998). Organizational differences also can create constraints on international collaboration. Achieving common goals in border regions is difficult when agencies in each country have contrasting mandates and opposing views of management. Likewise, in common with ecological conservation, infrastructure planning in border regions is often neglected, because in most cases borderlands are viewed as marginal and unimportant by central administrators (Timothy 2001) unless they possess some kind of intrinsic value (e.g., oil and mineral deposits) or when the physical periphery forms part of the functional core (e.g., Canada; Bratislava, Slovakia; Basle, Switzerland).

Conclusion

Despite traditions of institutionalized barriers, today most countries have begun to see the value of working together in many developmental areas, including tourism. As a matter of fact, tourism itself has been a major force in the economic and social globalization that has evolved in conjunction with global and regional tourism and trade alliances. Indeed, many of the concepts, issues, and applications agreed upon in supranational alliances have direct implications for tourism, in particular trade in goods and services, movement of people, conservation, promotion, and infrastructure and transportation, and they are key in supporting the notions of sustainability and peace-building.

Despite the importance that peace and sustainability bring to bear on cross-frontier partnerships, they are not always guaranteed to succeed. One or more obstacles may stand in the way. Issues of sovereignty and national protectionism, asymmetrical levels of economic development, political and cultural dissimilarities, and the peripheral status of border regions can thwart the success of cross-boundary partnerships.

Scale is a very influential factor in the success of international alliances, even though it has not been well addressed in tourism research. While there are considerable constraints on international cooperation, and indeed even some potentially negative outcomes, the most common and effective form of cooperation in tourism is on a small scale at the local level where adjacent communities or areas who share much in common, frequently including culture, language, trade, and ethnic traditions, are separated by human-created and often arbitrary political divides. Local-level collaborative efforts are more manageable than broader supranational coalitions and in most cases face fewer obstacles. Although the barrier effect of the border may impede some elements of local cooperation (and in some cases entirely restrict it), there is generally a higher degree of willingness and a desire on both sides to form partnerships. In most borderlands of the world sovereignty is an ambiguous notion, and there may be a mutual sentiment of marginality where strength is gained through collaborative efforts. Even in non-marginal border communities, complementary, rather than competitive, relations regularly exist – commonly evidenced through small-scale informal (or formal) trade and tourism.

It is often noted that small-scale efforts are among the most effective in achieving goals of sustainability and neighborly goodwill. Local cooperative efforts are also commonly attributed to the growth of greater events to come. "Strategies for accomplishing cross-border or international planning have tended to develop informally in local communities sharing a border; some techniques have been institutionalized into more formal mechanisms at various levels of planning" (Richard 1993: 601). The question of scale needs to be addressed in future research on international cooperation, and national governments who desire to participate in supranational alliances may want to consider encouraging more local-level cross-border cooperation as an antecedent to broader collaborative ventures.

REFERENCES

Anderson, J., and O'Dowd, L. (1999). Borders, border regions and territoriality: Contradictory meanings, changing significance. *Regional Studies* 33(7), 593–604.

Apostolopoulos, Y., and Sönmez, S. (2000). New directions in Mediterranean tourism: Restructuring and cooperative marketing in the era of globalization. *Thunderbird International Business Review* 42(4), 381–92.

Aulakh, P. S., Kotabe, M., and Sahay, A. (1996). Trust and performance in cross-border marketing partnerships: A behavioral approach. *Journal of International Business Studies* 27(5), 1005–32.

Bach, D. C. (1999). *Regionalization in Africa: Integration and Disintegration.* Bloomington: Indiana University Press.

Balassa, B. (1961). *The Theory of Economic Integration.* Homewood, IL: Richard D. Irwin.

Bertram, H. (1998). Double transformation at the eastern border of the EU: The case of the Euroregion pro Europa Viadrina. *GeoJournal* 44(3), 215–24.

Bhalla, A. S., and Bhalla, P. (1997). *Regional Blocs: Building Blocks or Stumbling Blocks?* London: Macmillan.

Blake, G. (1994). International transboundary collaborative ventures. In W. A. Gallusser (ed.), *Political Boundaries and Coexistence* (pp. 359–71). Berne: Peter Lang.

Blatter, J. (1997). Explaining crossborder cooperation: A border-focused and border-external approach. *Journal of Borderlands Studies* 12(1/2), 151–74.

Bufon, M. (1994). Local aspects of transborder cooperation: A case study in the Italo-Slovene border landscape. In W. A. Gallusser (ed.), *Political Boundaries and Coexistence* (pp. 19–29). Berne: Peter Lang.

Church, A., and Reid, P. (1996). Urban power, international networks and competition: The example of cross-border cooperation. *Urban Studies* 33(8), 1297–1318.

Church, A., and Reid, P. (1999). Cross-border co-operation, institutionalization and political space across the English Channel. *Regional Studies* 33, 643–56.

Dupuy, P. M. (1982). Legal aspects of transfrontier regional co-operation. *West European Politics* 5, 50–63.

Fineberg, A. (1993). *Regional Cooperation in the Tourism Industry.* Jerusalem: Israel/Palestine Center for Research and Information.

Gaines, S. E. (1995). Bridges to a better environment: Building cross-border institutions for environmental improvement in the U.S.–Mexico border area. *Arizona Journal of International and Comparative Law* 12(2), 429–71.

Gradus, Y. (1994). The Israel–Jordan Rift Valley: A border of cooperation and productive coexistence. In W. A. Gallusser (ed.), *Political Boundaries and Coexistence* (pp. 315–21). Berne: Peter Lang.

Graizbord, C. (1986). Trans-boundary land-use planning: A Mexican perspective. In L. A. Herzog (ed.), *Planning the International Border Metropolis: Trans-Boundary Policy Options in the San Diego–Tijuana Region* (pp. 13–20). San Diego: University of California.

Hall, C. M. (1994). *Tourism and Politics: Policy, Power and Place.* Chichester: John Wiley.

Hall, C. M. (2000). *Tourism Planning: Policies, Processes and Relationships.* Harlow: Prentice Hall.

Hall, C. M. (2001). Tourism and political relationships in southeast Asia. In P. Teo, T. C. Chang, and K. C. Ho (eds), *Interconnected Worlds: Tourism in Southeast Asia* (pp. 13–26). Oxford: Pergamon.

Hall, C. M., and Lew, A. A. (eds) (1998). *Sustainable Tourism: A Geographical Perspective.* Harlow: Longman.

Hansen, N. (1983). International cooperation in border regions: An overview and research agenda. *International Regional Science Review* 8(3), 255–70.

Herzog, L. A. (1991). USA–Mexico border cities: A clash of two cultures. *Habitat International* 15(1/2), 261–73.

Hussain, R. M. (1999). SAARC 1985–1995: A review and analysis of progress. In E. Gonsalves and N. Jetley (eds), *The Dynamics of South Asia: Regional Cooperation and SAARC* (pp. 21–39). New Delhi: Sage.

Ingram, H., Milich, L., and Varady, R. G. (1994). Managing transboundary resources: Lessons from Ambos Nogales. *Environment* 36(4), 6–38.

Jessop, B. (1995) Regional economic blocs, cross-border cooperation, and local economic strategies in postcolonialism. *American Behavioral Scientist* 38(5), 674–715.

Johnstone, N. (1995). International trade, transfrontier pollution, and environmental cooperation: A case study of the Mexican-American border region. *Natural Resources Journal* 35(1), 33–62.

Kliot, N. (1996). Turning desert to bloom: Israeli–Jordanian peace proposals for the Jordan Rift Valley. *Journal of Borderlands Studies* 11(1), 1–24.

Leimgruber, W. (1989). The perception of boundaries: Barriers or invitation to interaction? *Regio Basiliensis* 30, 49–59.

Parent, L. (1990). Tex-Mex Park: Making Mexico's Sierra del Carmen sister park to Big Bend. *National Parks* 64(7), 30–6.

Parsonage, J. (1992). Southeast Asia's "Growth Triangle": A subregional response to global transformation. *International Journal of Urban and Regional Research* 16(2), 307–17.

Renninger, J. P. (1979). *Multinational Co-operation in West Africa.* Oxford: Pergamon Press.

Richard, W. E. (1993). International planning for tourism. *Annals of Tourism Research* 20(3), 601–4.

Saba, R. P. (1999). From peace to partnership: Challenges of integration and development along the Peru–Ecuador border. *Journal of Borderlands Studies*, 14(2), 1–22.

Saint-Germain, M. A. (1995). Problems and opportunities for cooperation among public managers on the U.S.–Mexico border. *American Review of Public Administration* 25(2), 93–117.

Scott, J. W. (1998). Planning cooperation and transboundary regionalism: Implementing policies for European border regions in the German-Polish context. *Environment and Planning C: Government and Policy* 16(5), 605–24.

Sönmez, S., and Apostolopoulos, Y. (2000). Conflict resolution through tourism cooperation? The case of the partitioned island-state of Cyprus. *Journal of Travel and Tourism Marketing* 9(3), 35–48.

Teye, V. B. (1991). Prospects for regional tourism cooperation in Africa. In S. Medlik (ed.), *Managing Tourism* (pp. 286–96). Oxford: Butterworth-Heinemann.

Teye, V. B. (2000). Regional cooperation and tourism development in Africa. In P. U. C. Dieke (ed.), *The Political Economy of Tourism Development in Africa* (pp. 217–27). New York: Cognizant Communication Corporation.

Timothy, D. J. (1995). Political boundaries and tourism: Borders as tourist attractions. *Tourism Management* 16(7), 525–32.

Timothy, D. J. (1999). Cross-border partnership in tourism resource management: International parks along the US–Canada border. *Journal of Sustainable Tourism* 7(3/4), 182–205.

Timothy, D. J. (2000a). Tourism and international parks. In R. W. Butler and S. W. Boyd (eds), *Tourism and National Parks: Issues and Implications* (pp. 263–82). Chichester: John Wiley.

Timothy, D. J. (2000b). Tourism planning in Southeast Asia: Bringing down borders through cooperation. In K. S. Chon (ed.), *Tourism in Southeast Asia: A New Direction* (pp. 21–35). New York: Haworth Hospitality Press.

Timothy, D. J. (2001). *Tourism and Political Boundaries*. London: Routledge.

Timothy, D. J. (2002). Tourism in borderlands: Competition, complementarity, and cross-frontier cooperation. In S. Krakover and Y. Gradus (eds), *Tourism in Frontier Areas* (pp. 233–58). Lanham, MD: Lexington Books.

Timothy, D. J., and Boyd, S. W. (2003). *Heritage Tourism*. Harlow: Prentice Hall.

Williams, A. M. (1994). *The European Community*. Oxford: Blackwell.

Williams, A. M., Baláž, V., and Bodnárová, B. (2001). Border regions and trans-border mobility: Slovakia in economic transition. *Regional Studies* 35(9), 831–46.

Williams, A. M., and Hall, C. M. (2002). Tourism, migration, circulation and mobility: The contingencies of time and place. In C. M. Hall and A. M. Williams (eds), *Tourism and Migration: New Relationships between Production and Consumption* (pp. 1–52). Dordrecht: Kluwer.

Wu, C. T. (1998). Cross-border development in Europe and Asia. *GeoJournal* 44(3), 189–201.

Chapter 47

GIS Applications in the Planning and Management of Tourism

Yianna Farsari and Poulicos Prastacos

Introduction

A geographic Information System (GIS) is a database and mapping computer technology that is used to store and analyze geographical data. Geographical data include information about the location, characteristics, and relationships among places distributed over the earth's surface. A GIS is an information system which has the capability to handle spatially distributed data, relate them to other numerical or descriptive data, and present the data visually on a map. The ultimate goal of GIS, like any other information system, is to convert data into meaningful information available to support a number of actions and decisions (Benyon 1990; Cowen and Shirley 1991). GIS technology is the most common tool used today for natural resource management, urban land-use management, land development, and transportation planning.

Tourism is essentially a spatial phenomenon which, at a minimum, involves a home place, a destination place, and people moving from one of these to the other. However, the number of GIS applications for tourism planning has not mushroomed as the technology has in other fields.

The lack of GIS applications in tourism is most evident in managing mass tourism in existing destinations. Sustainable tourism management of highly developed, popular destinations has not received much attention and such practices have been rather rare. A reason for this failure has been the fact that for many years sustainable tourism was considered the opposite of mass tourism and there were already inherent difficulties in managing large-scale activities such as mass tourism. Moreover, sustainable tourism remains a vague, not clearly defined concept jeopardizing movement towards its implementation (Hunter and Green 1995; Butler 1998, 1999).

In this chapter the potential contribution of GIS technology to tourism planning and management is discussed, including its applications to tourism and sustainable development (which is defined more comprehensively elsewhere in this volume). It is our aim to highlight the need to exploit the capabilities offered by this technology in sustainable tourism policy-making. We argue that there are many advantages which have not been exploited, while solid and rational methodologies should be developed for designing systems for sustainable tourism. An extensive review of the literature on GIS applications in tourism and recreation will identify current trends and areas of future research, with the aim of pinpointing key features of GIS that may be used for tourism development planning. To better illustrate these features, examples of GIS applications are categorized according to the generic questions the technology is often used to answer.

GIS Applications in Tourism

Rhind (1990) categorized GIS applications in a structured approach according to the generic questions which GIS is frequently used to investigate. Bahaire and Elliott-White (1999) related these categories to basic GIS functions and their potential applications in tourism (table 47.1). The examples in the table demonstrate the range of tourism and recreation management and planning applications that can benefit from using GIS technology. Some of the key capabilities of GIS that could benefit tourism planning include: the ability to manipulate data and spatial attributes (Boyd and Butler 1996); the ability to provide value-added information (Bahaire and Elliott-White 1999; McAdam 1999); the ease with which resources can be allocated resources between what are often conflicting demands and to test "what if" scenarios (Townshend 1991; Williams, Paul, and Hainsworth 1996); adaptability to requirements, needs, and data changes over time (Beedasy and Whyatt 1999); and the ability to identify patterns or relationships based on particular criteria to support decision-making (McAdam 1999).

Although the number of GIS applications in tourism and recreation management and planning have been increasing, there are still many more potential opportunities

Table 47.1 GIS capabilities and tourism applications

Functional capabilities of GIS	Basic questions that can be investigated using GIS		Examples of tourism applications
Data entry, storage, and manipulation	Location	What is it?	Tourism resource inventories
Map production	Conditions	Where is it?	Identifying suitable locations for development
Database integration and management	Trends	What has changed?	Measuring tourism impacts
Data queries and searches	Routing	Which is the best way?	Visitor flows and management
Spatial analysis	Pattern	What is the pattern?	Analyzing relationships associated with resource use
Spatial modeling	Modeling	What if?	Assessing potential impacts of tourism development
Decision support			

Source: After Rhind 1990; Bahaire and Elliott-White 1999.

that have yet to be explored (Boyd and Butler 1996; Porter and Tarrant 2001). In the following section some examples of tourism GIS applications that have been proposed are reviewed. These are categorized based on the examples in table 47.1. It should be stressed that most GIS applications in tourism involve more than one of the categories cited below and their boundaries are not always clear. Nonetheless, it was felt that categorization of the examples was necessary to place them in a context and to facilitate the understanding and identification of their usefulness.

Tourism resource inventories

Resource inventories are undertaken to manage and control tourism development by taking into account conflicting or complementary land uses and activities, infrastructure available, and natural resources, through which the capabilities and capacities of an area are defined (Butler 1993; Bahaire and Elliott-White 1999). A well-known example of this application is the identification of areas suitable for ecotourism development. Boyd et al. (1994) and Boyd and Butler (1996) illustrated a methodology for identifying areas with potential for ecotourism in northern Ontario, Canada. First, a resource inventory and a list of ecotourism criteria were developed. At the next stage, GIS techniques were used to measure the ranking of different sites according to a set of pre-defined criteria, resulting in the sites with "best" or "highest" potential. Minagawa and Tanaka (1998) used GIS to locate areas suitable for tourism development at Lombok Island in Indonesia.

Another dimension of tourism resource inventories is to provide information about tourist destinations over the internet. Map-based information for tourists that may be found on websites or at computer information kiosks is a popular application of GIS. An ever-increasing number of destinations are promoted via the internet using this technology. Depending on the application, these maps may be static or interactive, allowing limited real-time operations to be handled online. Kirkby and Pollitt (1998) reported the development of a spatial information system on the web which provides information of interest to both ecotourists (e.g., accommodation, tours, cultural sites, road access) and the managers who monitor the local natural environment.

Location suitability

Location suitability analysis is perhaps the best known and most widely developed application of GIS. Tourism could not be excluded from this application, and many tourism examples are related directly or indirectly to identifying locations suitable for tourism development. Conflicting or complementary land uses and activities, infrastructure availability, and enabling or limiting natural resources are basic geographic variables used to determine the potential and the capacity of a place or area to be developed as a tourist destination (Butler 1993; Bahaire and Elliott-White 1999).

Berry (1991) used an area in the US Virgin Islands as a demonstration site to highlight the use of GIS in spatial analysis. Using three models, he defined conservation areas, ecological research areas, and areas of residential and recreational development, while a fourth model was used for conflict resolution among competing uses. Boyd et al. (1994) and Boyd and Butler (1996) illustrated a methodology for identifying areas with potential for ecotourism in the context of northern

Ontario, Canada. At first, a resource inventory (see above) and a list of ecotourism criteria were developed. GIS techniques were then used to measure the ranking of different sites according to the set criteria and thereby identify those with the "best" potential for development. Minagawa and Tanaka (1998) used this GIS approach to locate areas suitable for tourism development at Lombok Island in Indonesia. The main objective was to propose a methodology for GIS-based tourism planning. Using map overlay and multiple criteria evaluation, a number of potential sites for tourism development were identified. Joerger, DeGloria, and Noden (1999) advocated the advantages of using GIS for hotel site planning in Costa Rica, allowing complex criteria, which would otherwise not be readily apparent, to be taken into account.

Measuring and monitoring tourism impacts

This category of applications, as Rhind (1990) illustrated (table 47.1), involves the tracing of trends and answering the question, "What has changed?" It is therefore related to the monitoring of selected parameters over time and across space, rather than predicting potential impacts, which is covered in the next example. In the case of sustainable tourism development, where environmental, social, and economic information is required, GIS technology permits the integration and management of the various data. Butler (1993) points out that such integration capabilities facilitate the identification and monitoring of key indicators. Moreover, exploitation of the analytical and modeling capabilities that GIS offers can provide complex measures and indicators which are often required for monitoring sustainable development.

McAdam (1994) reported the case of a GIS prototype application developed for monitoring the impacts resulting from the increasing number of trekking and special interest tourists in a remote region in Nepal. Shackley (1997), based on her involvement in regional and site tourism management issues of the Himalayan kingdom of Lo (Mustang), Nepal, newly opened to visitors, suggested the development of a GIS-based multimedia cultural archive. This archive, with data collected at an early stage of tourism development, could serve as a baseline to monitor changes through time.

Visitor flows and management

This category refers to what Rhind (1990) described as routing applications answering to the question, "Which is the best way?" The best way may be determined on the basis of diverse criteria such as the shortest path, or the way that combines passing through various key points. In tourism applications this is mostly related to tourist time-space analysis. Tourist time-space analysis aims at understanding the behavior of tourists or visitors. Traditionally this has been accomplished by analyzing the static numbers of tourists or visitors and their socioeconomic and demographic characteristics (Dietvorst 1995). GIS can be a powerful tool in such analysis, offering a better understanding of tourist flows in a given region or area. A better understanding of tourist behavior may lead to better infrastructure and activities management, protection of the environment, and the spreading of benefits such as economic gains. Tourist time-space analysis is also related to the next category, analyzing relationships associated with resources, as it involves understanding visitors' behavior with respect to the use of available resources.

Dietvorst (1995) used a survey-based time-space analysis at a theme park in the Netherlands to better understand visitors' preferences among the various attractions in the park. GIS was used to assess the coherence between the various attractions and other elements of the park. The findings were then used for a more balanced diffusion of visitor streams and a better routing system. Van der Knaap (1999) used GIS to analyze tourist movement through, and their use of, the physical environment in order to promote sustainable tourism development. Bishop and Gimblett (2000) presented a case study at Broken Arrow Canyon, Arizona where, using rule-driven autonomous agents moving in a GIS-based landscape, the movement patterns of the visitors were simulated.

Relationships associated with resource use

Analyzing relationships associated with resource use answers the question "What is the pattern?" Scientists, planners, and decision-makers may undertake pattern detection to identify phenomena, their occurrence and their distribution. GIS can be used to delineate areas that should be undisturbed by tourism or any type of development activity. Impact analysis is related to this category as GIS can be used to identify patterns and the interaction between different components and evaluate the potential impact of tourism development on the natural environment (Bahaire and Elliott-White 1999). Another issue here is environmental justice, a topic that has been growing in importance over the last decade and which is related to equity in the distribution of impacts among various populations, and the costs and benefits resulting from the location of certain activities, such as tourism. Usually, the issue of environmental justice arises when undesirable land uses, such as pollution sources, are found to impact low-income communities at higher than average rates. Although tourism and recreation facilities often represent desirable land uses, with recreation opportunities and positive economic impacts as their main benefits, environmental justice can still be an issue since the positive impacts may not benefit all population groups in a similar way. The spatial character – and thus the GIS use – is strongly present in such evaluations.

Gribb (1991) described the planning effort that took place at the Grayrocks reservoir in Wyoming, integrating visitor surveys and environmental factors in a GIS. The aim was to come up with a recreation development plan that would contribute at the same time to environmental conservation of the reservoir. Nepal and Weber (1994) described the identification and delineation of buffer areas for biodiversity conservation in Nepal. Fishwick and Clayson (1995) used GIS in the Lake District National Park, UK, to exclude certain areas from tourism development because it was deemed this would be detrimental to the quality of those areas. They also identified areas adjacent to the lakes that suffered noise disturbance from power boats. Carver (1995) described the development of a "wilderness continuum map" showing areas designated as wilderness in the UK, and its use to identify areas of potential risk from recreational development.

Porter and Tarrant (2001) used GIS within the framework of environmental justice to determine whether certain socioeconomic and racial groups are discriminated against in the distribution of government tourism and recreation sites in Appalachia in the US. Nicholls (2001) illustrated an application in which the accessibility and distributional equity in the park system of Bryan, Texas, was examined. The author illustrated how GIS can help leisure service professionals visualize and measure levels of accessibility and equity. Using GIS, the author was able to measure accessibility in ways other than straight-line distance measures, thereby achieving much better accuracy and reducing errors.

Tourism marketing is a dimension of GIS applications related to this category. Elliot-White and Finn (1998) advocate geodemographics and lifestyle analysis utilizing GIS, which they believe could make a significant contribution to the needs of "postmodern" tourism marketing. Postmodern tourism is characterized by a move away from mass tourism and toward smaller and more personalized forms of tourism. Despite its potential benefits, GIS applications in tourism marketing seem rather rare. As Sussmann and Rashad (1994) pointed out in their study on the level of GIS awareness among managers of tourist areas, this may be the result of lack of capital, training, and qualified personnel.

Assessing potential impacts of tourism development

This category includes applications that integrate several or all of the previously mentioned uses of GIS, and which employ many of the more complex analytical capabilities of GIS. The "What if?" question refers to the development and evaluation of different change scenarios. Visual impact analysis (predicting how a proposed change will be seen in the landscape) is an example of an approach that may be undertaken in tourism planning projects, especially in the case of environments with scenic or high aesthetic value (Millar et al. 1994).

Selman et al. (1991) produced a Digital Terrain Model (DTM) for the Aonach Mor in Scotland which was used to assess the visibility of the development ski facilities. The impacts of the development on vegetation and on competing land uses were also considered in this GIS. Millar et al. (1994) developed an application, which among other things provided a scenery and visual impact assessment in the Cairngorm Mountains in Scotland. The Lake District National Park Authority (1995) used GIS to identify the areas from which proposed forestry schemes within the national park and wind farms outside the park would be visible. SpaME (Beedasy and Whyatt 1999) is a spatial decision support system for tourism planning on developing islands which contains a major visibility analysis component. As the authors argue, it is important to explore the visual qualities and examine the visual impacts of developments as the competitiveness of tourism sites depends on the scenic landscapes and natural attractions they provide.

Community involvement and participation application are also related to this category. Sustainable development considers community participation as an important factor in asserting some degree of local control over decisions on development plans (Mowforth and Munt 1998) and in enhancing commitment to their implementation. Moreover, in tourism planning which involves various agencies and organizations, the participation of groups or individuals from different disciplines may be necessary. However, participatory processes using GIS as a facilitator is not free from criticism. It is often suggested that traditional GIS do not provide the mechanisms for multiple-user access and for incorporating the diverse priorities in the evaluation and should therefore be expanded to encompass the necessary methods and tools for group decision-making (Carver 1991; Armstrong 1994; Feick and Hall 2000). Bahaire and Elliott-White (1999) cite the Brecon Beacons

National Park project, in which a GIS was used to provide the maps to facilitate discussion between locals and planners and to provide a focus at public meetings. The TourPlan system (Feick and Hall 2000) is a GIS-based decision-support system designed to assist individuals and groups in exploring alternative development strategies while building consensus and identifying conflict in land-use planning for tourism. A sample application was conducted in West Bay District of Grand Cayman involving four basic types of participant: government, non-government, private sector, and the general public.

Ultimately, the "What if?" question, along with the modeling and analytical capabilities of GIS, refers to decision-making support. Although GIS is not widely considered a decision support system (DSS) in itself, its contribution in supporting decision-making has been acknowledged (Nicholls 2001). As Boyd et al. (1994) state, GIS is a method for providing information in a format upon which decisions can be based rather than a decision-making tool. McAdam (1999) recognized GIS's contribution to decision-making in its ability to provide value-added information. This value-added information is a product of the system's ability to identify patterns or relationships based on particular criteria through its graphical display, data manipulation, spatial analysis, and spatial modeling functions.

Beedasy and Whyatt (1999) developed a decision support system (SpaME) to assist sound tourism planning in Mauritius. SpaME was designed to take into account all criteria simultaneously and to facilitate the user's understanding of the problem, as well as of the interactions that may take place between these criteria in a dynamic environment. The system's analytical capabilities were further enhanced using appropriate models and multi-criteria evaluation techniques. Feick and Hall (2000) describe the development of TourPlan, a GIS-based decision support system designed to allow multiple participants from various sectors to explore alternative land-related development strategies in small island states.

GIS and Sustainable Tourism

The evolution of GIS applications in tourism follows closely the three phases of GIS applications development described by Crain and MacDonald (1984). First there were the *inventory applications* for assembling and organizing features of interest, and which performed mainly simple data queries, such as location and condition questions. This evolved into *analysis applications*, in which more complex analytical operations were undertaken. In the final stage, more comprehensive *management applications* were developed, which supported decision-making. It is in this last phase that GIS has the greatest potential to support sustainable development approaches to tourism planning, development, and management (also known as "sustainable tourism"). Unfortunately, most of the GIS management applications in tourism are related to identifying suitable locations for developing tourism activities. Other important issues, such as the contribution of GIS to the management of existing destinations and to the implementation of sustainable tourism principles, have been neglected.

Malczewski (1999) identified GIS contributions in all the three phases of a planning and decision-making process: the *intelligence* phase for identifying opportunities or problems; the *design* phase for the development and analysis of possible alternatives to the problem(s) identified; and the *choice* phase for evaluation of the alternatives. All three of these phases necessitate the identification and use of sustainable tourism indicators for assessing the present situation, identifying weaknesses, monitoring change, and evaluating alternatives. GIS could be the lead technology to use for identifying and monitoring these sustainability indicators.

It can be argued that the potential of GIS in tourism development and management has not yet been fully explored; nor have the capabilities of GIS been fully exploited. A considerable number of the aforementioned applications have actually been developed for recreation rather than tourism. One reason for this is that they were related to the environmental management of national parks and other attractions. GIS has been extensively used for the management of the environment and are considered an essential tool for its protection, monitoring, resource use optimization and allocation, and zoning of activities (Aronoff 1991). Although the environment is a critical factor and resource for tourism development, GIS has not been widespread in environmental management within the tourism sector. Another contradiction lies in the fact that GIS is the principal technology specialized in handling geographical data and thus facilitate the study of geographic phenomena. Thus tourism, which has a very strong geographic character, could benefit from the use of this form of information system.

The capability of GIS to integrate different data sets – qualitative and quantitative, spatial and non-spatial – has already been highlighted in the applications presented here. This capability is especially important within the context of sustainable tourism, which calls for a balance between economic growth, environmental costs, and benefits for society. What needs to be underlined, however, is the ability of GIS to relate different data and generate new information (Cowen 1988). Furthermore, they also have the capability of relating various parameters and attributes to their spatial context, facilitating the analysis and implications of proposed changes within a sustainability context. As McAdam (1999) pointed out, the significant value of GIS technology lies in its ability to provide desktop mapping through the graphical display and manipulation of data in order to identify patterns or relationships based on certain criteria and thus provide enhanced information for further analysis. Finally, additional analysis is enhanced by the ability of GIS to integrate with other technologies (Malczewski 1999). Remote-sensing satellite imagery and global positioning systems (GPS) can both be used to acquire detailed and tailored spatial information for GIS analysis.

A widely acknowledged capability of GIS is visualization of the results of data entry and analysis. Visualization may be offered either in more common formats, such as tabular displays, or in the more specialized form of map display. Both forms facilitate the communication of results between interested parties, as well as adding to the analysis process itself through visual comparison – for example, between tourism resources and resources needed for other activities (Williams, Paul, and Hainsworth 1996). Thus, visualization can facilitate certain parts of the decision-making process and, importantly, enhance efforts toward sustainable development. As mentioned in the applications section above, GIS and its visualization capabilities were used in a number of cases to facilitate and enhance citizen and stakeholder participation. This aspect can be a significant contribution, as participatory processes are considered essential in achieving sustainable development (Harris et al.

1996; Nicholls 2001). Related to this is the form of planning for sustainable development. Bottom-up hierarchies are preferred from a sustainability perspective and GIS technology can be a tool to support the decentralization of planning and policy formulation. Standalone systems or distributed systems may be available for one or more users performing relevant tasks. Thus, depending on what is needed and what is legitimized, local authorities may use their own information systems, or use them in conjunction with other agencies or the central government.

Another competitive advantage of GIS technology lies in its adaptability in adding or removing thematic layers, constraints, and data. It is thus a dynamic tool for planners rather than a static one, capable of being adjusted as new data become available and as tastes and preferences in demand change over time (Beedasy and Whyatt 1999). This characteristic could be of particular importance in sustainable tourism decision-making as both preferences and targets may change in the course of development and in the course of operationalizing the concept of sustainable tourism.

Limitations

Millar et al. (1994) argue that a GIS may support a decision-making process based on the sensitive use of resources and local needs. However, as Bahaire and Elliott-White (1999) note, a GIS is just a tool, and does not by itself ensure fairness, equity, and compatibility with sustainability principles. They continue that GIS is not "asocial" or "neutral." It may be manipulated to support policies of certain interests. As Pickles (1996) argues, although GIS can enhance access to information and therefore enhance democratic practices, it can also be used to promote the interests of particular groups having access to the technology. In any case, GIS does not make the decision itself, it may facilitate data-processing and analysis as well as communicate results, but, according to Bahaire and Elliott-White (1999: 171), it is "unlikely to alter the political character of policy making and thereby produce a more sustainable tourism planning practice." It could thus be argued that those techniques and methods which would safeguard the compatibility of both the process followed and the results should be identified and integrated into a system for decision support for sustainable tourism.

The software advances which have been seen during the last decade have not managed to alter perceptions of GIS, which is still considered a quite complicated technology necessitating more advanced skills than simple word processing. This is one of the main reasons identified by McAdam (1999) in his research about the failure of GIS to be incorporated in tourism planners' decision-making process. Thus it could be argued that there is a need for a system which will be easy for non-GIS experts to use, which still incorporates all the necessary policy-making and sustainability procedures and tools, and which can be operated by users from diverse backgrounds.

Further limitations arise from the concept of sustainable development itself. As already mentioned, the concept of sustainable tourism is still vague, and implementational aspects are not yet fully elaborated. Moreover, the multidimensional character of sustainable tourism means that we need diverse kinds of data for planning and management, and these are not available in most cases. However, as mentioned in the previous section, awareness of the potential benefits of systems for supporting decision-making in sustainable tourism could act as a stimulus for further research in the field, as well as for the establishment of the procedures and the mechanisms to provide the context for policy-making and data collection.

Conclusions

This review of GIS applications in tourism implies that the technology has evolved from simple mapping systems to complex systems that support decision-making effectively and in an integrated way. The latter, however, have not been widely utilized in tourism destination management, and more effective decision support applications of GIS need to be developed and adopted. This is even more challenging in respect to the implementation of sustainable tourism, and especially in existing mass tourism destinations. GIS technology can provide a basis for the development of systems to support decision-making for sustainable tourism. Such systems should be integrated and capable of identifying weaknesses in the developments used, evaluate alternatives, and monitor change.

For developing such systems there is an apparent need to identify methods and techniques that will safeguard the evaluations made, in all the detection, scenario, and monitoring phases, and ensure they are consistent with sustainable tourism principles. In operational terms, this would include, at the first stage, the identification of proper indicators, criteria, and policy goals for sustainable tourism development. Modeling for sustainable tourism should also be a consideration in case that simulation is needed.

REFERENCES

Armstrong, M. (1994). Requirements for the development of GIS-based group decision-support systems. *Journal of the American Society for Information Science* 45(9), 669–77.

Aronoff, S. (1991). *Geographic Information Systems: A Management Perspective*. Canada: WDL Publications.

Bahaire, T., and Elliott-White, M. (1999). The application of geographical information systems (GIS) in sustainable tourism planning: A review. *Journal of Sustainable Tourism* 7(2), 159–74.

Beedasy, J., and Whyatt, D. (1999). Diverting the tourists: A spatial decision-support system for tourism planning on a developing island. *ITC-Journal* (3–4), 163–74.

Benyon, D. (1990). *Information and Data Modelling*. Oxford: Blackwell Scientific Publications.

Berry, J. K. (1991). GIS in island resource planning: A case study in map analysis. In D. Maguire, M. Goodchild, and D. Rhind (eds), *Geographical Information Systems*, vol. 2: *Applications* (pp. 285–95). Harlow: Longman.

Bishop, I. D., and Gimblett, H. R. (2000). Management of recreational areas: GIS, autonomous agents, and virtual reality. *Environment and Planning B: Planning and Design* 27(3), 423–35.

Boyd, S. W., and Butler, R. W. (1996). Seeing the forest through the trees: Using GIS to identify potential ecotourism sites in Northern Ontario. In L. C. Harrison and W. Husbands (eds), *Practicing Responsible Tourism: International Case Studies in Tourism Planning, Policy and Development* (pp. 380–403). New York: John Wiley.

Boyd, S., Butler, R., Haider, W., and Perera, A. (1994). Identifying areas for ecotourism in Northern Ontario: Application of a geographical information system methodology. *Journal of Applied Recreation Research* 19(1), 41–6.

Butler, R. (1993). Alternative tourism: The thin edge of the wedge. In V. Smith and W. Eadington (eds), *Tourism Alternatives* (pp. 31–46). Chichester: John Wiley.

Butler, R. (1998). Sustainable tourism: Looking backwards in order to progress? In M. Hall and A. Lew (eds), *Sustainable Tourism: A Geographical Perspective*. London: Longman.

Butler, R. (1999). Sustainable tourism: A state-of-the-art review. *Tourism Geographies* 1(1), 7–25.

Carver, S. J. (1991). Integrating multi-criteria evaluation with geographical information systems. *International Journal of Geographical Information Systems* 5(3), 321–39.

Carver, S. J. (1995). Mapping the wilderness continuum. In *Proceedings of the GIS Research UK 1995* (p. 15). Newcastle: University of Newcastle.

Cowen, D. J. (1988). GIS versus CAD versus DBMS: What are the differences? *Photogrammetric Engineering and Remote Sensing* 54, 1551–4.

Cowen, D. J., and Shirley, W. L. (1991). Integrated planning information systems. In D. J. Maguire, M. F. Goodchild, and D. W. Rhind (eds), *Geographical Information Systems*, vol. 2: *Applications* (pp. 297–310). Harlow: Longman.

Crain, I. K., and MacDonald, C. L. (1984). From land inventory to land management. *Cartographica* 21, 40–60.

Dietvorst, A. G. J. (1995). Tourist behaviour and the importance of time-space analysis. In G. J. Ashworth and A. G. J. Dietvorst (eds), *Tourism and Spatial Transformations: Implications for Policy and Planning* (pp. 163–81). Wallingford: CAB International

Elliott-White, M. P., and Finn, M. (1998). Growing in sophistication: The application of GIS in post-modern marketing. *Journal of Travel and Tourism Marketing* 7(1), 65–84.

Feick, R. D., and Hall, B. (2000). The application of a spatial decision support system to tourism-based land management in small island states. *Journal of Travel Research* 39, 163–71.

Fishwick, A., and Clayson, J. (1995). *GIS Development Project: Final Report to the Countryside Commission*. Kendal: Lake District National Park Authority.

Gribb, W. (1991). Integrating visitor surveys, environmental factors, and GIS into recreation planning: Site development at Grayrocks reservoir, Wyoming. In *GIS/LIS '91 Proceedings* (vol. 1, pp. 177–86). Maryland: American Congress on Surveying and Mapping.

Harris, T. M., Weiner, D., Warner, T., and Levin, R. (1996). Pursuing social goals through participatory GIS: Redressing South Africa's historical political ecology. In J. Pickles (ed.), *Ground Truth: The Social Implications of Geographic Information Systems* (pp. 196–222). New York: Guilford Press.

Hunter, C., and Green, H. (1995). *Tourism and the Environment: A Sustainable Approach*. London: Routledge.

Joerger, A., DeGloria, S. D., and Noden, M. A. (1999). Applying geographic information systems: Siting of coastal hotels in Costa Rica. *Cornell Hotel and Restaurant Administration Quarterly* 40(4), 48–59.

Kirkby, S. D., and Pollitt, S. E. P. (1998). Distributing spatial information to geographically disparate users: A case study of ecotourism and environmental management. *Australian Geographical Studies* 36(3), 262–72.

Lake District National Park Authority (1995). *Tourism in the Lake District*. Kendal: LDNP.

Malczewski, J. (1999). *GIS and Multicriteria Decision Analysis*. New York: John Wiley.

McAdam, D. (1994). Mustang 2: The silk road project. *Association for Geographical Information Systems Conference Proceedings 1994*, paper 4.1.

McAdam, D. (1999). The value and scope of geographical information systems in tourism management. *Journal of Sustainable Tourism* 7(1), 77–92.

Millar, D. R., Morrice, J. G., Horne, P. L., and Aspinall, R. J. (1994). The use of geographic information systems for analysis of scenery in the Cairngorm mountains, Scotland. In M. F. Price and D. I. Heywood (eds), *Mountain Environments and GIS* (pp. 119–32). London: Taylor & Francis.

Minagawa, M., and Tanaka, N. (eds) (1998). *Application of Geographic Information Systems to Tourism Development Planning: A Case Study of Lombok, Indonesia*. Research Report 27. Nagoya, Japan: UNCRD.

Mowforth, M., and Munt, I. (1998). *Tourism and Sustainability: New Tourism in the Third World*. London: Routledge.

Nepal, S. K., and Weber, K. E. (1994). A buffer zone for biodiversity conservation: Viability of the concept in Nepal's Royal Chitwan National Park. *Environmental Conservation* 21(4), 332–41.

Nicholls, S. (2001). Measuring the accessibility and equity of public parks: A case study using GIS. *Managing Leisure* 6(4), 201–19.

Pickles, J. (ed.) (1996). *Ground Truth: The Social Implications of Geographic Information Systems*. New York: Guilford Press.

Porter, R., and Tarrant, M. (2001). A case study of environmental justice and federal tourism sites in southern Appalachia: A GIS application. *Journal of Travel Research* 40, 27–40.

Rhind, D. W. (1990), Global databases and GIS. In M. F. Foster and P. J. Shands (eds), *The Association for Geographic Information Yearbook 1990*. London: Taylor & Francis.

Selman, P., Davidson, D., Watson, A., and Winterbottom, S. (1991). GIS in rural environmental planning: Visual and land-use analysis of major development proposals. *Town Planning Review* 62(2), 215–23.

Shackley, M. (1997). Saving cultural information: The potential role of digital databases in developing cultural tourism. *Journal of Sustainable Tourism* 5(3), 244–9.

Sussmann, S., and Rashad, T. (1994), Geographic information systems in tourism marketing. In C. Cooper and A. Lockwood (eds), *Progress in Tourism, Recreation and Hospitality Management* (vol. 6, pp. 250–8). London: Belhaven Press.

Townshend, J. R. G. (1991). Environmental data bases and GIS. In D. Maguire, M. Goodchild, and D. Rhind (eds), *Geographical Information Systems*, vol. 2: *Applications* (pp. 201–16). Harlow: Longman.

Van der Knaap, W. (1999). Research reports: GIS-oriented analysis of tourist-space patterns to support sustainable development. *Tourism Geographies* 1(1), 59–69.

Williams, P. W., Paul, J., and Hainsworth, D. (1996). Keeping track of what really counts: Tourism resource inventory systems in British Columbia, Canada. In L. C. Harrison and W. Husbands (eds), *Practising Responsible Tourism: International Case Studies in Tourism Planning, Policy and Development* (pp. 404–21). New York: John Wiley.

Part IX Conclusions

Chapter 48

Contemporary Themes and Challenges in Tourism Research

Allan M. Williams, C. Michael Hall, and Alan A. Lew

Beginnings and Endings

As comprehensive and far-reaching as this volume has been, in many ways it only scratches the surface of the geographic approach to understanding tourism. It is not a comprehensive state-of-the-art review of tourism geography, let alone tourism studies. It was also not an attempt to delineate the complex evolution of tourism studies, nor to define an agenda for research. Finally, it was not an attempt to provide a rationale for the way tourism is, or should be, structured for academic study. Tourism is such a complex and evolving phenomenon that no single volume could hope to achieve these objectives. However, we do believe that the contributors to this project have made a significant contribution toward each of these goals.

In the introduction we explored three areas of concern: issues relating to the definition of tourism and hence how it is studied; the key themes and issues which have emerged in tourism as a field of social scientific endeavor; and the ebb and flow of research themes. Amongst the key points to emerge from that brief review were the futility of trying to pin down precise definitions of tourism studies, the growing institutional strength of tourism studies, though accompanied by the blurred and shifting nature of disciplinary boundaries and fields of study, and the changing objects of study of both tourism geography and tourism studies. However, if only one message emerges from the introduction and subsequent chapters, it is quite simply that this book has been a celebration of the richness and diversity of tourism studies.

If this volume does contribute to the definition of either the geography of tourism, or tourism studies more generally, then it is through the voices of its scholars. Of course, there are shared approaches and concerns amongst many of the contributors, but there are also different theoretical and methodological orientations, possibly even distinct communities of scholars. Within these tensions and contradictions there is also much fruitful pollination. For example, the interests of critical social science often stand in marked contrast to those concerned with the policy and practical implications of tourism knowledge. Yet there is also the emerging development of policy analysis in tourism that stands within the critical science tradition, but which may be of utility to policy-makers as they seek policy alternatives. There are also different theoretical perspectives which can still be crystallized around positivism/behavioralism, political economy and postmodern/cultural interpretations. But these should not be understood as simple, homogenous, and mutually exclusive categories, as individual researchers have attempted to bridge the divides between them. Instead, each can be seen as a fertile and increasingly porous avenue for innovative research, providing for new and insightful analytical frameworks and perspectives.

The book also celebrates the diversity of disciplinary boundaries. The authors who have contributed to this volume were invited to do so on the basis of their previous contributions to research on the key themes that concern tourism geography – at least as the editors perceived these. The outcome is a collection of authors who have varying degrees of formal training within geography as a discipline, may or may not be situated within geography departments, and who publish papers with varying degrees of explicit reference to geography and the geography of tourism. More than anything else, this illustrates the blurred and shifting boundaries of tourism studies and of the traditional academic disciplines such as geography, sociology, economics, and psychology as they relate to tourism studies. This is cause for celebration rather than concern, for the most original "blue skies" research is often found at the borders of established research areas, or when links are made between previously disconnected areas of inquiry. This point was stated forcibly by Prentice (chapter 21), when he called for greater willingness amongst academics in tourism to question what have become implicitly established ways of thinking. Although referring specifically to studies of motivation, his comments have more general purchase.

The above comments lead us to emphasize that this book is as much about beginnings as about endings. It looks backwards and forwards, establishes the lineage of particular themes, current concerns, and future possibilities. Readers may find it both optimistic and pessimistic – so much begun, so much still to do. There are areas bursting with new ideas, while others are characterized by incremental learning. Disciplinary boundaries are crossed with ease, unthinkingly even, in some areas of research, but still seem to regiment knowledge in others. And the contributions to this volume, while including a range of researchers from many parts or the world, also barely extend outside the English-language community of scholars in the developed world, let alone the less developed world. Therefore, the scope for beginnings and new lines of research is immense. Below we explore further some of the themes that have emerged from the essays.

Tourism: A Fruitful Arena of Social Science Endeavor

The celebration of diversity, which we consider to be one of the hallmarks of this volume, necessarily poses difficulties when trying to identify some of the key themes which have emerged of continuing and potentially new areas of research. The following review, therefore, makes no claim to be comprehensive, but rather is illustrative. That is to say, the themes discussed below identify some of the key debates within tourism geography and, to some extent, tourism studies, and illustrate how these are engaging tourism researchers in some of the wider concerns of social science endeavor.

The cultural shift

One of the most persistent themes in this volume is the need for more culturally informed approaches. Many of the contributions are, of course, firmly located within poststructuralist and cultural theory frameworks. But the "cultural turn" is also informing other theoretical frameworks, notably political economy (Lee and Wills 1997), leading to greater incorporation of discourses about non-material relationships into economic analyses. Ateljevic and Doorne (chapter 23), for example, argue that the cultural practice of tourism, viewed as performance, provides a perspective for analyzing the circuits of production and consumption in tourism. Paradis (chapter 16) makes a telling distinction between heritage theming and enterprise theming, drawing on Robins (1999). This interweaving of cultural perspectives can also be found in discourses about behavioral research. For example, Crouch (chapter 7) calls for approaches to motivation and behavior that are better informed by discourses of practice and performance. There is a danger here, of course, of falling into the trap of cultural hegemony, ignoring material relationships, regulatory frameworks, and the value of behavioral research methods. But this "trap" may be weaker in tourism than in some other fields of study, for tourism research has a long tradition of engaging with the cultural, perhaps reflecting the relatively early and influential role of anthropologists and sociologists such as Graburn (1976, 1983a, 1983b), Smith (1977, 1979), and Cohen (1974, 1979). Recent contributions by cultural geographers (Cartier and Lew 2004; Crang, chapter 6) are extending this tradition in new directions.

Scale

Scale constitutes one of the abiding concerns of geographers, including tourism geographers. Recently this has become focused on debates about global–local relationships. Indeed, Meethan (chapter 9) argues that one of the distinctive features of tourism activities is that they are highly globalized while necessarily being bound to the specificities of place. Indeed, tourism research has become increasingly concerned with global–local relationships, although arguably rather uncritically. There are widespread debates as to the multiple and contested meanings of globalization (Held 2000) that only now are percolating into the tourism literature (e.g., Cooper and Wahab 2001). Moreover, there is increasing criticism of the notion of the global–local as a dichotomy; the local is not separately constituted but is shaped by how the global and the local are interrelated in particular places (Smith 2001). Again, this is hardly new in tourism studies and d'Hauteserre (chapter 19), for example, in the context of postcolonialism, reminds us of researchers' concerns for how economic, cultural, and other forces originating from metropolitan centers become hybridized when brought into different places. However, considerable challenges remain with respect to how tourism researchers engage with current debates about scale (Herod and Wright 2002). This is a point powerfully made by Church (chapter 44) when arguing that tourism geographers need to examine how the continual rescaling of governance and the development of multiscalar policies are shaping power relations.

Spaces and flows

Massey's (1994: 154) view that places are constituted of local and more spatially stretched relationships, that is that they are "articulated moments in networks of social relations and understandings," has particular resonance for tourism geography. Of course, tourism researchers have long been interested in tourist flows in their own right (Pearce 1987; McKercher and Lew, chapter 3), but for some tourism geographers the central interest lies in Allen's emphasis on the implication that social relationships are – at least temporarily – locked into particular places (Allen et al. 1998). These are the moments in which host–guest, guest–guest, and host–host relationships are made and remade, thereby contributing to how places and spaces are constituted.

Recently, tourism researchers have shown greater awareness of how tourism is situated in a complex continuum of mobility (Williams and Hall 2002; Hall et al., chapter 1), and that there is a need to understand how different flows are interrelated in particular spaces. This is at the heart of Müller's assertion (chapter 31) that emerging new geographies of human mobility pose profound questions for how we conceptualize places and identities. Crang (chapter 6), within a different theoretical perspective, also argues the need to see how the meanings of place are constructed "through actors and discourses that are both local and distant." Elsewhere in the book, Coles (chapter 29) argues for research that looks "beyond the transaction," which can be extended into a call for research that situates tourism relationships in the framework of the articulation of spaces and flows. One of the particular tasks that faces tourism geographers is to delineate and understand the shifting temporalities and spatialities that characterize these.

The environment

As indicated in the introduction (tables 1.2 and 1.3), the environment has long been a central concern for tourism researchers in general, and tourism geographers in particular. However, the research agenda in this area has been dominated in recent years by the concept of sustainability (Hall and Lew 1998). That literature has been long on case studies and advocacy, and short on critical social science content. And yet there is a need to link debates on sustainability to those on social welfare, social and territorial justice, and the geographies of power and democracy amongst others. Hughes (chapter 40) makes a significant contribution to this re-theorizing of the ambiguous, and sometimes vacuous, notion of sustainability, with his concept of the "reflexive tourist." There is also a need to inform our understanding of sustainability with some of the discourses on what Macnaghten and Urry (1998: 1) term "a diversity of contested natures." The latter leads Saarinen (chapter 35) to argue for greater consideration of the ideologies which inform representations of nature and how these are deployed in tourism. There is also a need for more sophisticated research with respect to the environmental impacts of tourism (Wong, chapter 36). Whilst environmental impacts are a long-established research concern in tourism studies, much of the research is poorly informed by natural science research (Butler 2000). Echoing our comments above (and in chapter 1), this re-emphasizes the fact that the potential for innovative research is often strongest at the boundaries between disciplines or, in this case, between science and social science. Technological developments, especially those involving remote scanning and recording, global positioning systems, and GIS, offer new possibilities for research on environmental impacts, but their full potential can only be realized when we have the appropriate theoretical frameworks for analysis.

Non-chaotic conceptualization

It was de Kadt (1979) who urged recognition that "tourism is not a unique devil," a reference to the need to set evaluations of tourism in the context of other processes of economic and social change. This is a call echoed by Wong (chapter 36) in respect of comparing the environmental impacts of tourism to those associated with other forms of economic activity. Tourism researchers have, to some extent, responded to such calls in recent years, and have increasingly sought to socially situate their research. For example, behavioral studies have examined how holiday behavior relates to other forms of leisure behavior (Prentice, chapter 21). Political economy studies have examined how firms are embedded in local economies, and Riley (chapter 11), for instance, has posed some penetrating questions as to the relationships between tourism and other labor markets. Most obviously, postmodernist studies have made the blurring of divides between social practices one of the central motifs of their research. Terkenli (chapter 27), for instance, argues that this is driven by the tendency for all landscapes to be constituted, at least in part, as landscapes of tourism. Together these amount to a clarion call for research which places tourism in, rather than abstracts it from, wider social relationships, and for a less chaotic approach to conceptualization. This is a process which should lead to genuine dialogue between tourism and other fields of study. Oakes and Minca (chapter 22), reinforce this point, when arguing that tourism presents an enormous range of "field sites" for postmodernist studies.

Multiple voices

In common with much of social science, some voices have been much louder than others in tourism studies. Quite apart from fundamental notions of equity, this implicitly means that our understanding of tourism is less complete than it should be. This informs Pritchard's (chapter 25) call for the tourism academy to incorporate *both* feminine and masculine voices if it is to become less partial and unrepresentative. The contents of tourism journals (see chapter 1 and table 1.3) suggests that there is increased concern with gender and sexuality issues, although there is still considerable progress required in this, as there is in the organizations and institutions of tourism. Other voices also have to be heard more clearly. For example, Hinch (chapter 20) notes that one of the ironies of most research on indigenous peoples is the dominance of non-indigenous voices. Ashworth and Tunbridge (chapter 17) make a similar point when calling for a form of heritage and heritage tourism that better represents those who are currently un- or under-represented.

The above discussion can be read negatively as a commentary on the "failings" of tourism research, but it also highlights tourism as an area of and for fruitful social science endeavor. The agenda for this research continues to shift in response to discourses within tourism studies and other field of study, but also – as we argue in the next section – in response to the challenges of a changing external environment.

Challenges of a Changing External Environment

The dynamics of change in tourism studies are to be understood not only through reference to academic discourses, but also through engagement with actual changes in tourism practices. The literature on tour operators can be traced to particular concerns with the emergence of mass tourism (Turner and Ash 1975), the literature on mega-events is related to the increased scale and commodification of the Olympic Games and other major happenings (Hall 1992), and the sustainable tourism literature followed hard on the heels of the Brundtland declaration (Hall and Lew 1998). The objects of tourism study are constantly changing, presenting new and shifting challenges for academic research. We outline below some of the current and emerging concerns of tourism research, not so much delineating an agenda for future research as illustrating the nature of the challenges facing researchers.

Risk and uncertainty

The first and perhaps the most obvious of these changes was touched on in the introduction (chapter 1), that is the growing concern with *risk and uncertainty* in response to a variety of challenges, including terrorism, war, the increasingly rapid and internationalized diffusion of infectious diseases, and economic uncertainty. As Hall and Jenkins (chapter 42) argue, the media have had a particularly strong impact on how policy-makers have responded to increased risks. Indeed, we can liken the media to a lens which both enlarges and distorts perceptions of risk and uncertainty. The net outcome has been a shift from the emphasis on year-on-year growth of international tourism, and forecasts of near exponential growth, to stuttering or declining levels of international travel, and gloomy prognoses for future trends. Neither vision of the trajectory of tourism is entirely appropriate of course. Growth and decline, fueled by shifts in tastes and fashions, as well as relentless competitive pressures, are inherently uneven, both temporally and spatially. The challenge for tourism researchers is to unravel some of the complex ways in which these mega-shifts are realized on the ground, in particular places. This requires careful study of all forms of tourism and leisure activities, and of both complementarities and substitutions.

Changing conditions

Secondly, *the conditions of tourism production and consumption are subject to change* emanating from globalization, technological innovations, and changes in the costs of production factors such as capital and labor. On the one hand, there has been seemingly relentless deregulation, hand in hand with privatization. This is most starkly evident in the air travel sector. However, the reality is not so much deregulation as re-regulation, with the emergence of new forms of governance, partnerships, and state entrepreneurship (see Hall and Jenkins (chapter 42), Williams (chapter 5), Church (chapter 44), and Bramwell (chapter 43), respectively). The challenge for tourism researchers is to understand how re-regulation relates to the circuits of production and consumption (Shaw and Williams 2004; Ateljevic and Doorne, chapter 23). And, in particular, we need to better understand the process of change as one of innovation, whether incremental or paradigm-changing (Hjalager

2002). That requires far more sophisticated approaches than hitherto to the study of the socio-psychological, technological, and organizational determinants of innovation. This is essential if we are to have a better understanding of why both public and private tourism initiatives sometimes result in replication and uniformity. Given the sharp changes in how the industry is organized, and especially the impact of new technologies, we very much concur with Debbage and Ioannides' (chapter 8) appeal for tourism geographers to embrace Britton's (1991) call for a more critical examination of the tourism production process. That includes the need for a more critical approach to new technologies (see Milne et al., chapter 15), which recognizes the highly uneven impacts this has on firms, individual tourists, and places.

Socially divided/dividing world

Finally, there is a need to address more explicitly that tourism not only occurs in a *socially divided and dividing world*, but actively contributes to such processes. There are sharp divisions in access to, and participation in, various forms of tourism. These divisions are articulated both socially and spatially, in the north–south divide, and in regional divides, as much as in class, gender, racial, and age differences. Given that tourism constitutes an important element in quality of life, this inevitably means that tourism practices serve to reproduce these inequalities. Moreover, tourism production in capitalist economies necessarily generates further unequal social relationships between and within factions of capital and labor. The future challenges of tourism development cannot adequately be faced unless tourism research explicitly acknowledges such deep and persistent inequalities. For example, the growing number of international tourists has led to calls to limit tourism growth, and especially international travel. This may result in policies which aim at various forms of rationing, to be realized through price mechanisms or regulatory controls. The outcomes will not be socially neutral. Instead, most such interventions will likely reproduce or deepen social inequalities in tourism practices. There is probably no greater challenge for critical tourism studies than the analysis of these inequalities.

ACKNOWLEDGMENTS

David Crouch, Andrew Church, T. C. Chang, Keith Debbage, David Edgell, Don Getz, Shirlena Huang, Dimitri Ioannides, Bob McKercher, Tim Oakes, Richard Prentice, and P. P. Wong all provided useful suggestions of themes for future research.

REFERENCES

Allen, J., Massey, D. B., Cochrane, A., and Charlesworth, J. (1998). *Rethinking the Region*. London: Routledge.

Britton, S. (1991). Tourism, capital and place: Towards a critical geography of tourism. *Environment and Planning D: Society and Space* 9, 452–78.

Butler, R. W. (2000). Tourism and the environment: A geographical perspective. *Tourism Geographies* 2(3), 337–58.

Cartier, C. and Lew, A. A. (eds) (2004). *Seductions of Place*. London: Routledge.

Cohen, E. (1974). Who is a tourist? A conceptual clarification. *Sociological Review* 22(4), 527–55.

Cohen, E. (1979). Rethinking the sociology of tourism. *Annals of Tourism Research* 6, 18–35.

Cooper, C. and Wahab, S. (eds) (2001). *Tourism in the Age of Globalisation*. London: Routledge.

de Kadt, E. (ed.) (1979). *Tourism: Passport to Development*. Oxford: Oxford University Press.

Graburn, N. (1976). *Ethnic and Tourist Arts: Cultural Expressions from the Fourth World*. Berkeley: University of California Press.

Graburn, N. (1983a). The anthropology of tourism. *Annals of Tourism Research* 10, 9–33.

Graburn, N. (1983b). Tourism and prostitution. *Annals of Tourism Research* 10, 437–43.

Hall, C. M. (1992). *Hallmark Tourist Events: Impacts, Management and Planning*. London: Belhaven.

Hall, C. M., and Lew, A. (eds) (1998). *Sustainable Tourism: A Geographical Perspective*. London: Longman.

Held, D. (2000). Introduction. In D. Held (ed.), *A Globalizing World? Culture, Economics, Politics* (pp. 1–12). London: Routledge.

Herod, A. and Wright, M. W. (eds) (2002). *Geographies of Power: Placing Scale*. Oxford: Blackwell.

Hjalager, A.-M. (2002). Repairing innovation defectiveness in tourism. *Tourism Management* 23(5), 465–74.

Lee, R. and Wills, J. (eds) (1997). *Geographies of Economies*. London: Arnold.

Macnaghten, P., and Urry, J. (1998). *Contested Natures*. London: Sage.

Massey, D. (1994). *Place, Space and Gender*. Minneapolis: University of Minnesota Press.

Pearce, D. G. (1987). *Tourism Today: A Geographical Analysis*. Harlow: Longman Scientific and Technical.

Robins, K. (1999). Tradition and translation: National culture in its global context. In David Boswell and Jessica Evans (eds), *Representing the Nation: A Reader* (pp. 15–32). London: Routledge.

Shaw, G., and Williams, A. M. (2004). *Tourism, Tourists and Tourism Spaces*. London: Sage.

Smith, M. P. (2001). *Transnational Urbanism: Locating Globalization*. Oxford: Blackwell.

Smith, V. L. (ed.) (1977). *Hosts and Guests: The Anthropology of Tourism*, 1st edn. Philadelphia: University of Pennsylvania Press.

Smith, V. L. (1979). Women the taste-makers in tourism. *Annals of Tourism Research* 6, 49–60.

Turner, L. and Ash, J. (1975). *The Golden Hordes: International Tourism and the Pleasure Periphery*. London: Constable.

Williams, A. M., and Hall, M. (2002). Tourism, migration, circulation and mobility: The contingencies of time and place. In M. Hall and A. M. Williams (eds), *Tourism and Migration: New Relationships Between Production and Consumption* (pp. 1–52). Dordrecht: Kluwer.

Index

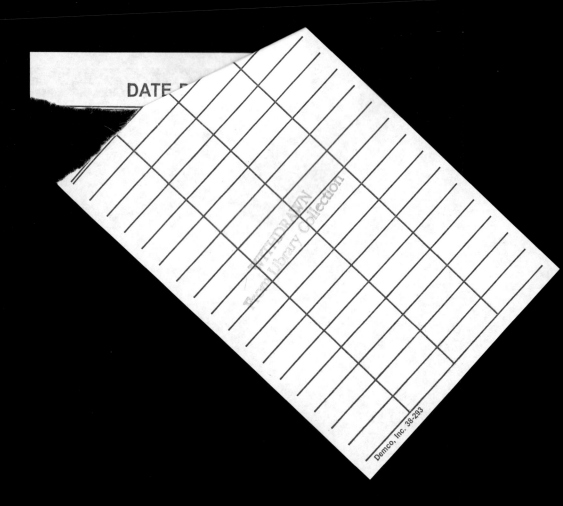